Internet Starter Kit

for Macintosh
2nd Edition

D1415804

Internet Starter Kit for Macintosh

2nd Edition

Adam C. Engst

Hayden Books

Internet Starter Kit for Macintosh, 2nd Edition

Library of Congress Catalog No.: 94-75944

ISBN: 1-56830-111-1

96   95   4

Interpretation of the printing code: the rightmost double-digit number is the year of the book's printing; the rightmost single-digit number the number of the book's printing. For example, a printing code of 94-1 shows that the first printing of the book occurred in 1994.

The Hayden Books Team

Publisher

David Rogelberg

Managing Editor

Karen Whitehouse

Development Editor

Brad Miser

Copy Editors

M.T. Cozzola, Brian Gill

Publishing Coordinator

Stacy Kaplan

Interior Designers

Barbara Webster, Kevin Spear

Illustrators

Kathy Hanley, Kevin Spear

Cover Designer

Jay Corpus

Production Team

Gary Adair, Dan Caparo,
Brad Chinn, Kim Cofer, Lisa
Daugherty, Jennifer Eberhardt,
Mark Enochs, Beth Rago,
Bobbi Satterfield, Kris Simmons,
Carol Stamile, Robert Wolf

Indexers

Greg Eldred, Michael Hughes

*Composed in Palatino and Futura
by Hayden Books*

License Information

To Our Readers

Dear Friend,

Thank you on behalf of everyone at Hayden Books for choosing *Internet Starter Kit for Macintosh* to enable you to explore the Internet. The Internet is the fastest growing, and most exciting, aspect of our modern society. Without the right guide, participating on the Internet can be difficult. We have carefully crafted this book and disk to enable you to both learn about the Internet and actually get on it. We wish you the best in your explorations and hopefully, we'll meet you there soon!

What you think of this book is important to our ability to better serve you in the future. If you have any comments, no matter how great or small, we'd appreciate you taking the time to send us email or a note by snail mail. Of course, we'd love to hear your book ideas.

Sincerely yours,

David Rogelberg
Publisher, Hayden Books and Adobe Press

You can reach Hayden Books at the following:

Hayden Books
201 West 103rd Street
Indianapolis, IN 46290
(800) 428-5331 voice
(800) 448-3804 fax

Email addresses:

America Online:	Hayden Bks
AppleLink:	hayden.books
CompuServe:	76350,3014
Internet:	hayden@hayden.com

Dedication

To my lovely and talented wife, Tonya, without whose patience and editing skills I would certainly have gone stark raving mad.

About the Author

Adam C. Engst

Adam C. Engst is the editor and publisher of *TidBITS*, a free electronic newsletter distributed weekly on the world-wide computer networks. After graduating from Cornell University with a double-major in Hypertextual Fiction and Classics, he worked as an independent consultant in Ithaca, New York, where he started *TidBITS* in April of 1990. He now lives in Renton, Washington, with his wife, Tonya, and cats, Tasha and Cubbins, but seems to spend most of his time corresponding via electronic mail with friends and associates around the globe. After writing the first edition of *Internet Starter Kit for Macintosh* (released in September of 1993), he was somehow rooked into co-authoring *Internet Explorer Kit for Macintosh* with Bill Dickson, and *Internet Starter Kit for Windows* with Cory Low and Mike Simon. These titles were published in April of 1994.

Like anyone who attempts to condense the immensity of the Internet into a single book, he is certifiably crazy. His favorite quote (which reportedly comes from Alan Kay, an Apple Fellow and Xerox PARC alumnus) is: "The best way to predict the future is to invent it."

Contents at a Glance

Table of Contents

Introduction

Before anything else, please believe me when I say that this book is not a manual to be ignored after you've removed the disk from the back cover and stuffed it in your Macintosh. Using the Internet is not like using a word processor. There are some quirks and confusions that I explain, but which may frustrate you to no end if you don't bother to read the sections about using the different programs. Also, if you don't bother to read the instructions provided for, say, connecting to an Internet provider, and then you call the provider for help, you cannot expect them to be all that happy about explaining over the phone what I've already explained in the book.

That said, I want to tell you a little about how I designed *Internet Starter Kit for Macintosh*, because I think it will help you make the most of the book in the limited time that we all have. As with any broad subject, some parts of the Internet won't interest you in the slightest, and that's fine. However, I feel that it's important to cover many of these topics even if they won't interest all of my readers. So, let's look quickly at each of the four parts that make up this book, and I'll tell you what to expect.

Part I: Introduction and History

This part stays fairly general, introducing you to the book and to the Internet, and trying to offer a way of looking at the world through Internet-colored glasses. Chapter 1, "Welcome," serves as the introduction. Chapter 2 seeks to answer the question, "Why is the Internet Neat?" The third chapter, "What is the Internet?," tackles a more difficult issue and attempts to explain just what the Internet is. Next, "The Internet Beanstalk" traces a line down the history of the Internet, branching off to look briefly at other topics of potential interest. If you're new to the Internet, you should definitely read the first three chapters, and if you're at all interested in a historical perspective, read the fourth.

The fifth chapter, "Exploring the Internet," is excerpted from *Internet Explorer Kit for Macintosh*. I wanted to provide a sense of what life is like on the Internet, so I talked my co-author on that book, Bill Dickson, into putting together this chapter with me. If you like chapter 5, you may want to get *Internet Explorer Kit* in a bookstore—it contains lots of great stuff we couldn't fit into the excerpt.

Part II: Internet Foundations

The second part is required reading for novices, because it covers network foundations in terms of basic usage and social customs. It's important because it provides much of the information that is simply known on the Internet. If you want to know how email is constructed, for example, or when you should avoid using FTP, you should read this part. Community knowledge can be difficult to pick up without spending a lot of time on the Internet, so these chapters can save you a lot of time and trouble (and money!).

Chapter 6 covers the basics of "Addressing and Email," and handles mailing lists, as well. Chapter 7, "Usenet News," is devoted exclusively to Usenet news. Chapter 8 describes "Internet Services," those being services that require a full Internet connection, such as Telnet, FTP, WAIS, Gopher, and the World-Wide Web, and also discusses the many file formats you find on the Internet.

Part III: Connecting to the Internet

The third part is big, really big. I apologize for that, because concise explanations are generally good. On the other hand, everything I cover is necessary to understand each method of connection.

Six chapters make up Part III. The first five examine four different methods of accessing the Internet, and the sixth walks you through using the most popular MacTCP-based applications. Chapter 9, "Commercial Services," starts things off by looking at the easiest and least interesting method of Internet access, using a commercial online service such as CompuServe or America Online. Chapter 10, "Shell Access," tackles the next step up in Internet access, the Unix command line. It tells only what you need to know to get around (and not much more—this is *not* the book for you if you only want to learn how to use Unix programs on the Internet). Chapter 11, "UUCP Access," explores an older but still useful method of access that provides only electronic mail and news, the UUCP connection.

Chapters 12, "MacTCP, PPP, and SLIP," and 13, "MacTCP-based Software," look in depth at the newest and coolest Internet connection, MacTCP. Although the other methods of connection are important and useful (and often the most cost-effective), nothing competes with the range and quality of software available for Macs connected to the Internet and running MacTCP. Chapters 12 and 13 are important enough that Hayden Books licensed MacTCP from Apple and included it on the disk that comes with this book, along with other programs that you need to start using a MacTCP connection via your modem right away.

Finally, chapter 14, "Step-by-Step Internet," takes a bare bones approach to teaching you how to use the most popular MacTCP-based programs, some of which are included on the disk. If you're uncertain how to perform basic tasks with these programs, this chapter is for you.

You don't have to read every one of these chapters; in fact, I don't recommend it, because the information is a lot to wade through in one sitting. Instead, concentrate on the method of access that most interests you. I'll talk more about the different types of access and which might be most appropriate for you, in the introduction to Part III.

Appendixes

The fourth part of this book is a collection of appendixes for browsing and skimming, not for reading.

Appendix A, "Internet Resources," is a list of resources that was compiled primarily by Ken Stuart. One of the major problems with the Internet is that it doesn't have a card catalog, so it can take some time to find out about enough resources that you learn how to find new ones. This list, although by no means comprehensive (that would be utterly impossible and foolish to attempt), should provide a push in the right direction, and show you some of the more interesting resources currently available. Special thanks are due to Ken for compiling this list—I couldn't have done it without him.

Appendix B, "Newsgroup List," from Gene Spafford and David Lawrence, is a massive list of Usenet newsgroups, complete with descriptions. Turn here to see which newsgroups might interest you, before you're boggled by the choices that confront you when you actually connect and start paging through the thousands available.

Appendix C, "PDIAL List," and appendix D, "Supplementary PDIAL List," list public access providers. You can use them to find out who provides Internet services in your area and around the world.

After those lists of information, you'll see appendix E, "Glossary," which briefly explains common terms and acronyms. That's followed by appendix F, "Special Internet Access Offer," which provides information on a special connection offer. Finally, appendix G, "The Internet Starter Kit Disk," looks in detail at the contents of the disk. Last, but not least, comes the ever-popular index.

At the back of the book are a coupon for discount access to a great Internet provider as well as a sheet on which you can record all your online data.

Welcome to *Internet Starter Kit for Macintosh*, welcome to the Internet, and please, make yourself at home.

Adam C. Engst

June, 1994

I

Introduction and History

In this part of *Internet Starter Kit for Macintosh*, I introduce myself and give you a look at what the Internet is, why it's so neat, where it came from. I also give you a glimpse of what life on the net is like. These five chapters convey the proper mindset for thinking about the Internet, a mindset without which you may find the Internet an overwhelming place.

Chapter 1, "Welcome," starts out slowly to allow us to introduce ourselves to one another. It also lays out the basic requirements for using the Internet. Chapter 2, "Why Is the Internet Neat?," talks about what makes the Internet a special place, and chapter 3, "What Is the Internet?," supports that by attempting to define the Internet. Chapter 4, "The Internet Beanstalk," provides a brief look at the past and future of the Internet, although if you don't like reading about history, feel free to skip this one. (If you find yourself condemned to repeat history at some later time, though, don't blame me, since chapter 4 provides the background you need to understand why the Internet is the way it is and how it works politically.) Finally, chapter 5, "Exploring the Internet," actually gives a feel for what life on the net is really like. It's an excerpt from my book *Internet Explorer Kit for Macintosh* (Hayden Books, 1994), co-authored with Bill Dickson.

Welcome

Welcome to the *Internet Starter Kit for Macintosh, 2nd Edition*. I have two goals for this book, at least one of which hopefully applies to you as either its prospective buyer or proud new owner. First, I want to tell you about the Internet—what it is and why it's so wonderful (and I mean that in all senses of the word, especially the bit about becoming filled with wonderment)—and introduce you to a number of the services and resources that make it one of humankind's greatest achievements. Second, I want to show you how to gain access to the Internet and use many of the Macintosh tools available for working with it. In fact, I've even included some of these tools on the disk that comes with this book so you can get started right away. For those tools for which I didn't have room on the disk, I tell you where on the Internet to go to get them. But before I start, let's skip the small talk and introduce ourselves.

Who Are You?

I haven't the foggiest idea who you are. That's not true, actually; I can make a couple of guesses. You probably are a Macintosh user, because if you aren't, only about half of this book will hold your interest. You probably are also interested in the Internet; otherwise, only about 2 percent of the book is worth your time. Given these minor prerequisites, this book should provide hours of educational entertainment, just like Uncle Milton's Ant Farm. The major difference is that the Internet Ant Farm is worlds bigger than Uncle Milton's, and if you go away on vacation, all the Internet ants won't keel over—though you may be tempted to do so when you get back and see how much you have to catch up on. The Internet never stops.

I've written this book for the individual, the person behind that most personal of personal computers, the Macintosh. In the process, I undoubtedly will disappoint the die-hard Unix system administrators and network gurus who talk about X.400 and TCP/IP in their sleep (which doesn't come often because of the amount of Jolt cola they consume). I'm also aiming this book at students and staff at universities, which often have wonderful connections to the Internet, but seldom provide any guidance about what's out there. And I'm aiming at user groups, who can teach their members about the Internet with the aid of a good book and disk resource. I'm also aiming at ordinary people who have a Mac, a modem, and the desire to start using the Internet. And, yes, I'm even aiming at those Unix system administrators, because what better way to get those annoying Macintosh users off your back than by giving them this book?

I should note that this book will not particularly help you learn how to become a provider of information, a publisher if you will, on the Internet. That's an entirely separate topic that deserves its own book, which I may someday write. This particular book is for Internet consumers, not publishers.

What Do You Need?

This book, of course—why do you think I wrote it? But beyond that. . .

First, you need a Macintosh. That's not absolutely true, because you can use any sort of computer to access the Internet, but to get the most out of this book you should use a Macintosh. (For those of you who use Windows, check out *Internet Starter Kit for Windows*.) You don't need a fast Macintosh, although it would be nice. When I wrote the previous edition of this book, I used an elderly SE/30, and although I've since moved up to a Centris 660AV, most things I do on the Internet haven't changed much with the faster Mac.

Second, you need some type of physical connection to the Internet. This connection may take the form of a local area network at work or, more likely, a modem. A 2,400 bps modem works, though only barely, and the faster the better. If you start out with a 2,400 bps modem, be prepared to buy a new one soon. That speed will become intolerable quickly, and why make something as fascinating as the Internet intolerable?

Third, I recommend that you use System 7 or later, if only because I haven't used System 6 in more than three years and have no idea whether the software included on the disk works under System 6. That's not entirely true—some of the basic programs will work—but many others, including the best ones, now require System 7. All of my instructions assume you are using System 7. If you need to upgrade, talk to your dealer.

Fourth, you need an account on a host machine somewhere. In the introduction to Part III, I cover how to find an appropriate account for your needs.

Fifth, you need a certain level of computer experience. This stuff simply is not for the Macintosh novice. If you don't know the difference between a menu and a window, or haven't figured out how to tell applications and documents apart, I recommend you visit your local user group and ask a lot of questions. A number of excellent books also are available. My favorite is *The Little Mac Book,* by Robin Williams. You can also read your manuals but frankly, as good as Apple's documentation is, Robin does a better job.

Finally, you may need to adjust your expectations. The Internet is not a commercial service like America Online or CompuServe. Customer service representatives are not available via a toll-free call 24 hours a day. The majority of people on the Internet have taught themselves enough to get on or have been shown just enough by friends. The Internet is very much a learning experience; even with as much information and guidance as I provide in this book, there's simply no way to anticipate every question that might come up through those first few days. The Internet is what you make it, so don't be shy. No one greets you on your first dip in, but at the same time, people on the Internet are some of the most helpful I've ever had the pleasure to know. If you are struggling, just ask and someone almost always comes to your aid. I wish that were true outside of the Internet as well.

Who Am I?

"Who am I?" is a question that I often ask myself. In the interests of leaving my autobiography for later, I must limit the answer to the parts that are relevant to this book. My name, as you probably figured out from the cover, is Adam Engst. I started using computers in grade school and had my first experience with a mainframe and a network playing Adventure over a 300 baud acoustic modem (you know, where you dial the number and stuff the receiver into the modem's rubber ears) on a computer my uncle used in New York City. I used microcomputers throughout high school, but upon entering Cornell University learned to use their mainframes. In my sophomore year, I finally found the gateway to BITNET (the "Because It's Time" Network) in some information another user had left behind in a public computer room. Finding that initial bit of gateway information was like finding a clue in Adventure—but don't worry, it's not that difficult any more. From BITNET I graduated to using a computer connected to Usenet (the User's Network, generally synonymous with "news") and around the same time learned about the vast Internet, on whose fringes I'd been playing.

After graduating from Cornell in 1989, I set up my own Internet access using QuickMail for Macintosh. QuickMail was overkill for a single person because it's designed to be a network electronic mail program, so I eventually switched to a more appropriate program called UUCP/Connect. Several years ago, my wife and I moved from Ithaca, New York, where we had grown up and where Cornell is located, to the Seattle, Washington area. In the process I learned more about finding public-access Internet hosts in a place where you know no one in person. In many ways the Internet kept me sane those first few months.

Throughout this Internet odyssey of the last eight years, I've used the nets for fun, socializing, and general elucidation. In the last four years, I've also written and edited a free, weekly, electronic newsletter called *TidBITS*. It focuses on two of my favorite subjects: the Macintosh and electronic communications. *TidBITS* is both a product and citizen of the Internet. It has grown from a 300-person mailing list that once crashed a Navy computer running old mail software, to an electronic behemoth that lives on every network I can find and boasts an estimated 100,000 readers in some 46 countries.

So that is the reason I'm writing this book (well, there are those incriminating photographs of publishing industry VIPs that I have digitized and poised to distribute to the net at large). Any questions? I hope so, but hold off until you've finished the book. And for those of you already marking things up with those nasty yellow highlighters, don't; I promise there is no quiz awaiting you.

Changes

Keep in mind that the Internet changes quickly and constantly, and trying to capture it in a snapshot requires high-speed film. I've got that film, so the image of the Internet that I present here isn't blurry or out of focus, but it's impossible to cover, or even discover, everything that deserves to be in *Internet Starter Kit for Macintosh*. If, in the course of your travels on the Internet, you find a neat resource or piece of software that I overlooked, send me electronic mail (email) at **ace@tidbits.com**, and I'll take a closer look for future editions.

This book has evolved and grown along with the Internet, and is now in its second edition. I've left in place the best parts of the first edition, inserted some new ways of explaining the Internet, updated the software discussions to cover the latest releases, and added in some great new programs that have appeared since the first edition hit the shelves.

The first edition of *Internet Starter Kit for Macintosh* distinctly changed my life, for the better. I've been asked to speak at conferences, interviewed via email and on the radio, filmed for TV, and fed food that was pre-chewed, for my convenience, by weasels on interminable cross-country airplane flights. But the reason I put up with all the hassle is that I truly love the Internet and believe it's worth preserving, protecting, building, and explaining. If I can infect others with my enthusiasm for the Internet, I think the world becomes a better place. And that's the goal in the end.

Thanks

Many people have helped me throughout the writing of the book. I certainly want to thank my wife Tonya, who edited everything and put up with me during the final few weeks. I also thank David Rogelberg, Karen Whitehouse, and Brad Miser of Hayden Books, all of whom went out of their way to help make the book a success. Thanks also to my mother, who went from using WordPerfect 5.0 on an aging IBM PC to using a Quadra 700 and running a Gopher server, and my father, who has become quite fond of Eudora on their LC II and is contemplating a PowerBook purchase. I'd also like to thank all the readers of *TidBITS* because they have kept me going these last four years. If I've forgotten anyone, my apologies and thanks for your help.

Thanks are due as well to all the people who helped edit portions of the book, including the following:

Bill Dickson, for general comments and Internet kibitzing that led him to co-author my second book, *Internet Explorer Kit for Macintosh*

Sandro Menzel, Werner Uhrig, and Herb Effron, for general comments about the book and the state of the Internet

Chuck Shotton, for the World-Wide Web sections

Geoff Duncan, for his Unix comments and many Internet discussions

Harry Morris and Franklin Davis, for checking out the WAIS sections

Mark H. Anbinder, for extensive help with the glossary and contributing to *TidBITS* in my time of need

Ross Scott Rubin, for fact-checking the chapter about the online services

Mark McCahill and the Gopher Team, for clarifying the Gopher sections

Mark Williamson, for providing much-needed information about LISTSERV

Steve Dorner, for checking the Eudora section

Jeff Needleman, Cary Lu, and Bill Lipa, for checking sections on Prodigy, eWorld, and Outland

Rusty Tucker, Bill Gram-Reefer, Peter Broadribb, James Skee, and Jeff Steele, for comments on the BBS section

Amir Rosenblatt and Drummond Reed, for checking the Pipeline and TIA sections

Paul Celestin, Leonard Rosenthol, and Brian Hall, for checking the information about terminal emulators

John Mah, Roy Wood, and Jim O'Dell, for comments about UUCP

Jim Matthews and Roger Brown, for their help with the MacTCP chapter

John Norstad, Jonathan Lundell, and Peter Lewis, for providing necessary technical details about MacTCP

John Hardin, for checking the MacWeb section

Liam Breck, for helping with `ftp.tidbits.com`

And, of course, thanks to those people who provided text for the Appendixes, including the following:

Gene Spafford and David Lawrence, creator and maintainer of the newsgroups list

Peter Kaminski, author of the PDIAL list

Ed Morin, Ralph Sims, Michael Tardiff, Scott Anderson, and Jeanne Talich, of Northwest Nexus

Finally, although I don't have room to acknowledge individually the programmers of all the software I mention in the book, I do want to thank those who graciously allowed me to include their programs on the disk, including the following:

All the folks at Aladdin Systems, for StuffIt InstallerMaker

Garry Hornbuckle and the MacTCP team at Apple Computer, for MacTCP

Larry Blunk and Merit Network, for MacPPP

InterCon Systems (and especially Duncan Briggs), for InterSLIP

Peter Lewis, for Anarchie

Steve Dorner, for Eudora

The entire Gopher Team, for TurboGopher

John Hardin of MCC's EINet group, for MacWAIS and MacWeb

Charles Cooper of OneWorld, for hosting the Web page

Separately, I want to thank Ken Stuart for creating the resource section, and Bill Dickson for helping with the disk installer, editing the excerpt from *Internet Explorer Kit for Macintosh*, and generally helping out. I couldn't have done it without either of them.

Why Is the Internet Neat?

Unless you've just idly picked up this book based on its cool cover while waiting for your spouse to choose the right gift for Aunt Millie's birthday, you probably have some sense that you should be interested in the Internet. Given the Clinton administration's emphasis on a national data highway system, many a poor reporter has written or broadcast a story on this Internet thing.

Those stories almost always make those of us who live and breathe the Internet cringe because they almost always miss the point. The stories either crow about the technological achievement and vast worldwide coverage of the Internet (while failing to explain that it is definitely not a commercial service staffed by friendly nerds in white coats, and ignoring its human dimension), or they provide a gratuitous human interest story about how two people met on the Internet and got married eleven days later because typing to each other was such a moving experience. Sure, this stuff happens, but such gee-whiz stories never touch on the commonplace parts of the Internet: the discussion groups, information databases, and selfless volunteer work that keeps the whole thing running. That's a shame, and I vow to avoid that slippery slope.

But I should be talking about why you should be interested in the Internet, instead of ragging on the mediocre descriptions from people who apparently aren't. Keep in mind that I may miss your favorite reason to use the Internet—one woman's Brownian motion generator is another man's cup of tea. In addition, remember that technology is seldom used for its intended purpose. The Internet started as a method of linking defense researchers around the country, and has grown beyond that use in ways its creators never could have imagined.

Electronic Mail

For many people, electronic mail (or email) is the primary reason to get on the Internet; they simply want to be able to send mail to someone else on the Internet. Once you're on, though, you're likely to strike up many new friendships and end up with a long list of electronic correspondents. Email is an excellent way to stay in touch even with people whom you regularly talk to on the phone because it's quick and easy. Even though I talk to my parents often, I also send them email because it's more appropriate for quick notes. Email messages are even better than an answering machine for conveying simple information. At one point, for example, the local Macintosh user group held steering committee meetings at my house. I could have called all the steering committee members before each meeting to remind them about it, but because all I wanted to say was, "Don't forget the meeting tomorrow night," contacting them was easiest via email.

Email sometimes gains the least likely converts. One friend of mine is best described as a telephobe—he hates talking on the telephone and only has one at his house, out of necessity. He had been equally disparaging of computers and email until he was forced to try it, after which he became an instant email proponent. He discovered that with email, no longer did he have to play telephone tag with coworkers or try to arrange meetings to talk about simple topics. Email enabled him to work more flexible hours because he didn't care when his coworkers were present and their email was waiting whenever he wanted to read it.

Discussion Groups

A large number of people read and participate in the twenty-odd discussion groups, also called *newsgroups*, about the Macintosh, and far more people contribute to thousands of other non-technical discussions. Several years ago, when I went away on a bike trip, my Macintosh started sounding the Chords of Death and displaying the sad Mac face along with an error code. My wife couldn't contact me to tell me about it, but she posted a help message on one of the Macintosh discussion groups. Within a few days she had received answers from Macintosh experts around the world, all telling her that that code meant we had a bad memory card. (Luckily, the card turned out to be only badly seated.)

Similarly, when we were in the process of buying a car, I started reading appropriate messages on one of the discussion groups dedicated to talking about cars. The messages were of some help, but I wish I had known then that there was an entire discussion group devoted to Hondas, the make we were looking at most.

Software

For many Macintosh users, some of the most immediately useful and interesting things about the Internet are the *file sites*. File sites are computers on the Internet that are accessible to everyone (more or less) and store thousands of the latest and greatest *freeware* and *shareware* (where you pay the author if you use the program) programs for the Macintosh. An equal or greater number of file sites exist for other platforms, most notably for the omnipresent PCs from IBM, Compaq, Dell, and the other seventeen million clone makers. Finding specific numbers is difficult, but I think it's safe to say that thousands of people download files every day from the most popular *archive sites* (just another name for file site).

Information at Your Electronic Fingertips

The popularity of email and newsgroups notwithstanding, the massive databases of information impress some people the most. Recently, a friend came over to look at a QuickTime movie of the Knowledge Navigator film clip. The Knowledge Navigator is ex-Apple CEO John Sculley's idea of what information access will be like in the future—an anthropomorphic "talking head" that acts as an *information agent*, searching through massive databases of information at the user's command. The Knowledge Navigator film portrays a professor preparing for a class discussion about deforestation in the Amazon rainforest by looking at data retrieved by his electronic agent.

The film is fairly neat, but after watching it, I remembered that I also wanted to show my friend Wide Area Information Server (WAIS). Using the Macintosh WAIS software, we connected to WAIS and typed in our query, "Tell me about deforestation in the Amazon rainforest." After about 10 seconds, WAIS returned a list of 15 articles from various sources that dealt with just that topic, sorted by relevance. Talk about knocking someone's socks off—my friend was staring, mouth open, tongue lolling, and completely barefoot, so to speak. Although WAIS doesn't have an infinite number of databases, it does have more than 500 (including *TidBITS*), and more appear all the time. I list some of the more popular databases later in the book, and it's usually fairly easy to search for the databases themselves.

Although I have no numbers to back this up, I get the impression that the largest quantity of raw information is available via FTP (File Transfer Protocol). The freeware and shareware programs for the Mac that I mentioned previously are available via FTP, as are electronic editions of books, newsletters such as *TidBITS*, fiction magazines such as *InterText*, and huge numbers of other files.

Gopher, another method of transferring information over the Internet, is rapidly increasing in popularity. It's easy to set up a Gopher server, so anyone who has good information can do it. WAIS databases require high-powered computers, whereas a ten dollar shareware program from Australian programmer Peter Lewis enables someone to set up a Gopher server on a Macintosh (I've done it for some friends here in Seattle—it took about an hour all told). More than 1,500 Gopher servers exist today, and the information available on them ranges from Macintosh price lists at major universities (they often contain Apple's prices as well, making them useful for comparison even if you don't attend a university), Internet statistics, tech support information from Apple, and press releases from the U.S. government.

Finally, a vast amount of information is appearing on a daily basis on the World-Wide Web, a service created by CERN, the high-energy physics research lab in Switzerland. Other methods of providing information over the Internet have been pretty much restricted to text until the data is downloaded to a Mac or PC, but the World-Wide Web supports text with fonts, sizes, and styles; graphics within the text, sounds, animations, and movies; and all of it is interconnected with hypertext links. For many folks with information to provide to the Internet, the World-Wide Web is the only way to go. For instance, I've seen a beautiful collection of fractals (some even animated) on the Web, the University of California at Berkeley has made available a wonderful museum-style paleontology exhibit there, and a group called INFACT Online has an extensive Web server devoted to a campaign to stop tobacco companies from marketing cigarettes to children.

The Lemming Factor

Aside from the personal communications, the discussions on every imaginable subject (and some you'd never imagine), and the databases of information, the Internet is neat for yet another reason: It's what I sometimes call the "lemming factor." That is, if so many people from so many cultures and walks of life are connecting to the Internet, something has got to be there. Don't scoff; no one makes all these people log on every day and spend time reading discussion lists and sending email. People aren't forced to increase Internet traffic at a whopping rate of 15 percent per month. They use the Internet because they want to, and few people are happy when they lose Internet access for any reason. And as much as "lemming factor" may imply people are getting on Internet because their friends are, they aren't doing it from peer pressure (well, okay, so I hassled my parents into getting connected, but they love it now). People connect to Internet because it is becoming more than just an elite club of technoweenies—it has become a virtual community in and of itself.

The allure of the Internet sets it apart from other communities such as religious, charitable, or humanitarian groups. No implied theological punishment exists for avoiding the Internet, and although its attraction somewhat resembles that of volunteer groups such as the Red Cross, those organizations often depend on people's belief systems. The Internet continues to thrive because of the volunteer labor pumped into it; but also important is the fact that it provides as much information as an individual can handle, and in this day and age, information is power.

The Internet is What You Make of It

Whatever advantage you want to take of the Internet, remember two things: First, the information available on the Internet has generally avoided the processing introduced by the mass media. If you want some unfiltered opinions on both sides of any issue ranging from the death penalty to abortion to local taxes, people usually are discussing the issue at length somewhere on the net. Because of the lack of filtering, you may read a bit more about any one subject than you do in the mass media.

Second, you get only the information you want. For about a year, my wife and I followed a weekly routine with the Sunday *Seattle Times*. First, we'd compete for the comics and then for the *Pacific Magazine,* which has in-depth articles. Then we'd settle down: I'd read the sports section and the business section, and my wife proceeded to the Home & Garden section. Good little stereotypes, weren't we? The point is that I was completely uninterested in reading at least three-quarters of the two-inch thick stack of paper, and so was my wife. So why were we paying for the entire thing only to bring it home and recycle half? A good question, and one that newspaper publishers should get their duffs in gear and answer.

Tonya and I answered it by ceasing to bother with the Sunday paper most weeks. Not only was it a waste of paper resources, especially considering that we didn't read most of it, but it was a waste of time to flip through much of the parts that we did read. Instead, I've started getting most of the news I want on the Internet, through a combination of mailing lists and newsgroups that cover my interests closely. I can't get all the comics that I'd like to read yet, but *Dilbert* from Scott Adams, an Internet-only cartoon called *Dr. Fun,* and some of the *Slugs!* cartoons that my friend Dominic White drew for *Internet Explorer Kit for Macintosh,* have all appeared in recent months.

The same problem applies to junk mail. I instantly throw out about 90 percent of the *snail mail* (the Internet term for paper mail) I get, whereas almost all email I get is at least worth reading.

On the Internet, when all is said and done, I get only what I ask for. Periodically, my interests change so I switch things around, but I don't have to read, or even deal with, topics that either bore or irritate me—such as anything unpleasant happening in Northern Ireland or Beirut. Try avoiding such topics in the mass media. It's just not possible.

Now that I think of it, there's a third point I want to make about information on the Internet. Most of it, as I said, is free of media-processing. That's because most of the information comes from individuals and small groups rather than large publishing conglomerates that own hundreds of newspapers and maga-zines around the world. Even though I'm not going to tell you anything about how to set up an Internet machine to provide information over the Internet, be aware that you as an individual don't necessarily need your own machine. You could run a small mailing list from a Mac, and could easily post a newsletter or report of some sort to discussion lists without a dedicated machine. And, if what you want to do requires an FTP site or mainframe that can run mailing list software, ask around; someone might be willing to provide that sort of access to you. This is how I've published *TidBITS* for the last four years, so as long as you're providing useful information for free, you'd be surprised how many people may step forward to help you.

Champing at the Bit

I know you're all excited about the Internet now that you know why it is so neat. But, you're probably saying to yourself, "Self, it sure sounds like I can do lots of cool things on the Internet, but just what the heck is this Internet thing, any-way?" Glad you asked yourself that question because that's precisely what we will talk about next.

What Is the Internet?

What is the Internet? That question is tremendously difficult to answer because the Internet is so many things to so many different people. Nonetheless, you need a short answer to give your mother when she asks, so here goes:

The Internet consists of a mind-bogglingly huge number of participants, connected machines, software programs, and a massive quantity of information, spread all around the world.

Now, let's see if I can put those various parts into some kind of meaningful context.

Size

To say the Internet is big—in terms of people, machines, information, and geographic area included—is to put it mildly. How big is it? Let's take a look and see.

People

The Seattle Kingdome seats approximately 60,000 people for a sellout Seahawks football or Mariners baseball game (once-in-a-lifetime experiences for those teams). That's about the same number of people who read a single, mildly popular newsgroup on the Internet. If all 23 million people on the Internet were to get together, they'd need almost 400 stadiums, each the size of the Kingdome, to have a party. I could calculate how many times that number of people would reach to the moon and back if we stacked them one on top of another, but I think I've made my point.

Machines

In the infancy of the computer industry, IBM once decided that it did not need to get into the computer business because the entire world needed only six computers. Talk about a miscalculation! Many millions of computers of all sizes, shapes, and colors have been sold in the decades since IBM's incorrect assumption. An estimated 2.3 million of these (2,300,000 for those of you who like the digits) are currently connected to the Internet. I keep having trouble with these numbers since they change so frequently. In the first edition, I used 1.7 million computers as the basic number, but I had to change that at the last minute, since the manuscript I'd sent to Hayden used 1.3 million, the number from a few months before. When we published *Internet Starter Kit for Windows,* I updated the number to 2.2 million, and here I am, just a few months later, updating to 2.3 million.

Information

I can't pretend that the Internet offers more pieces of useful information than a good university library system, but that's only because a university has, in theory, a paid staff and funding for acquisitions and development. Information on the Internet is indeed vast, but finding your way around in it proves a daunting task. However, neither could I pretend that finding a given piece of information in a large research library would be any easier without the help of a skilled reference librarian.

Information on the Internet also changes and seems to appear more quickly than in a physical library, so you never know what's arrived since your last visit. Also, keep in mind that Internet information is more personal and fluid than the information in a library. Although you may not be able to look up something in a reference work on the Internet, you can get 10 personal responses (some useful, some not) to almost any query you pose.

Geographic Size

Explaining the geographic size of the Internet is difficult because, in many ways, messages traveling over the network connections don't give a hoot where they are going physically. Almost every industrialized nation (that's some 60 countries) has at least one machine on the Internet, and more countries come online all the time. But geographical distance means little on the net. For example, I mail issues of *TidBITS* to our mailing list on Monday night. People down the road from me find it in their mailboxes on Tuesday morning, as do subscribers in New Zealand and Norway (Norway apparently has the highest per-capita density of Internet machines). A friend described the Internet as ranging from Antarctica to the space shuttles, from submarines to battle tanks, from a guy riding a bicycle around the globe to others crossing oceans in a yacht, from kids in kindergarten to the most eclectic gathering of brains.... Well, you get the idea.

Perhaps the best way of wrapping your mind around the Internet is to recall the old joke about blind men all giving their impression of an elephant based on what they can feel. Like that elephant, the Internet is too large to understand in one mental gulp (see figure 3.1).

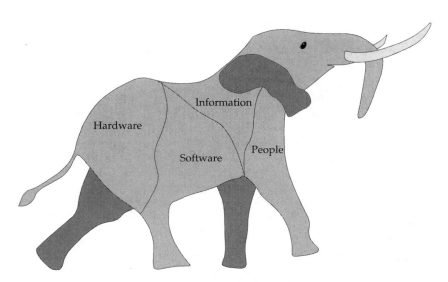

Figure 3.1   *The Internet Elephant*—Elephantidae **internetus**

Some people may think of the Internet in terms of the people that are on the net (this is my favorite way of looking at it). Technical people may insist that the machines and the networks that comprise the physical Internet are the crux of the matter. Software programmers may chime in that none of it works without software. Others may feel that the essence of the Internet lies in the information present on it.

In fact, all of these people are equally right, although as I said, I personally prefer to think of the Internet as millions of people constantly communicating about every topic under the sun. The amount and type of information, the hardware and software will all change, but the simple fact of people communicating will always exist on the Internet.

People—Doing What They Do Best

The most important part of the Internet is the collection of many millions of people, *homo sapiens*, all doing what people do best. No, I don't mean reproducing, I mean communicating.

Communication is central to the human psyche; we are always reaching out to other people, trying to understand them and trying to get them to understand us. As a species, we can't shut up. But that's good! Only by communicating can we ever hope to solve the problems that face the world today. The United Nations can bring together one or two representatives of each nation and sit them down with simultaneous translations. But via the wire and satellite transmissions of the Internet, anyone can talk to anyone else on the Internet at any time—no matter where they live.

I regularly correspond with friends (most of whom I've never met) in England, Ireland, France, Italy, Sweden, Denmark, Turkey, Russia, Japan, New Zealand, Australia, Singapore, Taiwan, Canada, and a guy who lives about 15 miles from my house. (Actually, my wife and I finally broke down and went to visit the guy down the road, and he's since become one of our best friends in Seattle.) I've worked on text-formatting issues over the networks with my friend in Sweden, helped design and test a freely distributable program written by my friend in Turkey, and co-wrote software reviews with a friend in New Zealand, who'd been one of my Classics professors back at Cornell. On the net, where everything comes down to the least common denominator of ASCII text, you don't worry about where your correspondents live. Although people use many languages on the net, English is the de facto language of the computer industry, and far more people in the world know English than English speakers know other languages.

During the Gulf War, while people in the U.S. were glued to their television sets watching the devastation, people in Israel were sending reports to the net. Some of these described the terror of air raid sirens and worrying about SCUD missiles launched from Iraq. No television shot of a family getting into their gas masks with an obligatory sound bite can compare with the lengthy and tortured accounts of daily life that came from the Israeli net community.

The Internet also helped disseminate information about the attempted coup in the former Soviet Union that led to its breakup. One Internet friend of mine, Vladimir Butenko, spent the nights during the events near the Parliament. When everything seemed to be clear, he went to his office, wrote a message about what he'd seen, and sent it to the Internet. His message was widely distributed at the time and even partially reprinted in the *San Jose Mercury News*.

Although people on the Internet are sometimes argumentative and contentious, is that entirely bad? Let's face it, not all the events in the world are nice, and people often disagree, sometimes violently. In the real world, people may repress their feelings to avoid conflict, and repression isn't good. Or people may end up at the other extreme where the disagreement results in physical violence. On the Internet, no matter what the argument (be it about religion, racism, abortion, the death penalty, the role of police in society, or whatever else), there are only three ways for it to end. First, and mostly likely, all parties involved may simply stop arguing through exhaustion. Second, both sides may agree to disagree (although this usually only happens in arguments where both sides are being rational about the issues at hand). Third, one person may actually convince another that he is wrong; though I doubt this happens all that often since people hate to admit they're wrong. But notice, in none of these possibilities is someone punched, knifed, or shot. As vitriolic as many of these arguments, or flame wars, can be, there's simply no way to compare them to the suffering that happens when people are unable to settle their differences without resorting to violence.

Most of the time on the net, an incredible sense of community and sharing transcends all physical and geopolitical boundaries. How can we attempt to understand events in other parts of the world when we, as regular citizens, have absolutely no clue what the regular citizens in those other countries think or feel? And what about the simple facts of life such as taxes and government services? Sure, the newspapers print those info-graphics comparing our country's tax burden to that in other countries. But this information doesn't have the same effect as listening to someone work out how much some object, say a Macintosh, costs in France once you take into account the exchange rate and add an 18 percent VAT (value added tax), which of course comes on top of France's already-high income taxes. It makes you think.

If nothing else, that's the tag line I want to convey about the Internet. It makes you think.

Maybe with a little thought and communication, we can avoid some of the violent and destructive conflicts that have marked world affairs. Many of the Internet resources stand as testaments to the fact that people *can* work together with no reward other than the satisfaction of making something good and useful. If we can translate more of that sense of volunteerism and community spirit back into the real world, we stand a much better chance of surviving ourselves.

Hardware

Getting down to the technical data, more than 2.3 million computers of all sizes, shapes, and colors make up the hardware part of the Internet. In addition to the computers are various types of network links, ranging from super-fast *T-1* and *T-3* lines all the way down to slow 2,400 bps modems. T-3 was also the code name for Microsoft Word 6.0—but I digress. That often happens when I'm talking about relatively boring things like networks, because what's important is that the Internet works. Just as with your telephone, you rarely notice its technical side unless something goes wrong.

Computers

The computers that form the Internet range from the most powerful supercomputers from Cray and IBM all the way down to your friendly local Macintosh and garden-variety PC clone. You can split these machines into two basic types: *host* computers and *client* computers. Host computers are generally the more powerful of the two and usually have more disk space and faster connections. Although, I don't want to imply that host machines must be fancy, expensive computers; Apple's popular FTP site at one point ran on an aging Mac II (however, it did use Apple's implementation of Unix, called A/UX).

Similarly, client machines can also be large, powerful workstations from companies like Sun and Hewlett-Packard. Because their task of sending and receiving information for a single person (as opposed to many people) is more limited, clients generally require less processor power and storage space than host machines. Basically, it can be a waste to use a $10,000 Unix workstation as an Internet client (although they can make great client machines, if you have the money to throw around). In my opinion, microcomputers—Macs in particular—make the best clients. Why spend lots of money and a large amount of configuration time when an inexpensive, simple-to-set-up Macintosh does the job as well or better?

I look only at client hardware and software in this book. The gritty details of setting up an Internet host and the many programs that run it aren't all that interesting to most people, not to mention the fact that I haven't the foggiest idea of how to configure a Unix workstation to be an Internet host. I'll leave those tasks to the wonderful people who are already doing them. (First rule of the Internet: Be extremely nice to your system administrator.) If you want to get into the administration end of things, O'Reilly & Associates publishes a long line of books on Unix and network administration.

Note

You don't absolutely need to use Unix on an Internet host, and in fact you can run an FTP, Gopher, or World-Wide Web server on a Mac with no trouble. But this setup requires a fast and constant connection to the Internet, and again, I'm aiming this book more at users of Internet information, not information provider wanna-bes. Maybe the next book.

Networks

In basic terms, two computers attached together form a *local area network*, and as that network grows, it may become connected to other independent local area networks. That configuration is called an *internet*, with a small *i*. The Internet, with a capital *I*, is the largest possible collection of inter-connected networks. I could spill the gory details of what networks are connected to the Internet and whether they are true parts of the Internet (as defined by using a set of *protocols* called *TCP/IP*, or Transmission Control Protocol/Internet Protocol, the language that Internet machines speak), but that information wouldn't be very useful to you.

Note

An Internet old-timer once commented that "Internet" technically only applies to machines using TCP/IP protocols. He said the term once proposed for the collection of all the interconnected networks, no matter what protocols they used, was "WorldNet." That term seems to have faded into obscurity—unfortunately, since it's rather apt. Common usage now includes "Internet" (the safest term, though it's technically inaccurate), "the net" (sometimes capitalized), and "cyberspace" (a heavily overused term from William Gibson's science-fiction novel Neuromancer, *which, ironically enough, he wrote on a manual typewriter with images of video games, not the Internet, in his head). Lately, the term "information superhighway" (an unfortunate term that has spawned imagery of toll booths, speed bumps, on-ramps, and road kill, but which means almost nothing in the context in which it's generally used) is in vogue.*

Worrying about the specific protocol details is generally pointless these days because many machines speak multiple languages and exist on multiple networks. For instance, my host machine speaks both TCP/IP as an Internet client and *UUCP* (Unix to Unix CoPy) as a UUCP host. My old machine at Cornell existed in both the Internet and in the BITNET worlds. The distinctions are technical and relatively meaningless to the end user.

Modems and Phone Lines

For most people using a microcomputer such as a Macintosh, a *modem* generally makes the necessary link to the Internet. Modem stands for modulator-demodulator (glad you asked?), and it enables your computer to monopolize your phone, much like a teenager. You may not need a modem if you study or work at an institution that has its local area networks attached to the Internet. If you are at such a site, count yourself lucky and ignore the parts of this book that talk about finding connections and using the modem. But remember those sections exist; one day you may leave those connections behind, and nothing is more pitiful than someone pleading on the nets for information on how to stay connected after graduation.

Certain new types of connections, including high-speed ISDN (Integrated Services Digital Network) may be the death of the modem as we know it. However, even ISDN connections require a box called a terminal adapter to enable the computer to appropriately pass data over the ISDN lines. In addition, even for folks with normal telephone line connections to the Internet, the modem itself may fade into the background—or rather, into the innards of the computer. It's already possible to almost completely emulate a modem in software on Apple's Macintosh 660AV, 840AV, and Power Macintosh computers. Eventually, wireless modems may become common, so the details of making a connection may fade away entirely. Or at least that's what I hope happens.

Note

In a exaggerated show of acronym making, normal phone service is known as POTS, or Plain Old Telephone Service. Don't the people who came up with this stuff have anything better to do with their time?

It's beyond the scope of this book to tell you what sort of modem to buy, but most reputable modem manufacturers make fine modems with long or lifetime warranties. Some companies sell extremely cheap modems which often work well in most cases, but you may also get what you pay for.

Note

I don't want to bash specific manufacturers, but many Macintosh users have had good luck with modems from Supra and Global Village, and I personally have owned modems from Telebit and Practical Peripherals. Apple's Express Modem can be a bit flaky at times, but it's one of only two choices for the PowerBook Duos (Global Village makes the more-expensive PowerPort/Mercury Duo).

Suffice it to say that you want the fastest standard modem you can lay your hands on, and as of this writing, the fastest standard means that you want a modem with the magic word *v.32bis* stamped prominently on its box. That word, which says that the modem supports a certain standard method of transmitting information, ensures that your modem talks to most other modems at a high rate of speed, generally 14,400 bits per second (bps). (This speed, although fast for a modem, doesn't even approach that of a local area network [the standard LocalTalk networking built into every Macintosh runs at 230,000 bps].)

Modem manufacturers often make claims about maximum throughput being 57,600 bps, but real speeds vary based on several variables such as phone line quality and the load on the host. Modems never (well, almost never) reach the promised maximum speed. The main point to keep in mind is that it takes two to tango; the modem on either end of a connection drops to the slowest common speed (usually 2,400 bps) if they don't speak the same protocols. Just think of this situation as my trying to dance with Ginger Rogers—there's no way she and I could move as quickly as she and Fred Astaire did.

Note

You may see such terms as v.34, v.fast, and v.terbo (or v.turbo), but remember what I said about needing two to tango. If your provider doesn't use modems that also support these new semi-standards, there's no point in worrying about anything beyond v.32bis for right now.

Actually, there are more caveats to the modem question than I'd like to admit. Modems work by converting digital bits into analog waves that can travel over normal phone lines, and—on the other end—translating those waves back into bits. Translation of anything is an inherently error-prone process, as you know if you've ever managed to make a fool of yourself by trying to speak in a foreign language.

A large percentage of the problems I've seen people have since the first edition of this book came out, were related to their modems. Modem troubles are exacerbated by the fact that modem manuals are, without a doubt, the worst excuse for technical writing that I've ever seen. They're confusing, poorly written, poorly organized, and usually concentrate on the commands that the modem understands without providing any information as to what might go wrong. So, as much as I'd like to pretend that modems are all compatible, and that setting one up to communicate with an Internet host is a simple process, it might not work right away. If you encounter problems after first checking all the settings to make sure you've done everything right, you should check the settings in your modem manual; see whether they match the settings you can get if you ask the people who run the machine to which you connect.

I can't tell you how unhappy I am to have written that last paragraph, but it's just how the world is. You probably didn't get a driver's license without passing a written test, practicing with an adult, taking Driver's Ed, and finally passing a practical test. Perhaps more apt, you probably weren't able to find anything in a school library until one of the teachers or librarians showed you around. If your modem works on the first try, great! If not, don't get depressed—not everything in this life is as easy as it should be. If it were, we'd have world peace.

Anyway, modems connect to phone lines, of course, and residential phone lines are generally self-explanatory, although at some point you may want to get a second line for your modem. Otherwise, those long sessions reading news or downloading the latest and greatest shareware can irritate loved ones who want to speak with you. (Of course, those sessions also keep telemarketers and loquacious acquaintances off your phone.) I also thoroughly enjoy being able to search the Internet for a file, download it, and send it to a friend who needs it, all while talking to him on the phone.

Not all telephone lines are created equal, and you may find that yours suffers from *line noise*, which is static on the line caused by any number of things. Modems employ error correction schemes to help work around line noise, but if it's especially bad, you may notice your modem slowing down as it attempts to compensate for all the static. When it's really bad, or when someone induces line noise by picking up an extension phone, your modem may just throw up its little modem hands and hang up on you. You can complain to the phone company about line noise; as I understand it, telephone lines must conform to a certain level of quality for voice transmissions. Unfortunately, that level may not be quite good enough for modems, especially in outlying rural areas, but if you're persnickety enough, you can usually get the phone company to clean up the lines sufficiently.

Note

If you connect from home and order a second line from your phone company, don't be too forthcoming about why you want the second line. Business rates are higher than residential rates, although they provide no additional quality or service. Some phone companies are sticky about using modems for non-business purposes, which is why this point is worth mentioning. If you connect to the Internet from your office, there's no way around this situation.

Software

As for the software, the programs that probably come to your mind first are the freeware and shareware files stored on the Internet for downloading—things such as games, utilities, and full-fledged applications. I'll let you discover those files for yourself though, and concentrate on the software available for connecting to the Internet, much of which is free. Other programs are shareware or commercial, although most don't cost much. I'll talk about pretty much every piece of software I know about for connecting to the Internet in Part III of this book. Although there's no way for the book's discussion to keep up with the rate at which new and updated programs appear, I provide the latest versions of all the freeware and shareware programs on my file site, `ftp.tidbits.com`. Don't worry about the details now—I'll get to them later in the book.

For the time being though, I want to hammer home a few key points to help you understand, on a more "gut" level, how this setup all works. First, the Internet machines run software programs all the time. When you use electronic mail, Telnet, or most anything else, you are actually using a software program, even if it doesn't seem like it. That point is important because as much as you don't need to know the details, I don't want to mystify the situation unnecessarily. The Internet, despite appearances, is not magic.

Second, because it takes two to tango on the Internet (speaking in terms of host and client machines), a software program is always running on both sides of the connection. Remember the client and host distinctions for machines? That's actually more true of the software, where you generally change the term *host* to the term *server*, which gives the broader term *client/server computing*. So, when you run a program on the Mac, say something like Fetch (an FTP client that retrieves files), it must talk to the FTP server program that is running continually on the remote machine. The same is true no matter what sort of connection you have. If you're using a Unix command-line account and you run a program called Lynx to browse the World-Wide Web, Lynx is a client program that communicates with one or more World-Wide Web servers on other machines.

Note

Think of a dessert cart filled with luscious pastries. You're not allowed to get your grubby hands on the food itself, so the restaurant provides a pair of dessert tongs that you must use to retrieve your choice of desserts. That's exactly how client/ server computing works. The dessert cart is the server—it makes the data, the desserts in this example, available to you, but only via the client program, the dessert tongs. Hungry yet?

Third, FTP and Fetch are the high-level programs that you interact with, but low-level software also handles the communications between Fetch and an FTP server. This communication at multiple levels is how the Internet makes functions understandable to humans and still efficient for the machines, two goals that seldom otherwise overlap.

So, if you can cram the idea into your head that software makes the Internet work on both a high level that you see and a low level that you don't, you'll be much better off. Some people never manage to understand that level of abstraction, and as a result, they never understand anything beyond how to type the magic incantations they have memorized. Seeing the world as a series of magic incantations is a problem because people who do so are unable to modify their behavior when anything changes, and on the Internet, things change every day.

Information

More so than any other human endeavor, the Internet is an incredible, happy accident. Unlike the library at Alexandria (the one that burned down) or the Library of Congress, the Internet's information resources follow no master plan (although the Library of Congress, as do many other large university and public libraries, has its catalog and some of its contents on the Internet). No one works as the Internet librarian, and any free information resources that appear can just as easily disappear if the machine or the staff go away. And yet, resources stick around; they refuse to die—in part because when the original provider or machine steps down, someone else generally feels that the resource is important enough to step in and take over.

Andy Williams at Dartmouth, for instance, runs a mailing list devoted to talking about scripting on the Macintosh, specifically about AppleScript and Frontier (an Apple event-based scripting program from UserLand Software). Andy also originally made sample scripts and other files pertaining to Frontier available, but he was not able to keep up with the files and still do his real job (a common problem). Luckily, Fred Terry at the University of Kansas quickly stepped in and offered to provide a Frontier file site because he was already storing files related to two other Macintosh programs, QuicKeys and Nisus. (Fred also rescued the Nisus mailing list when Brad Hedstrom, the list creator and administrator, had to bow out, and Fred's probably a sucker for stray dogs too.) Fred felt that keeping the information available on the Internet was important, and the sacrifice was sufficiently small that he was able do it.

Just to fill in more of the story, Fred was actually running a list about AppleScript on his site, along with lists about QuicKeys and Nisus, and when it became clear that discussions about scripting on the Macintosh overlapped both the AppleScript and the Frontier list, Fred and Andy got together and created that single list at Dartmouth, today's MacScripting list.

Andy's something of a sucker for resources in need of a home, as well. When a man named Bill Murphy came up with a method of translating our issues of *TidBITS* into a form suitable for display on the World-Wide Web, he ran into the problem of not having a sufficiently capable machine to provide that information to the Internet community. Who should step in but Andy, who offered the use of a World-Wide Web server that he runs at Dartmouth. Between Bill's and Andy's selfless volunteer efforts, the Internet had yet another information resource for anyone to use.

These are just a few examples of the way information can appear on the Internet. Damming the Internet's flow of information would be harder than damming the Amazon with toothpicks. In fact, some of the Internet's resiliency is due to the way the networks themselves were constructed, but we'll get into that later on. Next, let's look at the main ways information is provided on the Internet.

The Internet Post Office

You can think of an Internet host machine as a post office, a rather large post office in a large metropolitan area. In that post office, huge quantities of information are dispensed every day, but it doesn't just gush out the front door. No, you have to go inside, sometimes wait in line, and then go to the appropriate window to talk to the proper clerk to get the information you want. You don't necessarily pick up mail that's been held for you at the same window as you purchase a money order. Internet information works in much the same way. But on an Internet host, instead of windows, information flows through virtual ports (they're more like two-way television channels than physical SCSI ports or serial ports). A port number is, as I said, like a window in the post office—you must go to the right window to buy a money order, and similarly, you must connect to the right port number to run an Internet application. Luckily, almost all of this happens behind the scenes, so you seldom have to think about it. See table 1.1 for a list of some common port numbers.

Table 1.1
A Few Common Port Numbers

Port Number	Description
20, 21	File Transfer Protocol (data on 20, control on 21)
23	Telnet
25	Simple Mail Transfer Protocol
53	Domain Name Server
70	Gopher
79	Finger
80	World-Wide Web
110	Post Office Protocol - Version 3
119	Network News Transfer Protocol
123	Network Time Protocol
194	Internet Relay Chat Protocol

Note

I found this information in RFC (Request for Comment) 1340 via Gopher at **is.internic.net**. *All of the RFCs that define Internet standards are stored there, should you want more technical information about how parts of the Internet work at their lowest levels.*

So, in our hypothetical Internet post office, there are seven main windows that people use on a regular basis. There are, of course, hundreds of other windows, usually used by administrative programs or other things that people don't touch much, but we won't worry about them. The main parts to worry about are email, Usenet news, Telnet, FTP, WAIS, Gopher, and the World-Wide Web. Each provides access to different sorts of information, and most people use one or more to obtain the information they need.

Now that I've said how they're all similar, in the sense of all working through connections to the proper ports, there are some distinctions we must make between the various Internet services.

Email and Usenet news (along with MUDs and Internet Relay Chat) are forms of interpersonal communication—there is always a sender and a recipient. Depending on the type of email message or news posting, you can use different analogies to the paper world, and I'll get to those in a moment.

All of the information made available through other main parts of the Internet such as Telnet, FTP, WAIS, Gopher, and the World-Wide Web, is more like information in libraries than interpersonal communication, in the sense that you must visit the library specifically, and once there, browse or search through the resources to find a specific piece of information. These services have much more in common with traditional publishing than email and news do.

Note

I should note that, in my eyes, the difference between browsing and searching is merely that when you're browsing, you're not looking for a specific piece of information. Perhaps you only want some background, or simply want to see what's out there. When you're searching, you usually have a particular question that you want answered.

No matter what you use, there is still some sort of communication of information going on. With email and news, it's generally informal and between individuals, whereas with the rest of the Internet services, the information is usually more distilled—that is, someone has selected and presented it in a specific format and in a specific context. None of these distinctions are hard and fast, and much informal information is available via Gopher, for instance. It's certainly easy enough to find distilled information via email. I'll try to give you a sense of what each service is good for when talking about them later on.

Electronic Mail

Email is used by the largest number of people on the Internet, although in terms of traffic, the heaviest volumes lie elsewhere. Almost all people who consider themselves connected to the Internet in some way can send and receive email.

As I said above, most personal exchanges happen in email since email is inherently an interpersonal form of communication. All of your email comes into your electronic mailbox, and unless you let them, no one else can easily read your mail. When you get a message from a friend via email, it's not particularly different than getting that same message, printed out and stuffed in an envelope, via snail mail. Sure, it's faster and may have been easier to send, but in essence, personal email is just like personal snail mail.

Because it's trivial to send the same piece of email to multiple people at once, you can also use email much as you would use snail mail in conjunction with a photocopy machine. If you write up a little personal newsletter about what's happening in your life and send it to all the relatives at Christmas, that's the same concept as writing a single email message and addressing it to multiple people. It's still personal mail, but just a bit closer to a form letter.

The third type of email is carried on *mailing lists*. Sending a submission to a mailing list is much like writing for a user group or alumni newsletter. You may not know all of the people who will read your message, but it is a finite (and usually relatively small) group of people who share your interests. Mailing list messages aren't usually aimed at a specific person on the list, but are more intended to discuss a topic of interest to most of the people who have joined that list. However, I don't want to imply that posting to a mailing list is like writing an article for publication, since the content of most mailing lists more resembles the editorial page of a newsletter than anything else. You'll see opinions, rebuttals, diatribes, questions, comments, and even a few answers. Everyone on the list sees every posting that comes through, and the discussions often become quite spirited.

The fourth type of email most resembles those "bingo cards" that you find in the back of many magazines. Punch out the proper holes or fill in the appropriate numbered circle, return the card to the magazine, and several weeks later you'll receive the advertising information you requested. For instance, I've set up my

Macintosh to send an informational file about *TidBITS* automatically to anyone in the world who sends email to a certain address (**info@tidbits.com**, if you're impatient and want to try something right away). A number of similar systems exist on the Internet, dispensing information on a variety of subjects to anyone who can send them email. A variant of these auto-reply systems is the *mailserver* or *fileserver*, which generally looks at the Subject line in the letter or at the body of the letter and returns the requested file. Mailservers enable people with email-only access to retrieve files that otherwise are available only via FTP.

Usenet News

Like email-based discussion lists, Usenet news is interpersonal information—it comes from individuals and is aimed at thousands of people around the world. Unlike email, even unlike mailing lists, you cannot find out who makes up your audience. Because of this unknown audience, posting a message to Usenet is more like writing a letter to the editor of a magazine or major metropolitan newspaper with hundreds of thousands of readers. We have ways of estimating how many people reach each of the thousands of Usenet groups, but the estimates are nothing more than statistical constructs (though hopefully accurate ones).

Almost everything on Usenet is a discussion of some sort, although a few groups are devoted to regular information postings, with no discussion allowed. The primary difference between Usenet news and mailing lists is that news is more efficient because each machine receives only one copy of every message. If two users on the same machine (generally multi-user mainframes or workstations at this point) read the same discussion list via email, getting the same information in news is twice as efficient. If you have a large mainframe with 100 people all reading the same group, news suddenly becomes 100 times as efficient because the machine stores only the single copy of each message, rather than each individual receiving her own copy.

In many ways, Usenet is the kitchen table of the Internet—the common ground where no subject is taboo and you must discuss everything before implementing it. In great part because of the speed at which Usenet moves (messages appear quickly and constantly, and most machines don't keep old messages for more than a week due to lack of disk space), finding information there can be difficult. Think of Usenet as a river, and you must dip in to see what's available at a specific point in time because that information may disappear downstream within a few days.

Note

The speed at which messages disappear from Usenet varies by group and by the machine you use. Each administrator sets how long messages in a group will last before being expired (deleted) from the system. Messages in newsgroups with many postings per day may expire after a day or two; messages in groups with only a few postings per week may last a month. Since Usenet traffic is about 50M of information each day, you can see why short expiration times are essential.

You can, of course, always ask your own question, and you usually get an answer (though it may be one you don't like), even if it's the sort of question everyone asks. Common questions are called Frequently Asked Questions, or *FAQs*, and are collected into lists and posted regularly for newcomers. Luckily, the cost of disk storage is decreasing sufficiently so that some people and organizations are starting to archive Usenet discussions. These enable you to use WAIS or Gopher to go back and search for information that flowed past in a mailing list or newsgroup a long time ago.

Telnet

Telnet is a tough thing to describe. The best analogy I can think of is that Telnet is like an Internet modem. As with a standard modem, Telnet enables your computer to communicate with another computer somewhere else. Where you give your modem a phone number to dial, you give Telnet an Internet address to connect to. And just like a modem, you don't really do anything within Telnet itself other than make the connection—in the vernacular, you *telnet* to that remote computer. Once that connection is made, you're using the remote computer over the Internet just as though it were sitting next to you. This process is cool because it enables me to telnet to the mainframes at Cornell University, for example, and use them just as I did when I was actually in Ithaca, not 3,000 miles away in Seattle.

Note

Telnet, FTP, and Gopher can all work as nouns describing the service or the protocols, and as verbs describing the actions you perform with them. If Telnet or Gopher is capitalized in this book, it's a noun describing the service; if it's in lowercase, it's a verb describing the action. (FTP is always capitalized in the book, since it's an acronym.) Unfortunately, others on the Internet aren't as consistent (and they don't have editors checking their text) so this isn't a universal convention.

I realize I'm supposed to talk about information in this section, but Telnet is such a low-level protocol that it's impossible to separate the information that's available via Telnet from the protocol itself.

Most people don't have personal accounts on machines around the world (and I never use the Cornell mainframes any more), but a number of organizations have written special programs providing useful information that anyone can run over the Internet via Telnet.

Say I want to search for a book that's not in my local library system. I can connect via Telnet to a machine that automatically runs the card catalog program for me. I can then search for the book I want, find out which university library has it, and then go back to my local library and ask for an inter-library loan.

Or, for a more generically useful example, if you telnet to **downwind.sprl.umich.edu**, you reach the University of Michigan's Weather Underground server, with gobs of data about the weather around the entire country.

Note

Sure you could telnet to the Weather Underground. Or, if you have a MacTCP-connection to the Internet, you could download the fascinating Blue Skies application and get a graphical interface that makes the weather a lot more interesting. See the chapter about MacTCP-based software for details about Blue Skies.

File Transfer Protocol (FTP)

FTP feels like it's related to Telnet, but in fact that's an illusion—the two are basic protocols on the Internet, but are not otherwise related. Where Telnet simply enables you to connect to another remote computer and run a program there, FTP enables you to connect to a remote computer and transfer files back and forth. It's really that simple.

More data is transferred via plain old FTP than by any other method on the Internet, and it's not surprising since it's a least-common denominator that almost every machine on the Internet supports. Like Telnet, you must be directly connected to the Internet while using FTP, although there are a few special FTP-by-mail services that enable you to retrieve files stored on FTP sites by sending specially formatted email messages to an FTP-by-mail server.

There are probably millions of files available via FTP on the Internet, although you may discover that many of them are duplicates because people tend to want to give users more than one way to retrieve a file. If a major file site goes down for a few days, it's nice to have a *mirror site* that has exactly the same files and can take up the slack.

Note

Mirror sites are important because as the Internet grows, individual machines become overloaded and refuse to accept new connections. As with anything that's busy (like the phone lines on Mother's Day, the checkout lines at 5:00 P.M. on Friday afternoons at the grocery store, and so on) it always seems that you're the one who gets bumped or who has to try over and over again to get through. Don't feel special—hundreds of other people suffer exactly the same fate all the time. Mirror sites help spread the load.

In the Macintosh world, several sites with lots of disk space (several gigabytes, actually) store a tremendous number of freeware and shareware programs along with commercial demos and other types of Macintosh information. If you think your local BBS has many files, wait until you see the two main file sites for the Mac, `mac.archive.umich.edu` and the Info-Mac site at `sumex-aim.stanford.edu`. The file that lists the names of all the files stored in the Info-Mac archive is 323K alone (as of early May), and contains listings for almost 6,300 files. I would estimate that between 20 and 50 new files appear in the Info-Mac archive every week—certainly enough to keep you busy if you enjoy exploring freeware and shareware software for the Macintosh.

The vastness of the number of files stored on FTP sites may stun you, but you have access to a tool that helps bring FTP under control. *Archie* takes the grunt work out of searching numerous FTP sites for a specific file. You ask Archie to find files with a specific keyword in their names, and Archie searches its database of many FTP sites for matches. Archie then returns a listing to you, providing the full file names and all the address information you need to retrieve the file via FTP.

Note

If you have MacTCP access to the Internet, you can use Anarchie, an FTP and Archie client program for the Mac. Just ask Archie to find a file, and when the results come back, double-click on the file to retrieve it. And people complain about how hard the Internet is!

WAIS

I mentioned using WAIS to search for information about deforestation in the Amazon rainforest in the preceding chapter, but that's only the tip of the iceberg. WAIS originated from a company called Thinking Machines, but has now split off into its own company, WAIS, Inc. Using the tremendous processing power of Thinking Machines' Connection Machine supercomputer or another powerful computer, WAIS can quickly (usually under a minute) return a number of articles to English-language queries, sorted by the likelihood that they are relevant to your question. WAIS is limited only by the information that people feed into it.

Last I counted, there were more than 500 sources available for searching within topics as diverse as Buddhism, cookbooks, song lyrics, Supreme Court decisions, science fiction book reviews, and President Clinton's speeches. For all the sources on non-technical topics, I'm sure an equal number exist about technical topics in many fields.

Note

People talking about WAIS (pronounced "ways," I hear) tend to use the terms "source," "server," and "database" interchangeably, and so do I.

Perhaps the hardest part about WAIS is learning how to ask it questions. Even though you can use natural English queries, it takes your question quite literally, and only applies it to the selected sources. So, if you asked about deforestation in the Amazon rainforest while searching in the Buddhism source, I'd be surprised if you found anything. Perhaps the most generically useful server is the Connection-Machine server, which includes the 1990 CIA World Factbook, a few patents, some biology abstracts, the King James Version of the Bible, the NIH Guide to Grants and Programs, the PARIS manual for programming the Connection Machine, a number of public mailing lists including *TidBITS* and the Info-Mac Digest, and a couple of months of the *Wall Street Journal* (but the issues are old).

Gopher

Gopher, which originated with the Golden Gophers of the University of Minnesota, is an information browser along the same lines as FTP, but with significant enhancements for ease of use and flexibility. Numerous sites—more than 1,500 at last count—on the Internet run the host Gopher software, placing information in what are colloquially called *gopher holes*. When you connect to a Gopher site, you can search databases, read text files, transfer files, and generally navigate around the collection of gopher holes, which is itself called *Gopherspace*.

I find Gopher to be the most useful of the Internet services in terms of actually making information available that I need to answer specific questions. Part of the reason for my opinion is *Veronica*, and to a lesser extent *Jughead*, which enable you to search through Gopherspace as Archie enables you to search for files on anonymous FTP servers.

Note

Veronica *and* Jughead *were both named to match* Archie *(from the Archie comics), but Veronica's creators at the University of Nevada came up with an acronym as well—Very Easy Rodent-Oriented Net-wide Index to Computerized Archives. Jughead stands for Jonzy's Universal Gopher Hierarchy Excavation And Display. Glad you asked?*

Veronica searches through all of Gopherspace, which is useful, although badly phrased searches (Veronica doesn't use natural English, as WAIS does) can result in hundreds of results. Jughead searches a subset of Gopherspace and can thus be more accurate, though less comprehensive.

One of the special features of Gopher is that it provides access to FTP (and Archie) and WAIS, and can even run a Telnet program to provide access to resources only available via Telnet. Gopher can also work with other programs to provide access to special data types, such as pictures and sounds. When you double-click on a picture listing in Gopher, it downloads the file and then runs another program to display the picture. This sort of integration doesn't generally work all that well if all you have is Unix command-line access to the Internet.

World-Wide Web

When I wrote the first edition of this book, the World-Wide Web existed, but lacked a good client program on the Macintosh. I managed to write a paragraph or two about NCSA Mosaic, the *Web* browser that was officially released a few months after I finished the book, but there simply wasn't much I could check out on the Web at that point.

Note

You may see the World-Wide Web referred to as simply "the Web," "W3," or sometime as "WWW."

Everything about the Web has changed since then. It's become much, much larger, and the resources available on it have become incredibly diverse and far more useful.

The Web brings a couple of very important features to the Internet. First, unlike Gopher or anything else, it provides access to full fonts, sizes, and styles for text, and can include images onscreen with no special treatment. Sounds and movies are also possible, though often too large for many people to download and view. Second, the Web provides true hypertextual links between documents anywhere on the Web, not just on a single machine. For those unfamiliar with hypertext, it's a powerful concept that enables the reader to navigate flexibly through linked pieces of information. If you read a paragraph with a link promising more information about the topic, say results from last winter's Olympic Games, simply click on the link, and you'll see the results. It really is that simple, and the World-Wide Web is indeed the wave of the future for the Internet. Nothing touches it in terms of pure sexiness, although many Web servers that you see suffer from the same problem that many publications did after the Macintosh made desktop-publishing popular: they're designed by amateurs and are ugly as sin.

Summing Up

I've tried to answer one of the harder questions around, "What is the Internet?" The simple answer is that the Internet is a massive collection of people, machines, software programs, and data, spread all around the world and constantly interacting. That definition, and the explication I've provided about the various parts of the Internet elephant, should serve you well as we look next at the history of this fascinating beast.

The Internet Beanstalk

Unlike the Greek goddess Athena, the Internet did not spring from the head of some Zeusian computer scientist. It was formed by a process of relatively rapid accretion and fusion (but keep in mind that this industry is one in which computer power doubles every few years). In 1980, there were 200 machines on the Internet—that number is now more than 2.3 million. The grain of sand that formed the heart of this giant electronic pearl came from the U.S. Department of Defense (DoD) in 1969. I'm pleased to be older than the Internet, having been born in 1967, but I'm not enough older to talk authoritatively about world conditions at that time. So, please bear with my second-hand retelling.

Cold War Network

In the 1950s, the Russian Sputnik program humiliated the United States. To better compete in the space race, the U.S. space program (at the time under the auspices of the military) received major government funding. That funding came from the DoD under its Advanced Research Projects Agency (ARPA). In the early 1960s, the space program left the military to become NASA, but ARPA remained, and as with many government programs that have seemingly lost their reason to exist, so did its funding. What to do with the money?

The DoD was, at the time, the world's largest user of computers, so J.C.R. Licklider and others proposed that ARPA support large-scale basic research in computer science. ARPA didn't originally require that the research it supported be either classified or directly related to military applications, which left the door open for far-reaching research in many fields. In 1963, ARPA devoted a measly $5 to $8 million to its computer research, the Information Processing Technologies Office (IPTO), first under Licklider, and then subsequently under the 26-year-old Ivan Sutherland, who had developed an early (perhaps the earliest) graphics program at MIT. After Sutherland, a 32-year-old named Robert Taylor headed IPTO. Taylor managed to double IPTO's budget in a time when ARPA's overall budget was decreasing, and even admitted to diverting funds from military-specific projects to pure computer science.

Around this time, the ARPAnet (Advanced Research Projects Agency Network) got its start, connecting various computers around the country at sites performing research for ARPA. Computers were expensive, and sharing them was the only way to distribute the resources appropriately. Distribution of cost via networks proved to be an important force in the development of the Internet later on as well. Proponents like Taylor ensured the early survival of the fledgling ARPAnet when it was all too vulnerable to governmental whimsy.

In 1969, Congress got wind of what ARPA was up to, in terms of funding basic research with money from the defense budget. Three senators, including the still-active Edward Kennedy, pushed through legislation requiring that ARPA show that its programs were directly applicable to the military. In the process, ARPA's name changed to reflect its new nature; it became the Defense Advanced Research Projects Agency, or DARPA. (Years later, the name changed back to ARPA again, just to confuse the issue.) Bob Taylor became entangled in some unpleasant business reworking military computers in Saigon during the Vietnam War and left DARPA shortly thereafter. He was succeeded by Larry Roberts, who worked a large part in getting the then two-year-old ARPAnet up and running. Stewart Brand, founder of *The Whole Earth Catalog*, wrote at the time:

> At present some 20 major computer centers are linked on the two-year-old ARPA Net. Traffic on the Net has been very slow, due to delays and difficulties of translation between different computers and divergent projects. Use has recently begun to increase as researchers travel from center to center and want to keep in touch with home base, and as more tantalizing sharable resources come available. How Net usage will evolve is uncertain. There's a curious mix of theoretical fascination and operational resistance around the scheme. The

resistance may have something to do with reluctance about equipping a future Big Brother and his Central Computer. The fascination resides in the thorough rightness of computers as communication instruments, which implies some revolutions. (Stewart Brand, in *II Cybernetic Frontiers*, Random House, 1974)

So if DARPA had to justify the military applications of its research, what survived? Well, the ARPAnet did, and here's why: As leaders of the free world (pardon the rhetoric), we needed the latest and greatest methods of killing as many other people as possible. Along with *offensive* research must perforce come *defensive* research; even the DoD isn't so foolish as to assume we could wage a major war entirely on foreign soil. For this reason, the tremendous U.S. interstate highway system served double duty as distribution medium for tanks and other military hardware. Similarly, the Internet's precursor was both a utilitarian and experimental network. ARPAnet connected military research sites (hardware was expensive and had to be shared) and was an experiment in resilient networks that could withstand a catastrophe—including, in the imaginations of the DoD planners of the day, an atomic bomb.

Interestingly, the resiliency of the ARPAnet design, as carried down to the Internet, has led some to note that the Internet routes around censorship as it would route around physical damage. It's a fascinating thought, especially in regard to Stewart Brand's earlier comment about Big Brother. If anything, the Internet actually has served to reduce the threat of a Big Brother, because it makes communication between people so fluid and unrestricted. But, I anticipate myself.

Gateways

As a result of the machinations described previously, the Internet Protocol, or IP (the second half of TCP/IP) was created. Essentially, the point behind IP systems is that each computer knows of, or can determine, the existence of all the others and thus route packets of information to its destination via the quickest route. While doing this, they are able to take into account any section of the network that's been bombed out or has merely been cut by an over-enthusiastic telephone repairperson. This design turns out to work well; more importantly, it makes for an extremely flexible network. If your computer can get a properly addressed packet of information to a machine on the Internet, that machine will worry about how to deliver it, translating as necessary. That's the essence of a *gateway*—it connects two dissimilar networks, translating information so that it can pass transparently from one to the other.

In the early 1980s, the military began to rely more and more heavily on the ARPAnet for communication, but because the ARPAnet still connected a haphazard mix of research institutions, businesses doing defense work, and military sites, the military wanted its own network. And so the ARPAnet split in half, becoming the ARPAnet and the Milnet (Military Network). The ARPAnet continued to carry traffic for research sites, and even though the military now had its own Milnet, traffic passed between the ARPAnet and the Milnet by going through gateways.

The concept of gateways proved important in the history of the Internet. Alongside the development of the Internet came the development of a number of other, generally smaller, networks that used protocols other than IP, such as BITNET, JANET, and various others. These also included some like Usenet and CSNET that didn't care what protocols were used. These networks were regional or dedicated to serving certain types of machines or users.

Perhaps the largest driving force behind the Internet is that of the need to connect with other people and other networks. The grass is always greener on the other side of the fence, and gradually gateway sites sprung up so that email could pass between the different networks with ease.

Usenet

I'm going to take a brief break from the Internet itself, because at approximately the same time the ARPAnet split, a whole host of other networks came into being, probably the most interesting of which was Usenet, the User's Network.

Usenet started in 1979, when two graduate students at Duke decided to link several Unix computers together in an attempt to better communicate with the rest of the Unix community. The system they created included software to read news, post news, and transport news between machines. To this day, that simple model continues, but whereas once two machines were on Usenet, today there are hundreds of thousands. The software that transports and displays Usenet news now runs on not just Unix machines, but on almost every type of computer in use on the networks. The topics of discussion have blossomed from Unix into almost any conceivable subject—and many inconceivable ones. Like all the other network entities, Usenet quickly grew to be international in scope and size.

Unlike many of the other networks, Usenet truly grew from the bottom up, rather from the top down. Usenet was created by and for users, and no organization—commercial, federal, or otherwise—had a hand in it originally. In many ways, Usenet has provided much of the attitude of sharing that exists on the Internet today. In the past, you usually got a Usenet *feed* (that is, had another machine send news traffic to your machine) for free (other than your telephone charges) as long as you were willing to pass the feed on to someone else for free. Due to commercial pressures, the days of the free feeds are essentially no more, but the spirit of cooperation they engendered remains in much of what happens on the Internet.

I don't want to imply that Usenet is this happy, carefree network where everything is free and easy, because in many cases it's a noisy, unpleasant network that exists because of the utility of some of the information that it carries. Despite the attitude toward sharing, the survival of Usenet is due in large part to the resourcefulness of network administrators at major sites. Faced with mounting telephone charges for long distance calls between Usenet hosts, these administrators found a way to carry Usenet news over the TCP/IP-based Internet rather than just the previous modem-based UUCP connections. Thus, they prevented the costs of carrying Usenet from coming to the attention of the bean counters poised to strike unnecessary expenses from their budgets. The TCP/IP connections of the ARPAnet, and then the Internet, were already paid for. So, by figuring out how to carry Usenet over those lines, the network administrators managed to cut their costs, keep users happy, and save Usenet from itself in the process. In other words, Usenet may be an anarchy, but it wouldn't stand a chance without some occasional help from high places.

BITNET

Shortly after Usenet took its first faltering networked steps, Ira Fuchs of City University of New York and Gleydon Freeman of Yale University decided to network their universities using IBM's then-new NJE communications protocol. Although this protocol later expanded to support Digital Equipment's Vaxen running VMS and even some implementations of Unix, the vast majority of machines on BITNET (the "Because It's Time" network) have always been IBM mainframes. Fuchs and Freeman made their connection in the spring of 1981. BITNET grew rapidly, encompassing more than 100 organizations on 225 machines by 1984, and reaching the current level of 1,400 organizations in 49 countries around the world. Most BITNET sites are at universities, colleges, and other research institutions.

BITNET has always been a cooperative network; members pass traffic bound for other sites for free, and software developed by one has been made available to all. Unlike Usenet, however, BITNET developed an organizational structure in 1984. This took the form of an Executive Committee, made of up representatives of all the major nodes on the network. Also in 1984, IBM provided a large grant that provided initial funding for centralized network support services. This grant, coupled with the fact that most of the machines on BITNET were IBM mainframes, gave rise to the erroneous rumor that BITNET was an IBM network. In 1987, BITNET became a nonprofit corporation. In 1989, it changed its corporate name to CREN, the Corporation for Research and Educational Networking, when it merged its administrative organization with another of the parallel educational networks, CSNET (the Computer+Science Network). Today, BITNET is in something of a decline, due in large part to the nonstandard NJE protocol in an increasingly IP world.

NSFNET

The next big event in the history of the Internet was the creation of the high-speed NSFNET (National Science Foundation Network) in 1986. NSFNET was developed to connect supercomputer sites around the country. Because supercomputers are terribly expensive, the NSF could afford to fund only five (and even then they received some major financial help from companies like IBM). With this limited number, it made sense to network the supercomputers so that researchers everywhere could use them without traveling great distances. At first, the NSF tried to use the ARPAnet, but that attempt quickly became bogged down in bureaucracy and red tape.

The NSF therefore decided to build its own network. Merely connecting the five supercomputer sites wasn't going to help the vast majority of researchers, of course, so the NSF created (or used existing) regional networks that connected schools and research sites in the same area. Then those networks were connected to the NSFNET.

To quote from W.P. Kinsella's *Shoeless Joe,* "If you build it, they will come." Perhaps not surprisingly, once all of these networks were able to communicate with one another, the supercomputer usage faded into the background. Other uses, most notably email, became preeminent. One of the important features of the NSFNET was that the NSF encouraged universities to provide wide access to students and staff, so the population of and traffic on the net increased dramatically.

In 1987, the NSF awarded a contract to a group of companies to manage and upgrade the NSFNET. This group was made up of IBM, MCI, and Merit Network, which ran the educational network in Michigan. The group dealt with the massive increase in traffic by replacing the old lines with much faster connections.

Eventually, the NSFNET had entirely supplanted the ARPAnet, and in March of 1990, the ARPAnet was taken down for good, having played the starring role for

21 years. Similarly, another national network, CSNET, which had connected computer science researchers around the country, closed its electronic doors a year later, all of its traffic having moved to the faster NSFNET.

NREN

The NSFNET is all fine and nice, but in many ways it discriminated against "lower" education—two-year colleges, community colleges, and the much-maligned K–12 schools. To save the day, then-Senator Al Gore sponsored a bill, passed in December of 1991, called the "High-Performance Computing Act of 1991." Gore's legislation created a new network on top of (and initially using) the NSFNET. This new network is called the interim NREN, for National Research and Education Network. Along with providing even faster speeds when feasible (at which point the "interim" will go away), the NREN specifically targets grade schools, high schools, public libraries, and two- and four-year colleges. In working with the thousands of people who subscribe to *TidBITS*, I see a lot of email addresses, and it's clear to me that these educational institutions are joining the Internet in droves. A day rarely passes when I don't see something from someone whose address clearly labels him or her as a teacher at a grade school or even a student in a high school.

Alert readers probably have noticed that NREN looks a lot like CREN, and in fact, the acronyms are similar—with reason. CREN recognizes the need for an integrated National Research and Education Network. In fact, as the IBM-created NJE protocol gradually disappears in favor of the more powerful and popular IP, CREN has said it will disband, merge with NREN, or cooperate with it as appropriate—though only when NREN exists with access rules, funding, and usage policies that allow a clean transition. Currently, CREN feels that the interim NREN, the NSFNET, does not provide consistent policies regarding these issues. And, of course, what happens if commercial organizations end up running some large part of the NREN?

Who Pays?

Along with the NREN taking over the part of the Internet that was the NSFNET, more and more of the Internet is being created and run by commercial organizations. All a commercial provider has to do is to pay for its part of the network, just as universities pay for their connections and government departments pay for theirs. The difference is that, unlike universities or government organizations, commercial providers want to make money, or at least break even, so they in turn sell access to their machines or networks to other providers or to end users.

The gut reaction to the commercialization of the Internet from the old-timers (who remember when you could get a Usenet feed merely by asking) is often negative, but most people believe that the Internet must accept commercial traffic. In part, this response is true because the only alternative to accepting commercial traffic is actively rejecting it, and no one wants to sit around censoring the Internet, if that was even possible.

Commercialization also allows small organizations to create the equivalent of wide-area networks that previously only large businesses could afford. A company such as Microsoft can spend the money to install an international company network, but few companies are so large or so wealthy. Many may not need such an international network, but may need enhanced communications. Email can be a powerful medium for business communication, just as it is for personal communication. And, if transferring a file via FTP or email can save a few uses of an overnight courier, the connection can pay for itself in no time.

In addition, whereas in the past you had to work at a large business or university to gain Internet access, it has become far easier for an individual to get access without any such affiliation, although the costs are, of course, more obvious. Easier independent access couldn't have happened without increased participation by commercial interests.

The commercialization issue has another side. The U.S. government still runs the interim NREN, which is a large portion of the Internet and connects many of the major educational sites. As more commercial providers get into the business and see the massive interest in the Internet, they increasingly think that the government should turn the public portions of the Internet over to them. This thought has much support because the commercial providers could make money, which is what they want to do, and the government could save money, which is what many people want the government to do.

In fact, as I wrote the first edition of this book, an impassioned plea was zapping around the Internet. This plea, poorly worded and ambiguous, claims that the government is indeed proposing to sell off the Internet—lock, stock, and barrel—which, the message claims, may result in millions of people losing free Internet access. Coincidentally, as I write this second edition, another such message has just appeared, although this time from the Taxpayer Assets Project (TAP), a non-profit government-watch organization. The TAP letter claims the National Science Foundation is proposing to contract with four telephone companies to provide the high-speed Internet backbone, and—the claim continues—that usage-based pricing will appear on the Internet as a result, harming the Internet in the process. In an informal rebuttal posted to a Cornell mailing list, M. Stuart Lynn, currently the head of Cornell Information Technologies, noted that the Internet is a global network and some countries, such as New Zealand, already have usage-based pricing. So even if the NSFNET moved to usage-based pricing, most of the Internet wouldn't be affected. Stuart Lynn also commented that the federal subsidy is trivial to many institutions, and at Cornell is equivalent to two cans of beer per student per year. In other words, even if Cornell had to rely on a completely commercial network (which might or might not be usage-based), its costs would not change noticeably.

Note

It's worth noting that people like flat-rate fees for most things (telephone service and cable service come to mind), and most personal Internet accounts from commercial providers have been usage-based, with only a recent trend toward flat-rate service in the past year. I believe the increasing number of flat-rate SLIP and PPP accounts from various commercial providers was helped in part by the first edition of this book, with its flat-rate offer for SLIP access from Northwest Nexus. I'm unaware of any other widely available flat-rate accounts that predate the offer from Northwest Nexus. Of course, I could be wrong, but I like to think I had a positive influence.

Such dire warnings of impending Internet doom—some real, most not—appear every few months. It's difficult to determine which you should act on. My advice is: do nothing until you have sufficient facts to cause you to believe that the danger is indeed real. Regarding the government sell-out scare, no contact information or pointers to current legislation exist, which makes it hard to believe without more corroboration. The TAP claim seemed more serious until I saw Stuart Lynn's message discussing how this wouldn't affect Cornell (and presumably, many other institutions) at all.

The trick is to remember that someone always pays for the Internet. If you have a free Internet account thanks to your school, remember that the institution is paying for that connection and funding it in part from your tuition. If your workplace offers Internet access and doesn't limit your use of it, consider that a benefit of working there, along with retirement and health benefits. And an increasingly large number of people, like me, pay directly, usually somewhere between $5 and $30 per month. Sure beats cable television.

Remember how I previously said that the NSFNET was created to carry supercomputer traffic but soon found itself being used for all sorts of tasks? That's another basic principle to keep in mind about how the Internet is funded. The network links were created for a specific reason (supercomputer access), and because of that reason, the money necessary to create and maintain those links was allocated in various budgets. Thus, when traffic unrelated to the supercomputer access travels on the same network, it's piggy-backing on the lines that have already been paid for out of existing budgets. So it seems free, and as long as the ancillary traffic doesn't impinge on the supercomputer access, no one is likely to complain. It's much like using your friend's Mac's processing power to generate processor-intensive pictures when he's not using his Mac. As long as your use doesn't slow down the things he wants to do, he probably won't mind, especially if it helps you finish your work sooner. But, if your use prevents him from doing his own work, he'll probably become less generous about it.

So, if the Internet did indeed move from governmental to private control, most people would not see the difference because their organizations would continue to foot the bill, especially if the costs didn't change. The danger is to poorly funded organizations such as grade schools and public libraries, which may only be able to afford their Internet connections with help from the government. Oh, and where do you think the government gets the money? Taxes, of course. So you end up paying one way or another.

Politics

After all of this discussion, you're probably confused as to who runs what on the Internet. Good, that's the way it should be, because no one person or organization runs the Internet as such. I think of the Internet as a collection of fiefdoms that must cooperate to survive. The fiefdoms are often inclusive as well, so one group may control an entire network, but another group controls a specific machine in that network. You, as a user, must abide by what both of them say, or find another host.

I don't mean to say that there aren't some guiding forces. The NSF exercised a certain influence over much of the Internet because it controlled a large part of it in the NSFNET. Thus, the NSF's Acceptable Use Policies (which state that the NSFNET may not be used for "commercial activities") became important rules to follow, or at least keep in mind, and I'll bet that many commercial providers used them as a starting point for creating their own less restrictive, acceptable use policies.

Several other important groups exist, all of which are volunteer-based (as is most everything on the Internet). The Internet Architecture Board, or IAB, sets the standards for the Internet. Without standards, the Internet wouldn't be possible, because so many types of hardware and software exist on it. Although you must be invited to be on the IAB, anyone can attend the regular meetings of the Internet Engineering Task Force, or IETF. The IETF's meetings serve as a forum to discuss and address the immediate issues that face the Internet as a whole. Serious problems, or rather problems that interest a sufficient number of volunteers, result in working groups that report back to the IETF with a recommendation for solving the problem. This system seems haphazard, but frankly, it works, which is more than you can say for certain other organizations we could probably name.

Other networks undoubtedly have their controlling boards as well, but the most interesting is Usenet, which has even less organization than the Internet as a whole. Due to its roots in the user community, Usenet is run primarily by the community, as strange as that may sound. Every network administrator controls what news can come into her machine but can't control what goes around her machine. The converse applies as well—if a sufficient number of network administrators don't approve of something, say a newsgroup creation, then it simply doesn't happen. Major events on Usenet must have sufficient support from a sufficient number of people.

Of course, some people's votes count more than others. These people are sometimes called *net heavies* because they often administer major sites or run important mailing lists. The net heavies consider it their job (who knows how they manage to keep real jobs with all the work they do here) to keep the nets running smoothly. Even though they often work behind the scenes, they do an excellent job. Shortly after I started *TidBITS*, for instance, I was searching for the best ways to distribute it. I wasn't able to run a mailing list from my account at Cornell, and *TidBITS* was too big to post to a general Usenet group every week. After I spoke with several of the net heavies, they allowed me to post to a moderated newsgroup, `comp.sys.mac.digest`, that had, up to that point, been used only for distributing the Info-Mac Digest to Usenet.

If you want to get involved with what little organization there is on the Internet, I suggest that you participate and contribute to discussions about the future of the nets. Gradually, you'll learn how the system works and find yourself in a position where you can help the net continue to thrive.

You should keep one thing in mind about the Internet and its loose controlling structure: It works, and it works far better than do most other organizations. By bringing control down to almost the individual level, but by requiring cooperation to exist, the Internet works without the strong central government that most countries use and claim is necessary to avoid lawlessness and anarchy. Hmm . . .

The Internet makes you think, and that's good.

Oh, and remember Bob Taylor, one of the early heads of ARPA? Several years later he helped found Xerox PARC, which employed luminaries such as Douglas Englebart (inventor of the mouse), Alan Kay (a current Apple Fellow), Bob Metcalfe (inventor of Ethernet and current publisher of *InfoWorld*), and Larry Tesler (who was, and may still be, head of Apple's Advanced Technology

Group). And, of course, Xerox PARC was where Steve Jobs saw the Xerox Alto workstation and its graphical interface, and at that moment, in many respects, the Macintosh was born.

The Future

I hope this chapter has provided a coherent view of where the Internet has come from, along with some of the people and networks that were instrumental in its growth. After any history lesson, the immediate question concerns the future. Where can we expect the Internet to go from here?

I'm an optimist. I'm sure you can find someone more than happy to tell you all the horrible problems—technical, political, and social—facing the Internet. I don't hold with such attitudes, though, because something that affects so many people around the world didn't appear so quickly for no reason. In one way or another, I think most people understand on a visceral level that the Internet is good, the Internet is here to stay, and if they want to be someone, they would do well to get access today and contribute in a positive fashion. Of course, books like this one only encourage such utopian attitudes.

In any event, I predict that the Internet will continue growing at an incredible rate. You might make an argument for the rate of growth slowing from its 15 percent per month rate based on the fact that it's silly to assume that anything can continue to grow at such a breakneck speed. A naysayer also might point at the massive influx of novices as endangering the Internet, or point at the increased level of commercialization as a major problem. I feel that such growth is self-propelling and that bringing more people and resources onto the Internet only further fuels the expansion. I think growth is good—the more people, the more resources, the more opinions, the better off we all are.

I also expect to see the Internet continue to standardize, both officially and informally. At lower levels, more computers will start to use IP instead of BITNET's NJE or the aging UUCP protocols. It's merely a matter of keeping up with the Joneses, and the Joneses are running IP. At a higher level, I think that using various network resources will become easier as they start migrating toward similar interfaces. Just as it's easy to use multiple applications on a Mac because you always know how to open, close, save, and quit, so will it be easier to use new and enhanced services on the Internet because they will resemble each other more and more. Even now, people rely heavily on network conventions such as prefixing site names to indicate what services they provide, like `ftp.tidbits.com` for FTP, `gopher.seattle.wa.us` for Gopher, and `www.wired.com` for the World-Wide Web.

And yes, I fully expect to see the Internet become more and more commercial, both in terms of where the service comes from, and in terms of the traffic the Internet carries. However, we must remember the old attitudes about commercial use of the Internet. In the past, commercial use was often acceptable if it wasn't blatant, was appropriately directed, and was of significant value to the readers. In other words, I'll be as angry as the next person if I start receiving automatically generated junk email every day, just as I receive junk mail via snail mail. If such things start happening, the course of action will be the same as it always has been: politely ask the originator to stop once, and then, if that doesn't work, flame away—that is, send back an outrageously nasty message.

Even though I'm optimistic, I know problems will occur. For example, consider the so-called Green Card debacle. In the spring of 1994, the husband and wife law firm of Canter & Siegel posted a blatantly commercial message advertising a green card lottery and immigration services. That wasn't the problem. The problem was that they posted it to all 5,000 Usenet newsgroups, an act called *spamming*. Discussions about Celtic culture, Macintosh communications (where I first saw it), and Washington state politics were all interrupted, along with thousands of others completely apathetic about anything to do with immigration. Or at least they were apathetic until they were bludgeoned repeatedly with Canter & Siegel's post. All of a sudden, everyone cared a great deal about immigration, and sent 30,000 flame messages (more than 100 megabytes of text) to the offenders. That many messages was far more than Canter & Siegel's provider, Internet Direct, could handle, and their machine went down like a boxer on the wrong end of a knock-out punch.

The aftershocks keep coming, with Internet Direct suing Canter & Siegel for violating acceptable use policies (it seems that Canter & Siegel never signed the terms and conditions form) and for the detrimental effect the post had on business. In return Canter & Siegel counter-sued for loss of business, claiming some ludicrous percentage of the messages were requests for more information (though they refuse to provide any verifiable data). Internet Direct disabled their account immediately, and details about Canter & Siegel's history began to surface. They'd been kicked off of other providers for similar smaller-scale posts in the past, they'd been suspended from the bar in Florida in 1987 for conduct the Supreme Court of Florida deemed "contrary to honest," and so on. Canter & Siegel garnered a huge amount of press (most of it negative, but as the saying goes, "I don't care what you say about me as long as you spell my name right."). They even announced in a newspaper interview that they were setting up a company to provide services to other companies who wanted to flood Usenet with advertising, and that they were going to write a book about how to advertise on the Internet. That's a bit like serial cannibal Jeffrey Dahmer writing a book about preserving meat.

The Canter & Siegel fiasco raises the question of how the Internet should be policed. In the past, and the present, any transgression has been dealt with much as it might have been in the perhaps-fictional view of the American Old West. Everyone takes justice into his own hands, and if a few innocents are hurt in the process, well, it was for the greater good. When Canter & Siegel spammed Usenet, thousands of people spammed them back.

This process is more commonly known as *mail bombing*. Mail bombs are generally small Unix programs (before you ask, I don't know of any for the Mac) that simply send a user-configured number of messages (using a specified file as the message body) to a given address, potentially ensuring that none of the mail bomb messages come from real addresses. A better solution came from a Norwegian programmer, who created a spambot (his term, not mine) program that somehow figures out which newsgroups Canter & Siegel spammed (yes, it happened again, although on a smaller scale) and bounces the spamming message back to them, along with a short note daring them to sue him, since he's in Norway.

Frontier justice sounds like great fun, especially when slimy lawyers are on the other end, but it raises some interesting issues. Mail bombing a machine doesn't affect just that machine—it affects many of the machines nearby on the Internet. In the case of a public machine like Internet Direct's **indirect.com**, it also hurts an innocent business and hundreds of innocent users who also use that machine. And, although the Internet as a whole can deal with the occasional mail bomb attack, if such things happened every day, they would seriously impair Internet communications. Such possibilities raise the specter of regulation, something that most Internet users disapprove of (though certain usage regulations are built into the service agreements of almost every Internet provider for liability reasons). So, will the government get involved and lay down the law about inappropriate Internet use? Probably not. The people who must do the regulation are the providers themselves—there's no way to prevent everyone from retaliating against such spam attacks as Canter & Siegel's, so the best place to stop them is at the level of the providers. They can simply refuse to give problem users an account or remove accounts when abuse occurs. But the government itself? I certainly hope not.

I don't believe that the Internet will ever be governed to a much greater extent than it is now (at least in the U.S.), simply because I don't believe it's feasible. How can you govern something that spans the globe or police something that carries gigabytes of data every day? The U.S. government could easily ban pornographic postings, say, but how does that affect someone from a different country? Or how does that affect U.S. users retrieving the pornographic images from another country? Remember, the Internet can just route around censorship. It's all very confusing, and it will be some time (if ever) before the government understands all of the issues surrounding the Internet sufficiently to produce reasonable legislation. Of course, that begs the question of unreasonable legislation, but that's always a fear.

The way the government as a whole currently views the Internet reminds me a bit of the joke about how to tell if you have an elephant in your fridge. The answer is by the footprints in the peanut butter—it's the middle of the night, and the government is standing at the open door, yawning and blinking at those massive footprints. Luckily, different parts of the government are starting to wake up, which should help dispel the dangerous ignorance that has marked certain past government Internet actions. For example, there was the Steve Jackson case, in which the CIA completely inappropriately confiscated the computer systems of a popular publisher of role-playing games. The damage award from that case enabled Steve Jackson Games to create an Internet provider called Illuminati Online (`io.com`). Perhaps the greater problem now with the government's view of the Internet is that it seems more concerned with regulating occasional outrageous behavior, than with using the power of the Internet to further the public good. Personally, I prefer my government to be more interested in helping than in regulating. Of course, then there are the people who would prefer that the government just stayed out of the way, but somehow I doubt that will happen any time soon.

Past and Future—Next, the Present

I've tried to give a glimpse of the history of the Internet, from its first stumbling steps as the military- and research-based ARPAnet to the swift NSFNET and the commercial providers of today. If nothing else, it's worth noting that those who ignore history are condemned to repeat it, and by paying attention to the mistakes of the past, perhaps we can avoid making them again in the future. The future will also bring new problems and new opportunities, but for the moment we can only speculate as to what those might be. But put all that out of your mind, because the next chapter takes you on a tour of the Internet of today.

Exploring the Internet

Before I dive into the "hows" of the Internet, I'd like to take a chapter to discuss the "whys." I spend most of the rest of this book talking about how to do things—how to use Anarchie to retrieve a file, how to use Eudora, how to use NewsWatcher, what's neat about MacWeb, and so forth. But, it makes sense to spend a little time first talking about why you would want to use email, read news, talk to people via IRC (Internet Relay Chat), or browse the World-Wide Web.

The problem with attempting to give you a sense of why you would want to do these things is that for most readers, I don't know you personally. Any specific example I give might or might not interest you, so I instead talk about the things that I do on the Internet and the kinds of ways I use the Internet in my daily life. Although you and I are undoubtedly interested in different subjects, if you just sit back in a comfortable chair and read through this chapter, I hope you'll get a better sense of what life on the Internet is really like.

Don't sweat the details in this chapter. It's not meant to be technical at all, and you've got the rest of the book to answer any niggling details. If you don't recognize a program name or an Internet service, don't worry about it—just mentally note it and come back after you've read the later chapters. As odd as it may sound, consider this chapter a work of fiction. It's not that the subject matter is contrived, but instead that you must suspend disbelief and just flow with the text. After all, you don't worry about how Ian Fleming enabled his fictional master spy, James Bond, to drive a car that could metamorphose into a submarine, right?

After you've read the rest of the book and gotten on the Internet, you might come back to this chapter and see if you can perhaps duplicate some of the examples that follow. You never know what you might find when you retrace the steps of a fictional, or not so fictional, character.

Actually, I've already written an entire book, called *Internet Explorer Kit for Macintosh*, devoted to this less-technical subject matter. My co-author on that book, Bill Dickson, has graciously agreed to join me for a chapter to go over some of the material we cover in *Internet Explorer Kit for Macintosh*. Hi, Bill!

`Bill: Hi, Adam! Hello, Readers!`

Adam: You'll notice that we've just switched over to a dialog format. In keeping with the more informal nature of this setting, we'll present this chapter as a sort of extended conversation. It worked well in *Internet Explorer Kit for Macintosh*, as we were able to draw on each other's experience with different aspects of the Internet, and interject with questions where appropriate.

`Bill: Think of it as a quick spin around the Internet in the back seat of a Macintosh convertible, with Adam and I sitting up front and taking turns driving. Kick back and relax, and we'll see if we can show you something interesting.`

Adam: And I suppose the first thing we'll do is what most people do when they get their first car—we'll go visit some friends.

People

Adam: News stories about the Internet love to quote big numbers, since big numbers impress people. I suspect that's mostly because few people have ever sat down and counted to a million, or even much past a hundred. Today's youth probably consider it sufficient to watch that many digits flash by on the computer screen, muttering that if Zeus had intended us to count to a million, he would have given us a million toes—and wouldn't that have made "This little piggy" difficult?

So, you hear a lot about how there are more than two million computers on the Internet and how the growth rate increases at some 15 percent per month. It's equally *chic* to talk about the hardware and software and the myriad of protocols, each with an acronym like FTP or HTTP, all of which mean little to the average person, even to the average Internet user.

Let's face it, a vast number of people drive cars in the world, and I'm willing to bet that almost none of them know how powerful their cars' engines are in terms of horsepower. Here's the important fact about the Internet: people.

The Internet is about people. The actual number is unknown, and relatively unimportant, other than the number of zeros, since estimates place the population of the Internet between 20 and 50 million people worldwide. That's a large pool, and there's a pretty good chance that someone you know, or even many people you know, have access to the Internet.

```
Bill: The first thing many of us do when we arrive on the
Internet is look for our friends. It's only natural; it's harder
to make new friends than to stick with old ones. So, we sit down
at our computers, try to imagine who we know, anywhere in the
world, who might be able to receive email over the Internet, and
we start hunting around for them.

This can be a great deal harder than it sounds. Paradoxically,
the Internet — one of the greatest tools for the exchange of in-
formation devised since Gutenberg starting mashing ink onto paper
with wooden blocks — can't keep track of who is using it. Or
rather, it could, but nobody's ever bothered to tell it how. So,
silly as it may sound, there is no comprehensive directory of
Internet users. Not even close. Some sites maintain their own
directories, but the information can be pretty dated, and you've
still got to know where to look.
```

Adam: To illustrate this fact, we're going to look around for Bill. Now, you may think this is strange, even pointless, as Bill is obviously pretty close by or he wouldn't be able to raid my fridge for beer while writing this chapter.

```
Bill: Hey! It's my beer, bucko!
```

Adam: What dark secrets does the Internet hold? Perhaps the Whois server can provide some details on one William R. Dickson, possibly exposing his sordid past as the illegitimate son of a third world dictator. Let's find out.

First, we'll try a little UNIX program called Whois. It turns up a William E. Dickson, but no William R. Dickson. Even if it had found him, all that Whois provides is an address, phone number, and email address, which aren't enough to suspect illegitimacy (see figure 5.1).

You must be careful when finding people in this manner since some names are relatively common. You might be embarrassed if you send an intensely personal letter to an old flame you located on the Internet, only to find out that you'd found somebody else's old flame.

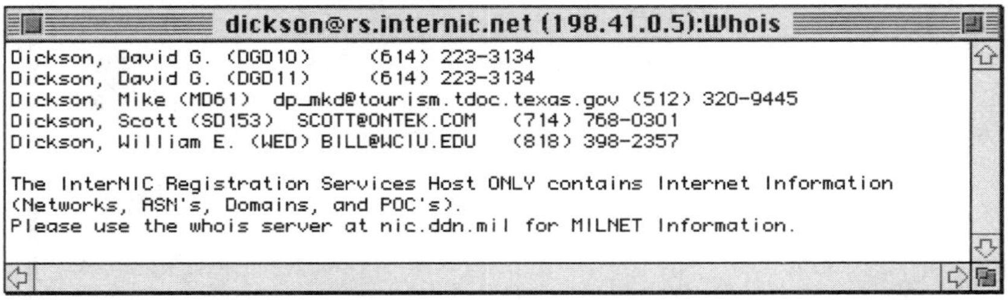

```
┌─────────────────────────────────────────────────────────────────┐
│ ▦▦    dickson@rs.internic.net (198.41.0.5):Whois    ▦▦ │ ⇧
├─────────────────────────────────────────────────────────────────┤
│ Dickson, David G. (DGD10)    (614) 223-3134                       │
│ Dickson, David G. (DGD11)    (614) 223-3134                       │
│ Dickson, Mike (MD61)  dp_mkd@tourism.tdoc.texas.gov (512) 320-9445│
│ Dickson, Scott (SD153)  SCOTT@ONTEK.COM   (714) 768-0301          │
│ Dickson, William E. (WED)  BILL@WCIU.EDU   (818) 398-2357         │
│                                                                   │
│ The InterNIC Registration Services Host ONLY contains Internet Information │
│ (Networks, ASN's, Domains, and POC's).                            │
│ Please use the whois server at nic.ddn.mil for MILNET Information.│ ⇩
├─────────────────────────────────────────────────────────────────┤
│ ⇦                                                             ⇨ ▦ │
└─────────────────────────────────────────────────────────────────┘
```

Figure 5.1   *Probably not the illegitimate son of a third world dictator; also, not our man*

But I don't give up easily, and I do want to see if I can turn something up on Bill. I like to use Gopher, which is a program created by the University of Minnesota to provide access to all sorts of information on the Internet. Gopher knows about a number of ways of searching for people, so first I'm going to try something called Netfind (see figure 5.2).

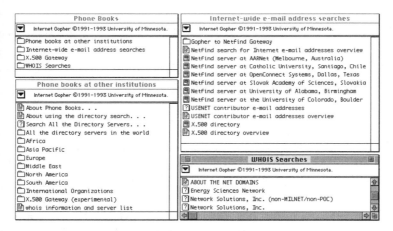

Figure 5.2   *The many tentacles of G.O.P.H.E.R.*

Netfind only works if your target works at a large business or university, and Bill's workplace—a Popular Copy Shop—isn't included. Strike two (Whois was strike one). Next up is something called X.500, which sounds like a robot but turns out to be a large white pages database maintained by some organization in England. It wants tons of information, including department and organization, that Bill doesn't have, so that's a strike as well. Ah, but now I see something that searches Usenet contributor email addresses, and I know that Bill occasionally posts to the Usenet newsgroups—maybe that will find him. Blast it, Gopher reports, "Could not connect," which means that the machine that runs that service or the network to that machine is down—maybe it's frozen. Strike four. Internet machines go down fairly frequently, but don't worry about it—they usually come back up in a few hours or the next day, so there's no need to panic and ask if the site has gone away. Just try again later.

I'm beginning to worry that I can't find Bill at all on the Internet. I know he exists, since he raids my fridge, but is it possible that he has erased all trace of his existence from the nets, in an attempt to cover up his horrible past? Hm, I just found an item called something like, "Search all the directory servers in the world." Unfortunately it doesn't know of any Dicksons. Hey, wait a minute, it doesn't know about any Smiths, either. I wonder what world it's on? Strike five.

Next up is a service called Veronica which knows how to search through all the Gopher databases in the world (or at least, a lot of them) to find files matching the search term. I start a Veronica search on "Dickson" and am immediately rewarded with lots of… information that I don't want, including reviews of Gordon Dickson's books and a report (co-authored by a professor I knew) about computers in a dorm at Cornell University, Clara Dickson Hall. It's a small world, but, sigh, strike six (see figure 5.3).

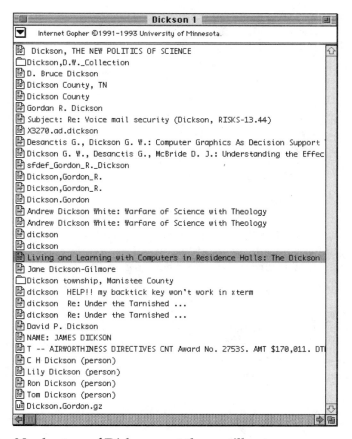

Figure 5.3 *No shortage of Dicksons out there, still not our man*

This is beginning to annoy me. Two outs later, and my reputation as an Internet guru is at stake. I have one last trick to find some record of Bill on the Internet. I know he uses a Macintosh, and thus very well may read and contribute to the Info-Mac Digest, which is a discussion list about things Macintosh. I also happen to know that the entire list is archived and indexed in WAIS, which stands for *Wide Area Information Servers,* and contains many massive databases of information on all sorts of topics. Last I checked, there were more than 500 databases in WAIS, so I'm going to check the `macintosh-news.src` database for some sign of Bill (see figure 5.4).

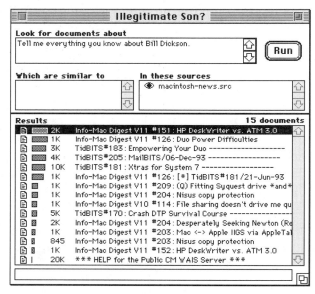

Figure 5.4   *Captured at last—the elusive Bill Dickson*

You readers can't see this because I didn't want to embarrass Bill by showing his posting in public, but take my word for it, the selected posting (and some of the others) in figure 5.4 are from Bill, and it comes complete with his email address.

`Bill: Argh! Found me!`

Adam: I assure you that it isn't always this hard. On the other hand, it isn't always this easy, either. Sometimes finding people works immediately and at other times it's almost futile. Don't worry, just don't rely on these methods. I certainly don't. The telephone is almost always the most reliable method of finding someone's email address—just call and ask them.

Net Alter Egos

Adam: Superman, Batman, the Black Cat, Spiderman, Phoenix—all of these comic book heroes and heroines share one feature other than great bodies and skintight uniforms that show every curve. They all have alter egos who can mix in normal society without anyone else's realizing their true identities. One minute, mild-mannered reporter Clark Kent is being brow-beaten by Lois Lane, the next minute (and a phone booth later), Superman is saving the world from the latest crazed super villain. Bruce Wayne and Batman, Peter Parker and Spiderman… Can anyone who has read comic books not have wanted an alter ego at some point? Our alter egos could do what we didn't want to, and would be stronger, smarter, and always ready with a clever comeback to any insult from dastardly villains of every ilk.

The Internet doesn't change your physical appearance or capabilities, but because of the lack of visual interaction, it enables you to portray yourself in any manner you so choose. Some people might become crusaders for truth and justice, albeit in a single discussion list, whereas others might turn into psychotic lunatics in a subconscious rebellion against abusive parents or whatever. I doubt that most people change all that radically in their net personas, but keep in mind that you can never know what any given net citizen is like in person, without a face-to-face meeting.

There is another phenomenon that relates to this concept of net alter egos—that of amplification. Because the Internet enables any single person to send a message to tens of thousands of other people around the world and to maintain intellectual discussions with numerous people on a number of different topics, the Internet *amplifies* the individual, or enables her to do far more than any single person could do outside of the Internet.

The Internet thus enables the individual to become more important and more influential than would otherwise be possible in real life. Of course, the extent to which this happens is directly related to the level of interest and utility of your postings. Those who do good stuff are respected, whereas those who merely clog the Internet with garbage are universally reviled. Well-known, yes, but infamous.

```
Bill: There's something about the Internet that makes some people
cut loose a little bit. Not everybody; Adam's email, for in-
stance, conveys his real personality fairly accurately.
```

Adam: I'm not sure if he's flattering me or being subtly underhanded. Must be his background as the illegitimate son of a third world dictator.

Bill: We'll never know, will we? But, many people have an "electronic personality" that is distinctly different from their "real" personality.

It bothers me when people put quotation marks around words that don't need them, so let me assure you that I mean it in this case. The question that arises here is, given that the pressure of face-to-face interaction (and the possibility of embarrassment that goes along with it) are largely absent on the Internet, does a person behave more or less naturally when they communicate this way?

Well, the answer, of course, is both. There, that clears it right up, doesn't it?

Let's take as an example one form of human interaction that's in abundant supply on the Internet: flirtation. People love to flirt electronically! Since it's so unlikely that you'll ever actually meet the target of your wiles, there's no fear of rejection; since you're judged entirely by your words (and skillful use of smileys), you don't need to worry about your weight or your hair. So, what you'll find is that people who couldn't possibly force themselves to buy somebody, anybody, a drink in your typical cocktail bar become remarkably fluent in the language of romance when you put them behind a keyboard and monitor. Which is the real person? Hard to say. Obviously, the talent for personal interaction is there, but that talent seems to take a vacation when there's another person around to actually interact with.

Likewise, you'll find people on the Internet telling total strangers things they'd never say to many of their friends if they had to say them face-to-face. Incredibly personal information will find its way into your email from surprising sources. People are willing to bare their souls, revealing aspects of themselves you'd never see in person.

There are also people who would be polite in person, but who may, since they need not worry about getting punched in the mouth, sound off in an abrasive manner about anything that bothers them—which frequently turns out to be rather a lot.

This stuff is all very interesting and could probably be the subject of many studies involving mazes and cheese and spilled ink. But there's another sort of alter ego you'll encounter on the Internet, and that's the deliberate role of an actor. People actually construct a part for themselves to play, and present that character as their network personality. Some do so as a disguise, playing the role as if it were a real person. Others make no secret of the fact that they are playing a part. The role may be played for the network at large, in discussion groups and correspondence, or only for a specific group of people in some corner of the Internet where such role-playing is the norm.

This is one of the most fascinating things about the Internet for me, and I've wholeheartedly participated from time-to-time. I currently play several roles, including a six-foot anthropomorphized pickle in a virtual community called FurryMUCK, a nigh-omnipotent (but highly irresponsible) Author in the Author's Altiverse of Superguy Digest, and a Supreme Court Justice on the Politics list. It may sound weird to you, but it all makes perfect sense to each of those three groups of people.

Adam: Bill?

Bill: Yes?

Adam: You're really strange.

Bill: Yes. But lovably so. Net personalities can manifest in some unusual ways, even if you don't turn into a giant walking pickle. Sometimes it takes the form of an affected quirk: there are three people on the Politics list who refuse to use capital letters. One of them explained her reasons to me; she is a relatively shy person, and feels that lowercase conveys her personality more accurately by implying a small, quiet speaking voice.

Adam: Although most people are extremely pleasant in email because they know that email lacks the body language and intonations of normal speech, there are exceptions. I suspect that most of these occur simply as a matter of limited time to answer email messages, or perhaps as a subconscious response to the frustration of being asked the same question over and over again. Recently I received more than 100 copies of the same message from different *TidBITS* readers, all of whom forwarded it to me because it raised some serious questions about an article I had written. I had actually seen the message before publishing the article, but failed to mention that fact within the article itself, so I shouldn't have been the slightest bit upset with any of the individuals who tried to warn me about a potentially bad situation. Nonetheless, I was a bit peeved at having to deal with more than 100 of these messages, so I decided to write a single reply that was sufficiently generic, and then to send it back to each person. That allowed me to stay pleasant, whereas if I had had to reply to each message individually, by the end I would undoubtedly have been writing, "You're wrong—and probably stupid. -Adam." That's not a particularly nice way to respond to someone who was just trying to help, and it seldom helps to be testy.

```
Bill: I've got another specific example. Norman is a long-stand-
ing member of the Politics discussion list, to which I've be-
longed on-and-off since, oh, 1988 or 1989. Norman's politics are
almost always diametrically opposed to mine, and he's extraordi-
narily outspoken about them—sometimes to the point of offending
many list members. He can be abrasive, and more than a few people
have called him obnoxious.
```

Adam: He sounds like real winner.

```
Bill: Well, early in my career on Politics, he and I got into a
nice little row over something I can't even remember anymore. It
was extraordinarily heated online, flames going back and forth
like there was no tomorrow. Neither of us was especially civil.
So you can imagine my surprise when the phone rang one day, and
there at the other end of the line was Norman.

We talked some, and he was surprisingly pleasant. We talked about
the car I was about to buy, life in general, a bit of political
stuff, things like that. Although I still disagreed with him
strongly, I found it hard to dislike him after that.

Basically (as later correspondence with him suggested), I think
he just likes to argue. The volatile arguments on Politics are
fun for him. Not that he doesn't believe what he's saying, he
does; but he gets a blast out of intense argument, and writes
accordingly. It's his Internet personality.
```

Adam: Of course, these examples prove nothing, since it's equally common for people to interact better remotely than they do in person. There have been a number of occasions on which I've conversed quite happily with someone via email, and then, when the time came to meet them, found that I wasn't all that fond of them. Usually, the meeting also dampened later email conversations, since it's difficult to communicate with someone you've met without recalling your impressions of that meeting.

In one respect, I like this facet of Internet communication more than any other, because it says that when we communicate purely on a conscious, intellectual level, we can often do so far better than when we're staring into each other's faces. I see the Internet as important not only because of the information available on it, but because of the ways it opens channels of communication between people who would never otherwise talk due to barriers of language, geography, religion, or even philosophy.

It's interesting, because people can find almost any excuse to avoid talking to one another in person, whereas online you can't pry them apart with an electronic crowbar. Although I won't pretend that talking on the Internet could solve the world's problems, the model of communication where anyone can say anything and is allotted attention commensurate with the coherence and interest of the message, is one I would love to see more of in the world.

```
Bill: Net personalities are part of life on the Internet, and you
get used to them. Eventually, you begin to learn where you can
expect to find certain kinds of personalities, much in the way
you learn which bars to visit on a Saturday night to find your
kind of crowd.

The personalities you'll encounter will be many and varied.
People can be pretty much anything they want to be on the Net.
Superheroes are favorites, along with many other fictional char-
acters. Some people even choose the names of real, more famous
people. This, of course, raises a little question. If you're
chatting on the Fly Fishing channel on IRC, and suddenly "Ma-
donna" signs on, how do you know it's not… well, it couldn't
really be… Nah.

Could it?
```

Celebrities

Adam: Last summer I watched a multi-part PBS television series called "Fame in the Twentieth Century." It used fabulous old photographs, newspapers, and newsreel footage to make the point that, although initially an event might give someone fleeting fame, only the mass media could provide lasting fame. In the process of working its way through each decade of the twentieth century, the show examined the lives of people like Al Capone, who was addicted to his media-reflected fame, Charles Lindbergh, who tried to escape it only to become all the more famous for attempting to avoid the spotlight, and Madonna, whose fame is the result of being one of the most skilled self-promoters in the world today.

How does this all apply to the Internet? I'm not completely certain, except to note that the concept of fame seems to translate directly to the Internet as another medium of information exchange. The icons of popular culture are starting to appear in various ways on the Internet, which is an interesting process to note in its own right, since that which makes one popular in *People* very well may turn you into a laughingstock on the Internet. This is not to imply that the Internet rejects all the heroes of popular culture, or that there are no home-grown Internet legends. Both traditional celebrities and Internet celebrities exist on the nets, but the Internet being what it is, you can never quite predict how people will react to the arrival of a celebrity.

```
Bill: There's no telling how many celebrities are lurking on the
Internet. Some say Harry Anderson of Night Court fame is out
there somewhere on the Internet, possibly reading rec.arts.magic.
Rush Limbaugh is on CompuServe, and Tom Clancy supposedly is
connected through America Online. Of course, if Harry Anderson
has an America Online account, does that mean he uses the
Internet, or is even aware that he can send mail to it? Not nec-
essarily.
```

```
It's sort of interesting, seeing who chooses to make him- or
herself known. You generally won't find big-name mass-appeal
celebrities, but you can find many, many people who would be
considered celebrities in certain circles. Game designers and
writers can often be found mingling with the people who buy and
play their games, getting feedback on the Internet. I wouldn't
know them if I tripped over them, but they're well known in the
gaming community. On the Mac newsgroups, asking a question about
a program will often bring you an answer from its author.
```

Adam: While some people have brought their fame to the Internet, there are a number of people whose fame has yet to spread beyond the Internet. In the Macintosh world of the nets, one of the most famous net denizens, John Norstad, hails from Northwestern University. Although he no longer works on it except when events require him to, John is best known for his free anti-virus program called Disinfectant. John created Disinfectant in response to early Macintosh viruses (evil little programs designed to reproduce themselves within other files on your computer, making you feel unclean, and sometimes causing damage in the process) and continued to improve it over the years. It has become a commercial-quality piece of software, and being free, is something that I recommend that every Macintosh user have and use periodically.

More recently, John turned his attention to his current project, a Macintosh program called NewsWatcher that enables Macintosh users with full Internet access to read and reply to messages on Usenet, which is home to the many thousands of newsgroups, or discussion lists, on almost every imaginable topic.

NewsWatcher had actually been started, and then dropped, by Steve Falkenburg, a programmer from Apple. John picked up the program from Steve and enhanced it significantly, turning it into what I feel is the best of the Internet news readers on the Macintosh. Once again, NewsWatcher remains completely free to users everywhere, and although he retains final control over what goes in, John has had help from numerous people on the nets. In essence, then, NewsWatcher has become a community project, something to which any programmer can contribute and which any Macintosh user connected to the Internet can use and enjoy.

In real life, John works at Northwestern University, so I asked him via email just why he works on projects like Disinfectant and NewsWatcher and if he minds being an Internet celebrity. I'll let him answer those questions in his own words.

John Norstad: That's a hard question, and I get asked it a lot. I'll try to give a serious answer, at the risk of being pretentious.

I am passionate about free software. For me, developing free software in my spare time is more than just a hobby. I'm also passionate about the Mac. It's so incredibly clear to me that the Mac is the very best computer anywhere, period. I don't understand why there's any controversy at all about this. I'm also passionate about the revolutionary potential of the Internet, and the Mac's role on the Internet. It has certainly changed my life, and with the right software and services and access, it can change other people's lives, too.

The best kind of programming is an act of artistic creation. Truly great programs are works of art. They have beauty and elegance and truth and purity. They are much, much more than just a random collection of features. Writing this kind of program is much, much more than just "software engineering."

For me, the only way to even attempt to create this kind of software is to have total freedom and complete control over the entire development process. My best programs are the ones I've written on my own time, not as official projects as part of my job.

I've discovered over the 30 years I've been a programmer that as soon as money is involved in any way with the software I write, I in some way lose some significant amount of control over the software. By developing free software, I retain complete control. I don't have to respond to market pressures, or to often-misguided customer complaints and requests, or to lawyers or marketing people, or to bosses, or to magazine reviewers, or to shipping deadlines, or to financial pressures, or to anyone or anything else. If you don't like one of my free programs, tough. I'll give you double your money back.

There's no question that the extent to which my programs are good and even begin to approach being in any sense the works of art I want them to be is because of this freedom.

In short, "free" software = "freedom" for the software creator. For me, this freedom is what it's all about. Sure, I'd like to be rich, but I've got enough money to support my family well, and it's more important to have the freedom.

Programming as an act of creation is an addiction. The only reason I write Mac programs is because of this urge to create. I don't do it because my bosses tell me to do it, or for money, or as a public service, or for fame. I do it to feed the monkey on my back.

This is nothing new or startling or unique. Any good programmer who really cares about his or her work will tell you much the same thing.

I'm very fortunate to find myself in a working environment that makes this all possible. I have a good job with good pay, and Northwestern gives me a very large amount of control over my work and encourages and supports my independent projects like Disinfectant and NewsWatcher. Few people are so lucky.

Adam: And as far as being a celebrity?

John Norstad: It's very much a mixed blessing.

I get way too much mail and way too many phone calls. Way too many people want me to do way too many things. Email is sometimes like a Chinese water torture. I have to keep up with it every day, or I get hopelessly behind. If I leave town for three days or a week, when I get back it takes a whole day or two just to get caught up. I sometimes have to be ruthless and quite rude when I reject requests for help or requests to speak or requests for interviews or requests for whatever. This is unpleasant, because I don't like being nasty to people.

But overall, becoming a minor "celebrity" in the Mac world (a somewhat larger than average fish in a rather small pond) has been very pleasant. The very best thing that has happened is that it has given me the opportunity to become friends and colleagues with some of the best Mac programmers in the world. It's also very pleasant to have people recognize and appreciate my work. I really enjoy getting simple thank you notes via email and postcards from all over the world and having strangers come up to me and thank me at conferences and all that sort of thing.

Awards are nice, too. I recently went to San Francisco to receive this year's MacUser Editors' Choice John J. Anderson Distinguished Achievement award. It was a very fancy black tie affair. I got to give a short speech, and I brought home an incredibly large and beautiful Eddy statue. This was definitely the thrill of a lifetime.

Finally, I have to admit that my "celebrity" status is pretty cheap, and is entirely due to being lucky enough to have written Disinfectant in the late 1980s, just when the virus problem was becoming more serious and seriously over-hyped by the press. Sure, it's a very good program, and I'm a very good programmer, and viruses are a serious problem, and my program is a serious and successful attempt to deal with the problem, but it's still just one program, and I'm still just one programmer. There are many, many developers in the Mac world who have done much more work and much better work and much more significant work and are much smarter than I am, but who haven't gotten anywhere near the same recognition as I have.

Finding Your Niche

Adam: The first task that faces any Internet newcomer, or *newbie*, in Internet parlance, is finding the group of people with whom you want to hang out. This of course assumes that you're not an antisocial hermit who doesn't want to have anything to do with other people. Don't become discouraged if it takes you some time to find just the right place. If you were anything like me, it took years during adolescence to do the same thing in real life, and I can guarantee that it won't take that long on the Internet.

As with anything on the Internet (and in real life, for that matter), many ways of finding your future group of friends exist. They range from extremely low-tech methods, such as asking someone in person or looking in a book, to the high-tech methods of running complicated searches in WAIS databases.

```
Bill: One of my main social groups on the Internet is the Poli-
tics list, a group devoted to the discussion of current events,
political theory, and all those other government-related topics
that make you unpopular at parties.
```

Adam: If the conversation turns to education reform in Nicaragua, you know it's not going to be one of those parties where people balance spoons on their noses.

```
Bill: Well… don't be too sure. I wound up as part of the Politics
crowd through a rather complicated series of events. Around that
time in my college career, I signed up for a Political Science
minor, and I was quite fascinated with much of what I was learn-
ing. It's been so long now that I don't remember the exact de-
tails, but one of the various people who I'd met through
entirely different channels on the Internet told me about the
Politics list. He wasn't subscribed to it, but he thought it
might interest me, and pointed me in the right direction. I
signed up, and I've been there every since. In fact, I am now a
Supreme Court Justice.
```

Adam: You are not. You're lying.

```
Bill: Am too! Within the context of the Politics list, anyway.
There are three Supreme Court Justices, and I'm one of them.
```

Adam: OK, say I wanted a cabinet position. How would I find the Politics list?

```
Bill: Well, I can't be sure you'd be offered one, but let's say
you are interested in Politics anyway, and you decide to look
around for it. If you don't know where to look—or even what
you're looking for—how can you hope to find it in the vast sea
of Internet resources?
```

Well fortunately, the LISTSERV programs that run many of the
mailing lists themselves are pretty helpful. They maintain a
complete list of lists, called (not surprisingly) LISTSERV Lists.
You can retrieve this list fairly easily from any LISTSERV, such
as **listserv@ricevm1.rice.edu**, by sending email to it with the
words "LIST GLOBAL" in the body of your message.

Adam: If you don't want to keep your own copy of the list of mailing lists, but
do want to be able to get at it when you need it, you can find it in numerous
places online. Beware that it's a lot of data, so the files are large and sometimes
unwieldy. One place that I like to look for this sort of thing is in the newsgroup,
news.lists, which contains periodically updated lists of lots of useful information, along with some utter trivia such as the most prolific Usenet poster of the
month (see figure 5.5).

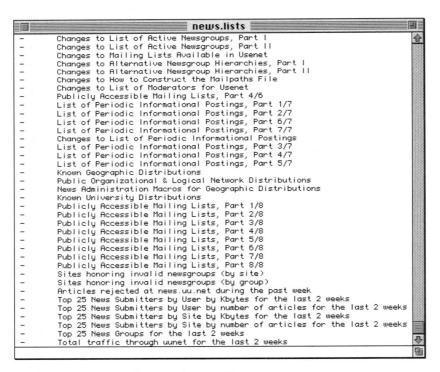

Figure 5.5   *Lists, lists, lists; we've got lists*

As you can see, there are a number of postings for the "Publicly Accessible Mailing Lists." That's because the entire list is too large to put in a single message. Just download all of the messages if you want to keep your own copy for searching, but remember that the details change frequently.

Lurking

Adam: The next trick, once you've found a group that interests you, is learning how to assimilate without seriously offending your new-found acquaintances. The first thing most people do, or at least should do, is lurk. Don't worry, we're not suggesting that you spend your spare time in dark alley ways, frightening passersby. On the Internet, lurking is an innocuous occupation practiced by the vast majority of Internet users. It simply means that you read and observe the goings-on without actually contributing to the group. Think of the old adage about how children should be seen and not heard. On the Internet, no one even sees the lurkers, and there's nothing to hear from a lurker, either.

```
Bill: Let's take a newsgroup on which I lurk as an example. The
group comp.sys.powerpc is devoted to discussion of the new
PowerPC machines from IBM and Apple. People talk about everything
from the number of transistors on the chip to the speeds we can
expect from it in the next year to the reasons it may or may not
wipe the floor with its Intel competition. Much of this informa-
tion and conversation is extremely technical, far more technical
than I am. I can understand much of it, but I sure don't know
enough to contribute intelligently to the conversation. So I just
sit there and read and soak it in—the possibilities offered by
these new machines interest me, but I don't know enough about
them to post constructively.
```

Adam: I do much the same thing that Bill does, with a list called Newton-L that comes from **listserv@dartmouth.edu**. I have absolutely no use for one of Apple's Newton MessagePads, because I seldom go anywhere and I write a great deal, so I don't need the ability to communicate with people via email or fax while on the road, and I could never write quickly enough with the stylus. Nonetheless, I think some of the Newton technology represents the future of computing in terms of intelligent assistance, so I like to stay up to date on what people say about the MessagePad.

Chapter 5
Exploring the
Internet

Introducing Yourself

Adam: Once you do decide to participate in the discussions, and we strongly recommend that you do so when you feel you have something useful to add, be careful at first, since people are often judged on first impressions on the Internet. If you act as though you're Zeus's gift to the nets, people will quite correctly consider you to be a serious jerk. I suppose that if "serious jerk" describes you well, you might want to stick with that tone in your posts, but if you want anyone to listen to you and respond in a thoughtful and intelligent manner, you should pick up a little humility at the 7-Eleven.

Bill: `And some beef jerky while you're at it.`

Adam: Bill, you're a vegetarian.

Bill: `I'm not positive that beef jerky contains animal products.`

Adam: Good point—do vegetarians eat petrochemicals? In general, discussion lists are little worlds all to themselves, so what you've done or said in one group generally won't be known in another. This can be both good and bad—if you were a major contributor to one group and move to another, your reputation probably will neither precede nor follow you. You must prove yourself all over again, although I'd hope that you would know how to go about it more quickly the second time. However, if you managed to become known as a major drip on one list, you can move to another and enjoy a clean slate.

One of the Gang

Adam: We've talked about the processes of finding the group of people with whom you want to hang out, how not to offend them immediately, by lurking and watching what goes on, and some basics about introducing yourself to the list. But what about the majority of the time you spend on the list? How do you assimilate into the day-to-day conversations that ebb and flow across the wires? How do you become one of the gang, and how do you ascend to a chair on the front porch from which you can sit and spit while trading tall tales? Hopefully, it's mostly a matter of being your normal friendly self, but here are a few other things to consider.

Bill: `The means of becoming accepted in your group varies quite` `a bit. I believe my acceptance into a social group called the` `Pink Iguana Tavern began the day I started a pie fight. It began` `simply enough—I chose a safe target, the woman who had intro-` `duced me to the group in the first place. I knew that planting a` virtual pie in her face wouldn't upset her greatly, so she was my target. Of course, she had other friends present on Relay (the precursor to Internet Relay Chat, the interactive chatting part of the Internet) that night, and one of them, Frank, I think, sprang to her defense by informing me that I had just received a banana cream pie pressed firmly against my face. Somebody else who had probably been just looking for an excuse to get Frank leapt to my defense, and soon the proprietor had wheeled in the virtual dessert cart. The rest is history.

Adam: Sounds virtually messy.

Bill: Yes, but virtually tasty too. Of course, not every group will accept you on the basis of your written slapstick skills.

Adam: Since many of the discussion lists and Internet groups exchange useful, at least to the participants, information, making yourself useful always speeds the assimilation process. The more I learn about the business world, the more I realize it's not so much what you know, it's who you know. On the Internet, however, that doesn't fly. No one gives a hoot who you know, but if your knowledge is valuable to the members of the group, they appreciate it.

Bill: It is usually best to let others decide whether your knowledge is valuable to the members of the group, rather than deciding yourself, if you truly want to get along with them.

Adam: You must still dole out your knowledge with the online equivalent of a smile, since no one likes a know-it-all in the real world or on the Internet, even if you do. Know it all, that is.

I've tried to practice what I'm preaching here on the main groups in which I participate currently, the Info-Mac Digest and the **comp.sys.mac.comm** newsgroup. The Info-Mac Digest carries general Macintosh discussions, and since I know that there are plenty of knowledgeable and helpful folks on the list, I don't attempt to answer every question to which I happen to know the answer. However, if a question comes up in one of my fields of expertise, such as MacTCP connections to the Internet, Nisus (the word processor I use), recent events in the industry, or certain PowerBook issues, I try to jump in and help out. Much of the research I do for articles in *TidBITS* aids me in this process, so even if I decide not to write an article about something, I often share the knowledge I picked up on Info-Mac. As I see it, if I know an answer that no one else on the group is likely to know, it's my duty to my friends to pass on that bit of information.

Signal-to-Noise

Adam: One of the reasons for the proliferation of Usenet newsgroups is that they tend to split into much smaller groups to bring the signal-to-noise ratio back into line.

Bill: Whack! Two-minute penalty for jargon.

Adam: Humph. Let me explain, will you? *Signal-to-noise* is a phrase that probably comes from a field like electrical engineering or something, but it's quite simple with regard to information on the Internet. *Signal* is information that interests you, and *noise* is information that you would prefer never darkened your monitor. The concept applies well to many fields—for instance, in terms of music, for me, Leonard Cohen is signal, whereas Kate Bush is noise.

Bill: Hey!

Adam: Knew that would get a rise out of you. Note that I didn't say that signal was information that was generally interesting, since it's not. Signal is information that interests you, and possibly no one else. What interests Bill may bore me stiff, and vice versa. That's why we participate in different groups on the Internet. But, in fact, any group talks about a large number of different topics, and as an individual, you may find yourself utterly uninterested in most of them. That's fine—there's no one checking up on you to see if you read all the messages in a group.

Of course, if you have a technical bent, you'll consider any socializing to be noise, since it doesn't convey useful information for you. And, for the socialites (or is it socialists?), the socializing might be all you want from life.

Bill: The concept of signal-to-noise doesn't apply everywhere, of course. You need a focus of some kind in order for noise to interfere with it. The Pink Iguana Tavern, for instance, was entirely a social group—everything we talked about could be considered signal. Or noise, if you prefer. But nothing was outside the intended topic of discussion, since there wasn't one.

Interactive Internet

Adam: OK, here comes a fun section.

Bill: Yes, this one should really irritate our production folks. That's great fun. "Wow," I'll say, "how can we ever make something like this look good?" "Don't worry about it," Adam will

respond. "That's why Hayden has production people!" Then we attempt to laugh in a sinister manner, like the late Mr. Vincent
Price would.

Adam: Most people communicate on the Internet through email or Usenet
postings. These are roughly analogous to letters and telegrams—the sender
sends when she's ready, and the recipient collects the mail when he's ready.
Eventually, the process reverses and then repeats itself, and thus is a conversation born.

Bill: If you're better about writing your mail than I am, anyway.
But there are other ways to communicate and interact on the
Internet that involve live, real-time conversations. This is
analogous to the telephone or, to be more specific, the party
line. You actual carry on your conversations with people as you
sit at your terminal, typing what you want to send as you read
what other people are saying to you. If it sounds confusing, just
wait a few paragraphs and all should become clear.

Adam: First, we plan to visit several areas—they're called "channels"—on IRC,
which stands for *Internet Relay Chat*. We're not going to settle for attempting to
tell you about IRC; we'll let the people who hang out there tell you themselves.

Bill: And then we'll pay a quick visit to FurryMUCK, an example
of a multi-user role-playing environment where everyone pretends
to be anthropomorphized animals. Except me, of course. I'm a six-
foot tall anthropomorphic pickle.

Adam: Sigh, leave it to me to find the one guy who can't even act weird in synch
with everyone else.

Bill: Damn straight.

Adam: Bear in mind that we've edited *very* heavily. There was far too much
material to include here; we've only taken excerpts, and even those were edited
for content and appearance.

Bill: But in some sense, our editing better retains the proper
flavor of the discussions than the original transcripts do. After
you've spent some time on IRC or on a MUD, your brain filters out
much of the extraneous garbage that we've filtered for you here,
and starts putting together fragments of conversation into a
coherent whole.

Adam: Let's get started with our first stop on IRC, the #superguy channel.

IRC— #superguy

Bill: I suppose that in this section, since I actually know everyone who participates, I should provide a cheat sheet, so our readers know which person matches to which nickname.

Adam: Yeah, I could have used that to begin with.

Bill: OK, **Rubicon** is Eric Burns, **Superuser** is Bill Paul (commonly known as the Man with Two First Names), and **the_Swede** is Gary Olson. You'll see us refer to each other by all these names and by others in this conversation.

Adam: Keep in mind, folks, that Bill knows these people pretty well. As a result, a lot of the silliness is the product of years of practice.

Bill: And beer.

Adam: I guess. First, let's take a picture so you can see what's happening.

*** Server:	AdamEngst has joined channel #superguy
*** Server:	BillDcksn has joined channel #superguy
<BillDcksn>	All right, everybody, Adam's going to switch into greyscale and take a snapshot.
<AdamEngst>	Smile for the snapshot...
<the_Swede>	heh...
<Superuser>	Won't that hurt?
<the_Swede>	my, i feel so... grey...
<Rubicon>	Cheese!!!!!!!!!! <Bill's, that is>
<the_Swede>	beeeer!
<Superuser>	Prozac!!!

Bill: In the ensuing pandemonium, we did manage to take a snapshot. Notice the nice interface in Homer, and the fact you can even see pictures for some of us (see figure 5.6).

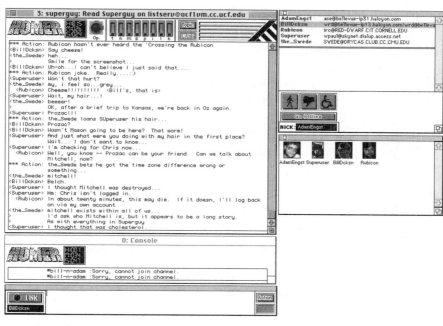

Figure 5.6   *Superguy authors; yes, they are really that weird*

<AdamEngst>   OK, after a brief trip to Kansas, we're back in Oz again.

<Superuser>   Wait, my hair...!

                *** Action: the_Swede loans Superuser his hair...

<Superuser>   And just what were you doing with my hair in the first place? Wait... I don't want to know...

  <Rubicon>   Well, you know — Prozac can be your friend.

<Superuser>   I thought that was cholesterol.

<BillDcksn>   So didn't we have some interview questions or something?

<AdamEngst>   OK, first question - perhaps stupid. Do you get anything "productive" done on IRC? Or is email more useful? Obviously it depends on your definition of productive.

<the_Swede>   what... this isn't productive?

<Superuser>   Well, we collaborate a lot on Superguy writing, and it's easier to discuss things live than via mail.

<Rubicon>   Productive... well, as a co-writer of Superguy, I'd have to say yes. It's a place where I can contact other of my Superguy authors and discuss upcoming events and the like

<the_Swede>   the only time i recall ever doing something productive here is while the bills and i were working on a storyline back in december...

<Superuser>   In case you haven't guessed, we don't use IRC for work purposes.

<the_Swede>   i don't have net access at work, as they expect me to do actual work or something...

<Superuser>   The fiends.

<BillDcksn>   Well, unless we can turn Superguy into a meal ticket...

<Superuser>   I just had a meal, thank you...

<Rubicon>   Well — I can list some 'practical' applications.

<Superuser>   Go ahead: I dare you.

<Rubicon>   In my guise as a mild-mannered English Lit type person, I have had actual scholarly discourse on here — and therefore I have found productive use of IRC. Nah nah nah

Bill: Eric's comment touched off a massive dose of silliness that has been edited out for brevity. However, you can find much more of its kind in *Internet Explorer Kit for Macintosh*, where this very conversation is reproduced in all of its glory.

Adam: Well, most of its glory, anyway. We next tried to get back onto an interview question...

<BillDcksn>   OK, guys, this is for Adam's benefit. And don't try to lie, because I know the answer:

<the_Swede>   awww... telling the truth's no fun...

```
<Superuser>    No, you can't borrow any money.

 <Rubicon>     So what's the next question, o Writer-types? :)

<BillDcksn>    Would you say your electronic persona, in an
               environment like IRC, is different from your
               real-life persona?

<Superuser>    What real-life persona...

<BillDcksn>    Oooooo, good answer :)

<Superuser>    Hell[tm], I barely have a real-life, let alone a
               persona...
```

Adam: Is Hell trademarked?

Bill: In the Superguy universe, Hell™ is actually a corporation, and yes, the name is trademarked. The main offices are in Fong's Enchilada Emporium, a Mexican restaurant staffed by the souls of the damned.

Adam: Why is it that every time I ask you a question about Superguy, I wish I hadn't?

```
<the_Swede>    in IRC? not really... i'm not on often enough
               for that... on the muck, yes...

 <Rubicon>     Ooo... tough question...

<Superuser>    Dowh!

<the_Swede>    okey dokey...:)

 <Rubicon>     I would say my electronic persona is very like
               my real persona — my friends who I have met
               online and then met in life say I'm a lot like
               who I say I am on the net :)

<Superuser>    Except that in real-life, Eric looks like a hot-
               dog vendor. :)

<BillDcksn>    Two points!

<the_Swede>    or, without his beard, like one of the super
               mario brothers...

 <Rubicon>     Hey, Bill — they know what I look like. I'm on
               their screen, remember?
```

```
<BillDcksn>    Adopts an interviewer persona. "So then, would
               you say that people sign onto IRC to insult each
               other?"

<Superuser>    %^&^#&*(%*(O^*!

<the_Swede>    *^(&*^%%$#%&*(%*&%^&^$&#^!

<AdamEngst>    Seems the answer is yes.

<the_Swede>    umm... well, actually, not really...

<Superuser>    Hmm... you are going to edit all this before
               putting it into the book, yes?

<AdamEngst>    Maybe. They're going to like the insulting parts
               of the book, Bill.

<Superuser>    I thought we were the insulting parts of the
               book.

<the_Swede>    hey, readers! your mothers dress you funny!
```

Adam: Hmm, on that note, let's move on to another channel.

IRC— #macintosh

Bill: Next, we figured that we would drop in on what might be a
more technical channel, one perhaps more aimed at talking about
a specific subject, rather than one that's purely for social
chatting.

Adam: Since we're both Macintosh users, it seemed only natural to drop in on
the #macintosh channel. Maybe we'd even know someone there. Bill's friends
had all been told to meet us in the #superguy channel, so that wasn't spontane-
ous. Maybe this one would be different.

```
*** Server:    AdamEngst has joined channel #macintosh

*** Server:    BillDcksn has joined channel #macintosh

<BillDcksn>    Hey there!

   <ackpht>    AdamEngst: as in TidBITS?

<AdamEngst>    Yup, that's me.

   <ackpht>    cool

<tHINGLES>     wow... adam engst...
```

```
      <GreenGoo>    tidbits?

      <tHINGLES>    and bill... the dude that the dialog is with in
                    the new book about the internet?

      <BillDcksn>   Bingo. Guess why we're here?

      <tHINGLES>    ahh... the book? :)

      <BillDcksn>   We're on our IRC chapter :). Thought this would
                    be a good place to stop in.

            <rvf>   hey adam

      <AdamEngst>   Bill's showing me around IRC - I've basically
                    never used it before.

      <tHINGLES>    which is a shame... :)

      <BillDcksn>   If you guys don't mind, we'd like to talk about
                    it with you...

      <AdamEngst>   Not enough time in the day to do all the things
                    I already do, which is the main problem. :-) I
                    get hammered in email.

   *** Action:      tHINGLES ups the notch for net.celebrities
                    coming into #macintosh

            <rvf>   that is a shame... but everyone's got to learn
                    sometime

      <GreenGoo>    its the perfect thing to prevent anyone from
                    doing REAL work

            <rvf>   I can believe it...
```

Bill: Serendipitously, we were almost instantly presented with an example of how someone can get useful information on IRC. And Adam even got to participate!

```
   *** Server:      SpYcE has joined channel #macintosh

         <SpYcE>    do you think i should sell my Quadra 700 and get
                    a Q650???

      <AdamEngst>   Nah, I'd hold on to the 700.

         <SpYcE>    why is that?

      <AdamEngst>   I'm hearing good things about the PowerPC up-
                    grade cards that you should theoretically be
                    able to put in a Q700.
```

```
    <tHINGLES>    me 2. don't do anything with your apple labeled
                  CPU's for the next month

      <SpYcE>     hmm. i can get a 650 for about $1300

   <AdamEngst>    You'll be able to boot under either PowerPC or
                  68040 modes, and it's unclear if the performance
                  might not even be better in some cases due to
                  the 1 MB cache RAM.

      <SpYcE>     so i should wait... how about if i buy the 650
                  and keep the 700 as well ;)

   <AdamEngst>    A 650 isn't a significant enough improvement
                  over the 700 to bother until the Power Macs
                  settle in.

   <AdamEngst>    Of course, if you just want more Macs, that's
                  fine. :-)

      <SpYcE>     well i must go watch a movie... thanx for the
                  help

*** Server:       Signoff: SpYcE (Leaving)
```

Adam: That was enough to show a bit of contrast, I think. Now that we've had a taste of IRC, let's take a look at another form of live interpersonal interaction on the Internet.

MUCKing with the Furries

Bill: Adam and I are now going to enter a different sort of interactive setting, known as a MU*.

Adam: A what?

Bill: A MU*. The asterisk is a wildcard, allowing the term to stand for MUD, MUCK, MUSH, or whatever the latest variety is. MUDs were the first of this set of programs, and the term stands for *Multi-User Dungeon* or *Multi-User Dimension*, depending on who you're talking to and perhaps on the MUD in question.

Adam: This sounds like a different type of IRC. Similar idea, correct?

Bill: Well, on a basic level, yes. It's a program that enables numerous people on the Internet all to interact with each other in real time. But MUDs and their ilk open up a whole new realm of possibilities.

Adam: I've heard that MUDs are an environment of sorts, in which you can move about and role-play, much like a game.

Bill: Yes, but in many of them the role-playing is much more like theatre than like a game of Acuras & Attorneys.

Adam: Is that a real game?

Bill: Good lord, no.

Adam: Phew!

Bill: A MUD has another important feature—it is user-modifiable. If you join a MUD and create a character, and the owners of the MUD permit it, you can build your own home and describe it. Other characters (and, by proxy, their players) can then visit and explore your home, experiencing it as you have defined it. There is a very real sense of space on a MUD.

Adam: That's difficult to wrap the mind around. What do you mean by the character's home? The character is just an artificial construct, right?

Bill: Not if you're a good enough actor. But I realize this can be confusing to talk about, so I'm not going to try to explain it further. It would be far better simply to show you.

We'll visit a MUCK known as FurryMUCK. The concept is a bit interesting: the characters are all anthropomorphized animals, creatures known as "furries."

Adam: Oh, great... you're going to introduce me to something I don't understand, using as an example, something else I don't understand.

Bill: Yup! Brace yourself... we're going to jump right into an interesting bit of the conversation we had while we were visiting, in which our hosts discussed the differences they see between MUDs and IRC.

```
          _____              _ _  _  _ _  _  _   ,
       / '                  ' ) ) ) ' ) / / ) ' ) /
    ,-/-, . . __  __  __  , / / /  / / /     /-<
   (_/   (_/_/ (_/ (_/ (_/ / ' (_  (__/ (__/  /   )
                        /
                        '
```

AdamEngst says, "We've just spent some time on IRC - how do you think the socializing here is different? Do you use IRC at all?"

Mer'rark walks in from Sable Street.

Mer'rark says, "Slice was telling me there's some guys writing a book about this place?"

FoxTrot yaps, "Here it is a little different then IRC because people have characters they use to express themselves."

Triggur whickers, "This environment is much richer than IRC. Less artificial."

ErmaFelna says, "There's more of a sense of *place* here... you can move around, have a distinct concept of rooms and objects... this is much more of a game as well."

Dekhyr says, "Never been on IRC. Or any 'social MUD' for that matter, except this one. And this one only two weeks ago. Used to play hack-n-slash MUDs. Got bored of it. Socializing this way for some reason seems to be better than the pot-luck I tend to get in RL."

FoxTrot yaps, "Also, IRC is highly topic oriented, here, you can go somewhere and the topic will change a lot."

Kimiko nods at FoxTrot.

ErmaFelna says, "This place is much more flexible than IRC; it's a lot easier for the players to modify the general environment. Anyone can add new commands for people to use, or reprogram portions of the setup. I've written programs to do anything from making a lock that only lets the people inside choose who can come in, to creating an object that can be used as a container."

Dekhyr says, "Probably the thing I like about Furry most of all is that you *need* a kind of extroverted imagination to even play a furry in the first place."

Adam: As it happens, we visited FurryMUCK very shortly after a rather unflattering description of the place appeared in *Wired* magazine. Our hosts took the opportunity, while talking to us, to rebut the article, fairly convincingly. A little bit of that conversation:

```
AdamEngst says, "What do furries generally think about the out-
                side view of MUDs and this MUCK in specific? Is
                that view unrealistic or off-base?"

Triggur whickers, "Uhhhh... 'too kyoot' is a common reaction :)
                lots of outsiders think this place is too sticky
                sweet, especially from a MUD standpoint."

FoxTrot yaps, "They are quite often biased towards one activity,
                as WIRED illustrates."

Dekhyr says, "I think everyone latches on to the erotic sector of
                MUCK. Too emotionally charged."

Dekhyr says, "Some people couldn't imagine playing a MUD. They
                feel it's a waste of time."

Lynx purrs, "Dunno, you tell me, what's the outside view of MUDs
                and MUCKs?"

AdamEngst says, "Well, the addictive nature of MUDs is certainly
                mentioned a lot."

Kimiko nods, they ARE addictive... worlds can be created here...

Lynx nods. This is true. Stay away, AdamEngst, you'll find your
                free time slipping away...

ErmaFelna says, "This particular MUCK has a very general theme,
                which means that things tend to be extremely
                free-form. What big events do happen tend to be
                very fast versions of co-operative story-tell-
                ing, with a lot of the same difficulties: one
                person can Deus Ex Machina the plotline and ruin
                it for everyone else."

Pickle declares, "Erma, is there a set of rules to guide things
                like that?"

ErmaFelna says, "Rules? Not really... just politesse and some
                general guidelines."

Triggur whickers, "thank GOD there's no rules :)"
```

```
Kratsminsch says, "I've also used the MUCK to contact experts in
             certain fields, when I got lost trying to fix
             something RL."
```

```
Kimiko does that too! (have a computer Q? @shout for an answer!)
```

```
Bill: And finally, in one of my favorite moments, we got to see
that old-timers like to berate the newcomers on MUDs, just like
in real life:
```

```
Pickle declares, "How long has Furry been around?"
```

```
ErmaFelna says, "It's been around a little over three years, now.
             Of course, some of us have been MUDding since
             before Furry existed."  She nods over to Lynx.
```

```
Lynx mumbles something about how when HE was a kit, we had to
             telnet 12 miles uphill through thick snow and
             line noise to get to a MUD, and then we
             telnetted 12 miles back the other way, also
             uphill, to get a response back, and we LYKED yt.
```

```
Bill: And on that note, I think it's time to move on.
```

Browsing the Second-Hand Bookstore of the Internet

Adam: The Internet is many things to many people, but when we were trying to think about how to express the range of information available on the Internet, all we could think of was a second-hand bookstore.

```
Bill: That's because in a second-hand bookstore, you're likely to
wander around, gazing aimlessly at the books until something
catches your eye, at which point you'll pick it up and browse
through it.
```

Adam: And even if you're looking for something about cooking, say, you don't go to a second-hand bookstore with a specific idea of what you want to buy. You go thinking, "Maybe I'll buy a cookbook today." If you want Julia Child's *The Way to Cook* specifically, you'll go to a fancy new bookstore.

```
Bill: We're going to wander aimlessly on the Internet for a
while, seeing what we may see.
```

Adam: And then we'll look for some general categories of information, just so you can see the sorts of things that are out there. Once again, don't worry about the technical details of what we do here. Just file them away in the back of your mind, and once you've played with some of the Macintosh programs yourself, perhaps read this section again to get a feel for how people actually use the Internet.

Aimless Wandering

Bill: Some days you get up and realize you want to do something, but you're not at all certain exactly what. I do, anyway. This is the sort of day that often leads me into one of the more active parts of town, window shopping and hanging out in bookstores, thumbing through anything that catches my eye, or in music stores, flipping through all the compact discs from A to Z.

While I'm looking around, I often find one or two items of inter-est that I want to take home with me. I find many other things that have an interesting cover or a nice store display, but which completely fail to live up to the initial intrigue. But I never feel I've wasted my time, because of the unexpected finds.

We're now going to take a semi-random drive through some of the information you can find on the Internet. At first, we're going to use a program called Mosaic that simplifies browsing on the World-Wide Web.

Adam: Let me explain a little bit about the World-Wide Web that we're traveling on before I go much further. The World-Wide Web is made up of many docu-ments that include text, graphics, sounds, and even movies, but most impor-tantly, these documents contain links to other documents scattered around the world. As I write this, there is no way to see a list of everything that exists on the Web.

Not only can you not see a list of all the documents on the Web, or even a list of all the machines that are part of the Web, there is currently no way to search for any specific item on the Web. Because of this fact, numerous sites have created sets of links that collect and categorize various different types of information. You might think of these sites as live encyclopedias—as new resources appear, the people who run these encyclopedia sites check out the new resources and add them to the encyclopedia.

There are two basic groupings that I've seen in encyclopedic sites—chronological and topical. The NCSA What's New page is an example of a *chronological* listing—the only way you can find resources in it is to browse through them. And, if the resource you're looking for appeared before the current month, you have to switch to a different What's New page for the month in which that resource appeared. It's great for browsing and lousy for searching.

Bill: We're going to take a quick spin around the Web now, with Adam driving. Let's see if he can take us somewhere fun, shall we?

Adam: I'm starting my trip at the National Center for Supercomputing Applications, mostly because that's where their slick NCSA Mosaic program takes you first, by default.

Bill: Just to clarify—Mosaic is what we call a *client program*. The World-Wide Web isn't a program, *per se*, though there are programs that make it perform different functions. These are called *server programs*, and their job is to offer up the Web's information using standard procedures. A client program familiar with these procedures is required in order for you, the user, to obtain and make use of the information.

You might think of the server software as being a dessert cart; you're not allowed to put your filthy paws on the pastries, so you need a client, a set of tongs, perhaps, to obtain that tasty éclair. Mosaic is our set of tongs. There are other tongs now available, such as MacWeb.

Adam: Nice simile, Bill, but now I'm getting hungry. All right, I'm going to act on whim now and use a link on the NCSA Home Page to go back in time and look at the old What's New page from November. I remember some good stuff from back then.

Hmm, here's something that sounds interesting. What do you suppose the Fractal Microscope is, Bill?

Bill: No idea. How would they get a fractal onto the slide? Do you need a cover slip? If you cut a fractal in half, will both halves regenerate?

Adam: Ahem. It seems to be in some way related to a program, written by NCSA for schools, with which students can explore fractals, and thus the art and science of mathematics. I think it runs on a supercomputer, which means that it's really fast. But for the life of me, I can't find anything that lets us play with it. That's why I wasn't a biology major at Cornell—they wouldn't let me play with the electron microscope freshman year. And now I appear to be too old to play with the Fractal Microscope.

Bill: Salescritters often use fractal programs to show off the graphics capabilities of a computer. There must be some out there for the Mac—want to find one?

Adam: Sure—we'll use WAIS for this one. I'm going to search in the macintosh-news database, since it stores all of the Info-Mac Digests, where most new programs are announced (see figure 5.7).

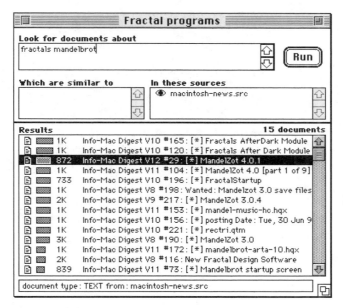

Figure 5.7   *Plenty of them out there*

Bill: Pretty cool. Can we actually see any of these images on the Internet?

Adam: It appears so—at the Fractal Microscope server I see a link to a gallery of fractal images located in France. Going there we first see a link to the image of the guy who maintains this server. The server also claims to have animations as well as static images, but let's stick with the pictures, since animations are often quite large and will take a long time to download so we can view them (see figure 5.8).

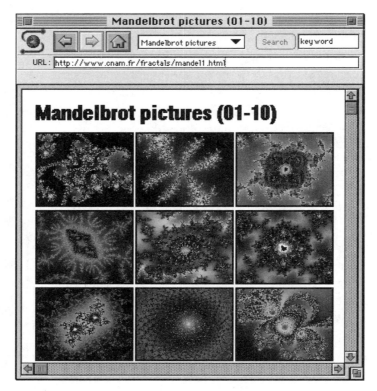

Figure 5.8   *The tenth image removed for symmetry's sake*

Adam: Time to switch back to the What's New page and browse some more. Here's something for the online activists to get their teeth into—a server called INFACT Online.

Bill: What's that stand for?

Adam: I don't know—they don't seem to say. It appears to have something to do with an anti-tobacco campaign. Let's go there and read more about it. Yes, it is indeed true Internet activism, and their specific mission is to store information relating to the campaign to force tobacco companies to stop marketing cigarettes to children (see figure 5.9).

Figure 5.9   *Smoke; Look cool, smell bad*

Poking around some more on this server turns up an open letter to the Internet so you can learn more about what they're trying to do and why, and here are some form letters that you can download, fill in, and mail to the chief executive officers of various tobacco companies. I like the logos (see figure 5.10).

Figure 5.10   Say it ain't so, Joe

Bill: This server seems to be quite a bit better-organized than most. Who set this thing up?

Adam: Judging from the home page, it's maintained by a man named Tom Boutell. He's even provided a link to his own home page.

Bill: Let's go there. I'm jealous—I've always wanted my own home page.

Adam: It includes a picture of him and even a sound that says, "I live in Seattle. I telecommute to New York. It's a hell of a drive."

Bill: Hey, another Seattlelite. Where does he live?

Adam: Wait a minute—here's a pointer called "Where I live." Clicking on that takes us to, hmm, looks like a site run by Xerox PARC (Palo Alto Research Center), home of many Very Smart Folks who have come up with ideas like the graphical interface for computers, which has evolved into the Macintosh and Windows interfaces.

The Xerox PARC site shows a map of the Northwest with Seattle roughly in the center, but it's not particularly detailed (see figure 5.11).

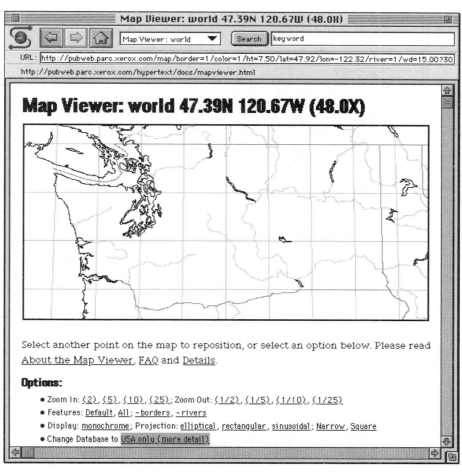

Figure 5.11   Our little corner of the world

There seem to be various controls for zooming in—Awk! The host machine at Xerox just went down. Blast it, just as it was getting interesting. Humph, we'll have to come back later when the machine is back up. That sort of thing happens on the Internet, and you never know whose fault it is. Thus, it's best to just assume that not everything is perfect and avoid stressing out over machines that you can't connect to.

Bill: Such is life.

Adam: Let's try another link from the What's New page. I've always been a sucker for dinosaur exhibits in museums, so let's take a peek at the University of California at Berkeley Paleontology Exhibit—I've heard other people say that it's well done.

It has a nice entry page that I can't show you because the picture was too large to fit into a reasonable figure. Those of you who can, just go there yourself and browse around. Instead, let's check out the About page (see figure 5.12).

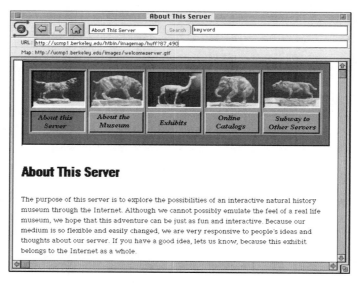

Figure 5.12   *They have the best icons of anything I've seen yet*

Adam: In this case, they have all sorts of statistics about how many people have stopped in for a look around. In January, the UC Berkeley Paleontology exhibit served 1,242,427,149 bytes of information contained in 98,401 files. That's more than 1.2 gigabytes of information, and when you average it out, it comes out to 3514 files of 44,372,398 bytes (44M) per day.

Bill: That's a lot of information to send around the world on the Internet.

Adam: And it's growing all the time. In the first nine days of February, the site averaged more than 62 megabytes of data each day. I've heard statistics that say that traffic on the World-Wide Web increases at more than 300 percent per month. We're probably boring our nice readers with all these numbers, so let's go check out the exhibits (see figure 5.13).

Bill: Ooo, good stuff.

Adam: I see that I can quite easily spend the rest of my afternoon here, browsing through the exhibits, and all without hurting my feet. So let's stop wandering and see if we can find something specific.

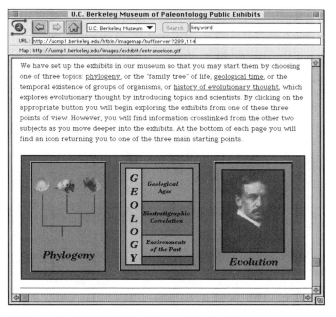

Figure 5.13   *Where to start, that's always the problem*

I Wonder If

Adam: Although the World-Wide Web is the best place for aimless wandering, it's currently pretty much useless if you want to find information on a given topic. I expect that will change, but as it stands, you have to know how to find something on the Web, or at least stumble across it once while exploring. In order to find out what information is available on some general topic, I usually turn to WAIS databases and Gopherspace.

Bill: What about Archie?

Adam: Archie is also a good tool for answering a nagging curiosity, although Archie's information generally seems to be less useful to me than what I find via WAIS and Gopher, mostly because all Archie finds is files, and then you must transfer them to your Mac before you can find out whether there's anything useful inside. Anyway, let's start with penguins.

Bill: Penguins? You're going to use the most powerful information tool in history to search for flightless waterfowl?

Adam: Smile when you say that. Just to placate you, I'll start with an Archie search via Anarchie. It finds a good number of files (see figure 5.14) with the word "penguin" in the title, although there are number of duplicates, and most of the rest appear to be graphics files, including a scan of the cover from Berke Breathed's *Penguin Dreams and Stranger Things*.

Name	Size	Date	Zone	Host	Path
penguin-dreams.jpg	155k	10/14/93	5	ftp.sunet.se	/pub/pictures/comics/Bloom.County/penguin-dreams.jpg
penguin-dreams.txt	1k	10/14/93	5	ftp.sunet.se	/pub/pictures/comics/Bloom.County/penguin-dreams.txt
penguin-registration-nums.hqx	23k	9/18/91	1	wuarchive.wustl.edu	/systems/mac/info-mac/Old/card/penguin-registration-nums.hqx
penguin-serial-numbers.hqx	34k	6/29/91	1	wuarchive.wustl.edu	/systems/mac/info-mac/Old/card/penguin-serial-numbers.hqx
penguin-utilities.hqx	116k	6/29/91	1	wuarchive.wustl.edu	/systems/mac/info-mac/Old/card/penguin-utilities.hqx
penguin.bitmap	6k	6/3/92	1	sumex-aim.stanford.edu	/pub/exp/images/penguin.bitmap
penguin.icon	2k	7/29/88	1	emx.cc.utexas.edu	/pub/mnt/images/icons/SunView/penguin.icon
penguin.pcx	4k	4/16/92	1	hpcsos.col.hp.com	/mirrors/.hplb0/hp951x/pcx/penguin.pcx
penguin.tar.Z	591k	10/6/93	2	ftp.cpsc.ucalgary.ca	/pub/blob/papers/penguin.tar.Z
penguin.txt	4k	2/20/91	1	ftp.nevada.edu	/pub/ocsd/ANTARCTICA1/penguin.txt
penguin.uss.tek.com	-	8/11/93	1	ftp.uu.net	/published/usenix/faces/penguin.uss.tek.com
penguin.uss.tek.com	-	8/21/93	1	ftp.cs.umn.edu	/pub/doc/published/usenix/faces/penguin.uss.tek.com
penguin.Z	1k	1/21/94	1	csd4.csd.uwm.edu	/pub/optimus/Graphics/animals/penguin.Z
penguin1.jpg	170k	7/30/92	5	sauna.cs.hut.fi	/pub/store/jpg/Misc/penguin1.jpg
penguin2.jpg	177k	7/30/92	5	sauna.cs.hut.fi	/pub/store/jpg/Misc/penguin2.jpg
penguins	-	4/10/93	1	ftp.luth.se	/pub/misc/lyrics/p/penguins
penguins	-	11/5/93	1	ftp.uwp.edu	/pub/music/artists/p/penguins
penguins.msa	284k	11/10/92	1	wuarchive.wustl.edu	/systems/atari/umich.edu/Games/penguins.msa
rsp-penguin.icon.Z	1k	4/17/88	5	huon.itd.adelaide.edu.au	/pub/sun-icons/rsp-penguin.icon.Z
rsp_penguin.gif	1k	1/5/93	1	ee.lbl.gov	/poskbitmaps/sun_icons/rsp_penguin.gif

Figure 5.14   *Penguin files on the Internet*

Bill: What's that one that lives in a "lyrics" folder?

Adam: I suspect it's the lyrics to a song done by a group called The Penguins. Let's retrieve the file and take a look. Whee—it seems to be the lyrics to "Earth Angel." We'll spare you.

Bill: Kate Bush it's not.

Adam: Enough of these files, and I'm not sure that I want to delve any further in that group's lyrics. Next up is a swing through Gopherspace, using TurboGopher and searching via Veronica. Although it often makes a difference how you search for things in Veronica, in this case I think "penguin" will probably find most everything we could want. The range of penguin items in Gopherspace is much broader than the range of files that merely have the word "penguin" in their names (see figure 5.15).

Look at all those books written for penguins. You never realized that penguins were such literary birds, did you Bill?

Bill: Those are books from the publishing house called Penguin Books.

Adam: Oh. Are you sure?

Bill: Positive. But what's that bit about penguin events at Cornell?

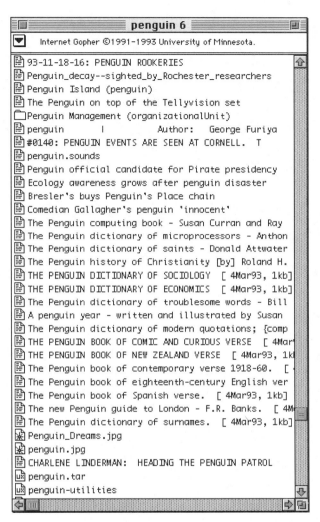

Figure 5.15   *Penguins in Gopherspace*

Adam: A friend told me about that a while back. It's some thoroughly obscure physics thing where the Feynman diagram of it looks vaguely like a penguin.

Bill: Oh, come now. You're making that up.

Adam: No, I'm not. Take a look at figure 5.16.

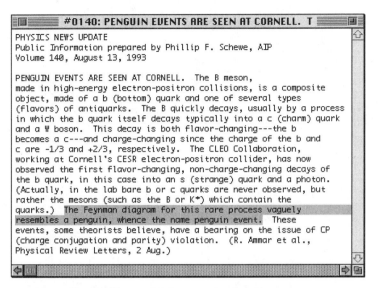

Figure 5.16　*Penguins infiltrate high-energy physics*

Bill: Say, what have we got out there on movies? I need some information for my Lambada film festival.

Adam: First, Bill, that's a terrible idea. Second, you should save it for later, when we find specific things. Third, umm, what's a Lambada?

Bill: True, that's a bit more specific than we want right now. The Lambada is a type of dance, Brazilian I believe, in which the partners get extraordinarily close. It makes for terrible movies. How about just general movie information?

Adam: That, we've got (see figure 5.17).

Bill: Well, I think that's an adequate warm-up. We've browsed and searched on general topics just to see if they're out there. I think now it's time we work on something a bit more practical.

Adam: Yes. Lest our readers begin to think that the Internet is useful only to browsing bookworms with time on their hands, let's see if it can answer some specific questions for us. Will we be able to find what we're looking for? Will any good information exist? Will our editor tell us we're blathering too much? Is there any other way I can create some suspense?

Bill: Only way to find out is to try it. Let's go dig for some answers.

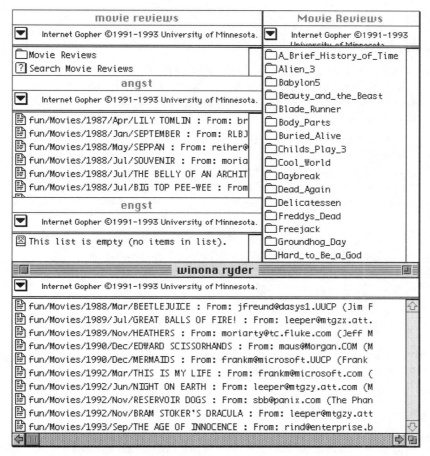

Figure 5.17   *The electronic Siskel and Ebert*

Looking for Files in All the Wrong Places

Bill: We've separated the things we're going to look for into two groups we're going to call "files" and "facts." A *file* is any given thing that you want to obtain—a program for your computer, for instance, or a back issue of an electronic journal you can obtain over the Internet, such as *InterText* or *Møøse Droppings*.

You might also find the lyrics to that song that's been driving
you crazy for the past 36 hours, such as the theme to "Gilligan's
Island."

Adam: Whatever you do, folks, don't think about it! Just drive the millionaire
and his wife straight from your mind. Don't let it take hold! Don't think about
the theme to "Gilligan's Island"! Just relax, and sit right back, and you'll hear a
tale, a tale of a fateful trip…

Bill: Adam, that was a terrible thing to do! Folks, I apologize.
After we've gone out onto the Internet and located some files,
we'll start looking for facts. A *fact* is any piece of information
that you can locate on the Internet—the answer to a riddle, help
on a specific problem you may be having, or perhaps a concert
date.

Let's get started; maybe we can distract you so you don't think
about the theme to "Gilligan's Island" too much. We're going to
be downloading a few things, so I'll want to make some room. Hold
on while I clean up my desktop a bit here…

Adam: Wait, how did you do that?

Bill: Do what?

Adam: You dragged that icon into your menu. The Mac doesn't normally allow
that.

Bill: Oh, that's MenuDropper, by David Winterburn! I couldn't
live without it, and as freeware, you can't beat the price.

Adam: Well, let's go get it. This is a case where a direct approach could work
well: I know MenuDropper's name, and I know where Macintosh utilities are
stored. I could probably find it relatively quickly by browsing through the
directories on **sumex-aim.stanford.edu**.

Bill: But you can never get into that site these days. It's become extremely popular, and tends to be completely filled with as
many users as it can support, all the time. So we're probably
going to have to find another source.

Adam: True, and that's a good use for Archie, since we can ask Anarchie to
search for the file and tell us where it lives. A double-click later and it will be on
my hard disk.

Bill: I should note once again that Archie is the name of the
program that runs on the Internet machine, whereas Anarchie (pronounced like "anarchy," not "an archie") is a Macintosh program
that talks to the remote Archie program.

Adam: I'm going to take advantage of a small piece of information I happen to know from having been around for a while. There are two main sites that archive Macintosh files, and they have slightly different naming schemes. The Info-Mac folks like putting dashes between words, whereas the administrators of the site at **mac.archive.umich.edu** don't use any separator at all. Since we're searching for a file called MenuDropper, I suspect that it will be called either "menu-dropper" or "menudropper" so I'll search on both of those words.

Bill: And the winner is...?

Adam: Anarchie was able to find a number of sites that carry the same file. In this instance, I'm afraid we're going to have be rude and request a file from overseas, since I know for a fact that the U.S. sites that we've found are down (see figure 5.18).

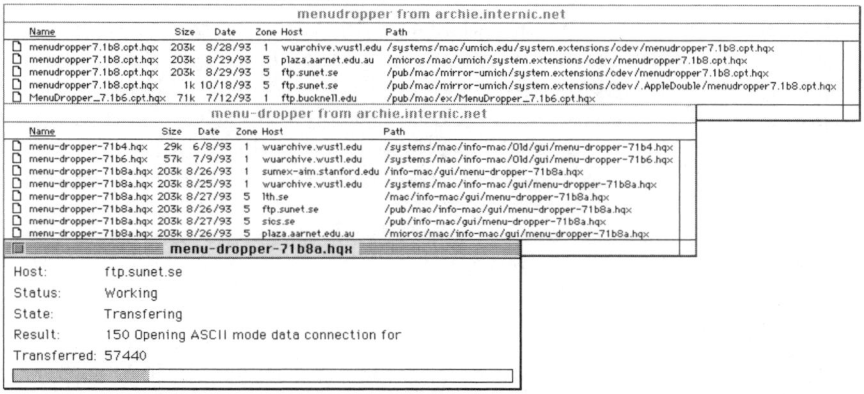

Figure 5.18   *The Scandinavian version of MenuDropper*

Adam: Luckily, it's early evening here in Seattle, which means that it should be the middle of the night in Sweden, where the file we're snagging lives. If you must use a site on the other side of the ocean, please try to do so in the middle of the night there, when you aren't likely to interrupt people trying to do real work.

Bill: I've heard of a game called Bolo that can supposedly be played over the Internet. You can locate ongoing games and join in, teaming up with and fighting against people you've never met. Could be fun.

Adam: Sounds like you've been watching too much violence on television again. But sure, let's see if we can find it.

Chapter 5
Exploring the
Internet

Bill: Shall we do an Anarchie search? We know what we're after,
and it's a program, so we know it'll be stored at an FTP site.
This kind of search is what Archie was made for, and Anarchie
will make it easy to retrieve the file once we've found it.

Adam: In many cases, you'd be right about a situation like this. But Bolo's
extremely popular, and there has been an awful lot of Bolo-oriented stuff
produced. I suspect you may be disappointed by Archie on this one.

Bill: Good lord, you're right. Anarchie was set to tell us about
the first 100 items it found with "bolo" in their names, and it
did that admirably—unfortunately, the actual game itself didn't
turn up in the list! We'd have to boost that 100-item limit way
up to find the program, I bet.

Adam: I can't quite say why, but this feels like a job for Veronica. Since it's just
as easy to retrieve files via TurboGopher as with Anarchie, there's no real reason
not to search with Veronica and, if it finds anything, download directly in
TurboGopher. The only thing I don't like about downloading files in
TurboGopher is that it doesn't tell you how large the file is, so you don't know
how long it will take, or how far along you are at any given time. Nevertheless,
there are a ton of Bolo folders and one of them contains Bolo 0.99.2, which I
believe is the latest version (see figure 5.19).

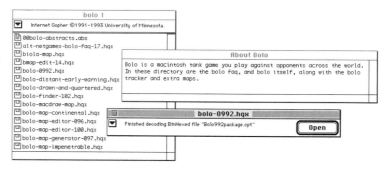

Figure 5.19   *More than one way to skin a tank game*

Adam: For our last "thing" search, let's find a weather map. I'm pretty sure
some of those exist on the Internet, and it would be nice to see what sort of
weather we're having right now.

Bill: Why don't you look out the window?

Adam: Because it's dark.

Bill: Oh, right, you live in the 'burbs. There aren't many streetlights outside of the city.

Adam: OK, let's see if we can figure out what sort of weather system is over the East coast, hammering on our parents.

Bill: For the reader at home, it's hard to tell, but this is taking a while. If you like, I could entertain you with my rendition of various pirate songs from *Peter Pan* while we wait.

Adam: No, wait! I've found a weather map. It wasn't as easy as I thought it should have been, though. I did a Veronica search on "weather map" but every one of the folders of weather maps that it found turned out to be a bum steer.

Bill: Interesting mental picture on that phrase. So that's what was happening when you were downloading that file for 20 minutes. I thought you were downloading Willard Scott himself for a while there.

Adam: Yeah, I didn't time it, but the file was almost two megabytes large and was a gorgeous satellite picture of the planet, complete with white parts that might have been clouds.

Bill: Oh, yeah, I see it. It's pretty, why don't we use that figure?

Adam: Because you can't tell from the picture what part of the planet you're even looking at.

Bill: Hmm. True. In fact, you can't even tell which planet it is. How do weatherbeings interpret this stuff? You might as well hand them a Picasso.

Adam: No kidding. But I did eventually figure out how to find a better map of the United States. I remember seeing something about weather once in a list of Internet resources maintained by Scott Yanoff. You can get a copy of this list from Scott's machine, and you can find out what machine that is by using Finger on Scott's address. I've done this before, so my copy of Finger remembered it.

Bill: Lucky.

Adam: I prefer to think of it as foresight. Anyway, once I retrieved the entire Special Internet Services list, I found a site mentioned as having weather information, so I went there with TurboGopher, found the maps, and downloaded one (see figure 5.20).

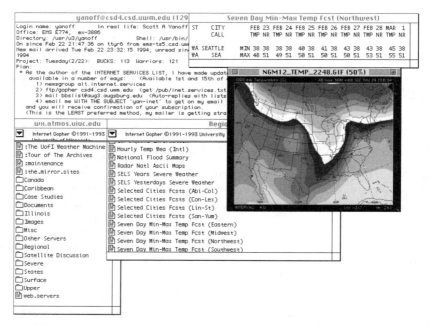

Figure 5.20   *50 percent chance of something in your area tonight*

Adam: Moving on to less concrete problems, here's a question that has always bothered me.

Bill: What's that?

Adam: What are the risks of buying gas at a gas station with a credit card from one of those automated pumps? I like using them since they're a lot faster than dealing with the cashier, particularly if they make you pay first and go back for change. But, at the same time, I've seen a bunch of receipts just lying around, which says to me that people don't particularly protect their credit card numbers.

There's a fabulous mailing list called Risks Digest that focuses on the risks of technology, and I'll bet this is the sort of thing that they've talked about at some point. I've noticed postings from that group come up when I search the Connection Machine Server via WAIS, so let's see if there is anything on this (see figure 5.21).

Bill: That's one thing I like about WAIS, the ability to use real English sentences as you did there, "Tell me about using a gas pump and a credit card." But I've never seen anything in that "Which are similar to" box before. What's that for?

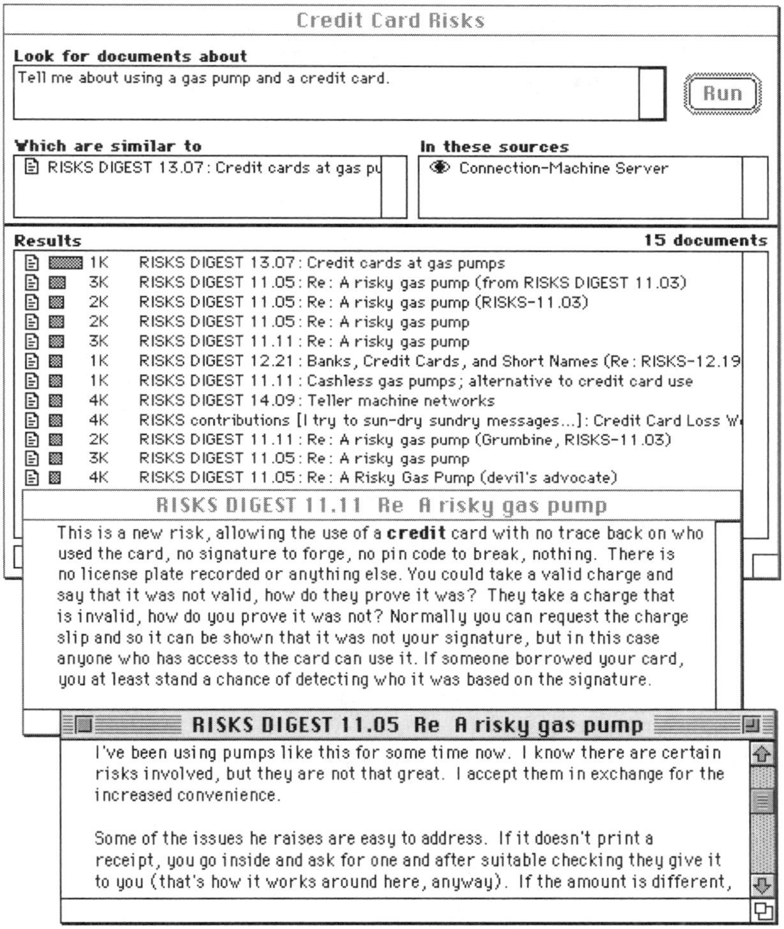

Figure 5.21   *Name, number, and expiration date, please*

Adam: Glad you asked. That box provides a truly interesting part of WAIS called "relevance feedback." *Relevance feedback* is a phrase that basically means: "Show me more like this one." So, in the example above, I first searched for the search phrase alone and found a few articles that matched what I wanted, but there were also some that were far from the subject. By asking WAIS to find me more like the article I dropped in the relevance feedback box, I narrowed the search and found more articles that were on the topic I wanted. You can do that with either an entire article, as I did above, or with just a part of an article.

```
Bill: Clever. That would allow you to narrow the search, as you
did, or broaden it by loosening the original parameters while
allowing the relevance feedback to keep the answers on track.
```

Adam: Relevance feedback requires a good WAIS program on the Mac or PC, though, and although you can search through a WAIS database from within Gopher or the World-Wide Web, clients for those two generally don't support WAIS's fancier features, like relevance feedback. That's why I generally prefer to use MacWAIS or WAIS for Mac whenever I'm searching in WAIS. The same principle applies elsewhere, so, for instance, although you can retrieve files stored on an FTP site with TurboGopher, it's not as good at doing so as Anarchie or Fetch from Dartmouth College. Similarly, even though the World-Wide Web servers can show you the contents of Gopher sites, Mosaic isn't nearly as slick as TurboGopher when it comes to navigating through Gopherspace. There's always a right tool for the job.

Owning an Internet Press

Adam: Since the beginning of time, or at least since Gutenberg first stamped out his Bible, people have wanted to publish. After all, someone clever said that freedom of the press goes to those who have a press. The obstacles to becoming a publisher are vast, but generally boil down to money, as so much does these days. To publish a simple newsletter today you must pay for design and production and printing and distribution, and you probably even must buy a mailing list from some guy wearing a trench coat in a dark alley.

```
Bill: But on the Internet, many of these problems disappear, or
are at least made far more manageable. Newsletters, magazines,
fiction and the like abound, all published by people who probably
couldn't dream of being able to publish their work in the stan-
dard way.
```

Adam: As this is a topic that is near and dear to my heart, we'll start by talking about newsletters, and my very own *TidBITS*.

Newsletters

Adam: I'm not quite sure of the technical difference between a newsletter and a magazine, but it seems to be related primarily to length. Newsletters are generally under 20 pages or so, and magazines usually seem to check in closer to 100 or more pages. The small size of newsletters makes them easy to distribute through email and Usenet news, which is a big plus. This is the route Tonya and I took with *TidBITS*.

Bill: Of course, even if you paid for nothing else to put out your newsletter, there's still the question of your own time. Do you make any money on *TidBITS* to compensate for the time you spend on it?

Adam: We do, although it was hard to decide how to go about it. After much thought, we settled on a Public Broadcasting-style sponsorship program for *TidBITS*. We set it up so that our sponsors can distribute more information directly to interested readers via email—those who are interested send an email message to a specific address mentioned in the issue, and the information comes back automatically.

Bill: Pretty neat setup. Why don't you tell us more about *TidBITS* itself? I'd like to show our readers what these publications are like, not just the logistics of publishing them over the Internet.

Adam: OK. In *TidBITS* we cover all sorts of news related to the world of the Macintosh, although the actual mission statement is to report on anything computer-related that interests me, which often includes information on the Internet and electronic communications.

Bill: Egotist.

Adam: Realist. If it doesn't interest me, I won't write about it well. I also have a short attention span and become interested in lots of different topics. Every now and then I worry that no one is interested in what I'm writing, but the reader-ship continues to grow and provide positive feedback, so I guess that's not a major problem.

At first, being personally interested in every topic was especially important, since I wrote 90 percent of the articles in the first year, and although I continue to write a large number, many other people help out. We encourage other people to submit articles.

Bill: As a matter of fact, even I've contributed an article or two. You didn't pay me anything, though—does anyone earn any-thing from writing for *TidBITS*?

Adam: Not directly, since we don't earn anything from the direct distribution of each issue either—the sponsorships are for the act of publishing *TidBITS* so they pay for the hardware, software, and connection expenses that we incur, not to mention the long hours I put in each week researching articles, writing articles, editing articles, and generally putting the entire issue together. Tonya contrib-utes articles occasionally, and edits each issue, which makes the issues much better than they would be otherwise.

However, if you've ever tried to submit an article to *MacUser* or *Macworld*, you know how hard that is. I'm not nearly as picky as they are because I don't have a staff that's paid to write. I also don't pretend to be an expert on every topic, so although I'll happily write about Internet topics, say, I try to get other people to write about high-end desktop publishing or databases, about which I know little. So, writing for *TidBITS* is a way to practice writing, assuming you have some valuable knowledge to share, of course, a way to see how your writing might be edited, and a way to become published.

Bill: Speaking from the point of view of somebody who's just breaking into this professional writing stuff, is an article for *TidBITS* going to look as good on a resume as an article for *Macworld*?

Adam: That I don't know, since I'm not the sort who particularly cares about where someone has been published before. If you're an expert about something and you write well, I couldn't care less if you've been published somewhere. I think it's generally a matter of someone who's paying for an article wanting to know that some other publication took a risk on paying you for a different article. I hope that some of the people who write for *TidBITS* get to use us as proof that they're good writers. Hey, it worked for you.

Bill: Oh. Did it?

Adam: Sure, it's not as though I ever read your newsletter, *Møøse Droppings*, or *Superguy Digest*—I knew you could write your way out of a paper bag because of the stuff you did for *TidBITS*. And the email we've exchanged, of course, but that's slightly different.

Bill: Oh. I'll consider myself flattered. How else is *TidBITS* different from a normal newsletter?

Adam: The part that I both love and hate is that it's really easy for most of our readers to reply to articles that they read in *TidBITS*. I enjoy this immensely when they pass on information I didn't know, or make insightful comments, or even just write to say that they appreciate *TidBITS*. It's good for the psyche.

Bill: And the bad part?

Adam: Do you know how hard it is to reply to more than 100 personal messages each day? Some days I spend so much time replying to email that I have no time to even think about writing new articles for the next issue of *TidBITS*. I also don't like it when time constraints force me to be more terse than I'd like. I prefer to explain fully when answering a question, but it's gotten so that it takes too long.

The other reason for keeping *TidBITS* relatively small is that I'm sure most of our readers are busy people, too, and they probably allot a certain amount of time to read *TidBITS* each week. If I doubled the size one week, they'd have to spend twice as much time reading. It's easier to stick with the formula that has worked for so many years, streamlining and enhancing when appropriate, but not for the sake of change alone.

Bill: The small size also helps in distribution, of course.

Adam: Definitely. At 30K per week, *TidBITS* fits in email relatively well and also traverses Usenet in the **comp.sys.mac.digest** group. If it were a couple of hundred kilobytes large, I wouldn't be able to use the newsgroup for distribution as easily, and people would dislike receiving it in email as well. *TidBITS* is also available on the World-Wide Web and Gopher servers.

Collaborations

Bill: Let's move on now to our next type of Internet publication, and my specialty for the time being, which I like to call collaborative fiction. I suppose it is possible that somebody on the Internet is writing some collaborative non-fiction, or some collaborative poetry, or even some collaborative biographical studies of Orville and Wilbur Wright, but if they are, I've never heard of them. So we're going to stick with collaborative fiction.

Adam: If I might interject for a moment, Bill, would you mind explaining just what you mean by collaborative fiction? I know you have multiple people writing stories in a similar setting, but I don't really understand how it works.

Bill: Gladly! Since I'm most familiar with it, I'm going to use *Superguy Digest*, a collaborative fiction project based around humorous superhero fiction, as my example throughout this section.

The concept of collaborative fiction is quite simple. Each author has one or more characters of his or her own. The author develops what we call a storyline, a continuing series of episodes starring a reasonably consistent set of characters. Thus, my first storyline was the Dangerousman series, starring Dangerousman and his faithful car, Lulu the Dangerousmobile.

Each storyline is essentially self-contained. My characters are mine, your characters are yours. My storylines will not generally involve your characters directly. However, because we are both writing in the same world, a world we refer to as the Superguy Altiverse, there is a certain degree of interaction between our storylines. When Dangerousman blew up Mudclump, Arkansas on his

first adventure, it could be reasonably expected that characters
in other storylines would hear about it happening—so Wonder
Grunion could read about it in the paper, for instance, and if
his author so desired, he could react to the event in some way.

Adam: It sounds like a logistical nightmare. How do you coordinate this? Do
you all take turns writing?

Bill: No, although there is a subset of collaborative fiction
that does work that way, known as a *round robin*. No, I write
Dangerousman when I want, and everybody else writes their stories
when they want. Obviously, this can lead to some temporal problems—if I take a month to write a plotline that encompasses
three days of fictional time, and somebody else has covered two
weeks of fictional time over the course of that same month, it
can be a bit problematic to cross-reference between the two
storylines. But there are ways to write around these problems.

Adam: Excuse me? A plotline?

Bill: I'm sorry, a *plotline* is essentially a series of episodes
that make up a single, unified story within the larger context of
the storyline. Interactive fiction must be thought of episodi-
cally, or else you'll never understand it. It's not usually like
today's television, where each episode tells a single story. It's
more like the old "Green Hornet" or "Rocky and Bullwinkle" seri-
als, where you have to wait for the next episode to find out what
happens next. Our stories often come complete with cliff-hangers
and teaser questions: "Will Ramrod and High Jinx destroy the
Giant Robot Cow? Will the National Guard manage to evict the
pirates from the Space Needle?" That sort of thing.

Adam: So far, though, it doesn't sound very collaborative. Where does all this
interaction come in?

Bill: Well, in the early *Superguy* stories, and in the beginning
of the evolution of most storylines, interaction is mostly limited to casual cross-references—things like newspaper and television reports, and casual mentions. But as time goes on, things
can become much more complex, and much more interesting.

The primary cohesive force that binds all our stories together
into a single unified world is the Pool of Villains. Although
heroes are generally the property of a single author, villains
are usually available for common use. Thus, when Rob Furr is done
using FlatPhoot, the archless-enemy of all superheroes, in his
storyline, I can have FlatPhoot hatch a nefarious scheme in my

storyline. There's a good-sized pool of villains to draw from, and also a smaller pool of minor heroes, so we have a constant flow of characters between different storylines.

Second, we have a set of conventions, or commonly-used devices, that every author can draw on. It can range from a running gag, such as the Peter Noone joke ("Noone noticed that the child was missing." "Peter Noone?"), to a single prison used for supervillains, known as the Really Really Hard To Get Out Of Place. Everybody, whenever possible, follows the word "suddenly" with the phrase, "and without warning," as a tribute to the in-fluential humor of Dave Barry. If anybody refers to the weather in Bob City at night, it's raining. Hell" is trademarked. And most importantly, Superguy himself, the mightiest superhero in the world, is never, ever seen.

Adam: Then how do you know he exists?

Bill: He leaves notes. You know, things like: "Dear heroes, I was passing by and saw that you were doing a great job with the oil spill, but I wasn't sure you'd have time to clean up all the sea gulls so I took care of them. I'll have the Department of Wild-life check on them for a few weeks to make sure they're eating. Keep up the good work! —Superguy."

There are countless more like this, some major and some minor. Apart from the one about never seeing Superguy, none of them were deliberately thought up—they just develop over time, until ev-erybody is using them. That's a strong unifier in the various storylines.

Third, an author might borrow another author's characters. I'll be writing a story soon in which I need to use one of Gary's characters, so he and I worked out a point in time when she could reasonably be away from his storyline without interfering with it, and I can work her into my plotline. I was once able to bor-row IgnorantMan for a three-episode team-up with Dangerousman. This allows us to build relationships between our characters, improving the cohesion further. Relativity Woman, another of my characters, is very close to The Dash, one of Eric Burns's char-acters.

And finally, we reach the most complex form of interaction, the crossover series. This is when two or more authors actually put their heads together and write a single plotline that spans two or more storylines.

Adam: You write the whole thing together, like we've done with this section?

Bill: No, not really. We plan the whole thing together, determining what must happen and when it must happen—a good use for IRC—and then we separately write toward a sort of nexus point, where all the storylines come together, at which point we usually collaborate on a single climactic episode wrapping it all up. An epilogue usually follows, again with each author writing separately, but still coordinating matters so it all works together as part of the same story.

Adam: That sounds like actual work!

Bill: It sure can be. Sometimes it's relatively simple, like the four-issue softball game between Team Cynical and the Awesome Force that my roommate Dominic and I wrote last year. But other times, it can be complex. Obviously, we can't just skim over little issues like time in a case like this, because the coordination has to be tight for the story to work properly. But the rewards, the sense of satisfaction and accolades, can be well worth it. Gary Olson, Bill Paul, and I shared a Golden Grunion award for last year's biggest crossover, "Songs of Darkness." Our audience is pretty small, but it still felt good to be appreciated like that.

Adam: It sounds like you guys put an awful lot of work into something that is essentially a lark. Why do you do it?

Bill: Well, I can only speak for myself here, but I do it because I love it. It's a chance to write for an audience, albeit a small one, and to work with some people I think rather highly of.

Adam: You realize that they're never going to let you live that down.

Bill: Yeah. It's a wonderful writing exercise—the concept of *Superguy* is pretty silly, of course, but the execution of it can be taken seriously. We do not have a captive audience—can we write well enough to keep their interest? Can we write the same set of characters for 100 episodes, and do it with enough humor and consistency to make it worth reading? We're constantly looking for feedback, and the responses can be extremely enlightening.

Adam: It sounds almost as if you use it as a workshop, then.

Bill: I do, in a way. It isn't as organized as a writing workshop; our feedback is pretty minimal most of the time, and it comes only from our fellow authors, not from readers. But I

```
couldn't imagine becoming this attached to a writing workshop.
We've actually tossed around a few ideas on how to make Superguy
a paying project, but I think most of us wouldn't give up writing
for the list for free, regardless of what happened.
```

Magazines and Books

Adam: There are an increasing number of paper magazines that have in some way expanded to the Internet. They don't usually publish the full text of their articles on the Internet, and none attempt to recreate the entire look of the magazine online. That may change, although I expect that the reluctance is entirely due to the fact that they cannot easily charge for the magazines on the Internet.

```
Bill: There are also some technical problems, of course. Some new
software would permit easy electronic transmission of magazines
while retaining the original look of the publication, but those
programs aren't free and are far from widespread.
```

Adam: And besides, people aren't accustomed to paying for Internet services and most likely would decide that there are plenty of other good things to check out instead of the commercial resource.

```
Bill: That makes sense. I wouldn't pay for most things on the
Internet, not because they aren't good, but, as you say, because
there are plenty that are good and free. Many of these are maga-
zines and journals that exist solely on the Internet, with no
paper counterpart.
```

Adam: *Wired* magazine, one that does cross over between the Internet and standard print media, appeared about a year ago and has grown quickly in popularity, being as someone in IRC said, "the tabloid of the electronic geek set." Another friend said something to the effect of *Wired's* motto being, "The world is ending, but you can buy cool stuff." Apparently, *Wired's* editor didn't think this was particularly funny, which may indicate the existence of a grain of sand from which can grow a pearl of truth.

```
Bill: Pithy. A tortuous metaphor, but pithy.
```

Adam: Thanks. I think. I like reading the magazine though, because, more so than most of the ones I get, there are actual honest-to-goodness ideas in *Wired*. At this point in my life, I have a voracious appetite for ideas, and even if I don't always agree with *Wired's* articles, I find them interesting. That FurryMUCK article was pretty one-sided, though, and with the headline, "MUDS: Sex with the FurryMUCKers" on the cover, rather unfair, I thought.

Bill: It certainly distressed enough people—er, furries on
FurryMUCK itself, as we could plainly see when we visited.

Adam: *Wired* has done quite well, nonetheless, at putting its Internet access
where its mouth is, so to speak.

Bill: I suppose it does sound rather hypocritical to wax lyrical
about the coolness of the Internet but not provide any Internet
resources.

Adam: Precisely. *Wired* has set up rather well-designed World-Wide Web and
Gopher servers for anyone to use, and it has released the full text of articles in
back issues of the magazine. Good thing, since two of mine were lost in the mail
at some point while moving last year (see figure 5.22).

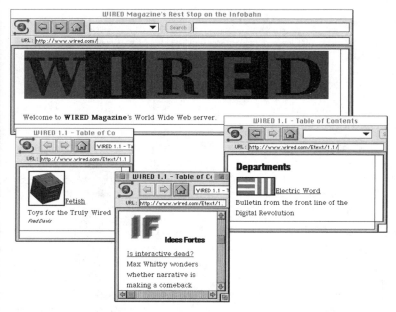

Figure 5.22 *Better graphics than most Web sites*

Bill: Magazines and other periodicals are one thing, but what
about those of us who prefer to read novels? Are there any actual
books available on the Internet?

Adam: Absolutely. One of the most fascinating and ambitious projects on the
Internet has to be Project Gutenberg, conceived of, and ably directed by, Michael
Hart. Project Gutenberg's goal is to give away one trillion electronic texts by
December 31, 2001.

Bill: That's a lot of electronic books!

Adam: Yup, but Project Gutenberg only anticipates distributing 10,000 separate titles—its one trillion number comes from the one hundred million people it anticipates will read its texts by that time. I don't believe it has any way of tracking how many readers it gets.

Bill: Even still, 10,000 is a lot. How are they managing it?

Adam: It's quite clever, actually. Project Gutenberg started many years ago, in the early 70s, and it works on a doubling scheme, so in 1993 it released four books each month, and in 1994, it hopes to release eight books each month. It's like that game on a checkerboard, where you put down a penny on the first square, two pennies on the second square, four pennies on the third square, and so on. It adds up to a huge amount of money, and similarly Project Gutenberg will end up with a huge number of electronic texts.

Bill: Where does it get its material? Electronic texts don't grow on directory trees, you know.

Adam: Perhaps the most impressive part of the entire project is that it's done entirely with volunteer labor by hundreds of people around the world. For instance, you could type a book into the computer, proofread it, and submit it to Project Gutenberg, assuming of course, that it was out of copyright or that it was done with permission. I suspect that most people use scanners to capture the pages of the book and then use optical character recognition software to turn it into editable text.

Bill: Working in a Popular Copy Shop has taught me that copyright can be a very tricky business. How does it handle it, making sure that a book is indeed in the public domain?

Adam: There are some basic rules, although I gather that copyright searches make up a large portion of the work for Project Gutenberg volunteers now. Needless to say, such a loose organization cannot afford to be sued by a large publisher for copyright infringement. The rule they use the most states that works first published before January 1, 1978 usually enter the public domain 75 years from the date copyright was first secured, which usually means 75 years from the date of first publication. There are a number of other variations on this, and in other countries the general rule is the life of the author plus 50 years. But exceptions exist, and even today, the electronic version of *Peter Pan* comes with a note that says it may not be downloaded outside of the United States due to some strange copyright deal.

Bill: That raises the question of foreign language texts. Do they work with them at all? And how do they feel about some of the alternative distribution methods we talked about above?

Adam: They only concern themselves with English language texts, and prefer to use straight text since it's universal. However, when you're in the position of Project Gutenberg, if someone wants to give you a copy of an electronic text in, say, Acrobat format, you're not going to turn it down. And although it primarily makes its works available in text format, I imagine that's primarily a limitation of volunteer labor—they would love to be able to make versions available on the World-Wide Web and in Acrobat format, and so on.

Bill: Project Gutenberg is extremely impressive, and highly ambitious. It sounds like a huge amount of work. What keeps it going?

Adam: It's hard to say for sure, since I'm sure everyone does it for a slightly different reason. I don't know if Michael and Project Gutenberg will reach their goals, but I do know that they have provided a storehouse of useful and interesting information for today's Internet. Also, the volunteers who make Project Gutenberg happen stand as a shining example of what normal people can do on the Internet if they want to. Perhaps that's what impresses me the most about many of these publishing projects—it's amazing what the human mind can do if it merely wants to, and is given the freedom to express itself widely via the Internet.

Moving On

Adam: Now that we've had a quick little jaunt around the Internet, let's move on to discussing some of the nuts and bolts of how the Internet actually works. Keep what you've seen here in mind; when I explain specific tools to you later on, think about how they can help you explore the Internet and find your own way through the maze of information.

Bill: And hey, if you liked this chapter, check out our other book! That will help me eat something besides microwave burritos from time-to-time!

Adam: That may be the most blatant plug I've ever seen, Bill.

Bill: True. I have no shame. 'Bye, folks, and enjoy the rest of the book!

Adam: Thanks for the help, Bill!

II

Internet Foundations

So far, we've looked at the Internet in the abstract only, and it's important that you have an overview of the world you are entering. Like all things electronic, however, the Internet is terribly picky about the details; you must know exactly what to type and where to click. Moreover, unlike on your friendly local Macintosh, on the Internet real people see what you type, so I also talk about the social customs of the Internet, the manners and mores that everyone eventually learns. And, because I hope the Internet becomes something about which you talk with friends, I try to pass on some of the jargon and modes of speech.

First off, then, you look at names, addresses, and email, in chapter 6, "Addressing and Email." This is followed by an exploration of Usenet news in chapter 7, "Usenet News." Part II ends with chapter 8, "Internet Services," where I cover services available only if you have a full connection to the Internet. These are services such as FTP, Telnet, WAIS, Gopher, and the World-Wide Web (although I also pass on some handy tricks for using Usenet, FTP, and Archie through email).

Keep in mind that this information is all background—I don't tell you the specific details of how to deal with programs on the Internet or anything like that, until Part III.

Text Styles

As a convention, I write all network addresses, whether they are only machine names or full email addresses; in this `monospaced font`. Note also that any punctuation following the address is not part of the address itself; instead, it's required by my seventh grade English teacher, who was adamant about ending clauses with commas and sentences with periods. Every now and then, I'd leave off a period when it confuses an address that ends a sentence, but the thought of her beet-red face (I'm sure she was very nice, but she reminded me of a lobster) looming over me always makes me add that period. So remember that addresses *never* have any punctuation at the end.

Commands that you type exactly as written **look like this**; when there is a variable that you have to fill in, it *looks like this*. So, **TYPE** *this* means to type the word **TYPE**, followed by whatever is appropriate for *this*: your name, a filename, a directory name, a machine name, or whatever.

Finally, any text that shows up as though it scrolled by on a terminal window connected to a Unix machine, appears in its own monospaced font, line-by-line, much like the following two lines.

```
To: The Reader <reader@iskm.book.net>

Subject: Style conventions...
```

Addressing and Email

Before I can tell you about email, retrieving files via FTP, or much of anything else, I must discuss how email addresses and machine names are formed, where they come from, and that sort of thing. After that, I'll discuss the wide world of email in greater depth, relating some of the uses and customs that you encounter.

Addressing

A rose may be a rose by any other name, but the same is not true of an Internet computer. All Internet computers think of each other in terms of numbers (not surprisingly), and all people think of them in terms of names (also not surprisingly). The Internet uses the *domain name system* to make sense of the millions of machines that make up the Internet. In terms of the numbers, each machine's address is composed of four numbers, each less than 256. People are generally bad about remembering more than the seven digits of a phone number, so a *domain name server* was developed. The domain name server translates between the numeric addresses and the names that real people can remember and use.

Despite the fact that all Internet numeric addresses are sets of four numbers, the corresponding name can have between two and five sets of words. After five, it gets out of hand, so although it's possible, it's not generally done. For instance, the machine I use now is called **tidbits.com** (two words), and the machine I used at Cornell was called **cornella.cit.cornell.edu** (four words). The domain style addresses may look daunting, but in fact they are quite easy to work with, especially when you consider the numeric equivalents. Each item in those addresses, separated by the periods, is called a *domain*, and in the following sections, you are going to look at them backward, or in terms of the largest domain to the smallest.

Note

A random aside for those of you who are students of classical rhetoric: The process of introducing topics A, B, and C, and then discussing them in the order C, B, and A is called chiasmus. This little known fact is entirely unrelated to the Internet, except that after the first edition of this book I took a lot of good-natured ribbing on the Internet about my classical education, so I figured I should at least pretend to know something about the topic.

Top-level Domains

In any machine name, the final word after the last dot is the *top-level domain*, and a limited number of them exist. Originally, and this shows the Internet's early Americo-centric view, six top-level domains indicated to what type of organization the machine belonged. Thus, we ended up with the following list:

- **com** = commercial
- **edu** = educational
- **org** = organization, usually nonprofit
- **mil** = military
- **net** = network
- **gov** = government

That setup was all fine and nice for starters, but as the number of machines on the Internet began to grow at an amazing rate, a more all-encompassing solution became necessary. The new top-level domains are based on countries, so each country has its own two-letter domain. Thus, the United Kingdom's top-level domain is **uk**, Sweden's is **se**, Japan's is **jp**, Australia's is **au**, and so on. Every now and then another country comes on the Internet, and I see a domain code that totally throws me, as Iceland's **is** code did the first time. The United States has this system, too; so, for example, The Well, a popular commercial service with links to the Internet, is **well.sf.ca.us**. Unfortunately, because so many sites already existed with the old domain names, it made no sense to change them. Thus, we have both types of top-level domain names here in the U.S., and you just have to live with it.

You may see a couple of other top-level domains on occasion, **bitnet** and **uucp**, such as in **listserv@bitnic.bitnet** or **ace@tidbits.uucp**. In both of these cases, the top-level domain indicates that the machine is on one of the alternative networks and may not exist directly on the Internet (otherwise, it would have a normal top-level domain such as **com** or **uk**). This setup isn't a big deal these days because so many machines exist on two networks that your email gets through just fine in most cases. In the past, though, few connections existed between the Internet and BITNET or Usenet, so getting mail through one of the existing gateways was more difficult. Keep in mind that because a machine whose name ends with **bitnet** or **uucp** is not usually on the Internet, you cannot use Telnet or FTP with it.

My current machine name, **tidbits.com**, is as simple as it gets: a machine name and a top-level domain. Many other addresses are more complex because other domains are in the middle. Think of an address such as **cornella.cit.cornell.edu** as one of those nested Russian dolls (see figure 6.1). The outermost doll is the top-level domain, the next few dolls are the mid-level domains, and, if you go all the way in, the final doll is the userid (which I'll explain soon enough).

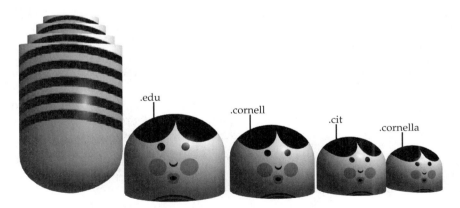

Figure 6.1   *The Russian doll approach to Internet addresses*

Mid-level Domains

What do these mid-level domains represent? It's hard to say precisely, because the answer can vary a bit. The machine I used at Cornell, known as **cornella.cit.cornell.edu**, represents one way the mid-level domains have been handled. As a recap, the machine name is **cornella**, and the top-level domain is **edu**, because Cornell claims all those undergraduates are there to get an education. The **cit** after **cornella** is the department, Cornell Information Technologies, that runs the machine known as **cornella**. The next part, **cornell**, is obvious; it's the name of the overall organization to which CIT belongs. So, for this machine anyway, the hierarchy of dolls is, in order, machine name, department name, organization name, and organization type.

In the machine name for The Well, **well.sf.ca.us**, you see a geographic use of mid-level domains. In this case, **well** is the machine name, **sf** is the city name (San Francisco), **ca** is the state name (California), and **us** is the country code for the United States.

Mid-level domains spread the work around. Obviously, the Internet can't have machines with the same name; otherwise, chaos would erupt. But because the domain name system allows for mid-level domains, the administrators for those mid-level domains must make sure that everyone below them stays unique. In other words, I could actually name my machine **cornella.com** because that name is completely different from **cornella.cit.cornell.edu** (though why I'd want to, I don't know). And, if they wanted, the administrators at CIT could put a new machine on the net and call it **tidbits.cit.cornell.edu** without any trouble, for the same reason. More importantly, the administrators don't need to bother anyone else if they want to make that change. They control the **cit** domain, and as long as all the machines within that domain have unique names, there aren't any problems. Of course, someone has to watch the top-level domains because it's all too likely that two people may want **tidbits.com** as a machine name (but I've already got it, so they can't have it). That task is handled by the Network Information Center, or NIC. As a user, you shouldn't have to worry about naming problems, because everyone should have a system administrator who knows who to talk to, and you need the cooperation of your provider anyway—you can't set up a domain on your own.

There is yet another way to handle the mid-level domains, this time in terms of intermediate computers. Before I got my current address, I had a feed from a machine called **halcyon**, whose full name was **halcyon.com**. My machine name was **tidbits.halcyon.com**. In this case, **tidbits** was my machine name, **halcyon** was the machine through which all of my mail was routed, and **com** indicated that the connection was through a commercial organization. I realize that this example is a bit confusing, but I mention it because it's one way that you can pretend to have an Internet address when you really have only a UUCP connection (a different sort of connection that transfers only email and news). All my mail and news came in via UUCP through **halcyon**, so by including **halcyon** in my address, I created an Internet-style address.

The other way of pretending that a UUCP connection is a real Internet connection for address purposes, is to have your host set up an *MX record* (where MX stands for Mail Exchange). An MX record is a pointer on several true Internet machines to your site. That's what I use now, but because **tidbits.com** is actually a UUCP site, theoretically you also can reach me by sending email to **ace@tidbits.uucp**. Mail sent that way isn't as quick or reliable, however.

Note

*This means that you cannot FTP to **tidbits.com**, something which has confused people who don't notice that my FTP site is a different machine, called **ftp.tidbits.com**.*

Machine Name

The next part of my machine name is the machine itself, **tidbits**. In my case, the machine is a Macintosh 660AV, but people use all sorts of machines, and because the system administrators often are a punchy, overworked lot, they tend to give machines silly names. Large organizations with more centralized control lean more toward thoroughly boring names, like the machine at Cornell, which was called **cornella** (as opposed to **cornellc** and **cornelld** and **cornellf**). One of the reasons for boring names is that in the early days, machines on BITNET had to have names with between six and eight characters. Coming up with a meaningful unique name within that restriction became increasingly difficult. Usenet doesn't put a limit on the length of names but requires that the first six characters be unique.

If you remember that machines often exist on the Internet as well as on one of these other networks, thereby blurring the distinctions, you'll see the problem. Internet machines don't, as far as I know, have any rigid limitations on names, so any alternative connections dictate what names are acceptable. Although possible (another machine at Cornell was called **crnlvax5** on BITNET and **vax5** on the Internet), most machines have only one name. This convention makes life easier.

There is one caveat to the multiple name issue: Often, special services keep their names even when they move to different machines or even different organizations. Because of this situation, a machine that runs a service may have two names, one that goes with the machine normally and one that points solely at that service. For instance, the anonymous FTP site that I use to store all the software I talk about in this book is called **ftp.tidbits.com**. But in fact, it runs on a machine called **ftp.halcyon.com**, and I could move it to any other machine while still retaining the **ftp.tidbits.com** name. This situation is not a big deal one way or another.

To summarize, you can have multiple domains in an address, and the further you go to the right, the more general they become, often ending in the country code. Conversely, the further you go to the left, the more specific the domains become, ending in the userid because that part of the address is the most specific. And so it's time to talk about the userid.

Userid

Now that you've looked at the machine name, you can move on to the *userid* or *username*, which identifies a specific user on a machine. Both terms are equally correct (with two exceptions—the commercial online service GEnie and the FirstClass BBS software both treat userids and usernames separately) and commonly used. If you set up your own machine, or work with a sufficiently flexible provider, you can choose your own username. Choosing your own name is good because then your correspondents can more easily remember your address, assuming of course that you choose a userid that makes sense and is easy to type. If I made my address **ferdinand-the-bull@tidbits.com**, people who typed the address slightly wrong and had their mail bounced back to them would become irritated at me.

Unlike Macintosh filenames (and America Online and eWorld userids), Internet userids cannot have spaces in them, so convention dictates that you replace any potential spaces with underscores, dashes, or dots, or omit them entirely. Other reasonable userids that I could use (but don't) include **adam_engst@tidbits.com** or **adam-engst@tidbits.com** or **adam.engst@tidbits.com** or **adamengst@tidbits.com**. However, all of these names are more difficult to type than **ace@tidbits.com**, and because I have good initials, I stick with them.

Unfortunately, there are a limited number of possible userids, especially at a large site. So Cornell, for instance, with its thousands of students and staff, has opted for a system of using initials plus one or more digits (because initials aren't all that unique, either—in fact, I once asked for my initials as a userid on one of Cornell's mainframes and was told that ACE was a reserved word in that machine's operating system, though no one could tell me what it was reserved for).

Microsoft uses a different scheme yet: first name and last initial (using more than one initial to keep the userids unique). As Microsoft has grown, common names such as David have been used up, so the company has started other schemes such as first initial and last name. Why am I telling you this? Because knowing an organization's scheme can prove useful at times if you're trying to figure out how to send mail to someone at that organization, and so that I can note a societal quirk. At places like Microsoft where people use email so heavily, many folks refer to each other by email names exclusively. When my wife, Tonya, worked at Microsoft, she had a problem with her username, **tonyae** (first name and last initial) because it looked more like TonyAe than TonyaE to most people.

The real problem with assigned userids comes when the scheme is ludicrously random. Some universities work student ID numbers into the userid, for instance, and CompuServe userids are mere strings of digits like 72511,306. I believe the scheme has something to do with octal numbers or some such technoweenie hoo-hah. I don't speak octal or septal or any such nonsense, and as a result, I can never remember CompuServe userids.

Remember that email addresses point at an individual, but when you're using Telnet or FTP, no individual is involved. You simply want to connect to that machine, and you have to connect *sans* userid. This restriction may seem obvious, but it often trips people up until they get used to it. For example, it seems that you could just FTP to **anonymous@space.alien.com**. The system doesn't work that way, though, and you FTP to **space.alien.com**, and once there, log in as **anonymous**. More about FTP in later chapters.

Punctuation

Enough about userids. What about all this punctuation? Better known as SI (on U.S. keyboards anyway), the **@** symbol came into use, I imagine, because .. a single character that generally means "at" in traditional usage. The **@** symbol i. generally universal for Internet email, but not all types of networks have always used it. For instance, some BITNET machines once required you to spell out the word, as in the command **TELL LISTSERV AT BITNIC HELP**. Luckily, almost everything uses the **@** symbol with no spaces these days, which reduces four characters to one, and probably has saved untold person-hours worth of typing over the years.

As long as you're learning about special characters, look at the dot. It is, of course, the period character on the keyboard, and it serves to separate the domains in the address. For various reasons unknown to me, the periods have become universally known as dots in the context of addresses. When you tell someone your email address over the phone, you say (or rather I'd say because it's my address), "My email address is ace at tidbits dot com." The other person must know that "at" equals the **@** symbol and that "dot" equals the period. If he's unsure, explain yourself.

Alternative Addresses

You may see two other styles of addressing mail on the Internet, both of which work to sites that aren't actually on the Internet itself. The first, and older, of the two is called *bang* addressing. It was born in the early days when there were relatively few machines using UUCP. Not every machine knew how to reach every other machine, so the trick was to get the mail out to a machine that knew about a machine that knew about a machine that knew about your machine. Talk about a friend of a friend! So, you could once have sent email to an address that looked like **uunet!nwnexus!caladan!tidbits!ace**. This address would have bounced the mail from **uunet** to **nwnexus** to **caladan** to **tidbits** and finally to my userid on **tidbits**. This approach assumes that your machine knows about the machine **uunet** (run by the commercial provider UUNET) and that all of the machines in the middle are up and running. All the exclamation points are called "bangs," appropriately enough, I suppose. On the whole, this style of addressing is slow and unreliable these days, but if you use a machine that speaks UUCP, you can occasionally use it to your advantage. For instance, every now and then, I try to send email to a machine that my UUCP host, **nwnexus.wa.com**, for some reason can't reach. By bang-routing the mail appropriately, I can make another Internet machine try to send the mail out, sometimes with greater success.

The other sort of special addressing is another way to get around the fact that your machine, or even your network, isn't connected to the Internet as such. In this case, you must provide two addresses: one to get to the machine that feeds your machine, and one to get to your machine. The problem here is that Internet addresses cannot have more than one **@** symbol in them. You can replace the first **@** symbol with a **%** symbol, and the mailers then try to translate the address properly. My old address, **ace@tidbits.halcyon.com**, could also have been **ace%tidbits.uucp@halcyon.com**. These tricks are ugly and awkward, but sometimes necessary. Luckily, as the Internet grows and standardizes, you need fewer and fewer of them.

Electronic Mail

Electronic mail is the most pervasive application on the Internet, and for good reason. What better way to communicate with so many people so quickly? But to use and understand email properly, I must show you how it's constructed, the relevant social mores and pitfalls, and the uses to which you can put it.

Email Construction

What makes up an email message? Most messages have two important parts, with a third part that doesn't have to appear. The first two parts are the *header* and the *body* of the message, and the third, non-essential part, is the *signature*. For simplicity's sake, let's work backward.

Signature

Many email programs, including Eudora, which I've included on the disk, provide a facility for creating signatures. Signatures are just about what you'd expect—some text that goes at the bottom of every message you send. Most people include their names (real or pretend) in their signatures; it's considered good form to include your preferred email address in your signature as well, just in case the address in the header isn't useful for some reason or another. After you get past the basics of name and email address, however, you can put anything you like in your signature. Many people lean toward clever quotations or manage to express some sporting partisanship of their favorite team, usually with an erudite "Go Weasels '94" or some such. It's hard to grunt in ASCII. I prefer clever quotations, especially so if changed once per day—not that I have time or energy to think them up or type them in every day. Here is a signature that must have taken some time to create, because all the lines and dashes had to be typed in the right place:

```
 / =======================================================================\
 ||                                                                     ||
 || _                                                                   ||
 || *  \            Sorry, a signature error has occurred.              ||
 ||   _!_                                                               ||
 ||  /   \      /===========\              /==========\                 ||
 || |     |     ¦   Resume   ¦             ¦  Restart ¦                 ||
 ||  \_____/     \ — — — — —/              \— —¦\— —/                  ||
 ||                                           ¦  \                     ||
 \=============================================¦   _\==================/
                                               ¦/\ \
                                                \_\
```

(Courtesy of A. Marsh Gardiner, `gardin@harvarda.harvard.edu`)

Many people also use signatures to disclaim their messages. The signature acts as a disclaimer, usually stating that the opinions and facts stated in the preceding message have no relationship to the organization paying for the account or employing the individual. Disclaimers are important online because readers have no context in which to take postings. If Ferdinand the Bull posts a glowing review of specific species of cork tree, for example, he should also note at the bottom of his review that he is a paid consultant of Corking Good Times International and is therefore biased. More common are glowing reviews from users who "have no relationship with Corking Good Times International, other than as a satisfied customer." Disclaimers also serve to ensure that no one takes the words of a single employee as the policy of the entire organization. Marketing departments hate that. "But Joe said online that Apple was going to give free Macs to everyone whose birthday falls on the second Tuesday of odd months this year." "Yeah, sure buddy."

One warning, though. Mailing lists that are published as *digests*—that is, lists in which a moderator collects the day's messages and concatenates them into a single file—frown on or even reject postings with multiple line signatures. This suggestion makes sense, if you think about it. A large digest file can have 50 messages in it, and if every person has a four-line signature, the digest suddenly becomes 200 lines longer than necessary.

Body

What you put in the body of your letter is your business. I can recommend several practices, however. First, get in the habit of pressing the Return key twice between paragraphs to insert a blank line between paragraphs; that additional white space makes email messages much easier to read. Nothing is harder to read than page after page of unbroken text.

Actually, something *is* worse than unbroken text, and that's page after page of unbroken text in capital letters. DON'T USE ALL CAPS BECAUSE IT LOOKS LIKE YOU'RE SHOUTING! No one uses all capital letters for long because everyone hates reading it and will tell you, nicely the first time, to stop.

I suppose now is a good time to talk about manners in terms of the sorts of things you should consider when writing email. Email differs from normal mail in many ways. Think of the difference between a short note to your mother, a memo at work, and a formal business letter. Most email falls somewhere between the short note and the memo, and seldom do you ever see an email message with the formality and rigidity of a business letter. Although I'm giving this information in the context of email, it applies equally as well to postings on Usenet; if you like, reread this section, substituting posting for email everywhere.

How do you start these messages? In many ways, email acts as the great equalizer. Most of the time, you know someone's name and email address when you send email to him, nothing more. Someone with the address **joeschmoe@alien.com** could be a janitor, a summer student intern, or the president of a Fortune 500 firm. Similarly, any address ending in **edu** can link to a student, some member of the staff, a world-renowned professor of underwater basket weaving, or the president of the university. You have no way of knowing, unless that fact somehow comes up in conversation.

Most people react to this lack of context by treating everyone with the same level of polite, but informal, respect. Seldom do people use their titles, so equally seldom do correspondents use those titles in email. Everyone is on a first-name basis. I once took a class with the astronomer and science advocate Carl Sagan while I was at Cornell, and the first day of class, an awed undergraduate (but braver than the rest of us) asked, "How should we address you, Dr. Sagan?" He replied, "You can call me Mr. Sagan, Professor Sagan, Dr. Sagan, or Herr Doktor Professor Sagan," he paused, "or you can call me Carl." Carl it was then, and the class benefited greatly from that level of informality, just as the Internet does.

In light of this knowledge, when I started using email I thought about the differences between email and paper mail (hereafter called by its true name in the Internet community, snail mail). The standard salutation of "Dear" sounds inappropriately formal and stilted to my ears (apologies to Miss Manners). Since email more closely resembles spoken communication than written, I opted for the less formal and more colloquial "Hi," which has served me well. Some people forego the salutation completely, relying solely on the first name, but that approach feels abrupt to me, as if someone called me on the phone and stated my name without a "Hello" or so much as a questioning tone. Do what you like, though; no one has laid down rules on this matter.

What you say in the letter itself deserves more thought, however. Because email is so quick and it's so easy to respond without thinking, many people often reply hastily and less politely than they would had they taken a moment to consider. Remember, you want to achieve a certain effect with an email message, just as you do with any form of communication. If you simply whack your first thoughts into a message, it probably won't properly convey your true feelings. If you want information from someone, phrasing your request politely only increases your chances of getting that information, and if you wish to comment on someone else's words, doing so in a reasoned and level-headed manner ensures that that person won't immediately consider you a serious jerk.

You also must remember that informal though email may be, it lacks most of the nonverbal parts of communication that we seldom consider in normal speech. All inflection, body language, and facial expressions disappear, and it doesn't help one whit if you make them while composing the letter. Email is ASCII text only, and only two ways exist to convey inflections such as sarcasm or irony that would be obvious in spoken conversation. First, polish your writing skills. There

Chapter 6
Addressing and Email

is no substitute for clear and coherent writing. Many people find writing difficult, but I recommend that you don't think of composing email as writing, but as speaking to someone who sees your words but cannot see or hear you. Most people who claim they can't write have little trouble making themselves understood when speaking.

Second, utilize *smileys*, or as they are sometimes known, *emoticons*. Smileys are strings of punctuation characters meant to be viewed by tilting your head (which is usually easier than tilting your monitor) to the side. (If they still look wrong, try tilting your head to the *other* side.) People have come up with literally hundreds of different smileys, and you can find lists containing them on the Internet. Seth Godin has even compiled many of them into a book, *The Smiley Dictionary*, published by Peachpit Press (and there is at least one other book, published by O'Reilly & Associates, on the same somewhat silly topic). I take the view that only two, or maybe three, smileys are at all useful in normal email. The first is the happy face **:-)**, which implies that what you just said was meant as humor or at least shouldn't be taken too seriously. I often use it to imply that I would have said that bit with a smile. A variant of the happy face uses the semicolon instead of the colon **;-)** and (because of the wink) implies that the preceding sentence was somewhat sarcastic or ironic. Finally, the frowning face **:-(** implies that you aren't happy about whatever you just said.

I use smileys relatively heavily in email, where I don't have time to craft each letter as carefully as I would like. I miss not being able to use them (I could, but no one would understand) in snail mail occasionally, and I actively try to avoid using them in *TidBITS*, favoring instead words that convey my feelings without the smiley crutch. When in doubt, use smileys. If I say in email, "Well, that was a stupid thing to do," the message is much more offensive than if I say, "Well, that was a stupid thing to do. :-)" Believe me, it is.

I may have given the impression that the Internet is this utopia where everyone always behaves nicely and ne'er is heard a discouraging word. Unfortunately, that's not so, and in reality you see plenty of *flaming* on the nets. Flaming happens when, in a PC discussion list, you innocently mention that you like your Macintosh, and seventeen people immediately jump on you in email and pummel you within an inch of your electronic life for saying something so obviously stupid and incorrect when everyone knows that only weenies, wimps, and little wusses use those toy Macintosh computers, which are good only for paperweights—and expensive paperweights at that, because you can buy three completely configured, top-of-the-line Pentium-based PCs for the same price as a used Macintosh Classic—without a hard drive. And by the way, did I mention that your mother wears combat boots and your father wears ballet slippers? :-)

The preceding paragraph is flaming (except for the smiley, which I threw in to indicate that I was kidding about your parents' footwear), and if you must respond to an inflammatory message, which I don't recommend, do it in email.

No one else wants to read your flames. Think before you lower yourself to flaming; it never solves anything. I have found in almost every case that replying calmly and clearly embarrasses anyone (assuming that person is normal and rational, which is not always a good assumption) so thoroughly that she immediately apologizes for being such a jerk. And yes, I know how hard it is not to just tee off on someone. Restrain yourself and rest assured that everyone who sees your restraint will think more highly of you for it.

Note

My favorite method of responding to long and vitriolic flames is to send back a single-line message reading, "You may be right. -Engst." I heard about this technique in an interview with Tom Brokaw, I think, and it works extremely well, confusing the recipient to no end and generally putting a stop to the flaming.

Often, people flame companies or large organizations that are doing stupid things. Various governments are favorite, though slow-moving and not very challenging, targets. This sort of flaming is more acceptable, although you may start a *flame war* if other people don't share your opinions on some major topic, such as whether the Mac is better than Windows. As a spectator, you may enjoy watching the occasional flame war, as I do, but again, they never solve anything, and they waste a huge amount of *bandwidth* (which is composed of transmission time, people time, and disk storage throughout the world).

Note

Actually, I've decided that in some respects a certain amount of flaming can be positive, because there are only three ways of ending an argument on the Internet. Agree to disagree, win your opponent over to your side, or stop from exhaustion. In no case does anyone get knifed or shot, and if participating in a flame war lets someone blow off some steam, that's better than their going home and abusing their children. Everything is relative.

Keep in mind that no matter what you say, it may not be private. Always assume that gobs of people can and do read every message you send. These people include your coworkers, your system administrator, system administrators on other machines through which your email travels, random pimply-faced fools who like poking around in other people's email, and last, but certainly not least, the government, probably in the form of the CIA, FBI, or National Security Agency. I realize this sounds alarming, and it is most certainly not completely true, but the possibility exists for all of these people to read your email.

In reality, email carries significant privacy, but because you have no guarantee of that privacy, you should stay aware of what you're saying. This suggestion is especially true if you use email at work, where you could lose your job over ill-considered remarks in email. It's always a good idea to check on your employer's policy about email privacy.

Note

There have been a number of court cases regarding ownership of email (Does it belong to you? Does it belong to your employer?) at large companies like Epson and Borland, and as far as I know the issue has yet to be settled for good. Since it comes down to a matter of their lawyers being meaner than your lawyers, don't push it.

This lack of privacy carries over to mailing lists and Usenet news (where you want people to read your messages, but you may not want the government to keep tabs on your postings). In fact, some people have gone so far as to include inflammatory keywords in otherwise innocuous postings, just to trip up the rumored government computers scanning for terrorists, assassins, space aliens, nudists, vegetarians, people who like broccoli, and other possible undesirables.

I almost forgot about *attachments*. Many people like to send each other files in email, and although you can do this by simply encoding the file as BinHex or uucode (which I'll talk about in a few chapters) and pasting it into the body of the message, modern email programs instead enable you to merely attach the file to the message with a specific command.

That's all fine and nice if your recipient also uses an email program that knows how to deal with the attachment, but if not, your friend sees the file, usually encoded in BinHex or uucode, at the end of the message in the body (but before the signature). Large email files can be a pain to deal with unless your email program supports attachments.

Header

Okay, I admit it; I've been avoiding talking about the header so far. I did so because the message header generally looks like a lot of gobbledygook to the novice user, and in fact, it should. The header exists for the computers, not for the users, and you're lucky that you can read it as well as you can. In some programs you can see an abbreviated header, which is good, and in some you can ignore the header altogether, which can be a little dangerous because it may not be clear who receives a reply to that message.

As much as the header is technoweenie information that exists primarily for the computers to route mail to you, I recommend that you choose an abbreviated header display if you have one. An abbreviated header shows you information that can be useful, such as who sent the email to you, when it was sent, what the subject of the message is, and to whom it was sent (not always only you—it's easy to send the same piece of email to multiple people).

Take a look at a typical header, culled just now from one of my archived pieces of email (see figure 6.2).

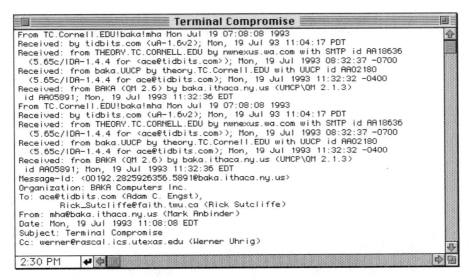

Figure 6.2   *A sample header*

Let's take a spin through all the different parts of the header, explaining each one along the way and starting with the glop at the top.

```
From TC.Cornell.EDU!baka!mha Mon Jul 19 07:08:08 1993

Received: by tidbits.com (uA-1.6v2); Mon, 19 Jul 93 11:04:17 PDT
Received: from THEORY.TC.CORNELL.EDU by nwnexus.wa.com with SMTP id AA18636
    (5.65c/IDA-1.4.4 for <ace@tidbits.com>); Mon, 19 Jul 1993 08:32:37 -0700
Received: from baka.UUCP by theory.TC.Cornell.EDU with UUCP id AA02180
    (5.65c/IDA-1.4.4 for ace@tidbits.com); Mon, 19 Jul 1993 11:32:32 -0400
Received: from BAKA (QM 2.6) by baka.ithaca.ny.us (UMCP\QM 2.1.3)
    id AA05891; Mon, 19 Jul 1993 11:32:36 EDT
```

The preceding lines are merely routing information that tell you where a message went and when it arrived there. You have to read it backwards to follow the flow, so this message traveled from the QuickMail server at BAKA Computers to the UMCP Bridge (**baka.ithaca.ny.us**), which acts as a gateway for QuickMail messages destined for the Internet. From there it traveled to Cornell's Theory Center, **theory.tc.cornell.edu**, and from the Theory Center, the message bounced almost instantly to **nwnexus.wa.com**, which is my Internet host, and then several hours later to my machine, **tidbits.com**.

You generally can ignore this part of the header, although it can be fun to see where your message went at times. If your message *bounces*—that is, if it fails to go through for some reason and comes back to you—looking at this part in the header helps you determine how far it got and which machine didn't like it. More about how to handle bounces in a bit.

```
Message-Id: <00192.2825926356.5891@baka.ithaca.ny.us>
```

The Message-Id line uniquely identifies each message. It's generally of no use at all, and although it looks like an email address, it's not.

Note

Only once have I found the Message-Id information useful. For some reason, one of my hosts was duplicating some files that went out, and often the only difference between the messages was that at a certain point they started having different Ids. Unfortunately, I never figured out how to solve the problem; I just switched to another host.

```
Organization: BAKA Computers Inc.
```

The Organization line identifies the organization of the sender, as you might suspect. Individuals often have a good time with this line because they don't have real organizations to put down and can thus include fake organizations like "Our Lady of the Vacant Lot Enterprises."

```
To: ace@tidbits.com (Adam C. Engst),
        Rick_Sutcliffe@faith.twu.ca (Rick Sutcliffe)
```

The To line can have one or more entries, and it specifies, reasonably enough, who the mail was sent to. The recipient may not be you because you might be the person mentioned in the Cc line or even the Bcc line (which you don't see because Bcc stands for Blind Carbon Copy). Most of the time you see a name before or after the email address, but it's not mandatory.

```
From: mha@baka.ithaca.ny.us (Mark Anbinder)
```

The From line indicates who sent the email and is self-explanatory.

```
Date: Mon, 19 Jul 1993 11:08:08 EDT
```

The Date line lists the date that the email was sent originally, not the time you received it or read it, and should usually indicate the time zone in which the sender lives. Even then I find it difficult to keep track of what time it is in other countries. Do you know the local time in Turkey right now? Some messages use a number, either positive or negative, and the acronym GMT, which stands for Greenwich Mean Time. Unfortunately, this use requires that you know what time it is in Greenwich, England, and that you know how your local daylight savings time is involved. Date lines usually just confuse me.

Note

The best way to determine what time it is in another part of the world is to open the Map control panel, click on the appropriate spot on the map of the world, and look at the time display. Finding the appropriate spot is up to you. I hope you paid attention in geography class in grade school.

```
Subject: Terminal Compromise
```

The Subject line should give a clear and concise description of the contents of the email message. In practice, this description often isn't true, especially after a discussion proceeds, changing topics occasionally, with everyone using the reply function to keep the Subject the same. After a while the Subject line bears no resemblance to the contents of the message, at which point it's time to change the line.

```
Cc: werner@rascal.ics.utexas.edu (Werner Uhrig)
```

The Cc line lists all the people who received copies of the message. There is no functional difference from being on the To line or the Cc line, but in theory if you receive only a copy, the message shouldn't concern you as much. In practice I notice little difference.

An abbreviated header probably just shows the last five lines and avoids displaying the routing information at the top of the header.

You also may see other lines in the header that identify which program mailed the message, to whom the recipients should reply, the type of data included in the message, how the data is encoded, and that sort of thing. In general, you don't have to worry about anything in the header very much, but it's worth taking a look every now and then to see if you can tell what's going on in there.

Bounces

In a perfect world, all email would get through to its destination quickly and reliably. But just as with snail mail, which can take one to five days to appear, and which sometimes never appears at all, email isn't perfect, and sometimes will bounce back to you. Some of the time the machine that bounced the mail back to you will give you a hint as to what went wrong, but more often you're on your own.

The most common reason for a bounced message is a typo somewhere in the address. That's one reason that short email addresses are good—they're easier to type and thus less likely to be mistyped. The first thing to do when you get a bounce is to look through the header of the original message (the full headers are usually returned to you) and make sure you typed the address properly. Everyone makes this mistake on occasion.

A common error message in bounced email is "User unknown." This means that the email arrived at the proper machine, which searched through its list of users and decided that it didn't have a user with the name you used. Again, this is most commonly due to a typo in the userid, although sometimes there are problems on the destination machine that have caused it to forget about a user, possibly temporarily. After checking the address, try resending the message, especially if you've gotten mail through to that address before.

Along with unknown users, you may see error messages complaining about "Host unknown." This is a more serious error that's more difficult to work around if it's not simply a typo. The basic problem is that for some reason one machine, perhaps your host machine or perhaps one further along in the path to the destination, was unable to contact the destination machine. There's not much you can do in this case other than try again a little later, in the hope that the machine you're mailing to has come back up.

One thing to watch out for is that sometimes the header provides an incorrect address to your email program, but the person includes the proper one in their signature. If you have trouble replying to a message, and the address you're replying to is different from an address listed in the signature, try using the signature address instead.

Note

I find this trick especially useful if the address in the signature is simple, whereas the address from the header is long and convoluted. Simple addresses seem to be more reliable, on the whole, although that's not a hard and fast rule.

Using Email Programs

All email programs share some basic features that you need in order to read quickly and efficiently, reply to, and store your email. However, after these basic commonalities, the differences between programs mount quickly, so I concentrate on those differences when I talk about each program later in the book. For the moment, though, look at what an email program must do at a minimum.

Reading Email

An email program should enable you to display and scroll through an email message easily. Because you're using the Macintosh, you should be able to do all the standard Macintosh things to text in a window, such as copying and pasting into a different program, resizing the window to display more text, selecting all the text with a single command, and that sort of thing.

Although you usually can choose the font and size in which you view messages in Macintosh email programs, I recommend that you stick to a monospaced font such as Monaco or Courier. People on the Internet must format tables and graphics with spaces, and monospaced fonts such as Monaco and Courier display these tables and graphics properly. Proportionally spaced fonts such as Times and Helvetica don't work as well because the characters in these fonts can have different widths, with a lowercase *i* being thinner than an uppercase *W*. Few of these features are generally available with a Unix mail program; that's one of the major advantages of using the Mac.

Note

Some email or communications programs come with special monospaced fonts that are supposedly easier to read than the standard Monaco and Courier. If you see fonts like TTYFont, VT100, or Mishawaka, they're designed for displaying Internet email on the screen. I personally prefer Monaco 9 point.

Navigating and Managing Email

Another important feature of an email program is the manner in which it enables you to move between messages, save messages in different mailboxes, and delete unwanted messages after you've read them. Most email programs display a list of the messages in an In Box area, and some indicate which messages you have already read, replied to, or saved to disk. Opening a message usually opens a new window to display the message, and sometimes closing the window (with or without deleting the current message) opens the next unread message, a nice feature for those who receive a great deal of mail. Being able to sort the list of messages is useful on occasion, and you should be able to select multiple messages at once to move them to another mailbox or delete them.

Note

Some of these navigation features may not exist in the email program you use, but with a macro program like CE Software's QuicKeys, you may be able to simulate them.

Speaking of multiple mailboxes, all email programs should support them, though unfortunately not all do. Most people want to save some of the messages they receive, so a program should allow you to create your own mailboxes for filing away messages on different topics. Of course, if you can create a new mailbox, the email program should enable you to do everything you can do in your In Box to the messages stored in a personal mailbox.

Note

Perhaps the worst, and most surprising, offender in the multiple mailbox world is Apple's PowerTalk (released in late 1993), which puts a single mailbox on your Mac's desktop, but loses any mail-related information like sender, subject, and date if you copy the messages out of the mailbox to a folder.

While you're managing your email, you will undoubtedly want to delete many of the messages you receive. This area may seem straightforward, but the better email programs follow Apple's lead with the Finder and enable you to trash a file without actually immediately deleting it. The easier it is to delete a message (and it should be very easy since you're likely to eventually want to delete most of the mail you receive), the more likely you will eventually delete something accidentally. If the email program deletes immediately, your message is toast. The other advantage of the two-stage (where a message is put in a trash can before being deleted later) or a delayed delete (where a message is marked as being deleted but isn't actually deleted until you close the mailbox) is that you then don't have to put up with an annoying confirmation dialog every time you delete a message.

Some of your messages may, in fact, contain programs or other files that you want to save to a normal Macintosh file. A few email programs automatically detect attachments encoded in certain formats (more about file formats later, when I talk about FTP and other ways of receiving files) and decode such messages on their own. But one way or another, you need a simple way to save the message you're looking at without copying and pasting the entire thing into a word processor.

Replying to Email

Much of the mail you receive requires a reply of some sort, so an email program should make replying extremely easy, either with a command key shortcut or a single click on an icon. An email program should also facilitate *quoting* the original message, or prefixing each line with one or two special characters, usually a greater-than symbol and a space. Using quoting, you can easily include some of the message you're replying to so that the recipient has some context to know what you're talking about. A nice feature is the ability to select just a certain part of the original message and have the email program quote only that selected text in the reply and ignore the rest of the original message (see figure 6.3).

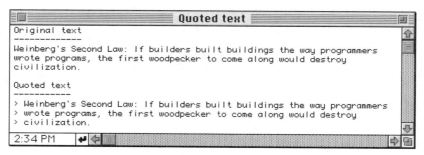

Figure 6.3   Original text and quoted text

Note

Rick Holzgrafe has written a clever little $10 shareware utility called SignatureQuote that enables you to quote messages properly even if your email program doesn't support it. SignatureQuote supports two quoting styles, two signatures that you can paste in, and can join and split text. It's a must-have if you're locked into a lousy email program.

Because an email message may have originally been sent to several people, an email program should give you the option of replying only to the sender or to all the people to whom the message originally went. At the same time, it ideally should make sure that you see the salient lines in the header. I've spawned a couple of embarrassing scenes by forwarding a message to a friend, and when my friend replied to me, his email program saw that mine had included the original message's address in the Reply-To line in the header. So his reply, instead of going just to me, went back to the sender, which was a mailing list that went to thousands of people. Oops! Luckily, I didn't say anything embarrassing and neither did he, so we were safe, but that's a good example of how two computer professionals who know better could have been thoroughly embarrassed in public. Think of this situation as standing up in a crowded restaurant and shouting loudly that your underwear has holes. You get the idea.

More powerful email programs provide features that automatically can mark or reply to email based on the contents of the header or the body of the incoming message. They often generalize these features so that you can essentially run a *mailserver*, which sends out requested information automatically via email. You can also use this sort of feature to run a simple mailing list, which takes a message to a certain local address and forwards it automatically to a list of subscribers.

Note

> *To answer a frequently asked question on the nets, I know of no Macintosh program that enables you to run a full-fledged mailing list, complete with automated subscription and sign off features. Maybe someday soon, but until then you need a Unix machine at minimum. (See later discussion for information on the three main mailing list managers.)*

New Email

Both when replying to email and when creating new mail, an email program should provide all the features you're used to when you're writing in a Macintosh word processor. In my opinion (which is by no means universal), the standard editors in the character-based Unix world stink (yeah, I know those are fighting words), and I spend so much time writing and editing my email that I couldn't possibly put up with anything other than a decent Macintosh editor. However, because every email program implements text entry and editing on its own, none of them compare to a full-fledged word processor, and a few barely even compete with the free TeachText and certainly not its fancier successor, SimpleText. My dream, which isn't all that far off, is to be able to use Nisus, the word processor with which I'm writing this book, for all of my email. With the growing acceptance of Apple events, this change will happen. I just hope it happens sooner rather than later.

I may be odd in this respect, but I think that any email program should make it easy to save a copy of everything you write, preferably automatically. I send more email than most people, often as many as 1,000 messages per month, but I like to be able to go back on occasion and see what I said, forward a message to someone who lost it, or just browse through the thoughts that appeared in my writings at that time. Why bother to keep a diary if you're writing about most of what happens in your life in email to friends?

Finally, whenever you create email, your email program should enable you to send the mail to a *nickname* or *alias*, which is merely another, easier-to-remember form of an email address. So instead of typing **ferdinand-the-bull@cork.tree.com** every time you want to send that person email, you can type the shorter **Bull**. Be careful with nicknames because it's easy to create more than you can easily remember, at which point they don't particularly help any more. Defining nicknames for everyone you might ever send email to is a waste of time; settle for defining a nickname only after you decide that you are likely to send that person email frequently.

Note

You want to be slightly careful with nicknames, because occasionally the recipient sees the nickname as well as the address. A friend once created a nickname DA BOSS for our supervisor, who thought it was funny when she saw it. I can think of some less humorous situations.

Finding People

Now you know how an email program should work and how to read email addresses when you see them littering up this book and the nets in general. But how do you find people to write to? Finding people to write to depends on what you're looking for. Hmm? What does he mean by that?

Assume that there are two types of people, those you already know and those you haven't yet met. The latter group makes up most of the world, and in some respects are the easiest to find and talk to because you don't really care who specifically you end up talking to. After all, you don't know any more about one stranger over another, so who you talk to makes no difference.

Friends

When I first started using the networks way back when, few of my friends had accounts, and of them, only my best friend from high school ever managed to send me email more than once. I think I got a total of three messages from him. I tried to convince them, but I just couldn't get my friends to use email. Finally, I decided they all truly hated me (a logical conclusion for a 17-year-old college freshman) and gave up on them. My ego has recovered some since then, because I've found that convincing people to start using email just to talk to me is almost impossible. This argument worked with my parents, after a while, especially after my sister also started using email heavily at Cornell. But otherwise? I can't think of a single person whom I've convinced to use email for my sake. I don't even attempt to convince my grandparents. The moral of the story is that you should assume that you can talk only to people who already use email.

Okay, so once past that reality check, how do you find the address of someone who you know uses email? The simplest and most effective method seldom occurs to many net denizens—use the telephone and ask them. This method, low-tech though it may be, has the advantage of being quick, accurate, and easy. Of course, it does ruin the surprise value of that first email note. Such is life. You do need to know your friend's telephone number, or failing that, her address so you can call the all-knowing information computers at the phone company. If you don't even know where your friend lives, she may be trying to hide from you anyway after that ugly incident a while back.

"Aha!" you say, "If the all-knowing phone company computers can give me my friend's telephone number, aren't there all-knowing computers on the Internet that can give me my friend's email address?" Nice try, and good question, but the answer is, unfortunately, maybe. Some computers know what users they support, and you can find some information via services called *Finger*, *Whois*, *X.500*, *Knowbot*, and various others, but that information doesn't help unless you already know what machine to search. Several attempts have been made at linking various directory services on different machines, but I've never found them in the slightest bit useful. The problem is twofold. First, hooking a local directory of users to an Internet-wide directory requires some effort and certain standards, and inertia being what it is, that effort isn't always made and the standards don't exist. Second, many organizations shield their users from the outside world for reasons of security and privacy. These shields also make it difficult to determine how many people actually use the Internet because one machine name may have two users, like **tidbits.com**, or many thousands of users, like **microsoft.com**.

Note

*Frankly, because I find these services so completely useless, I'm not going to bother to discuss them further. That said, if you crave some frustration, go to the University of Minnesota's Gopher server at **gopher.tc.umn.edu** (the Home Gopher server by default, if you use TurboGopher), select Phone Books, and then check out the various different options available for searching for Internet email addresses. If you know the organization in question, and they have a Phone Book server, that's the best start—otherwise you're on your own. The main thing you miss via the Gopher route is the Knowbot Information Service—to access it, telnet to **info.cnri.reston.va.us 185** and type **help** to see the possible commands.*

Acquaintances

As I said earlier in this chapter, finding new friends is easy on the Internet. You don't know people beforehand, so communicating with them in a discussion list via email or news requires nothing in terms of opening lines or trivial small talk about the fallibility of weather forecasters. If you have something to contribute to a discussion, or perhaps if you merely want to make a private comment to one of the people in the discussion, meeting him is as easy as replying to his message. Whether that first contact grows beyond a one-time message depends on many variables, but with so many people, finding correspondents on the net doesn't take long.

As much as meeting people may be easy, finding them again after some time often proves more difficult. You may not remember where a person lives, if you ever knew, and if it's in the United States at all; you probably don't know his telephone number; and frankly, you may not even remember how to spell his name. And yet, all too often I've had long, involved conversations that eventually trail off after several weeks or months, and then I don't hear from that person again. If I haven't saved a message (which contains the all-important email address in the header) or recorded his email address somewhere, I have to hope that my friend has better organizational systems than I do.

I suggest that you figure out some way to keep track of your correspondents' email addresses. Nickname features work well although they may prove unwieldy as a storage mechanism later on. If that's true, I recommend using a standard database or address book program that can handle extra fields for email addresses. This advice may sound obvious, but I can't tell you how many times I've lost an address that I wanted several months later. These days I keep a copy of every piece of email I send, in part so I can search that file, large though it may be, for email addresses that have escaped my short-term memory.

Mailing Lists

There's no accounting for taste, and similarly, there's no accounting for different interests. I may be interested in electronic publishing, tropical fish, and competitive distance running, whereas the next person might favor *The Simpsons*, aviation, and Irish culture. As a result, discussion groups have sprung up around almost every imaginable topic, and if your area of interest isn't represented, it's not too difficult to start your own group. These groups take two forms: mailing lists and Usenet newsgroups. I talk more about Usenet in the next chapter; for now I'll concentrate on mailing lists.

The beauty of mailing lists is that they cover specific topics and they come straight to you, without any extra work on your part. If you find yourself interested in a topic, you can subscribe to the appropriate mailing list, and all the traffic comes directly to your electronic mailbox. This system makes participating in many mailing lists easy, even if you have only email access to the Internet; Usenet access may require more money and effort. Luckily for those of you who cannot get Usenet access, many mailing lists and newsgroups mirror each other.

Mailing lists have several other advantages over Usenet news. Email is ubiquitous on the Internet, whereas access to news is far less common (although certainly widespread). Because of the way Usenet news propagates throughout the nets, mailing lists often arrive faster than any given posting in a newsgroup might. Because mailing lists arrive in your electronic mailbox, they may seem less intimidating than large newsgroups with many participants. And frankly, many of us who lead busy lives find mailing lists easier to keep up with because we don't have to run another program to read the list, whereas reading news always requires leaving that ubiquitous email program and running a newsreader.

There are a number of programs that operate mailing lists, the most well-known of which are LISTSERV, ListProcessor, and Majordomo. They all support similar commands; I'll get into those in a moment. LISTSERV is a commercial program from Eric Thomas of LSoft and currently requires an IBM mainframe running VM/CMS (although versions for VMS, Unix, and Windows NT are in the works). The Unix-based ListProcessor comes from Anastasios Kotsikonas and is now owned by CREN (remember them from chapter 4?). The Unix-based Majordomo is free as far as I can tell.

Note

I said previously that there is no software for managing mailing lists on a Mac, but I've learned that Majordomo is written in a powerful Unix scripting language called perl. There exists a version of perl for the Mac, called MacPerl. In theory (I haven't heard of anyone trying this yet), you could port the Majordomo perl code over to MacPerl and use it to run a mailing list on a Mac. Let me know if you do this, and I'll publicize it in TidBITS.

There are also many mailing lists that are run through hacks to the Unix mailer software—these generally require some sort of human intervention for subscribing and signing off, although sometimes they use non-standard commands that do the same thing. Have I mentioned yet that I dislike programs that don't work in standard ways? They make life even more confusing than it already is.

Note

You may wonder why LISTSERV doesn't have an E at the end and why it is spelled with all capitals. LISTSERV software has existed for some time on IBM mainframes that run the VM/CMS operating system. This operating system limits userids to eight characters (hence the missing E), and because the operating system itself was not case sensitive, all commands and program names have traditionally been typed in uppercase only. The name also may have had something to do with early computer terminals not supporting lowercase, but I can't prove that theory. Just believe me—by convention, LISTSERVs are always addressed in the uppercase, although it doesn't matter any more.

Along with the different mailing list manager programs, you may have to deal with two other variables related to mailing lists—moderation and digests. Each of these possibilities slightly changes how you interact with the list, so let's look at each in turn and then go over the basics of using the list manager software as a subscriber.

Moderated vs. Unmoderated

I suspect many mailing lists started out *unmoderated*, which means that anyone was able to send a message on any topic (whether or not it was appropriate to the group) to the list. The list software then distributed that message to the entire list. You see the problem already—no one wants to read a bunch of messages that have nothing to do with the topic or discussion at hand. Similarly, if a discussion is spinning out of control and turning into a flame war, it's just a waste of time for many people.

Thus was born the concept of the moderated mailing list. To stem inappropriate postings, a moderator reads all the postings before they go out to the group at large and decides which are appropriate. Moderated groups tend to have less traffic, and the messages that go through are guaranteed by the moderator to have some worth. This system is good.

Note

The Info-Mac Digest is a prominent example of a moderated group in the Macintosh world. Although they're usually fairly lenient, moderators Bill Lipa, Liam Breck, Igor Livshits, and Gordon Watts do an excellent job, and their efforts are much appreciated by all.

On the downside, moderated groups occasionally run into sticky issues of censorship because the moderator may not always represent the views of the majority of the readers. Moderator positions are volunteer only; I've never heard of a mailing list that elected a moderator, although it's certainly possible, particularly among lists that carry traffic associated with a professional organization.

I see no reason to choose to read or not read a mailing list based on its moderation until you've spent a while seeing what goes on in the group. I subscribe to various lists, some moderated, some not, and on the whole, both have their place. Keep in mind, though, that if you post to a moderated list, the moderator may reject your posting. Don't feel bad, but do ask why so that your future submissions stand a better chance of reaching the rest of the group. On the other hand, when posting to an unmoderated group, try to stick to appropriate topics because people hate hearing about how you like your new car in a list devoted to potbellied pigs. Too many misdirected postings to a list, and the list members may start agitating for a moderator to limit the discussion.

Individual Messages vs. Digests

When the number of messages in a mailing list increases to a certain level, many lists consider creating a digest version of the list. A digest is simply a single message that contains all the individual messages concatenated in a specific way. Why bother with a digest? Depending on how your email program works, you might find it awkward to receive and read as many as 30 messages a day, especially if your email service, such as AppleLink, charges you a per-message fee to receive email. Just think how many messages you may have waiting after a week of vacation. If the messages are sent in digest form, a mailing list becomes easier to handle for some people because you get one big message instead of lots of little messages.

Unfortunately, digests have problems too. Some email gateways to commercial services (notably AppleLink) limit the size of incoming email messages. Thus, digest mailing lists like the Info-Mac Digest, one of the most popular Macintosh mailing lists, can range in size from 30K to more than 100K, so very few issues of the digest sneak through the gateways with size limitations. In addition, you may find it easier to read (or skip through) small individual messages, whereas scrolling through a 100K file can take quite a bit of time and be extremely awkward with some email programs. To add to the complication, certain email programs (I'm not aware of any on the Mac that do this) can break up a digest into its individual messages for easier viewing. I'm talking the email equivalent of digestive enzymes here.

You must decide for yourself whether a digest is easier or harder to work with, but only with some groups do you have any choice. The LISTSERV and ListProcessor software sometimes provide an option that you can set to switch your subscription to a mailing list from individual messages to a single, usually daily, digest. I don't believe you can toggle this option for Majordomo-based lists, but Majordomo list administrators can set up a separate list that sends out a digest—you would simply subscribe to the separate (digest) list instead. These separate digest lists in Majordomo generally have "-digest" appended to the listname.

Mailing List Managers

Mailing list managers sport many sophisticated features for managing large mailing lists, and these features have made the programs popular among the people who start and run mailing lists (you didn't think lists just worked on their own, did you?). For instance, you can easily and automatically subscribe to and sign off from mailing lists run with a mailing list manager without bothering a human (in most cases). This significantly reduces the amount of work the list administrator has to do. These programs generally also have provisions for tracking the subscribers to a list, and for those who want to remain unknown, concealing certain subscriptions.

Mailing list managers can prevent unauthorized people from sending messages to the list. The *TidBITS* list works this way in theory because only I can send a message, in this case an issue of *TidBITS*, to the list. I say "in theory" because in practice the safeguards have broken down twice, resulting in confusing messages going to the entire list. The LISTSERV that runs the *TidBITS* list also knows to route all replies to postings on the list to me directly, which is normally good, but when these two accidental postings got through the safeguards, I received hundreds of messages from confused readers who didn't know why they had gotten this message. It was a major hassle.

The LISTSERV software knows about other LISTSERVs running on other machines around the world, and uses this knowledge to limit network traffic. For instance, I send a single message from my machine to a mainframe at Rice University in Texas that runs the LISTSERV handling the *TidBITS* list. Once the message arrives at Rice, the LISTSERV software checks to make sure it came from me and then sends it out to the thousands of readers on the *TidBITS* subscription list.

The LISTSERV is smart, however. It doesn't blindly send out thousands of messages, one per user, because that would waste network bandwidth, especially on expensive trans-oceanic satellite or cable links. Instead, the LISTSERV determines how to enlist the help of certain other LISTSERVs running around the world. If it knows of a LISTSERV site in Australia, for instance, it sends a single copy of the message to Australia along with the list of Australian readers to distribute to. If 100 people in Australia subscribe to the *TidBITS* list, only one message crosses the Pacific instead of 100 identical copies of the same message. That's elegant.

I gather that ListProcessor and Majordomo, Unix mail-based mailing list managers, don't have as many features as the LISTSERV software, but that's more from an administrator's point of view. Users generally shouldn't care which they use. Don't worry about it one way or another; you have no choice when picking mailing lists to subscribe to. And despite the added features of the LISTSERV software, the thing that makes the administrative details of a list easy to deal with is the administrator, not the software.

Note

ListProcessor used to be called Unix-Listserv and was distributed freely (version 6.0c is still free, even now that CREN has bought it and will be selling future versions), but after some unpleasantness regarding the term "Listserv," Anastasios Kotsikonas decided to rename it to avoid confusion. So, if you see references to Unix-Listserv, they're talking about ListProcessor.

Using LISTSERVs

Most people find dealing with LISTSERVs quite easy; however, you should watch out for a few common pitfalls while working with LISTSERV-based mailing lists. Many of the commands and pitfalls below apply to lists run by the other mailing list managers as well, so it's worth reading through the LISTSERV section even if, for instance, you're dealing with a ListProcessor list.

Every LISTSERV list has two email addresses associated with it: the address for the LISTSERV itself, and the address for the mailing list. Why the dichotomy? Well, the LISTSERV address handles all the commands, things such as subscriptions and requests for lists of subscribers and the like. The mailing list address is where you send submissions to the list, assuming of course that it's that sort of list. Here, I use the *TidBITS* list as an example for my illustrations of the basic tasks you do with a LISTSERV-based mailing list. (The only difference between the *TidBITS* list and many others is that if you send mail to the mailing list address, it doesn't go to everyone else on the list because the *TidBITS* list is dedicated to distributing *TidBITS*, not to discussion, as are most lists. Any mail sent to the mailing list address comes to me, which is fine, because such messages are usually comments on articles.)

If you want to send the LISTSERV that handles the *TidBITS* list a command, such as your subscription request, you send it to **listserv@ricevm1.rice.edu**. Notice that nowhere in the address is *TidBITS* mentioned, which is a hint that you have to specify *TidBITS* somewhere else. LISTSERVs ignore the Subject line entirely, so don't worry about filling it in at all. In the body of the message, though, you can put one or more commands, each on its own line.

To subscribe to the *TidBITS* list, you send the preceding address a message with the following command on one line in the body of the message: **SUBSCRIBE TIDBITS *your full name***, where you replace ***your full name*** with your real name, not your email address or some cute nickname. If the list administrator has to contact you about a problem, she probably doesn't appreciate having to address you as "Dear Swedish Chef Fan Club Ork Ork Ork." To clarify the preceding command, to subscribe to any LISTSERV mailing list, you send the **SUBSCRIBE** command, a space, the name of the list you want to subscribe to, a space, and then your full name, which must be at least two words. I don't know how rock star types like Cher or Prince manage with LISTSERVs, although I did once get mail from someone who really only had one name. I advised him to use "No really, I only have one name" as his last name (see figure 6.4).

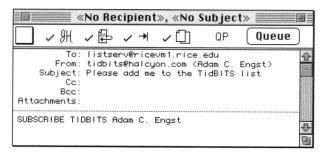

Figure 6.4   *Subscribing to* TidBITS

Note

I hear that Prince has legally changed his name to a single character that looks like a little stick figure person. Such characters are called dingbats in the publishing world, so I vote that we simply refer to Prince as Dingbat, or perhaps Prince Dingbat to be unambiguous. Needless to say, there's no way to subscribe to a mailing list using a single non-alphabetic character as your name.

The LISTSERV always returns a welcome note after you have subscribed successfully. Keep that note! It lists various useful commands, such as how to sign off from the list, and it usually provides the address of the list administrator. You can contact the list administrator to handle any problems that the automated program chokes on.

After you have subscribed to a list, you mainly want to read messages (which is easy) and post occasional messages to the rest of the people on the list. Once again, to post a message you send it to the mailing list address, which is always the name of the list at the same machine. If, for example, you want to send mail to the *TidBITS* list (which comes only to me), you send the email to **tidbits@ricevm1.rice.edu**. I realize I've almost beaten this particular horse to death, but I can't emphasize enough the difference between the LISTSERV address and the mailing list address. You send commands to the LISTSERV, and submissions to the mailing list address. Perhaps the most common problem I see on LISTSERV mailing lists is that people forget to send commands to the LISTSERV address and instead fill up the mailing list with the electronic equivalent of junk mail that no one wants to see. And, of course, sending commands to the mailing list address isn't just annoying and flame-provoking, it's futile because the LISTSERV doesn't respond to them there.

After you've been on a list for some time, the LISTSERV may ask you to confirm your subscription. I set this option with the *TidBITS* list to clean the deadwood from the list every year. Students graduate, employees move on, bulletin boards close up, and those addresses don't always go away, so the LISTSERV wastes network resources sending to a non-existent person, much like talking to a politician. After you have received *TidBITS* for a year from the LISTSERV, it sends you a message asking you to confirm that you still want to get the newsletter. If you don't respond within seven days, the LISTSERV removes you from the list, assuming that you don't want to continue receiving email from it. If you respond, you must respond with a command so that you send it to the LISTSERV address, not the mailing list address. The command is simply **CONFIRM TIDBITS** (or the name of the list you are asked to confirm).

A portion of the time this confirmation process fails. As I'm sure you noticed in the preceding paragraphs, nowhere do you provide your email address to the LISTSERV, which is supposed to determine it from the header of your message. This idea seems excellent at first because the header should, in theory, have your email address correct, and it doesn't suffer from typos or simple human mistakes that you might make if you type it in by hand. However, depending on the routing that your mail takes and how you or your system administrators have your system set up, your address as it appears in the header may change from time to time. Those changes play havoc with the LISTSERV, which is a very literal program. Therefore, when you confirm a subscription, if that confirmation comes from an address the LISTSERV doesn't recognize, poof, it doesn't work. You probably still receive mail to the original address just fine because the address is usually merely a variant on the theme, so many people sit helplessly by as the LISTERV asks for confirmation, rejects it, and then calmly deletes them from the list.

Note

This situation is a perfect example of why computers should never be given direct control over human lives. If you don't properly match for some reason, you're just another file to be deleted.

There is a simple fix. Just resubscribe as soon as the LISTSERV sends either the confirmation rejection or the message saying that it has deleted you from the list. You may get duplicates of everything for a few days, but then the LISTSERV deletes your old address and continues to send to your new one.

If you blow it and misspell your name while subscribing, or perhaps decide to change your name for one reason or another, you can always change your name (only) with the LISTSERV by sending another **SUBSCRIBE** command. The danger here, as discussed in the preceding paragraphs, is that if your address looks at all different from when you originally subscribed, the LISTSERV happily adds you to the list again, and you receive duplicates of everything. Now is a good time to ask the list administrator for help because the LISTSERV recognizes only your new address, so you can't delete your old address. Bit of a Catch-22 there.

This Catch-22 can apply to trying to sign off from a list normally, as well. Under standard circumstances, if you send the command **SIGNOFF TIDBITS** to the LISTSERV address, it removes you from the list. If your address in the header has changed, however, it doesn't recognize you as a current subscriber and thus doesn't let you sign off. Once again, if you need help beyond what the LISTSERV program can provide, don't hesitate to ask the list administrator, but ask nicely. These people don't get paid to take abuse, and in fact, they don't get paid to administrate a list at all. I'll tell you how to contact a list administrator in a moment.

The reason for this seemingly irritating address feature is that administrators realized early on that it would be way too much fun to sign someone else up for mailing lists if you really don't like him. You could, for example, sign him up for all the special offers in the back of *The National Enquirer*. Some friends of mine once had a war with that game, but one was declared the loser when he received bronzed baby shoes and a free subscription to a white supremacist newsletter, or some such nonsense. I'm sure it would be great fun to sign Bill Gates up for a really far-out mailing list, but it gets old after a while, and is generally considered abuse of the networks.

Some LISTSERVs can send you files if you send them proper commands in a message. The LISTSERV at Rice, `listserv@ricevm1.rice.edu`, is one of these sites. In fact, it stores Macintosh files that also exist on the popular FTP site `sumex-aim.stanford.edu`. You can find site-specific information by sending a **HELP** command to any LISTSERV, and for the standard LISTSERV information, send **INFO REFCARD**.

LISTSERVs support a number of other commands, of which only a few are generally useful. If you want to see a list of all the people who have subscribed to a LISTSERV list, you can use the **REVIEW** command. For instance, if you want to receive a 500K message listing all the subscribers to *TidBITS* (and I don't really recommend you do so unless you like reading lists of names and addresses), send email to the LISTSERV address, `listserv@ricevm1.rice.edu` with the following line in the body of the message: **REVIEW TIDBITS COUNTRIES**. I threw in the **COUNTRIES** modifier (it's not necessary) because it instructs the LISTSERV to sort the subscribers by country and to include a count of subscribers for each country at the bottom, which is neat.

The other utility of the **REVIEW** command is that it includes the address of the list administrator at the top, so it's a good way to find out who to ask for help. Using the **REVIEW** command is a good way to see what address the LISTSERV thinks you used to subscribe and then ask the administrator for help. For just the administrator address, you can change the command to **REVIEW SHORT**.

Note

Budding direct marketers should be aware that if you request a bunch of subscriber lists and use them for nefarious marketing purposes, the following will occur: (a) that feature will be immediately turned off in most lists, and (b) I will personally lead the flamethrower crews on a mission to turn you into fine electronic ash. That sort of opportunism doesn't fly on the Internet.

To switch a LISTSERV subscription (you must already be subscribed) from individual messages to a digest format, send the LISTSERV address the command **SET** *listname* **DIGEST**. To switch back to individual messages, send it command **SET** *listname* **MAIL**.

Most of the other commands that LISTSERVs support aren't as interesting, or as much fun to write about, so I'll refrain and let you find them on your own.

Using ListProcessor

Working with a mailing list run by the ListProcessor program is remarkably like working with a mailing list run by the LISTSERV program. The similarity isn't coincidental—ListProcessor started out as a clone of LISTSERV, not in terms of the code, but in terms of the command structure. Thus, the few differences between the two are minimal, especially in the basic functions.

Just as LISTSERVs have a `listserv@domain.name` address, ListProcessors are generally referred to as `listproc@domain.name`, although a number of them may still use the `listserv@domain.name` address left over from when ListProcessor was called Unix-Listserv. And just as the mailing list itself has a different address from the LISTSERV address, something like `listname@domain.name`, so too do ListProcessor lists. In other words, the confusing dichotomy between the ListProcessor address and the list address exists, just as it does with LISTSERV lists. You send commands to the ListProcessor address (in the body of the message—the Subject line doesn't matter) and submissions to the mailing list address. I'm really beginning to feel sorry for this poor horse, since I keep beating it, but I can't tell you how many people fail to understand this basic distinction, and in the process irritate thousands of other people on numerous lists.

To subscribe to a ListProcessor-based mailing list, send **subscribe** *listname your full name* to the ListProcessor address. Just as with the LISTSERV mailing lists, replace *listname* with the name of the list you wish to subscribe to and use your real name in place of *your full name*. ListProcessor figures out your email address from the header of the message.

You leave a ListProcessor-based mailing list by sending the command **unsubscribe** *listname* to the ListProcessor address. The command **signoff** *listname* does exactly the same thing. Just like the LISTSERV lists, if your address has changed, the automated process very well may not work, at which point you must talk to the list administrator.

The command to switch a ListProcessor subscription from individual messages to digest format differs slightly from LISTSERV—send the command **set** *listname* **mail digest** to the ListProcessor address. Frankly, I can't see from the instructions how to switch back to individual messages.

If all else fails, try sending the ListProcessor the **help** command for a simple reference card that explains the options.

Using Majordomo

This is getting kind of boring, but Majordomo works pretty much like the other two mailing list managers. There are two addresses—the Majordomo address to send your commands to (often `majordomo@domain.name`), and the mailing list address to send submissions to (`listname@domain.name`). You may also (if they're running a recent version of Majordomo) be able to send commands to `listname-request@domain.name`.

To subscribe to a Majordomo-based list, send email to the Majordomo address with the command **subscribe** *listname*. Majordomo differs slightly from the other two mailing list managers in that you don't have to specify your full name, and if you like, you can append an email address to the subscription command. This enables you to subscribe someone else to a mailing list, which can be handy—just don't abuse it. The same structure applies to removing yourself or someone else from a list—send **unsubscribe** *listname* to the Majordomo address (**signoff** *listname* works as well).

An easier method of subscribing and unsubscribing to Majordomo-based lists is to send email to **listname-request@domain.name** with either the **subscribe** command or the **unsubscribe** command in the body of the message. Since you've made it clear which list you want to subscribe to with the address, there's no need to include it in the subscription command.

Finally, you can send Majordomo a **help** command to see what other options are available. I always recommend that you do this, just so you know how and so that you see what's possible.

Neither Rain, Nor Snow...

I believe I promised early on in this book that there would be no quiz, but if I were going to break my promise, this is probably the chapter I'd do it in. You cannot get around on the Internet unless you understand how machine names and email addresses are put together. And, quite frankly, since you're likely to use email heavily, I hope you've gotten a sense for how it works, the sorts of things you shouldn't do with it, what an email program should do for you, and what it makes possible in terms of mailing lists. Enough about mailing lists— let's move on to the next sort of discussion lists, the Usenet newsgroups.

Usenet News

I've talked generally about the thousands of Usenet newsgroups that hold fast-moving discussions on every imaginable topic. My host machine, for example, carried more than 5,000 of them at last count, and that's nowhere near the entire list. Hundreds of thousands of people read Usenet every day. It's certainly one of the most interesting, although strange, parts of the Internet.

Note

Prompted by a problem posed by Nicholas Negroponte, head of the MIT Media Lab, Eric Jorgensen of MIT did a survey in early 1994 to determine the average age and gender of Usenet readers. Jorgensen received 4,566 responses to his survey. He figured out that the average age of the Usenet reader is 30.7 years old (with a standard deviation of 9.4). Eighty-six and a half percent of the replies came from men, 13.5 percent came from women, and 0.1 percent came from, well, not men or women. Although most newsgroups he surveyed were heavily male-dominated, `misc.kids` *(71 percent female),* `rec.arts.tv.soaps` *(91 percent female), and* `rec.food.sourdough` *(50 percent female) were notable exceptions. You may be able to find more information about the survey and the full results in:*

```
http://www.mit.edu:8001/people/nebosite/home-page.html
```

How is Usenet different from the mailing lists we've just looked at in the last chapter? I see two primary differences, neither of which has to do with the information that flows through them.

First, although mailing lists may be faster to propagate because they go directly to the subscriber, they can be extremely inefficient. If only one person on a machine reads a mailing list, one copy comes in. If, however, 100 people on that machine all read the same mailing list, then 100 identical copies of each posting must come in, eating up disk space and slowing down other tasks. This is bad. In contrast, only one copy of every Usenet message goes to each machine, and any number of people on that machine can read it. So, assuming that both contained an identical posting (which in reality occurs only occasionally), you could greatly reduce your machine's storage load by reading the Usenet newsgroup instead of the mailing list.

Second, many people like mailing lists because they always read their mail but may not always run a separate newsreading program. This situation actually works in favor of news as well. Most email programs are designed for a relatively small number of messages, each completely different and unrelated. In contrast, most newsreaders concern themselves with large numbers of messages, many of which are related, or in a *thread*. So, if you read the news and come across an interesting posting, reading the next posting in that thread is easy (or should be), whether or not the posting is the next one in the list. Following threads in an email program is generally difficult or impossible.

Given those advantages, how does Usenet work, what do the messages on it look like, and how do you generally interact with it?

Usenet Plumbing

For the most part, knowing how Usenet actually works isn't even slightly important to daily life. However, the basic principles may help you to better cope with some of its quirks and limitations.

The entire concept of Usenet is based on one machine transferring postings to another. Scale that up so that any one machine carrying Usenet messages talks to at least one other machine carrying Usenet messages, and you start to see how this simple idea can become an immense and powerful reality. We're talking about thousands of machines and millions of people and megabytes of data per day.

If you post a message in a Usenet group, your machine passes the message on to all the machines it talks to, both *upstream* and *downstream*. Upstream loosely refers to the machines that your machine generally gets all of its news from. Downstream loosely refers to the machines that get all of their news from your machine. In either case, those machines continue to propagate your message throughout the network, with the Usenet software that controls the system making sure your message isn't duplicated *ad infinitum* (Latin for "a hell of a lot of times, which irritates everyone").

The actual process by which your message travels is equally simple, at least in UUCP. The Usenet software creates a batch of messages to go out and compresses the batch to reduce transmission time. When the next machine receives the batch, it unbatches the messages, placing the files in directories in which the news-reading software knows to find them. One testament to the simplicity of this scheme is that not all implementations have to use this technique. (In fact, NNTP, another common method of transferring news, sends only the text of articles a specific reader requests while reading news.) InterCon's UUCP/ Connect, for example, creates a single file for each newsgroup and appends new messages to that single file. However, most Unix machines store the messages as individual files within specific directories, and those directories are directly related to the names of the newsgroups, which you look at next.

Newsgroup Innards

Just as email addresses make sense after you know all the parts, so do the Usenet newsgroup names. Although they resemble email addresses, the basic principles are a bit different.

Note

Although, like email addresses, Usenet newsgroups use periods to separate different parts of the name, people tend not to use them in conversation. If, for example, you were to tell a friend about an interesting discussion on `comp.sys.mac.misc`*, you'd say "Check it out on comp sys mac misc." Part of the problem may be the linguistic clumsiness of saying all those "dots," but I suspect more of the reason is that precision isn't nearly as necessary. Unlike email addresses, you seldom type out newsgroup names. It may also have to do with the fact that newsgroup names are all unique and easily parsed.*

The premise of the Usenet newsgroup naming scheme is that of a hierarchy. The naming scheme makes figuring out how to name new groups easy. More importantly, it maps over to a hierarchical directory (or folder) structure. On the Unix machines that hold the newsgroups, therefore, you find a directory called **news**. Inside that directory sit other directories corresponding to the top-level parts of the hierarchy—**alt**, **comp**, **misc**, **news**, **rec**, **sci**, and so on. These directories are abbreviations for alternate, computers, miscellaneous, news, recreation, and science, respectively.

Note

*I could attempt to create a table listing all the top level hierarchies, but it's a pointless task. There are many local hierarchies that I have no way of finding (just as many other machines probably don't carry the **halcyon** or **seattle** hierarchies that I can see), and I couldn't begin to guess which hierarchies your machine might carry.*

Let's dissect the name of **comp.sys.mac.misc**, a popular newsgroup. If we first look into the **comp** directory, we see more directories corresponding to **lang**, **sys**, and so on. Under **sys** we find many directories, one for each computer system. There are **atari**, **amiga**, **ibm**, **mac**, and gobs of systems that you may never have even heard of. (I certainly haven't heard of all of them.) After we go into the **mac** directory, we find the lowest level directories that correspond to the individual topics about the Mac. These include **advocacy**, **apps**, **databases**, **games**, **hardware**, **misc**, **portables**, **system**, and others. Once inside those directories (feel like you're in a Russian doll again?), you find the files that hold the text of the messages (see figure 7.1).

This system may seem a tad clumsy, but remember, as a user you never have to traverse that entire directory structure. It exists to categorize and classify newsgroups, and to provide a storage system that maps onto a Unix directory structure.

Message Construction

On the surface, a Usenet posting looks much like an email message (see figure 7.2).

Figure 7.1   *An abbreviated Usenet hierarchy tree*

The posting's header holds a From line, a Subject line, and a fair amount of other stuff. Then comes the body of the message, and a signature.

The header has a few new lines that you might find interesting.

```
Newsgroups: comp.sys.mac.misc
```

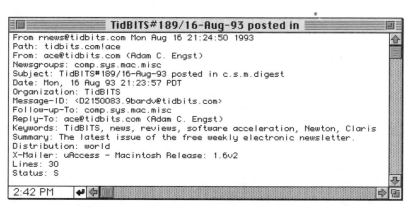

Figure 7.2   A Usenet header

First comes the Newsgroups line. It lists, separated by commas, all the newsgroups to which the message is posted. You can post a message to more than one group at a time by putting more than one group in the Newsgroups line. At that point, an article is *cross-posted*. If you must post an article in several groups (which is generally frowned on as a waste of bandwidth), make sure to post via the Newsgroups line and not through individual messages. Individual messages take up more space, because a machine stores only one copy of a cross-posted article along with pointers to it from different groups.

```
Follow-up-To: comp.sys.mac.misc
```

The next Usenet-specific line is the Follow-up-To line, which usually contains the name of the newsgroup in which the article appears. Sometimes, however, you want to post an article in one group, have a discussion, then move back to another group. In this case you put the second group in the Follow-up-To line, because whenever anyone posts a follow-up to your article, the news software makes sure that it ends up in the proper group.

```
Reply-To: ace@tidbits.com (Adam C. Engst)
```

The Reply-To ensures that all email replies come back to me. It makes it easier for people to respond directly rather than cluttering the group with personal messages.

```
Keywords: TidBITS, news, reviews, software acceleration, Newton, Claris

Summary: The latest issue of the free weekly electronic newsletter.
```

Sometimes you see a Keywords and/or Summary line as well. Although not universal or enforced, it's often a good idea to fill in these lines for your article before you post it. That way, people who have set up their newsreaders properly can more effectively filter articles based on keywords. In addition, some newsreaders show only the header and first few lines of an article, and then let the reader decide whether she wants to read the whole thing. A few well-chosen keywords or a concise summary can help make that decision easier.

```
Distribution: world
```

Many articles are only relevant in specific geographic areas. You have two ways to handle this situation. First, if you're selling a car in, say, Seattle, you should post to a specific group that goes only to people in Seattle (more or less, anyway), such as **seattle.forsale**. Many of these site-specific groups exist, even down to the machine. There's a group, **halcyon.slip**, for example, for discussion about issues affecting SLIP and PPP users of the **halcyon.com** machine.

The other way to handle this situation is to use the Distribution line. This enables you to limit the area to which your message is distributed, even if the group encompasses all of Usenet. So, if you want to post a notice about a Seattle British Car Show in **rec.autos**, you should put **seattle**, or possibly **pnw** (for Pacific Northwest) in the Distribution line.

```
Subject: TidBITS#189/16-Aug-93 posted in c.s.m.digest
```

And of course we have the ubiquitous Subject line. Much as it is courteous for you to provide a descriptive Subject line in an email message, it's imperative in a Usenet posting. Most newsreaders these days show the user a list of the messages and their subjects. If you don't provide a good Subject line, far fewer people even notice your message. For example, each week I post an announcement of each issue of *TidBITS* in the **comp.sys.mac.misc** group. Instead of a general Subject line such as "TidBITS posted," I enter "TidBITS#189/16-Aug-93 posted in c.s.m.digest." This tells the reader in precise terms what I posted and where she can find it.

The Newsgroup Stork

Now that you know something about how messages travel from machine to machine and how the naming system works, you may wonder where new newsgroups come from. Whenever I've talked about the range of Usenet groups, I've said something to the effect of "and if there isn't one that matches your interests, you can create one." That is true, but the process is not trivial.

Note

Although I summarize the process below, if you want to see all the gory details, check out two periodic postings in **news.announce.newusers**. *Both "How to Create a New Usenet Newsgroup" and "The Usenet Newsgroup Creation Companion" are required reading for anyone seriously considering creating a new group.*

The first rule in creating new groups is: Don't do so unless you are absolutely sure no appropriate group already exists. Usually, you simply haven't found the right group. Once you do, the need to create a group disappears. The Usenet structure lends itself to talking about almost any subject in an existing group. For instance, you can talk about anything Macintosh-related in **comp.sys.mac.misc**. Thus, the second rule of creating a new group: Don't create a group until the traffic in a more general group has grown unmanageable, and stayed that way for some time. As a rule of thumb, wait six months. And, one way or another, make sure you have a Usenet old-timer on your side, to help with the details and steer you clear of any egregious mistakes.

After you are sure the world really does need a group dedicated to discussion of the psychology of smelling flowers from under cork trees, you write a proposal. This *Request for Discussion*, or *RFD*, states what the group is called, what its purpose is, why no existing group serves the need, and so on. Then your job as agitator begins, as you distribute the RFD to groups where interested parties might hang out. Be sure to place the **news.announce.newgroups** group first in the Newsgroups line (so the moderator can correct any problems in the RFD before posting it to **news.announce.newgroups** and the others for you) and to set the Follow-up-To line so that the discussion takes place in **news.groups**. Then you encourage discussion of the topic for 30 days in **news.groups**, all the while collecting responses and modifying the proposal, called a *charter*, accordingly.

After 30 days, if people don't agree on the charter, you must start the RFD process again—with a new and improved proposal, of course. If everyone does agree on the charter, the time has come for a *Call For Votes*, or *CFV*, with clear and unbiased directions on how to vote.

The CFV goes, once again, to all the interested newsgroups, with **news.announce.newgroups** first in the Newsgroups line. It lasts between 21 and 31 days, and you must include the exact end date in the CFV. Once again, your job is to collect and tally the votes via email. (Don't even think of stuffing the electronic ballot box—there's little the Usenet community hates more than a cheat.) You must record each voter's email address along with his Yes or No vote, for later use. You can re-post the CFV during the vote to keep up awareness, but only if you don't change anything from the original CFV.

At the end of the voting period, you post the results—including the total number of votes, and the vote and email address for each—to **news.announce.newgroups** and the other interested newsgroups. Then everyone waits five days, which provides enough time to correct any mistakes or raise serious objections. You need to meet two separate goals to justify a newsgroup. A sufficient number of votes and, within that number, a sufficient number of YES votes. If you have at least 100 more YES votes (for creating the newsgroup) than NO votes, and at least two-thirds of the votes are YES votes, then the group passes the vote.

If, of course, you don't get the required number or percentage of votes, the group doesn't get created. There's no shame in not having your group created. You can even try again in six months if you want to and interest seems to have increased since the original failure. If you fail more than twice, give it up and form your own mailing list. You don't need anyone's cooperation to do that.

If the vote comes out positive, someone (often the moderator of **news.announce.newgroups**) can create the group, sending out the newsgroup control message. Gradually, the group is created at different sites and propagates through much of the network. Why not the entire network? Well, nothing says a machine has to carry every Usenet group in existence. If a system administrator decides that talking about smelling flowers is offensive, she might decide not to carry the group. None of the machines that rely on her machine for news will have the group, either. Nonetheless, groups focusing on technical issues enjoy relatively complete propagation. Even those discussing topics that some people find offensive enjoy wide propagation, and often greater readership, than the technical groups.

Using Usenet

No matter what software you use to access Usenet, you must be aware of some basic concepts, tasks, and features. When I evaluate different newsreaders such as UUCP/Connect and NewsWatcher in later chapters, I tell whether the newsreader in question does a good job of handling these tasks and features for you.

Subscribing to Groups

When you first invoke a newsreader, you must subscribe to the groups you want to read. Occasionally, the newsreader automatically subscribes you to a couple of basic groups, such as **news.newusers.questions** and **news.announce.newusers**. For the most part, however, the thousands of available newsgroups are in the unsubscribed category. Appendix B, "Newsgroup List," lists and briefly describes many available newsgroups. You can flip through the appendix to see which you might want to read.

Most machines don't carry all of the Usenet groups. Numbers vary, but there are somewhere between 5,000 and 7,000 groups, all told. If your machine doesn't carry a group you want, you can either ask the system administrator to get it, or go to a machine that lets anyone read news on it. These sites are called *public NNTP sites*. Be forewarned, however: Only a few public NNTP (Net News Transport Protocol) sites still exist, and even fewer of those allow posting.

Note

Finger **lesikar@tigger.stcloud.msus.edu** *for a list of public NNTP sites, but be aware that, as with all Internet services, this one may not be there forever.*

Generally, the first time you start up, a newsreader takes a long time because you have to go through all the groups and figure out which ones to subscribe to.

The better newsreaders allow you to sort through the list at different times. In the past, you had to sit for an hour or more just unsubscribing from all the groups you didn't want to read. It was a major hassle. Even now, allot plenty of time to your first session if you're doing it interactively. (Note: This rule doesn't apply to a UUCP connection, where you request only specific groups.)

Reading Articles

After you subscribe to a group, it's time to read the articles. Obviously, the first time you read, all the articles are new to you. After that, you want to make sure that you read only previously unread articles. Most newsreaders are extremely good about keeping track of what you've read already. In the Unix world, the `.newsrc` file tracks what you've read. Advanced users can edit that file manually with a text editor, to subscribe or unsubscribe from several groups at once. The Macintosh newsreaders make that task, on the whole, unnecessary.

You've learned what the header for a Usenet article might look like, but many newsreaders hide most of the header from you. This is generally helpful, although it can be a pain at times.

Discussions happen in threads, which are groups of related articles, generally with the same or very similar Subject lines. Threads are important because they group both discussions that you want to read and those you don't want to read. Believe me, threads are a very big deal when you have to handle the kind of volume that passes through a popular newsgroup.

When it comes to newsreaders, there are two basic philosophies. The first, which is older, assumes that you want to read 90 percent of the information in a newsgroup. Therefore, the newsreader tries to show you the text of every article unless you explicitly tell it to skip that article or thread. This method may have worked better in the days when Usenet traffic was relatively sparse, but in these modern times, the traffic comes fast and thick. I liken this method to trying to drink from a fire hose.

The second philosophy believes that you want to read only 10 percent of the articles in any given group. With the exception of moderated groups or low-volume groups where every message counts, this assumption is far more realistic. Newsreaders built on this philosophy usually provide a list of the unread messages in a newsgroup, then let you pick and choose which to read. Some newsreaders force you to read each message or thread as you pick it. Others make you pick a whole bunch of them at once and then read them after you've sorted through the entire newsgroup. Both methods have their advantages, and a good newsreader lets you work either way.

Note

One of the most frequently asked-for programs in `comp.sys.mac.comm` *is an off-line newsreader, a program that enables you to save articles to disk and then read them when you aren't connected to the Internet. There are a few ways of getting this capability in a newsreader (UUCP is inherently off-line, for instance), and I discuss them later in this book.*

Navigation

After you start reading a set of messages, you need tools for navigating among them. Navigation tools were more important back in the days when character-based Unix newsreaders were all we had. Today, many of the Macintosh newsreaders replace the navigation commands with mouse actions. However, many people (myself included) find the keyboard to be more efficient than the mouse for navigating through news, so perhaps there's still room for some of the old tools.

The most common navigation capability takes you to the next unread message, whether or not it is in the same thread as the message that preceded it. Closely related is the capability to move to the next unread message in the same thread, even if it's not next to the message you were just reading. In a well-designed newsreader, these two capabilities are closely intertwined, so you don't have to know whether or not you're in a thread.

Note

Often, these navigation features are encapsulated in a single command linked to the Spacebar, which thus serves as an unusual computer command. Essentially, it says to the newsreader, "Do whatever makes the most sense right here." Computers hate those sort of commands, but the concept works extremely well in a newsreader. The Spacebar scrolls down the page; when you hit the bottom of the article, you probably want to read the next article in the thread, so the Spacebar takes you there. When you finish all the articles in that thread, you probably want to go back up and read the next thread, so the Spacebar takes you back up. Finally, after you read everything in a newsgroup, the Spacebar assumes that you want to read the next newsgroup you subscribe to. By making intelligent guesses, a number of commands can be subsumed under that one key. Too bad not all newsreaders subscribe to this concept.

You want to group discussions into threads so that you can easily read an entire one, even when it spans a fair amount of real world time. You also want to group discussions so you can ignore them more easily. Despite the fact that people should include descriptive Subject lines in their postings, they don't always. If you see a long thread called "Cool Stuff," you have no idea what it's about. It may pique your curiosity, though, so you start reading, only to find out that it's another "my computer is better than your computer" flame war. Now you need a way to kill the entire thread. Good newsreaders make that effort easy.

An even neater feature is the ability to create a list of Subject lines or topics about which you never want to read. This capability usually applies to anything in the header and sometimes to information in the body of the messages, too. It's extremely useful for customizing your Usenet reading experience. Currently, only one program on the Mac, the HyperCard stack NewsFetcher, supports this kind of feature.

To go even one step further, a few newsreaders provide a feature to only read articles that match certain topics. These are ideal for the very busy user.

After you read all the messages that interest you, it's generally a good idea to mark the rest of them as read (even though you didn't read them). This way, you don't see them again the next time you read news. Some newsreaders handle this option automatically, whereas others make you mark them manually. Sometimes, especially if you just returned from a vacation, you may want to mark everything as read without even trying to read the waiting messages. Marking everything lets you start with a clean slate and with a manageable number of messages the next day, and is generally referred to as *catching up*. There's no difference between a "catch up" feature and a "mark all as read" feature, but you may see both in different programs.

Now you know all about navigating around Usenet and reading articles. Many people never move past that point, and are called *lurkers*. The term has no negative connotation, it simply means people who only read and never post.

rot13

I almost forgot. You might occasionally run across articles that are completely unreadable. They may be in a newsgroup specific to a language you don't understand, but the newsreader can't help with that problem. It can (or should be able to) help you with messages coded in the *rot13* format. Rot13 is a simple coding scheme that assigns a number to each letter of the alphabet, starting with 1 for A, 2 for B, and so on, for every character in a message. It then adds 13 to each number and converts back into letters. The result is an utterly unreadable message, which the poster usually intended because some people might find the message offensive. If you see such a message and are easily offended, don't read it. No one forces you to use the rot13 decoding feature that exists in most newsreaders. If you do, you can't very well complain about the contents. I usually see most rot13 encoded postings in joke newsgroups, protecting the innocent from really sick jokes (see figure 7.3).

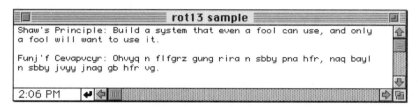

Figure 7.3   *Normal text versus rot13*

Replying to Articles

In the course of reading Usenet news, you often see messages that aren't quite clear or that catch your interest for some reason or another. When you see such a message, you may want to send email to the poster. You could, of course, copy down the poster's email address from the header onto a little piece of paper, and when you finished reading news, use your email program to send him a message. However, that process is a pain and wastes lots of little pieces of paper, so most newsreaders support sending mail replies while you're reading news.

Use email replies whenever the rest of the group won't give a hoot about what you have to say. Most of us feel that our words are pearls of wisdom and should be distributed to the widest possible audience. But, try to step back and think about whether your reply is best directed at the individual making the posting or the group as a whole.

People often ask questions on Usenet, saying that you should reply directly to them and that they plan to summarize to the net. Listen to what these people have to say. They only want replies via email, and because they've promised to post a summary of the replies, you don't need to ask for a copy personally (unless perhaps you don't stand a chance of seeing the summary in the newsgroup; even then, ask nicely). If you ever post a question and promise a summary, live up to your promise, even if you get only a couple of responses. No matter how many responses you get, format them nicely with quote characters before each quoted line so that they are easy for readers to understand; messages are often confusing as to who wrote what in a summary. Never re-post entire headers.

As far as what to say when you reply to postings on Usenet, re-read what I said about email manners in the last chapter. The same rules apply here. If you must carry out a flame war, do it in email; but if possible, don't do it at all.

Follow-ups

Discussions are the entire point of Usenet, of course, so you eventually gather the courage to post something to a newsgroup. For most people, the easiest way to post a message is to reply to another message, an action called *following up*. A follow-up is easier for the novice because the newsreader fills in most of the lines in the header for you; the lines for Subject, Newsgroups, Distribution, and so on are generally determined by the message you reply to.

Just as in email, you should be given the chance to quote the previous message so that readers can understand the context of your reply. Some newsreaders are picky about the proportion of quoted text to new text, and for good reason. No one wants to read a two-screen quoted letter only to see at the bottom a few words from you: "I agree with all this." Even in newsreaders that don't prevent you from over-quoting, be careful. Try to edit out as much of the quoted text as possible. Remember that most people have already seen that message in its original form, so you're simply jogging their memory. Definitely remove signatures and unnecessary previously quoted text.

Note

Using Usenet as a method of getting a message to a specific individual is considered extremely bad form, even if you can't seem to get email to that person. Imagine, everyone's discussing nuclear disarmament, and you suddenly see a message from a college friend. Your note discussing old times at Catatonic University will hold absolutely no interest for the rest of the group. If you find yourself being flamed, suffer and don't do it again.

Posting an Article

If you really have something new to say, or a new question to ask, don't insert it into an existing thread just because it's easier than posting a new one. Posting a new message should be simple enough in any decent newsreader.

Note

If you cannot post from a newsreader (because you only have a CompuServe account, for instance), you can still send messages to a Usenet newsgroup. Two email posting services exist: **news-group@cs.utexas.edu** *and* **news-group@pws.bull.com**. *Do not send email to* **news-group**, *but to the name of the group to which you want to post, replacing the dots in the group name with dashes. So, for example, to post to* **comp.sys.mac.comm**, *send email to* **comp-sys-mac-comm@cs.utexas.edu**. *Make sure to ask for replies via email.*

In general, you should avoid posting a few things. Avoid copyrighted works such as magazine articles or newspaper stories. Although it's unlikely that anyone could sue the Internet (it would be a bit like boxing with a dense mist), that person might sue you for copyright infringement. Besides, posting copyrighted work is not polite. Simply post the complete reference to the article or whatever, along with a summary or selected quote or two if you want to pique some curiosity.

Note

Interestingly, recipes in cookbooks are not copyrighted because they are essentially lists of instructions. However, the instructions for creating the recipe may be protected if they contain anything other than the bare bones instructions, and any preface explaining or describing the recipe is definitely protected. People often post a recipe or two from a cookbook they particularly like so that others can see whether they like the recipes enough to buy the book.

Perhaps the least obvious but most important works to avoid posting are pictures scanned in from magazines or videos digitized from TV or videotape. Most of the scanned pictures are varying degrees of erotic images, and unfortunately, most are blatant examples of copyright infringement. The magazines, *Playboy* in particular, don't look kindly on this sort of thing, and legal action might result. Besides, pictures suck up disk space, and the quality of a scanned image doesn't even begin to approach the high-quality photography and printing of most magazines.

In general, you should not post headline events that everyone can read about in the newspaper or possibly in ClariNet (which I talk about in a bit). I don't mean to imply that you can't talk about these events, but because news travels relatively slowly to all parts of the net, announcing the results of an election or a similar event is just silly. People already know about the event, and if they don't, they'll figure it out from the ensuing discussion.

Finally, don't post personal email that you receive unless the sender gives you explicit permission. As with most things on the Internet, posting personal email is a legally murky area, but the etiquette is crystal-clear: It's rude.

ClariNet

Along with all the discussion groups about computers and recreational activities and whatnot, you may see a hierarchy under **clari**. You've found ClariNet. Unlike Usenet, ClariNet doesn't carry any discussions, and in fact, I don't believe that you can post to any ClariNet groups. Instead ClariNet is dedicated to distributing commercial information, much of it the same stuff that you read in your newspaper or hear on the radio. ClariNet claims 60,000 daily readers, which isn't too bad in terms of circulation.

Also unlike Usenet, ClariNet isn't free. A site must pay a certain amount to receive the ClariNet news feed, which uses the same transport protocols and newsreaders as Usenet. Sites that receive the ClariNet feed cannot redistribute that feed on to other machines unless those machines pay for it as well. Because of ClariNet's commercial nature, I can't predict whether you even have access to it. It's strictly up to each site.

Much of the ClariNet information comes from press wires like UPI, along with NewsBytes computer articles, and various syndicated columnists such as Dave Barry, Mike Royko, and Miss Manners. A recent arrival is *Dilbert*, the cartoon by Scott Adams (although you have to download each installment and view it in a graphics program, since there isn't a newsreader around that can view graphics internally). Although you can probably find much of the information in a standard newspaper, ClariNet organizes it extremely well, making reading about a single topic much easier. For instance, some groups carry local news briefs for each state, some carry only news about Apple Computer, and there are groups with tantalizing names like **clari.news.goodnews**, which indeed includes only articles that are good news. (Depressingly, that newsgroup sees very little traffic.)

ClariNet was founded a few years ago by Brad Templeton, who is also well known as the creator of the moderated group **rec.humor.funny**, which accepts only jokes that he thinks are funny (actually, someone else does the selection now). ClariNet is an important experiment, because it is specifically commercial traffic flowing via the same methods and pathways as Usenet, perhaps the most rabidly anti-commercial part of the Internet. I don't know the business details of ClariNet, but it has been around long enough that I suspect it's a financial success, and the news that it brings is certainly welcome.

Enough Usenet

Well, that's enough on Usenet. You're ready to move on to the services that require a full connection to the Internet, such as FTP, Telnet, WAIS, Gopher, and the World-Wide Web.

Internet Services

I must tread a fine line when talking about Internet services, because the level of connection (and thus the level of service) varies widely. People who can send Internet email, for instance, may not be able to use Gopher or the World-Wide Web. The services I talk about in this chapter (except for FTP and Archie via email) all require a full TCP/IP connection to the Internet.

URLs

Before I get into the various different TCP/IP-based Internet services, I want to explain *URLs*, or Uniform Resource Locators. These constitute the most common and efficient method of telling people about resources available via FTP, the World-Wide Web, and other Internet services.

A URL, quite simply, is a method of uniquely specifying the location of a resource on the Internet. Depending on how you break it down, there are three main pieces you must know in order to retrieve any given resource. First, you have to know how to access the resource, be it on FTP, Gopher, or the World-Wide Web. Second, you must know the machine on which the resource lives. Finally, you must know the full pathname to the information you want.

Note

Uniform Resource Locators have become so popular, the Library of Congress has added a subfield for them when it catalogs electronic resources.

The description I just gave you is an oversimplification, because the subject of URLs is extremely complex. The point I want to make is simply that URLs are an attempt to provide a consistent way to reference objects on the Internet. I say "objects" because you can specify URLs for email addresses, Telnet sessions, and stranger things that may not even seem like "objects."

Table 8.1 shows the main URL types that you're likely to see.

Table 8.1
Common URL Types

Name	Internet Protocol	Sample Client
ftp	File Transfer protocol	Anarchie
gopher	Gopher protocol	TurboGopher
http	HyperText Transfer Protocol	MacWeb
wais	Wide Area Information Servers	MacWAIS

If you see a URL that starts with **ftp**, you know the file specified in the rest of the URL is available via FTP, which means that you could use FTP under Unix, FTP via email, or a MacTCP-based FTP client such as Anarchie or Fetch to retrieve it. If the URL starts with **gopher**, use TurboGopher or another Gopher client. If it starts with **http**, use NCSA Mosaic or MacWeb. And, finally, if a URL starts with **wais**, you can use MacWAIS or other WAIS browser.

Note

You can actually use NCSA Mosaic or MacWeb to access any of the URLs in Table 8.1, although they're not ideal for anything but information on the World-Wide Web itself.

After the URL comes a colon (**:**) and two slashes (**/ /**). These separate the type from the second part of common URLs. This second part is the name of the machine that contains the information you're seeking.

Note

In some rare circumstances, you may need to use a username and password in the URL as well. A URL with a username and password might look like this:

```
ftp://username:password@domain.name/pub/
```

The last part of the URL is the path to the directory of the file you're looking for. This is separated from the machine name by a slash (/). When used with WAIS or various other protocols that don't simply point at files, the path may specify other types of information. You may not have to specify the path with some URLs, such as FTP or Gopher URLs, if you're only connecting to the top level of the site.

Note

If an FTP or Gopher URL ends with a slash, that means it's pointing at a directory and not a file. If it doesn't end with a slash, it may or may not point at a directory. If it's not obvious from the last part of the path, there's no good way of telling until you go there.

All of these details aside, how do you use URLs? Your mileage may vary, but I use them in three basic ways. First, if I see them in email or in a Usenet posting, I often copy and paste them into Anarchie (if they're FTP URLs) or Mosaic or MacWeb (if any other type). That's the easiest way to retrieve a file or connect to a site if you have a MacTCP-based Internet connection.

Second, if for some reason I don't want to use Mosaic or MacWeb (I prefer Anarchie for FTP, for instance), sometimes I manually decode the URL to figure out which program to use and where to go. This method takes more work, but sometimes pays off in the end.

Third and finally, and this is where you come in, whenever I want to point someone at a specific Internet resource or file available for anonymous FTP, I give them a URL. URLs are unambiguous, and although a bit ugly in running text, easier to use than attempting to spell out what they mean. Consider the example below:

```
ftp://ftp.tidbits.com/pub/tidbits/issues/1994/TidBITS#228_30-May-94.etx
```

To verbally explain the same information contained in that URL, I would have to say something like: "Using a FTP client program, connect to the anonymous FTP site **ftp.tidbits.com**. Change directories into the **/pub/tidbits/issues/ 1994/** directory, and once you're there, retrieve the file **TidBITS#228_30-May-94.etx**." A single URL enables me to avoid such convoluted (and boring) language; URLs are in such common use on the Internet, you might as well get used to seeing them now.

Note

Frankly, I'm a little worried that some of the longer URLs in this book may be messed up in the book production process, so if you see a hyphenated URL that doesn't look or work right (hypens should only appear between words, never in the middle of a word as you would normally see at the end of a line in running text), assume that the hyphen is an artifact of the production process.

So, from now on, whenever I mention a file or a Web site, I'll use a URL. If you try to retrieve a file or connect to a Web site and are unsuccessful, chances are either you've typed the URL slightly wrong, or the file or server no longer exists. It's *extremely* likely that many of the files I give URLs for will have been updated by the time you read this, so the file name at the end of the URL may have changed. So if a URL doesn't work, try removing the file name from the last part of the URL and look in the directory that the original file lived in for the updated file. If, after all this, you'd like to learn more about the technical details behind the URL specifications, check out:

```
http://info.cern.ch/hypertext/WWW/Addressing/URL/Overview.html
```

Note

I find that URLs don't always work well for files stored on Gopher servers, since Gopher allows spaces and other characters that URLs don't accept. Thus, spaces are encoded in Gopher URLs with %20 to indicate that there's a space there. Similarly, WAIS sources usually are easier to simply refer to by name—using a WAIS client such as MacWAIS makes it easy to use sources without worrying about all the additional information in a URL.

FTP

Despite the occasionally confusing way people use the term both as a noun and a verb, most people don't have much trouble using FTP. FTP stands for *File Transfer Protocol*, and not surprisingly, it's only good for transferring files between machines. In the past, you could only use an FTP client to access files stored on FTP servers. Today, however, enough other services such as Gopher and the World-Wide Web have implemented the FTP protocols that you can often FTP files no matter what service you happen to be using. Heck, you can even FTP files via email. I'll get to the specifics of the different clients in later chapters; for now, here are a few salient facts to keep in mind regarding FTP.

FTP Manners

The Internet does a wonderful job of hiding geographical boundaries. You may never realize a person with whom you correspond lives on the other side of the globe. When using FTP, however, try to keep the physical location of the remote machine in mind.

First, as with everything on the Internet, someone pays for all this traffic. It's probably not you directly, so try to behave like a good citizen who's being given free access to an amazing resource. Show some consideration by not, for example, using machines in Australia when one in the same area of your country works equally well. Because trans-oceanic traffic is expensive, many machines mirror others; that is, they make sure to transfer the entire contents of one machine to the other, updating the file collection on a regular, often daily basis.

Here's an example. Because the Info-Mac archive site at `sumex-aim.stanford.edu` is popular and kept up-to-date, other sites carrying Macintosh software don't want to duplicate the effort. It's much easier to set up a mirror to `sumex` so that machines in Australia and Scandinavia can have exactly the same contents as `sumex`. Mirroring not only saves work, it enables users in those countries to access a cheaper, local site for files. Everyone wins, but only if you, the user, utilize local sites whenever possible. You can usually tell where a site is located by looking at the two-letter country domain at the end of the address.

Sometimes, of course, the file you need exists only on a remote site in Finland, for example, so that's where you must go to get it. Another point of etiquette to keep in mind, wherever the file may be, is sensitivity to the time of day at the site from which you retrieve it. Like most things in life, other than universities during exams, more people use the Internet during their daytime hours than at night. Thus, it's generally polite to retrieve files during off hours; otherwise, you're preventing people from doing their work. That's not polite, especially if the file you're retrieving is a massive QuickTime movie or something equally frivolous.

Notice that I said "their daytime hours." Because the Internet spans the globe, it may be 4:00 A.M. where you are, but it's the middle of the day somewhere else. You can figure out the local time by using the Map Control Panel that comes with your Mac.

One final piece of FTP etiquette: Don't use someone else's FTP site as a temporary dumping ground for junk that you either can't store on your account or don't want to download directly.

FTP Clients

FTP is inherently simple to use, but there's plenty of room for FTP client software to make your life miserable. The following sections, therefore, describe several benefits and features to look for in an FTP client.

Connecting

Most of the time, people use an FTP client program to log on to a remote FTP site, find a file or two, download them, and then log off. As such, a disproportionate amount of your time is spent connecting and navigating to the files you want.

A good FTP client enables you to define shortcuts for frequently used FTP sites, along with the userid and password necessary for connecting to them. This benefit is minor but makes a big difference when repeated numerous times. I can't tell you how much I hate typing **sumex-aim.stanford.edu** on a Unix command line when I'm trying to connect to that site with FTP.

Navigating

Once you're on, the FTP client program should make it very easy to move between directories (or folders, in Mac jargon). Most programs do this by emulating the Standard File Dialog used on the Mac to open and save files, which is a good start (although the Standard File Dialog is one of the most confusing parts of the Macintosh interface). It's helpful when the client program remembers the contents of directories. That way, if you go back to one you've already visited, you don't have to wait for it to refresh.

Note

In the first edition of this book, I commented that I'd like to see an FTP client program emulate the Finder instead, so you could use familiar techniques for opening and closing folders and retrieving files. Since then, Peter Lewis has released Anarchie, a fabulous FTP client that works with MacTCP-based connections. It looks and works much like the Finder in Name view. If you have the proper system software, you can even drag and drop files from Anarchie windows into Finder windows. See chapter 13 for details about Anarchie.

A useful variant of shortcuts (also known as bookmarks) to FTP site names is the addition of directory information to the site name. Say, for instance, you want to retrieve something from `ftp.tidbits.com`. Not only do you have to enter the host name, userid, and password, but you must also go to the proper directory, which is `/pub/tidbits`.

Listing Style

In Unix, you can choose among several different methods of viewing files. Some show you more information, such as file size and creation date, and others show you less, in order to fit more entries on the screen. Although the Mac doesn't have the problem of trying to fit multiple columns in a list (no Macintosh program uses multiple column lists), not all the FTP clients are good about showing you the entire filename, size, or date. I think this failure is inexcusable, because you need to know how large a file is before you spend an hour retrieving it—especially if you're connecting at a slow speed. Make sure the program you use provides this information.

Recognizing File Type and Decoding

Much of the time, an FTP client can figure out what sort of file you're retrieving by looking at the extension to the filename. This being the case, the client can make sure it is transferring the file in the proper format. If you're lucky, it even decodes some of the common formats you see on the Internet.

"Wait a minute," you say. "He didn't mention strange file formats before." Sorry about that. I'll get to file formats later on in this chapter, after I've discussed the various different ways files might appear on your machine. But first, let's look at how you can retrieve files from FTP sites armed only with an email program.

FTP by Email

One of the problems with FTP is that it requires your attention—in fact, pretty much your full attention. In addition, you must have a TCP/IP connection to the Internet. If you're connecting via CompuServe or UUCP, you simply cannot use FTP normally.

Note

If you're clever and are able to do a little scripting with AppleScript or Frontier, you can script Anarchie to retrieve files automatically. Unfortunately, the only FTP client that can do this internally, XferIt, hasn't been updated in years.

There is a solution, although not a terribly good one. You can retrieve files remotely, using only your email program, in two different ways. The most generic way by using one of the *FTPmail* or *BITFTP* servers. The other way is to use a specific mailserver program that only knows how to serve a specific site, sometimes as part of a mailing list manager such as LISTSERV, ListProcessor, or Majordomo. Let's look at the generic way first.

FTPmail and BITFTP

Using FTPmail or BITFTP isn't particularly difficult, but can be extremely frustrating. The problem is twofold. First, the main FTPmail server is seriously overloaded. Because it's a free service that someone at DEC runs in their machine's spare time, FTPmail is a low priority. It can take a week for your file to come back. I've even had requests seemingly disappear into the ether. Second, talking to an FTPmail server is like playing 20 Questions—unless you know precisely what you're looking for, where it is, and are able to enter the commands perfectly, you'll get an error message back. And, if that message comes back a week later, you may not even have the original information with which to correct your mistake.

Note

Often when you use email to retrieve files stored on FTP sites, the files are split into chunks. Usually you can control the size of the chunks, but manually joining them in a word processor can be difficult. Some email programs, such as Eudora, and various utilities make joining file chunks easier. If you don't use Eudora, check out ChunkJoiner and BinHqx (if the file is a BinHex file). You can find them at:

```
ftp://ftp.tidbits.com/pub/tidbits/tisk/utilities/binhqx-102.hqx
```

```
ftp://mac.archive.umich.edu/mac/util/diskfile/chunkjoiner1.1.sit.hqx
```

Talking to an FTPmail or BITFTP server feels much like logging into an FTP site, changing directories, and finally retrieving the file. The only problem is, you must type in the commands all at once. So, to get a file from the main FTPmail server, you would send email to **ftpmail@decwrl.dec.com**, put something in the Subject line (it doesn't care what, but dislikes empty Subject lines), and then, in the body of the message, put a set of commands like this:

```
help
connect ftp.tidbits.com
chdir /pub/tidbits/misc
get easy-view.hqx
quit
```

So, in English, what you're doing is first getting the help file from FTPmail, then connecting to the anonymous FTP site at **ftp.tidbits.com**, then changing into the **/pub/tidbits/misc/** directory, then retrieving the file called **easy-view.hqx**, and finally quitting. If you wanted, you could retrieve more files. And, if you included an **ls** command, FTPmail would return the directory listing to you, enabling you to see what's there before requesting specific files. The resulting email message looks like that in figure 8.1.

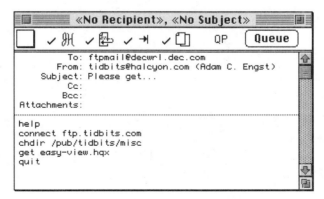

Figure 8.1 *FTPmail sample in Eudora*

Needless to say, there are a number of other commands that FTPmail accepts, and you will probably want to use some of them (see table 8.2).

Table 8.2
Basic FTPmail Commands

Command	Function
ascii	Tells FTPmail that the files you're getting are straight ASCII files, which is true of BinHex and uuencoded files (see file format section later in this chapter).
binary	Tells FTPmail that the files you're getting are binary files and should be encoded in ASCII before sending. The default format for encoding is btoa, but you can set it to uuencode as well (see next item). You must specify either btoa or uuencode or the request will fail.
btoa	Tells FTPmail to mail binary files in btoa format.
chdir *directory*	Changes into the specified directory.
chunksize *size*	Splits files into chunks defined by the number of bytes in *size*. The default is 64,000 bytes (64K).
compress	Tells FTPmail to compress the files before sending with Unix Compress (discussed later).
connect *domain.name*	Tells FTPmail to connect to the specified host.
dir *directory*	Returns a long directory listing.
get *filename*	Gets a file and mails it to you.
help	Sends back the help file.
ls *directory*	Returns a short directory listing.
quit	Quits FTPmail and ignores the rest of mail message.
reply *your-address*	Gives FTPmail your address, since it may not be able to determine it from the header.
uuencode	Tells FTPmail to mail binary files in uuencode format.

I only know of one other FTPmail server. It's in Ireland and uses a somewhat different command set, so I don't recommend using it unless you're in Europe. If you want to find out more about it, send email to **ftpmail@ieunet.ie** and put the single command **help** in the body of the message.

I know of three BITFTP servers. One is in the U.S., another in Germany, and the third in Poland (see table 8.3). Don't use the ones in Europe unless you too are in Europe—it's a waste of net bandwidth, and probably won't result in particularly good service anyway.

Table 8.3
BITFTP Servers

Server name	Location
bitftp@pucc.princeton.edu	U.S.
bitftp@vm.gmd.de	Germany
bitftp@plearn.edu.pl	Poland

Note

BITFTP stands for BITNET FTP, or something like that. Machines that are only on BITNET cannot use FTP normally, so some enterprising programmers created the BITFTP program to enable BITNET users to retrieve files stored on FTP sites. I had thought these servers were restricted to BITNET users, but couldn't find any mention of that restriction in the help file.

Retrieving a file from a BITFTP server works similarly to retrieving a file from FTPmail, but the commands are somewhat different. Here's how you retrieve the same file (along with the help file again) we snagged before. Send email to **bitftp@pucc.princeton.edu** and put these commands in the body of the letter:

```
help
ftp ftp.tidbits.com
user anonymous
cd /pub/tidbits/misc
get easy-view.hqx
quit
```

Enough about BITFTP. You can probably figure out the rest on your own, with the aid of the help file. I wouldn't want to spoil all the fun of figuring some of this stuff out for yourself!

Mailservers

More common than FTPmail or BITFTP programs that serve everyone are mailserver programs that provide email access to FTP archives on a specific site. There are many of these mailservers around, although finding them can be a bit difficult, and I cannot tell which FTP sites that might interest you also have mailservers. I can, however, tell you of a few mailservers you may find useful. Each has its own command structure.

BART, the mailserver for the massive Macintosh software archives at `mac.archive.umich.edu` is an extremely useful way to access many Macintosh files, especially since the load on the machine via FTP is often so great that you cannot easily connect.

Note

BART *is short for* Brode's Archive Retrieval Thang. *Glad you asked?*

BART only provides access to the files stored on `mac.archive.umich.edu`. If you want more general access via email, you must use one of the FTPmail or BITFTP servers mentioned previously. Luckily, because BART is so specific, its command structure is relatively simple (see table 8.4).

Table 8.4
BART Commands

Command	Function
help	Retrieves a help file.
index	Asks BART to send you a complete index of all the files available on the site. This file is more than 1,000K, so be prepared for one big file or lots of little ones.
path *your-address*	Tells BART where to send the results of your request if it cannot figure out your return address from the header of your message.

Command	Function
chunk *size*	Tells BART how large a message you can accept in kilobytes. BART breaks files into chunks of *size* K. The larger the chunk, the less work it is for BART, so use the largest possible size. The default is 25K.
send *pathname*	Asks BART to send you a file. You can only retrieve Macintosh files, so you only must specify hierarchies under /`mac`.

For instance, to retrieve help and Easy View from BART, I would send email to `mac@mac.archive.umich.edu` and in the body of the message put the following commands:

```
path tidbits@halcyon.com
help
chunk 100
send util/text/easyview2.44.sit.hqx
```

That's about it. BART limits you to 1,500K and five files per day (the list of files isn't currently considered against your quota), so you can't abuse it. Your quota is cleared every day at midnight (Eastern Daylight Time). Perhaps the main problem with BART is that if there's something wrong with your request, it tends to ignore the request entirely and not send any error messages. So, for instance, if you surpass your quota, BART simply throws out any additional requests and you must send them again after midnight when your quota has been cleared.

Note

You may run into trouble with certain files if you use Eudora to retrieve them via BART. If the submitter also used Eudora or a compatible program to attach the file, here's what will happen: Eudora will start downloading the first chunk from BART, see that it contains an attachment, and then complain when it sees the attachment is too short (since the other parts aren't included). Simply tell Eudora to fetch the attachment again as a normal message, and it will work fine.

Mailing list manager programs such as LISTSERV, ListProcessor, and Major-domo also often provide access to files, although these files aren't always available via FTP. Most often, the files in question are logs of mailing list discussions, but in a few instances, they're more interesting.

The LISTSERV at Rice University, which helps distribute the Info-Mac Digest, also provides access to all of the files stored in the Info-Mac archives at **sumex-aim.stanford.edu**. Using it is simplicity itself. The LISTSERV doesn't care about directory paths, chunks, or anything like that. You need not specify your email address, or tell the LISTSERV how to encode the files. Instead, all you do is send **listserv@ricevm1.rice.edu** a message with one-line commands that look like any of the following:

```
$MAC HELP
$MAC GET easy-view-244.hqx
$MAC GET tidbits-228.etx
```

Actually, I'm oversimplifying slightly. There are four commands, all told (see table 8.5).

Table 8.5
LISTSERV File Retrieval Commands

Command	Function
$MAC IND *ALL*	Gets list of recent or all files
$MAC DIR *directory*	Gets subdirectory contents
$MAC GET *name.type*	Gets Info-Mac archive file
$MAC HELP	Gets help information

The LISTSERV limits you to 250K per day, although if you request a single file larger than that, it won't refuse that single request. Since all new files in the Info-Mac archives are announced in the Info-Mac Digest, you can easily copy the filenames out to a file request message as you're reading, send off the message when you're finished, and have files coming back quite quickly.

Enough about FTP by email. It's like playing Pin the Tail on the Donkey with a donkey the size of... Nah, I'll avoid the easy shot at some sleazy politician. Let's talk next about how you find files via FTP. The answer is Archie.

Archie

Archie is a remarkable example of what happens when you apply simple technology to a difficult problem in an elegant way. Here is the problem: How do you find any given file on the nets if you don't already know where it's located? After all, in comparison with finding a single file on several million machines, the proverbial haystack looks tiny, and its cousin, the proverbial needle, sticks out like the sore thumb you get when you find it. In a nutshell, Archie uses normal FTP commands to get directory listings of all the files on hundreds of anonymous FTP sites around the world. It then puts these file listings into a database and provides a simple interface for searching it. That's really all there is to Archie. It's amazing that no one thought of it before.

Note

Archie was developed in early 1991 by Alan Emtage, Peter Deutsch, and Bill Heelan from the McGill University Computing Center, Canada. Development now takes place at a company founded by Deutsch and Emtage, Bunyip Information Systems. Although the basic Archie client software is distributed freely, Bunyip sells and supports the Archie server software. If you have questions about Archie, you can write to the Archie Group at **archie-group@bunyip.com**.

You can access Archie via Telnet, email, Gopher, the World-Wide Web, and special Macintosh client programs. Some Unix machines may also have Unix Archie clients installed. It seems to me there are two basic goals an Archie client should meet. First, it should be easy to search for files, but when you want to define a more complex search, that should be possible as well. Second, since the entire point of finding files is so that you can retrieve them, an Archie client ideally should make it very easy to retrieve anything that it finds. This second feature appears to be less common than you would expect. On the Mac, only Anarchie can retrieve found files with just a double-click.

Note

Archie isn't an acronym for anything, although it took me half an hour searching through files about Archie on the Internet to determine that once and for all.

Accessing Archie via email is extremely easy, although the Archie server offers enough options (I'll let you discover them for yourself) to significantly increase the complexity. For a basic search through, merely send email to **archie@archie.internic.net** and put in the body of the message lines like the following:

```
help
find easy-view
find easyview
```

In a short while (or perhaps a long while, depending on the load on the Archie server), the results should come back—the help file that you asked for and the results of your search for "easy-view" and "easyview." However, if the Archie server you chose is down, or merely being flaky (as is their wont) you might want to try another one. There are plenty. Simply send email to the userid **archie** at any one of the Archie servers from the list in table 8.6. As usual, it's polite to choose a local server.

Table 8.6
Current Archie Servers

Server Name	Server IP Number	Location
archie.au	139.130.4.6	Australia
archie.edvz.uni-linz.ac.at	140.78.3.8	Austria
archie.univie.ac.at	131.130.1.23	Austria
archie.uqam.ca	132.208.250.10	Canada
archie.funet.fi	128.214.6.100	Finland
archie.th-darmstadt.de	130.83.22.60	Germany
archie.ac.il	132.65.6.15	Israel
archie.unipi.it	131.114.21.10	Italy
archie.wide.ad.jp	133.4.3.6	Japan
archie.kr	128.134.1.1	Korea
archie.sogang.ac.kr	163.239.1.11	Korea
archie.rediris.es	130.206.1.2	Spain
archie.luth.se	130.240.18.4	Sweden
archie.switch.ch	130.59.1.40	Switzerland
archie.ncu.edu.tw	140.115.19.24	Taiwan
archie.doc.ic.ac.uk	146.169.11.3	United Kingdom
archie.unl.edu	129.93.1.14	USA (NE)
archie.internic.net	198.48.45.10	USA (NJ)

Server Name	Server IP Number	Location
archie.rutgers.edu	128.6.18.15	USA (NJ)
archie.ans.net	147.225.1.10	USA (NY)
archie.sura.net	128.167.254.179	USA (MD)

Telnet Usage

Because Telnet is similar to FTP in the sense that you're logging in to a remote machine, the same rules of etiquette apply (although running a program over Telnet usually places less stress on a machine). As long as you try to avoid bogging down the network when people want to use it for their local work, you shouldn't have to worry about it too much. When you telnet to another machine, you generally telnet into a specific program that provides information you want. The folks making that information available may have specific restrictions on the way you can use their site. Pay attention to these restrictions. The few people who abuse a network service can ruin it for everyone else.

What might you want to look for in a Telnet program? That's a good question, I suppose, but not one that I'm all that qualified to answer. For the most part, I avoid Telnet-based command-line interfaces. Thus, in my opinion, you should look for features in a Telnet program that will make using it, and any random program that you might happen to run on the remote machine, easier to use.

It's useful to be able to save connection documents that save you the work of logging into a specific machine (but beware of security issues if they also store your password). Also, any sort of macro capability will come in handy for automating repetitive keystrokes. Depending on what you're doing, you may also want some feature for capturing the text that flows by for future reference. And, you should of course be able to copy and paste out of the Telnet program.

IRC

IRC, which stands for *Internet Relay Chat*, is a method of communicating with others on the Internet in real time. It was written by Jarkko Oikarinen of Finland in 1988 and has spread to 20 countries. IRC is perhaps better defined as a multi-user chat system, where people gather in groups that are called *channels*, usually devoted to some specific subject. Private conversations are also possible.

Note

IRC gained a certain level of fame during the Gulf War, when updates about the fighting flowed into a single channel where a huge number of people had gathered to stay up to date on the situation.

I personally have never messed with IRC much, having had some boring experiences with RELAY, a similar service on BITNET, back in college. I'm not all that fond of IRC, in large part because I find the amount of useful information there almost nonexistent, and I'm uninterested in making small talk with people from around the world. Nevertheless, IRC is one of the most popular Internet services. Thousands of people connect to IRC servers throughout any given day. If you're interested in IRC, refer to the section on it back in chapter 5, the excerpt from *Internet Explorer Kit for Macintosh*. That should give you a sense of what IRC is like. You can find more information in the IRC tutorials posted for anonymous FTP in:

```
ftp://cs.bu.edu/irc/support/
```

Client programs for many different platforms exist, including two for the Macintosh called ircle and Homer. Much as with Telnet, you're looking for features that make the tedious parts of IRC simpler. I could blather on about all the features you might want, but frankly, if you're using a Macintosh with either a Unix shell account or a MacTCP-based account, just get Homer. It has more features than one would think possible, and can even—in conjunction with Apple's PlainTalk software—speak some or all of the text that flows by.

MUDs

MUD, which stands for *Multi-User Dungeon* or often *Multi-User Dimension*, may be one of the most dangerously addictive services available on the Internet. The basic idea is somewhat like the text adventures of old, where you type in commands like "Go south," "Get knife," and so on. The difference with MUDs is that they can take place in a wide variety of different realities, basically anything someone can dream up. More importantly, the characters in the MUD are actually other people interacting with you in real time. Finally, after you reach a certain level of proficiency, you are often allowed to modify the environment of the MUD.

The allure of the MUDs should be obvious. Suddenly, you can become your favorite alter-ego, describing yourself in any way you want. Your alternate-reality prowess is based on your intellect, and if you rise high enough, you can literally change your world. Particularly for those who may feel powerless or put upon in the real world, the world of the MUD is an attractive escape, despite its text-environment limitations.

After the publication of an article about MUDs, the magazine *Wired* printed a letter from someone who had watched his brother fail out of an engineering degree and was watching his fiancée, a fourth-year astrophysics student, suffer similar academic problems, both due to their addictions to MUDs. But don't take my word for it; read the letter for yourself on *Wired's* Web server:

```
http://www.wired.com/Etext/1.4/departments/rants.html
```

I've seen people close to me fall prey to the addictive lure of MUDs. As an experiment in interactive communications and human online interactions, MUDs are extremely interesting, but be aware of the time they can consume from your real life.

I don't want to imply that MUDs are evil. Like almost anything else, they can be abused. But in other situations, they have been used in fascinating ways, such as to create an online classroom for geographically separated students. There's also a very real question of what constitutes addiction and what constitutes real life. I'd say that someone who is failing out of college or failing to perform acceptably at work because of a MUD has a problem, but if that person is replacing several hours per day of television with MUDing, it's a tougher call. Similarly, is playing hours and hours of golf each week any better than stretching your mind in the imaginative world of a MUD? You decide, but remember: there are certain parts of real life that we cannot and should not blow off in favor of a virtual environment.

Although MUDs are currently text-only, rudimentary graphics will almost certainly appear at some point, followed by more realistic graphics, sound, and video, and perhaps some day even links to the virtual reality systems of tomorrow. I don't even want to speculate on what those changes might mean to society, but you may want to think about what might happen, both positive and negative.

MUDs generally run under Unix, but you could run your own with a Macintosh port of a MUD, called MacMud, and connect to other Unix MUDs with a simple MUD client program, MUDDweller. Even more interesting is the program Meeting Space from a small company called World Benders. Meeting Space is billed as a virtual conference room, and is marketed to large businesses as money- and time-saving alternative to business trips. However, it's actually a business MUD with a snazzy Macintosh interface and hefty price tag. Meeting Space works over any Macintosh network, including the Internet, and although I don't know of any public Meeting Space servers yet, some were being discussed earlier in the year. For more information about Meeting Space, send email to **wb-info@worldbenders.com** and check out the discussion of it in chapter 13.

WAIS

Unlike almost every other resource mentioned in this book, the *WAIS*, or *Wide Area Information Servers*, project had its conception in big business and was designed for big business. The project started in response to a basic problem. Professionals from all walks of life, and corporate executives in particular, need tremendous amounts of information that is usually stored online in vast databases. However, corporate executives are almost always incredibly busy people without the time, inclination, or skills to learn a complex database query language. Of course, corporate executives are not alone in this situation; many people have the same needs and limitations.

In 1991, four large companies—Apple Computer, Dow Jones & Co., Thinking Machines Corporation, and KPMG Peat Marwick—joined together to create a prototype system to address this pressing problem. Apple brought its user interface design expertise, Dow Jones was involved because of its massive databases of information, Thinking Machines provided the programming and expertise in high-end information retrieval engines, and KPMG Peat Marwick provided the information-hungry guinea pigs.

One of the initial concepts was the formation of an organizational memory—the combined set of memos, reports, guidelines, email, and whatnot—that make up the textual history of an organization. Because all of these items are primarily text and completely without structure, stuffing them into a standard relational database is like trying to fill a room with balloons. They don't fit well, they're always escaping, and you can never find anything. WAIS was designed to help with this problem.

So far I haven't said anything about how WAIS became one of the Internet's primary sources of free information. With such corporate parentage, it's in some ways surprising that it did. The important thing about the design of WAIS is that it doesn't discriminate. WAIS can incorporate data from many different sources, distribute them over various types of networks, and record whether the data is free or carries a fee. WAIS is also scaleable, so that it can accept an increasing number and complexity of information sources. This is an important feature in today's world of exponentially increasing amounts of information. The end result of these design features is that WAIS works perfectly well for serving financial reports to harried executives, but equally well for providing science fiction book reviews to curious undergraduates.

In addition, the WAIS protocol is an Internet standard and is freely available, as are some clients and servers. Anyone can set up her own WAIS server for anyone with a WAIS client to access. Eventually, we may see Microsoft, Lotus, and WordPerfect duking it out over who has the best client for accessing WAIS. With the turn the Internet has taken in the past year, however, it's far more likely that we'll see Microsoft, Lotus, and WordPerfect (now a division of Novell) competing with World-Wide Web clients.

At the beginning of this section, I mentioned the problem of most people not knowing how to communicate in complex database query languages. WAIS solves that problem by implementing a sophisticated natural language input system, which is a fancy way of saying that you can talk to it in English. If you want to find more information about deforestation in the Amazon rainforest, you simply formulate your query as: "Tell me about deforestation in the Amazon rainforest." Pretty rough, eh? In its current state, WAIS does not actually examine your question for semantic content; that is, it searches based on the useful words it finds in your question (and ignores, for instance, "in" and "the"). However, nothing prevents advances in language processing from augmenting WAIS so that it has a better idea of what you mean.

In any database, you find only the items that match your search. In a very large database, though, you often find far too many items; so many, in fact, that you are equally at a loss as to what might be useful. WAIS attempts to solve this problem with *ranking* and *relevance feedback*. Ranking is just what it says. WAIS looks at each item that answers the user's question and ranks them based on the proximity of words and other variables. The better the match, the higher up the document appears in your list of found items. Although by no means perfect, this basic method works well in practice.

Relevance feedback, although a fuzzier concept, also helps you refine a search. If you ask a question and WAIS returns 30 documents that match, you may find one or two that are almost exactly what you're looking for. You can then refine the search by telling WAIS, in effect, that those one or two documents are "relevant" and that it should go look for other documents that are "similar" to the relevant ones. Relevance feedback is basically a computer method of pointing at something and saying, "Get me more like that."

The rise of services such as WAIS and Gopher on the Internet will by no means put librarians out of business. Instead, the opposite is true. Librarians are trained in ways of searching and refining searches. We need their experience, both in making sense of the frantic increase in information resources and in setting up the information services of tomorrow. More than ever, we need to eliminate the stereotype of the little old lady among dusty books and replace it with an image of a person who can help us navigate through data in ways we never could ourselves. There will always be a need for human experts.

Note

The WAIS folks discourage the use of the term keywords *because keywords imply that the databases are indexed, and unless you type in a keyword that matches an index term, you cannot find anything. In fact, keywords and Boolean queries (where you say, for instance, "Find* Apple *AND* Computer*") were both methods of getting around the fact that, until recently, we didn't have the computer power to search the full text of stored documents. Nor did we have the computer power to attempt natural language queries and relevance feedback. Now we do, and it's a good thing.*

When you put all this information together, you end up with a true *electronic publishing system*. This definition, pulled from a paper written by Brewster Kahle, then of Thinking Machines and now president of WAIS, Inc., is important for Internet users to keep in mind as the future becomes the present: "Electronic publishing is the distribution of textual information over electronic networks." (Kahle later mentions that the WAIS protocol does not prohibit the transmission of audio or video.) I emphasize that definition because I've been fighting to spread it for some years now because of my role with *TidBITS*.

Electronic publishing has little to do with using computer tools to create paper publications. For those of you who know about Adobe Acrobat, Common Ground from No Hands Software, and Replica from Farallon, those three programs aren't directly related to electronic publishing because they all work on the metaphor of a printed page. With them, you create a page and then print to a file format that other platforms can read (using special readers), but never edit or reuse in any significant way. We're talking about electronic fax machines. We should enjoy greater flexibility with electronic data.

So, how can you use WAIS? I see two basic uses. Most of the queries WAIS gets are probably one-time shots where the user has a question and wants to see whether WAIS stores any information that can provide the answer. This use has much in common with the way reference librarians work—someone comes in, asks a question, gets an answer, and leaves.

More interesting for the future of electronic publishing is a second use, that of periodic information requests. As I said earlier in this book, most people read specific sections of the newspaper and, even within those sections, are choosy about what they do and don't read. I, for instance, always read the sports section but am interested only in baseball, basketball, football to a lesser extent, and hockey only if the Pittsburgh Penguins are mentioned. Even within the sports I follow closely, baseball and basketball, I'm more interested in certain teams and players than others.

Rather than skim through the paper each Sunday to see whether anything interesting happened to the teams or players I follow, I can instead ask a question of a WAIS-based newspaper system (which is conceivable right now, using the UPI news feed that ClariNet sells via Usenet). In fact, I might not ask only one question, but might gradually come up with a set of questions, some specific, others abstract. Along with "What's happening with Cal Ripken and the Baltimore Orioles?" could be "Tell me about the U.S. economy."

In either case, WAIS would run my requests periodically, every day or two, and indicate which items are new in the list. Ideally, the actual searching would take place at night to minimize the load on the network and to make the search seem faster than the technology permits. Once again, this capability is entirely possible today; all that lacks for common usage is the vast quantities of information necessary to address everyone's varied interests. Although the amount of data available in WAIS is still limited (if you call 500-plus sources limited), serious and important uses are already occurring.

Note

A friend at Thinking Machines related a story about a friend who used WAIS to research his son's unusual medical condition and ended up knowing more than the doctor. Sounds like it's time to look for another doctor, but you get the point.

In large part due to its corporate parentage, the WAIS project has been careful to allow for information to be sold and for owners of the information to control who can access the data and when. Although not foolproof, the fact that WAIS addresses these issues makes it easier to deal with copyright laws and information theft.

Because of the controls WAIS allows, information providers are likely to start making sources of information more widely available. With the proliferation of these information sources, it will become harder for the user to keep track of what's available. To handle that problem, WAIS incorporates a Directory of Servers, which tracks all the available information servers. Posing a question to the Directory of Servers source (WAIS calls sets of information *sources* or *servers*) returns a list of servers that might have information pertaining to your question. You can then easily ask the same question of those servers to reach the actual data.

Most of the data available on WAIS is public and free at the moment, and I don't expect that arrangement to change. I do expect more commercial data to appear in the future, however.

In regard to that issue I want to propose two ideas. First, charges should be very low to allow and encourage access, which means that profit is made on high volume rather than high price. Given the size of the Internet, I think this approach is the way to go, rather than charging exorbitant amounts for a simple search that may not even turn up the answer to your question.

Second, I'd like to see the appearance of more "information handlers," who foot the cost of putting a machine on the Internet and buying WAIS server software and then, for a percentage, allow others to create information sources on their server. WAIS, Inc. already provides this service, but I haven't heard of much competition yet. That service enables a small publisher to make, say, a financial newsletter available to the Internet public for a small fee, but the publisher doesn't have to go to the expense of setting up and maintaining a WAIS server. This arrangement will become more commonplace; the question is when? Of course, as the prices of server machines, server software, and network connections drop, the number of such providers will increase.

WAIS has numerous client interfaces for numerous platforms, but you probably can use either a simple VT100 interface via Telnet or, if you have a MacTCP link to the Internet, one of several slick WAIS clients. When evaluating WAIS client programs, keep in mind my comments about the two types of questions and the relevance feedback. A WAIS client should make it easy to ask a quick question without screwing around with a weird interface, and it should also enable you save questions for repeated use (as in the electronic newspaper example). Similarly, with relevance feedback, that act of pointing and saying, "Find me more like this one that I'm pointing at" should be as simple as possible without making you jump through hoops.

Finally, something that none of the WAIS clients I've seen do well is provide a simple method of keeping track of new sources as they appear, not to mention keeping track of which sources have gone away for good.

Gopher

In direct contrast to WAIS, Gopher originated in academia at the University of Minnesota, where it was intended to help distribute campus information to staff and students. The name is actually a two-way pun (there's probably a word for that) because Gopher was designed to enable you to "go fer" some information. Many people probably picked up on that pun, but the less well-known one is that the University of Minnesota is colloquially known as the home of the Golden Gophers, the school mascot. In addition, one of the Gopher Team members said that they have real gophers living outside their office.

Note

Calling yourself the Golden Gophers makes more sense than calling yourself the Trojans, not only considering that the Trojans were one of the most well-known groups in history that lost, but also considering that they lost the Trojan War because they fell for a really dumb trick. "Hey, there's a gigantic wooden horse outside, and all the Greeks have left. Let's bring it inside!" Not a formula for long-term survival. Now, if they had formed a task force to study the Trojan Horse and report back to a committee, everyone wouldn't have been massacred. Who says middle management is useless? Anyway, I digress.

The point of Gopher is to make information available over the network, much in the same way that FTP does. In some respects, Gopher and FTP are competing standards for information retrieval, although I'm sure there are more FTP sites than Gopher sites. I'm equally sure that Gopher is far cooler than FTP and stands to completely supplant it at some point in the future.

Note

Actually, FTP probably will never go away, because it's such a low-level standard on the Internet. Also, Gopher only works for retrieving data; you cannot use it to send data. Finally, there's no easy way to give Gopher users usernames and passwords so only they can access a Gopher site.

Gopher has several major advantages over FTP. First, it provides a much friendlier interface than the standard command-line FTP client. The Macintosh TurboGopher client is certainly on a par with Fetch, the main Macintosh FTP client.

Second, Gopher provides access to far more types of information resources than FTP. Gopher provides access to online phone books, online library catalogs, the text of the actual files, databases of information stored in WAIS, various email directories, Usenet news, and Archie.

Third, Gopher pulls all this information together under one interface and makes it all available from the basic menu system.

Note

Menu items on a Gopher server are not Macintosh menus, but list items in a Macintosh window under TurboGopher. Keep that in mind, and you'll be fine.

If you retrieve a file via FTP and the file gives you a reference to another FTP server, you as the user must connect to that site separately to retrieve any more files from there. In contrast, you connect to a single home Gopher server, and from there, wend your way out into the wide world of Gopherspace without ever having to consciously disconnect from one site and connect to another (although that is what happens under the hood). Gopher servers almost always point at each other, so after browsing through one Gopher server in Europe, you may pick a menu item that brings you back to a directory on your home server. Physical location matters little, if at all, in Gopherspace.

Gopher has also become popular because it uses less net bandwidth than standard FTP. When you connect to a Gopher server, the Gopher client software actually connects only long enough to retrieve the menu, and then it disconnects. When you select something from the menu, the client connects again very quickly, so you barely notice that you weren't actually wasting net bandwidth during that time. Administrators like using Gopher for this reason. They don't have to use as much computing power providing files to Internet users.

> ### Note
>
> *There's actually no reason FTP servers couldn't be rewritten to work this way, as well. Jim Matthews, the author of Fetch, is always going on about how writing an FTP server that used something called* lightweight threads *would make FTP more efficient. In the meantime, Peter Lewis's Anarchie FTP client for the Mac works much like a Gopher client in that it is continually connecting again and again to your target FTP site, enabling you to perform more than one FTP task at a time.*

Several Gopher clients exist for the Macintosh. The one written by the Gopher programmers themselves is arguably the best Gopher client for any platform. They claim it's the fastest over slow connections, and although I haven't used clients on other platforms, TurboGopher is certainly fast. You can also access Gopher via Telnet and a VT100 interface. It's nowhere near as nice (it's slower, you can only do one thing at a time, and you cannot view pictures and the like online), but it works if you don't have MacTCP-based access to the Internet.

Veronica

The most important adjunct to Gopher is a service called Veronica, developed by Steve Foster and Fred Barrie at University of Nevada. Basically, Veronica is to Gopher what Archie is to FTP—a searching agent; hence, the name.

Note

> *Veronica stands* for Very Easy Rodent-Oriented Net-wide Index to Computerized Archives, *but apparently the acronym followed the name.*

Veronica servers work much like Archie servers. They tunnel through Gopherspace recording the names of available items and adding them to a massive database that is 1.3G large (and growing at such a rate that it will reach 5.6G by April of 1995).

You usually find a Veronica menu within an item called Other Gopher and Information Servers, or occasionally simply World. When you perform a Veronica search, you either look for Gopher directories, which contain files, or you look for everything available via Gopher, which includes the files and things like WAIS sources as well. There are only a few Veronica servers in the world (between four and six, depending on which machines are up), so you may find that the servers are heavily overloaded at times, at which point they'll tell you that there are too many connections and that you should try again later. Although it's not as polite as I'd like, I find that using the European Veronica servers during their night is the least frustrating (see table 8.7).

Table 8.7
Current Veronica Servers

Server Name	Location
NYSERNet	U.S.
University of Texas, Dallas	U.S.
SCS Nevada	U.S.
University of Koeln	Germany
University of Pisa	Italy
UNINETT/University of Bergen	Norway

It's definitely worth reading the "Frequently Asked Questions about Veronica" document that lives with the actual Veronica servers. It provides all sorts of useful information about how Veronica works, including the options for limiting your search to only directories or only searchable items. You can use Boolean searches within Veronica, and there are ways of searching for word stems—that is, the beginning of words. So, if you wanted to learn about yachting, you could search for "yacht*." The possibilities aren't endless, but Veronica is utterly indispensable for navigating Gopherspace and for searching on the Internet in general.

Jughead

Getting sick of the Archie Comics puns yet? They just keep coming and, like Veronica, I somehow doubt that this acronym came before the name. *Jughead* stands for *Jonzy's Universal Gopher Hierarchy Excavation And Display*. Jughead does approximately the same thing as Veronica, but if you've ever done a Veronica search on some generic word, you know that Veronica can provide just a few too many responses (insert sarcasm here). Jughead is generally used to limit the range of a search to a certain machine, and to limit it to directory titles. This makes Jughead much more useful than Veronica if you know where you want to search, or if you're only searching on a Gopher server that runs Jughead.

I don't use Jughead all that much, because what I like about the massive number of Veronica results is that they often give me a sense of what information might exist on any given topic. I suppose that if I regularly performed fairly specific searches on the same set of Gopher servers, I'd use Jughead more.

Note

The best way to find a Jughead server that's generally accessible is to do a Veronica search on "jughead -t7." That returns a list of all searchable Jughead servers, rather than all the documents and directories in Gopherspace that contain the word "jughead."

World-Wide Web

The World-Wide Web is the most recent and ambitious of the major Internet services. The Web was started at CERN, a high-energy physics research center in Switzerland, as an academic project. It attempts to provide access to the widest range of information by linking not only documents made available via its native *HTTP* (*HyperText Transfer Protocol*), but also additional sources of information via FTP, WAIS, and Gopher. Gateways also exist to Oracle databases and to DEC's VMS/Help systems, among many others. The Web tries to suck in all sorts of data from all sorts of sources, avoiding the problems of incompatibility by allowing a smart server and a smart client program to negotiate the format of the data.

Note

CERN doesn't stand for anything now, but once was an acronym for a French name.

In theory, this capability to negotiate formats enables the Web to accept any type of data, including multimedia formats, once the proper translation code is added to the servers and the clients. And, when clients don't understand the type of data that's appearing, such as a QuickTime movie, for instance, they generally just treat the data as a generic file, and ask another program to handle it after downloading.

The theory behind the Web makes possible many things, such as linking into massive databases without the modification of the format in which they're stored, thereby reducing the amount of redundant or out-dated information stored on the nets. It also enables the use of intelligent agents for traversing the Web. But what the Web really does for the Internet is take us one step further toward total ease of use. Let's think about this evolution for a minute.

FTP simply transfers a file from one place to another—it's essentially the same thing as copying a file from one disk to another on the Mac. WAIS took the concept of moving information from one place to another, and made it possible for client and server to agree on exactly what information is transferred. When that information is searched or transferred, you get the full text without having to use additional tools to handle the information. Gopher merged both of those concepts, adding in a simple menu-based interface that greatly eased the task of browsing through information. Gopher also pioneered the concept of a virtual space, if you will, where any menu item on a Gopher server can refer to an actual file anywhere on the Internet. Finally, the World-Wide Web subsumes all of the previous services and concepts, so it can copy files from one place to another; it can search through and transfer the text present in those files; and it can present the user with a simple interface for browsing through linked information.

But aside from doing everything that was already possible, the World-Wide Web introduced four new concepts. The first one I've mentioned already; it's the capability to accept and distribute data from any source, given an appropriately written Web server.

Second, the Web introduced the concept of rich text and multimedia elements in Internet documents. Gopher and WAIS can display the text in a document, but they can't display it with fonts and styles and sizes and sophisticated formatting. You're limited to straight, boring text (not that it was boring when it first appeared, I assure you). With the Web, you can create *HTML* (short for

HyperText Markup Language) documents that contain special codes that tell a Web browser program to display the text in various different fonts and styles and sizes. Web *pages* (that's what documents on the Web are generally called) can also contain *inline graphics*—that is, graphics that are mixed right in with the text, much as you're used to seeing in books and magazines. And finally, for something you're not used to seeing in books and magazines, a Web page can contain sounds and movies, although sound and movie files are so large that you must follow a link to play each one.

Link? What's a link? Ah, that's the third concept that the Web brought to the Internet. Just as an item in a Gopher menu can point to a file on another Internet machine in a different country, so can Web *links*. The difference is that any Web page can have a large number of links, all pointing to different files on different machines, and those links can be embedded in the text. For instance, if I were to say in a Web page that I have a really great collection of penguin pictures stored on another Web page (and if you were reading this on the Web and not in a book), you could simply click on the underlined words to immediately jump to that link. Hypertext arrives on the Internet.

Hmm, I should probably explain hypertext. A term coined by Ted Nelson years ago, *hypertext* refers to nonlinear text. Whereas you normally read left to right, top to bottom, and beginning to end, in hypertext you follow links that take you to various different places in the document, or even to other related documents, without having to scan through the entire text. Assume, for instance, that you're reading about wine. There's a link to information on the cork trees that produce the corks for wine bottles, so you take that link, only to see another link to the children's story about Ferdinand the Bull, who liked lying under a cork tree and smelling the flowers. That section is in turn linked to a newspaper article about the running of the bulls in Pamplona, Spain. A hypertext jump from there takes you to a biography of Ernest Hemingway, who was a great fan of bull fighting (and of wine, to bring us full circle). This example is somewhat facetious, but hopefully it gives you an idea of the flexibility a hypertext system with sufficient information, such as the World-Wide Web, can provide.

Fourth, the final new concept the Web introduced to the Internet is *forms*. Forms are just what you would think, online forms that you can fill in, but on the Internet, forms become tremendously powerful since they make possible all sorts of applications, ranging from surveys to online ordering to reservations to searching agents to who knows what. Until very recently, there were only forms-capable Web browsers for X Windows and Windows, although the forms-capable version of Mosaic for the Mac is in testing now, and a new Web browser with forms capabilities called MacWeb recently appeared. Forms are extremely useful, and although I have almost no experience with them currently, I expect to use them heavily now that I can do so on the Mac.

For some time, the Web lacked a searching agent such as Archie or Veronica, a major limitation because the Web is so huge. However, a number of searching agents have appeared, and although they simply don't feel as successful as Veronica yet, I suspect that's merely because I'm less used to them. You can find a list of the Web searching agents (and a ton of other useful pointers) at:

```
http://www.ncsa.uiuc.edu/SDG/Software/Mosaic/MetaIndex.html
```

You can access the Web via a terminal and a VT100 interface, or reportedly even via email (which would be agonizingly slow), but for proper usage, you must have a special browser.

When you're evaluating Web browsers, there are a number of features to seek. The most important is one that seems obvious: an easy way to traverse links. Since the entire point of a Web browser is to display fonts and styles in text, a Web browser should give you the ability to change the fonts used to ones on your Mac that you find easy to read. HTML documents don't actually include references to Times and Helvetica; they encode text in certain styles, much like a word processor or page layout program does. Then, when your Web browser reads the text of a Web page, it decodes the HTML styles and displays them according to the fonts that are available. Sometimes the defaults are ugly, so I recommend playing with them a bit. Many, if not most, Web pages also contain graphics, which is all fine and nice unless you're the impatient sort who dislikes waiting for the graphics to travel over a slow modem. Web browsers should have an option to turn off auto-loading of images. You should be able to do anything you can do in a normal Mac application, such as copy and paste. You should be able to save a hotlist of Web sites that you'd like to visit again. Finally, you should be able to easily go back to previously visited pages without having to reload them over the Internet.

As I said previously, there are a number of ways to access the Web; but frankly, if you use a Mac but don't have access to a MacTCP-based connection, you'll miss out on the best parts, even if you can see the textual data in a VT100 browser such as Lynx.

Well, that's enough about all the Internet services. But, before we go on and talk about ways you can get Internet access, I should explain about all the different file formats that you run into on the Internet. They're a source of confusion for many new users.

Chapter 8
Internet
Services

File Formats

On the Macintosh, we're all used to the simple concept of double-clicking on a document icon to open it in the proper application. The Macintosh keeps track of which documents go with which applications by type and creator codes. Thus, we tend not to think about file formats as much as people who use other operating systems that lack the Mac's elegance. Nonetheless, every Mac file does have a format, and if you've ever seen the "Application not found" message, you may have wished for an easier way to determine any given file's format.

Note

Various utility programs such as Apple's free ResEdit and PrairieSoft's commercial DiskTop can show you the type and creator codes that the Mac's Finder uses to link documents and applications. You can find ResEdit at:

```
ftp://ftp.apple.com/dts/mac/tools/resedit/resedit-2-1-1.hqx
```

On the Internet, there is no way to store the type and creator codes for each file, and there are so many types of computers accessing files that it's a pointless exercise anyway. When you start exploring, you quickly discover that most files have filename extensions, as is standard in DOS. Unlike DOS, Unix allows long filenames, so you don't have to think of meaningless eight-character names for everything. Extensions are extremely useful on the Internet because they identify what sort of file you're looking at. On the Mac, you see a different icon, or you can double-click on the file and see what program launches, but on the Internet, all you get is the filename and extension.

Unlike standard DOS usage, where every program seems to have at least one or two extensions for its documents (.WK1, .WKS, .DOC, .WP, .DBF, .NDX, .IDX, and other thoroughly memorable three-letter combinations), a limited set of extensions is in common use for files that a Mac user may care about. These extensions fall into three basic categories: those used to indicate *ASCII* encoding; those used to indicate compression formats; and several others used to mark certain types of text and graphics files.

ASCII Encoding

Programs and other binary data files (files with more than just straight text in them) contain binary codes that most email programs don't understand, because email programs are designed to display only text. Binary data files even include data files such as word processor files, which contain formatting information or other non-printing characters. Most programs enable you to save your files in a variety of formats, including text. If you don't explicitly save a file in some kind of text format, then it's probably a binary data file, although there are exceptions.

Note

The main exceptions to this are Apple's TeachText and SimpleText and Nisus Software's Nisus word processor. TeachText and SimpleText can only save text files. Nisus saves its files in such a way that all other programs see them as text files (the formatting lives in the file's resource fork, if you were wondering).

Computers of different types generally agree on only the first 128 characters in the ASCII character set. (*ASCII* stands for *American Standard Code for Information Interchange*.) The important fact to remember is that after those first 128 characters, which include the letters of the alphabet and numbers and punctuation, a Mac's accented letter may be a DOS machine's smiley face.

Still, people want to transfer files via email and other programs that cannot handle all the possible binary codes in a data file or application. Programmers therefore came up with several different ways of representing 8 bits of binary data in 7 bits of straight text. In other words, these conversion programs can take in a binary file such as the Alarm Clock desk accessory, for instance, and convert it into a long string of numbers, letters, and punctuation marks. Another program can take that string of text and turn it back into a functioning copy of the Alarm Clock desk accessory. I'll leave it to the philosophers to decide whether it is the same program.

Once encoded, that file can travel through almost any email gateway and be displayed in any email program, although it's worthless until you download it to the Mac and decode it. The main drawback to this sort of encoding is that you must always decode the file before you can work with it, although many programs on the Mac decode for you automatically. In addition, because you move from an 8-bit file to a 7-bit file during the encoding process, the encoded file must be larger than the original, sometimes by up to as much as 35 percent.

Now that you understand why we go through such bother, the Internet uses three main encoding formats (see table 8.8): *BinHex, uuencode,* and *btoa* (read as "b to a").

Table 8.8
ASCII Encoding Formats

Format	Advantages	Disadvantages
BinHex	Macintosh standard	Least efficient
uuencode	Most common in Unix	Less common on Mac
btoa	Most efficient	Least common

BinHex

BinHex is by far the most common format you see in the Macintosh world, because it originated on the Mac. In fact, it's basically used only on Macintosh computers. You can identify most BinHex files by the **.hqx** extension they carry. I haven't the foggiest idea why it is **.hqx** instead of **.bhx** or something slightly more reasonable. Keep in mind that BinHex is another one of these computer words that works as a verb, too, so people say that they binhexed a file before sending it to you.

There are two flavors of BinHex, but they aren't interchangeable. The BinHex 4.0 format was originally created by Yves Lempereur and has been around forever. BinHex 5.0, which also came from Yves, is more recent but unfortunately causes massive confusion because it doesn't turn binary files into ASCII. Ignore BinHex 5.0 entirely, because everyone else does. I've never heard of any versions of BinHex before 4.0, although it's fair to assume that some existed. Ignore them, too, if you run across them. The only format that matters now is BinHex 4.0. Got it?

Note

BinHex 4.0 is a file format, and numerous programs can encode and decode that format. Yves wrote a program called BinHex 4.0 years ago, but it has some known bugs and should be avoided. I recommend that you use Aladdin's free StuffIt Expander for debinhexing files, especially because it can also expand various compression formats.

Every BinHex file starts with the phrase **(This file must be converted with BinHex 4.0)** even if another program actually did the creating. Then comes a new line with a colon at the start, followed by many lines of ASCII gibberish. Only the last line can be a different length than the others (each line has a hard return after it), and the last character must be a colon as well (see figure 8.2). Occasionally, something happens to a BinHex file in transit, and one line is shortened by a character or two or even deleted. When that happens, the file is toast.

Figure 8.2 *Example of BinHex*

BinHex suffers from only two real problems, other than that of having a vaguely confusing name. It is perhaps the least efficient of the three encoding formats, which means that we Macintosh users must waste more space on our FTP sites and in our email when transferring files. Oh well, just because something is the standard doesn't mean it's the best. Its other real problem is that even though tools exist for debinhexing files on other platforms, they aren't common. Use uuencode if you plan to send binary files to a user on another platform.

Note

Under Unix, you must use a program called mcvert *to debinhex files. If you wish to encode or decode BinHex files on a PC, you can find a PC version of BinHex at:*

```
ftp://boombox.micro.umn.edu/pub/binhex/MSDOS/binhex.exe
```

uucode

In the Unix world, uucode (also called uuencode) is the most common format. You can identify a uuencoded file by its **.uu** extension. Although not in common usage in the Macintosh world, uucode is seen frequently enough that a number of Macintosh programs have sprung up to encode and decode this format. These include StuffIt Deluxe, UULite, and UMCP Tools, among others. You're unlikely to run across uuencoded Macintosh files frequently. You may run across slightly different extensions on occasion; I've also seen **.uud** and **.uue**. They're all the same thing.

Note

By default, most LAN-based email programs (such as Microsoft Mail) that have Internet gateways encode binary files sent across the Internet in uucode format, since it's the most common.

Most uuencoded files start with **begin 644**, followed by the filename. From that point on, they look a lot like BinHex files: rows upon rows of ASCII gibberish with each line being the same length. (Actually, these lines may not all look the same length when you're viewing them on the Mac because Unix machines use the ASCII 10 linefeed character instead of a carriage return, which the Mac uses to end a line.)

Note

Because the number 644 is related to Unix file permissions (don't ask), other numbers are possible in uuencoded files, although I see them less frequently.

All uuencoded files end with a linefeed, a space, the word **end**, and another linefeed (see figure 8.3).

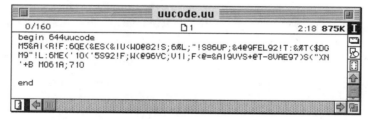

Figure 8.3   Example of uuencode

btoa

Frankly, I don't know a lot about *btoa*, which stands for *binary to ASCII*. This format (see figure 8.4) is supported by a complementary atob convertor, which translates ASCII files back into binary. It is the most efficient of the three, so btoa files are slightly smaller than the equivalent uuencode or BinHex file. Despite this seemingly major advantage, btoa doesn't appear nearly as frequently in the Unix world as uuencode, and appears rarely in the Macintosh world. As far as I know, the only program that can decode the btoa format on the Mac is StuffIt Deluxe, through one if its many translators.

Figure 8.4   Example of btoa

Compression Formats

Along with the various ASCII encoded formats, on the Internet you frequently see a number of file extensions that indicate that the files have been compressed in some way. Almost every file available on the Internet is compressed, because disk space is at a premium everywhere.

Unfortunately, because the majority of Macintosh files stored on the Internet are binhexed after being compressed, you don't see the full benefit of the compression. Nevertheless, if your original file is 200K and a compression program reduces it to 75K, you're still on the winning side if binhexing the file increases it back up to 100K.

The folks who run the Internet file sites like two things to be true about a compression format. They want it to be as tight as possible, so as to save the most space, and they want to be sure that the files stored in that format will be accessible essentially forever, which requires the format of the compressed files to be made public, so that in theory any competent programmer can write a program to expand those files should the company go out of business or otherwise disappear.

This second desire has caused some trouble over the years, because the compression market is hotly contested. Companies seldom want to put their proprietary compression algorithms (the rules by which a file is compressed) into the public domain, where their competitors can copy them. For a while there was a project on the Internet to create a public format based on some other public compression formats, but it never saw the light of day. As it is, the only compression format widely available in the Macintosh world that is also public domain is that used by StuffIt 1.5.1, an older and less-efficient version of the now-proprietary StuffIt 3.0 format.

Most people on the Internet compress Macintosh files in one of three ways: StuffIt, Compact Pro, or as a self-extracting archive. In addition, there are at least three or four other programs that can compress files, but few people ever use them for files posted on the Internet, other than for self-extracting archives.

StuffIt 3.0

Perhaps the most popular Macintosh compression format on the nets today is StuffIt 3.0, which is used by a family of programs—some free (StuffIt Expander), some shareware (StuffIt Lite), and some commercial (StuffIt Deluxe)—from Aladdin Systems. StuffIt files always have the **.sit** extension. The only confusion here is that the StuffIt file format has gone through three main incarnations: 1.5.1, 2.0, and 3.0. The latest versions of all the StuffIt tools can read all of those formats, but not surprisingly, StuffIt 2.0-class tools can read only files created in 2.0 or 1.5.1, and StuffIt 1.5.1 can read only files in its specific format.

This limitation leads to the common problem on the nets whereby someone downloads a file in StuffIt 3.0 format, assuming he can expand it with his StuffIt 2.0-class program because of the **.sit** extension. Unfortunately, because all three file formats use the **.sit** extension, the extension provides no useful indication, and StuffIt 2.0 spits up all over a StuffIt 3.0 file. The simple solution to this problem and most other compression problems is—and listen carefully— StuffIt Expander.

StuffIt Expander can expand any StuffIt format, it can expand Compact Pro archives, and as an added bonus, it can debinhex files as well. It slices, it dices, and no one should be without StuffIt Expander. Thanks are due to Aladdin Systems for making such a useful tool available for free. You can find the latest versions of StuffIt Expander and StuffIt Lite online as well in the directory:

```
ftp://ftp.tidbits.com/pub/tidbits/tisk/utilities/
```

Compact Pro

Compact Pro, a shareware compression utility from Bill Goodman, is almost as popular as the StuffIt family in the Macintosh world. Functionally, StuffIt and Compact Pro do the same thing—create a compressed archive of one or more files. In my experience, either utility does an admirable job, so personal preference and other features may sway you one way or the other.

Compact Pro files are always identified by their **.cpt** extension. You may see an earlier version of Compact Pro floating around on the nets as well. It's called Compactor and uses the same file format as Compact Pro, so you don't have to worry about which version created a given file. Compactor is just an older version of Compact Pro, but Bill Goodman had to change the name for legal reasons. You can find Compact Pro online at:

```
ftp://ftp.tidbits.com/pub/tidbits/tisk/utilities/compact-pro-134.hqx
```

Self-extracting Archives

What if you want to send a compressed file or files to a friend who you know has no compression utilities at all? Then you use a *self-extracting archive*, which is hard to describe further than the name already does. Most compression programs on the market can create self-extracting archives by compressing the file and then attaching a *stub*, or small expansion program, to the compressed file. The self-extracting archive looks like an application to the user, and if you double-click on a self-extracting archive, it launches and expands the file contained within it. Internet file sites prefer not to have many files, particularly small ones, compressed in self-extracting archives because the stubs are a waste of space for most people on the nets, who already have utilities to expand compressed files.

You can always identify self-extracting archives by the `.sea` extension. You can tell by the icon which compression program created any given self-extracting archive, but on the whole it makes no difference. The only exceptions to this naming scheme are self-extracting archives created by Alysis's SuperDisk program, which automatically appends a `.x` to the end of its self-extracting archives. You don't see many, if any, of those.

Unix Compression

Unix has a built-in compression program, called, in an uncharacteristically straightforward fashion for Unix, Compress. Compress creates files with the `.Z` extension (note the capital Z—it makes a difference). Although you don't see files with that extension too often in Macintosh file sites, plenty of them exist on the rest of the net. Both StuffIt and a program called MacCompress can expand these files, should you need to do so.

Note

Incidentally, MacCompress was written by Lloyd Chambers, who later went on to write DiskDoubler and AutoDoubler, starting the transparent compression market in the Macintosh world.

As far as I know, Compress works only on a single file, but you often want to put more than one file in an archive. All of the Mac compression programs both archive and compress in a single step. Under Unix, however, you need to perform the archiving step before you compress the file (and of course, if you want to mail it to someone, then you need to uuencode it). A program called Tar (which stands for *Tape archive*) archives under Unix, and files archived with Tar get a `.tar` extension. If you archive a bunch of files with Tar, then shrink them with Compress, and then uuencode the compressed file to send to someone, the resulting filename ends with `.tar.Z.uue`, to indicate what you've done to it and in what order.

Recently, a new format, called *gzip*, has started to appear in the Unix world. It's marked by the `.z` or `.gz` extension. Gzip is the free GNU version of ZIP, a popular PC compression format. A Macintosh version, called *MacGzip*, recently appeared to decode these files. You can find it online in:

```
ftp://ftp.tidbits.com/pub/tidbits/tisk/utilities/mac-gzip-02.hqx
```

Note

> *What's GNU? Not much, what's GNU with you? Sorry, but my editor made me put that in. GNU stands for the paradoxical "GNU's Not Unix" and is a project to create a fully functional version of Unix that you are free to do with as you please.*

The Rest

You may run across several other compression formats in your net travels. Few people use these formats for files distributed to the world, but a few do, so the rest of us have to stay on our toes. DiskDoubler, from Symantec, can create "combined files" that generally have a `.dd` extension. Symantec makes a free DDExpandOnly application available for people who don't own DiskDoubler. Alysis's SuperDisk can create its own `.x` self-extracting archives. Now Compress, from Now Software, can make stand-alone and self-extracting archives. If you run into one of the stand-alone files, look for the free Expand Now application from Now Software.

Note

> *Don't be confused about DiskDoubler's company, because it changed since the first edition of this book. Lloyd Chambers wrote DiskDoubler for his company, Salient Software, which was then purchased by Fifth Generation Systems. Then, Symantec bought Fifth Generation Systems, getting DiskDoubler and the other Salient utilities in the bargain.*

If you run across a very old archive, it might have a `.pit` extension, which means that it was created by an old program called PackIt (which I haven't seen in years). Don't bother looking for PackIt, and if you find it, don't create any files with it because it's a dead format. Several of the compression utilities (I don't have a PackIt file to even test this) claim to be able to expand PackIt files, but frankly, no one much cares anymore.

DOS Compression

Unfortunately, you are bound to run into some files compressed with DOS programs at some point. In most cases these files are text files that you can easily read on a Mac, as long as you can expand them. The most common DOS format is the ZIP format, which uses the `.ZIP` extension. Several shareware tools exist for unzipping these files, and StuffIt Deluxe also includes a translator for unzipping files.

Less common these days is the `.ARC` extension, which was a common format several years ago, so there were several DOS programs that created and expanded `.ARC` files. Once again, if you see one of these extensions on the Mac, try using StuffIt's translators.

Other File Types

You may want to keep in mind a number of other file type issues, relating both to formatting text files for different systems and to graphics files that you find on the Internet.

Text Files

Text files are universally indicated by the `.txt` extension, and after that, the main thing you have watch for is the end-of-line character.

Unix expects the end-of-line character to be a linefeed (LF, or ASCII character 10), which usually shows up on the Mac as a little box because it's a nonprinting character in most fonts. The Mac prefers to end its lines with carriage returns (CR, or ASCII character 13), and to further confuse the issue, DOS machines straddle the fence and use a carriage return and linefeed combination (CR/LF).

Because the Internet is nondenominational when it comes to computer religion (that is, the Internet as a whole; almost every individual is rabid about his choice of computer platform), most communication programs are good about making sure to put any outgoing text into a format that other platforms can read. Most programs also attempt to read in text and display it correctly no matter what machine formatted it to start with. Unfortunately, as hard as these programs may try, they often fail, so you must pay attention to what sort of text you send out and retrieve—via email, FTP, Gopher or whatnot.

When you're sending files from a Mac, the main thing to remember is to break the lines before 80 characters. "Eighty characters," you say, "how the heck am I supposed to figure out how many characters are on a line without counting them all? After all, the Mac has superior proportionally spaced fonts. Humph!"

Yeah, well, forget about those fonts when you're dealing with the Internet. You can't guarantee that anyone reading what you write even has those fonts, so stick to a monospaced font such as Monaco or Courier. I personally recommend Monaco 9 point if your eyes don't mind. Then, I recommend setting your word processor's ruler (if that's where you're typing the file) to approximately 6.25 inches. That way, you have around 64 characters per line, give or take a few. Finally, if you're using a sophisticated word processor such as Nisus, you can run a macro that replaces spaces at the end of each line with hard returns. If you don't use Nisus, you can probably find an option that enables you to Save As Text, and that inserts returns at the end of each line in the process.

Note

There are also several utilities, including one called Add/Strip, that add returns for you. You can find Add/Strip on the Internet quite easily. Search with Archie or Veronica for "add-strip" and it should turn up.

After your lines have hard returns (carriage returns on the Mac) at the end, you usually can send a file properly, because most communications programs can handle replacing carriage returns with linefeeds or perhaps simply adding linefeeds. If you don't add returns and someone tries to read your text file under DOS or Unix, the file may or may not display correctly. There's no telling, depending on that person's individual circumstances, but you usually hear about it if you screw up. Test with something short if you're unsure whether you can send and receive text files properly.

Often, the Internet client program automatically strips and replaces linefeeds with carriage returns on files coming in from the Internet. If that doesn't happen, you either can use Add/Strip or one of its compatriots, or just run a Find and Replace in your word processor.

Note

If you search for the linefeed (by copying the little box from the document into the Find field in your word processor) and replace it with the carriage return, the file still has hard returns at the end of every line. Instead, try this: Search for two linefeeds; replace them with some special character that doesn't otherwise exist in the document (I usually use Option-8, the bullet); then search for one linefeed and replace it with a space; finally, replace your bullets with carriage returns. As a result, you get nicely wrapped text (assuming of course, that there were blank lines separating paragraphs in the original file).

The other reason to view files from the Internet in a monospaced font with lines delimited by hard returns is that people on the Internet can be incredibly creative with ASCII tables and charts. Using only the standard characters you see on your keyboard, these people manage to create some extremely complex tables and graphics. I can't say they are works of art, but I'm always impressed. If you wrap the lines and view in a proportionally spaced font, those ASCII tables and graphics look like textual garbage.

setext

One other note on text formatting on the Internet. Ian Feldman, with megabytes of comments from me and several others, has defined a "structure-enhanced text" format specifically for electronic periodicals. Files encoded in *setext* format should have the `.etx` extension. *TidBITS* was the first publication to use setext, but more are switching to it every day. Setext has the advantage of being eminently readable online, where it conforms to the least-common denominator of Internet machines (less-than 70 character-long lines, only the standard character set, and so on), but special front-end programs enable you to browse a setext file, adding structure, navigational capabilities, and enhanced display features such as fonts and styles. The idea is to profit from the best of both worlds, the online text-based platforms and the graphically oriented client machines many of us use.

The trick setext employs to remain so unobtrusive online while retaining a format that special browsers can read is making the code implicit in the text and using accepted online styles when possible (see figure 8.5). The title of a setext file, for instance, is a line of characters followed by another line of the exact same number of equal signs, effectively forming a double-underline. Subheads are similar, but they are followed by lines of dashes, forming a single underline. Words that should be bold when decoded are sandwiched by asterisk pairs like **this**, and words that should be underlined are sandwiched by underscores like _this_.

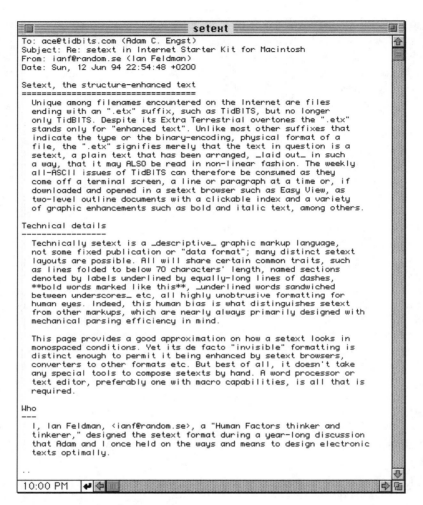

Figure 8.5   Example of setext

It's best to read a setext in a browser such as Akif Eyler's Easy View (primarily a Macintosh browser, although versions are available for Unix and Windows). Easy View can replace the awkward underscores and asterisks with bold and underline styles, and can break up a setext into its sections, displaying each subhead separately. But if you can't or don't want to use a program such as Easy View, any program that can display a text file will suffice. You can find Easy View online at:

```
ftp://ftp.tidbits.com/pub/tidbits/tisk/utilities/easy-view-244.hqx
```

Graphics

For a long time, graphics files weren't commonly posted on the Internet except for use by users of a specific machine, because Macs were not able to read PC graphic file formats and vice-versa. Now, however, you can view some common formats on multiple platforms.

First among these formats is *GIF*, which stands for *Graphics Interchange Format*. GIF was originally created by CompuServe. GIF files almost always have the extension `.gif`. They are popular on the Internet because the file format is internally compressed. When you open a GIF file in a program such as Giffer or JPEGView (postcardware from Aaron Giles), the program expands the GIF file before displaying it.

Note

It seems that almost no one can agree on how to pronounce GIF, either with a hard G sound or with a J sound. Take your pick; I won't argue with you either way.

The second type of file format you may see is *JPEG*, which stands for *Joint Photographic Experts Group*. JPEG files, which are generally marked by the `.jpeg` extension, use a different form of compression than GIF. JPEG file compression reduces the image size to as much as one-twentieth of the original size, but also reduces the quality slightly because it actually throws out parts of the file that you generally can't see. You can view JPEG files with JPEGView, which is available on the Internet at:

```
ftp://ftp.tidbits.com/pub/tidbits/tisk/utilities/jpeg-view-33.hqx
```

Sound and Video

With the advent of the World-Wide Web, sound and video files have become far more common on the Internet, although they're so large that most people using a modem won't want to spend the hours required to download a short sound or video clip. But, if you have either a fast connection or patience, there are several file formats that you should watch for.

Sound appears to come primarily in the *Ulaw* format. Files in this format have the `.au` extension. I know very little about the Ulaw format except that there are two programs on the Mac capable of playing it, UlawPlay and SoundMachine, both written by Rod Kennedy. Both are free, and seem to work fine, although

SoundMachine has a far more sophisticated interface. It wouldn't take much—UlawPlay merely accepts a file dropped on it, launches, plays the file, and quits. You can find both on the Internet at:

```
ftp://ftp.tidbits.com/pub/tidbits/tisk/utilities/Ulaw1.4.sit.hqx
```

```
ftp://ftp.tidbits.com/pub/tidbits/tisk/utilities/SoundMachine.sit.hqx
```

There are two video formats that you should know about, *MPEG* and *QuickTime*. MPEG stands for *Motion Picture Experts Group*. It's actually a compression format, much like JPEG, although one optimized for compressing video rather than still images. MPEG files generally have the extension `.mpeg`, as you might expect. The only Macintosh program I know of that can play MPEG files is Maynard Handley's free Sparkle. You can find Sparkle on the Internet at:

```
ftp://ftp.tidbits.com/pub/tidbits/tisk/utilities/Sparkle.sit.hqx
```

The confusing part is that QuickTime, Apple's multimedia file format, reportedly will be able to use MPEG-compression late in the summer of 1994, when version 2.0 arrives. So eventually, any QuickTime-aware application should be able to play MPEG movies along with normal QuickTime movies.

Note

Just to confuse the matter further, QuickTime movie files can contain just sound tracks, making them yet another method of transmitting sounds, although I haven't seen this happen yet.

The most common application for playing QuickTime movies is Simple Player, which comes with the QuickTime distribution from Apple. Many other applications can play QuickTime movies as well, but Simple Player works sufficiently well for basic QuickTime movies. You can find it, along with the necessary QuickTime extension on the Internet, on **ftp.apple.com** or at the following (sorry for the mega-long URL—that's what happens when Apple uses long directory names and buries things deeply):

```
ftp://ftp.austin.apple.com/Apple.Support.Area/Apple.SW.Updates/
Supplemental.System.SW/QuickTime.1.6.2/quicktime1.6.2.sea.hqx
```

Wrapping Up

That should do it for the background material about the various TCP/IP
Internet services, such as FTP, Telnet, Gopher, WAIS, the World-Wide Web, and
a few other minor ones like IRC and MUDs. Feel free to flip back here and
browse if you're confused about basic usage or what might be important to look
for in a client program. Lastly, I looked at the many file formats you may run
into and the programs that you must use to decode or display them. Let's move
on, and look at the four common methods of connecting to the Internet.

Chapter 8
Internet
Services

III

Connecting to the Internet

Finally, it's time to talk about how you get Internet access and what it looks like. You have four basic ways to connect to the Internet, each with pros and cons, costs and confusions. First comes email-only access, followed by Unix shell accounts, then a UUCP connection, and finally, a MacTCP-based connection. Don't worry about the terms and acronyms just yet; I explain them in the following chapters.

I don't expect you to read each of these chapters in detail right off. The following descriptions are meant to help you figure out which sort of connection method is best for you, and thus which chapter should be first on your agenda.

Chapter 9, Commercial Services

At the most basic level, you can use email-only access via a commercial service, a local BBS, or a gateway from a LAN-based email package at work. This type of service is easy to find because commercial services such as CompuServe, America Online, and Delphi have local phone numbers in many locations. When I talk about the commercial services, I provide contact information so you can find out whether there's a local number in your area. Some of the commercial services have added more Internet services in the past year, so you may even be able to do more than just email.

More and more local bulletin boards also have Internet access now (often via the worldwide BBS network called FidoNet). Because many boards are free, that route may be the least expensive, although potentially the least reliable as well. Finding a local BBS can be a daunting task, because most communities don't have listings of them in the newspaper or anywhere else for that matter. The best place to start is at your dealer or any local computer store. These people can often point you to some-one on the staff who uses bulletin boards, or they might direct you to local user groups that often operate bulletin boards.

Another way to obtain access is through your job. As more and more businesses find themselves needing to connect to other locations, they are setting up gateways between the Internet and internal network mail packages such as QuickMail and Microsoft Mail. This type of access is also generally free to you, but it requires that you work for an organization that provides such a service. The only way to find out about this type of connection is to ask the person who takes care of your network. I can't really help you with this type of access, since it varies significantly based on how your network is set up and administered.

Chapter 10, Shell Access

This is it, the dreaded command line of the Unix shell account. I assume that because you use a Mac, you're not all that interested in typing long strings of commands or remembering cryptic Unix abbreviations. Nonetheless, one of the most common ways you can gain Internet access is through an account on a public access machine, usually running some form of Unix.

Finding a public access Unix site is far more difficult than joining a commercial service, although Phil Eschallier has compiled a list of sites, called the nixpub list, that can help. To receive the latest copy, send email to **mail-server@bts.com** using either **get PUB nixpub.long** or **get PUB nixpub.short** in the body of the message. Any Subject line works. The long list is approximately 60K (in two parts), and the short list is approximately 14K—the difference lies in the amount of detail provided. The PDIAL list, from Peter Kaminski, which lists only public providers that have a full connection to the Internet, is also a good source. A copy of the PDIAL list is in appendix C, but if you want the latest edition, send email to **info-deli-server@netcom.com**, using **Send PDIAL** in the Subject line. What you put in the body of this message doesn't matter.

Also, try calling the help desks at any local universities or colleges, because some provide limited access to their machines. If you work at a university or large computer-oriented business, of course, you probably simply have to ask the right person, so start with the help desk or the person who takes care of your computers. I should be honest—the hard part is not finding access but finding affordable access, preferably through a local telephone call.

If you end up with terminal access, you have little choice about using the command line and typing out every command by hand. I recommend this sort of access only if you have no choice or don't mind learning and using Unix. If you decide to take this route, I recommend either Harley Hahn and Rick Stout's *The Internet Complete Reference* (Osborne) or Ed Krol's *The Whole Internet User's Guide and Catalog* (O'Reilly & Associates). Both provide more complete information on this topic. Ed does a great job of explaining in detail how to work with the Internet on a Unix machine, whereas I restrict myself to talking about what you absolutely must know to get by. Besides, Ed's a great guy, and he uses a Macintosh PowerBook Duo and Eudora in real life. You can play a couple of graphical tricks on a straight Unix connection with Eudora and a newsreader called MacNews or a special version of NewsWatcher, but on the whole, you're going to be typing your fingers off.

Chapter 11, UUCP Access

Although UUCP access gives you only email and news, I prefer it to shell access, if only because you can use free and shareware programs (or one very good commercial program) that provide decent Macintosh interfaces, as opposed to the cruel command line. UUCP (Unix-to-Unix CoPy) is a protocol that copies files corresponding to email messages and news postings from your UUCP host to your machine. Therefore, everything happens on a schedule, and you don't interact with the remote machine. I approve of automation of email and news, because you can automatically call out several times a day, send outgoing mail and receive incoming messages, and then read and reply to the messages at your leisure. This arrangement makes for efficient use of your time, the remote machine, and your phone line, because your computer can transfer messages faster than you can read and reply online.

Finding a site that gives you a UUCP newsfeed is more difficult than finding terminal access, although the process is similar, especially in terms of consulting the nixpub list and the PDIAL list. In my experience, the help desks at universities seldom know about UUCP, even though Unix machines located in the Computer Science or Engineering departments often support it. You might ask around to find out who administrates those computers, then ask nicely whether they provide any UUCP feeds. UUCP is enough more efficient than the other methods that a long distance call might make financial sense, especially if you don't subscribe to a large newsgroup or receive large programs in email.

Chapter 12, MacTCP, PPP, and SLIP

Ah, the cream of the crop. Students and staff at universities often have Macs connected to a local network, and, with Apple's MacTCP (included on the disk that comes with this book), can connect directly to the Internet through the campus network. Most of us aren't so lucky, and even people with full network access at work or school may want to call in from home as well. To use MacTCP via modem, you use either PPP (Point to Point Protocol) or the older but more common SLIP (Serial Line Internet Protocol), which an increasing number of sites offer. Included among them is Northwest Nexus, a Bellevue, Washington-based Internet provider that offers a special flat-rate connection offer to readers of this book (see appendix F for details). The disk included with this book contains both MacPPP, a free implementation of PPP from Merit Networks, and InterSLIP, a free implementation of SLIP from InterCon Systems, along with various MacTCP-based software.

Finding a provider with SLIP or PPP access can be difficult. Such providers aren't yet as common as providers of terminal access or UUCP access, but consult the PDIAL list (appendix C) and check which providers in your area offer SLIP access. Long distance calls, such as to Northwest Nexus, are always a possibility, but a few providers offer 800 number access for a fee. If you must call long distance, talk to your provider about ways of lowering your costs through special calling plans offered by your long distance carrier. If you can get 50 percent off on the one number you call the most frequently, or some such deal, you can significantly reduce your costs.

Chapter 12 covers the installation and configuration of MacTCP, PPP, and SLIP in great detail, more so than any other source that I know.

Chapter 13, MacTCP-based Software

The combination of SLIP or PPP and MacTCP lets you run great Macintosh programs that enable you to do everything on the Internet with a Macintosh interface. Gone are the days of the command line (well, almost); now you can use programs such as Eudora for email, Anarchie for FTP, NCSA Telnet, NewsWatcher, InterNews, or Nuntius for reading news, and a slew of other wonderful applications such as TurboGopher, MacWeb, Finger, and MacWAIS. If you can get a PPP or SLIP account and use it, go for it. It's the best way to experience the Internet.

This chapter covers as many of the MacTCP-based programs that I could find on the nets, and a few commercial programs that you won't find there, but are often worth the price.

Chapter 14, Step-by-Step Internet

New to this edition of *Internet Starter Kit for Macintosh* is chapter 14, in which I walk you through the basic tasks that you perform in the most common of the MacTCP-based programs. If, for example, after reading the description of Fetch in chapter 13, you're still a bit confused about how to retrieve a file, check out the instructions in chapter 14. I don't show you how to do much, just enough to get started using each of the most popular programs. After following the instructions in chapter 14, you should be able to go on to perform other tasks that interest you.

Reality Check

At this point, you need to think carefully about what you really want to do on the Internet, because that decision will help you figure out what sort of access is right for you.

I received a call the other day from a man who had been referred to me by my Internet provider. He had a Macintosh and wanted Internet access for his business (supplying peripherals to users of Sun workstations, which run Unix). He said that he knew a little about how to use Unix, so I immediately started telling him about Eudora, UUCP, and SLIP. After we talked for a while, though, it became clear that he only wanted to send and receive email, and that he wasn't interested in learning new stuff on his Mac right now. So, with a heavy heart, I recommended that he simply get a shell account on a Unix machine and use what he knew. Luckily, this particular Unix machine does work with Eudora, so I hope that at some point he'll wean himself away from the familiar, if ugly, Unix command-line environment to a slick Macintosh program.

Similarly, you must think carefully about what you want. If you only want email, and the speed doesn't matter (as it did with my new acquaintance, who didn't want to wait more than an hour or two for mail to come in or go out), a commercial service or a local BBS with an Internet feed may make the most sense. Also consider the costs involved. If you want full Internet access with FTP and Telnet, and you can get a Unix account for, say, a $240 per year flat rate, that may be a better deal than a SLIP or PPP account, which provide nice graphical interfaces but charge by the hour. I understand the concept of not having any money, so please, only do what you can afford, no matter how cool the more expensive options may seem. Credit card debt is an ugly thing.

Commercial Services

There are three easy ways to gain limited Internet access: through one of the numerous commercial services; through a local BBS with an Internet feed; or, if you're lucky, through a gateway maintained by your employer that connects to your network email system.

First, the commercial services. These companies, such as CompuServe, America Online, and GEnie, provide their own fee-based services such as email, computer and non-computer related discussions, file libraries, and databases of information. And, just to ward off this question right away, no, you cannot access files or databases on a commercial service via a normal Internet account. If you could, then the commercial service couldn't squeeze any nickels from you, and what fun would that be?

Note

You can access some of the commercial services over the Internet instead of over a modem, but this still requires you to have an account on that service.

Commercial services offer two main advantages over finding a real Internet site. First, because they have deals with international commercial network carriers such as SprintNet and Tymnet, finding a local phone number is usually easier. But, you pay for that easier access, usually with the connect-time fee for the commercial service. Second, the commercial services find it easier to offer commercial-quality information, because they can charge users to access that information and then pay the information provider. Hence you find, for example, full-text databases of computer magazines on CompuServe, but you pay extra for any searches in those databases, with the revenue going to the magazine publishers. Remember, to paraphrase the Bard, "All the world's a marketing scheme."

In the last year or so, all the commercial services have added Internet email gateways, which means that you can use these services to send and receive Internet email. With a few exceptions, comprised of Delphi, BIX, and, most recently, America Online, the commercial services are limited to email-based Internet access. Some place additional restrictions on email, such as limiting the size of files you can receive, or charging extra for Internet email (as opposed to Internal email on that service).

Note

Absolutely none of the commercial online services properly handle quoting for email. When offering quoting at all, they, like AppleLink, append the original letter to your reply, which makes it difficult to refer to different parts of the original in context. If you use any of these services and aren't happy with the lack of decent facilities, get and use Rick Holzgrafe's SignatureQuote. You can find it at:

```
ftp://ftp.tidbits.com/pub/tidbits/tisk/utilities/signature-quote-10.hqx
```

In this chapter, I discuss each of the major commercial services. I mention the features and limitations of each, so that you can decide whether any satisfy your Internet needs. Keep in mind that rates change frequently on these services, to accommodate market pressures and the marketing whim of the day, so the rates mentioned throughout may not always be accurate.

Having an account on one of the commercial services can be a good way to ease into the Internet because you can send and receive email. Being able to send and receive email enables you to request automated information from the major

Internet providers, which makes finding a local connection much easier. In addition, many of the online services provide decent graphical interfaces that are easier to use than character-based interfaces.

Note

Some of the services that have only character-based interfaces might work with the Loran module provided with the MicroPhone II terminal emulation program; it's worth checking out.

Before I get into specifics, take a look at table 9.1 which summarizes the syntax for sending email between each service and the Internet.

Table 9.1
Commercial Online Service Addressing*

Service	To the Internet	From the Internet
America Online	user@internet.com	user@aol.com
AppleLink	user@internet.com@internet#	user@applelink.apple.com
BIX	user@internet.com	user@bix.com
CompuServe	>INTERNET:user@internet.com	77777.777@compuserve.com
Delphi	user@internet.com	user@delphi.com
eWorld	user@internet.com	user@eworld.com
GEnie	user@internet.com@inet#	user@genie.geis.com
MCI Mail	user@internet.com	user@mcimail.com
Prodigy	user@internet.com	user@prodigy.com

Note: none of these are real addresses—substitute the username for "user**" and the full domain name for "**internet.com**" as in **ace@tidbits.com***

America Online

America Online (see figure 9.1), commonly known as AOL, has been around only since 1989 but has always boasted one of the best graphical interfaces for browsing files and sending email. The way its software handles discussions, however, leaves much to be desired.

Figure 9.1   *America Online Welcome Window, set for TCP Connection*

In the spring of 1992, AOL opened an Internet gateway, and its popularity grew quickly. In early 1994, AOL added additional Internet services, including access to Usenet newsgroups and limited access to some Gopher and WAIS servers. In the spring of 1994, AOL started testing TCP/IP connections that enable you to connect to AOL over an Internet connection and run the America Online software at the same time as other MacTCP-based programs. Connecting to AOL via the Internet requires version 2.1 of the America Online software.

Note

The term "America Online" refers to both the service and to the special software it provides for accessing the service. Sorry if it's confusing.

Connections

As I said, you can now connect to America Online over the Internet if you have MacTCP-based Internet access, either through a network or through SLIP or PPP. Of course, this does you no good if you don't already have an AOL account. You can sign up online if you download their software (I'll tell you where to get it in a second).

Needless to say, you can't simply telnet into America Online. You need special software, and that software (in beta form, so this information is likely to change) is currently available at:

```
ftp://ftp.aol.com/mac/TCP-for-Mac-AOL-2.1.sea
```

Once you download and expand the self-extracting archive, you are left with three main files: a Telnet tool called TCPack for AOL, a file called TCP Connection, and another called TCPack. Drag the Telnet tool onto your System Folder so it lands in your Extensions folder, and put the other two files in your Online Files folder inside the America Online folder. The instructions then recommend setting the preferred memory requirements for AOL's application to 1024K, after which you can launch America Online. Then, from the Locality pop-up menu, you choose TCP Connection.

Note

Although the TCP Connection script comes hard-coded to use the TCPack Telnet tool, with a properly written script you can use a different Telnet tool. Why would you want to? Choice. It's The American Way™.

Once you have everything configured correctly, make sure you're properly connected to the Internet (if you use SLIP or PPP), and then click on America Online's Sign On button. The login process proceeds normally, but since you've already made the connection to the Internet, it's quite a bit faster. After you're on, everything works pretty much as normal. I connect over a 14,400 bps PPP connection, so the speed was not significantly different from the normal 9,600 bps modem connection I used with AOL. Windows seemed to open a little faster, but uploads took a bit longer. Overall, I found reliability better with the Internet connection, but I've been having major communications trouble with AOL lately, so I may not be a good judge.

I see several advantages to using the Internet access method over the normal modem connection. Many people may only have Internet access at work, so connecting from there is not only possible, but much faster if you have a fast

Internet connection. In other cases, Internet access may be cheaper if you must otherwise call AOL long distance (the actual cost of using AOL is the same no matter how you connect). Also, because of the standard way Macintosh Internet programs work, you can use any number of them simultaneously. This simply isn't possible if one application hogs the modem, as is normal with AOL. Finally, Internet access makes it far easier for non-U.S. users to connect.

Disadvantages to connecting to AOL over the Internet as opposed to a normal modem connection? There are a lot of access numbers for AOL around the U.S., certainly more than Internet access numbers. If that's true in your area, there may be no reason to bother with the Internet access. But enough about the connection. On to the Internet services that AOL provides.

Internet Services

I may have quibbles with the way they implement things, or how long they take to do so, but AOL deserves major points for providing as much access to the Internet as they do. You can get to the Internet Center (see figure 9.2) to read more about it by going to the Go To menu and choosing Keyword. In the Keyword dialog box, type **Internet** and press Return.

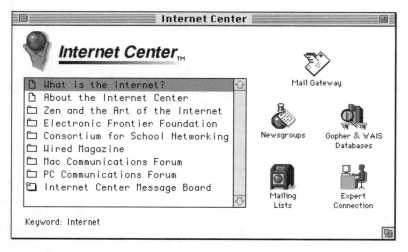

Figure 9.2   America Online Internet Center

America Online has promised to support FTP and Telnet in the future, although it mentions no specific time frame. The problem with using this service for all of your Internet activities is that you're limited by what's available. For instance, unless AOL adds support for a Web browser, you won't be able to access anything on the World-Wide Web. I'd be surprised if that wasn't on its list of things to work on, but less obvious applications, such as an Archie client that can retrieve the files it finds via FTP, probably aren't, yet. And, even if AOL eventually supports everything you can do on the Internet, the best software for using the Internet will always appear first for MacTCP-based connections.

Note

The feature that I most want from AOL, and which they've promised for some future date, is the capability to forward all of my email to my Internet address. If nothing else, it's a pain to log on to AOL to read the mail there when I already get so much email at my Internet account.

Advantages

America Online doesn't charge for internal email or for email that goes in or out through its Internet gateway. This has endeared this service to budget-conscious online users. In addition, AOL has reasonable monthly base rates of $9.95 for the first five hours and $3.50 per hour for each hour after that. You can often get special sign-up deals that offer even more free time for the first month.

Email

America Online's Internet email gateway is one of the easiest to use, due in no small part to the simple interface for sending email. If you can send email on America Online to another AOL user, you can send email to anyone on the Internet with no additional work. In addition, AOL makes it relatively easy to send email to a number of people all at once for the same amount of connect time that you might spend to send the message to one person. This service is handy, for instance, if you write a fairly general letter to a friend and want to send it to two other friends at the same time. Simply put multiple addresses in the To and/or CC fields, and your message goes to all of them (see figure 9.3).

Although it seems somewhat apologetic about not doing so, AOL doesn't reformat incoming Internet email. This means that you may have to expand the size of your email window to accommodate the longer line lengths Internet email tends to have. An advantage of not reformatting incoming email is that to do so would undoubtedly destroy most ASCII graphics and hand-coded ASCII tables.

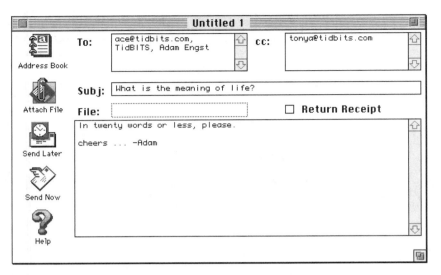

Figure 9.3   *America Online Mail window*

Note

If you mainly receive Internet email on AOL, you may wish to stick with a monospaced font such as Monaco or Courier for viewing your email, since proportionally spaced fonts such as Times and Helvetica won't work with ASCII tables.

In the Internet Center, clicking on the Mailing Lists button presents you with a window of information about mailing lists (see figure 9.4), and, most importantly, a button called Search Mailing Lists. It's essentially a simple search in the List of Lists, and AOL thoughtfully provided a Compose Mail button for subscribing on the spot. Had they also created a mailing list subscription manager, which would handle all your subscriptions and provide single-click access to the standard mailing list function, it would have been truly impressive.

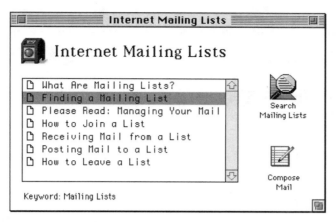

Figure 9.4 *America Online Internet Mailing Lists window*

Usenet News

Along with email, America Online now provides access to Usenet news. Although the interface provided for reading news does work, it's about as bare bones as you get. When you click on the Newsgroups button in the Internet Center window, you see the Newsgroups window (see figure 9.5), complete with handy buttons. These enable you to read the newsgroups you've subscribed to, add more newsgroups to your subscription list, check new newsgroups, and search through the list of newsgroups for those that might interest you.

AOL does a decent job of displaying the newsgroups and opening a new window for each level of hierarchy. However, I find it extremely irritating to have to constantly click on the More button when AOL doesn't list all of the items in a hierarchy. This is a major problem with how AOL handles lists in general, so I doubt it will be fixed any time soon. Being able to search for newsgroups is also useful, although both the basic list and the search feature limit the results to newsgroups that AOL finds "acceptable." If you wish to read any "unacceptable" newsgroups (the entire **alt.sex** hierarchy falls in this category, although there are other sex-related groups that slip through), click on the Expert Add button in the Newsgroups window and type in the name of the group you want to read (see figure 9.6).

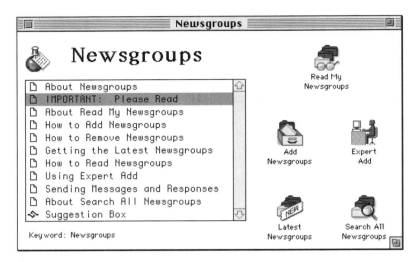

Figure 9.5   *America Online Newsgroups window*

Figure 9.6   *America Online Expert Add window*

This is also the fastest way to subscribe to newsgroups if you have trouble, as I do, translating from the expanded names America Online has given the newsgroups back to the proper Usenet names. Part of the problem with AOL's expanded names is that they seldom convey anything about the hierarchy of the group in question. Hierarchies can make a difference when you're trying to figure out what to read or where to post (see figure 9.7).

Subscribing to a newsgroup generally requires double-clicking on the newsgroup name in the list, clicking on the Add button in the newsgroup description window, and then confirming three or four times that you really want to do this.

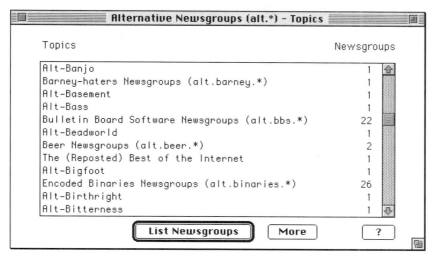

Figure 9.7   *List of* **alt** *groups*

Note

AOL is obsessive about making you confirm your actions; it drives me nuts. If I click on a button, there's a pretty good chance I meant to click on it, and if I confirm that I want to do something, there's an excellent chance that I know it is going to happen. No need to tell me that I actually did indeed click on that OK button. Sorry for the rant.

Once you've subscribed to a few newsgroups (and AOL subscribes everyone to a few newsgroups, although I'm not sure which ones any more), click on the Read My Newsgroups button to see to which groups you are subscribed (see figure 9.8).

I find the Internet Names button a bit irritating, since it "translates" the names that AOL has made up for the newsgroups into the groups' real names. This provides the ever-so-useful information that "Comp-Sys-Mac-Comm" is really the newsgroup called **comp.sys.mac.comm**. Do you feel enlightened?

Anyway, the buttons here are fairly obvious. List Unread (or double-clicking on a group name) opens the group and lists the messages you haven't yet read; List All lists all the messages; Remove unsubscribes you from the selected newsgroup; More displays any groups that aren't yet showing; and the ? button displays help. Once you open the list of the messages in a group, you must again double-click on a message title or click on the Read Messages button to read the messages in a thread. It's good that AOL groups messages in a thread, although there is no method of marking which threads to read and which to kill. Similarly, when you get into the actual newsreader, all you can do is move forward and backward one article, post a new message, and send a response. We're not talking about a particularly impressive interface here (see figure 9.9).

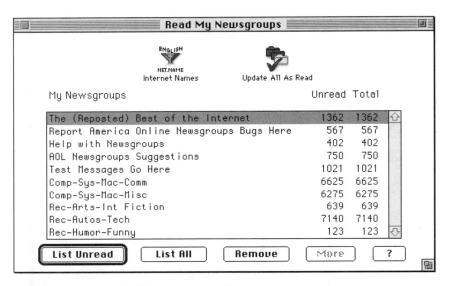

Figure 9.8   America Online Read My Newsgroups window

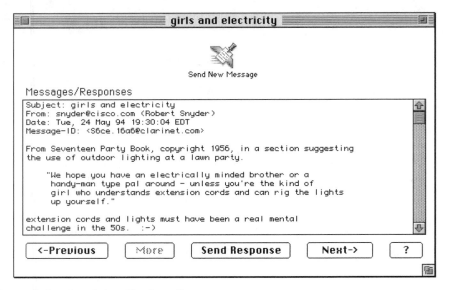

Figure 9.9   A minimalist interface

But enough ragging on AOL's Usenet interface. It works, it's somewhat graphical, and AOL is more accessible than Internet providers for many people. One recommendation: If you're only used to AOL, or are new to the whole shooting match, please read the newsgroup **news.announce.newusers**.

Gopher and WAIS

Along with Internet email (which can provide access to FTP and Archie, as you learned in chapter 8, "Internet Services"), AOL provides limited access to Gopher servers and WAIS sources. Once again, I'm not all that impressed with the interface AOL provides, compared to the MacTCP-based clients for Gopher and WAIS, but we can't have everything. Clicking on the Gopher & WAIS Databases button in the Internet Center window brings up the Gopher and WAIS window (see figure 9.10).

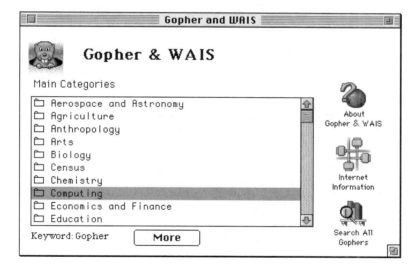

Figure 9.10   *America Online Gopher and WAIS*

Delving into the topics that America Online presents is much like working with a normal Gopher server, with WAIS and searchable Gopher items represented by little book icons (see figure 9.11).

There are several major limitations to AOL's implementation of WAIS, and—somewhat more so—Gopher. Most importantly, you can only retrieve text items. There is simply no way to download a file of any other type, as far as I can see. I'm also bothered by the selection of Gopher and WAIS items that AOL includes. There's nothing wrong with it, but it makes it downright difficult to get out to the normal Other Gopher and Information Servers item that you get to with TurboGopher. What you must do is click on the More button in the Gopher and WAIS window to display all the categories. At the bottom is Other Gopher and Information Servers. Double-click on that to open its window. But that's not it, yet. Finally, click on the More "Other Gopher" button to bring up the More "Other Gopher" Resources window. It shows you the full geographical hierarchy of Gopher servers that can be handy for finding a new Gopher server (see figure 9.12).

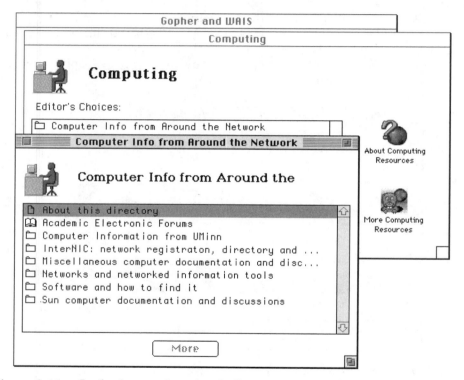

Figure 9.11   Gophering on America Online

Luckily, using Veronica to find something isn't nearly so hard, since there's a Search All Gophers button on the main Gopher and WAIS window that brings up a search window for searching with Veronica. AOL has set up a private Veronica server so response is generally pretty good (see figure 9.13).

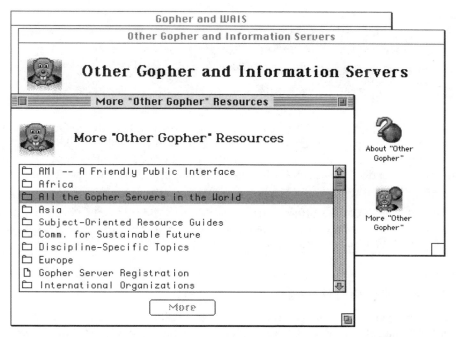

Figure 9.12   *Finally made it to Other Gopher and Information Servers*

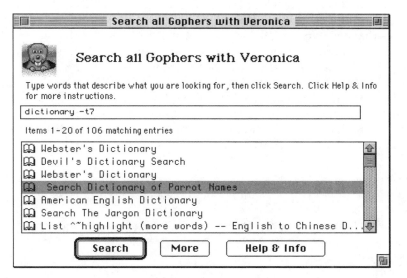

Figure 9.13   *America Online Searching in Veronica*

Note

*You can even use the **-t** switches that limit the search results to certain types of information. Use **-t1** to limit the results to directories, and **-t7** to limit the results to searchable items.*

My main irritations with America Online's Veronica, and with the Gopher interface in general, are the irritating More button and the slow speed. In time, all of that is bound to improve. And, I expect that once FTP access appears, you will be able to download other file types from Gopher, since the basic technology should be the same.

Finally, America Online offers a discussion area in the Internet Center about the Internet. If you use Internet services from AOL regularly, stop in and check it out for the latest information on the Internet connection.

Disadvantages

If you plan to use AOL for serious Internet email, let me dissuade you somewhat. AOL limits the size of outgoing mail to the amount of text that can fit in its software's message box. According to my testing, that's exactly 24,000 characters. You cannot send attached files through the gateway (it's technically feasible, but would increase the traffic significantly), and AOL splits large email messages that come in from the Internet at about 25K each. (This file splitting is actually a major advance for America Online. In the past, it truncated incoming messages at 27K, which was a major headache for many people.) Finally, although you can type special characters such as the bullet (•) or the trademark symbol (™) in the AOL email window, the Internet gateway software replaces some special characters with reasonable replacements, and others with spaces or nonsensical replacements. It would be far better if it did an intelligent replacement, so the trademark sign was converted to something like [tm].

Note

Interestingly, it's hard to tell how long it takes for messages to travel to and from AOL. I sent my AOL account a message from my Internet account, and a few minutes later, sent my Internet account a message from my AOL account. The message from AOL to the Internet was delivered essentially instantly. It took about half an hour for the Internet message to arrive at AOL. Go figure.

Although AOL's software is fine for a message or two a day, if you anticipate joining a mailing list that could generate up to 30 messages a day (which is easily possible), its interface for reading mail can quickly make your life miserable. AOL opens messages slowly, and makes you confirm your actions when you delete a message or reply to a message off-line. I gather that your mailbox can only hold 500 messages, which may seem like a lot, but if you participate in a few high-volume mailing lists and then go on vacation, it's not unthinkable that your mailbox would fill up. Mail that you've read is deleted from your online mailbox in a week; unread mail sticks around for five weeks before being deleted automatically.

Although I believe it has fixed most of the problems, AOL has developed a reputation for having vaguely flaky connections. As a result, sometimes Internet email arrives immediately, whereas other times something delays it for up to several days. This problem isn't serious for the casual email user. It can quickly become frustrating, however, if you're having a conversation with someone via email or depend on your email for business reasons.

Finally, although AOL has finally implemented 9,600 bps access, it's not available for everyone yet, and using AOL at 2,400 bps is a touch painful. (The people I really envy are those with fast Internet connections, since they can get approximately 56,000 bps speeds through the Internet connection.)

Addressing

To send email from America Online to the Internet, you don't have to do anything special. Simply type the Internet address in the To field, and fill in the Subject field and the body of the message as you do when sending email to another AOL user.

To send email from the Internet to a user on AOL, you must remember a few simple rules. First, you need to know the person's username. Second, type the username in lowercase letters, because some email packages on the Internet are picky about upper- and lowercase. Third, remove any spaces in the name. Fourth, append an **@** and the machine name and domain to the end of the address; for AOL, it's **aol.com**. For example, my username on AOL is **Adam Engst**. To send email from the Internet to my AOL account, you would address your message to **adamengst@aol.com**.

Connecting

You need America Online's special software to log on to the service, but it distributes it for free. Simply call 800-827-6364, and ask the operator to send you the software. Alternatively, if you have a friend who already uses AOL, that person can ask AOL to send you the software, and she receives some free time online when you first log on.

If you have an account somewhere that enables you to send Internet email, you can send email to **joinaol@aol.com** and ask for a free AOL software kit, or, if you have FTP access, it's at:

```
ftp://ftp.aol.com/mac/Install-AOL-v2.1.sea
```

AppleLink

Until recently, Apple didn't encourage normal people to use AppleLink, Apple's internal online support service. Apple developers all use AppleLink, though, and most companies in the Macintosh market have AppleLink accounts. As a result, there is a fair amount of Macintosh industry and support information on AppleLink that doesn't exist elsewhere. AppleLink has all the basic features of a commercial online service, including discussion forums and email. Apple has begun inviting normal users on to AppleLink, and to entice them has added a couple of services such as weather information. AppleLink's Internet gateway has been in place for quite some time.

Advantages

AppleLink requires graphical software, so it's a little easier to use than some, and you can get 9,600 bps access. It's often the only way to send email to companies that make Macintosh hardware and software. Besides that, all I can say is that AppleLink works.

Disadvantages

Disadvantages of AppleLink abound. Starting from the top, AppleLink is perhaps the most expensive service around. The software you need to access AppleLink costs $70, and the connection time rate is $37 per hour for 9,600 bps access, or $12 per hour for 2,400 bps access, in addition to charges for the number of characters you transmit. Add to that $0.50 per Internet message, incoming or outgoing. Remember the mailing list that might generate 30 messages each day? Is it worth $15 per day to belong to that list? If cost alone isn't enough to sway you, you obviously have too much money for your own good, so let me tell you about AppleLink's other problems.

AppleLink allows only messages under 32K to go out, because that's all the text that fits in the mail software's text box. AppleLink also only accepts incoming messages under 30K (this amount would also be 32K, but headers steal that extra 2K or so). And, AppleLink's email interface is extremely bare, although it does come with a nice address book feature (see figure 9.14).

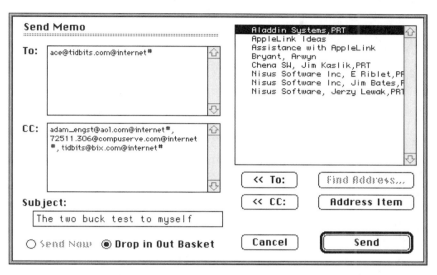

Figure 9.14 *AppleLink address book*

AppleLink enables you to attach files to messages that go out to the Internet, but in all my years of working with them, I have successfully decoded only one. AppleLink first turns the normal Macintosh file into a format called *Apple Single.* That's assuming the user hasn't compressed the file into an *AppleLink Package.* If he has, AppleLink then uses another coding scheme, uucode, to turn the message from a binary file that cannot travel through Internet mailers into a text file that can. Confused yet? I still am. In theory, when you get the text file that results from all these changes, you can use StuffIt Deluxe to first uudecode the file, then decode from Apple Single back into a normal Macintosh file, and, if necessary, expand the AppleLink package (StuffIt Expander 3.0.7 can do this, as can the AppleLink application itself). Nice idea, but usually it doesn't work—at least, not for me.

Finally, AppleLink uses a weird addressing scheme that not only looks funny but conflicts with other Internet addressing rules. Actually, the final disadvantage to using AppleLink for an Internet connection is that it is slated to eventually disappear in favor of Apple's new online service, called eWorld, which is based on the same software that AOL uses.

Addressing

If you want to send email to the Internet from AppleLink, you have two choices. First, you can get someone to send you email from the Internet first, and then you can reply to it. That's the practical choice, but if it's not possible, here's how you address an Internet message from AppleLink. First, take the Internet address, `ace@tidbits.com`, for instance, and then append `@internet#` to it. My address from AppleLink looks like `ace@tidbits.com@internet#`. Putting double `@` signs in confuses anyone who has used real Internet email and knows that you're never allowed to have two `@` signs in an address. And that `#` sign on the end? Who knows where that came from. I'm sure there's a rationale for it, but it's ugly and cumbersome.

There's another quirk. AppleLink cannot send mail to addresses longer than 35 characters. Luckily, my Internet address from AppleLink is only 15 characters all told, but it chokes on `ferdinand-the-bull@large.cork.tree.com@internet#`, which checks in at 38 characters for the part before the `@internet#`. If Ferdinand the Bull sends you email from the Internet, however, you can reply with no trouble. AppleLink waves a magic wand and modifies the address temporarily so that it works fine on the way back out. (Ferdinand's long address may seem like an uncommon occurrence, but wait until you see some of the German Internet addresses; they're sometimes longer than you can imagine.)

Sending email from the Internet to AppleLink, however, is easy. Just take the userid, which sometimes resembles a name or word and other times is just a letter plus some numbers, and append `@applelink.apple.com`. So, Ferdinand's AppleLink userid being `FERDINAND.BULL`, you can send email to him at `ferdinand.bull@applelink.apple.com`.

Connecting

As I said, you need to buy AppleLink's special software. You do this by visiting your friendly local Apple dealer, where you fill out a form online that must be sent in on AppleLink by the dealer. Hmm, does this system sound like the way to attract users to your service? Not exactly. You can try calling the Apple Online Services HelpLine at 408-974-3309, or send Internet email to `alink.mgmt@applelink.apple.com`, but I don't know whether or not your attempts will do any good.

BIX

BIX is one of the oldest of the commercial online services, and until it was purchased by General Videotext Corporation a while back, it was the online arm of *BYTE* magazine. Because of its association with *BYTE*, BIX boasts an eclectic group of technically minded subscribers, although its Macintosh services don't appear to be as popular as those serving other platforms.

BIX has been accessible from the Internet for quite some time, but through a relatively odd gateway, that wasn't common knowledge. BIX has a direct connection to the Internet, which makes it much easier to send and receive Internet email. As an added bonus, you can FTP files from Internet hosts, telnet into BIX from the Internet, and read news with the popular Unix nn newsreader. Other outbound services, such as Finger and Telnet, have arrived more recently.

Advantages

BIX boasts reasonable addressing schemes and an interesting group of subscribers. Its support of FTP and other Internet services, such as Usenet news, Telnet, and Finger, is also a major plus. Those with local Internet access can even telnet to BIX over the Internet, saving on the costs because BIX charges less for Telnet access than for dial-in access. You can telnet into BIX by logging into an Internet machine, typing **telnet x25.bix.com**, and replying **BIX** to the Username prompt before logging on normally.

Note

The login message that appears when you telnet to BIX warns you that uploading to BIX over the Telnet link doesn't usually work. Downloading requires making sure your Telnet session is in binary mode and isn't using the escape character.

I won't talk here about reading Usenet news with nn, since there's a whole section on that in the next chapter on Unix. Suffice it to say that nn was a good choice of character-based Unix newsreaders for BIX to pick. Finger seems to work just as you would expect, and so does Telnet, assuming that you expect to be using the Unix command-line. Again, check out the next chapter for more information on these programs.

BIX provides a great deal of Internet hand-holding in its Internet message areas (try typing **join internet** or **join ask.bix/internet**). Although getting the hang of the massively strange interface may take you some time (you reply to a message online with the **comment** command, for example), the hand-holding and constant advice are a great help. The Internet discussion areas on BIX are an excellent place to talk about exploring the Internet.

As it currently stands, FTP on BIX works rather oddly. Because you don't have a full Unix-like account, BIX had to come up with a way to get the files from the remote Internet machine to your Mac. The manner in which it sends these files is interesting, although occasionally confusing. Instead of storing the file on the BIX host machine and requiring an extra step to download it, BIX set it up so that files are automatically dumped to your Mac via ZMODEM or whatever transfer protocol you normally use to download files from BIX.

I can't decide whether this system is good or bad, although I like the way it queues up files and then downloads them when you're done. That approach can be more efficient than your sitting through each successive download, especially if you have a slow modem. Check out the following FTP session transcript to see how it works. I recommend using ZMODEM if you can; I accidentally got sucked into XMODEM, and it wasn't nearly as clean a process. Setting up BIX to use ZMODEM requires you to look in the Options area.

Note

If you plan on downloading files from BIX via FTP and a transfer protocol like ZMODEM, you won't be able to use the free NCSA Telnet over a MacTCP-based connection. For that sort of connection, I recommend a Communications Toolbox-aware terminal emulator such as SITcomm, MicroPhone Pro, or Communicate.

```
:ftp ftp.tidbits.com

Connected to ftp.halcyon.com.
220 ftp FTP server (Version wu-2.1c(2) Fri Sep 24 14:51:24 PDT 1993) ready.
Name (ftp.tidbits.com:anonymous): <— hit Return to accept "anonymous"
331 Guest login ok, send your complete e-mail address as password.
Password (tidbits@BIX.com): <— hit Return to accept default password
230-Please read the file 00-README
230-  it was last modified on Sat Sep 25 03:57:27 1993 - 251 days ago
230 Guest login ok, access restrictions apply.
Remote system type is UNIX.
Using binary mode to transfer files.

Type "help download" to find out how to download files
from an Internet host computer using BIX end-to-end ftp.

BETA TEST FTP!! Questions? Bugs? Contact peabo in ask.bix/internet!
Sorry, Kermit is not supported in this version; please use X-, Y-, or
ZMODEM to download.  Uploading is not supported at all yet.
```

```
ftp> cd /pub/tidbits
250 CWD command successful.
ftp> ls
200 PORT command successful.
150 Opening ASCII mode data connection for /bin/ls.
total 113
-rw-r—r—  1 1961    235          903 Feb  8 13:47 .message
-rw-r—r—  1 1961    235        42432 Mar 11 11:56 fulldirlist.txt
drwxr-xr-x 7 1961   235          512 Jan 11 15:22 issues
drwxr-xr-x 2 1961   235          512 Jun  2 10:14 misc
drwxr-xr-x 2 1961   235          512 May 16 10:55 private
drwxr-xr-x 2 1961   235         1024 Jun  1 14:53 select
drwxr-xr-x 2 1961   235          512 May  1 23:26 thewordbook
drwxr-xr-x 7 1961   235          512 Sep 29  1993 tisk
drwxr-xr-x 2 1961   235          512 Jun  1 15:01 www
226 Transfer complete.
ftp> get fulldirlist.txt
get fulldirlist.txt
Starting a new queue of files to be downloaded; type "help download"
if you need assistance using BIX end-to-end ftp.
Download queued files? y
Download file: fulldirlist.txt
Get ready to receive using XMODEM/checksum....
[ bytes: unknown, blocks: unknown, block size 128 ]
Forgetting files previously queued.
221 Goodbye.
```

Disadvantages

I must admit that BIX bothers me. I have major trouble with the custom command-line-based interface, and I'm always fighting to end up in the proper place. For instance, to go to the section where I upload *TidBITS*, I must type **join mac.hack/tidbits**, something that I seem incapable of doing reliably. Although graphical front ends to BIX exist for Windows, no program has yet migrated to the Macintosh. A graphical front end would go a long way toward assuaging my complaints.

Note

There is an off-line-reader package called Semaphore II available for CIX, a British service that uses the same software as the BIX host machines and partially works with BIX. You can find Semaphore II on the Internet as:

```
ftp://ftp.tidbits.com/pub/tidbits/tisk/bbs/semaphore-110.hqx
```

In addition, BIX has relatively high rates of $13 per month, supplemented by a connect-time charge ranging from $1 per hour for Telnet access to $9 per hour for dial-up access via SprintNet or Tymnet during weekdays. The standard non-prime time rate that you most likely pay is $3 per hour. You don't pay extra for 9,600 bps access, luckily, and Internet email is free until you have sent and received 10M-worth in one month, after which BIX charges $1 for each subsequent 100K. That rate is fair for Internet email.

If you plan to use BIX heavily, there's a 20/20 plan that costs $20.00 and provides 20 hours of connect time. This charge is in addition to your $13.00 per month membership fee. Time more than the 20 hours is charged at $1.80 per hour, or $1.00 per hour if you telnet in.

Addressing

BIX does addressing right. To send email to someone on the Internet, you type his Internet email address instead of his BIX username. To send mail to me from BIX, for example, you type **mail: to ace@tidbits.com**.

Sending mail to BIX is equally easy. Simply append **@bix.com** to the end of the BIX username and send it. My address on BIX is simply **tidbits@bix.com**.

Connecting

The sole advantage of a command-line environment is that it makes signing up for the service easy. To get an account on BIX, have your modem dial 800-695-4882 or 617-491-5410 (use 8 data bits, no parity, 1 stop bit, full duplex). Press Return a few times until you see the Login: (enter "bix") prompt, and then type **bix**. At the Name? prompt, type **bix.net**. If you prefer, you also can telnet to BIX to sign up, following the instructions in the preceding "Advantages" section.

CompuServe

Although not the cheapest of the services, CompuServe has recently put more reasonable rates into place. CompuServe has had an Internet gateway for some years, and in the last year or so has removed the file size limitation on incoming mail (it previously refused incoming mail larger than 50K). CompuServe has promised to add Usenet news, FTP, and outgoing Telnet support in the future, although it's entirely unclear when those features will actually arrive. I also wonder how expensive using them will turn out to be.

Advantages

Although you can use CompuServe's menu-based interface from any terminal program such as ZTerm, it makes my teeth hurt. The only reason to use the menu-based interface these days is that CompuServe has made it possible to telnet in at the same rates as local dialup, which can make for easier and cheaper access, especially for people in other countries.

Note

As with BIX and Delphi, if you telnet into CompuServe, make sure you use a program that supports standard transfer protocols such as XMODEM, YMODEM, and ZMODEM, or in CompuServe's case, its B-protocol.

CompuServe sells two graphical applications that make using CompuServe's services easier and cheaper. Even if you only anticipate using email on CompuServe, I recommend that you get either Navigator or CompuServe Information Manager (CIM).

Mike O'Connor designed Navigator specifically to save users' money when using CompuServe. You tell Navigator what you want to do in terms of reading mail, sending mail, reading discussions on CompuServe, downloading files, and so on, and then you tell Navigator to log on and do everything for you. Because it works quickly by itself off-line, like UUCP, it stays on for a shorter time than you normally would and thereby saves you money. That's good. However, Navigator was designed for reading discussions on CompuServe, so it's clumsy for email use. Every item, mail or otherwise, is appended to a Navigator session file that rapidly grows large and cumbersome to navigate when searching for old mail that you haven't yet replied to (see figure 9.15).

In contrast, CIM works much better for email because it too can transfer all mail quickly and automatically, but also shows you a nice list of all your mail and enables you to sort it in several different ways (see figure 9.16). I seldom mess with the sorting, but listing mail makes much more sense than forcing the user to scroll through each message, as Navigator does.

I often find myself receiving email that I don't have time to respond to immediately, or perhaps the message requires enough research that I don't want to respond for a day or two. In either case, it's easy to lose email in Navigator, whereas in CIM you can easily see which messages need a response. CIM also makes it easy to save copies of outgoing messages (useful for those times when you want to say, "I didn't write that!" in a hurt tone). Also, you can file messages in different folders, essential if you receive email about different projects.

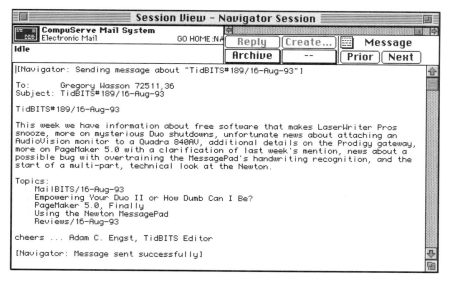

Figure 9.15   Navigator Session window

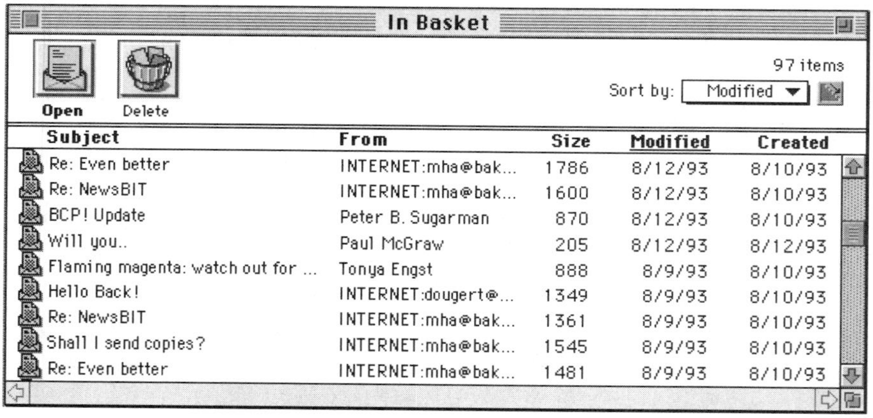

Figure 9.16   CIM In Basket

Overall, I strongly recommend that you purchase CIM if you intend to use CompuServe email seriously. Navigator is a good value only if you intend to read many of the discussion sections on CompuServe itself (possibly worthwhile, but out of the scope of this book).

Telnetting to CompuServe

You can use CIM to telnet into CompuServe if you have a Unix shell account, thus avoiding CompuServe's unpleasant character-based interface. This process does not currently work if you have a MacTCP-based connection to the Internet, but I assume that CompuServe will fix the problem relatively soon.

To telnet to CompuServe using CIM, go to the Special menu and choose Connection from the hierarchical menu. Make sure the Network pop-up menu is set to CompuServe, and the Dial Type menu is set to Direct Connection. Click on the OK button to save your changes (see figure 9.17).

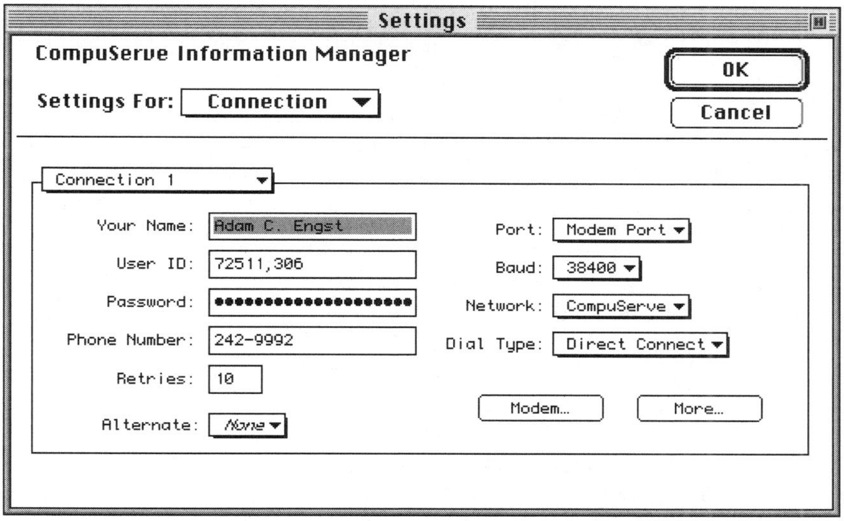

Figure 9.17   *CIM Settings window*

Next, go to the Special menu and choose Terminal. Make sure the Manual Connect checkbox is checked, and then click on the Connect button to open the terminal window. At this point you must use the Hayes AT commands to call your Internet account and login normally. Once you're logged in, type **telnet -E compuserve.com**. The -E option tells the Telnet program not to use escape characters, which are what screw up CIM if you try to use one of the existing Telnet tools over a MacTCP-based connection. Believe me, I tried them all with all the options, and I couldn't find any way of making the connection.

Anyway, once you've telnetted to CompuServe, enter **CISAGREE** at the Host Name prompt. Then type **9600** or whatever speed you wish to be charged for at the Baud Rate prompt. When you see the User ID prompt, close the terminal window, since CIM can handle the rest on its own if you do something like choose Send & Receive All Mail from the Mail menu. (Special thanks to Paul Celestin of Celestin Company for providing these instructions. If only they worked with a Telnet tool...)

Note

CompuServe reportedly limits the speed at which you can connect to the speeds supported by its modems, even if you happen to have a much faster Internet connection. I don't have that fast a Internet connection to test with, but intentionally throttling back throughput irritates me.

Disadvantages

I don't want to imply that CompuServe is the ideal service for Internet email, although it may sport the best combination of features among the commercial online services. CompuServe's failings fall in the areas of cost, receiving, and weird addressing formats.

Cost-wise, CompuServe no longer holds the title as the most expensive service, although it is aiming for one of the most confusing pricing structures around. CompuServe introduced a new Standard Pricing Plan, which allows unlimited access to a limited set of CompuServe services (most of which aren't the ones you as a Macintosh user might find interesting) for $8.95 per month. Internet email is not included in the Standard Pricing Plan, and services that aren't included are billed at an hourly rate of $4.80 per hour for 2,400 bps access or $9.60 per hour for 9,600 bps access. With the monthly fee, you get a $9.00 credit toward email, which is billed at a rate of $0.15 for the first 7,500 characters and $0.05 for every 2,500 characters after the first 7,500. Confusing the issue even further, those mail charges apply to sending all mail, but only to reading email from the Internet. You don't pay for reading CompuServe email.

The Alternative Pricing Plan costs only $2.50 per month, and has a higher connect charge, but doesn't charge extra for Internet email. The hourly rates for the Alternative Pricing Plan are $12.80 for 2,400 bps access and $22.80 for 9,600 bps access.

Also, CompuServe requires an irritating addressing scheme in which you must prefix `>INTERNET:` to the beginning of each Internet address you use. Internet addresses are enough to remember on their own without CompuServe adding its own oddities.

I've also heard of a bug with Navigator that prevents it from sending email to long Internet addresses. I haven't tested to find out what that length is exactly, but watch those interminable German email addresses.

Addressing

You must know the magic words to add to an Internet address for CompuServe to behave properly. It's not difficult, only obscure and easy to type incorrectly. If you want to send email to my account on the Internet, **ace@tidbits.com**, you prefix **>INTERNET:** to my address, so the ungainly end result looks like **>INTERNET:ace@tidbits.com**. Easy enough, but people often type the address slightly wrong. It doesn't seem to make a difference whether a space lives between the colon and the start of the Internet address, but remember that spaces are verboten within an Internet address. To further complicate matters, when you receive Internet email in CIM or Navigator, they both politely strip the **>** symbol from the beginning of the message. "Oh no," you think, "then replying won't work." If you thought that, then you're quite clever, but wrong, at least for CIM. Don't ask why, but CIM doesn't mind not seeing the **>** symbol if it isn't present in a reply. Navigator at one point couldn't do that, so replying to Internet email without adding that **>** symbol manually didn't work. I believe it works fine now.

Luckily, sending email from the Internet to CompuServe poses fewer problems. You merely must follow two simple rules. First, all CompuServe addresses are pairs of octal numbers, or some such nonsense. My CompuServe address looks like **72511,306**. Commas aren't allowed in Internet addresses (they usually indicate a list of addresses), so you must change the comma to a period and then add **@compuserve.com**. My address, then, becomes **72511.306@compuserve.com**. Unless you have a better memory for octal numbers than I do, put CompuServe addresses in a nicknames file or address book.

Connecting

You must purchase a CompuServe Membership Kit to access CompuServe. You can order it from mail order vendors or directly from CompuServe. The package I've seen in a recent MacConnection catalog costs only $25 and includes CIM. You can call MacConnection at 800-800-2222, or contact CompuServe for more information at 800-848-8199. You can also get more information if you telnet to **compuserve.com**, send **CIS** to the Host Name prompt, and then ask for **HELP**. Among the documents you can check out is one that details how to sign up for CompuServe membership online, over your Telnet connection if you wish. If you download CIM from CompuServe itself in the CIM Support forum, you usually get the purchase price back in connect-time credit.

Delphi

I get the impression that at one time Delphi was more popular among the Macintosh online crowd than it is now. After some time in the doldrums, that popularity seems to be returning, due in part to Delphi's competitive pricing and full Internet access.

Advantages

Yes, you heard me right. Delphi—alone of the commercial services—boasts full Internet access. You can telnet in and out of Delphi and access remote FTP sites to your heart's content. Email in and out works just fine, and you can even read news there. What a deal! There's not really much point in talking about Telnet, FTP, and Gopher here because I cover those subjects from the command line in the next chapter. So keep reading if you want to find out how to use the Internet tools on Delphi.

Other advantages? Hm, because Delphi is completely connected to the Internet, email in and out should be as fast as possible. Also, like BIX, Delphi has an Internet Special Interest Group that talks about the Internet and the resources you can find on it. This is a big help for a newcomer.

Disadvantages

Delphi suffers from two problems in my estimation, though you may not agree with me on either. First, it appears that Delphi found it easy to add full Internet access, because it runs a custom menu-based system on top of DEC's VMS operating system, which is in relatively common use on the Internet. I'm not terribly fond of VMS, having had some bad experiences trying to use it in college, and Delphi's menu-based system is truly weird in places (especially in the file libraries). So, when I log in to Delphi, I either see a custom menu system I don't much like, or an operating system that irks me. Those irritations are of course due to personal preference, and you may feel differently. Many people like VMS just fine, and most of them manage to fit into normal society with only a little effort.

Second, Delphi has no decent graphical interface. I can't pretend that CompuServe's menu interface is any better or worse than Delphi's; that's not the point. However, CIM is a perfectly reasonable graphical window into CompuServe, and Delphi is hurting in this respect. One such program for Delphi, called D-Lite, does exist and as much as some people claim to have it working, when I try to use it I almost always end up mouthing obscenities. To make a long and painful story short, D-Lite has one of the worst interfaces I've ever seen on a Macintosh program. In addition, D-Lite works (theoretically) by typing in the proper response at the proper time, but that of course means anything that happens differently on the host confuses D-Lite. This problem always seemed to happen to me, and I wasn't using it for anything other than uploading *TidBITS* each week.

Addressing

Like BIX, Delphi doesn't do anything strange with addressing. You can send email to an Internet user by using her Internet address instead of the Delphi address in Delphi's mail program (which, for you mainframe buffs, is almost exactly like VMS mail). If you want to send email from the Internet to someone at Delphi, simply append **@delphi.com** to the Delphi userid. My address on Delphi looks like **adam_engst@delphi.com**.

Connecting

For information on connecting to Delphi, call 800-695-4005. Monthly rates are either $10.00 for four hours of use, with extra hours at $4.00 each, or $20.00 for 20 hours, with additional hours at $1.80 each. If your account has an Internet connection, you are charged an additional $3.00 per month. Delphi often offers five hours free so that you can try out the service, so ask about the current deal when you call. Delphi tends to advertise its Internet access heavily, but considering how much better (and, if you're a heavy user, cheaper), a MacTCP-based SLIP or PPP account at many providers is these days, I wouldn't crow so loudly. Let's face it, the future of computing does not lie in character-based interfaces. Existing graphical interfaces may not be perfect, but they're a heck of a lot better than most of the character interfaces I see out there.

eWorld

The most recent arrival in the commercial online service world is Apple's new eWorld service, which just opened to the public as I write this. Apple based eWorld heavily on AOL, using the same server and client software, but with various modifications and a somewhat different interface (see figure 9.18).

Unfortunately, eWorld has almost none of AOL's more interesting Internet features. In fact, about all you can currently do with the Internet on eWorld is send and receive email. However, the eWorld folks have announced that they will add Internet access similar to AOL's in 1995.

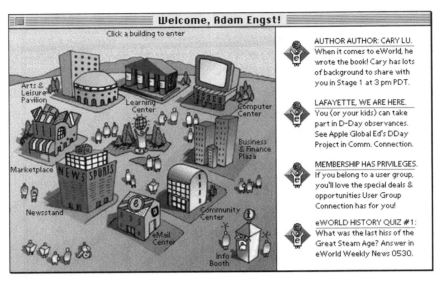

Figure 9.18   *eWorld Welcome screen (it's much nicer in color)*

Advantages

The main advantage to eWorld is that it provides a clean graphical interface for email, much as does AOL. Similarly, eWorld does not charge for email that goes in or out through its Internet gateway (see figure 9.19).

The Internet email gateway on eWorld allows you to forward messages to Internet users (easier than copying and pasting into a new message). You can also send email to a number of people simultaneously, saving connect time and thus cost (in contrast, CompuServe charges you for each recipient). But, all in all, the main advantage eWorld has is that it is slated to be the death knell for AppleLink and its $37 per hour charges (after a 15 month phase-out period).

Note

Apple claims to have reserved all of the AppleLink userids on eWorld and will transfer those accounts when it takes AppleLink down, which means that theoretically, if you know someone's AppleLink account, the same username should work if you want to send her Internet email on eWorld as well.

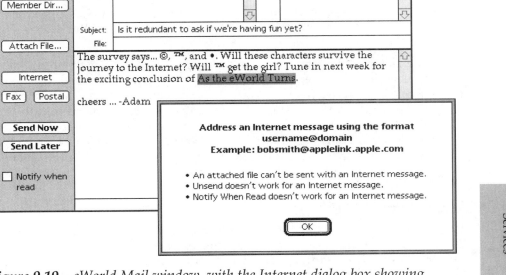

Figure 9.19 *eWorld Mail window, with the Internet dialog box showing*

Disadvantages

Not surprisingly, eWorld suffers from the same problems as AOL. Outgoing messages are limited in size to the amount of text that can fit in the software's message box (which in my testing is again exactly 24,000 characters). You can't send attached files through the gateway (it's technically feasible, but would increase the traffic significantly). eWorld splits large email messages that come in from the Internet at about 7K each, which is distinctly unreasonable, especially considering that AOL splits them at 25K. The reason for this small chunk size is that Apple actually runs its NewtonMail system on the same machines, and the 7K limit is necessary for Newtons.

Note

To give you an idea what a pain it would be, receiving TidBITS *on eWorld via the Internet gateway would result in five message chunks each week. Receiving something large like the Info-Mac Digest might result in 12 or more chunks.*

Addressing

To send email from eWorld to the Internet, you don't have to do anything special. You type the Internet address in the To field and fill in the Subject field and the body of the message, as you do when sending email to another eWorld user.

To send email from the Internet to a user on eWorld, you must remember a few simple rules. First, you need to know the person's username. Second, type the username in lowercase letters, to avoid offending email packages that are picky about upper- and lowercase. Third, remove any spaces in the name. Fourth, append an @ and the machine name and domain to the end of the address; for eWorld, it's **eworld.com**. My username on eWorld is **Adam Engst**, so to send me email from the Internet, you address your message to **adamengst@eworld.com**.

Connecting

Pricing for eWorld is $8.95 per month, which includes two free hours during evenings or weekends, with every hour after those two an additional $4.95. Daytime hours are an additional $2.95 per hour. Apple is making eWorld software available for free if you call 800-775-4556. In addition, the eWorld software is bundled with the definitive book on eWorld, called *eWorld: The Official Guide for Macintosh Users*, (Hayden Books, 1994), written by long-time author and Macworld editor Cary Lu along with John Milligan. Ask for it in your local bookstore.

GEnie

GEnie is yet another large commercial service. It claims to have 350,000 users, but GEnie is not a major hotbed of Macintosh activity. I've only used GEnie briefly with a friend, so I'm by no means an expert. However, I'm not all that impressed with what I've seen. To be honest, I haven't used GEnie's new graphical software, mostly since it took more than an hour to download at 2,400 bps and then failed. Maybe later. I have trouble believing that any graphical software can be all that usable at 2,400 bps, anyway—AOL certainly lagged seriously at 2,400 bps. There's also program called GEnieNav Lite that works with MicroPhone II or Pro to offer a graphical, off-line method to access GEnie. If GEnieNav Lite works well for you, there's also a more full-featured GEnieNav program that's commercial. I haven't used GEnieNav Lite, but it's available on the Internet at:

```
ftp://ftp.tidbits.com/pub/tidbits/tisk/bbs/genie-nav-lite-211.hqx
```

Advantages

GEnie has had Internet email access for some time now, but it seems to have added some additional Internet services, although in a tricky way. If you visit the Internet RoundTable (INTERNET-RT) on GEnie, you can discuss the Internet at length, browse through files that have been uploaded to GEnie, and even search the Internet for a file and request it.

```
GEnie                        INTERNET-RT                     Page 1405
                          Internet RoundTable

     1.    Internet Bulletin Board
     2.    Internet Conference Room
     3.    Internet Library of Files
     4.    About the Internet RoundTable
     5.    RoundTable News (940216)
     6.    Send Mail to RoundTable Staff
     7.    Internet Mail
     8.    Download Sysop's Pick File
     9.    Unix RoundTable
    10.    Search the Internet for a file
    11.    Request a file from the Internet
    12.    What is my Internet Address
    13.    Virus/Computer Security RoundTable

  Enter #, <P>revious, or <H>elp?
```

GEnie supports nothing but Internet email, so what it did is set up a system that accesses Archie via email, and uses a system similar to FTPmail for retrieving directories or actual files. Clever, if low-tech.

Disadvantages

In most locations, GEnie currently supports only 2,400 bps, which is a major pain in this age of 14,400 bps modems. There are a few 9,600 bps access numbers, and reportedly you can also access GEnie over SprintNet, which has a fair number of 9,600 bps access numbers. There may be an additional charge for using SprintNet.

Addressing messages to and from GEnie isn't terrible, but it could be easier. You can send messages to the Internet from either the GE Mail page or the Internet Mail Service page, but if you send the message from GE Mail, you must append **@inet#** to the end of the message. I don't know why there are two areas for sending email, especially since it seems you can also send email to another

GEnie user in the Internet Mail Service page. If you use the standard GE Mail page, GEnie doesn't prompt you for the required information, nor does it give the extra help text during the composition of your message. I think I'd prefer less help after using the Internet Mail Service page several times.

Addressing

To send email from GEnie to someone on the Internet, you can simply use the standard Internet address—if you're sending from the Internet Mail Service page. If you're sending the message from the GE Mail page, you must append **@inet#** to the end of the Internet address. To send email from the Internet to GEnie, append **@genie.geis.com** to your friend's GEnie address, making it look something like *username***@genie.geis.com**.

> ### Note
>
> *There is a difference between userid (or login name) and username on GEnie. Internet email must go to the username.*

Connecting

GEnie has a decent rate structure of $8.95 for the first four hours each month, with additional hours billed at $3.00 per hour. That was considered quite inexpensive at one time, but is not all that unusual today. You can get more information about GEnie by telephoning 800-638-9636.

Other Services and BBSs

I'm something of a completeness freak because every time I completely ignore various topics, I always end up answering questions about them. Therefore, although the following commercial online services and bulletin board systems (BBSs) aren't necessarily as common or useful for Internet access as those I've discussed already, I feel that they're worth mentioning.

MCI Mail

I'd hesitate to even mention a heavy-duty corporate, command line-based email system like MCI Mail, except for one thing. If you're clever, and can send email from another account, you can receive unlimited Internet email via MCI Mail and an 800 number for $35 per year! I know little about the system, other than the fact that MCI improved its speed in the past year or so, but I gather that MCI makes its money by charging heavily for the messages you send. Let's call MCI and see what they say.

If you dial 800-444-MAIL, you wait on hold for what seems like an eternity. But, as the nice recording says, MCI Customer Support (or at least its recording) is available 24 hours a day, seven days a week. In theory, if you wait long enough, someone will pick up the phone and tell you how to sign up for MCI Mail.

MCI Customer Support finally answered after ten minutes. I made the mistake of mentioning that I was writing the rate information down in a book, and immediately got the bubonic plague treatment. Public Relations didn't answer its phone, and the supervisor only faxed me a rate sheet (the background here is that I hate fax modems and they hate me). The moral of that story is, never tell people you're writing a book.

Will wonders never cease? On the third try, I managed to browbeat QuickLink II and my Telebit WorldBlazer into receiving the fax. It informed me (after six useless pages) that it costs $0.50 to send the first 500 characters of a message. The next 500 characters cost an extra $0.10, each subsequent set of 1,000 characters after that (up to 10K) is also $0.10, and each set of 1,000 characters after 10K is only $0.05. *Sheesh*, no wonder they didn't want to tell me over the phone. All those charges come on top of the $35.00 per year for the mailbox; so if you send much mail via MCI, the costs add up fast.

Here's a free idea that just might work. If you can download your MCI messages and convert them into a file in Unix mailbox format, Eudora can read them. Set Eudora so that messages appear to come from your MCI account (so that all replies go back to your MCI account). Then, even if you must call long distance to send mail with Eudora (which is easy enough with a number of providers), you could receive gobs of email via MCI and download it via that 800 number. But, of course, you didn't hear this suggestion from me. You figured it all out on your own.

As this book goes to press, MCI Mail has recently announced that it intends to add Internet access to its service. This isn't too surprising, since Vinton Cerf, president of the Internet Society, is also now a senior vice president for data architecture at MCI. All that Internet users will get, apparently, is access to additional MCI Mail services, such as electronic message transfer to letterhead, use of signature graphics, image transmission via fax, alternate addressing when sending a fax, and automatic retry for fax and telex. Frankly, I'm not impressed, but if you wish to find out more, send email to `mci-info-request@gatekeeper.mcimail.com`, and type **help** in the body of the message.

Outland

Outland is an unusual service, and one I know little about, in large part because it's very new. Outland is a nationwide commercial service dedicated to computer games. However, we're not talking just any computer games. It's specifically designed to support graphical multi-player games. Along with some of the standard board games, Outland offers a special version of Delta Tao's fabulous space opera game, Spaceward Ho!. See figure 9.20.

Figure 9.20   Outland Welcome screen

Why am I blathering about games here? Well, Outland is unusual (I know of only one other commercial game network) in that it is accessible via the Internet as well as modem. You must use Outland's special software, which is available for free, although actually playing the games costs money. Charges are $2.50 per hour for use of one game (while other players are present), and additional games are charged at $1.00 per hour. Those who call Outland directly with their modems rather than connect over the Internet are charged an additional $1.00 per hour, so the Internet connection is definitely a good deal. You can contact Outland for more information at 800-PLAY-OUT, or at **outland@aol.com**. You can retrieve the Outland software on the Internet as:

```
ftp://sumex-aim.stanford.edu/info-mac/game/com/outland-complete.hqx
```

Prodigy

Prodigy has a gateway for Internet email, but it requires special software for sending email, and that software doesn't yet exist for the Mac. Mac users can receive Internet mail on Prodigy, but it's a bit clumsy. The mail appears as a COD message and must be read by clicking on the Copy To Disk button in the mailbox (at which point you can view the files off-line). This is all part of Prodigy's standard software. However, until a version of Prodigy's DOS Mail Manager software is written for the Macintosh, you cannot reply to your Internet email. This software reportedly is in the works, but no beta versions have yet been sighted. To send email to a Prodigy user, append **@prodigy.com** to the user's Prodigy address.

Given that the Internet email costs are currently $0.10 for each 6,000-character block received, I doubt many people will use Prodigy for real Internet access, anyway. Spending $.50 for each 30K issue of *TidBITS* is too much. The cost would be astronomical if you tried to use FTPmail to retrieve a file via email to Prodigy. Although the Prodigy gateway can handle files up to 1M, a 1M file would cost, according to my calculations, more than $17. Ouch.

Prodigy has announced that it intends to offer full Internet access at some point. It has set up a bulletin board on Prodigy for discussing Internet access. To access it, **jump:internet bb** on Prodigy. In the past, Prodigy has been dogged by stupid policies toward censoring discussions (Prodigy was heavily in favor of it). Recent reports, however, indicate that Prodigy is trying to escape the burdens of censorship while still retaining a "family image." Its server software still automatically scans for naughty words, but Prodigy is trying to make the bulletin boards self-regulating, rather than having a censor wade through every posting to make sure it isn't actually a scrambled Satanic message. That's progress, but I still think full Internet access will force greater changes in the ways Prodigy and Prodigy members, accustomed to the filtered atmosphere, look at the world.

FirstClass

Without a doubt, one of the simplest methods of gaining limited access to the Internet is through a local bulletin board, often run by your local Macintosh users' group (see figure 9.21).

Until recently, none of the Macintosh BBS programs were able to communicate with an Internet host. With SoftArc's excellent FirstClass BBS software, and a special add-on gateway to the Internet, a Macintosh BBS can sport both a clean graphical interface and an email and Usenet news connection. Most of these sorts of Internet connections are handled through UUCP gateways, which means the FirstClass BBS calls an Internet host every few hours to transfer email and news.

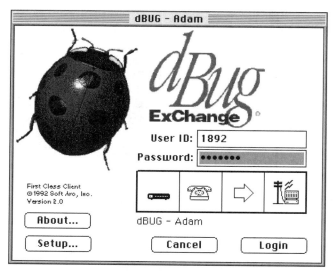

Figure 9.21   *FirstClass Login window*

Advantages

It's also possible, though currently unusual, for a FirstClass BBS to be accessible over the Internet. You can come in by way of a standard Telnet session or via the graphical FirstClass software, configured to use a Telnet tool, if you have MacTCP-based connection to the Internet.

Note

Apparently, SoftArc recommends that you use the VersaTerm Telnet tool, but I've successfully used the MP Telnet tool from MicroPhone Pro. It's certainly worth trying the free TGE TCP Tool, as well.

Configuring the FirstClass client software to use a Telnet tool is easy. Click on the Setup button in the main screen, and the Change button in the Connect Via part of the Connection Settings dialog. Then, in the Communications Setup dialog, choose Comm Toolbox from the Connect Via pop-up menu. Click on the Configure Tool button to choose your Telnet tool, and configure it with the

Internet address of the host BBS. OK, so it's not a one-step process, but it is straightforward, and I did it right on the first try. Once you connect to a FirstClass BBS over the Internet, it looks just like any other FirstClass BBS that you'd call via modem.

Disadvantages

FirstClass can receive Usenet newsgroups via the Internet gateway, which is an excellent way to bring more information into a fairly small BBS. Unfortunately, the current interface to reading news isn't as full-featured as I would like. Working with threads is difficult or impossible, and there's no easy way to skip an entire uninteresting thread (see figure 9.22).

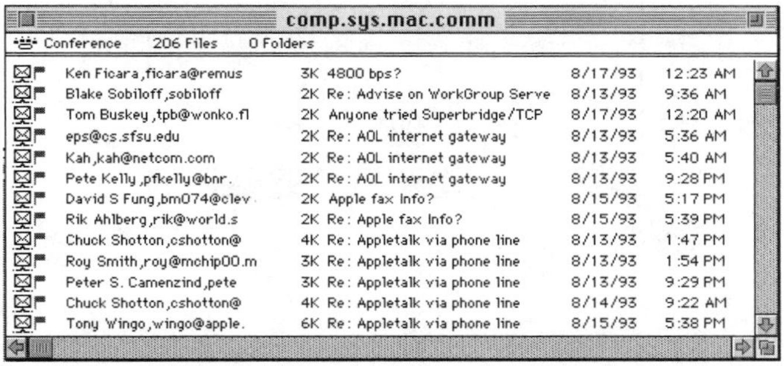

	comp.sys.mac.comm				
Conference	206 Files	0 Folders			
Ken Ficara ,ficara@remus	3K	4800 bps?	8/17/93	12:23 AM	
Blake Sobiloff ,sobiloff	2K	Re : Advise on WorkGroup Serve	8/13/93	9:36 AM	
Tom Buskey ,tpb@wonko.fl	2K	Anyone tried Superbridge/TCP	8/17/93	12:20 AM	
eps@cs.sfsu.edu	2K	Re : AOL internet gateway	8/13/93	5:36 AM	
Kah ,kah@netcom.com	2K	Re : AOL internet gateway	8/13/93	5:40 AM	
Pete Kelly ,pfkelly@bnr.	2K	Re : AOL internet gateway	8/13/93	9:28 PM	
David S Fung ,bm074@clev .	2K	Apple fax Info?	8/15/93	5:17 PM	
Rik Ahlberg ,rik@world.s	2K	Re : Apple fax Info?	8/15/93	5:39 PM	
Chuck Shotton ,cshotton@	4K	Re : Appletalk via phone line	8/13/93	1:47 PM	
Roy Smith ,roy@mchip00.m	3K	Re : Appletalk via phone line	8/13/93	1:54 PM	
Peter S. Camenzind ,pete	3K	Re : Appletalk via phone line	8/13/93	9:29 PM	
Chuck Shotton ,cshotton@	4K	Re : Appletalk via phone line	8/14/93	9:22 AM	
Tony Wingo ,wingo@apple.	6K	Re : Appletalk via phone line	8/15/93	5:38 PM	

Figure 9.22   *FirstClass newsgroups*

Addressing

Sending email on a FirstClass system is easy. Just go to the Message menu and choose New. FirstClass presents you with a message window (see figure 9.23).

To send a message to the Internet, type the Internet address and append **,Internet** to it. My Internet address from a FirstClass system looks like **ace@tidbits.com,Internet**. Because most FirstClass systems don't call out all that often to send and receive Internet email, don't expect immediate responses. Sending email to a FirstClass BBS is no different than sending to any other Internet site—you must know the username and sitename. In general, you can figure out usernames by taking the person's username on FirstClass and replacing the spaces with underscores. Making this change can result in some ugly addresses. If I am **Adam C. Engst** on a FirstClass board, for example, the

Internet form of my username on the local dBUG BBS (run by Seattle's downtown Business Users' Group) is **adam_c._engst@dbug.org**. Again, the sitename in the address is individual to each FirstClass BBS. It's also possible for the administrator to create aliases, so I could also be **ace@dbug.org** on the local BBS. The aliases are simply easier for others to use.

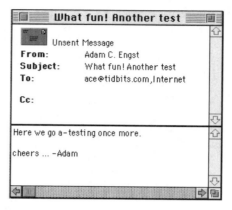

Figure 9.23   *FirstClass Mail window*

Note

*FirstClass distinguishes between usernames that identify you to other users (**Adam C. Engst**, for example) and userids that identify you to the software (mine on the local BBS is 1892). It's not a big deal, but if you want to be correct...*

Connecting

If you can find a local FirstClass BBS that's also in some way connected to the Internet, I recommend you try it out. It's a good interface for getting started with Internet email and news, and most BBSs have either minimal or nonexistent fees.

You can get more information about the FirstClass software from SoftArc by sending email to **sales@softarc.com**. You can download the free FirstClass client software from any FirstClass BBS, or on the Internet at:

```
ftp://ftp.tidbits.com/pub/tidbits/tisk/bbs/first-class-client-209.hqx
```

NovaLink Professional

Like most other BBS programs, I've seldom used NovaLink Professional and thus know little about it. It has a graphical interface called NovaTerm, and can support Internet email and Usenet news. It also can accept connections over the Internet, either in command-line mode (if you have a shell account) or with the graphical client (if you have a MacTCP-based Internet connection).

Note

Reportedly, having MacTCP 2.0.4 or later is important for making this connection.

You can connect to only a few NovaLink systems over the Internet. It's simply a matter of knowing the Internet address and switching to MacTCP in the Settings dialog. I presume that many more have UUCP connections to the Internet for retrieving Internet email and Usenet news (see figure 9.24).

Reportedly (I haven't tried this), if you connect to a NovaLink BBS that has full Internet connections, you can also telnet out of it, which is a nice touch—and a useful feature for a BBS to offer.

Note

*The public BBS that I connected to over the Internet, Global Democracy Network (**chrf.gdn.org**), is a non-profit human rights organization. It works with members of parliaments around the world to institutionalize human rights protections and increase democracy. Along the way, they're trying to get these members of parliament to become Internet users—a laudable goal. Two other NovaLink systems currently accessible on the Internet are **mpd.amaranth.com** and **infoport.com**.*

There's not much else to say about Internet connections via NovaLink systems, except that the process seems to work and is relatively speedy, considering the nice graphical interface. You can contact ResNova Software, the makers of NovaLink, at **sales@resnova.com** or **info@resnova.com**. You can get the NovaTerm client program from any NovaLink BBS, or on the Internet as:

```
ftp://ftp.tidbits.com/pub/tidbits/tisk/bbs/nova-term-31.hqx
```

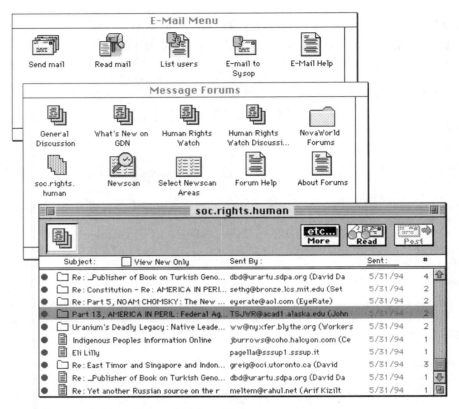

Figure 9.24 *Email and news in NovaLink*

Public Address

Public Address is a new BBS that, as we go to press, isn't out of beta testing yet. It sounds as though, for a character-based BBS, it will have some neat features, but what sets it apart from Hermes and Second Sight (the other major character-based BBS programs around) is that it can be accessed over the Internet via Telnet. There's not much more than that to say, until some bulletin boards using Public Address open up for Internet access.

TeleFinder

I haven't used TeleFinder much, mostly because I don't hang out on the BBS scene. It's a graphical interface BBS that (with additional software, called InterFinder, from Andreas Fink of Microframe) can connect to the Internet to send and receive email and news (see figure 9.25).

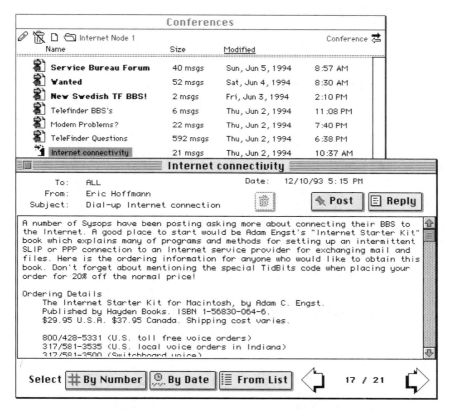

Figure 9.25 *TeleFinder Internet Connectivity discussion (and no, I didn't fake the screenshot—it really said that!)*

TeleFinder has one of the most interesting graphical interfaces I've seen—it actually takes over your monitor and sort of reproduces the way the Finder looks. It confused me a bit, at first. I have two monitors on my Mac, so TeleFinder Pro seemed to move a bunch of my desktop icons around whenever I was in the TeleFinder application.

Note

> The BBS package (host and client) is called TeleFinder Group Edition. The freely distributable client program that's generally customized for a specific BBS is called TeleFinder User. The more full-featured shareware ($20 if you want the documentation) client and terminal emulator is called TeleFinder Pro.

You can connect over the Internet to a TeleFinder BBS in command-line mode (all of these graphical BBS programs also offer straight character-based modes) by telnetting to **spiderisland.com**. You need special software to use the graphical interface over a MacTCP-based Internet connection (although Spider Island is working on eventually getting their graphical client software to work over a normal shell account). That software, called NetConnect TCP, creates a virtual "port" that you can select instead of the modem or printer port when you're configuring TeleFinder Pro (see figure 9.26). From the Special menu, choose Change Port after installing NetConnect TCP in your Extensions folder.

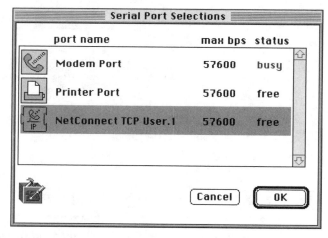

Figure 9.26   TeleFinder Pro's Change Port dialog

Once you've selected that port, you can configure TeleFinder Pro to "dial" a TeleFinder Pro BBS. Click on the port icon for NetConnect that appears in the lower left of the screen, and create a new Service. In the Service Information dialog, replace the phone number with either the IP number of the machine or the at sign and Internet name of that machine (see figure 9.27).

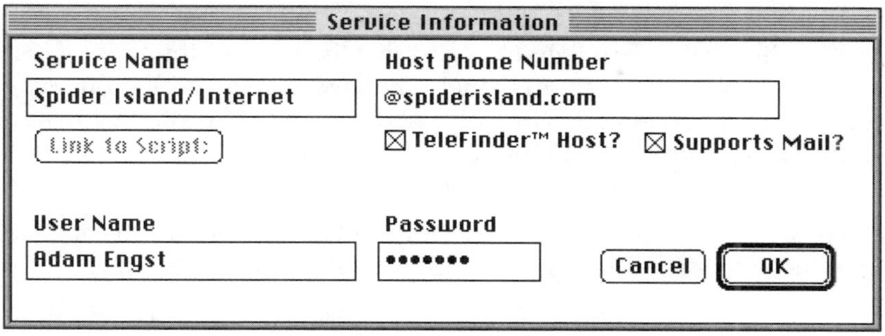

Figure 9.27   *Configuring TeleFinder Pro for the Internet*

So, to connect to Spider Island's own BBS over the Internet, I told the TeleFinder Pro software (via NetConnect TCP) to "dial" **@spiderisland.com**, which it did, complete with faked modem messages and everything. Once I was connected, everything worked as I expect it does when you dial in via modem. The speed, even over a relatively slow PPP connection, was quite good.

Eventually, Spider Island hopes to build the NetConnect TCP functionality into its program, so you don't have to mess around with installing additional software. As more inexpensive Internet connections appear, I expect we'll see many more of these graphical bulletin boards appearing on the Internet. If nothing else, supporting a number of modems and phone lines isn't cheap, so using the Internet might even be cheaper for many.

For more information about TeleFinder Pro, contact Spider Island Software at **support@spiderisland.com**. You can retrieve the TeleFinder Pro client software on the Internet at:

```
ftp://spiderisland.com/TFPro.2.2.3.sea
```

In theory, the NetConnect TCP software should also be at **spiderisland.com**, but it was in a beta revision when I was writing this, so I can't give you a URL for it.

Wrapping Up Commercial Online Services

Although I cannot recommend any of them as a replacement for a full MacTCP-based Internet connection, the commercial online services provide an easy way to dip into the Internet without diving headfirst. The liability of taking the dip in favor of the dive is that you'll quickly find that, in terms of Internet access, the commercial online services are extremely shallow. A number of bulletin boards have gained full Internet access in recent months, and I expect more to appear all the time. Since most bulletin board systems charge little or nothing for access, they can be a great way to obtain inexpensive Internet access.

Enough talking about limited access, though, let's move on to Unix shell accounts, which for Macintosh users, are as powerful as they are ugly.

Shell Access

Welcome to 1980! In this chapter I take you on a fast flight, first through the few Macintosh programs that can work over a Unix command-line interface (usually known as a shell account) and then through the Unix command-line interface itself, where I glance briefly only at the commands you absolutely need to know. Why the perfunctory look? Because to a novice user, Unix seems—to steal a quote—nasty, brutish, and short. I know only enough Unix to get by as a user; I never pretend to have more knowledge than that. The amount of Unix I know is what I've picked up here and there, often seemingly by osmosis. Once or twice I've come close to being sucked in by Unix's elegant power—elegant, that is, if you're a programmer, which I'm not.

Note

How can you tell if you already have a shell account? Simple. If you use a terminal emulator like MicroPhone or ZTerm to connect, once you're connected if you type Unix commands on a command-line, then you're using a shell account.

My mixed experiences with Unix have endeared me to the few programs that manage to work over the same connection that I would normally type cryptic commands—but let's take a look at them in a minute. First, I want to introduce you to a program that could seriously shake up the Internet world, The Internet Adapter, or TIA.

Note

If you don't intend to ever use Unix or get a shell account with an Internet provider, I strongly recommend that you skip this chapter, remembering only that it's here should you need it later on in your Internet wanderings.

The Internet Adapter

The Internet Adapter is so new that I had to sign a non-disclosure agreement even to talk about it with the folks who have created it. Luckily, it's due to be released between the time I write this and the time this book should hit the shelves, so Cyberspace Development gave me permission to write about TIA here.

On various different occasions, I've seen postings wondering why it is that someone hasn't written a program to enable graphical programs that normally require a MacTCP-based connection to work with a normal shell account. In fact, there are a number of these types of programs in the works, mostly from large Internet providers like Pipeline and Netcom, but they generally use a proprietary protocol for talking to the host machine, which means that you can't use the standard Macintosh Internet programs like Eudora, Anarchie, and MacWeb, which I talk about at length in chapter 13. Instead you must use the graphical client software provided by the same people who created the proprietary protocol.

I don't approve of this method of providing Internet access for two reasons. First, and most importantly, you're seriously limited in your choice of software for any particular task. With a full MacTCP-based connection, I can choose between Anarchie and Fetch, Mosaic and MacWeb, Eudora and VersaTerm-Link, NewsWatcher and InterNews and Nuntius. In fact, I may even use multiple programs for the same thing—I like and use both Anarchie and Fetch for different types of FTP tasks. You lose that flexibility when you're locked into a proprietary solution. Second, the Internet is a vast and fast-moving place, and new capabilities appear all the time, generally supported first, and often best, by freeware and shareware programmers. If you're locked into a specific proprietary program, there's no way you could use Cornell's Internet videoconferencing software, CU-SeeMe, play Stuart Cheshire's wonderful Bolo tank game, or check the weather with Chris Kidwell's MacWeather. All of those programs depend on the standard TCP/IP protocols that the Internet relies on, and these proprietary programs, useful as they may be, generally don't give you a standard TCP connection to the Internet.

TIA Basics

Such is not the case with The Internet Adapter. TIA is a relatively small (about 250K) Unix program that you run on your normal Unix shell account, and it acts as a SLIP emulator. In other words, after you install TIA on your shell account, running TIA turns your shell account into a SLIP account for that session. Although a TIA emulated-SLIP account is not quite the same as a real SLIP account, TIA's SLIP emulation is completely standard in terms of working with MacTCP-based software on the Mac (or WinSock if you use a Windows machine).

Just to repeat myself then, with the addition of a single Unix program that Cyberspace Development plans to sell for $25, you can turn your plain old shell account into a whizzy new SLIP account and use all of the MacTCP-based software I discuss in chapter 13. I realize this all sounds a bit like a Ginsu knife commercial (did I mention how TIA can cut beer cans too?), but if the reports I hear are true, TIA is going to seriously shake up the industry.

Note

To use the graphical software I discuss in chapter 13 with a TIA account, you must still have MacTCP and a version of SLIP installed. Don't worry about it because both MacTCP and InterSLIP come with this book!

Think about it. If a provider charges $20 per month for a shell account and $30 per month for a SLIP account, what response will they have to an individual buying a $25 piece of software to avoid giving the provider an extra $10 per month? Or more aptly, what about providers that charge $20 per month for a shell account but $2 per hour for the use of a SLIP account? Suddenly TIA could pay for itself in 13 hours of use for the individual, but the provider would lose big bucks. Of course, it wouldn't be technically difficult for the provider to outlaw (and erase copies of) TIA, but doing that would be horrible public relations and would alienate many users. The most rational approach I've heard yet came from a provider who plans to support TIA (small providers can purchase TIA for use by all users on a single machine for about $500), and charge a little more for a TIA emulated-SLIP account than a shell account, but less than a real SLIP account.

TIA will become popular instantly at sites that either aren't commercial, or that don't have much money to buy the expensive terminal servers that make real SLIP accounts easily possible. Since Cyberspace Development sells TIA to individuals, suddenly individual users have the choice of whether or not they get a SLIP account, whereas in the past, if the machine didn't support SLIP, that was the end of the story. I heartily applaud putting power in the hands of the individual.

TIA Details

Note

The details that follow about how TIA turns your shell account into a SLIP account may not make much sense if you haven't looked through chapter 12 yet—don't worry about it and just skip them unless you're interested in how TIA works.

Bear in mind that I haven't worked with TIA yet—it's not officially out, but it has been tested by many users at a large Internet provider. Nonetheless, here's what I know about how TIA works.

You do not get your own IP number that uniquely identifies your Mac on the Internet while you're connected, as you do with a real SLIP account. Instead, TIA uses the IP number of the machine your shell account is on, and "redirects" traffic back at you (this is the magic part). If you must enter an IP number in some software, any number like **1.1.1.1** should do fine—it's just a dummy address.

Note

The fact that you don't get your own IP number means that you cannot set your Mac up as an FTP server, for instance, since there's no IP number for an FTP client somewhere else to connect to.

Again, if you're not already familiar with SLIP and the like, this won't make much sense, but TIA's performance is reportedly good, faster than normal SLIP in fact, and about as fast as Compressed SLIP, or CSLIP. Future releases will support CSLIP and even PPP, and will reportedly increase speed by 10 to 20 percent. TIA doesn't create much of a load for the host machine, although slightly more than a real SLIP account, mostly because when you use SLIP, you're not usually running programs on the host machine, but are just using the network connection.

Installing TIA on your Unix shell account is not a trivial task, since you must install the proper version for the version of Unix running on your host machine. Cyberspace Development has ported TIA to a number of versions of Unix and many more are on the way. If you don't know what version of Unix is running on your shell account, Cyberspace Development has a simple program that can find out the information for you, or you can look up your provider's Unix type in a database it is building. Essentially then, you retrieve the proper version of TIA via FTP, Gopher, or the Web, and then launch it. (For evaluation purposes you can get a free version and test it for a while—contact Cyberspace Development for an evaluation code.) Needless to say, in normal usage, you would script your SLIP program to log in to your shell account, and then run TIA to start up the SLIP emulation, but it's possible to do it manually as well, I imagine.

You will be able to order TIA on the Internet itself if you wish, or other mechanisms will be available for those who dislike ordering on the nets. For more information, you can send email to **tia-info@marketplace.com** or connect to **marketplace.com** over the Web or via Gopher or FTP.

```
http://marketplace.com/
```

```
gopher://marketplace.com/
```

```
ftp://marketplace.com/
```

Serial Programs

Creating a program to act like a monkey and type the appropriate commands on the Unix command-line is quite a bit more difficult than it might sound. The main problem is that a surprising number of variations on Unix exist in the world, and even different sites running the same flavor of Unix may have their machines set up differently. The situation gets worse when new versions of Unix programs appear with slightly different commands or slightly different results to old commands. It's a programmer's nightmare.

Note

I use the term "serial program" to refer to any program not based on MacTCP that can dial an Internet host of some sort, log in, and then provide you with a graphical interface to an Internet service like email or Usenet news. These serial programs come in two main types—some work with normal shell accounts, whereas others require their own dedicated account of some sort.

Thus, the few programs that can exist in this harsh environment have evolved some similar methods of coping. Almost without exception, they work by relying on the user to get them properly connected to the remote system. From there they take over, usually connected directly to the appropriate server port for email or news or whatever. I say "whatever," but in fact, with one exception, the only two types of programs that work on Unix shell accounts are email programs like Eudora, a few newsreaders, and email and news modules in MicroPhone Pro. The exception is Homer, a client program for IRC, or Internet Relay Chat.

Actually, there are two other applications, WorldLink and Pipeline, that provide graphical Internet access without using MacTCP or any form of SLIP or PPP. WorldLink, from InterCon Systems provides Internet email, Usenet news, and anonymous FTP. Pipeline provides access to more Internet services than WorldLink, although not all the ones you might want to use. I talk about these programs first, because although they're not as flexible as a full shell account, they're easier to use and quite powerful for what they do. After that, I move on to the programs like Eudora and MacNews that can be configured to work with many existing shell accounts.

WorldLink

WorldLink is an oddity, in part because it has so many features for email and news, but provides no other Internet services past a form of FTP-via-email. It's also an oddity because it's both a software package and a ready-made account from PSI, one of the largest Internet providers, and comes complete with a long list of phone numbers you can dial anywhere in the world to connect to your WorldLink account. As I said, WorldLink does only email, news, and FTP, so if you want to use Telnet, Gopher, WAIS, or the World-Wide Web, move on because WorldLink doesn't support those protocols.

It's not surprising that WorldLink avoids the Internet services that require TCP/IP connections. Since it's a completely off-line application—you read and write email and news off-line, queue up FTP requests, and when you're ready, you connect and send them all out. At this point, the WorldLink software also retrieves any new email, news, or files waiting to come in. It's an efficient use of the modem and of the host computers, which is one reason the WorldLink accounts are so reasonable (ranging from $9 to $29 per month).

Installation and Setup

Configuring WorldLink is simple. Launch the program and fill in the fields for your userid, name, and modem configuration. If you click OK before finishing, never fear, you can always select Configure from the WorldLink menu later (see figure 10.1).

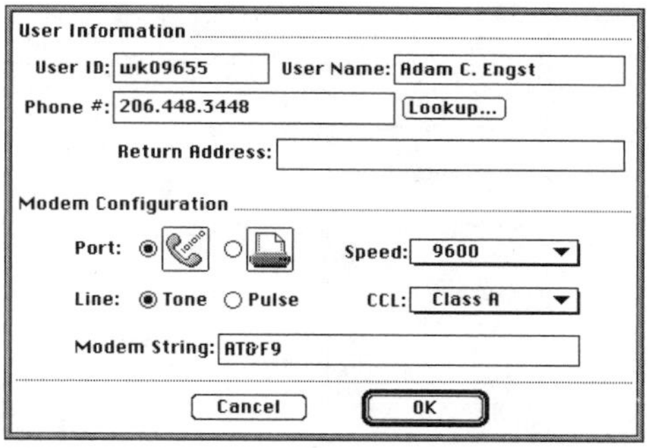

Figure 10.1   *WorldLink Configuration dialog*

One of the most interesting things about WorldLink is that it carries its own list of telephone numbers around with it. This not only makes finding your local telephone number simple, but also makes WorldLink an ideal package for someone who travels constantly—there's likely to be a local access number near you in most parts of the country (and possibly in many parts of the world, although those numbers cost more to use). You can limit the list by high speed numbers, low-speed numbers, the free Class A numbers, and so on; and you can sort the list in several different ways to make finding the right number easy (see figure 10.2).

While we're configuring things, go to the Edit menu and choose Subscribed Newsgroups. WorldLink brings up its News Groups window, and clicking on the triangles reveals the hierarchical structure of the newsgroups. When you see a group you want to read, click on it and drag it from the right-hand list into the left-hand list, as I've done for some of the Macintosh newsgroups (see figure 10.3).

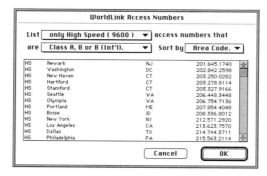

Figure 10.2   *WorldLink Access Numbers*

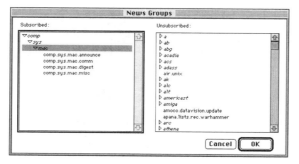

Figure 10.3   *WorldLink News Groups window*

Basic Usage

To create a new text document, email message, or news posting from the File menu, choose New. WorldLink brings up a dialog asking which of the three you'd like to create. Click on the Mail Message button and click OK. WorldLink then brings up a plain text window in which you can type your message. It's a basic text editor that isn't limited to 32K of text. (I pasted in 150K of this chapter just to see if it could handle that much. It could.) Once you've typed your message, click the Send button in the upper left-hand corner of the window to bring up the Send dialog box (see figure 10.4).

The Send dialog box has some nice features, like a pop-up menu for different signatures (you define them by choosing Message Signatures from the Edit menu), a pop-up menu to archive the message in a mailbox, and a scrolling list on the right-hand side of the dialog, which holds the contents of your currently selected address book. Once you're done addressing the message, click on the Send button to queue it up for sending.

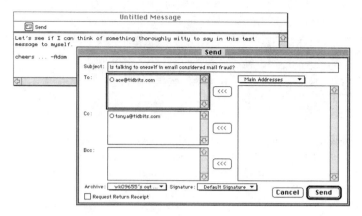

Figure 10.4   *WorldLink email message*

Posting a news article is essentially the same process, although the Post dialog looks rather different from the Send dialog to accommodate all of the different options for Usenet. You can either type in a newsgroup name manually, as I did for **halcyon.test**, or you can drag it over from the right-hand list of your subscribed newsgroups (see figure 10.5).

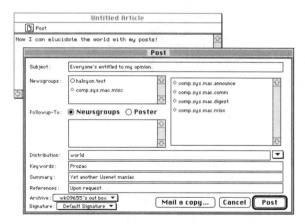

Figure 10.5   *WorldLink news article*

Note

If you've done something stupid, like I did in this message (posting a test message to **comp.sys.mac.misc***), you can't, as far as I can tell, delete a posted message from within WorldLink. If you switch to the Finder and look in the User folder (that lives in the same folder as the WorldLink application), you find an Articles To Be Posted folder that contains the errant posting. Just throw the bad posting in the trash from there. Also in the User folder is a Mail folder which contains a similar Messages To Be Sent folder.*

Reading messages in WorldLink is quite easy as well—from the Mailboxes menu, choose List Mailboxes. Double-click on a mailbox to open it then double click on a message in that mailbox to read it (see figure 10.6). From within the message you can print the message, refile it in a different mailbox, reply, forward or resend it.

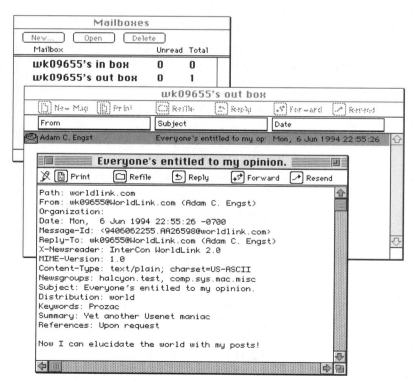

Figure 10.6   WorldLink mailboxes and messages

WorldLink has the capability to request files via FTP, and of course, you can always use Archie via email to help out. I tend to think that WorldLink's FTP feature is only slightly less frustrating than using an FTPmail program, because it's so hard to get everything just right when you can't see what you're looking for. If you know what you are looking for though, you can simply fill in the host name, path, and file that you want, click either the Text or the Binary button, and queue up your request (see figure 10.7).

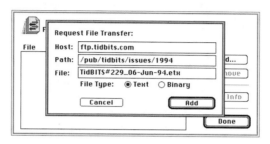

Figure 10.7   *WorldLink FTP requests*

Once you've created your mail and news article and queued up your FTP request, you must connect to the WorldLink host at PSI to send everything. From the WorldLink menu, choose Connect, at which point WorldLink presents you with the Connect dialog (see figure 10.8). It provides fields for username and password, and gives you options for what actions you'd like to perform upon connecting. For instance, if you're trying to catch a plane but must get some email out, you'd probably want to do nothing but send the email. Whereas if you're sitting bored in a hotel room, you may as well get and send everything you can. Clicking on the Connect button establishes the connection.

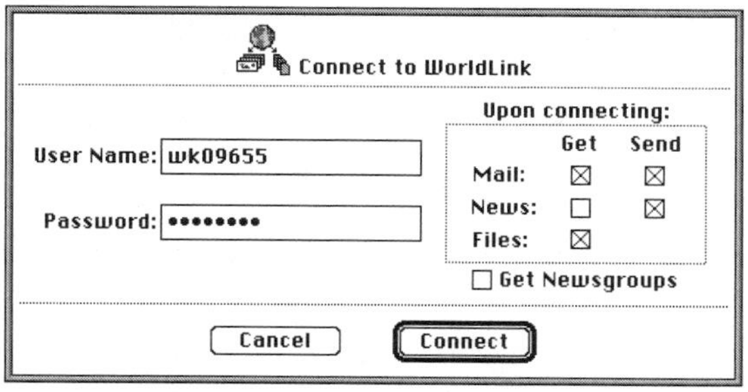

Chapter 10
Shell Access

Figure 10.8   *WorldLink Connect dialog*

Special Features

One of WorldLink's nicest features is its Global Mail Actions dialog (see figure 10.9). It enables you to filter incoming and existing messages based on information in the header and, if you want, the body of the message. You can check for mail from certain people, to certain people, about certain subjects, and so on. Once it has found them, WorldLink can mark those messages, delete them, move them, or copy them. All email programs should have such features, although as far as I can tell, WorldLink can't use actions on incoming news postings, which is where they're really necessary.

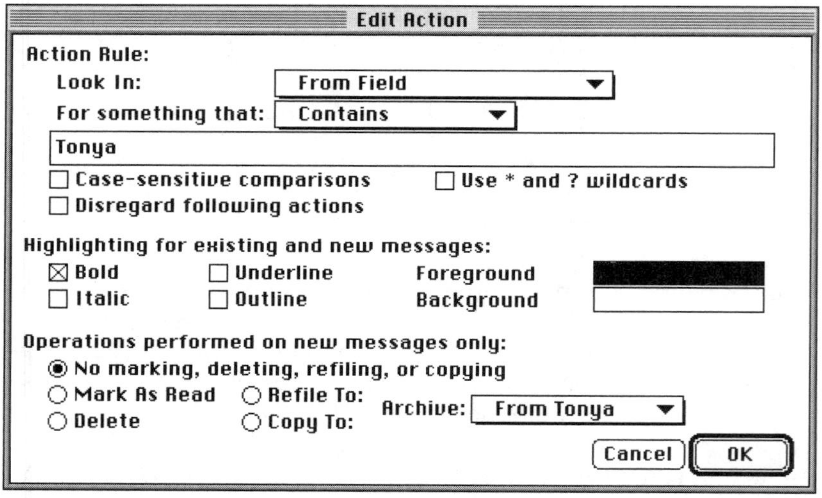

Figure 10.9   WorldLink Mail Actions dialog

Other nice features abound. You can open and edit text files of any size, which is often handy when working with email. You can even have WorldLink use Apple's PlainTalk technology to speak the text of your files and messages, which can either be a lot of fun, or a way to truly irritate the people on the plane next to you (if you're working on a PowerBook). You can change the font and size your messages display, and WorldLink includes a Find feature for finding text within a message.

WorldLink can automatically forward mail to a specified address (and can include a different return address) if you're using it as an auxiliary email program from home, for example, and want things to always end up in your office email.

You can have multiple mailboxes and move messages between them as you like. Within the mailboxes, you can search for messages and sort the existing ones by order received, date, from, subject, color, or even text style.

Finally, WorldLink provides a nice status window that tells you what it thinks is going on (see figure 10.10). I especially like the Misc Information field with the icon of J.R. "Bob" Dobbs of the Church of the Subgenius since it cycles between the time and date, disk usage, memory usage, and Bob saying, "Hi There."

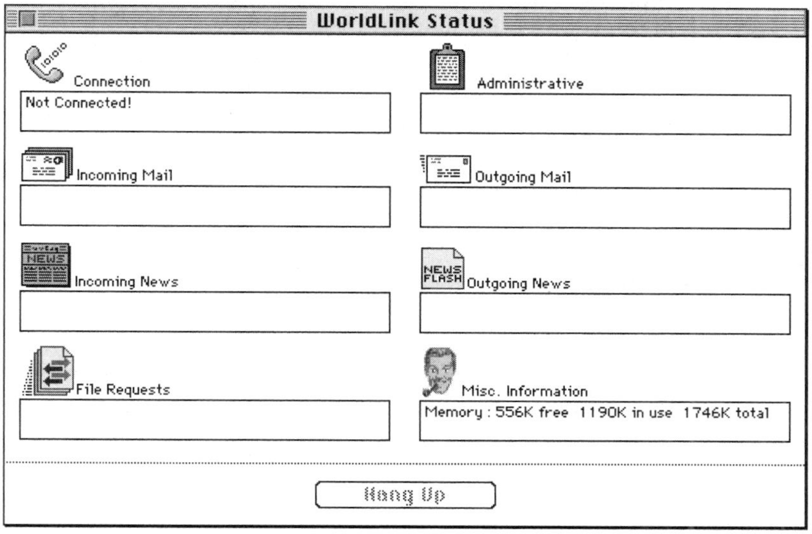

Figure 10.10 *WorldLink Status window*

Overall Evaluation

I admit it. I'm surprised at how nice WorldLink has become. It previously seemed like a stripped-down version of InterCon's TCP/Connect II package, but with the addition of a number of clever touches, I think it becomes something to seriously consider if you only want email, news, and the occasional file via FTP. If you travel frequently and have trouble staying in touch while on the road, I think WorldLink is the ideal way to go.

There are a few rough edges left in WorldLink. I occasionally had menus display the wrong information, and my Font menu never showed up at all. You have no choice about your userid, the assigned userids aren't easy to remember for your recipients, and they don't particularly have that cachet of exclusivity about them. But who cares about exclusivity when you have more or less unlimited usage for prices ranging from $9 to $29 per month?

Administrative details

WorldLink comes in both Mac and DOS flavors in the same box, which is unusual. Still, having both versions accessible could be handy at times in this increasingly cross-platform world. WorldLink's manual is in the process of being rewritten, so I'm not sure what it looks like, but the online documentation (which is what you'll have if you travel with it) is quite good. Until InterCon rewrites the documentation, the printed manual doesn't particularly apply—you can tell when the new documentation will start shipping with the package, because the manual will no longer provide both Mac and DOS information in the same book.

WorldLink costs about $30 (you can get it directly from Mac's Place at a discount), and there are several different monthly pricing schemes for access from PSI, based on what you get and at what speed you get it. The Lite service, which includes only email at 2,400 bps costs $9 per month, or $19 per month at 9,600 bps. Basic service including Usenet news and the anonymous FTP feature costs $19 per month at 2,400 bps and $29 per month at 9,600 bps. If you get more than 50M of news and files via FTP, PSI charges an additional $1 for each megabyte more than 50. For more information about WorldLink, contact InterCon at `sales@intercon.com` or at:

InterCon Systems Corporation
950 Herndon Pkwy., Ste. 420
Herndon, VA 22070
703-709-5500
703-709-5555 (fax)

Pipeline

Remember those proprietary protocol programs that I mentioned earlier? Well, one has just peeked into the Macintosh world, and although it's not quite available yet, I imagine it will be soon. Pipeline is the graphical client software for an Internet provider called Pipeline in New York City (they're in the PDIAL List in appendix C), and Pipeline has licensed its proprietary protocol and client software to a few other providers around the world. In addition, Pipeline is adding support for SprintNet, the telephone network that many of the commercial online services use, so you could access Pipeline's N.Y.C. service from anywhere in the country, although for a higher fee than a local call.

Pipeline mostly covers email, news, Talk, Archie, FTP, and Gopher, with some additional features thrown in to handle weather reports, Internet Relay Chat, and straight VT100 terminal emulation (see figure 10.11).

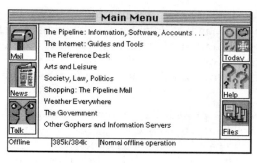

Figure 10.11   *Pipeline Main Menu window*

The basic choices in the middle of the Main Menu window are essentially Gopher items; clicking on them opens another window displaying the next Gopher menu, and so on. Displaying text items works as you'd expect, and should you download images in GIF or JPEG format, Pipeline automatically displays them for you.

Clicking the buttons on the side of the Main Menu window brings up additional windows dedicated to specific functions. A number of features weren't available in the beta version I used (and the interface may change slightly), but it appears that Pipeline has some nice touches, especially in the email section (see figure 10.12).

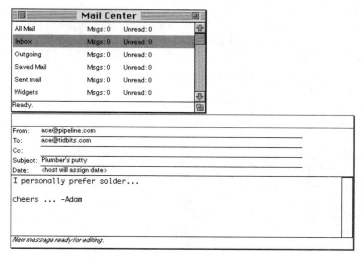

Figure 10.12   *Pipeline Mail windows*

Your Mail Center window provides access to multiple mailboxes, and the new message window has a clean look to it. Most interesting, though, are the Views, which enable you to sort and display mail according to various criteria. Pipeline can automatically uuencode or binhex binary files when they're attached to outgoing mail, and automatically decode them when they're attached to incoming mail.

The News Center window provides much the same display as the Mail Center window, but for newsgroups, of course. There also appears to be a fairly tight integration between the parts of the program that make sense to integrate. For instance, you can mail the contents of a Gopher window to someone with the Mail Contents command in the Readers menu.

My main complaint with Pipeline is merely that it's not a MacTCP-based application, so if you use it, you cannot browse World-Wide Web servers (until support for them is added to the Pipeline application).

Note

Apparently, the PC version of the Pipeline software is almost complete in terms of Web support, so it will probably migrate to the Mac version at some point.

Similarly, you'll probably never be able to play the Bolo tank game or use the CU-SeeMe videoconferencing application. And if you don't happen to like Pipeline's FTP interface as much as Anarchie's, too bad. That aside, it looks like Pipeline provides a nice interface to a subset of common Internet services, and if Pipeline support is all your local provider offers, Pipeline is definitely the way to go. Pipeline is slightly easier to configure than MacTCP and SLIP or PPP, because all you have to enter is the telephone number, modem initialization string, and username and password. But given the choice, I'd rather spend more time setting up MacTCP and friends to have increased flexibility.

Note

The Pipeline folks tell me that although the plans lie somewhere in the future, it's not technically all that difficult to modify the Pipeline software so it works with a Telnet tool over MacTCP-based connections. So perhaps one day my complaints will be moot.

Eudora

Steve Dorner's free Eudora email program easily wins the award as the most flexible of communications programs. I also mention it in chapter 11, UUCP Access, because it can work with a UUCP transport program to read and write email using UUCP. But for the moment, if your Unix host supports protocols called *POP* (Post Office Protocol) and *SMTP* (Simple Mail Transport Protocol), Eudora can work with the Communications Toolbox (standard in System 7) to dial your Unix host and send and receive email.

Note

Although the Communications Toolbox (CTB) code is built into System 7, the CTB tools necessary to use Eudora and many other CTB-aware programs are not included with System 7. You can get them from your Apple dealer, with many communications programs like SITcomm or MicroPhone II, or on the Internet at:

```
ftp://ftp.apple.com/dts/mac/sys.soft/netcomm/basic-conn-set-1-1-1-
image.hqx
```

This file is in Apple's disk image format, which requires a utility called Disk Copy to transfer to floppy before installing. Disk Copy is available at:

```
ftp://ftp.apple.com/dts/utils/diskcopy-4-2.hqx
```

Eudora was designed to work with MacTCP (and works best in that environment), so I don't explore the details of using the program until the MacTCP chapter. However, let's go over the details of setting it up to work over the modem. You might also want to refer to the excellent Eudora documentation, available at:

```
ftp://ftp.qualcomm.com/mac/eudora/documentation/
```

Also be sure to poke around in the folder dedicated to storing pre-configured plug-ins for different providers and types of server hardware at:

```
ftp://ftp.qualcomm.com/mac/eudora/dialup/
```

Installation and Setup

There are two drawbacks to using Eudora with the Communications Toolbox. First, it's slower than via MacTCP. Second, it's flakier. But if it's a choice between suffering with the Unix mail program or putting up with a few Eudora connection problems, I'll take Eudora any day.

Ask your system administrator if your Unix host supports POP for receiving mail and SMTP for sending mail, and if so, if he knows of anyone using Eudora on the Macintosh already. Once one person has customized Eudora to work on a specific machine, the customized file can work for everyone. Assuming that you're a pioneering sort and are the first one to attempt this task, read on.

To modify Eudora to work over a CTB connection, you first need a template called Unix Navs, which you can edit and place in your Preferences folder within the System Folder. It's available at:

```
ftp://ftp.qualcomm.com/mac/eudora/dialup/servers/unix.hqx
```

This template contains the conversation Eudora expects to have with your Unix host to set up everything. Such send-and-expect conversations are generally called *chat scripts,* and are most heavily used in the UUCP world. Unfortunately, you must use ResEdit, Apple's free resource editor, to edit the Direct Unix Navs file. If you don't have ResEdit, you might be able to get it from a power-user friend or your Apple dealer or from:

```
ftp://ftp.apple.com/dts/mac/tools/resedit/resedit-2-1-1.hqx
```

Launch ResEdit and from the File menu, select Open. Open the Unix Navs file. Double-click on the lone STR# resource, then double-click on the Navigate In resource, and the third window you see should have strings that you can modify (see figure 10.13).

If you have the Eudora manual, you can see that my settings differ from the standard ones that Steve Dorner provides. My Unix machine provided a different prompt, so I had to change the third string, and the program named srialpop in his example is named spop on my machine. You may or may not need to change those lines—I imagine many people don't.

The first line says Eudora should send two returns (the \r strings) and then expect (the \e string) to see the "login:" string. The second line says that Eudora should send your username (the \u string, determined from a setting inside Eudora itself) and a return, and then expect to see "ssword:", which is of course the tail end of "Password:". The third line says that Eudora should send your password (\p, again determined inside Eudora) and three returns; then expect to see the > sign at the end of the prompt (that's what my prompt looks like anyway; your prompt may look different). Once Eudora sees the prompt, you're properly logged in. The fourth line says Eudora should execute the spop program by sending "exec spop" and a return. You must ask your administrator what the name of the spop or srialpop program is on your machine if neither of those possibilities work.

Note

*You might be able to determine if your Unix machine uses either of these programs. Login normally, and when you're at the Unix prompt, type **srialpop** or **spop**. If the machine complains, "Command not found" you know that's not it. If it does something, like change the prompt, you may have hit the right program.*

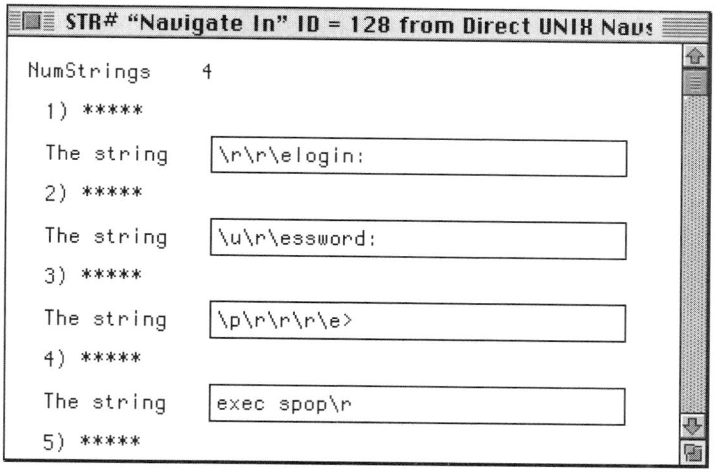

Figure 10.13 *Eudora Unix Navs config in ResEdit*

If necessary for your system, you can add another line by clicking on the five asterisks after a number, then going to the Resource menu and choosing Insert New Field(s). After you have configured these four strings to match your login procedure, save the file and quit ResEdit.

Next, launch Eudora. Go to the Special menu and choose Configuration (see figure 10.14).

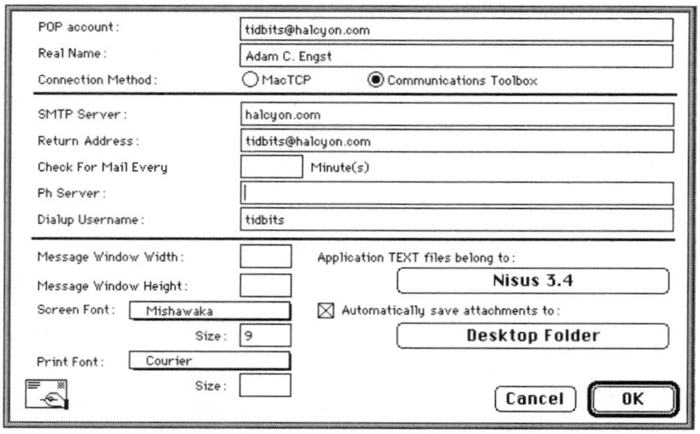

Figure 10.14   Eudora POP configuration

Although you see many fields here, you have to worry only about a few at the top. The POP account field holds your POP account, which is usually your email address on the machine running POP. I presume you can figure out what to enter in the Real Name field. Then click on the Communications Toolbox radio button because you want to connect via modem. You may also need to fill in the SMTP Server field, but in all likelihood this field is just the name of your host machine; Eudora can figure that out from the POP account if you leave the SMTP Server field blank. Finally, although I've filled in my Return Address field, you don't have to if it's the same as your POP account. Eudora fills in the address automatically.

Note

If you make a mistake in entering your email address manually into the Return Address field, no one can send you email until you fix it, because email will seem to come from an invalid address.

That's all the configuration that's necessary to basically use Eudora, so click the OK button to save the changes. From the Special menu again, choose Communications (see figure 10.15).

Eudora displays the standard Communications Toolbox configuration dialog. First, from the Method pop-up menu, choose Apple Modem Tool. If you don't have it, get it from a friend, your dealer, or the Internet because it's supposedly the only one that works with Eudora. It's hidden in with the Communicate Lite demo at:

```
ftp://ftp.tidbits.com/pub/tidbits/tisk/term/communicate-lite-demo-101.hqx
```

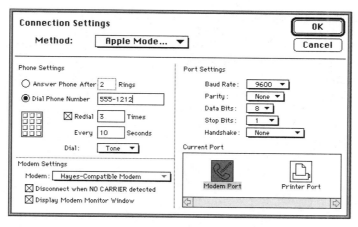

Figure 10.15   *Eudora Communications settings*

Type your host machine's phone number in the Dial Phone Number field. From the Modem pop-up menu, choose your modem or, if it's not listed, the closest one you can find. If all else fails, you can choose Custom and configure it yourself (this means figuring out the proper initialization string with the help of your modem manual). Finally, check the Port Settings to make sure your modem is talking at the right speed with No Parity, 8 Data Bits, 1 Stop Bit, and the appropriate Handshaking for your modem and cable. After you're done, click the OK button to save your settings.

Note

Three things are important for using Eudora in dialup mode. First, you must have a modem with either hardware or software error correction. Dropping a single character at the wrong time can kill the POP and SMTP protocols that Eudora relies on. Second, the remote host must have hardware flow control that actually works, which isn't always true, and unfortunately, you have little or no control over this. Third, you must configure the Mac properly and know your model's limitations. Steve Dorner suggests using software error control (even if the modem supports hardware error correction) on PowerBooks with high speed modems using the Apple Modem Tool 1.5 because the small hardware buffer in the serial chip can overflow at times.

Now comes the fun part—troubleshooting. From the File menu, choose Check Mail to make Eudora to dial out and retrieve your mail. Eudora displays a progress dialog at the top of the screen that shows what's happening, one line at a time. Those lines flash by quickly, though, so watch carefully so you can see where it might get stuck (if your host actually requires more information during login, for instance). If you're lucky, it works on the first try, but don't count on it. If it works, you should read the section on Eudora in chapter 13 to figure out how to use the rest of the program. If it doesn't work, retrace your steps, try to figure what's going wrong, and if all else fails, try asking on the newsgroup `comp.sys.mac.comm`. Many experienced Eudora users hang out there.

Other Options

Ray Davison of Simon Fraser University has modified a version of Eudora to be even more scriptable with the C- language. I haven't tried to use this version at all, since I had no trouble with Eudora's relatively simple setup. But if you have a particularly weird configuration that you must script around, it might be worth checking out at either:

```
ftp://ftp.tidbits.com/pub/tidbits/tisk/term/eudora-142-sfu.hqx
```

```
ftp://ftp.sfu.ca/pub/mac/eudora/
```

If all else fails, long-time Macintosh user and net citizen Murph Sewall posted this extremely clever suggestion. It's a major kludge, but if it works for Murph, it might work for you. First, download Tim Endres' Termy terminal emulator. It's at:

```
ftp://ftp.tidbits.com/pub/tidbits/tisk/term/termy-23.hqx
```

Then, configure both Termy and Eudora to use the Serial tool (not the Apple Modem Tool, as Eudora would normally want). When you want to connect, launch Termy, open a terminal window, and dial your modem by hand to connect with your Unix host. Proceed through the login normally until you get to the prompt that wants you to telnet to your POP server. Close Termy's terminal window. Since you're using the Serial tool, the modem should stay connected, and if it doesn't, check your modem initialization string to make sure the modem ignores DTR (usually something like &D0). After you close Termy's window, switch to Eudora, and use it as you normally would. Murph notes that you may have to use ResEdit to modify a resource that controls the format of the Telnet command—the instructions for that are in appendix D of the Eudora manual.

When you're done, you can either open a new terminal window in Termy to log out, or you may be able to get the Eudora NavigateOut resource properly configured to log out for you (but if you could do that, one would think you could get the NavigateIn resource properly configured as well). The more I think about it, the more I think this is a serious hack, but you might even be able to automate it with a program like QuicKeys if you have to use it.

Internet Email & Internet News

I cover MicroPhone Pro 2.0's Internet Mail and Internet News modules in this section because they have a number of features in common—most notably that both are written in MicroPhone Pro's scripting language, and both work over either a dialup connection to a shell account, or a MacTCP connection. (Since I consider them more important in their shell mode, I cover them here as opposed to in the MacTCP chapter.) Both are bundled with MicroPhone Pro 2.0 itself—there is no way to get them separately.

Installation and Setup

Since both Internet Mail and Internet News are MicroPhone Pro modules, double-clicking on either one launches MicroPhone Pro. The first part to configure is the Communications Settings; from the Settings menu choose Communications. When the Communications Settings dialog appears (see figure 10.16), choose the appropriate Method, Modem Driver, Port, and Port Settings for your modem (you can consult the MicroPhone Pro documentation if you have questions about these settings).

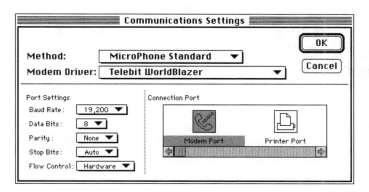

Figure 10.16   *Communications Settings dialog*

Once you've ensured that the settings are correct, close the Communications Settings dialog and double-click on Internet Mail in the Finder. Click on the Setup button in the Internet Mail window. Click the Use Communications Settings button, enter the appropriate phone number, login name, password, and host name.

Note

Although you can use the auto-connect feature and have it delete mail from the server, I recommend that you leave those settings off until you have everything working properly.

If you wish, click Edit Signature to create a signature file for your email messages. When you're done, click OK to save your settings (see figure 10.17).

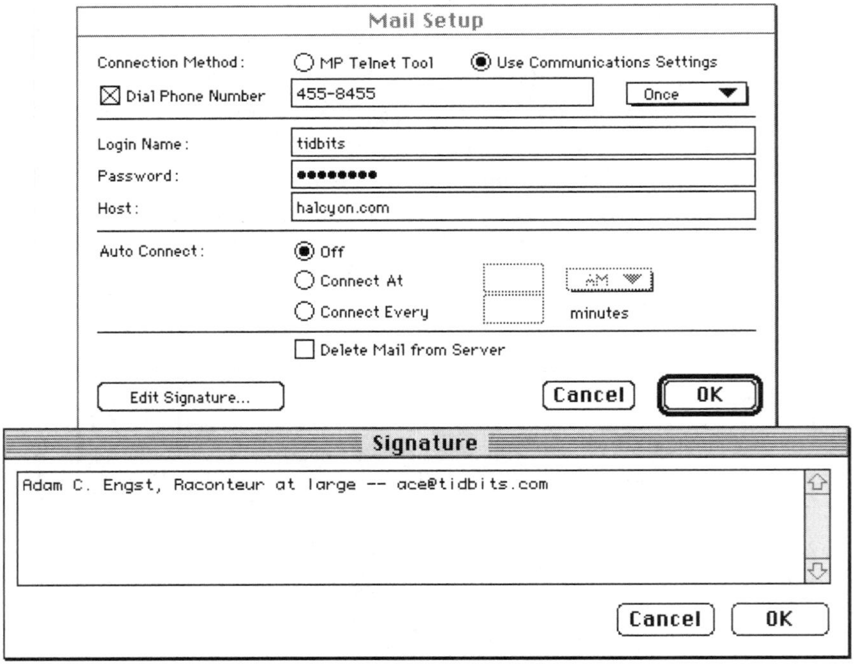

Figure 10.17 Internet Mail Setup

Next, double-click the Internet News icon in the Finder to launch it. Internet News brings up your Newsgroups window. Click Setup in the upper right-hand corner. In the Internet News Setup window that appears (see figure 10.18), click Use Communications Settings and fill in the appropriate information. You should know most of this information, except perhaps your NNTP Server (for Usenet news) and your SMTP server (for sending email). If you don't know what to enter, ask your system administrator for the names of your local NNTP and SMTP servers. Edit your signature if you want—the signature you used for Internet Mail is stored separately. When you're done, click OK to save your changes.

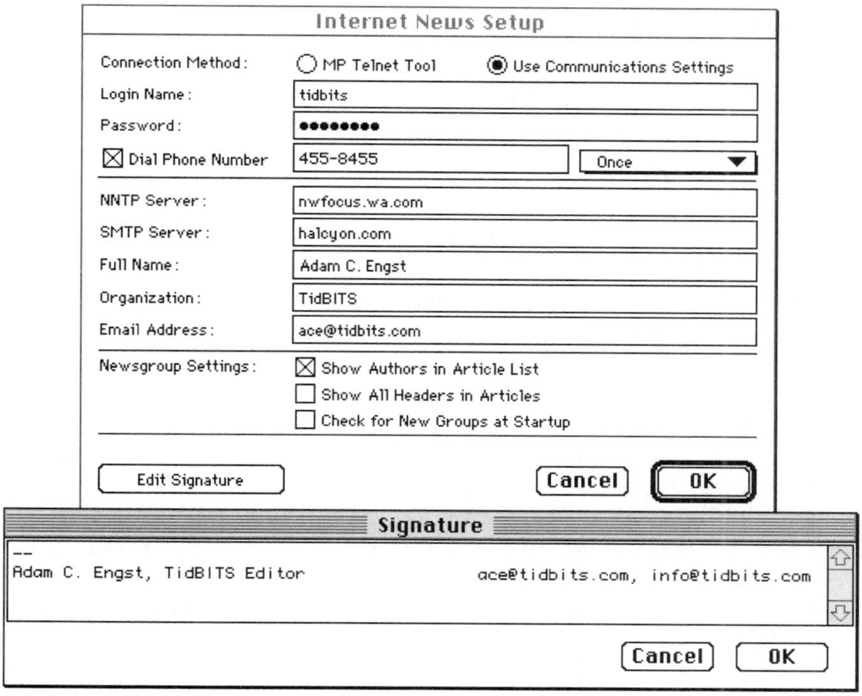

Figure 10.18   *Internet News Setup*

While we're configuring things, let's subscribe to some newsgroups. In the Newsgroups window, click the Edit button to bring up the Edit Newsgroups dialog (see figure 10.19).

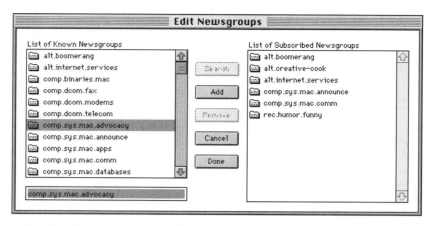

Figure 10.19   *Internet News Edit Newsgroups dialog*

Internet News only knows about a few newsgroups initially, although you can retrieve the entire list or search through all known newsgroups to find others. To subscribe to a newsgroup, select it in the left-hand list and click the Add button. If you know the name of the group you want, you can also type it in the text entry field and click the Add button to add it directly. When you're done, click the Done button to save your changes.

Basic Usage

Not surprisingly, Internet Mail and Internet News have relatively similar interfaces, and both are easy to use. You can almost completely ignore the menus for both—since they're MicroPhone Pro modules, the menus apply only to MicroPhone Pro itself and not to the modules. Also, Internet Mail is an off-line mail reader—you read and write email off-line and then connect to send replies and receive new messages. That's handy, especially if you pay for your connection time.

Internet Mail opens a Mail window when you launch it—you do almost everything from this mail window (see figure 10.20). The Mailbox menu enables you to switch between your multiple mailboxes (but there's no way to show more than one onscreen at a time), and all of the basic functions are handled by the buttons.

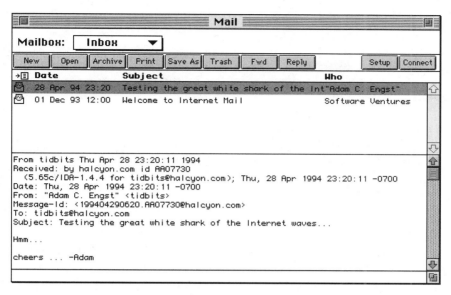

Figure 10.20 *Internet Mail main window*

For the most part, it's hard to explain the buttons any more than their names. The New button opens a new window for a new email message; the Open button opens the selected message in its own window (although just selecting the message displays the message body in the Mail window's lower pane); the Archive button brings up a dialog that enables you to save the message in one of your mailboxes (or create a new one); the Print, Save As, and Trash buttons do just what you'd expect; and the Fwd and Reply buttons are for your basic forwards and replies. Setup we've already seen, and I get to Connect in a minute. Let's look now at the New Message window created by clicking on the New button (see figure 10.21).

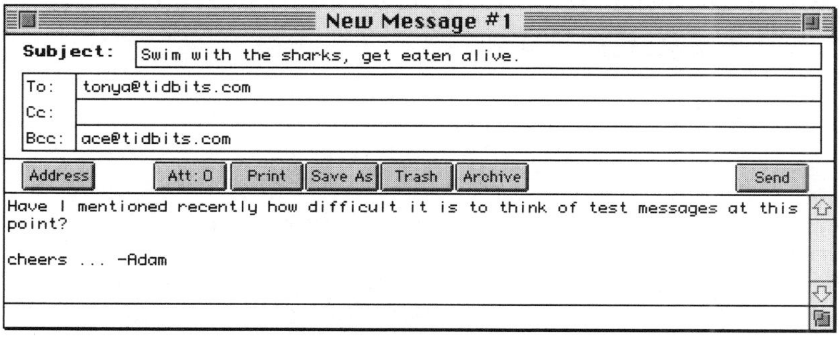

Figure 10.21 *Internet Mail New Message window*

The basic fields for email are all here, along with some familiar buttons (Print, Save As, Trash, and Archive) and a few new ones. The Address button opens a dialog containing your address book for storing frequently used addresses; the Att button, when clicked on, brings up a Standard File dialog for attaching a file to the message; and finally the Send button, once you're all done, queues the message for sending.

Note

Although not mentioned anywhere in the documentation, the Internet Mail attachment feature does automatically binhex binary attachments before sending them.

Once back in the Internet Mail window, click the Connect button to establish a connection and send your mail. Internet Mail prepares your mail for sending (I suspect it's inserting hard returns after wrapping the lines to the appropriate length, since its editor doesn't force you to enter them yourself), then sends the message. If you have an attachment, it uploads it with ZMODEM. The weird part comes next. Rather than rely on your host having a POP server (as Eudora does) to receive mail and give it to you when you log in, Internet Mail relies on your host using what's called a *mail spool* file, which is where POP would normally leave the mail anyway. Internet Mail downloads your mail spool file with ZMODEM and parses it back on the Mac to extract the letters. I don't know how many Unix machines have a mail spool file system for storing email that don't also have a POP server.

Note

Internet Mail tries to download with ZMODEM first, since it's the best protocol. If it can't find ZMODEM on the host, it tries Kermit, and if Kermit's not there, it uses the cat command in Unix, which just sends the file as text. A future version will reportedly support POP as well.

Unlike Internet Mail, Internet News is not an off-line newsreader. To do anything other than configure it or subscribe and unsubscribe to newsgroups, you must be connected to your host. When you click the Connect button in the Newsgroups window, Internet News connects to your host, then to the NNTP server and updates the list of new articles. If you've set it to do so, it also brings in a list of any new groups that have arrived and lets you subscribe to them if you wish. Once Internet News has finished updating the newsgroups, it displays the number of new articles in the Newsgroups window (see figure 10.22).

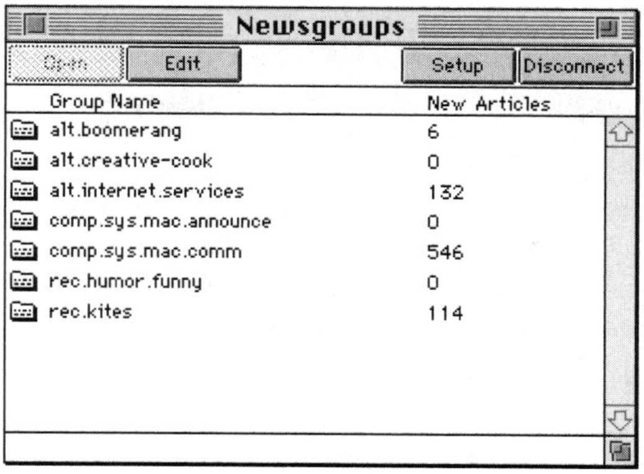

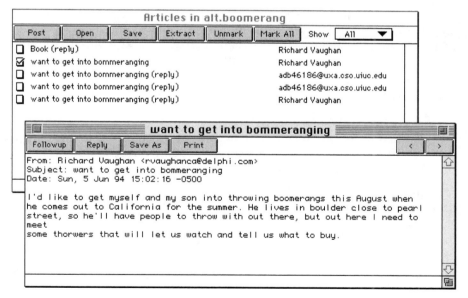

Figure 10.22 *Internet News Newsgroups window*

To read the messages in a group, select it and click Open, or double-click on the group name. Internet news goes out to the NNTP server and retrieves the subjects and authors of the new articles. Double-clicking on an article opens a new window and displays that article (see figure 10.23).

Figure 10.23 *Internet News Articles windows*

Once again, the buttons across the top of these windows are easy to figure out. The Post button opens a new window for you to create a new posting to that group; the Open button retrieves the article from the server and displays it; the Save button saves the text of the message to a file; the Extract button extracts a binary file; the Unmark button marks a message as unread; and the Mark All button marks everything in the group as read. In the window displaying the article itself, the Followup button posts a follow-up to the newsgroup; the Reply button replies via email, the Save As button saves the message to a file; the Print button prints the message; and the left/right buttons take you to the previous or next message.

Internet News is a simple newsreader without many features or quirks—there's nothing much hidden below the surface of the interface.

Overall Evaluation

MicroPhone Pro is a relatively expensive communications package, and I wouldn't buy it just for Internet Mail and Internet News. Although they seem to work pretty well, there are a number of rough edges (dialogs that aren't quite right) and other possible problems (the attachment that I sent to myself was corrupted during sending). More seriously, Internet Mail and Internet News, because of their heritage as MicroPhone Pro scripts, are slow as molasses, not in transfers so much, but in basic execution. There's no way around that. However, on the positive side, they're easier to set up than Eudora and most of the newsreaders, and if you do use MicroPhone Pro for other purposes, they're a welcome addition.

Administrative Details

You can purchase MicroPhone Pro 2.0 mail order for about $150, and if you have questions or comments about it, you can contact Software Ventures at `microphone@svcdudes.com` or at:

Software Ventures
2907 Claremont Ave.
Berkeley, CA 94075
510-644-3232
510-644-1325

MacNews

Matt Hall has created a clever $15 shareware application called MacNews, that gives you a graphical interface for reading Usenet news even, if you only have a shell account. The only requirements are that your machine run an NNTP (Net News Transport Protocol) server or that your machine be able to contact one over the Internet.

Note

*Finger **lesikar@tigger.stcloud.msus.edu** for a list of public NNTP sites, but be aware that, as with all Internet services, this one may go away at some point in the future.*

MacNews is decidedly a work-in-progress, and it lacks enough features that you may not want to lose all those you enjoy in a Unix newsreader like rn or nn in terms of reading and killing threads. On the other hand, the ability to use cut and paste and look at a Macintosh interface may outweigh the disadvantages. It's your call.

Installation and Setup

The first thing to configure in MacNews is the modem. From the Control menu, choose Modem. MacNews displays the Modem Settings dialog (see figure 10.24).

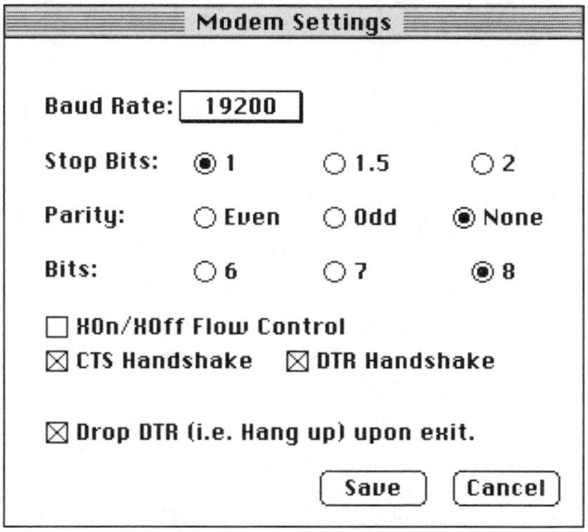

Figure 10.24 *MacNews modem settings*

You probably know how to set the appropriate speed and the rest of the options, but the standards are usually no parity, 8 data bits, and 1 stop bit. Handshaking settings depend entirely on your modem and cable. Click on the Save button to save your changes.

Then, if you know of a local NNTP site, choose Add Site from the Control menu and type its name (or IP number, if you know that). If you don't know about a local NNTP site, don't fret because the default settings list two sites that you can use, although they aren't guaranteed to work.

Basic Usage

To start a connection, go to the Control menu, and from the Connect To hierarchical menu, choose one of the sites listed. MacNews opens a dull-looking Console window that you can type in, and type in it you will, because MacNews has no facilities for automatically logging into your host machine. You probably know how to do this by now, but in general, you should initialize your modem, dial the phone, enter your username when connected, enter your password when asked, and make sure you're at the normal prompt. Then click on the Initialize button, at which point the Console window disappears, to be replaced by the Groups window, which lists the groups you read (see figure 10.25).

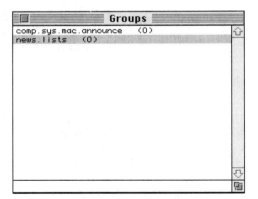

Figure 10.25   *MacNews Groups window*

If there aren't any groups listed, you can go to the Control menu and choose Newsgroup Maintenance, where you see one of the problems with MacNews. To subscribe to a group, you must type its name exactly into a text field and then click the Add button. (Check appendix B for a complete list of newsgroups to see what you might want to read and how their names are spelled.) You can also remove groups from this dialog.

Double-clicking on a group name brings up the Articles window (see figure 10.26).

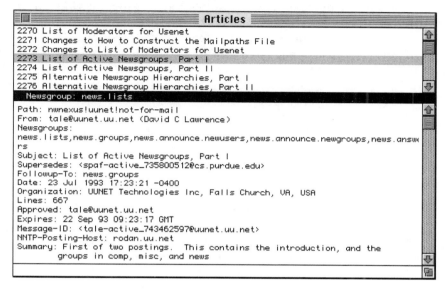

```
┌──────────────────────────────────────────────────────────┐
│ ☐ ▤▤▤▤▤▤▤▤▤▤▤    Articles    ▤▤▤▤▤▤▤▤▤▤▤                 │
│ 2270 List of Moderators for Usenet                    ⬆   │
│ 2271 Changes to How to Construct the Mailpaths File   ▓   │
│ 2272 Changes to List of Moderators for Usenet         ▓   │
│ 2273 List of Active Newsgroups, Part I                ▓   │
│ 2274 List of Active Newsgroups, Part II                   │
│ 2275 Alternative Newsgroup Hierarchies, Part I            │
│ 2276 Alternative Newsgroup Hierarchies, Part II       ⬇   │
│ ▬▬▬ Newsgroup: news.lists ▬▬▬▬▬▬▬▬▬▬▬▬▬▬▬▬▬▬▬▬▬▬▬▬▬▬▬▬▬   │
│ Path: nwnexus!uunet!not-for-mail                      ⬆   │
│ From: tale@uunet.uu.net (David C Lawrence)                │
│ Newsgroups:                                               │
│ news.lists,news.groups,news.announce.newusers,news.announce.newgroups,news.answe │
│ rs                                                        │
│ Subject: List of Active Newsgroups, Part I                │
│ Supersedes: <spaf-active_735800512@cs.purdue.edu>         │
│ Followup-To: news.groups                                  │
│ Date: 23 Jul 1993 17:23:21 -0400                          │
│ Organization: UUNET Technologies Inc, Falls Church, VA, USA│
│ Lines: 667                                                │
│ Approved: tale@uunet.uu.net                               │
│ Expires: 22 Sep 93 09:23:17 GMT                           │
│ Message-ID: <tale-active_743462597@uunet.uu.net>          │
│ NNTP-Posting-Host: rodan.uu.net                           │
│ Summary: First of two postings.  This contains the introduction, and the │
│          groups in comp, misc, and news              ⬇   │
└──────────────────────────────────────────────────────────┘
```

Figure 10.26   *MacNews Articles window*

If the newsgroup contains more than 50 articles, MacNews asks how many you want to bring in first (up to a maximum of 200). Its speed isn't amazing, but it was fast enough that I didn't mind waiting for it to bring in the 57 messages in **news.lists**.

The Articles window is divided into two panes. If you drag the black separator bar, you can resize the panes to your liking. There are no shortcuts for switching between articles yet, but the help, available in the Apple menu, mentions some shortcuts for scrolling through an article.

When you have a newsgroup window open, you can choose Post or Followup from the Control menu. Both ask you for some basic header information and open a text editing window for you to enter your message. Followup quotes the current article by default, although you can delete it if you want. Although it is not impressive by any stretch, you've got a Macintosh editing environment here, which is far easier to figure out and use than any of the Unix environments.

Overall Evaluation

Now you've learned about all there is to MacNews. As I said, it is a work-in-progress, and with a number of extra features and a cleaner interface, MacNews could become a popular program. But for the time being, it's an excellent start, and if Unix newsreaders give you hives, then it's worth checking out. And, of course, if you find it useful enough to use, pay your shareware fee so that Matt stays interested enough to keep developing MacNews.

Administrative Details

MacNews is $15 shareware, and you should send checks and money orders to:

Matt Hall
4 Wood Duck Lane
St. Paul, MN 55127

MacNews is available on the Internet at:

```
ftp://ftp.tidbits.com/pub/tidbits/tisk/term/mac-news-11.hqx
```

NewsWatcher SFU

Ray Davison of Simon Fraser University has modified a version of John Norstad's excellent NewsWatcher program to work over a serial line, much like Eudora. I haven't tried configuring it, in large part because it sounds like it's a bit harder than would be ideal, but it works on very much the same lines as Eudora and requires the same sort of chat script edited in ResEdit. For details on using NewsWatcher (note that this is an older version than I talk about later), check out the MacTCP chapter. You can contact Ray at **ray@sfu.ca** (and he specifically notes that any troubles you have with this version of NewsWatcher should be reported to him, not John Norstad). You can find the SFU version of NewsWatcher at:

```
ftp://ftp.sfu.ca/pub/mac/newswatcher/
```

```
ftp://ftp.tidbits.com/pub/tidbits/tisk/term/news-watcher-20d17-sfu.hqx
```

TheNews

I want to like Bill Cramer's TheNews because it's the most flexible of the newsreaders, and I approve strongly of flexibility. Like Eudora, it can work with shell accounts, UUCP accounts, and MacTCP-based connections. However, I just have trouble with TheNews every time I try to use it, so I won't look at it in detail. I cover using it in the UUCP chapter because UUCP is probably where it competes the best (its only competition being rnMac).

Configuring TheNews to work over a CTB-connection to a shell account isn't easy. It requires editing the program or its preferences file with ResEdit (you must set a "transfer media flag" in ResEdit before it even works in CTB mode) and bumbling through the same sort of chat scripts you must use in Eudora and the SFU version of NewsWatcher. I really wish these programs would come with simple interfaces for entering exactly the same information as you enter in ResEdit—it can't be that hard.

There's no point in me merely repeating what Bill outlines carefully in appendix F of the TheNews manual that you get with TheNews, so I'll settle for warning you that TheNews is slow to start up, at least over a MacTCP-based connection, because it seemingly downloads the full list of newsgroups every time you launch the program. It's also memory-hungry—it comes configured to use 1,300K in the Finder's Get Info window, but it crashed when trying to sort the full group list at that setting. I upped it to 2,000K. After I opened a newsgroup with about 30 articles in it and tried to read a small article, TheNews warned me that it was running out of memory. I then increased the memory allocation to 3,000K, and it seemed to behave a bit better, although I didn't test it extensively.

You can reach Bill Cramer via email at **cramer@world.std.com**, but he doesn't promise to reply to your message immediately. If you want to download TheNews 2.33 from the Internet, it's at:

```
ftp://ftp.tidbits.com/pub/tidbits/tisk/term/the-news-233.hqx
```

The standard shareware price for TheNews is $25 (although volume discounts are available), and shareware checks go to:

TheNews
1257 Worcester Road, Suite #196
Framingham, MA 01701

Homer

Homer comes in two forms—one for MacTCP-based connections and one for those who only have a Unix command-line account. I won't go into the details about Homer much here (check in the MacTCP chapter), but suffice it to say that if you plan on using IRC and you have a Mac, Homer is the way to go (see figure 10.27).

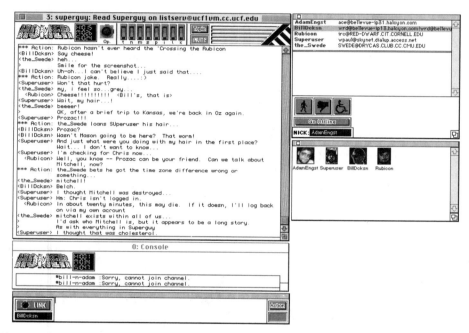

Figure 10.27 *Homer*

The serial version of Homer has a number of limitations not shared by the MacTCP version. First off, it's not compatible with the Communications Toolbox, which means you cannot use any Macintosh that uses a GeoPort Telecom Adapter instead of a modem (the GeoPort Telecom Adapter only works with the Communications Toolbox). Second, you must use a Unix account—no other operating systems will work—that can telnet out to a remote host. Third, some versions of Telnet simply don't cooperate with Homer and echo back everything you say and generally won't work properly.

To configure the serial version of Homer, launch the program, go to the Connection menu, then choose Communications Options to modify the communications settings to match your modem. After that, use the dumb terminal window (Homer automatically opens it at startup) to dial your modem, connect to your

Internet host, and login to your Unix account. Once you're in, from the Actions menu select Start IRC Session, at which point everything works as it normally does in Homer with the MacTCP version. However, when you're done, select Close IRC Session from the Actions menu rather than trying to quit IRC manually.

Homer is $25 shareware from Tob Smith, who you can reach via email at **tob@zaphod.ee.pitt.edu**. You can find Homer on the Internet at either:

```
ftp://zaphod.ee.pitt.edu/pub/
```

```
ftp://ftp.tidbits.com/pub/tidbits/tisk/term/homer-0934.hqx
```

Terminal Emulators

I don't want to get into reviewing all of the possible terminal emulation programs available for the Macintosh because there are a ton of them. However, you must have a terminal emulator to talk to a Unix machine, so here are those I've heard of and/or used.

Note

A number of these terminal emulators work through the Communications Toolbox and require CTB-tools. Luckily, except for Termy, they all ship with a full complement. You can find additional freely distributed tools in:

```
ftp://ftp.tidbits.com/pub/tidbits/tisk/ctb/
```

SITcomm

Aladdin Systems came out with SITcomm early in 1994, and it won a loyal following immediately because it's a small, relatively simple terminal emulator that still sports some neat features. SITcomm is completely CTB-aware, and comes with all the connection and transfer tools that you might want. Perhaps most importantly, though, SITcomm is completely Apple event-driven, which means that you can script it in either AppleScript or Frontier. And you can even record AppleScript or Frontier scripts from within SITcomm. SITcomm's cool features include a slick address book that simplifies connecting to many commercial services, automatic compression and expansion using Aladdin's StuffIt technology, and voice feedback. SITcomm costs about $50 mail order, and you can contact Aladdin at **aladdin@well.sf.ca.us**.

Note

Povl Pedersen has written a clever little AppleScript droplet that you can drop files onto, at which point the droplet launches SITcomm, logs on to your shell account, sends the files as news articles, and disconnects. You must have AppleScript, make some local changes inside the script, and create a new service called "SendNews" in SITcomm that uses the Text tool to send files. The droplet is on the Internet at:

```
ftp://ftp.tidbits.com/pub/tidbits/tisk/term/sitcomm-sendnews-as.hqx
```

MicroPhone

MicroPhone is probably the most popular terminal emulation package on the Macintosh and comes in a number of different forms, including MicroPhone LT for about $40, MicroPhone II 5.0 for about $120, and MicroPhone Pro 2.0 (which includes fax software and various Internet tools) for about $150. MicroPhone is a powerful, fully-laden terminal emulator with its own scripting language. Contact Software Ventures at **microphone@svcdudes.com**.

VersaTerm

VersaTerm has garnered a reputation among those who know, for having the most solid terminal emulations, especially for the stranger types of graphics terminals from Tektronix. The $120 VersaTerm itself supports a number of emulation modes, but the $170 VersaTerm Pro adds even more emulations. Both programs come with the VersaTilities, a collection of TCP/IP tools and utilities, which you can also buy separately for about $85 (all prices mail order). Contact Synergy at **maxwell@sales.synergy.com** for more information.

Crosstalk for Macintosh

I know little about DCA's Macintosh version of the popular PC Crosstalk communications programs, except for the fact that is CTB-aware and comes with a slew of CTB tools (22 tools for emulating different terminals and 15 tools for transfer protocols). If you're having trouble finding a terminal emulator to emulate a specific type of terminal, it might be worth checking out Crosstalk for Macintosh. Crosstalk also has its own powerful scripting language and generally costs about $120 (mail order).

Communicate & Communicate Lite

Communicate and Communicate Lite are relatively simple terminal emulators from Mark/Space Softworks that use the Communications Toolbox. Communicate Lite is pretty-much bare bones terminal emulation; the more-powerful Communicate adds features like an In/Out box for queuing up uploads and downloads, scripting via AppleScript or Frontier, automated virus detection, and spell checking via Apple events. Contact Mark/Space Softworks at **mspace@netcom.com**. There's also a version of Communicate localized for French, if you would prefer that. You can find a demo of Communicate Lite that has the Save, Save As, Open, and Session Directory commands disabled at:

```
ftp://ftp.tidbits.com/pub/tidbits/tisk/term/communicate-lite-demo.hqx
```

Termy

Termy is an extremely simple, free terminal emulator from Tim Endres, the programmer behind InterCon's UUCP/Connect and the free TGE TCP Tool. Termy doesn't do much on its own, but is CTB-aware, so if you have Communications Toolbox tools, you can use them with Termy for a basic terminal emulation solution. You can find the latest version of Termy at:

```
ftp://ftp.tidbits.com/pub/tidbits/tisk/term/termy-23.hqx
```

You will need the basic CTB tools for Termy, and you can find those at:

```
ftp://ftp.apple.com/dts/mac/sys.soft/netcomm/basic-conn-set-1-1-1-
image.hqx
```

ZTerm

Although not CTB-aware, ZTerm has gained a loyal following among telecommunications users because of its simple interface and speedy ZMODEM transfer protocol. ZTerm is shareware from Dave Alverson, and is available on the Internet at:

```
ftp://ftp.tidbits.com/pub/tidbits/tisk/term/zterm-09.hqx
```

That's about it for the Macintosh programs—let's turn now toward the Unix shell account's command-line and discuss the various Unix programs that you use there.

Using Unix

I first experienced Unix at Cornell's Theory Center on a machine that was alternately known as **tcgould** or **batcomputer**, although everyone preferred calling it the **batcomputer**. I figured out the rn newsreader fairly quickly (due in part to its built-in help), and eventually worked my way through mail. I handled changing and listing directories, but it took me the longest time to figure out how to delete files. Eventually, I realized that I was able to FTP to my **batcomputer** account from an account on a different mainframe and then use FTP's aptly named delete command.

In the end, I tracked down a friend and asked him. "I realize everything in Unix has to be as few letters as possible," I said, "so I've tried every possibility I can think of, including erase, delete, kill, er, de, dl, kl; you name it, I've tried it." My friend looked at me and said, "Oh, it's rm, you know, for remove." Sigh.

Keep in mind that many different implementations of Unix exist. Although I've tried to stick to the commands that should work everywhere, there's no telling if your Unix machine reacts in the same way as mine. Consider yourself warned; I don't go into details of different implementations or quirks when one version of a program doesn't talk to another version of the same program or anything like that. I can't believe Unix people complain about the Mac. Actually, I can. Operating systems are like religions, and you can't account for them.

As in previous chapters, commands that you type **look like this** (and variables that you type like *look like this*) within regular paragraphs and **bold monospaced** within onscreen messages, whereas I don't mark the general names of the programs in any special way because the text would become ugly fast.

Basic Commands

I assume you understand the basics of logging into an account; the hard part is that you often must press Return before you see the login prompt. Minor problem, but it throws a lot of people. When you see the login prompt, type your username, and when you see the password prompt, type your password, which probably doesn't show as you type it. Okay, you're logged on now.

But wait! Different machines provide different prompts by default, which isn't a big deal, but it means that you definitely won't see the prompt that I get on my Unix account. Don't worry about the difference, and if you want to poke around, you almost certainly can find a way to change it. Consider this as an exercise left for the reader.

ls

The first command you need to know is one you'd never think of if you've only seen Macintosh computers. Apple's programmers had the amazing insight that you always want to know where you are and what files there are. If you open a folder, therefore, the folder's name displays, along with all the files in the folder. The listing of files in that folder always stays up-to-date.

In Unix, as in most command-line operating systems, you must specifically request a file list using **ls**, and if something in that list changes, you must request the list again to see the change. In other words, I guarantee the **ls** command will become ingrained into the very flesh of your fingers.

Note

*As you can tell, **ls** stands for "list," although in true Unix fashion, they took out half the letters to make it easier to type. In this respect, Unix is the opposite of French, where you seemingly have twice as many letters as you need.*

For those of you who have used DOS on IBM-PC compatible computers, **ls** is essentially the same as **DIR**. A directory listing might look like the following:

```
/d/tidbits/> ls
Mail                                mail
News                                nn.help
big-dummys-guide-to-internet.hqx
```

Almost any Unix command gains extra functionality if you use various options. I suspect this capability happened because someone said, "But I'd like to see my directory listing in Esperanto," and an enterprising Unix programmer said, "Hey, I can do that." So from then on, you typed **ls -e** to output the listing in Esperanto. (I'm kidding; by the way, I haven't the foggiest idea what **ls -e** does.) Just for fun, let's see.

```
/d/tidbits/> ls -e
ls: illegal option — e
Usage: ls [-abcdgiklmnpqrstuxABCFGLNQRSUX1] [-w cols] [-T cols] [-I pattern]
       [—all] [—escape] [—directory] [—inode] [—kilobytes] [—literal]
       [—numeric-uid-gid] [—hide-control-chars] [—reverse] [—size]
       [—width=cols] [—tabsize=cols] [—almost-all] [—ignore-backups]
       [—classify] [—file-type] [—ignore=pattern] [—dereference]
```

```
[—quote-name] [—recursive] [—sort={none,time,size,extension}]
[—format={long,verbose,commas,across,vertical,single-column}]
[—time={atime,access,use,ctime,status}] [—no-group]
[—help] [—version] [path...]
```

Oops, the **-e** option is one of the few that doesn't, in some way, modify the functionality of **ls**. Despite Unix's obtuseness, don't feel shy about trying things. After a while, you may even start to understand it.

I generally don't tell you about any of the options because you seldom need to use them, and you'd forget by the time you needed them anyway. However, **ls** has several important options that you may want to use at various times: **-a**, **-s**, and **-l**.

- The **-a** option shows all files, including ones that start with a period and don't show up if you just use **ls**.

- The **-s** option shows you the names of the files and also the sizes (usually in kilobytes, although sometimes in half-kilobyte blocks on older systems), which I consider essential information.

- The **-l** option outputs the listing in a long format that shows all sorts of information, including directory privileges and dates.

In addition, you can combine the options. If you want a long directory listing showing invisible files and the file sizes, for example, type **ls -al**. The directory listings below, slightly edited for clarity, show the different results:

```
/d/tidbits> ls -a
.                 .gopherrc        .msgsrc          .oldnewsrc       Mail
..               2 .gopherrc~       .newnewsrc       .pinerc          News
.addressbook      .letter          .newsrc          .profile         gopher
.cshrc            .login           .newsrc.bak      .rnlast          mail
.elm              .mailrc          .nn              .rnsoft          nn.help

/d/tidbits> ls -s
total 4
    1 Mail          1 News           0 gopher          1 mail           1 nn.help

/d/tidbits> ls -l
total 4
drwx------   2 tidbits      512 Aug 13   1993 Mail
drwxr-xr-x   3 tidbits      512 Aug 13   1993 News
-rw-r--r--   1 tidbits        0 Aug 17   1993 gopher
drwx------   2 tidbits      512 Aug 13   1993 mail
-rw-r--r--   1 tidbits      467 Oct 20   1993 nn.help
```

```
/d/tidbits> ls -al
total 292
drwxr-xr-x   7 tidbits        1024 Jun  4 16:39 .
drwxr-xr-x459 root           10752 May 30 08:59 ..
-rw-r--r--   1 tidbits          32 Jul 16  1993 .cshrc
drwx------   2 tidbits         512 Aug 13  1993 .elm
-rw-r--r--   1 tidbits         295 Aug 25  1993 .letter
-rw-r--r--   1 tidbits         126 Aug 25  1993 .login
-rw-r--r--   1 tidbits          79 Jul 16  1993 .mailrc
-rw-r--r--   1 tidbits           2 Jul 16  1993 .msgsrc
-rw-r--r--   1 tidbits           0 Jan 23 15:28 .newnewsrc
-rw-r--r--   1 tidbits       89768 Apr 19 21:42 .newsrc
-rw-r--r--   1 tidbits       89756 Apr 19 21:40 .newsrc.bak
drwxr-xr-x   2 tidbits         512 Apr 19 21:42 .nn
-rw-r--r--   1 tidbits        1546 Aug 13  1993 .pinerc
-rw-r--r--   1 tidbits         198 Jul 16  1993 .profile
-rw-r--r--   1 tidbits          55 Jan 23 15:04 .rnlast
-rw-r--r--   1 tidbits        9146 Jan 23 15:07 .rnsoft
drwx------   2 tidbits         512 Aug 13  1993 Mail
drwxr-xr-x   3 tidbits         512 Aug 13  1993 News
-rw-r--r--   1 tidbits           0 Aug 17  1993 gopher
drwx------   2 tidbits         512 Aug 13  1993 mail
-rw-r--r--   1 tidbits         467 Oct 20  1993 nn.help
```

cd

Along with typing **ls** to see the files in a directory, you also must move between directories. On the Mac, moving between directories is as hard as double-clicking a folder or as easy as clicking once on an already-open window. In Unix, however, you find yourself continually typing **cd** *dirname*, where *dirname* is the name of the directory you want to enter. Unfortunately, **cd** *dirname* enables you to go down the hierarchy only; to traverse back up, you type **cd ..** (that's two periods, which indicates the parent directory or, in other words, the one just above this one). In these two respects, **cd** works just as it does in DOS.

```
/d/tidbits/> cd News
News> ls -l
total 120
-rw-r--r--   1 tidbits      108106 Aug 13  1993 rn.help

/d/tidbits/News> cd ..
/d/tidbits> ls
Mail    News    gopher   mail    nn.help
```

As you can see, with the second command, I moved up from the News directory into my home tidbits directory.

You can travel down multiple directories with one command, just as you can, for example, open your disk on the Mac desktop, open the Applications folder, open the Nisus folder, and finally open the Macros folders. To do the same thing with a single command in Unix, you type something like **cd harddisk/applications/nisus/macros**. Typing this command is much like how the command works in DOS, although DOS uses the backslash rather than the slash.

You may find this capability useful when you know the entire directory path; however, if you don't know the path, you must suffer with typing **cd** *dirname* to change directories, **ls** to list the files so you can see where to go next, **cd** *dirname* to go into the next directory, **ls** to see the files, and so on. If only **cd** automatically listed the files in the new directory (wait, let me guess, there's probably an option for it to do that)!

One final note about **cd**. You often may find that you want to go right to the top of the directory, the equivalent of the window you see when you open your hard disk on your Mac. This directory is usually called the *root directory* because it's the base from which all the others spring.

Note

Yes, I know that roots aren't usually at the top, but it makes sense to say that you are going down when you delve into subdirectories, so you then must go up to get back to the top. This is Unix, and it's not my fault.

You bounce all the way to the top by typing **cd /**, but be aware that typing this command may take you higher than you thought.

```
/d/tidbits> cd /
/> ls
Mail          e           i           news-db        usr
News          etc         j           opr            var
a             etc.native  k           rhosts.hold    vmunix
archive       f           l           scratch
b             ferry       lib         sys
bin           g           mail        tmp
dev           h           news        ultrixboot
```

As you can see, I ended up at the top of the machine's directory structure, not in the tidbits directory I see when I first log in. In actuality, the directory you see when you log in to a Unix machine (your *login directory*) is a subdirectory in a larger structure. Unix enables you to navigate to any point in that structure.

With all the possible directories, you can get thoroughly lost quite easily. An important thing to remember is that typing either **cd** or **cd ~** returns you to your login directory. In my case, typing **cd** returns me to **/d/tidbits** from anywhere else on the system.

rm

After you know how to move between directories and see what's in them, you might want to delete files. I like using **rm** because I'm a clean, orderly person, and I get irritated when I know junk files are littering my directories, even when I can't see them (without first executing an **ls** command). Just type **rm** *filename*, where *filename* is the name of the file to delete, and poof, the file is gone. Some Unix systems may be set up to prompt you whether you want to delete the file; just press **y** in response to delete the file. You can set an option to avoid that silly question if you so choose.

```
/d/tidbits> ls
Mail        News          junk.file  mail        nn.help
/d/tidbits> rm junk.file
/d/tidbits> ls
Mail        News          mail       nn.help
```

You can use **rm** in two other useful ways. If you want to delete several files at once, no problem. Just type **rm** *filename1 filename2 filename3*, and so on. Unlike the Mac, Unix filenames can't have spaces, which is why the space works as the delimiter between each filename. If you want to be destructive, you can use *wildcards*, which are like one-eyed jacks in poker. If you snag a bunch of files from an FTP site, they all probably have the same extension—that is, the same last three letters after a period. To delete **junk.sit**, **trash.sit**, **garbage.sit**, **refuse.sit**, and **waste.sit** all at once, type **rm *.sit**. This command tells the machine to delete all files in that directory whose names end in **.sit**, no matter what comes before the **.sit**.

Note

*Be forewarned, though, if you delete a file with **rm**, it's toast, unlike the Mac where you can pull the file out of the trash can if you haven't emptied the trash yet. (This warning is not entirely true because some systems may offer a **recover** or **undelete** command, but you're on your own there.)*

more

Before you delete a file, you might want to see what's in it, assuming that it's a text file. On the Mac, you generally double-click on a file, or open it from within a word processor, to read it. In Unix, you use a program called **more** to display it on the screen, pausing after every screen so you can read it. (And yes, there's another program, cleverly called **less**, that does the same basic thing but is undoubtedly far better.)

Just type **more** *filename*, where *filename* is the name of the file you want to view, and poof, the file appears on your screen. At the bottom of the screen, more says something to the effect of **— More — (21%)** to indicate that you have more to read, and you are 21 percent of the way through. At this point you have three basic controls. You press Return to advance one line, the Spacebar to advance to the next page, or the **q** key to quit reading. Generally, you simply page all the way through the file, after which you're back at the normal Unix prompt, whatever that may be on your system.

```
/d/tidbits> more nn.help
      Release 6.4.16                                        NN(1)


      NAME
           nn - efficient net news interface (No News is good news)

      SYNOPSIS
           nn [ options ] [ newsgroup ¦ +folder ¦ file ]...
           nn -g [ -r ]
           nn -a0 [ newsgroup ]...

      DESCRIPTION
           Net news is a world-wide information exchange service covering
           numerous topics in science and everyday life.  Topics are organ-
           ized in news groups, and these groups are open for everybody to
           post articles on a subject related to the topic of the group.

           Nn is a 'point-and-shoot' net news interface program, or a news
  —More— (0%)
```

man

Earlier in this chapter, I mentioned that **rm** has an option that tells it not to verify with you each file to delete. How do you find out about that option? You can try typing **help**, but there's no point because standard Unix machines don't have a help command. Unix programmers apparently thought that help is for weenies, so they didn't bother. However, Unix programmers (at least the ones I know) hate looking things up, and as a result, Unix has its manual online.

Note

The Unix manual is not the warm and fuzzy work of a professional writer. In fact, the Unix manual is one of the most user-hostile documents I've ever had the displeasure to read. It can't quite compete with IRS documentation because, as much as the IRS tries to include cute examples about Betsy's Sewing Shop, you always get the impression that they want to say, "And because Betsy's Sewing Shop failed to file Form 1,463,994 'Unearned Income of Deceased Persons Temporarily Living on Other Planets,' Betsy is now doing five-to-seven for tax fraud. So don't try anything, buster!"

The online Unix manual is commonly referred to as the *man pages*, mostly because the Unix programmers felt like stripping the last half of the word manual when creating the command. To get more information about any (well, almost any) command in Unix, type **man** *commandname*, where *commandname* is the command you want to figure out. Understanding what you see then is up to you; if I understood it better, I wouldn't be writing this book. For instance, here's the start of the man page for **rm**:

```
/d/tidbits> man rm
                                                                        rm(1)

    Name
          rm, rmdir - remove (unlink) files or directories

    Syntax
          rm [-f] [-r] [-i] [-] file-or-directory-name...
          rmdir directory-name...

    Description
          The rm command removes the entries for one or more files from a
          directory.  If there are no links to the file then the file is
          destroyed.  For further information, see ln(1).
```

```
         The rmdir command removes entries for the named directories,
         which must be empty.  If they are not empty, the directories
         remain, and rmdir displays an error message (see EXAMPLES).

         To remove a file, you must have write permission in its direc-
         tory, but you do not need read or write permission on the file
         itself.  When you are using rm from a terminal, and you do not
         have write permission on the file, the rm command asks for con-
  —More— (24%)
```

This method of invoking **man** assumes that you know the name of the program you want help with. That's often not true, and **man** has an option that can possibly help in this case. To use this option, type **man -k** (or sometimes **apropos**) and the term you want to explore. You may find lots of junk, but you also may find a useful command. Or, as in my case, you may find a command such as **ils**, which looks useful but in fact hangs your account. Oh well.

```
/d/tidbits> man -k directory
basename (1)                  - strip directory names from pathname
cd (1)                        - change current directory
chdir (2)                     - change working directory
chroot (1)                    - change root directory for a command
chroot (2)                    - change root directory
dcheck (8)                    - check directory consistency
dircmp (1)                    - directory comparison
dirname (1)                   - deliver directory names from pathname
dtree (1L)                    - display directory tree structures
getcwd (3)                    - get pathname of working directory
getdirentries (2)             - gets directory entries in a generic directory
format
getwd (3)                     - get current working directory pathname
ils (1)                       - interactive directory browser and visual shell
mkdir (2)                     - make a directory file
mklost+found (8)              - make a lost+found directory for fsck
mknod (2)                     - make a directory or a special file
pwd (1)                       - print working directory
rmdir (2)                     - remove a directory file
scandir (3)                   - scan a directory
statmon, current, backup, state (5) - statd directory and file structures
unlink (2)                    - remove directory entry
uuclean (8c)                  - uucp spool directory clean-up
vtree (1)                     - print a visual tree of a directory structure
whois (1)                     - DARPA Internet user name directory service
ypfiles (5yp)                 - Yellow Pages data base and directory structure
```

Other Basic Unix Programs

Unix supports thousands of additional programs, and you may find that some commands exist in one flavor of Unix (a version created by a specific company), but not in all flavors. Following are a couple of the most useful programs that I might use if I used Unix. Remember, no guarantees this software is installed on your Unix machine.

sz and rz

Instead of just looking at text files on your Unix account, you probably want to download them to your Mac. Assuming the Unix machine you use has been set up well, you should have access to the **sz** program, which stands for "send ZMODEM." If you haven't heard of it before, ZMODEM is a common file transfer protocol that is generally unequaled for performance and reliability. Other protocols you may run across include XMODEM, YMODEM, and Kermit. As with modems, you must match protocols on both the Unix machine and in your Macintosh terminal emulator, so check to make sure that your emulator handles ZMODEM.

Note

Most terminal emulators, with the notable exception of VersaTerm, handle ZMODEM just fine. VersaTerm can use ZMODEM transfer tools if you happen to have one from another program like Aladdin's SITcomm.

Unfortunately, my Unix-literate friend tells me that **sz** and **rz** are not common Unix programs, and in fact, there's no telling how you can get files from your Unix machine down to your Mac. He did provide some suggestions, so if your Unix machine doesn't have **sz** and **rz** installed, try some of these commands, matching with something your terminal emulator speaks, of course. For ZMODEM, also try typing **zm** or **zmodem**. For XMODEM, try **rz**, **xm**, or **xmodem**. It's always worth typing **kermit** to see if the froggy program exists. That said, let's pretend that you have **sz** and **rz** installed.

To use **sz**, simply type **sz** *filename*. Most, if not all terminal emulators, recognize when the Unix machine sends a file via ZMODEM and receives the file automatically. Most programs also either save the file in a specified folder or ask you where it should go. The following example file isn't big, but it illustrates the point:

```
/d/tidbits> ls
Mail         News         download.me  mail        nn.help
/d/tidbits> sz download.me
*z
### Receive (Z) download.me: 14 bytes, 0:00 elapsed, 14 cps, 0%
sz 3.24 5-16-93 finished.
```

The companion command to **sz** is **rz**, which, as more alert members of our Unix viewing audience have figured out, stands for "receive ZMODEM." You use **rz** on the Unix machine to receive a file sent from your Mac. The process for receiving a file on the Unix machine can be a little different. Not all implementations of **rz** under Unix recognize that a file is coming in automatically, as most Mac emulation programs do, which means that you may have to invoke **rz** on the Unix machine and then go back and choose Send ZMODEM from your terminal emulator on the Mac. You don't have to specify a filename in most cases because ZMODEM is smart enough to bring over the file. Sometimes, however, it's a good idea to give **rz** a filename as well because Mac filenames with spaces don't translate well to Unix filenames.

Here's what the file looks like when I ask ZTerm to send a file back to the Unix machine. Note that I didn't type any of this information; the programs did it all automatically.

```
/d/tidbits> rz
rz ready. Type "sz file ..." to your modem program
*B010000012f4ced
### Send (Z) download.me: 14 bytes, 0:01 elapsed, 12 cps, 0%
rz 3.24 5-5-93 finished.
```

Sometimes you must pay attention to how you send files to and from the Mac, but because these instructions vary from machine to machine, I can't predict what might go wrong. The Mac has three forms of ZMODEM: *Text, Binary,* and *MacBinary* (this information generally applies to XMODEM, YMODEM, and Kermit as well, should you be forced to use one of those transfer protocols). Leave your program set to download MacBinary ZMODEM, because that option works almost all of the time with almost all files. However, if a MacBinary transfer results in a damaged file, try one of the other two methods. Use Text if the file is a text file, like anything encoded with BinHex, and use Binary if the file is a non-Macintosh binary file such as something brought over from a PC. I can't be more explicit about the kinds of problems you're likely to run into here because it's impossible to tell what might happen.

finger

When you want to get information about someone, you finger them. The command syntax is simple, just type **finger** and then the userid, or for a list of users logged on to a specific machine, **finger** and then the machine name preceded by a @ sign.

```
/d/tidbits> finger yanoff@csd4.csd.uwm.edu
[csd4.csd.uwm.edu]
Login name: yanoff                      In real life: Scott A Yanoff
Office: EMS E774,  ex-3886
Directory: /usr/u3/yanoff           Shell: /usr/bin/tcsh
Last login Sat Jun  4 17:47 on ttyo0 from ems-ts3.csd.uwm.
New mail arrived Sat Jun  4 18:35:16 1994; unread since Sat Jun  4 18:25:08 1994
Project: Friday:  BREWERS: 4  Angels: 3  WP: Bones (5-4)  Save: Fetters (4)
Plan:
 * As the author of the INTERNET SERVICES LIST, I have made updates
    available in a number of ways:    (Available 1st and 15th of every month)
      1) newsgroup alt.internet.services
      2) ftp ftp.csd.uwm.edu  (get /pub/inet.services.txt)
      3) gopher csd4.csd.uwm.edu (select Remote Information Services...)
      4) mail bbslist@aug3.augsburg.edu  (Auto-replies with lists)
      5) URL: http://www.uwm.edu/Mirror/inet.services.html (for WWW, Mosaic)
      6) email me WITH THE SUBJECT 'yan-inet' to get on my email list
          and you will receive confirmation of your subscription.
          (This is the LEAST preferred method, my mailer is getting strained!)
```

```
Milwaukee, Wisconsin
        /'-_
       {    }/
        \  ./
        |___|

A Great Place On A
     Great Lake
```

Of course, Scott has particularly good information available for fingering (and I highly recommend that you check out his Internet Services List); most people—like me—don't have nearly as interesting stuff.

```
/d/tidbits> finger tidbits@halcyon.com
[halcyon.halcyon.com]
Login name: tidbits                 In real life: Adam C. Engst
Directory: /b/tidbits               Shell: /bin/csh
On since Jun  4 16:37:00 on ttyp1 from bellevue-ip29.ha
No Plan.
```

And, if you want to see whether a friend is logged in at the specific moment, you can check that too, via **finger**.

```
/d/tidbits> finger @halcyon.com
[halcyon.com]
Login      Name             TTY Idle    When         Office
breier     Breier William Schee 22      Fri 10:12
willhoek   Will Parker      23 1:00 Fri 10:40
craig      Craig Suhadolnik 24 1:18 Fri 09:25
nraven     Night Raven      25      Fri 12:32
davidr     David Rogers     26    2 Fri 12:26
sharpen    Sharpened Software 27    Fri 12:43
pat        Patrick Ryan     28      Fri 12:46
andy       Andy Teh         29    3 Fri 12:44
tsparks    thomas sparks    30      Fri 12:43
```

talk

Once you know if someone's logged in, you can talk to that person online, using the **talk** program. When you type **talk** and an email address, such as **talk tidbits@halcyon.com**, that user sees a message like the following one onscreen:

```
Message from Talk_Daemon@halcyon at 17:02 ...
talk: connection requested by ace@bellevue-ip29.halcyon.com.
talk: respond with:  talk ace@bellevue-ip29.halcyon.com
```

After the user answers by typing **talk** and your address, the screen splits into halves, separated by a line, and you each type in your own half. Once you hit the bottom of your half of the screen, **talk** starts overwriting the lines at the top. It's not terribly pretty, but it works.

```
[halcyon]:/b/tidbits> talk ace@bellevue-ip29.halcyon.com

[Connection established]
This is really schizophrenic, talking to onself.


_ _ _ _ _ _ _ _ _ _ _ _ _ _ _ _ _ _ _ _ _ _ _ _ _ _ _ _ _ _ _ _ _

Yup, you're right. Or rather, I'm right. Augh!
```

To get out of **talk**, press Control-Z. My major problems with **talk** are that you must be online at the same time as the other person, you never know whether you're bothering the other person (I usually hate when people talk to me while I'm online because I never know how to get out of what I'm doing fast enough), and frankly, typing constantly and quickly is a great way to encourage carpal tunnel syndrome, which can ruin your life. If possible, the telephone simply works better, although if you're talking to someone in another country, the expense probably outweighs the utility of the telephone. This is especially true for overseas discussions—I know someone who regularly converses via **talk** with a friend in Thailand, which would otherwise rack up a deadly telephone bill.

logout

I almost forgot this step. After you finish using your Unix shell account, you need to get out and hang up the modem. You can always just shut off the modem—that approach works, but it's not ideal. The universal command to log out under Unix is Control-D, but it's ugly and hard to remember. Different systems use different commands; because most systems respond to **logout**, try it first, followed by **exit**, followed by **logoff**. Strange systems use **bye** or **off**, but I've never seen them outside a custom BBS interface. One of those commands should work, and if all else fails, remember that you're in control of the hangup command in your terminal emulator and the power switch on the modem.

Good luck and feel free to ask someone on your system for help. I could tell you about all sorts of other great Unix commands that Unix wizards use all the time and that I may have even used once or twice. But in real life, assuming you don't aspire to Unix wizardhood, you need to know only about listing files, changing directories, deleting files, reading files, and exploring other Unix commands. Unix has a number of other programs, such as **mail**, **rn**, **nn**, **vi**, **FTP**, and **Telnet**, that you may want to use.

mail

Several Unix programs enable you to read and reply to email—so many that I don't stand a chance at mentioning them all. Instead, I tell you about **mail** because it's the standard Unix program and the only one guaranteed to be available on all Unix machines. If you plan to use a Unix email program exclusively, I highly recommend that you check out an alternative email program such as **elm**, **pine**, **mush**, or **mh**. There's no telling which of them your system administrator might have installed, so try typing the name on the command line, and for more information, use the man pages.

To send email from **mail**, type **mail**, followed by the email address of the person you want to reach. **Mail** then usually prompts you for the subject of the letter (some machines require the **-s** option, which makes the typed command look like **mail -s "Hi Self" ace@tidbits.com**). After that, you can type the body of the letter. Remember to press Return at the end of each line (you're not using a Macintosh editor, and you can't use the arrow keys to go back—only Delete works for editing). After you finish, press Return once to get to a new line and then press Control-D. Instead of Control-D, some machines use two blank lines, or perhaps two periods alone on a line. So, a simple **mail** session might look like the following:

```
/d/tidbits> mail ace@tidbits.com
Subject: Are we having fun yet?
Here's where I get to type anything I want, but since I'm talking
to myself, I can't think of anything to say. I guess that's good.

cheers ... -Adam
^d <— you don't really see this, but you do type it
Cc: tidbits@halcyon.com
```

Of course, sending mail is only half the game. You undoubtedly want to read mail, too. To display the messages in your mailbox (assuming you have any), type **mail**. You should see something like the following:

```
/d/tidbits> mail
Mail version 2.18 5/19/83.  Type ? for help.
"/usr/spool/mail/tidbits": 3 messages 1 new
     1 tidbits  Fri Aug 13 10:02  17/736 "Nothing like conversations wi"
     2 tidbits  Fri Aug 13 10:06  15/509 "Re:  Nothing like conversatio"
>N   3 tidbits  Fri Aug 13 12:09  15/484 "Are we having fun yet?"
&
```

At the **&** prompt, press Return to read the first new message, which is marked by an N (as message 3 is marked in the preceding onscreen mail). You also can type a number corresponding to any message to read that one specifically, as in the following:

```
& 1
Message  1:
From tidbits Fri Aug 13 10:02:19 1993
Received: by halcyon.com id AA09538
  (5.65c/IDA-1.4.4 for tidbits); Fri, 13 Aug 1993 10:02:15 -0700
Date: Fri, 13 Aug 1993 10:02:15 -0700
From: "Adam C. Engst" <tidbits>
Message-Id: <199308131702.AA09538@halcyon.com>
To: tidbits@halcyon.com
Subject: Nothing like conversations with oneself
Status: RO
```

There are a number of other commands you can use to navigate between messages and work with them. The easiest way to find these messages is to use the **?** command.

```
& ?
     Mail    Commands
t <message list>                        type messages
n                                       goto and type next message
e <message list>                        edit messages
f <message list>                        give headlines of messages
d <message list>                        delete messages
s <message list> file                   append messages to file
u <message list>                        undelete messages
r <message list>                        reply to messages(to sender and recipients)
R <message list>                        reply to messages(to sender only)
pre <message list>                      make messages go back to /usr/mail
m <user list>                           mail to specific users
q                                       quit, saving unresolved messages in mbox
x                                       quit, do not remove system mailbox
h                                       print out active message headers
!                                       shell escape
```

```
ch [directory]                  chdir to directory or home if none given
```

A <message list> consists of integers, ranges of same, or user names separated
by spaces. If omitted, Mail uses the last message typed.

A <user list> consists of user names or distribution names separated by spaces.
Distribution names are defined in .sendrc in your home directory.

Of these commands, you're most likely to use **n** to go on to the next message, **d**
to delete one or more messages, **r** or **R** to reply to messages, **h** to display your
list of messages, and **q** to quit mail.

```
& r
To: ace@tidbits.com tidbits
Subject: Re:  Are we having fun yet?
Cc: tidbits@halcyon.com

This is a reply to a message to myself, but once again, I'm suffering
from a complete block on what to say. Nine of ten people who do this
sort of thing eventually succumb to schizophrenia, so I'd better stop
soon.

cheers ... -Adam
Cc: tidbits@halcyon.com
```

If you type **h** to redisplay your messages, you see the following:

```
& h
      1 tidbits  Fri Aug 13 10:02   17/736 "Nothing like conversations wi"
      2 tidbits  Fri Aug 13 10:06   15/509 "Re:  Nothing like conversatio"
      3 tidbits  Fri Aug 13 12:09   16/495 "Are we having fun yet?"
 >N   4 tidbits  Fri Aug 13 12:26   17/581 "Re:  Are we having fun yet?"
```

Now, because talking to yourself in email is kind of sick, let's toast some of these
messages, as follows:

```
& d 2 4
& h
      1 tidbits  Fri Aug 13 10:02   17/736 "Nothing like conversations wi"
 >    3 tidbits  Fri Aug 13 12:09   16/495 "Are we having fun yet?"
```

You can easily mistype when you're deleting messages (you also can just type **d** after reading a message to delete that one), but you can recover the messages by using the **u** command.

```
& u
& h
    1 tidbits  Fri Aug 13 10:02  17/736 "Nothing like conversations wi"
    3 tidbits  Fri Aug 13 12:09  16/495 "Are we having fun yet?"
>   4 tidbits  Fri Aug 13 12:26  17/581 "Re:  Are we having fun yet?"
```

Using the **u** and **h** commands recovered only the most recently deleted message, though, and you want all of them back. You can type **u 2** to recover the second message, but using the * wildcard to recover all of them might be easier. The * wildcard also works if you want to delete all your messages, as in the following:

```
& u *
& h
    1 tidbits  Fri Aug 13 10:02  17/736 "Nothing like conversations wi"
>   2 tidbits  Fri Aug 13 10:06  15/509 "Re:  Nothing like conversatio"
    3 tidbits  Fri Aug 13 12:09  16/495 "Are we having fun yet?"
    4 tidbits  Fri Aug 13 12:26  17/581 "Re:  Are we having fun yet?"
& d *
& h
No applicable messages
```

Finally, as you can see in the following, you can easily delete or recover a range of messages by separating the numbers with a dash instead of a space:

```
& u 1-3
& h
    1 tidbits  Fri Aug 13 10:02  17/736 "Nothing like conversations wi"
    2 tidbits  Fri Aug 13 10:06  15/509 "Re:  Nothing like conversatio"
>   3 tidbits  Fri Aug 13 12:09  16/495 "Are we having fun yet?"
```

OK, that's enough about **mail**. Using **mail** frustrates me to no end. I can't recommend that you use it, but it should be available even if no other mail programs exist on your machine. There is something to be said for least common denominators, but utility is not usually among them. For novices, **elm** or **pine** are good choices because they provide full-screen interfaces that display the common commands at all times. They also enable you to select messages with the arrow keys and other seemingly obvious things like that. Remember, nothing is obvious in Unix.

Newsreaders

Now let's look at two of the popular newsreaders, **rn** and **nn**. They differ primarily in philosophy—**rn** assumes you want to read 90 percent of the news, whereas **nn** assumes you want to read 10 percent of the news. Which style you prefer depends on how much time you have to read news. Both programs are powerful and complex, and both have more options than anyone should be expected to remember, much less use regularly. In keeping with the focus of this book on Macintosh software, I'm going to give you only the briefest of looks at the two.

Before I discuss each program, let's talk about something they share—the `.newsrc` file. This file keeps track of which groups you subscribe to and which articles you've read in those groups. It also knows which groups you aren't subscribed to, which is the majority of them. Unfortunately, all of the newsreaders seem to want to subscribe you to everything when you start, which means your first session reading news is long and boring as you unsubscribe from groups that don't interest you.

You can avoid this situation. First, launch either **rn** or **nn** by typing **rn** or **nn**. Then quit immediately. In **rn** use the **q** command; in **nn** use the **Q** command (case is important). The act of starting and quitting leaves you with a fresh `.newsrc` file that assumes you want to read all the thousands of newsgroups that exist on your host machine. Download the `.newsrc` file to the Mac; then use your favorite word processor to change all the colons (:) to exclamation points (!). Newsreaders consider any newsgroup name ending in a colon to be subscribed and any name ending in an exclamation point to be unsubscribed. Now scroll through manually and change the exclamation point back to a colon for any group that sounds interesting. You can easily subscribe and unsubscribe from groups within a newsreader as well, but dealing with thousands of them is a major pain. Next, delete the `.newsrc` file on the Unix machine (don't worry—you can always have a newsreader create a new one if something goes wrong) by typing **rm .newsrc**. Then upload the edited `.newsrc` file and you're done.

I should note one potential problem. You may have trouble downloading and working with the `.newsrc` file on the Mac because filenames starting with periods on the Mac are drivers and are generally treated differently. It's not unthinkable that a communications application may refuse to create a filename starting with a period or fail to see it for uploading, although ZTerm didn't bat an eyelash when I tried it. If you encounter this problem, rename the file on the Unix machine before downloading and again after uploading. In standard Unix tradition, the **rename** command (which does exist) does something completely different; you need to use the **mv** command (which moves or renames files) to rename a file. First, rename the file:

```
/d/tidbits> mv .newsrc mynewsrc
/d/tidbits> ls
Mail        News        mail        mynewsrc  nn.help   rm.help
```

Then download it:

```
/d/tidbits> sz mynewsrc
*z
### Receive (Z) mynewsrc: 71255 bytes, 0:38 elapsed, 1834 cps, 127%
sz 3.24 5-16-93 finished.
```

Edit the file on the Mac (the smoke and mirrors part—I assume you know how to do a global search and replace in a word processor).

Next, upload the file to the Unix machine:

```
/d/tidbits> rz
rz ready. Type "sz file ..." to your modem program
*B010000012f4ced
### Send (Z) mynewsrc: 71255 bytes, 1:28 elapsed, 807 cps, 56%
rz 3.24 5-5-93 finished.
```

And finally, rename the file to the name the newsreaders expect: **.newsrc**.

```
/d/tidbits> mv mynewsrc .newsrc
```

Pretty neat, eh? I provided all that detail not so much because I expect everyone to go through the entire technique, but because it's a good review of some of the Unix commands I talked about earlier in the chapter.

rn

Now that you have a nicely edited `.newsrc` file, start up **rn** by typing **rn**. Here's what the screen looks like:

```
/d/tidbits> rn
Unread news in comp.sys.mac.comm                         417 articles
Unread news in comp.sys.mac.portables                   1131 articles

****** 417 unread articles in comp.sys.mac.comm — read now? [ynq]
```

You immediately see the first few newsgroups you subscribe to, and **rn** asks nicely if you want to read the first one. The letters in square brackets after the question indicate the question's most common answers: yes, no, and quit.

Whenever you learn a new program, figuring out how to look at the help is important, even if it's not very helpful. Even though typing **?** worked in mail, **rn** uses the **h** command. Type **h** and you should see something like the following (although I edited out the garbage you don't need now):

```
Newsgroup Selection commands:

y         Do this newsgroup now.
SP        Do this newsgroup, executing the default command listed in []'s.
=         Start this newsgroup, but list subjects before reading articles.
u         Unsubscribe from this newsgroup.
c         Catch up (mark all articles as read).
n         Go to the next newsgroup with unread news.
N         Go to the next newsgroup.
p         Go to the previous newsgroup with unread news.
P         Go to the previous newsgroup.
-         Go to the previously displayed newsgroup.
1         Go to the first newsgroup.
^         Go to the first newsgroup with unread news.
$         Go to the last newsgroup.
g name    Go to the named newsgroup.  Subscribe to new newsgroups this way too.
/pat      Search forward for newsgroup matching pattern.
?pat      Search backward for newsgroup matching pattern.
          (Use * and ? style patterns.  Append r to include read newsgroups.)
l pat     List unsubscribed newsgroups containing pattern.
m name    Move named newsgroup elsewhere (no name moves current newsgroup).
L         List current .newsrc.
q         Quit rn.
x         Quit, restoring .newsrc to its state at startup of trn.
^K        Edit the global KILL file.  Use commands like /pattern/j to suppress
          pattern in every newsgroup.
```

After you agree that you want to read the articles by answering yes (or actually, by typing **y**, because you don't type the entire word), **rn** displays the first unread message, which follows:

```
comp.sys.mac.comm #27410 (415 more)
Newsgroups:
comp.sys.mac.comm,comp.sys.mac.hardware,comp.sys.mac.system
From: lorenzo@spot.Colorado.EDU (Eric Lorenzo)
Subject: Did HSU 2.0 mess my serial ports?
Organization: University of Colorado, Boulder
Date: Thu Aug 05 23:42:11 PDT 1993
Lines: 21


What exactly does the serial driver update do?  I updated my C610 with
this option checked off and now my downloads are noticeably slower and
...
serial update?  I'm doing Zmodem transfers with Zterm.  Any help and
—MORE— (94%)
```

At this point in the middle of the article, you have more possibilities, none of which are addressed in the preceding help information. You're in a different mode now, so you need different help. Type **h** to check out the more useful commands.

```
Paging commands:

SP       Display the next page.
x        Display the next page decrypted (rot13).
d        Display half a page more.
CR       Display one more line.
^R,v,^X  Restart the current article (v=verbose header, ^X=rot13).
b        Back up one page.
^L,X     Refresh the screen (X=rot13).
```

The following commands skip the rest of the current article, then behave just as if typed after the "What next?" prompt at the end of the article:

```
n        Scan forward for next unread article.
N        Go to next article.
^N       Scan forward for next unread article with same title.
```

```
p,P,^P  Same as n,N,^N, only going backwards.
   -    Go to previously displayed article.
```

Press the Spacebar to finish reading the rest of the article, and poof, you're in yet another mode. Try getting help one more time, and you see another set of commands, as in the following:

```
Article Selection commands:

n,SP    Find next unread article (follows discussion-tree in threaded groups).
N       Go to next article.
^N      Scan forward for next unread article with same subject in date order.
p,P,^P  Same as n,N,^N, only going backwards.
_N,_P   Go to the next/previous article numerically.
   -    Go to previously displayed article.
number  Go to specified article.
/pattern/modifiers
        Scan forward for article containing pattern in the subject line.
        (Use ?pat? to scan backwards; append f to scan from lines, h to scan
        whole headers, a to scan entire articles, r to scan read articles, c
        to make case-sensitive.)
/pattern/modifiers:command{:command}
        Apply one or more commands to the set of articles matching pattern.
        Use a K modifier to save entire command to the KILL file for this
        newsgroup.  Commands m and M, if first, imply an r modifier.
        Valid commands are the same as for the range command.
f,F     Submit a followup article (F = include this article).
r,R     Reply through net mail (R = include this article).
s ...   Save to file or pipe via sh.
S ...   Save via preferred shell.
w,W     Like s and S but save without the header.
C       Cancel this article, if yours.
^R,v    Restart article (v=verbose).
^X      Restart article, rot13 mode.
c       Catch up (mark all articles as read).
b       Back up one page.
^L      Refresh the screen.  You can get back to the pager with this.
X       Refresh screen in rot13 mode.
m       Mark article as still unread.
k       Kill current subject (mark articles as read).
K       Mark current subject as read, and save command in KILL file.
^K      Edit local KILL file (the one for this newsgroup).
=       List subjects of unread articles.
u       Unsubscribe from this newsgroup.
q       Quit this newsgroup for now.
Q       Quit newsgroup, staying at current newsgroup.
```

Frankly, I think you mostly use the article selection commands because you spend most of your time moving from article to article, not searching for new groups or paging within an article.

Remember that the Spacebar performs the first command listed in the square brackets. Generally, that command is the one you want to execute because **rn** is good at reading your mind. Initially, the end-of-article line looks like the following:

```
End of article 27410 (of 27901) — what next? [npq]
```

The default action is **n**, for next, which takes you to the next unread article. However, you are likely to be either very interested in the subject of the article you just read or completely uninterested. The middle ground is less likely. If you are interested in the topic being discussed, you want to read the next article in the thread by using the Control-N command, generally abbreviated ^N. When you press Control-N at the end of an article, the end-of-article line looks like the following:

```
End of article 27458 (of 27901) — what next? [^Nnpq]
```

This line indicates that pressing the Spacebar enables you to read the next article in the thread, which is primarily what you want to do. If you realize that you aren't interested in a thread, of course, there's no reason to run into its uninteresting articles later on, so you can kill the entire thread temporarily by typing **k**. Use this command heavily.

After you've started reading in thread mode by using Control-N and you know to kill boring threads, you can zip through a newsgroup in no time. Because **rn** displays the number of unread messages left in the newsgroup at the top of each article, you can see how many articles you've killed with each successive use of **k**. I always find it gratifying when I kill an especially long and boring thread. (Hey, so what if I'm easily amused?)

Note

*It seems as though I'm glossing over parts of **rn**, and I am, but when I use **rn** for real, I start it up, use Control-N on the first article to get into thread mode, and then use the Spacebar to read within a thread and **k** to kill boring threads. When done with one newsgroup, **rn** moves on to the next. So despite **rn's** wads of commands, you can get along extremely well with a very few. If you do get into **rn** seriously, I recommend that you read over the man pages and the help carefully because some of the features, such as being able to search for articles containing specific text strings, are pretty neat, should you want to devote the time to learning how to use them effectively.*

As you can see in the preceding help text, you also can reply to messages by typing either the **r** or **R** command (depending on whether you want to include the text of the article in your email reply), follow up to an article by typing **f** or **F** (again, **F** includes the article in the followup to the newsgroup), save an article with or without its header, and quit by typing the **q** command. If you type **f** to followup to an article, **rn** (at least the version on my host's machine) asks if you want to start a new topic, which is one way to post a new message to a newsgroup.

The other way to create a new messages is the program **Pnews**, which walks you through the process of creating an article the first time.

```
/b/tidbits> Pnews
I see you've never used this version of Pnews before.  I will give you extra
help this first time through, but then you must remember what you learned.
If you don't understand any question, type h and a CR (carriage return) for
help.

If you've never posted an article to the net before, it is HIGHLY recommended
that you read the netiquette document found in news.announce.newusers so
that you'll know to avoid the commonest blunders.  To do that, interrupt
Pnews, get to the top-level prompt of [t]rn, and use the command
"g news.announce.newusers" to go to that group.


Newsgroup(s): halcyon.test

Your local distribution prefixes are:
    Local organization: halcyon
    Organization:       halcyon
    City:               seattle
    State:              wa
    Multi-State Area:
    Country:            usa
```

```
        Continent:          na
        Everywhere:         <null> (not "world")

Distribution (): halcyon

Title/Subject: Trying out Pnews

This program posts news to machines throughout the organization.
Are you absolutely sure that you want to do this? [ny] y

Prepared file to include [none]: <- Hit return to confirm no file.

A temporary file has been created for you to edit.  Be sure to leave at
least one blank line between the header and the body of your message.
(And until a certain bug is fixed all over the net, don't start the body of
your message with any indentation, or it may get eaten.)

Within the header may be fields that you don't understand.  If you don't
understand a field (or even if you do), you can simply leave it blank, and
it will go away when the article is posted.

Type return to get the default editor, or type the name of your favorite
editor.

Editor [/usr/ucb/vi]: <- Press Return to use vi, and then edit the post in vi.

(Here I edited the file in vi - see below for instructions on using it.)

Your article's newsgroup:
halcyon.test              [no description available]

Check spelling, Send, Abort, Edit, or List? send
```

Posting to a Usenet newsgroup is not meant to be a trivial operation, in large part because people who don't know *how* to post generally don't know *what* to post either. Nonetheless, after the first few times through posting, you should become comfortable with the quirks on your system. If it's any consolation, hundreds of thousands of people around the world have figured out how to muddle through the intricacies of **rn** and Unix.

nn

Unlike **rn**, **nn** assumes you don't want to read much of the news. Given the more than 5,000 newsgroups, many with hundreds of articles a day, that assumption is good for most. This assumption is also the one that most of the Macintosh newsreaders make, should you move from using Unix to a full Mac window on Usenet news.

The trick that **nn** uses to reduce the amount of newsgroup clutter in your life is that it forces you to select only the articles you want to read. In contrast, **rn** shoves all the articles at you, one thread at a time, and asks you whether you want to read that thread. In **nn**, you first scroll through all the articles in the newsgroup in selection mode, and then once you've selected the articles to read, **nn** drops into a reading mode that looks and works much like **rn**. In fact, many of the commands you use with **rn** work in **nn's** reading mode as well.

Launch the program by typing **nn**, and you should see something like the following:

```
Newsgroup: comp.sys.mac.comm                        Articles: 320 of 630/2

a Duncan Coward      42  >>>Apple MacTCP advertising bogosity!
b Lisa_R._Klein      10  Mac TCP help
c Edward Vielmetti 49    >
d BEN WOLFE          30  >
e E Kaftanski        27  >>IP tunneling from NetModem/E via FastPath?
f Michael Casteel  19    >>>
g James Skee          5  Hermes 2.5???
h James Skee         23  optimizing SLIP performance
i Edward Vielmetti 13    >
j Amanda Walker      11  >

 — 13:25 — SELECT — help:? — —Top 5%— —
```

The first line tells you what newsgroup you're in and how many articles are left to read of the total available. Then each detail line such as:

```
b Lisa_R._Klein     10  Mac TCP help
```

provides the article ID, which you use to select that article, the name of the poster, the number of lines in the message, and the subject of the message. Alert readers may no doubt ask immediately, "But what about lines like...?"

```
c Edward Vielmetti 49  >
```

Ah, here's the beauty of **nn**. It groups articles in the same thread automatically, unlike **rn,** and it makes it clear that the articles are all in the same thread by listing only the > (greater-than) sign under the first available article. You may see multiple > signs to indicate that the article is a follow-up on a follow-up on a follow-up, and so on. But that's not too important. What is important is that you can easily select the articles you want to read by typing the letter to the left of the poster's name. If you want to read the entire thread under an interesting-sounding article, just type * (an asterisk) after you type the letter that corresponds to that article.

Note

Assuming that your terminal emulator and Unix host are sufficiently advanced, you should see selected articles in reverse or high-intensity type.

If you change your mind and want to deselect an article or a thread, typing its letter (and optionally the asterisk) removes it from your selected articles.

In the preceding example, I deleted some of the bottom articles to save space, so you'll have to take my word for it that the articles went to the letter *s.* And yet, with hundreds of available articles, you'd obviously run out of letters fast in **nn's** selection mode. The program circumvents this problem by providing multiple screens of article titles, each listing articles from *a* to *s* (or a higher letter, if you have more lines available in your terminal definition). Pressing either Return or the Spacebar takes you to the next screen automatically, or you can move back and forth between screens with the < and > keys. If you want to read the messages you've marked right away, you can type **Z**.

Note

*Almost all commands in **nn** use uppercase letters because the lowercase letters are used for selecting articles.*

If you select an article and the rest in the thread with a letter and an asterisk, and you then use **Z** to display it immediately, your screen looks like the following:

```
Jack W. Howarth: MacTCP 2.0.3 upgrade path???????        16 Aug 1993 14:38
   I am thinking of ordering MacTCP 2.0.2. However, I always use SLIP
so I really want 2.0.3 which is the promised SLIP fix upgrade to 2.0.x.
```

My question is can anyone in the know explain how owners of 2.0.2 will
be able to upgrade to 2.0.4? I saw a blurb somewhere (MacWeek?) that
2.0.4 would be provided to 'developers' by ftp. What about 'the rest
of us'? Apple has never released patcher programs for updates before
although now might be a good time to start!
        Jack

—

Jack W. Howarth, Ph.D.   Univ. of Texas Medical School
Research Fellow   P.O. Box 20708
Department of Biochemistry   Houston, Texas 77225
— 17:30 —comp.sys.mac.comm— 8 MORE+next —help:?—All—

The line at the bottom of the message displays the time, the current newsgroup,
how many more messages you've selected, the shortcut for help, and finally, the
word **All**, which indicates that you've seen all of the article. If the article goes on
for several screens, **nn** places a number there to indicate how far it is into the
message. Some of the **rn**-style commands work in **nn's** reading mode as well, as
you can tell from the reading mode help screen:

```
SCROLLING                ABSOLUTE LINE              SEARCHING
SP        1 page forw    ^       top               /RE    find regular expr.
d         1/2 page forw  gNUM    line NUM           . //   repeat last search
CR        1 line forw    $       last line
DEL       1 page back    h       header             TEXT CONVERSIONS
u         1/2 page back  H       full digest        D      decrypt article (rot13)
TAB       skip section                              c      compress spaces
GOTO ANOTHER ARTICLE
SP        next (at end of current article)          CANCEL, SUBSCRIBE, KILL
n, p      next/previous article                     C      cancel article
l         mark article for later action             U      (un)subscribe to group
k         kill subject (not permanently)            K      kill/select handling
*         select subject
                                                    QUIT / ESCAPE
SAVE                                                 =      back to menu
s, o, w   save with full/short/no header            N      goto next group
:unshar :decode :patch   unpack article             X      as N, mark as read
                                                    !, ^Z  Shell escape, suspend
REPLY, POST                                          Q      quit nn
r         mail reply to author of article
m         mail (or forward article)                REDRAW
f         post followup to article                  ^P     Repeat last message
:post     post new article                          ^L, ^R Redraw screen
```

Note the **:post** command at the bottom of the help. If you type **:post**, **nn** asks you what it should put in each of the header lines like Newsgroup, Subject, Keywords, and Distribution, and then it dumps you into **vi**. (Read on for the minimal details on **vi**.)

If you learn how to select articles and threads, switch into reading mode, and kill nasty threads once in reading mode (by typing **k**, as in **rn**), you can get along fine in **nn**. Because you read many fewer messages, you either spend less time on the computer or you read a lot more newsgroups, your choice. Usenet is absolutely addictive though, so be careful.

vi

So far I've avoided talking much about posting news or replying to messages because of one unpleasant fact. Although starting is easy and involves answering a few questions by pressing Return, you then end up in a Unix editor, probably **vi**, and it isn't pleasant. O'Reilly & Associates sells a book called *Learning the vi Editor* by Linda Lamb; you might want to check it out. I think I'm justified in making unpleasant comments about a text editor that someone can write about for 192 pages. Put it this way, when I had to edit a special Unix file on my account named `.login`, I found it was easiest to write what I wanted in a word processor (making sure I had hard returns at the end of each line), copy it, invoke **vi** on a new version of the file, switch into insert mode, and then paste in my text. That's awful, and I'm thoroughly embarrassed about it, but Unix editors and I don't get along.

Here, then, are the absolutely basic commands you must know to use **vi**. You edit a file by typing **vi** *filename*, or you may be dumped into **vi** by **rn** or **nn** to edit a posting. In either case, you end up with the file listed at the top of the screen and a bunch of tildes (~) taking up any blank lines if the file isn't large enough to fill the screen. At this point, you're in a mode in which you can move around with the arrow keys.

```
To: noah@apple.com
Subject: Re: Q840av / AudioVision 14" Display don't work "out of the box"
Newsgroups: comp.sys.mac.announce
In-Reply-To: <noah-170893175443@90.130.0.233>
References: <1993Aug10.175723.5878@netcon.smc.edu>
Organization: "A World of Information at your Fingertips"
Cc:
Bcc:
```

```
        ~
        ~
        ~
        ~
"/d/tidbits/.letter" 10 lines, 295 characters
```

To start inserting text at the bottom of the message, use your arrow keys to move down to the line above the first tilde. You can't move any farther down, and keep in mind that you're not working on a Mac—moving all the way to the right does not wrap you around to the next line.

Type **i** to enter insert mode and type your text, pressing Return at the end of each line for safety's sake (the text might wrap, but I can't guarantee it). If you make a mistake, you can use Delete to go back and fix it, but don't try to use the arrow keys in insert mode because they don't work; they insert letters into your file instead.

Press Escape to return to the mode where your arrow keys work. At this point there are probably thousands of useful editing commands, but I'm going to tell you about only a few. Type **x** to delete the character that your cursor is on and type **dd** (type the two letters quickly) to delete the line you are on. If you just need to replace a single character, position your cursor over it, type **r**, and then type a single replacement character. If you make a mistake with any of these commands, undo the last change by typing **u**.

You can always go back into insert mode by positioning your cursor in the appropriate place and typing **i**. If you make a line too long, you can switch out of insert mode, move to the end using the arrow keys, switch back into insert mode, press Return to break the line, switch out of insert mode, and then type **J** to join the line you're on with the line below it.

After you finish editing the file, if you want to save it and quit, first make sure you aren't in insert mode; then type **ZZ**. If you don't want to save the changes, instead of **ZZ**, type **:** (a colon) and then, at the command-line prompt that appears at the bottom of the screen, type **quit!**. This series of commands exits you without saving your changes. I use **:quit!** heavily.

Note

*You might be able to get around using **vi** or another Unix editor much if you prepare files in a word processor on your Mac, then upload them to your Unix account. Much of the time when you're posting, the posting program gives you the chance to include a prepared file, which you could do to avoid the edit process at least some of the time.*

FTP

FTP, or File Transfer Protocol, is almost trivial to use, especially in comparison with other Unix programs. It does have a fair number of picky little options, however, and such nonsense that no one ever uses in daily life. I'm going to talk through the standard FTP commands and show you the results that come back from the FTP server.

To start, you invoke FTP and tell it where to go by typing **ftp** and the exact name of the file site. You must know the name of the site beforehand, and you must type it correctly; otherwise, FTP complains about an "unknown host." If you blow the name and end up at a blank **ftp>** prompt without connecting to a site, try typing **open** along with the correct file site name. Alternatively, you can swear at the machine, type **quit**, and try the original FTP command again. Here's what FTP looks like when you get it right:

```
/d/tidbits> ftp ftp.acns.nwu.edu
Connected to ftp.acns.nwu.edu.
220 casbah.acns.nwu.edu FTP server (SunOS 4.1) ready.
```

Next, FTP wants a login name, just as you need a login name or userid to log in to your Unix account. Unless you're logging into your own account at another machine (at which point you use your own userid), type the name **anonymous.** Again, you must spell it correctly, or FTP asks for a password that you don't know and then spits at you about an incorrect login or some such problem. If you spell the name wrong, your backup command is **user anonymous**, which lets you start the login process again.

```
Name (ftp.acns.nwu.edu:tidbits): anonymous
331 Guest login ok, send ident as password.
```

FTP responds to a successful anonymous login by asking for your identity as a password. I've never heard of anyone checking these things in FTP logs, but it's polite to enter your full email address. Like all good passwords, it doesn't appear as you type, which isn't a big deal because your email address isn't secret. However, if you make a mistake, don't sweat it; no one really cares. Well, almost no one. Some sites check the email address you enter against the name of the machine from which you use FTP and reject attempts that don't match properly. Therefore, typos may count! Also, even if you provide a good password, sites often don't allow more than a certain number of anonymous users to log in at the same time or at the same time from the same machine (causing trouble if someone else on your machine is using the FTP site already, for instance), so it may kick you out and tell you to try again later.

```
Password: tidbits@halcyon.com  <- this didn't really appear onscreen
230 Guest login ok, access restrictions apply.
```

Note

As a shortcut, or perhaps as a workaround for sites that don't like your real email address, try typing merely your userid and the @ symbol for the password. Mine would look like **ace@**.

Now that you've passed through the final set of locked FTP doors, you can get down to business. Simple or not, FTP suffers from the standard navigational problem of a command-line interface—you must list the directory to see where you are and what files are around; then you must change the directory, list the files to see what's around, and so on. Listing the directories is a drag (actually, I wish it was a drag—the sort associated with a click). First, list the files using the same command that lists files in Unix, **ls**:

```
ftp> ls
200 PORT command successful.
150 ASCII data connection for /bin/ls (198.137.231.1,1029) (0 bytes).
bin
dev
etc
private
pub
usr
226 ASCII Transfer complete.
34 bytes received in 0.06 seconds (0.55 Kbytes/s)
```

The preceding directories are standard Unix directories; you get used to seeing them. In general, you learn that you can usually look for stuff in the pub directory because it stands for public. Oh, how did I know they were directories? Experience. You can use the **dir** command to list the contents of the current directory as well, and then it is somewhat more obvious that these are directories.

Second, drop down into the next directory using the same command as in Unix, **cd**, along with the name of the directory you want to enter:

```
ftp> cd pub/newswatcher
250 CWD command successful.
```

OK, I cheated, I admit it. While I was online preparing this example, I switched down into the pub directory, then listed the files again, and saw the newswatcher directory. I didn't use that part of the transcript because I like falsifying the evidence (and it's as boring to read as it is to do). Specifying two or more directories is perfectly legal and an extremely good idea. Unfortunately, specifying directories requires that you know the path beforehand, which is seldom the case for me.

Now, see what's in this directory by typing **ls** again:

```
ftp> ls
200 PORT command successful.
150 ASCII data connection for /bin/ls (198.137.231.1,1037) (0 bytes).
newswatcher2.0d17.sea.hqx
readme
source2.0d17.sea.hqx
226 ASCII Transfer complete.
57 bytes received in 0.01 seconds (5.6 Kbytes/s)
```

Ah, that's what I wanted, the latest development version of John Norstad's excellent NewsWatcher (a cool newsreader for MacTCP; I talk about an even more recent version in chapter 13). Now that you can see what you want, you have to get it. That's all there is to it, just type **get** and the filename.

Note

*I like using Macintosh terminal emulators because they always enable me to copy the filename, type **get** and a space at the command line, and then paste in the name. It saves some typing.*

If you want to retrieve a set of files at once, type **mget** along with a list of filenames or a filename with a wildcard such as * in it. So, if you want to retrieve all the BinHex files in a certain directory, type **mget *.hqx**. Because I'm primarily looking at this situation from the consumer's point of view, I'll quickly mention that the complements to **get** and **mget** are **put** and **mput**. You're far less likely to **put** files than to **get** them.

```
ftp> get newswatcher2.0d17.sea.hqx
200 PORT command successful.
150 ASCII data connection for newswatcher2.0d17.sea.hqx
(198.137.231.1,1698)
226 ASCII Transfer complete.
local: newswatcher2.0d17.sea.hqx remote: newswatcher2.0d17.sea.hqx
291777 bytes received in 5.9 seconds (49 Kbytes/s)
```

The file has a final extension of .hqx, which means it's a BinHex file, and is thus text. Because I knew the type of file, I didn't have to change the file transfer mode because the default ASCII mode (see the third line, **ASCII data connection for...**) worked fine. However, if John had posted the smaller self-extracting archive without encoding it in BinHex format (the final extension would then have been **.sea**), I would have had to type the **binary** command to switch FTP into the mode where it can reliably transfer binary files such as self-extracting archives. The opposite of the binary command is the **ascii** command, which returns you to ASCII mode.

FTP doesn't display any feedback while it's working, although if you type **hash** before starting the transfer, FTP prints a hash mark (#) after transferring a block of data. Typing **hash** again toggles that setting off. I seldom have trouble with FTP, so I don't usually bother.

FTP then displays the specifics about the file transfer, noting that the throughput was 49K per second and it took six seconds to transfer. Just to compare, consider that it took me about three minutes to download this same file to my Mac using ZMODEM. That's right, once you have it on your Unix account, you next download it to your Mac. See the **sz** command earlier in this chapter for information on sending the file to your Mac—I'm sure you don't want to see the results of me typing **sz newswatcher2.0d17.sea.hqx** again.

I should mention that the file ends up in the current directory on your Unix account, which is most likely your main directory. However, if you changed directories before you invoked FTP, the file ends up in that directory instead.

Having retrieved your file, you have no reason to stick around, so type **quit** to get back to the Unix command line:

```
ftp> quit
221 Goodbye.
```

And that is that. FTP must have another 60 or 70 commands all told, but I've always been perfectly happy with the preceding subset, and I'll bet you will be happy too. To recap quickly (and in order that you can use them), table 10.1 lists the basic commands and the order in which you generally issue them.

Table 10.1
Basic FTP Command Sequence

Command	Function
ftp *sitename*	Connect to sitename
anonymous	Not a command, but the login name
email address	Not a command, but the password
ls	List the files and directories
cd *dirname*	Change the directory to dirname
get *filename*	Retrieve filename to your account
quit	Quit FTP

FTP is easily scripted with the scripting language of some terminal emulators. I once created a script in MicroPhone II, for instance, that read filenames from a text file that I made and then retrieved the files automatically by logging into an FTP server, changing the directory to the right place, getting the file, logging out, sending the file to my Mac, and then repeating the process. The script is a hack, and it's so poorly done that I'm too embarrassed to show it to you, but you can do the same with other scripting environments, such as AppleScript or Frontier.

Telnet

FTP may seem simple, but Telnet is a piece of cake because Telnet enables you to log in to another machine as though you dialed it locally. At that point, you're just using Unix or VMS or VM/CMS or some other nasty operating system in a different place, so you don't need to know much else. The other possibility is that you telnet into a special application, such as a library card catalog or a game, and that special application has its own interface. I can't help you there, but most of the applications provide some sort of help.

Aside from the standard method of telnetting, there are two quirks: specifying a port number, which some applications require, and telnetting to an IBM mainframe running a full-screen interface. I mention these quirks later, but first, the basic Telnet syntax.

Let's grab a hostname at random and peruse the InterNIC, or Internet Network Information Center. Several companies run this Internet service for the government, and there's good information there. The easiest way to invoke Telnet is to type **telnet** and the sitename, as in the following:

```
/d/tidbits> telnet rs.internic.net
Trying...
Connected to RS.INTERNIC.NET.
Escape character is '^]'.
```

As you can see, this machine didn't ask for any login or password information, but it could have required a special account like "guest." Usually a Telnet site tells you whether it wants you to use a special login name.

```
SunOS UNIX (rs) (ttyp1)

*********************************************************************
* — InterNIC Registration Services Center   —
*
* For gopher, type:                GOPHER <return>
* For wais, type:                  WAIS <search string> <return>
* For the *original* whois type:   WHOIS [search string] <return>
* For the X.500 whois DUA, type:   X500WHOIS <return>
* For registration status:         STATUS <ticket number> <return>
*
* For user assistance call (800) 444-4345 ¦ (619) 455-4600 or (703) 742-4777
* Please report system problems to ACTION@rs.internic.net
*********************************************************************
Please be advised that the InterNIC Registration host contains INTERNET
Domains, IP Network Numbers, ASNs, and Points of Contacts ONLY. Please
refer to rfc1400.txt for details (available via anonymous ftp at
either nic.ddn.mil [/rfc/rfc1400.txt]  or ftp.rs.internic.net
[/policy/rfc1400.txt]).
Cmdinter Ver 1.3 Wed Aug 18 00:36:31 1993 EST
[vt102] InterNIC >
```

This particular site also runs a number of other programs, including a WAIS client and a Gopher client. Because you're now playing by this machine's rules, type **gopher** and see what happens:

```
[vt102] InterNIC > gopher

                 Internet Gopher Information Client v1.03

                  Root gopher server: rs.internic.net

  —>  1.  Information about the InterNIC/
      2.  InterNIC Information Services (General Atomics)/
      3.  InterNIC Registration Services (NSI)/
      4.  InterNIC Directory and Database Services (AT&T)/

Press ? for Help, q to Quit, u to go up a menu      Retrieving Directory..-
```

Having invoked the local Gopher client, now you're playing by the Gopher's rules. To navigate, you move the **– >** pointer using the arrow keys, and either pressing Return or the right-arrow key moves you down into a subfolder, if you can call it that.

Almost all Telnet clients provide an easy way to leave, so if you get stuck or lost, try typing commands such as **quit**, **exit**, or **logout**. You also can try **help** or **?** to see what local commands might be available.

Let's explore how you telnet to a specific port number by telnetting to the Cookie Server. Watch closely:

```
/d/tidbits> telnet astro.temple.edu 12345
Trying...
Connected to astro.ocis.temple.edu.
Escape character is '^]'.
"Every time I think I know where it's at, they move it."
Connection closed by foreign host.
```

That's all there is to it—you simply append the port number, which you have found in some list or been told (I've never found an easy way to figure it out) to the standard **telnet** *sitename* command.

Note

It's possible that the Cookie Server has gone away—I couldn't connect to it when I tried again for the second edition.

Finally, what about full-screen IBM interfaces? Like many other things IBM has done, they don't get along well with the rest of the computing world, and in fact Telnet itself doesn't work well with an IBM mainframe running VM or MVS. For those machines, which usually identify themselves by mentioning one of their operating systems when you telnet to them, you need to use a related program, called **tn3270**. Otherwise, the program works about the same as Telnet; you just type **tn3270** *sitename*. After you get in, you must use the appropriate keys to send the key sequences that the IBM mainframe expects. Figuring out which keys on your keyboard map to the IBM keys is difficult, but I recommend trying the keypad keys or the combination of Escape and a number key. Good luck, you'll need it. This is a good question for a local administrator because she should know how the local system has been set up. In any event, here's what **tn3270** looks like:

```
/d/tidbits> tn3270 cornella.cit.cornell.edu
Trying...
Connected to cornella.cit.cornell.edu.
Unable to open file /etc/map3270
Unable to open file /etc/map3270
Using default key mappings.
```

I got stuck here and wasn't able to do much of anything. Oh well, I probably can't remember the password to that account any more anyway.

Now you've learned about all there is to using Telnet in the real world. Once again, if you want, you can check out the man pages for Telnet, or type **telnet** and then **help**, but you don't have to worry about most of Telnet's commands and options.

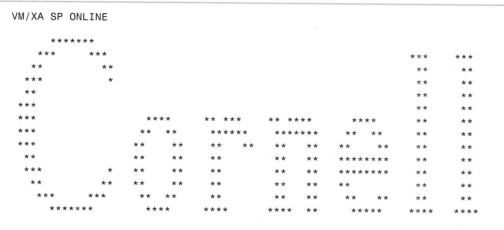

```
VM/XA SP ONLINE

          * * * * * * *
      * * *         * * *                                              * * *      * * *
       * *             * *                                              * *        * *
      * * *             *                                               * *        * *
       * *                                                              * *        * *
      * * *                                                             * *        * *
      * * *             * * * *      * *  * * *      * *  * * * *      * * * *      * *        * *
      * * *           * *    * *    * * * * * *    * * * * * * *    * *    * *     * *        * *
      * * *           * *    * *    * *    * *    * *    * *    * *      * *       * *        * *
       * *            * *    * *    * *             * *    * *    * * * * * * * *    * *        * *
      * * *       *   * *    * *    * *             * *    * *    * * * * * * * *    * *        * *
       * *           * *     * *    * *             * *    * *    * *             * *        * *
      * * *     * * *   * *    * *    * *             * *    * *    * *    * *     * *        * *
        * * * * * * *      * * * *      * * * *      * * * *   * *    * * * * *    * * * *    * * * *

              Cornell University Ithaca, New York

       This system is for authorized use only.  Type: CUINFO CIT ABUSE


     LOGON
                                                            RUNNING
       CORNELLA
```

Archie

Now that you've learned about Telnet, let's look at Internet services such as Archie, IRC, WAIS, Gopher, and the World-Wide Web, which you often use Telnet to access from a Unix shell account. The trick is, as I said, Telnet, because in each case you must telnet to another machine that runs a client for that service.

Note

> *You don't always have to telnet to a remote machine for things like Archie, since your host machine may run the client locally, at which point you could just type* **archie** *to search the Archie server. However, there's no telling what is installed on your Unix host, so let's pretend that the clients aren't installed. If they are, great, you're better off.*

First, let's explore Archie because it has almost no interface, although it's extremely useful for finding files available via FTP. You can telnet to a number of public Archie servers. Here, I pick a specific one in the U.S. to avoid burdening overseas connections.

To start, you connect to an Archie site:

```
/d/tidbits> telnet archie.sura.net
Trying...
Connected to yog-sothoth.sura.net.
Escape character is '^]'.
```

Then you log in to the Archie program by providing entering **archie** as the userid:

```
SunOS UNIX (yog-sothoth.sura.net)

login: archie
Last login: Wed Aug 18 01:55:47 from borris.eece.unm.
                Welcome to the ARCHIE server at SURAnet

Please report any problems to archie-admin@sura.net

PLEASE use the client software if you can. If things continue as they
are we will limit the number interactive logins.  Client software
is available on ftp.sura.net in /pub/archie/clients
```

Consider asking your system administrator to install the Archie client software on your machine so that you don't have to tie up the Archie servers around the world by logging into them. The Archie clients are more polite than a person can ever be.

```
Site update/change information should be sent to archie-updates@bunyip.com

SURAnet is trying out a new, experimental service called qarchie.
qarchie only supports doing searches on the database.  However queries
should complete much faster using the qarchie interface.  To try this out,
```

you can log into this machine as qarchie. Please use the qarchie service
unless there is a reason that you cannot. If you cannot, please send mail
to archie-admin@sura.net explaining why. Thanks.

The problem of the percentage becoming negative is a known problem which will
be fixed in the future.

```
        archie.ac.il               132.65.20.254     (Israel server)
        archie.ans.net             147.225.1.10      (ANS server, NY (USA))
        archie.au                  139.130.4.6       (Australian Server)
        archie.doc.ic.ac.uk        146.169.11.3      (United Kingdom Server)
        archie.edvz.uni-linz.ac.at 140.78.3.8        (Austrian Server)
        archie.funet.fi            128.214.6.102     (Finnish Server)
        archie.internic.net        198.49.45.10      (AT&T server, NY (USA))
        archie.kr                  128.134.1.1       (Korean Server)
        archie.kuis.kyoto-u.ac.jp  130.54.20.1       (Japanese Server)
        archie.luth.se             130.240.18.4      (Swedish Server)
        archie.ncu.edu.tw          140.115.19.24     (Taiwanese server)
        archie.nz                  130.195.9.4       (New Zealand server)
        archie.rediris.es          130.206.1.2       (Spanish Server)
        archie.rutgers.edu         128.6.18.15       (Rutgers University (USA))
        archie.sogang.ac.kr        163.239.1.11      (Korean Server)
        archie.sura.net            128.167.254.195   (SURAnet server MD (USA))
        archie.sura.net(1526)      128.167.254.195   (SURAnet alt. MD (USA))
        archie.switch.ch           130.59.1.40       (Swiss Server)
        archie.th-darmstadt.de     130.83.22.60      (German Server)
        archie.unipi.it            131.114.21.10     (Italian Server)
        archie.univie.ac.at        131.130.1.23      (Austrian Server)
        archie.unl.edu             129.93.1.14       (U. of Nebraska, Lincoln (USA))
        archie.uqam.ca             132.208.250.10    (Canadian Server)
        archie.wide.ad.jp          133.4.3.6         (Japanese Server)
```

Client software should be supported at all of these sites.

Telnet sites often provide a hefty chunk of information when you first log in so
that you know where you are and what's happening. In the case of telnetting to
an Archie server, the site tells you about the latest client software and all the
Archie servers around the world. If you see an Archie server nearer to you, you
should use it.

Now you can search for a file. I've stacked the deck on this search because I'm
searching for an issue of *TidBITS*, so I'm almost positive that it will turn up
somewhere on the nets.

```
archie> prog tidbits-222.etx
# matches / % database searched:   13 /-44%
```

I presume that **prog** stands for "program," but it would be nice if Archie used a standard term like "find." You can type a word after **prog**, or, if you know how, you can type a regular expression, which is a way of specifying patterns of text rather than specific text strings. Regular expressions are difficult to master, so don't worry about it now.

After it updates the **#** of matches and **%** of database searched for several minutes, Archie displays the matches, showing the site name, the IP number for that site, when the database at that site was last updated, and the full pathname of the file so you know where to get it via FTP.

```
Host akiu.gw.tohoku.ac.jp    (130.34.8.9)
Last updated 16:54  2 Jun 1994

    Location: /.u3/info-mac/per/tb
      FILE        rw-r--r--     30206  Apr 20 06:14    tidbits-222.etx

Host sics.se   (192.16.123.90)
Last updated 02:22 28 Apr 1994

    Location: /pub/info-mac/per/tb
      FILE        r--r--r--     30206  Apr 19 21:14    tidbits-222.etx

Host nctuccca.edu.tw   (192.83.166.10)
Last updated 21:08 26 Apr 1994

    Location: /Macintosh/info-mac/per/tb
      FILE        r--r--r--     30206  Apr 19  1994    tidbits-222.etx
```

I thought that this search string wouldn't turn up many responses, but you probably didn't want to see all 13 hits. One of the major problems with Archie is its enthusiasm; when you give it a common search string, it returns up to 1,000 hits on the database, which scroll by, out of control, for some time. Let's try to prevent this situation from happening:

```
archie> help

  Help gives you information about various topics, including all the
  commands that are available and how to use them.  Telling archie about
  your terminal type and size (via the "term" variable) and to use the
  pager (via the "pager" variable) is not necessary to use help, but
  provides a somewhat nicer interface.
```

```
Currently, the available help topics are:

    about    - a blurb about archie
    bugs     - known bugs and undesirable features
    bye      - same as "quit"
    email    - how to contact the archie email interface
    exit     - same as "quit"
    help     - this message
    list     - list the sites in the archie database
    mail     - mail output to a user
    nopager  - *** use 'unset pager' instead
    pager    - *** use 'set pager' instead
    prog     - search the database for a file
    quit     - exit archie
    set      - set a variable
    show     - display the value of a variable
    site     - list the files at an archive site
    term     - *** use 'set term ...' instead
    unset    - unset a variable
    whatis   - search for keyword in the software description database

For information on one of these topics type:

  help <topic>


A '?' at the help prompt will list the available sub-topics.


Help topics available:
        about    bugs     bye      email
        list     mail     nopager  pager
        prog     regex    set      show
        site     term     unset    whatis

Help topic?
```

I can't convey how I figured out which command might be the right one to explore further, but experience (you'll get it, don't worry!) claims that commands such as **set** generally work for changing settings. I see a few other interesting commands in this help screen: **mail**, **list**, and **whatis**. More on those commands later in this section.

```
Help topic? set

  The 'set' command allows you to set one of archie's variables.  Their
  values affect how archie interacts with the user.  Archie distinguishes
```

```
between three types of variable: "boolean", which may be either set or
unset, "numeric", representing an integer within a pre- determined
range, and "string", whose value is a string of characters (which may or
may not be restricted).

Currently, the variables that may be set are:


    autologout - numeric.    Number of minutes before automatic log out
    mailto     - string.     Address that output is to be mailed to
    maxhits    - numeric.    'prog' stops after this many matches
    pager      - boolean.    If set use the pager, otherwise don't
    search     - string.     How 'prog' is to search the database
    sortby     - string.     How 'prog' output is to be sorted
    status     - boolean.    Report how the search is progressing
    term       - string.     Describes your terminal


    Each variable has a corresponding subtopic entry under 'set'.  See them for
Press return for more:
    more details.  Also, see help on 'unset' and 'show'.


Subtopics available for set:
        autologout      mailto  maxhits pager
        search  sortby  status  term

'set' subtopic?
```

Yup, that's it, you want to find out more about the maxhits variable:

```
'set' subtopic? maxhits

'maxhits' is a numeric variable whose value is the maximum number of
matches you want the 'prog' command to generate.

If archie seems to be slow, or you don't want a lot of output this can be
set to a small value.  "maxhits" must be within the range 0 to 1000.  The
default value is 1000.

Example:

    set maxhits 100

'prog' will now stop after 100 matches have been found
```

Bingo! If you type **set maxhits 20** before you issue your **prog** command, Archie limits the results to 20 hits. You might not see what you want, but you should get a sense if you're on the right track.

But what about those other commands that sounded interesting? If you issue the **mail** command along with a userid after a **prog** command finishes, Archie mails the results of that search to the address you specify. This approach can be a good way to keep the list of hits for later perusal, or if you're searching for someone else, you can email that person the results.

The **list** command isn't necessarily useful, but you may find it fun to search the list of FTP sites in Archie's database. Try typing **list mac** to see how many sites have "mac" in their names.

Finally, the **whatis** command accesses a human-maintained database of file descriptions and searches it for files whose descriptions contain your search string. For instance, try the following:

```
archie> whatis stuffit
sit            produce StuffIt archives for downloading to the MacIntosh
```

It took me three or four tries using **whatis** before I found anything that matched, and as you can see, there's not much even for a near-ubiquitous program like StuffIt. (We must talk to someone about the spelling of Macintosh.)

Perhaps the only real problem with the Archie client available via telnet is that there's no link to an FTP client so that you can find a file and retrieve it immediately, without having to exit Archie and run FTP. For that you can use Gopher and Veronica, though, and they're coming later in this chapter.

IRC

IRC, which stands for Internet Relay Chat, consists of thousands of people talking to each other in real time over the network, and is one of the most heavily used Internet services. I've never much enjoyed talking to strangers online because every time I've tried, the discussions seem trivial and meaningless. My ego hasn't suffered because I don't notice the same problem in real life or email, so I always chalked it up to the fact that it's hard to have meaningful conversations with complete strangers using nicknames. That said, IRC is popular, and I'm sure many people find it an excellent way to meet others and exchange ideas. Because I'm obviously not qualified to speak about it at length, I just show you the online help that I got after typing **irc** and then **/HELP**.

```
*** Help on basics
Irc is a multi-user, multi-channel chatting network.  It allows
people all over the internet to talk to one another in real-time.
Each irc user has a nickname they use.  All communication with
another user is either by nickname or by the channel that they or
you are on.  All IRCII commands begin with a / character.
Anything that does not begin with a / is assumed to be a message
that is sent to everyone on your channel.  Here is a list of
basic commands to help you get started:

     /LIST               Lists all current irc channels, number of
                         users, and topic.
     /NAMES              Shows the nicknames of all users on each
                         channel
     /JOIN <channel>     Join the named channel.  All non-commands
                         you type will now go to everyone on that
                         channel
     /MSG <nick> <msg>   Sends a private message to the specified
                         person.  Only the specified nickname will
                         see this message.
     /NICK               Change your nickname
     /QUIT               Exits irc.
     /HELP <topic>       Gets help on all IRCII commands.
     /WHO <channel>      Shows who is on a given channel,
                         including nickname, user name and host,
                         and realname.
     /WHOIS <nick>       Shows the "true" identity of someone

These commands should get you started on irc. Use the /HELP command
to find out more about things on irc, or ask questions of people...
most would be happy to help you out.
```

There have been numerous problems with IRC users on local sites around here, so a number of them have shut off IRC access entirely. I won't get into the issue other than to note that you may be able to use an IRC server like **irc-2.mit.edu** if you want. I recommend that you use Homer instead of a character-based IRC client.

WAIS

To access WAIS from a Unix shell account, you once more rely on Telnet, although the interface completely changes when you arrive at the WAIS **swais** client, which was written by John Curran. Anyway, take a look.

```
/d/tidbits> telnet quake.think.com
Trying...
Connected to quake.think.com.
Escape character is '^]'.


SunOS UNIX (quake)
```

Accessing WAIS is a matter of telnetting to **quake.think.com** normally, no special port numbers or IBM mainframes here.

```
login: wais
```

You must log in to WAIS specifically; you aren't dumped in by default. No big deal, the login name is **wais**.

```
Last login: Wed Aug 18 09:47:29 from vax1.utulsa.edu
SunOS Release 4.1.1 (QUAKE) #3: Tue Jul 7 11:09:01 PDT 1992

Welcome to swais.
Please type user identifier (optional, i.e user@host):
ace@tidbits.com
```

Although you don't need a password as such for WAIS, it does ask you to identify yourself. You don't have to, but good net citizens do because they're using someone else's machine.

```
TERM = (vt100)

Starting swais (this may take a little while)...
This is the new experimental "wais" login on Quake.Think.COM

As the total number of sources has passed the 500 mark, we've found it's
become virtually impossible to find a source from the 25 screens of
sources.
```

```
I have decided that instead of presenting you with all the sources, I'll
just give you the Directory of Servers as a starting point.  To find
additional sources, just select the directory-of-server.src source, and ask
it a question.  If you know the name of the source you want, use it for the
keywords, and you should get that source as one of the results.  If you
don't know what source you want, then just ask a question that has
something to do with what you're looking for, and see what you get.

Once you have a list of results, you should "u"se the result you desire.
You can "v"iew a result before you "u"se it, paying close attention to the
"description".

Please let us know how you like this approach by sending feedback to
"wais@quake.think.com".

- WAIS at Think.COM

(press "q" to continue)
```

Press Return to agree that you're using a VT100 terminal and read through the welcome message that explains how using the site has changed. When you're done, press **q** to continue. It then takes a few seconds to run the **swais** program that displays the sources. After **swais** runs, the screen should display as follows (but with lots more blank lines than shown here):

```
SWAIS                        Source Selection                  Sources:  1
   #            Server                          Source               Cost
 001:      [  quake.think.com]  directory-of-servers               Free



Keywords:

<space> selects, w for keywords, arrows move, <return> searches, q quits, or ?
```

First off, press the Spacebar to select directory-of-servers. Then press **w** to move up into the Keywords field, and type **macintosh**. Press Return to search the Directory of Servers and the WAIS client goes out and finds nine sources that match the search string of "macintosh."

```
SWAIS                      Search Results                Items:  9
  #    Score      Source                    Title                 Lines
001:  [1000]  (directory-of-se)  macintosh-news                     13
002:  [ 942]  (directory-of-se)  macintosh-tidbits                  11
003:  [ 412]  (directory-of-se)  academic_email_conf                61
004:  [ 353]  (directory-of-se)  ANU-Asian-Computing                78
005:  [ 353]  (directory-of-se)  comp.sys.mac.programmer            12
006:  [ 353]  (directory-of-se)  internet-mail                     131
007:  [ 353]  (directory-of-se)  mac.FAQ                            15
008:  [ 353]  (directory-of-se)  merit-archive-mac                  15
009:  [ 353]  (directory-of-se)  nrao-fits                          76


<space> selects, arrows move, w for keywords, s for sources, ? for help
```

Now that we've found some sources, let's search for information about the MBDF virus, one of the Macintosh viruses. Information about Mac viruses is probably in the **macintosh-news** source—let's see what's type of information it holds. Highlight it by moving to it with the arrow keys and then press the Spacebar to display the description of the source.

```
SWAIS                      Document Display              Page:  1
(:source
  :version  3
  :ip-address "131.239.2.100"
  :ip-name "cmns-moon.think.com"
  :tcp-port 210
  :database-name "MAC CSMP TIDB"
  :maintainer "bug-public@think.com"
  :description
  "This source combines several publications of interest to Macintosh
   users: The info-mac digest (info-mac@sumex-aim.stanford.edu), Michael
   Kelly's comp.sys.mac.programmer digest, and Adam Engst's TidBITS
   electronic magazine for the Macintosh."

  )

Press a key to continue
```

Ah, this does look useful. Press any key to get back to the list of the found sources.

Note

> *One of the longest-standing computer jokes centers around the user who is having trouble and calls the tech support line. "Hello," says the user, "I'm having trouble with my new computer. It says 'Press any key to continue' but I can't find the Any key." OK, so it's a lousy joke.*

Once you're back at the list of the found sources, make sure the `macintosh-news` source is highlighted, and press **u** to use the source. If you wanted to use more than one source, just highlight another and press **u** again for each. Now press **s** to go back to the list of sources that you can search, and you see that `macintosh-news` has been added to your list.

```
SWAIS                    Source Selection          Sources:  2
  #            Server                   Source          Cost
001:  * [    quake.think.com]  directory-of-servers     Free
002:    [ cmns-moon.think.com]  macintosh-news           Free


Keywords: macintosh

<space> selects, w for keywords, arrows move, <return> searches, q quits, or ?
```

Note that the directory-of-servers source is still selected (see the asterisk next to it above?), so before we search the `macintosh-news` source, we must deselect `directory-of-servers` and select `macintosh-news`, both by highlighting and then pressing the Spacebar. After you do that, press **w** and change the Keywords field to include **MBDF** instead of `macintosh`.

Note

> *You should be able to delete **macintosh** with the Delete key, but if not, check your terminal emulator's settings to toggle the function of that key to Delete from Backspace.*

```
SWAIS                          Source Selection              Sources:  2
   #           Server                       Source                    Cost
001:    [      quake.think.com]  directory-of-servers                 Free
002:  * [ cmns-moon.think.com]  macintosh-news                       Free


Keywords: MBDF

<space> selects, w for keywords, arrows move, <return> searches, q quits, or ?
```

As you can see, there are a number of articles on the MBDF virus, including several articles in *TidBITS*.

```
SWAIS                          Search Results               Items: 40
   #   Score                       Title                           Lines
001:  [1000]  TidBITS#110: Request for MBDF damages  — — — — — — — —   98
002:  [ 966]  Info-Mac Digest V10 #49:  MBDF A Virus  Date: Thu, 20 Feb  54
003:  [ 966]  Comp.Sys.Mac.Programmer:   MBDF Protocol               78
004:  [ 949]  Info-Mac Digest V10 #62:  Request for MBDF Reports     99
005:  [ 897]  Info-Mac Digest V10 #46:  MBDF A Trojan Horse          34
006:  [ 897]  Info-Mac Digest V10 #49:  [*] MBDF Vaccine for Rival   20
007:  [ 863]  Info-Mac Digest V11 #219:  [!] New Macintosh Viruses Disco  195
008:  [ 845]  Info-Mac Digest V10 #246:  [*] TidBITS#146/12-Oct-92   33
009:  [ 845]  Info-Mac Digest V10 #217:  [*] TidBITS#141/07-Sep-92   31
010:  [ 845]  Info-Mac Digest V10 #53:  [*] TidBITS#108/24-Feb-92    41
011:  [ 845]  Info-Mac Digest V10 #51:  Sam Virus Clinic MBDF definition  30
012:  [ 845]  Comp.Sys.Mac.Programmer:   Patching MBDF              165
013:  [ 828]  Comp.Sys.Mac.Programmer:   Custom MDEF/Submenu woes..  73
014:  [ 811]  TidBITS#201: The Flu Season Returns  — — — — — — — —   61
015:  [ 811]  TidBITS#108: MBDF Virus  — — — —    Just after I wrote 1  89
016:  [ 811]  Comp.Sys.Mac.Programmer:   Patching GetResource      194
017:  [ 794]  Info-Mac Digest V11 #220:  [*] Disinfectant 3.3        47
018:  [ 794]  Info-Mac Digest V10 #60:  Comments about perpetrators and  37


<space> selects, arrows move, w for keywords, s for sources, ? for help
```

Here you have a good number of possibilities. Notice the Score column to the left of the Source column. The higher the number in this column, the more closely the article matches your search criteria. In theory, the articles at the top of the list should be exactly what you want, and the articles further down might or might not work out.

As before, the basic commands of the Spacebar and the arrow keys are listed for your reading convenience, but I bet more useful commands are hidden in the help. A quick **?** reveals the following:

```
SWAIS                          Search Results Help            Page:  1

  j, ^N              Move Down one item
  k, ^P              Move Up one item
  J                  Move Down one screen
  K                  Move Up one screen
  R                  Show relevant documents
  S                  Save current item to a file
  m                  Mail current item to an address
  ##                 Position to item number ##
  /sss               Position to item beginning sss
  <space>            Display current item
  <return>           Display current item
  |                  Pipe current item into a unix command
  v                  View current item information
  r                  Make current item a relevant document
  s                  Specify new sources to search
  u                  Use it; add it to the list of sources
  w                  Make another search with new keywords
  o                  Set and show swais options
  h                  Show this help display
  H                  Display program history
  q                  Leave this program
```

You might find many of these commands useful, especially the ability to mail information back to yourself. After you look at the results of your search, press the Spacebar to display the selected article, such as the abbreviated one that follows:

```
SWAIS                          Document Display              Page:  1
0000000708TIDB
920209
TidBITS electronic magazine for the Macintosh
Copyright 1990-1992 Adam & Tonya Engst. Non-profit, non-commercial
publications may reprint articles if full credit is given.

TidBITS#110: Request for MBDF damages

 _ _ _ _ _ _ _ _ _ _ _
   by Mark H. Anbinder — mha@baka.ithaca.ny.us
```

```
Good afternoon. I am a Macintosh technical consultant in Ithaca,
New York, where two Cornell University students were arrested last
month for allegedly creating and releasing the MBDF virus. I've
been asked to assist in collecting some information for an ongoing
investigation being conducted by Investigator Scott Hamilton of
Cornell's Department of Public Safety.

IF YOU WERE DIRECTLY AFFECTED by the MBDF virus, please send me a
detailed description of the damages and expenses incurred. See
below for details of what I need to know.

Press any key to continue, 'q' to quit.
```

If the article spans more than one screen, page through it by pressing the Spacebar after each screen. At the end of the article, the **swais** client returns the list of found articles so you can read another if you like. Pressing the **s** key takes you back to the list of sources if you wish to perform a different search or find more sources, and pressing **q** ends your session abruptly.

Note

*In many places in the WAIS client, if you press **q** it quits instantly, forcing you to log in again. The confusing part is that there are some points at which you press **q** to continue.*

My main opinion about the Telnet-accessible WAIS client is merely that it works. I find the interface confusing and awkward and strongly recommend that you use a MacTCP-based WAIS client if you can. They may not be perfect either, but they are a heck of a lot easier than the **swais** client.

Gopher

Tunneling through gopher holes of information in a character-based environment is harder than in a graphical environment because you must go up through the levels you go down. Gopher provides access to all sorts of information and files, and it links to anonymous FTP sites and WAIS for added utility. Gopher is inherently hierarchical, like folders on the Macintosh, but unlike folders, if you dive down into several levels, you must come back out the same way. The graphical MacTCP-based versions of Gopher don't suffer this problem because they generally provide windows for each level of the hierarchy, so you can always switch back to a different level by clicking on a different window. Although your local Unix machine can install the same client you see in the following, you can always telnet to a public Gopher server like this one. The effect is the same, but if you can use a local client (see what happens if you type **gopher** at the Unix prompt), that method is preferable for everyone.

```
/d/tidbits> telnet consultant.micro.umn.edu
Trying...
Connected to hafnhaf.micro.umn.edu.
Escape character is '^]'.

AIX telnet (hafnhaf)

N O T I C E : this system is very heavily used
For better performance, you should install and
run a gopher client on your own system.

Gopher clients are available for anonymous ftp from
boombox.micro.umn.edu

To run gopher on this system login as "gopher"


IBM AIX Version 3 for RISC System/6000
(C) Copyrights by IBM and by others 1982, 1991.
login: gopher
```

By now you're probably bored stiff with my explanations of logging in to a machine via Telnet, so I'll try to avoid sounding like a broken record. Like WAIS, Gopher wants you to log in to the machine with a special username, **gopher** in this case.

```
Last unsuccessful login: Mon Aug 16 09:57:11 1993 on pts/1 from
access.telecomm.umn.edu
Last login: Wed Aug 18 12:49:00 1993 on pts/18 from
gateway.cary.ibm.com
TERM = (vt100)
Erase is Ctrl-H
Kill is Ctrl-U
Interrupt is Ctrl-C
I think you're on a vt100 terminal
```

If you're not using a VT100 terminal, there's no telling if the client will work.

```
             Internet Gopher Information Client v2.0.15

              Home Gopher server: hafnhaf.micro.umn.edu

    —>  1.  Information About Gopher/
        2.  Computer Information/
        3.  Internet file server (ftp) sites/
        4.  Fun & Games/
        5.  Libraries/
        6.  Mailing Lists/
        7.  News/
        8.  Other Gopher and Information Servers/
        9.  Phone Books/
        10. Search Gopher Titles at the University of Minnesota <?>
        11. Search lots of places at the U of M <?>
        12. UofM Campus Information/

Press ? for Help, q to Quit                             Page: 1/1
```

After you're in the Gopher menus, move around with the arrows, press Return to select a menu item, and type **u** to move up a level. Notice that some of the entries end with **/**, which indicates they are directories, and other entries end with **<?>**, which indicates you can perform full text searches on them.

Veronica

Gopherspace is so huge these days that, although it's fun to browse through the various menus at times, if you want to find anything specific, you use Veronica, which is usually located under a menu called "Other Gopher and Information Servers" or "World."

```
             Internet Gopher Information Client v2.0.15

              Search titles in Gopherspace using veronica

    —>  1.
        2.  FAQ:  Frequently-Asked Questions about veronica  (1993-08-23)
        3.  Search Gopher Directory Titles via NYSERNet <?>
        4.  Search Gopher Directory Titles via SCS Nevada  <?>
        5.  Search Gopher Directory Titles via U. of Manitoba <?>
```

```
   6.  Search Gopher Directory Titles via U.Texas, Dallas <?>
   7.  Search Gopher Directory Titles via UNINETT/U. of Bergen <?>
   8.  Search Gopher Directory Titles via University of Koeln <?>
   9.  Search Gopher Directory Titles via University of Pisa <?>
  10.  Search gopherspace (veronica) via NYSERNet <?>
  11.  Search gopherspace (veronica) via SCS Nevada  <?>
  12.  Search gopherspace (veronica) via U. of Manitoba <?>
  13.  Search gopherspace (veronica) via U.Texas, Dallas <?>
  14.  Search gopherspace (veronica) via UNINETT/U. of Bergen <?>
  15.  Search gopherspace (veronica) via University of Koeln <?>
  16.  Search gopherspace (veronica) via University of Pisa <?>


Press ? for Help, q to Quit, u to go up a menu              Page: 1/1
```

I have no idea why item 1 is blank, but the important thing to note in the Veronica screen is that Veronica enables you to search two types of data within Gopherspace. Items 3 through 9 enable you to search for the names of other Gopher directories only, whereas with items 10 through 16 you can search for the titles of all items in Gopherspace, including individual files. Search directories first because the search is likely to narrow more quickly and be easier to wrap your mind around.

If you select item 15, you see a pseudo dialog box into which you can type the word you want to search for. In this case, I typed **tidbits**.

```
+— — — — —Search gopherspace (veronica) via University of Koeln— — — — —+
¦                                                                        ¦
¦ Words to search for                                                    ¦
¦                                                                        ¦
¦ tidbits                                                                ¦
¦                                                                        ¦
¦ [Help: ^-]  [Cancel: ^G]                                               ¦
+— — — — — — — — — — — — — — — — — — — — — — — — — — — — — — — — — — — — —+
```

And here's what Gopher came up with:

```
               Internet Gopher Information Client v2.0.15

        Search gopherspace (veronica) via University of Koeln: tidbits
```

```
—>   1.  TidBITS#59/AccessPC.etx.cpt <HQX>
     2.  tidbits-111-to-120.hqx <HQX>
     3.  tidbits-174.etx
     4.  tidbits-091-to-100.hqx  [ 1Aug92, 182kb] <HQX>
     5.  tidbits-161-to-170.hqx <HQX>
     6.  tidbits-061-to-070.hqx <HQX>
     7.  tidbits-199.etx
     8.  TidBITS#92/11-Nov-91.etx.cpt <HQX>
     9.  tidbits-175.etx/
    10.  TidBITS#66/Font_Converters..cpt <HQX>
    11.  tidbits-212.etx  [ 8Feb94, 29kb]
    12.  tidbits-021-to-030.hqx <HQX>
    13.  tidbits-212.etx
    14.  tidbits-223.etx
    15.  tidbits-217.etx
    16.  tidbits-211.etx  [ 1Feb94, 30kb]
    17.  tidbits-175.etx/
    18.  tidbits-111-to-120.hqx <HQX>

Press ? for Help, q to Quit, u to go up a menu          Page: 1/12
```

When you see a number of items that all look the same (which is all too common because of duplication of resources on the Internet), you can check where they live with the = command. If something seems slow, it may be because that particular Gopher server is located far away.

That's enough for now. You should be able to navigate through Gopherspace adequately by moving into and out of various menu levels and by using Veronica to search for specific Gopher servers and items in Gopherspace.

Oops, I almost forgot. One of Gopher's most impressive features is the way it links with Telnet to provide access to other, non-Gopher services. At the top level is an item called "Internet file server (ftp) sites," which takes you to any FTP site that you want. Gopher is an excellent way to FTP files because, for technical reasons, it puts less of a load on a server than FTP. The major problem with using Gopher to look for and snag files is that unlike FTP, it's impossible to determine file sizes unless the server is running the latest Gopher+ extensions.

Along the same lines of linking to other services, in the "Other Gopher and Information Servers" directory is an item for Terminal Based Information, which uses Telnet to access a number of campus-wide information systems and the like. Selecting one of these items drops you into whatever special Telnet interface the service uses.

```
            Internet Gopher Information Client v2.0.15

                     Terminal Based Information

  —>   1.  Appalachian State University <TEL>
        2.  CUline, University of Colorado,Boulder <TEL>
        3.  Columbia University - ColumbiaNet <TEL>
        4.  MIT TechInfo <TEL>
        5.  NYU ACF INFO system <TEL>
        6.  New Mexico State University NMSU/INFO <TEL>
        7.  North Carolina State University Happenings! <TEL>
        8.  Princeton News Network <TEL>
        9.  The GC EduNET System (A K-12 education resource) <TEL>
       10.  U of Saskatchewan Library INFOACCESS system <TEL>
       11.  University of New Hampshire's VideoTex <TEL>
       12.  University of North Carolina at Chapel Hill INFO <TEL>


  Press ? for Help, q to Quit, u to go up a menu        Page: 1/1
```

Another item in the "Other Gopher and Information Servers" directory enables you to access WAIS sources as though they were normal Gopher databases. If you found the awkward swais program daunting, you might consider using Veronica to search all of Gopherspace for a topic along with the keyword **.src** to indicate that you want to find only matching WAIS sources. I don't know whether that method is foolproof, but it works for me.

Enjoy Gopherspace, but don't let it overwhelm you. If you use a local Gopher client and you find a service within Gopherspace that you particularly like, you can mark neat items with bookmarks by typing **a** when pointing at that item. At any point, typing **v** displays your bookmarks so that you can jump to them without tunneling through Gopherspace.

HYTELNET

I'm not going to explore HYTELNET in depth, but suffice it to say that it stands for *hypertelnet* and provides a poor man's Gopher interface to information resources available via Telnet or **tn3270**. Like Gopher, HYTELNET enables you to select items from a menu by moving the cursor to them with the up- and down-arrow keys and then using the right- and left-arrow keys to move either to the next level down or back to the previous level. After you finally reach a description of a service, you can move to the Telnet command embedded in the description, and by selecting that command, HYTELNET actually telnets directly to that location. Because HYTELNET works with Telnet, of course, it provides yet another interface to Archie, WAIS, Gopher, and the World-Wide Web. Once you're in, you're still using a normal Telnet interface. Here's a partial HYTELNET session that I started by typing **hytelnet**:

```
                Welcome to HYTELNET version 6.6
                      October 10, 1993

            What is HYTELNET?        <WHATIS>
            Library catalogs         <SITES1>
            Other resources          <SITES2>
            Help files for catalogs  <OP000>
            Catalog interfaces       <SYS000>
            Internet Glossary        <GLOSSARY>
            Telnet tips              <TELNET>
            Telnet/TN3270 escape keys <ESCAPE.KEY>
            Key-stroke commands      <HELP>
.........................................................
Up/Down arrows MOVE     Left/Right arrows SELECT    ? for HELP anytime

      m  returns here    i  searches the index    q  quits
.........................................................

          HYTELNET 6.6 was written by Peter Scott
          E-mail address: aa375@freenet.carleton.ca
```

On this screen I moved down to the Other Resources item and used the right-arrow key to go into it.

```
              Other Telnet-accessible resources

        <ARC000>  Archie: Archive Server Listing Service
        <CWI000>  Campus-wide Information systems
        <FUL000>  Databases and bibliographies

        <DIS000>  Distributed File Servers (Gopher/WAIS/WWW)
        <BOOKS>   Electronic books
        <FEE000>  Fee-Based Services

        <FRE000>  FREE-NETs & Community Computing Systems
        <BBS000>  General Bulletin Boards
        <HYT000>  HYTELNET On-line versions

        <NAS000>  NASA databases
        <NET000>  Network Information Services
        <DIR000>  Whois/White Pages/Directory Services

        <OTH000>  Miscellaneous resources
```

Here I just stuck with the first item, Archie servers:

```
               Archie: Archive Server Listing Service

  <ARC005> Advanced Network & Services, Inc (USA)
  <ARC003> Deakin File Server (Australia)
  <ARC002> Finnish University and Research Network Server (Finland)
  <ARC008> Hebrew University of Jerusalem (Israel)
  <ARC006> Imperial College, London (England)
  <ARC016> InterNIC Directory and Database Server
  <ARC017> Johannes Kepler University, Linz, (Austria)
  <ARC001> McGill School of Computer Science Server (Canada)
  <ARC010> Melbourne (Australia)
  <ARC012> National Central University, Chung-li, (Taiwan)
  <ARC011> Rutgers University Archive Server (USA)
  <ARC014> Sogang University (Korea)
  <ARC004> SURAnet Server (USA)
  <ARC013> Technische Hochschule Darmstadt (Germany)
  <ARC015> University of Lulea (Sweden)
  <ARC007> University of Nebraska, Lincoln (USA)
  <ARC019> University of Quebec at Montreal
  <ARC009> Victoria University, Wellington (New Zealand)
  <ARC018> Vienna University (Austria)
```

Again, I used the right-arrow key to go into the first Archie server listed, one run by Advanced Network & Services, resulting in the following screen.

```
               Advanced Network & Services, Inc

  TELNET ARCHIE.ANS.NET or 147.225.1.31
  login: archie

  'help' for help
  Problems, comments etc. to archie-admin@ans.net

  Client software is available on ftp.ans.net:/pub/archie/clients, and
  documentation can be found in /pub/archie/doc on the same machine.

  Advanced Network & Services, Inc.   E-Mail: shiao@ans.net
  100 Clearbrook Road                 Office: (914) 789-5340
  Elmsford, NY 10523
```

If I wanted to show you more of the same Archie-via-Telnet, simply using the right-arrow key would invoke Telnet and take me to that Archie server.

There's nothing particularly wrong with HYTELNET, and it's a good, if basic, way of browsing through the Internet. Unfortunately, it just doesn't excite me. I don't find it any easier to use than Gopher, and Gopher provides access to the same sorts of things. I suppose your choice depends on how you work.

World-Wide Web

Using the World-Wide Web on a character-based account is a bit like going to the movies with cotton in your ears and wearing very dark glasses. You can sort of see what's happening and kind of hear what's going on, but you're pretty much in the dark. I know of two main ways of accessing the Web from a character-based terminal, one that's pretty bad and another that's surprisingly decent. First the bad news.

```
/d/tidbits> telnet info.cern.ch
Trying 128.141.201.214...
Connected to www0.cern.ch.
Escape character is '^]'.


UNIX(r) System V Release 4.0 (www0)

                                          Welcome to the World-Wide Web
                        THE WORLD-WIDE WEB

   This is just one of many access points to the web, the universe of
   information available over networks. To follow references, just type the
   number then hit the return (enter) key.

   The features you have by connecting to this telnet server are very primitive
   compared to the features you have when you run a W3 "client" program on your
   own computer. If you possibly can, please pick up a client for your platform
   to reduce the load on this service and  experience the web in its full
   splendor.

   For more information, select by number:

 A list of available W3 client programs[1]
 Everything about the W3 project[2]
 Places to start exploring[3]
 The First International WWW Conference[4]

   This telnet service is provided by the WWW team at the European Particle
   Physics Laboratory known as CERN[5]
      [End]
1-5, Up, Quit, or Help:
```

As you can see, this Web browser requires you to press a number to traverse a link. The numbers are bracketed and appended to the links, which hurts the readability of the page, and with a large page with many links, you find following them to be a pain at best. Let's not bother with this interface any more and instead go on to talk about Lynx. Although I won't pretend that Lynx in any way compares to NCSA Mosaic or MacWeb, it does OK.

Your Unix machine may have Lynx installed on it—if so, just type **lynx** to start it up. If not, telnet to **ukanaix.cc.ukans.edu**, login as **www**, and tell it you're using a VT100.

```
                          Lynx default home page (p1 of 2)

                  WELCOME TO LYNX AND THE WORLD OF THE WEB

      You are using a WWW Product called Lynx. For more information about
      obtaining and installing Lynx please choose About Lynx

      The current version of Lynx is 2.3. If you are running an earlier
      version PLEASE UPGRADE!

   INFORMATION SOURCES ABOUT AND FOR WWW
         * For a description of WWW choose Web Overview
         * About the WWW Information Sharing project
         * WWW Information By Subject
         * WWW Information By Type

   OTHER INFO SOURCES
         * University of Kansas CWIS
         * O'Reilly & Ass. Global Network Navigator
         * Nova-Links: Internet access made easy
         * NCSA: Network Starting Points, Information Resource Meta-Index
    — press space for more, use arrow keys to move, '?' for help, 'q' to quit
     Arrow keys: Up and Down to move. Right to follow a link; Left to go back.
    H)elp O)ptions P)rint G)o M)ain screen Q)uit /=search [delete]=history list
```

Note all the bold words. The VT100 terminal type may not be able to display fonts and sizes of text, but it can do bold, so bold words indicate the links in Lynx. Hmm, say that three times fast.

One problem Lynx faces is that it can only show one page at a time, so you must press the Spacebar (or the **+** key) to scroll to the second page of this screen. Pressing the **b** or **-** keys scrolls back up. The VT100 screen can also display a reverse text style, and that's how Lynx indicates over which of the links your "cursor" is positioned. The up and down arrow keys move you from one link to another, and the left and right arrow keys traverse links, with the right arrow following the link and the left arrow bringing you back. The **G** command enables you to enter a specific URL, although that feature is disabled in the version of Lynx that you can telnet to. On the whole, using Lynx, like any Web browser, is simple. All you generally do is move between links, reading the information you see, and moving on to other links. I was impressed to find that Lynx supports Web forms, which makes certain types of applications more useful such as the searchable CUI W3 Catalog, which I'm searching for mentions of *TidBITS* here.

```
                                              CUI W3 Catalog (p1 of 2)

                      CUI W3 CATALOG


        _____

        Provide a Perl regular expression as a search pattern. Submit
        tidbits_____
        NB: Searches are case-insensitive.


        _____

        Welcome to CUI's W3 Catalog, a searchable catalog of W3 resources.
        There are currently 7174 entries. You may also consult the list of
        recent changes.

        For information about the contents of this catalog, see the W3 Catalog
        overview.

        NB: For clients without support for forms, an alternative interface is
    (Text entry field) Enter text. Use UP or DOWN arrows or tab to move off.
                Enter text into the field by typing on the keyboard
        Ctrl-U to delete all text in field, [Backspace] to delete a character
```

When we actually make it to the *TidBITS* Web server at

```
http://www.dartmouth.edu/Pages/TidBITS/TidBITS.html
```

you see the main limitation Lynx faces on the Web—images.

```
                                                     TidBITS (p1 of 2)

    This TidBITS server is a work in progress. Feedback is encouraged.
    Also please note that it is not a good idea to have documents of your
    own point to subtopics within a given issue of TidBITS until I have
    finalized the format. The tag names are subject to change. (Bill)

                        [IMAGE] TIDBITS



    PLACES TO GO, THINGS TO SEE:
        * TidBITS-228.html is the most recent issue.
        * What is TidBITS?
        * The many and varied ways to get TidBITS...
        * Related stuff (links to ftp://ftp.tidbits.com/pub/tidbits)
        * TidBITS Index (starts with issue 200)



  — press space for next page —
    Arrow keys: Up and Down to move. Right to follow a link; Left to go back.
    H)elp O)ptions P)rint G)o M)ain screen Q)uit /=search [delete]=history list
```

There's no way for Lynx to display the image that goes with the headline, so it just tells you there's an image there. No way around that problem, short of being able to use a graphical browser like Mosaic or MacWeb. Lynx may not be able to handle images, but it can handle the other data types often accessible on the Web, things like FTP and Gopher servers. If you come across a file on an FTP or Gopher server, Lynx first tries to display the file, but if it can't, it offers you the option of saving it to disk (again, not available on the client you telnet to), or downloading via whatever protocols that machine supports.

```
                                                     Lynx Download Options

                        Download Options

              You have the following download choices
                        please select one

        Save to disk

        Use Kermit to download to the local terminal

        Use Zmodem to download to the local terminal
```

```
Commands: Use arrow keys to move, '?' for help, 'q' to quit, '<-' to go back
  Arrow keys: Up and Down to move. Right to follow a link; Left to go back.
  H)elp O)ptions P)rint G)o M)ain screen Q)uit /=search [delete]=history list
```

Ah well, enough fun with Lynx. Press **q** at any time to quit. I highly recommend that you use Lynx for browsing the World-Wide Web if you're limited to a shell account. Lynx may not compare to Mosaic or MacWeb, but it does display the vast quantity of text available on the Web, and there's far more text on the Web than you could ever read. And if you miss a few pictures... just think of it as radio.

Shell Shocked

If you've actually read through this entire chapter, award yourself a gold star and go rest your eyes for a while. I started out discussing some of the programs that put a graphical interface on a standard Unix shell account, touching on things like Eudora and MicroPhone Pro's Internet Mail and Internet News modules. I also talked about dedicated programs like WorldLink and Pipeline that require specific proprietary accounts. Next, I turned to the Unix command-line and talked about a few of the programs that you use in Unix. This has been a shallow look at Unix, which is an incredibly deep operating system, but it should be enough for you to get started.

It's time to move on to another way you can connect to the Internet, the UUCP account. Although old and a bit clunky, UUCP connections to the Internet are still a useful and extremely efficient way to use email and Usenet news.

UUCP Access

Although by no means the snazziest method of connecting to the Internet, UUCP access is often the most efficient for basic email and news, because it is inherently a non-interactive process. Your host machine sends messages to your Mac in the form of files, which the UUCP software then processes for display. This process accounts for the acronym as well. UUCP stands for Unix-to-Unix CoPy (the copy command in Unix is cp).

With a UUCP connection, you connect only to send or receive information. When you read news or write a reply to an email message, your modem is not connected and racking up connect charges. UUCP appeared in the days of the 300 bps modem; although it has scaled up just fine to faster connections, even direct Internet connections, it still works well at slower speeds, because the actual connection time is usually relatively short. Most people set up a UUCP connection on a schedule, but you also can connect on demand.

Note

If you plan to use UUCP primarily, you should find out whether your host uses modems from Telebit, a major modem manufacturer. Many UUCP hosts use Telebit modems because Telebit built hardware support for UUCP into their modems, and two Telebit modems with PEP (Packetized Ensemble Protocol) can achieve greater speed when transferring UUCP information than two straight v.32bis modems.

I am familiar with, and cover later, three UUCP implementations for the Macintosh. I'm not going to cover those implementations included in Apple's version of Unix, A/UX, or two other versions of Unix that run on the Macintosh, MachTen and Minix. I know A/UX supports UUCP, and believe the others do, but because they're all complicated enough to deserve their own books, I must ignore them.

The first implementation of UUCP for the Macintosh, Mac/gnuucp 6.09, carries a request for maintenance fees; the second, uupc 3.1b32, is free. It's based on public domain code that enterprising programmers ported to the Mac. The third program is commercial, and carries the hefty price tag of $295. It used to be called uAccess, but when InterCon Systems took over the marketing from ICE Engineering, the name changed to UUCP/Connect.

UUCP/Connect is more expensive because it implements far more than just the code necessary to talk to a remote UUCP program. Tim Endres of ICE added features galore, so UUCP/Connect can talk to remote UUCP programs, unbatch the incoming files, display and organize them into various mailboxes and newsgroups, and do most anything else you want. Added almost as an afterthought are file translation capabilities, a simple Communications Toolbox-based terminal emulator, the capability to run a fileserver, and the capability of acting as a UUCP host for other machines.

Note

Configuring UUCP under Unix is much more difficult than on a Macintosh, but you gain a certain level of flexibility with Unix.

UUCP Accounts

With any of these programs, you need a UUCP account on a host computer before you can connect. The hard part is finding a local host (although long distance calls aren't out of the question). Perhaps the best place to look for a UUCP host is in the list of public access Unix providers in Phil Eschallier's nixpub list.

UUCP accounts range from free to rather expensive, and you cannot necessarily equate price with quality. When I moved to Seattle, I found two sites willing to let me connect for free. Both provided excellent service and put up with the slow modem that I had. If possible, try to find an account that doesn't charge for connect time because that significantly reduces stress in your life, assuming that you don't have tons of money. If you're paying a flat fee, it's easy to budget, and you don't have to worry if someone sends you a 500K file in email without asking first.

When you call to get a UUCP account, make sure you can provide the nodename you want to use, the first six characters of which must be unique. The *nodename* is the name of your computer (mine is **tidbits** in **ace@tidbits.com**). Your system administrator can help you through this; it requires reading the UUCP maps, something that isn't inherently obvious. It doesn't matter what userid you choose. Someone can send mail to any userid at that machine and UUCP delivers it, whether or not there is a user with that userid. You should create or watch for email to **root** and **postmaster**, standard accounts that exist on almost all UUCP machines. You're likely to receive mail to those accounts occasionally.

Note

For organizations wanting to receive mail for various different employees, UUCP is often the easiest way to go, because it's so easy to add new users.

Your provider must give you a fair amount of information as well. Write all this stuff down, because you might need to refer to it at various times while you're setting up your account.

- Phone: What phone number should you call?
- Speed: What is the highest common speed your modem can use?
- Prompt: Does your UUCP program have to do anything special to get the login prompt?
- Login: What is the userid that your UUCP program should use to log in?
- Password: What is the password that your UUCP program should give when logging in?

You also should talk to your provider about how he has the host machine set up, in terms of domain names and mail routing. He may be able to give you a domain name or help you apply for one, but you can always settle for the **.uucp** top-level domain. It works, though not as quickly or reliably as a real domain, like **.com**. Now you know all there is to the generic UUCP account. Next, let's look at the specific programs for using your UUCP account.

Mac/gnuucp

Mac/gnuucp, from Jim O'Dell of Fort Pond Research, is based on the gnuucp code from the Free Software Foundation, an organization devoted to free software and source code. The word *free* refers not to the price of the software, but to what you can do with it. You cannot control what anyone else does with the software, including what they do to the source code. By agreeing to a GNU public license, you transmit complete rights so that other people are free to do what they want. If someone starts to sell a GNU-licensed program, someone else can get the sources and provide the same thing for less or no money. Mac/gnuucp's GNU heritage accounts for its low price, and Jim's real life accounts for its lack of much interface. Luckily, Mike Kazmierczak and later, Morgan Davis, helped out by creating a HyperCard stack, called Mac/gnuucp MailReader. It puts a friendlier face on the command-line environment that Jim ported from the Unix source code.

Note

What's GNU? Not much, what's GNU with you? Sorry, but my editor made me put that in. GNU stands for the paradoxical "GNU's Not Unix."

Earlier versions of Mac/gnuucp were dogged by performance problems that Jim claims he has solved in version 6.09. Time constraints prevented me from testing Mac/gnuucp seriously enough to determine how quickly Mac/gnuucp performs, but I did get it working, and sent and received email.

Note

I've used UUCP/Connect in its uAccess incarnation for several years now, so although I'm certainly no programmer or Unix wizard, I'm fairly good at configuring UUCP programs. Although the basic configuration is straightforward, any hitches are likely to be major and confusing. For instance, when I attempted to get Mac/gnuucp to dial my Telebit WorldBlazer with an appropriate configuration string to turn on the WorldBlazer's PEP mode (necessary for talking to my UUCP host), I was not able get it to dial the modem. On a hunch, I opened a terminal application, and lo and behold, it complained that something else was using the serial port. A restart cleared the serial port and allowed Mac/gnuucp to dial the modem successfully. If you have strange connection problems, your UUCP host's system administrator is a good person to turn to.

Installation and Setup

Installing Mac/gnuucp is rather simple and, at the same time, rather complex. You must configure two text files and the HyperCard stack that you use to read and write email. Luckily, although the documentation doesn't mention this capability, you can edit these files directly within the HyperCard stack. Before you start, be sure to make backups of the two text files and the MailReader stack. Name the copy of the stack with whatever you want to use for your userid. I named mine **ace**. Open the stack by double-clicking on it.

Note

> *Attention, new Mac users! These steps assume you have HyperCard, which no longer comes with every Macintosh. You may have an older version around from an old Mac. It's also possible that the MailReader stack works with the free HyperCard Player program that ships with new Macs.*

The main MailReader stack window displays your userid, your incoming mail, and control buttons (see figure 11.1).

The original stack doesn't have a User entry; you must add it first. Click on the Configure button and the Configuration window appears (see figure 11.2).

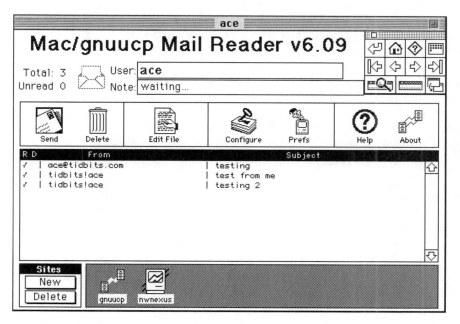

Figure 11.1   *MailReader main window*

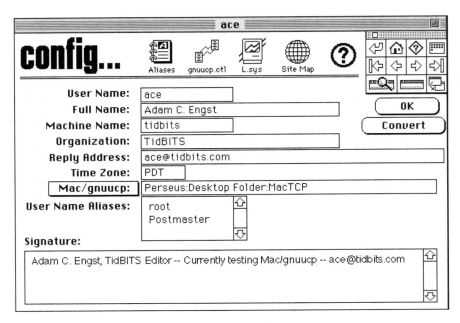

Figure 11.2 *MailReader Configuration window*

I've filled in the Configuration window with my information, but it should be fairly obvious what you should put in the different fields. The Time Zone field holds abbreviations such as EST for Eastern Standard Time and PDT for Pacific Daylight Time. The Mac/gnuucp button brings up a Standard File dialog when you click on it. Find the Mac/gnuucp program on your disk and select it, so that Mac/gnuucp knows where the program is. You don't have to fill in the User Name Aliases, but the two I've added are a good idea, so that you receive any administrative mail. And, finally, put anything you want in the Signature field, but keep it short—no more than four lines at most.

At the top of the Configuration window, you see buttons for Aliases, gnuucp.ctl, L.sys, Site Map, and Help (a question mark). Don't worry about the Aliases and Site Map buttons; you can play with them later. Click on the gnuucp.ctl button. MailReader brings up a text editing window so you can modify the **gnuucp.ctl** file (see figure 11.3).

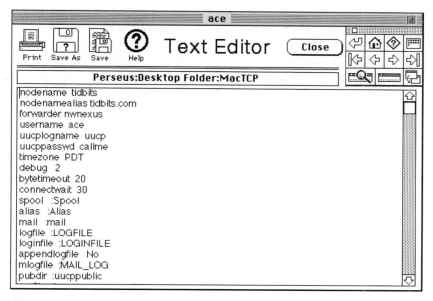

Figure 11.3 **gnuucp.ctl** *file*

The items to modify appear in the first three lines. Insert your nodename, an alias for your nodename if you have one, and your username, in place of the default values. You can see how I've configured the items. Once you get Mac/gnuucp working, you may want to set the debug value in the eighth line to 1; the higher the debug number, the more detail the program shows during connections. Detail is helpful in troubleshooting, but otherwise is a waste of time. Click on the Save button when you're finished; then click on the Close button to return to the Configuration window.

Next, click on the L.sys button to edit the **l.sys** file. The text editor window appears again (see figure 11.4).

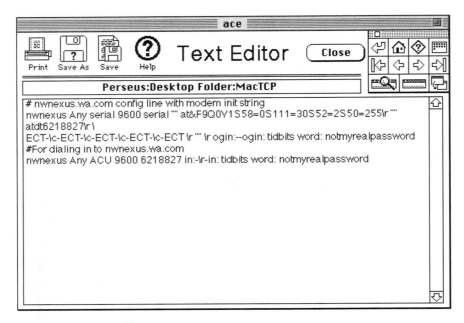

Figure 11.4   `1.sys` file

I've modified two of the sample strings that Jim O'Dell provides for the **`1.sys`** file. You can compare what I've done to the sample strings Jim provides, to get a better idea of how to configure the strings for your machine. Essentially, you enter your host's name, the connection type and speed, the phone number to call, and the login name and password. The tricky part is including a complex modem initialization string, which you can only do with the first string in the **`1.sys`** file. I'm not sure what all the parts are, but copy Jim's example closely, being careful not to introduce unnecessary characters. Save and close the **`1.sys`** file. Then, in the Configuration window, click on the OK button to return to the main window.

Next, create a site to call. Click on the New button in the lower-left corner of the window. In the dialog that pops up, type the name of your UUCP host exactly, just as you typed it in the **`1.sys`** file. UUCP is not forgiving of mistakes, so be careful. When you click on the OK button, an icon with the host's name appears next to the gnuucp icon. Clicking on the gnuucp button runs the Mac/gnuucp program, as if you had launched it from the Finder; clicking on the site button you just created runs Mac/gnuucp and feeds it the necessary command line to get it to call out. Unless you enjoy typing at a command line, you should click on the site icon.

Now you have the basic installation. There are more details, of course, and the documentation (in Microsoft Word format) covers most of what you need to know.

Note

Here's a good reason to have another Internet account of some sort available. While you're setting up Mac/gnuucp, you may want to send email or post a Usenet message asking for help. Without another account, getting help configuring an email program is hard.

Although the HyperCard stack eases the configuration process somewhat, I'd like to see it taken further. For instance, there's no reason the stack cannot provide one form for filling in the **gnuucp.ctl** and **l.sys** information, and then write to the appropriate text files. That also would make it easier to provide context-sensitive help on each field.

Basic Usage

Although a bit clumsy (because of its HyperCard roots), the MailReader stack provides almost every standard feature you might want from an email program (see figure 11.5). As you can see, it displays how many messages you have, how many of those are unread, whether you've read or deleted a message, the sender and the subject of each message, and buttons that enable you to create a new message or delete various marked messages. (Clicking on the Delete button enables you to delete all the read messages or all the messages marked for deletion.)

Clicking on any of the messages in the list in the MailReader main window takes you to that message (see figure 11.6).

MailReader displays both the header and the message (you can change the text font if you want to) and provides buttons for Reply, Forward, Save, Print, and Delete. You can navigate between messages by using the arrows and create new mail by using the Send button. Clicking the Close button returns you to the main screen or if you click the Reply button, MailReader sets you up to reply to the selected message by quoting the original message and filling in the header information (see figure 11.7).

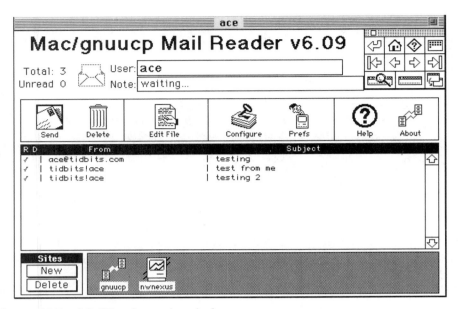

Figure 11.5   *MailReader main window*

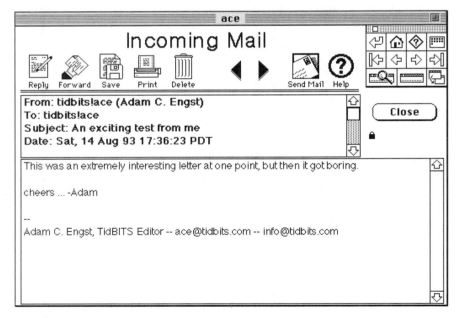

Figure 11.6   *MailReader Incoming Mail window*

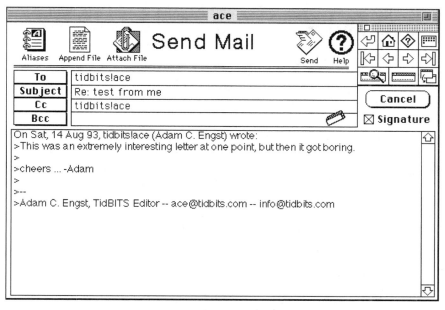

Figure 11.7   *MailReader Send Mail window*

Special Features

MailReader sports several interesting and unique email features. Most intriguingly, when you're reading email, a little lock icon appears above the message. The icon is normally locked, indicating that you cannot edit the text in the message. But, if you click on the icon, it opens up, allowing you to edit the text of the message. This capability can be useful when you receive a large file and only want to keep a few lines of it.

Also, when you're sending email, clicking on the To, Cc, or Bcc buttons brings up a scrolling list of all your aliases, which are short, easy-to-remember names that replace email address you often use. Although it would be nice to be able to select more than one at a time (something easy enough to script in HyperCard), this feature is a nice touch, especially considering that MailReader's aliases can contain one or more addresses.

You can attach text files to email messages with the Attach File button in the Send Mail screen. The documentation claims that a future version may enable you to attach binary files as well—it wouldn't be all that hard to do, although the stack would have to know how to binhex the file first. Given HyperCard's capabilities to send Apple events, MailReader could actually use a different program, such as Aladdin's StuffIt Lite, to do the binhexing. Currently, if you want to send a file, you must binhex it first, at which point there's no problem because a BinHex file is inherently a text file.

Overall Evaluation

I'm more impressed with the Mac/gnuucp package than I expected to be. My high opinion is mostly due to the MailReader HyperCard stack. Although suffering from a somewhat amateurish interface (these are hard to avoid with HyperCard), it manages to provide most of the features an email program should have. I'm concerned that MailReader might bog down if you try to keep a lot of email around. The Mac/gnuucp program itself is as ugly as possible. If you launch it manually rather than from the stack, it prompts you for a command-line entry, and its only other interface is a text window of scrolling diagnostic messages. But, it seems to work, and even allows other people to call your site for email. And frankly, Mac/gnuucp is cheap.

When I asked Jim O'Dell about Mac/gnuucp, he noted that it would be a much different program if he received lots of mail every day. For 10 to 20 messages a day, he feels that Mac/gnuucp is easier to use and set up than the main competition, uupc, and I have to agree with him on that. For those people who find the MailReader stack too limiting, Dave Platt, author of Fernmail, and Steve Dorner, author of Eudora, both claim that their email programs work with Mac/gnuucp, however the UUCP appendix in the Eudora manual mentions that there might be some problems.

Although Mac/gnuucp currently doesn't support unbatching and reading Usenet news that can come in through the same UUCP connection, Jim said he has all the code necessary to do so, and he is starting to write a newsreader. The major obstacle he faces currently is financial; if he receives enough from Mac/gnuucp, he can justify getting a Usenet news feed to work with. I guess improving this program is just another reason to pay for quality software that's distributed freely.

Administrative Details

To join the Mac/gnuucp mailing list and be informed of future developments, send $20 to Jim O'Dell. You can find the Mac/gnuucp 6.09 distribution file on the Internet at:

```
ftp://ftp.tidbits.com/pub/tidbits/tisk/uucp/gnuucp-609.hqx
```

If you have any questions or comments, you can reach Jim O'Dell of Fort Pond Research at **gnuucp@fpr.com**, or at the following address and phone number:

Fort Pond Research
15 Fort Pond Research
Acton, MA 01720
508-263-9692

uupc

Although the name may confuse you at first, uupc stands for *UUCP for PCs* and is a play on the standard term UUCP, which is short for *Unix to Unix CoPy*. Like Mac/gnuucp and UUCP/Connect, uupc is a UUCP transport program, and, like Mac/gnuucp, it only transports the UUCP files. It doesn't provide an interface to reading or writing email, although a related program that ships with uupc, pcmail, does provide email access. However, pcmail's email access is limited in such a way that I think I can safely say that no one will use pcmail for more than about ten minutes.

Uupc is a Macintosh port of publicly available source code, and versions exist for numerous platforms, including DOS, the Commodore Amiga, and the Atari ST. The original code apparently came from DOS, which accounts for some of the configuration quirks. The initial port to the Macintosh was performed by Stuart Lynne. Later, Dave Platt coordinated a group of Macintosh programmers on the Internet to come up with the most recent release, version 3.1b32.

Because uupc stems from public code and was created by a team of unrelated programmers, the uupc programmers encourage users to distribute the package for free, along with source code if you want. However, the programmers retain the copyright, which means that you cannot legally base a commercial program on the uupc source code without getting permission from each of the many authors first.

The most recent version of uupc is 3.1b32, but as you can tell from the number, it's a beta release and may contain bugs. It reportedly fixes some troublesome spots in 3.0, and the most notable addition is optional support for the Communications Toolbox. CTB support means that you can use any CTB tool with uupc, even (presumably) a Telnet tool such as the TGE TCP Tool from Tim Endres. You can also have uupc connect two Macs on the same network using the ADSP tool. I haven't tested these new features, but the documentation that comes with uupc 3.1b32 should help explain these features.

Installation and Setup

Installing uupc is trickier than installing Mac/gnuucp. Although you must provide the same sorts of information, the MailReader stack that comes with Mac/gnuucp makes entering it easier. To configure uupc, you need a copy of ResEdit, Apple's free resource editor. If you don't have ResEdit, or don't know what it is or how to use it, you probably don't want to attempt to install and configure uupc. However, you can get ResEdit on the Internet at:

```
ftp://ftp.apple.com/dts/mac/tools/resedit/resedit-2-1-1.hqx
```

Luckily, the documentation and examples that come with uupc are quite good and complete, although you must read carefully (especially in a few places to determine where to place certain files). In addition, the documentation includes a copy of the posting entitled "Becoming a USENET site." This is the standard document on the topic, and is posted to the **news.answers** newsgroup periodically. For those people who have never touched UUCP before, there are also references to three useful books: *Managing UUCP and USENET*, by Tim O'Reilly and Grace Todino, from O'Reilly & Associates; *Unix Communications*, by Bart Anderson, Barry Costales, and Harry Henderson, published by The Waite Group; and *Using UUCP and USENET*, by Grace Todino and Dale Dougherty, again published by O'Reilly & Associates.

To begin, make a copy of **Sample UUPC settings file**, rename it **UUPC Settings**, and place it in the same folder as the uupc program. Double-click on the file to open it in ResEdit, double-click on the STR icon, and you see a list of all the STR resources. Double-click on any of them, and you see another window for entering the actual string (see figure 11.8).

You must go through each of the STR resources and replace the sample information with the appropriate information for your setup. The only hard part is, you must provide full pathnames for the folder listed in HOME, MAILDIR, CONFDIR, and so on (uupc will create these folders later, so here you tell it where to do so). Macintosh users seldom have to deal with pathnames, but suffice it to say that a pathname is the name of the hard disk, a colon, the name of a folder, a colon, a name of another folder, and so on.

Note

Because you are hard-coding the pathnames to these folders, decide now where you want the uupc folder to live on your hard disk, and what you want it to be called. Also, keep in mind that if you change the name of the hard disk or any folder above the uupc folder, all hell will break loose.

Mac/gnuucp and UUCP/Connect both circumvent this pathname difficulty by enabling you to place the folders in the same folder as the program, then assume the special folders are there unless you state otherwise.

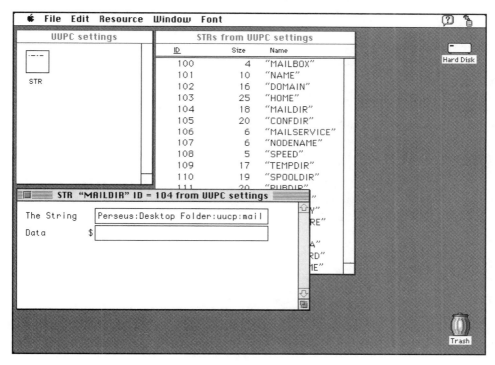

Figure 11.8 *uupc configuration in ResEdit*

Finally, if one of the folders above your destination folder is on the desktop, you must add **Desktop Folder** to the path after the hard disk name. So, for instance, my mail folder is called **Perseus:Desktop Folder:uucp:mail**. (The part of the path reading **uucp:mail** was created by uupc. The reversed *p*'s and *c*'s are not a mistake; uupc simply considers this your UUCP mail folder path.)

Just as with Mac/gnuucp, in uupc the values that you must provide in terms of username, nodename, and so on, are fairly obvious. The documentation describes each one. After you've added the names, double-click on uupc itself to launch it, and then quit immediately. Uupc creates the necessary folders for you in the places you've specified.

The **Systems** file is another story. Like the **l.sys** file in Mac/gnuucp, the **Systems** file contains the information necessary to call and negotiate a connection with a remote host. Even though uupc includes more examples than Mac/gnuucp, I had a lot more trouble getting it to connect and chat with various UUCP implementations. A **Sample Systems** file comes with uupc; copy it and shamelessly plagiarize the provided entries (use TeachText or SimpleText to edit the file). Be sure to rename your copy **Systems** and place it in the config folder that uupc created for you. Be prepared to edit that file continually as you troubleshoot your connection.

Basic Usage

After you have the **Systems** file in place, you can use pcmail to create a test message to send out and boomerang back. Double-click on pcmail. You should see a console window that looks amazingly like the command-line window that Mac/gnuucp uses. I suspect they were created with the same compiler (see figure 11.9).

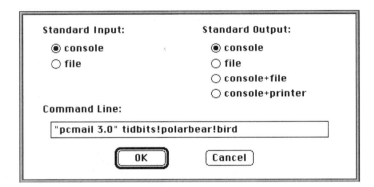

Figure 11.9   *pcmail console window*

To send a message out and receive it back again, you use a clever old trick called *bang-style addressing*. If you write an address listing your host's name, your machine's name, and your userid, all separated only by exclamation points, a UUCP program knows to send the message to your host, which then sees that it was destined for your machine and sends the message right back, and your machine sees that you should receive the message.

As you can see in figure 11.9, I've made up a new site called **polarbear**, and I'm using **tidbits** as my host (this setup actually worked—I had uupc running on my PowerBook 100, calling my SE/30 running UUCP/Connect on the second phone line).

Note

Of course, you see some smoke and mirrors here, because I wasn't able to get the nice gray-scale screenshots on the monochrome PowerBook 100 screen, but what is life without some mystery?

After you enter the address in that specific format, click on the OK button to enter the pcmail editing environment (see figure 11.10).

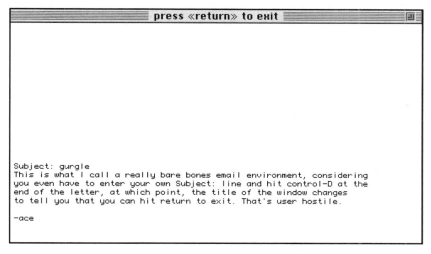

Figure 11.10   *pcmail editing environment*

The pcmail program makes mail under Unix seem friendly and full-featured. You must type your own header information, such as the Subject line, and when you're finished (making sure to press Return at the end of every line), you finish the message by pressing Control-D, just as in Unix. Of course, the title of the window changes to let you know how to exit the program. I think this feature qualifies as a negative interface, and that's the last thing I'm going to say about using pcmail, in part because that's all it does. I recommend ignoring it after your first test message.

Now, to send the message. Launch uupc by double-clicking on it. You should see a line saying "Welcome to uupc!" and another line with the current time and the word "Idle." From the File menu, select Debug Level and type **2** in the dialog (see figure 11.11).

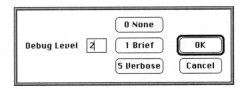

Figure 11.11   *uupc Debug dialog box*

Next, take a look at the Call menu. It provides excellent flexibility in terms of whom you call and when. If you've set up the features correctly, you should have one or more (uupc can easily handle calling multiple UUCP hosts) entries at the bottom of the menu (see figure 11.12).

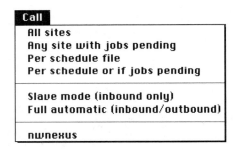

Figure 11.12   *uupc Call menu*

To test your configuration so far, select your host's name from the bottom of the menu. If all goes well, uupc dials the host, sends the waiting message, and retrieves any messages set to come in (not that there are likely to be any, yet). Because the host takes a few minutes to process the message, take a short break and then call again to receive it.

Unless you are extremely lucky or extremely talented, of course, your configuration won't work. My first attempt worked perfectly, but subsequent tries to different machines failed for hours (and, in fact, I never got any machine to work reliably in the limited time I had). If the configuration doesn't work for you, check the information in the **UUCP Settings** file. After that, puzzle over the variables in the **Systems** file. Problems usually appear in two areas: the modem configuration and the *chat script*. The modem configuration is a pain to figure out, but you can use any terminal emulator to log in to your UUCP host, trying different modem initialization strings until the two modems connect reliably. It's often a good idea to start at a least common denominator, such as 2,400 bps, and work up from that point.

A terminal emulator can help with the chat script as well. The *chat script* is the series of commands that the two machines pass back and forth to log in and start the UUCP conversation. In general, here's what happens: Your machine sends a return to wake up the host, the host replies with a login prompt, your machine sends the login name, the host asks for the password, your machine sends it, and then the host responds with a line starting with "Shere." If you get to that point, the two machines should start the UUCP conversation and start transferring files. Watching the debug messages can help determine where things are going wrong, although I often find the debug messages difficult to understand.

Special Features

The nicest part of uupc is its flexibility in terms of calling multiple hosts and running automatically at scheduled times. You can create a **Schedule** file (a sample is provided) that contains one or more lines listing the exact times and days that uupc should call out. Keep in mind that, in order for this exercise to work, uupc must be running, because it has no way of launching itself (QuicKeys from CE Software helps automate launching). Also, you want uupc to be in the foreground on your Macintosh. If it's running in the background, it may manage to dial out, but the performance is poor.

Note

*When you're configuring the **Schedule** file, each line must contain the minute, hour, day, month, weekday, and the host machine you want to call. The first five variables are all in numeric format, and you can provide multiple entries by separating them with commas; more importantly, if you replace the entry with an asterisk, the task happens every day, month, weekday, and so on. The documentation fails to make this point crystal clear, but it's a useful shortcut.*

The other advantage uupc has over Mac/gnuucp is that it works well with other email programs and can also easily transfer Usenet news. (Note, however, that it cannot process news in any way after transfering it; you need ToadNews, a separate program, to process the received news at that point.) Dave Platt, one of the primary authors of uupc, makes a shareware email program called Fernmail that works well with uupc and has a similar configuration scheme (which isn't good, but it is familiar). You also can use Steve Dorner's excellent Eudora email program. The combination of ToadNews and rnMac or TheNews enables you to read news transferred by uupc. All of these programs are either freeware or shareware, so you can put together a nice little package for a small financial investment. In terms of time, however, your investment may be fairly hefty.

Overall Evaluation

Uupc is definitely not for weenies or people who need hand-holding. Despite the added trouble I had setting it up on my system, though, I must say that it's a better choice for many people than Mac/gnuucp—especially for those with more than basic requirements, because of the combination of the flexibility in scheduling and the capability of working with powerful email programs such as Eudora.

I don't mean to imply that uupc is perfect in any way, shape, or form. One minor improvement would be to provide configuration assistance within the program, rather than requiring the use of ResEdit. Although ResEdit is free, it's not universally available or the configuration environment of choice. Since the first edition of this book, Mark Assad's UUPC Setup program has appeared, to simplify this task. See the section, "UUPC Setup," following.

Also, I found that the information provided with uupc was more useful than the relatively sparse documentation that came with Mac/gnuucp. This is due in part to the fact that uupc does more than Mac/gnuucp, but that's not the entire story. Of course, the additional information can potentially confuse the user more, because UUPC is, in fact, a rather complex and multifaceted transport protocol; trying to understand it beyond the basics can daunt even the most sophisticated novice.

Administrative Details

Aim questions or comments about uupc to Dave Platt via email at **dplatt@snulbug.mtview.ca.us**. Remember that because uupc is a free program, the support you get may reflect what you paid for the program. You can find uupc on the Internet at:

```
ftp://ftp.tidbits.com/pub/tidbits/tisk/uucp/uupc-31b32.hqx
```

UUPC Setup

As if in response to my complaints about the difficulty of setting up uupc (and ToadNews and rnMac, discussed later in the chapter), Mark Assad and Nathan Willis came up with UUPC Setup, a program that does just what anyone who sets up uupc would want. It asks appropriate questions and provides appropriate fields to fill in, and then goes off and creates the necessary folders and files.

Note

The first time I got to the end of using UUPC Setup, it froze my Mac, so I'd recommend saving any work before you launch it.

Using UUPC Setup is simple. Launch the program, and from the File menu, choose Set-up UUPC. UUPC Setup presents you with an initial dialog box for your host and basic setup (see figure 11.13).

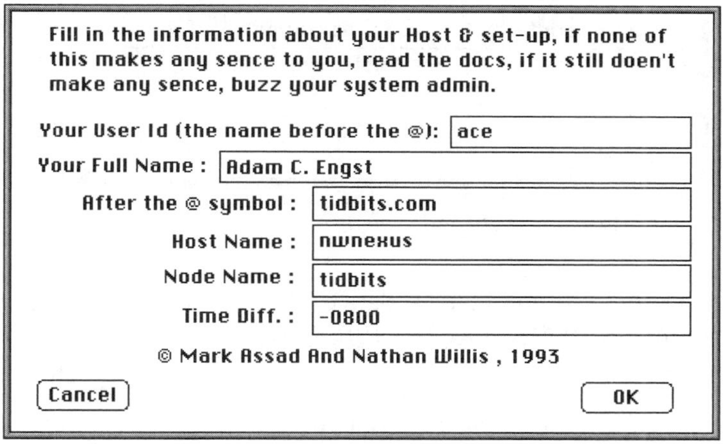

Figure 11.13   *UUPC Setup Host Info dialog*

After entering all of your information and clicking on the OK button, UUPC Setup moves on to the next dialog, in which you configure your modem (see figure 11.14).

The basic questions in the Modem configuration dialog are relatively easy. They ask about things like port, init string, speed, and phone number. The problem comes when you hit the Connect Script field, which is a major pain. The text that lives in that field before you edit it tells you that it wants "the last part of the **Systems** file... you know, the hard part." This is going to be difficult to trouble-shoot in your connection, and just entering it here won't make things any easier, since all UUPC Setup does is write the script into a **Systems** file that it creates for you. If you get the Connect Script field wrong, your connection won't work, but you can edit the **Systems** file manually for updates—that's easier than going through all of UUPC Setup again.

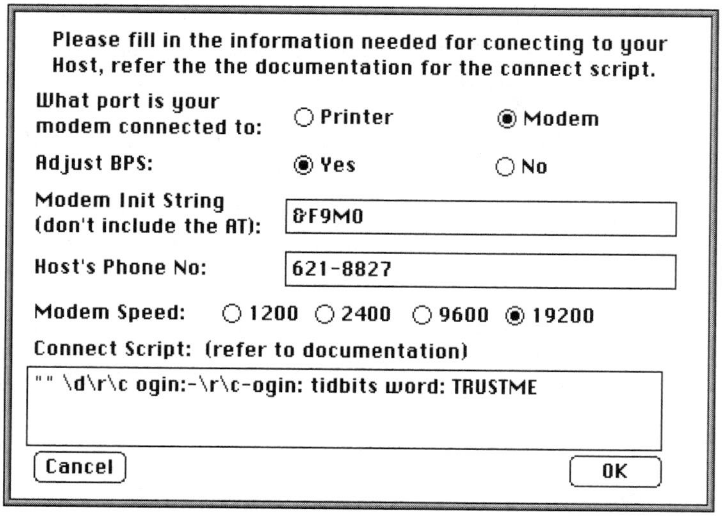

```
Please fill in the information needed for conecting to your
Host, refer the the documentation for the connect script.

What port is your
modem connected to:        ○ Printer           ◉ Modem

Adjust BPS:                ◉ Yes               ○ No

Modem Init String
(don't include the AT):    ⌈ &F9M0                        ⌉

Host's Phone No:           ⌈ 621-8827                     ⌉

Modem Speed:    ○ 1200  ○ 2400  ○ 9600  ◉ 19200

Connect Script: (refer to documentation)
⌈ "" \d\r\c ogin:-\r\c-ogin: tidbits word: TRUSTME        ⌉
⌊                                                         ⌋

⌈ Cancel ⌉                              ⌈   OK   ⌉
```

Figure 11.14   UUPC Setup Modem configuration

Clicking on the OK button in the Modem configuration dialog brings up the
News configuration dialog box (see figure 11.15).

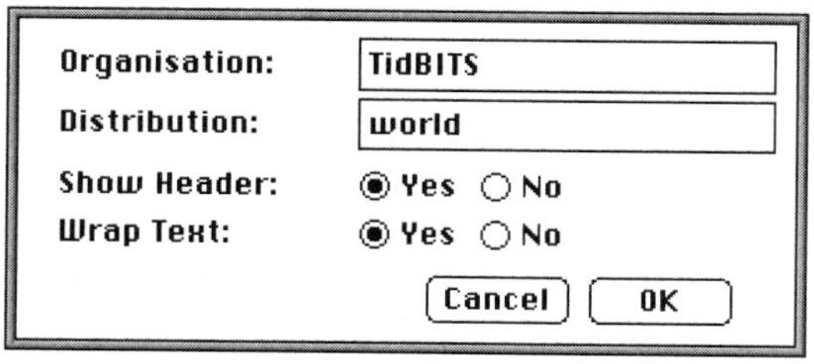

```
Organisation:   ⌈ TidBITS      ⌉

Distribution:   ⌈ world        ⌉

Show Header:    ◉ Yes ○ No
Wrap Text:      ◉ Yes ○ No

                ⌈ Cancel ⌉ ⌈  OK  ⌉
```

Figure 11.15   UUPC Setup News configuration

I presume that this information is meant for the fields that rnMac and/or
ToadNews want, since they're specifically things used by newsreaders and
nothing else. Clicking on the OK button next takes us to the Standard File
dialog, where we can save the UUPC folder and settings files that UUPC Setup
has created (see figure 11.16).

Remember to locate the folder uupc uses once and for all, since moving it can
cause all sorts of trouble. If everything works properly, UUPC Setup should pop
up a dialog saying that it has configured everything properly for you, and a
folder should appear on your hard disk in the location you specified with the
name you gave it (see figure 11.17). I stuck with the default name and put it on
my desktop.

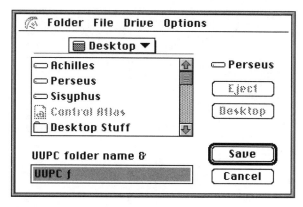

Figure 11.16 *UUPC Setup Save dialog*

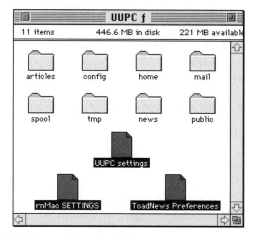

Figure 11.17 *UUPC Setup Results folder*

If you're the foolhardy sort, you could just assume that this has all been set up perfectly and dive right into launching uupc and the rest. However, if you did that, I suspect you'd be sorely frustrated, because as nice an idea as UUPC Setup is, it doesn't always work properly (see figure 11.18).

As you can see in figure 11.18, in the SPOOLDIR strings, UUPC Setup for some reason thinks my hard disk's name is "Perx" rather than the proper "Perseus" that you see in the MAILDIR string. Additionally, the DISTRABUTION string should have been "world" and not "TidBITS." Further, DISTRABUTION is spelled wrong and must be fixed; select it, go to the Resource menu in ResEdit and choose Get Resource Info to bring up a dialog in which you can change the name to DISTRIBUTION. I've heard other complaints about the job UUPC Setup does as well, so your experience may differ.

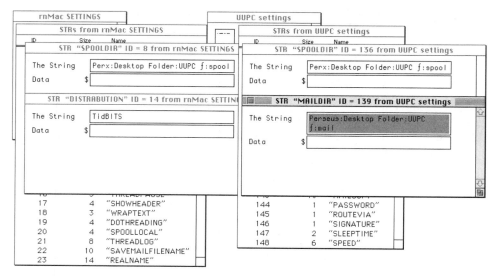

Figure 11.18   UUPC Setup errors

Overall Evaluation

The moral of the story, then, is to use UUPC Setup for what it's good for, but don't assume that the results will be perfect. Everything needs to be checked. Nonetheless, Mark and Nathan have made a nice start and I hope they clean it up a bit. I'd also greatly prefer it if they used modeless dialogs instead of modal. All too often, when you're filling in the fields, you want to switch out to another application to copy, say, the phone number, or perhaps that Connect Script, and there's currently no way to do that.

Administrative Details

As far as I can tell, UUPC Setup is freeware. You can contact Mark and Nathan at **massad@alsvid.une.edu.au** or **nwillis@alsvid.une.edu.au** if you have any questions or suggestions. You can retrieve UUPC Setup from the Internet at:

```
ftp://ftp.tidbits.com/pub/tidbits/tisk/uucp/uucp-setup.hqx
```

Fernmail

As long as I'm on the subject of uupc, I may as well cover Dave Platt's shareware Fernmail email program. Dave designed Fernmail for his own use with uupc, but it also works with Mac/gnuucp and with a program called UUMac, which apparently is yet another implementation of UUCP for the Mac. If I find a copy, I'll check it out for a future edition of this book. Because I had never heard of it until I read the Fernmail documentation, I assume that it's not widely used.

Like uupc, Fernmail is not for the novice. It requires ResEdit to configure, and Dave designed it to serve his own needs, which accounts for some of the nice features and for some of the omissions and oddities. Dave has added features to Fernmail based on suggestions from beta testers and registered users, but it's not as full-featured as some might like. The main things missing right now include more shortcuts, new mail notification, abbreviated header display, an Undo capability, and locks that enable you to read email from a mailbox file even while a UUCP program is delivering mail to that mailbox.

The latest version of Fernmail is 1.2 and sports several improvements. Most notably, it uses the TE32K editing package that enables it to display messages longer than 32K, a nasty limitation in other email packages. Finally, there are the usual bug fixes and performance enhancements, and luckily, the configuration process has stayed sufficiently the same. If you use Fernmail already, you can just use your old configuration file as a starting point. But you may have to do some work because there might be some new resources that don't exist in your current configuration file.

Installation and Setup

Dave must like ResEdit, because Fernmail's configuration process is almost identical to uupc's. You create a copy of the **Sample Fernmail config** file, rename it **Fernmail config**, and place it in the same folder as the Fernmail application. Unlike the **UUPC Settings** file, the **Fernmail config** file is not a ResEdit document, so double-clicking on it runs Fernmail, not ResEdit. Launch ResEdit separately then and open **Fernmail config**.

I'm going to assume here that you've already configured uupc and want to use it with Fernmail. It's a decent assumption, and there's a trick that saves you a bunch of time. If you also open the **UUPC Settings** file in ResEdit and then double-click on the STR resources in both files, you see that they look almost identical, at least at the beginning (see figure 11.19).

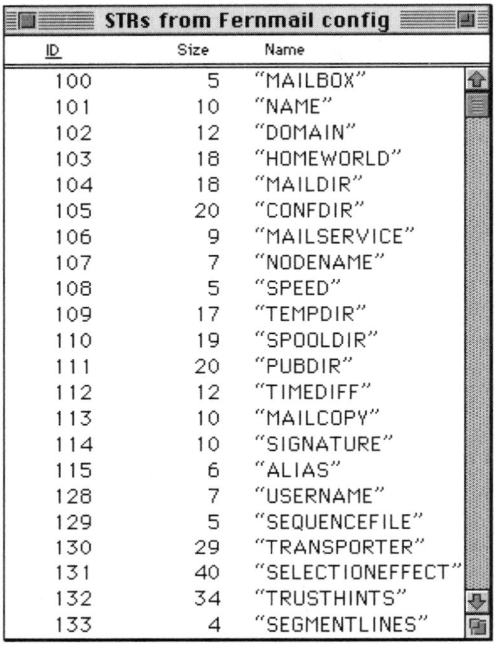

ID	Size	Name
100	5	"MAILBOX"
101	10	"NAME"
102	12	"DOMAIN"
103	18	"HOMEWORLD"
104	18	"MAILDIR"
105	20	"CONFDIR"
106	9	"MAILSERVICE"
107	7	"NODENAME"
108	5	"SPEED"
109	17	"TEMPDIR"
110	19	"SPOOLDIR"
111	20	"PUBDIR"
112	12	"TIMEDIFF"
113	10	"MAILCOPY"
114	10	"SIGNATURE"
115	6	"ALIAS"
128	7	"USERNAME"
129	5	"SEQUENCEFILE"
130	29	"TRANSPORTER"
131	40	"SELECTIONEFFECT"
132	34	"TRUSTHINTS"
133	4	"SEGMENTLINES"

STRs from Fernmail config

Figure 11.19   *Fernmail configuration in ResEdit*

Click on the STRs from **UUPC Settings** window; then from the Edit menu, choose Select All. Hold down the Command key and click once on the HOME, ROUTEVIA, PASSWORD, and SLEEPTIME resources, to deselect them. You should now have resources 100 through 115 selected, with the exception of 103, the HOME resource. From the Edit menu, choose Copy. Then click on the STRs from **Fernmail config** window, and from the Edit menu, choose Paste. ResEdit immediately warns you that you are about to overwrite resources with the same ID (see figure 11.20).

Here, you should replace the resources with the same IDs, so click on the Yes button. You've just replaced all the default values with the properly configured resources from your **UUPC Settings** file—no need to do the same work twice. You still must configure the HOMEWORLD resource (103) to have the same path as the other resources, and resources 128 and up still have the default values, but you can change them easily because they are similar to the ones you configured for uupc. Save the file and quit ResEdit to finish the basic configuration. If you want to get fancy, you can edit the **Sample Headers** and **Sample Aliases** files, but you don't need to do it immediately.

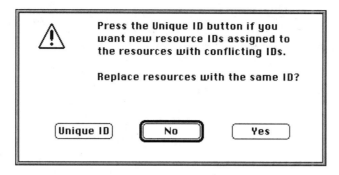

Figure 11.20   ResEdit warning

Basic Usage

Try sending some email to yourself in Fernmail to show off its basic features. From the File menu, choose Compose message. A text editing window appears, with two lines in the header and a line down the right side of the window (see figure 11.21).

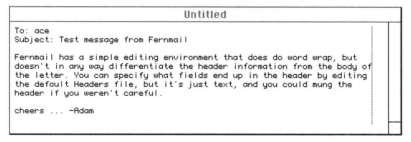

Figure 11.21   Fernmail Compose Message window

The header lines are the minimum necessary. You can provide a more complete header by modifying the **Headers** file. What's odd about Fernmail's headers is that they're just text; most email programs create special fields for you rather than letting you accidentally mess up the header while you edit the message. The line down the right indicates where the text wraps. Although it looks a little odd as you're typing—because the text goes out beyond the line and wraps down only when you finish a word—it does wrap correctly most of the time. The problem comes when you're editing something you've written in the middle of the line, because the edits usually cause wrapping problems. This is a shame, because making it easy to edit messages to prevent people from saying things they don't mean is important. Fernmail's Edit menu has a command to rewrap a paragraph, but manual rewrapping should be unnecessary in a Macintosh application (see figure 11.22).

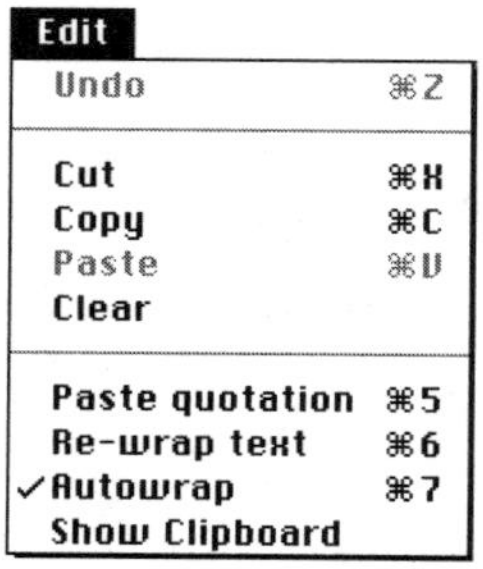

Figure 11.22　Fernmail Edit menu

Some of the commands in Fernmail's Outgoing menu help in editing, or at least they do if you're the sort who navigates around with Command-B to move back one character and Command-F to move forward one character (see figure 11.23).

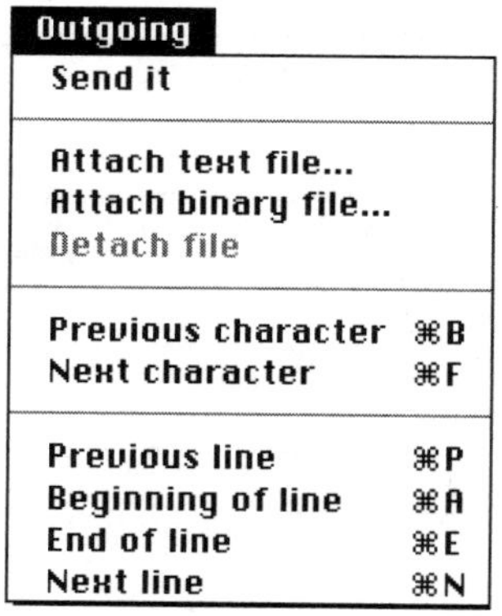

Figure 11.23　Fernmail Outgoing menu

The arrow keys work fine, too, so I have no idea why such commands ended up in Fernmail at all, much less as menu items. I can't imagine anyone ever selecting Back from the Outgoing menu to move the cursor back one character in the text.

Choose the Send it command to send your mail, or, if you're lazy like me, simply close the outgoing message window and answer Send when Fernmail asks if you want to Send, Save, or Discard the message.

Reading email in Fernmail is equally as quirky, but looks a bit snazzier (see figure 11.24).

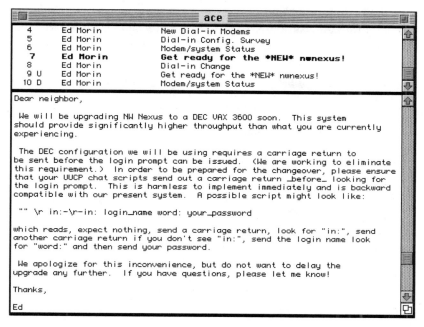

Figure 11.24 *Fernmail Mailbox window*

Fernmail has several nice features in the Mailbox window. The current message shows up bolded in the list, and the D and U markers next to other messages indicate which you have marked for deletion or have undeleted. Intriguingly, when you resize the window (as I've done in the previous figure), switching to any message prevents the header from being shown at all. Fernmail seems to calculate the screen display position for each message based on the window size. Although arrow keys don't move you among messages, you can use Command-N and Command-P to move to the next or previous message, respectively, instead of using the mouse.

When you look at the File menu, though, you see one glaring piece of weirdness (see figure 11.25).

Notice the first two commands, "Open my new-mail mailbox" and "Open my old-mail mailbox." Fernmail uses separate mailboxes, one to display your unread mail, the other to show mail you've already perused. You open the new-mail mailbox to check your mail, but as soon as you close it, even if you haven't replied to or filed any of the new mail, the new stuff moves to the old-mail mailbox. Very strange, especially considering Dave already has included the ability to mark messages with the D and U characters. I cannot imagine it would be difficult to create another character to indicate a new message. And, while I'm requesting features, I always like it when a message is marked so that I can tell that I've already replied to it, saved it to disk, or forwarded it to someone else. Also, although you can reply to the current message or save it to a file, there's currently no mechanism for forwarding a message to someone else.

File	
Open my new-mail mailbox	⌘I
Open my old-mail mailbox	⌘G
Open...	▶
Create mailbox...	
Compose message...	⌘M
Close	⌘W
Close and compact	
Save	⌘S
Save As...	
Page Setup...	
Print...	
Quit	⌘Q

Figure 11.25   Fernmail File menu

Special Features

Fernmail can create and display multiple mailboxes, and you can move messages from one to the other simply by dragging them. Fernmail never deletes anything (even moved messages) immediately. Instead, it marks them for deletion, and deletes when you choose Close and compact from the File menu. Holding down the Option key while you're dragging a message to another mailbox works the same as Option-dragging a file in the Finder, copying without deleting it from the source mailbox.

Fernmail can debinhex messages that you receive, and in a truly cool feature, it can debinhex multiple part messages (which you tend to get when someone sends you a file that is too large in a single part), prompting you to pick each part in turn.

By creating an alias file (or editing the sample file), you can use aliases for people or groups with whom you regularly correspond. This way, you can define a nickname for someone with a long address and also create a single alias for a whole bunch of people, simplifying distribution of the same message to a group.

Finally, if you communicate with one or more sites that can post Usenet news, Fernmail has a limited capability to create news postings. All you must do is create a message without a To line and with a Newsgroups line in the header.

Overall Evaluation

I'm of two minds about Fernmail. On the one hand, it makes pcmail look like trash, and it looks cleaner than Mac/gnuucp's MailReader stack. I also suspect that it handles large quantities of email better than MailReader. On the other hand, Fernmail doesn't compare with Steve Dorner's free Eudora, which, as it turns out, works as well with UUCP mail as it does with its native POP and SMTP mail. Before Eudora appeared, Fernmail certainly ranked right up there with the best of the freeware and shareware email programs. Of course, even if you use Eudora with uupc heavily, paying your shareware fee for Fernmail might be a good way to thank Dave Platt for all the good he's done the Macintosh world with uupc, Fernmail, and MandelZot, a snazzy Mandelbrot (fractal) program—which may have created the fractal fern that adorns Fernmail's icon and About box.

Administrative Details

You can reach Dave Platt at **dplatt@snulbug.mtview.ca.us**. Send a shareware payment of $20, if you use Fernmail actively for more than two weeks, to:

Dave Platt
Snulbug Software
1095 Burgoyne Street
Mountain View, CA 94043

Dave asks that you don't write to him and say, "I like Fernmail, and if you would only add features X, Y, and Z, I'll send in my shareware payment." Those sort of people seldom pay their fees. You should either pay for a shareware program if it is sufficiently useful to you in its current form, or stop using it. You can find the latest version of Fernmail at:

```
ftp://ftp.tidbits.com/pub/tidbits/tisk/uucp/fern-mail-12.hqx
```

Eudora

I mention Steve Dorner's Eudora whenever I talk about email programs because, frankly, it's just about the best out there, and it's free. Steve designed Eudora to work with MacTCP primarily, but along the way he added some clever features that allow it to work with UUCP as well. I refrain from talking about Eudora in depth here, because it's primarily a MacTCP program, but I want to touch quickly on the configuration issues so that UUCP users see how to set it up. After that, you can check out the section in chapter 13, "MacTCP-based Software," to learn why Eudora is so cool.

Since most of my mail comes into my Centris 660AV via a UUCP account to InterCon's UUCP/Connect, I set up Eudora in UUCP mode here at home so my wife Tonya could read mail on her Duo 230 without having to kick me off of my Mac. It works extremely well, so allow me to share how we did it. First, all of the mail to **tidbits.com** comes into my 660AV via UUCP/Connect, which stores messages in mailboxes corresponding to the userid in the message—hence all of my mail ends up in a mailbox called **ace**. We decided that Tonya's userid would be **tonya**, and simply advertised her address as **tonya@tidbits.com**, so all of her mail ends up in a UUCP/Connect mailbox called **tonya**. We have a LocalTalk network between my 660AV and her Duo 230, and System 7 File Sharing runs on my machine, so she can mount my hard disk on her desktop and use it just as though it were a local hard disk.

We configured Eudora to look for new mail in the mailbox called **tonya** on my hard disk, which as I said, she mounts over the network so that it looks like a local disk. We also set Eudora to send messages back into the UUCP/Connect spool:uucp folder, which is where UUCP/Connect processes all of its outgoing mail.

Tonya first makes sure my hard disk is mounted over the network, then tells Eudora to check for new mail. Eudora reads the contents of the **tonya** mailbox on my hard disk and brings the new messages into Tonya's In mailbox in Eudora. Tonya can then disconnect, and since she uses a Duo, go anywhere she chooses to read and reply to email. When she wants to send responses back out, she must connect to my machine over the network again, and tell Eudora to send the queued messages, which Eudora deposits in UUCP/Connect's outgoing mail folder.

We've run into two quirks so far. First, UUCP/Connect must be set not to be the domain nameserver for the **tidbits.com** domain (or it freaks, because it cannot find where the messages are supposed to go). Second, Tonya's messages must be processed by UUCP/Connect's command machine before they're actually sent out, since Eudora creates an intermediate file that requires processing. Since the UUCP/Connect command machine only runs when I send a message, or when new messages come in, it sometimes takes a little longer to send Tonya's messages that one might expect.

Although only Tonya reads mail using Eudora in this way on our network, there's no reason why it couldn't work for essentially any number of users with a single copy of UUCP/Connect on a server doing the mail transfer. I personally like Eudora more than LAN email packages such as QuickMail and Microsoft Mail, so it might be an excellent solution for a small office (but small offices are a topic for another book).

Installation and Setup

From Eudora's Special menu, choose Configuration. A large configuration dialog box appears, but if you use UUCP you can more or less ignore all but two fields (see figure 11.26).

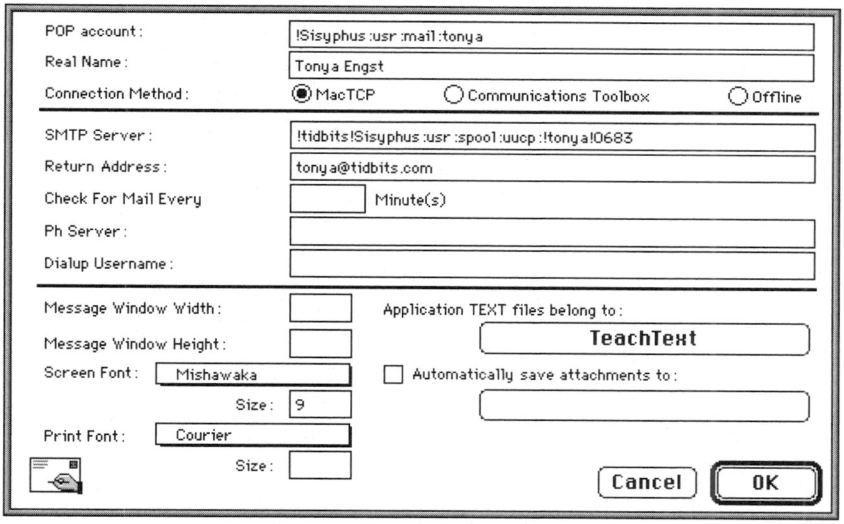

POP account :	!Sisyphus :usr :mail :tonya
Real Name :	Tonya Engst
Connection Method :	⦿ MacTCP ◯ Communications Toolbox ◯ Offline
SMTP Server :	!tidbits!Sisyphus :usr :spool :uucp :!tonya!0683
Return Address :	tonya@tidbits.com
Check For Mail Every	☐ Minute(s)
Ph Server :	
Dialup Username :	

Message Window Width:
Message Window Height:
Screen Font: Mishawaka   Size: 9
Print Font: Courier   Size:

Application TEXT files belong to:
TeachText
☐ Automatically save attachments to:

[Cancel]   [OK]

Figure 11.26   *Eudora's dialog configuration*

The first field, labeled POP Account, should contain an exclamation point and then the full pathname of the file that holds your email. This file is generally located in your mail folder and usually has the same name as your userid.

Next, in the field labeled SMTP Server, you must place four pieces of information, each starting with an exclamation point. Insert an exclamation point, then the UUCP name of your Mac, another exclamation point, then the full pathname of the folder where outgoing files should go (note that this pathname must end with a colon because it's a folder, not a file), another exclamation point, then your userid, a final exclamation point, and a four digit number that Eudora increments by one each time you mail a letter. Eudora must keep that number unique for each message to avoid confusing things. You may as well type four zeros for the sequence number. I don't know what happens when Eudora hits 9,999.

Note

In our Eudora setup, even though Tonya works on a different Mac, since she's essentially using my hard disk as hers, she uses **tidbits** *as the UUCP name of her Macintosh for the Eudora configuration.*

Although you should fill in the Real Name field, you can ignore the Connection Method buttons. And, other than Return Address, none of the fields in the middle section make any difference to a UUCP connection. The fields and buttons in the lower third of the dialog aren't necessary, but they affect UUCP users in the same way they affect everyone else. When you're finished, click on the OK button to save your configuration changes.

Basic Usage

The one quirk of using Eudora for UUCP is that you must remember that Eudora thinks it's connected to a network. Thus, depending on the way you've set various switches within Eudora, email doesn't automatically come in and go out. For instance, when I first tried it with UUCP, I had to use Check Mail from the File menu even though the mail was already sitting on my disk. When I wanted to send mail, I had to use Send Queued Messages, also from the File menu. This quirk is not a big deal, and you can easily set Eudora to send messages automatically when you finish them.

Overall Evaluation

If you use UUCP for email purposes, you owe it to yourself to check out Eudora. It competes well, even with commercial applications, and there are now two branches of Eudora evolution. The 1.4 series (now at 1.4.2) remains free, whereas the 2.0 series (now at 2.0.2) costs approximately $65 per copy (there are discounts for site licenses). The 2.0 series includes a few additional features, most notably, mail filtering options, which are extremely handy.

Administrative Details

You can retrieve Eudora from either of the following:

```
ftp://ftp.tidbits.com/pub/tidbits/tisk/tcp/mail/eudora-142.hqx
```

```
ftp://ftp.qualcomm.com/quest/mac/eudora/1.4/eudora142.hqx
```

If you want to sign up to receive more information about Eudora, send email to **eudora-info@qualcomm.com**. If you cannot use FTP or you want a nicely printed (and well-written) manual along with an original disk of Eudora, send a check for $30 (payable to QUALCOMM, Inc.) to:

QUALCOMM Inc.
c/o Eudora Package
10555 Sorrento Valley Road
San Diego, CA 92121

ToadNews

So what about reading Usenet news, anyway? I've danced around the subject for a while now because this territory can be fairly difficult to understand. Usenet news comes into your machine in batches (sometimes compressed) that a newsreader cannot understand. To convert these batches into usable files for a newsreader, you must have a program that can do the unbatching. Currently, the only stand-alone program that unbatches files (UUCP/Connect does it internally) is John Mah's ToadNews. ToadNews can handle either compressed or uncompressed batches, and the latest release, 1.1, can handle an external decompressor program as well.

Note

John added support for an external decompressor so that he'd be able to add support for gzip files later on.

ToadNews provides several administrative features. It not only unbatches news files and places them in the appropriate folders, but it also *expires* old news from your disk; that is, after a few days or weeks, it deletes old articles, thus saving hard disk space. ToadNews enables you to edit which newsgroups receive articles, and it can do all of its tasks quietly in the background.

Although ToadNews theoretically can work with other UUCP transport agents and other newsreaders, it has been closely integrated with uupc and Roy Wood's rnMac newsreader. It's also used in the MacTCP world, along with rnMac and a program called MacSlurp, which plays the role of the news transport agent, albeit over MacTCP-based connections rather than UUCP. Finally, John tells me that ToadNews can now process SOUP packets such as those generated by UQWK, a program that collects mail and news, and formats it for off-line reading. UQWK is mostly associated with certain BBS formats.

Installation and Setup

The first step in installing ToadNews is to create a folder in which it will work. Your news lives in this folder. The documentation recommends that you call this folder **News** and put it at the same level as the **spool** folder that uupc uses.

Actually, I lied. The first real step is to talk to your provider and arrange to have a newsfeed turned on. You must know which groups you want, because there's no way you can handle all of them. Check out the list of newsgroups in appendix B and pick a few to read before you ask your provider to send them to you. Although most administrators will happily change the set of groups you receive, they don't want to make changes frequently, so store them up and only ask every now and then.

ToadNews internally detects if the incoming news is compressed, so you don't have to set that manually, but you might want to mention to your system administrator that you can handle compressed news since it's so much faster to transfer.

Launch ToadNews. A log window appears, telling you nicely that you must configure the program before you do anything else. From the ToadNews menu, select the hierarchical Preferences menu and then Unbatcher Preferences. You see the Unbatcher Preference dialog (see figure 11.27).

In this dialog box, you must enter three items. Type the name of your UUCP host in the UUCP Name field. ToadNews accepts only eight characters here, which is odd because UUCP hosts can have names longer than eight characters (I cheated and took the screenshot before ToadNews complained to me). Next, click on the upper Select button. ToadNews displays a Standard File dialog so that you can find the directory in which news arrives. This **spool** folder is the same one uupc uses. Select the appropriate directory and then click on OK. Next, click on the lower Select button to choose the folder in which you want ToadNews to store messages after it unbatches the news file. You should have already created a **News** folder at the same level as your **spool** folder, so navigate to that folder and select it.

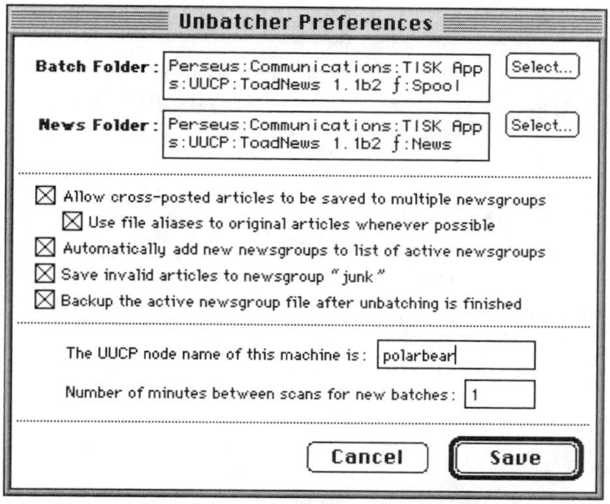

Figure 11.27   *ToadNews Unbatcher Preferences dialog*

The remaining options are more or less self-explanatory. ToadNews allows cross-posting, and even uses aliases for cross-posted articles, so you don't have to waste disk space on multiple copies of the same article. You almost certainly will want to raise the number of minutes between which ToadNews looks for new files unless you connect to your host every minute. Also, make sure that the checkbox to automatically add newsgroups is checked at first; otherwise, you have to add your newsgroups manually. After a while, you may want to shut off the automatic newsgroup-adding feature, because it gives you all the groups that people cross-post to as well. You might end up with **alt.sheep**, for example, if someone cross-posted there from **comp.sys.mac.comm**. Finally, a new option can save articles with an invalid format to the newsgroup called **junk**, for later perusal.

You also can configure the Expirer Preferences and the Window Preferences in that hierarchical Preferences menu, but because the defaults work fine, I'll let you play with them on your own. Basically, the Expirer Preferences enable you to set how quickly articles expire and when ToadNews should check for old articles. The Windows Preferences enable you to set which windows appear and what information is logged. In version 1.1, ToadNews has preferences for decompressing batches (you can use an external program if you want) and threading messages (again, you can use an external program). Finally, there are now preferences for the actions ToadNews should perform on startup (see figure 11.28).

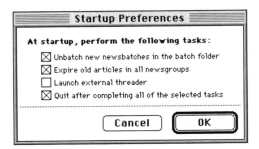

Figure 11.28   ToadNews Startup Preferences

Basic Usage

Most of the time you shouldn't have to mess with ToadNews too much, because it can quite happily work on unbatching and expiring news in the background while you work on other things. If you want to invoke it manually, you can either drag a newsbatch file onto the ToadNews icon (assuming you're using System 7 like a good Mac user) or from the File menu use either Unbatch or Unbatch Batch Folder (see figure 11.29).

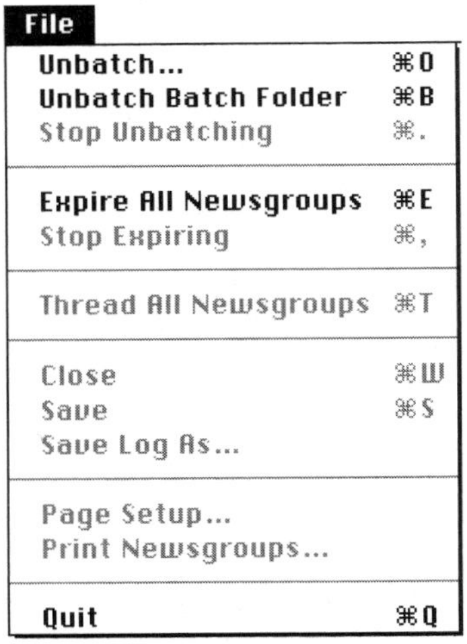

```
File
  Unbatch...                 ⌘O
  Unbatch Batch Folder       ⌘B
  Stop Unbatching            ⌘.

  Expire All Newsgroups      ⌘E
  Stop Expiring              ⌘,

  Thread All Newsgroups      ⌘T

  Close                      ⌘W
  Save                       ⌘S
  Save Log As...

  Page Setup...
  Print Newsgroups...

  Quit                       ⌘Q
```

Figure 11.29   ToadNews File menu

You can expire old news in all the active newsgroups by selecting Expire All Newsgroups. Choosing this option is a great way to clean up your hard disk quickly when you need some free space fast. New in version 1.1 is the option to schedule everything that ToadNews can do (see figure 11.30).

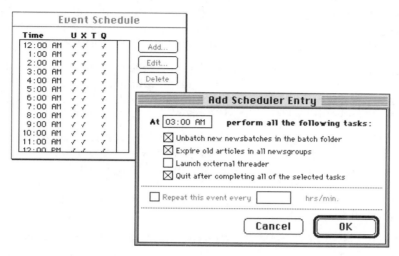

Figure 11.30 *ToadNews Scheduler*

The rest of the interaction you have with ToadNews is limited to the Active Newsgroups window, accessible when you choose Show Newsgroups from the Windows menu (see figure 11.31).

Newsgroup	First	Last	Total	Xpiry	Attr
alt.test	1	0	0	2	y
comp.lang.c	1	0	0	2	y
comp.lang.c++	1	0	0	2	y
comp.sys.mac.announce	1	5	5	2	y
comp.sys.mac.comm	1	23	23	2	y
comp.sys.mac.digest	1	0	0	2	y
comp.sys.mac.hardware	1	0	0	2	y
comp.sys.mac.misc	3	23	21	2	y
comp.sys.mac.programmer	1	0	0	2	y
comp.sys.mac.system	1	0	0	2	y
comp.windows.ms.programmer	1	0	0	2	y

Figure 11.31 *ToadNews Active Newsgroups window*

You can add newsgroups manually if ToadNews doesn't add them automatically. I've added some bogus newsgroups, and just for fun I modified a few article counts to make them look more real. Normally, you don't touch the article counts. You can also remove, edit, and expire newsgroups from this window.

Special Features

Because ToadNews mostly works unattended, it's hard for me to point at any special features that you might notice without your knowing more about the low-level Internet standards that ToadNews supports. Suffice it to say that ToadNews does some neat stuff at low levels that the user never sees.

Although it doesn't have extensive support for Apple events, ToadNews does support a few custom Apple events (and thus scripting programs such as AppleScript and Frontier) that help you automate tasks such as unbatching, expiring, and launching external threaders.

Speaking of the external threader, ToadNews enables you to select one for further processing of the news after ToadNews has unbatched it. At the moment, only rnMac can help here, but letting the newsreader do the threading generally enables the newsreader to run much faster. In theory, other programs could act as the external threader to provide access to the news in something like a Hermes BBS message file.

The latest version of ToadNews has a nice floating palette for unbatching and expiring progress bars.

I should also note that the combination of uupc, ToadNews, and rnMac consumes less RAM and disk space than UUCP/Connect, which merges the features of all three into a single program. If you don't have a large amount of disk space and one to two megabytes of RAM to devote to news, the freeware/shareware combination might be a better fit for you, and it's certainly cheaper. Depending on your specific setup, the combination of freeware and shareware might be more flexible as well, since you can pick and choose among several different transport mechanisms and newsreaders, all working more or less transparently with ToadNews.

Overall Evaluation

If you want to use UUCP but cannot afford UUCP/Connect, the combination of uupc, ToadNews, and (coming up next) rnMac provides an inexpensive way for you to read a small amount of news. Nothing else does what ToadNews does in the shareware arena, so if you need it, you need it. How's that for a nice tight tautology?

ToadNews was not designed for heavy duty newsfeeds. Therefore, if you plan to get a full feed of 4,000 plus newsgroups, don't even consider ToadNews. (For that matter, don't really even consider using UUCP/Connect—that kind of volume begs for Unix software.) In addition, ToadNews cannot forward news on to another person. In other words, with ToadNews you become a *leaf site*, a site that receives news and can send it back to the host but cannot pass it on. That capability would require ToadNews to batch news as well, something it doesn't do at the moment.

Administrative Details

ToadNews is shareware. It sells for $25 (in U.S. or Canadian dollars). If you are a programmer, John Mah will trade you for a copy of whatever program you've written. Otherwise, if you use ToadNews for three weeks, send John the money. You can contact him via email at `jpmah@undergrad.math.uwaterloo.ca`, and you can send shareware payments to:

John Mah
Toilets 'R Us Software
201 Riviera Dr.
Thunder Bay, Ontario, Canada
P7B 6H8

ToadNews is available on the Internet at:

```
ftp://ftp.tidbits.com/pub/tidbits/tisk/uucp/toad-news-11.hqx
```

rnMac

Roy Wood's rnMac is the third essential part of getting a UUCP newsfeed working without spending a lot of money. It is a fairly full-featured newsreader with a decent interface and low shareware payment of $25. With rnMac, you can read incoming Usenet articles and reply to them either via email or follow-up to the newsgroup. Newsreaders often have more functions, but when it comes right down to it, reading and replying are the two basic functions they must support to be useful.

Again, the combination of rnMac and ToadNews also works with MacSlurp, which is a MacTCP-based program for slurping in batches of news from an NNTP server, at which point ToadNews unbatches them and rnMac reads the news.

Installation and Setup

Roy Wood and Dave Platt should really get together. Although rnMac has a settings file that you can edit with ResEdit if you like (and it even resembles the uupc and Fernmail settings files), Roy also has provided a simple dialog that enables you to configure rnMac from within the program (see figure 11.32).

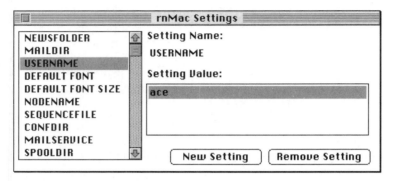

Figure 11.32   *rnMac Settings dialog*

I'm not going through all these items once again because, on the whole, they're the same sort that uupc and Fernmail require. The only confusing part is that you should use the same folders uupc uses rather than create another set, and rnMac may create a set of them for you automatically. Therefore, if you end up with two sets, you must trash one of them. Similarly, rnMac and ToadNews must agree where the spooled news lives and where to place the processed messages.

Note

You may wish to use aliases to the programs to make them more accessible, rather than having them all live in the same folder.

Basic Usage

After you have uupc, ToadNews, and rnMac set up, using rnMac is the least of your worries. The groups your machine receives show up in the omnipresent Subscribed Groups window. If there's nothing there, you must first subscribe to some groups. From the Groups menu choose List Active Newsgroups, then select a newsgroup in the Active Groups window, and select Subscribe from the Groups menu. Alternatively, you can simply double-click on a group in the Active Groups window to subscribe to it.

The number next to the group name indicates how many messages are in it. Double-clicking on a newsgroup brings up the newsgroup window. This window displays two scrollable panes, the sender and the subject of each message in one, and the text of the message in the other (see figure 11.33).

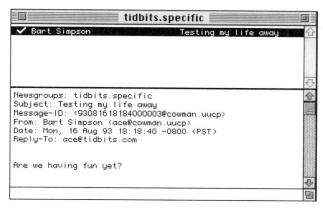

Figure 11.33   *rnMac Newsgroup window*

You can use the arrow keys to move up and down in the list of messages (which you do not see in the screenshot because I simulated only one message, and not very well at that—I forgot to change the default name and ended up with Bart Simpson).

Note

If Matt Groening's lawyers are reading this book, it was an accident!

If you look at the Articles menu, you can see the majority of rnMac's newsreading features, which are about all that you should need (see figure 11.34).

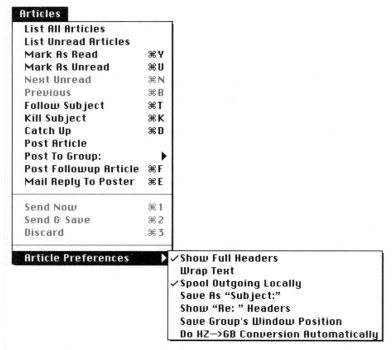

Figure 11.34   rnMac Articles menu

Most importantly, rnMac understands threads in newsgroups (by Subject/Date), so you can follow threads and kill them, two important features. With rnMac, you also can determine which articles show and which don't. It also makes marking articles as read or unread simple. The Post to Group hierarchical menu is a nice touch, too, because your subscribed newsgroups are in that menu for easy posting.

One unnerving aspect about rnMac is that it can handle threading in the background. That means that it scans the current articles constantly and determines which ones you've read and which should remain. This process results in an article occasionally disappearing from the upper article list in a newsgroup window, as rnMac realizes that you've read it. Yes, Virginia, there is a ghost in the machine.

Special Features

Along with its newsreading capabilities, rnMac includes a simple yet useful email feature. It uses an interface similar to the news and provides only a single mailbox, but if you have extremely small email requirements, it might suffice.

As in Fernmail, posting either news or email in rnMac opens a text window that has the header filled in for you but is completely accessible. Although I see that this feature is an easy way to build the header information, it makes me nervous because it's all too easy to edit something accidentally in the header and screw up the message.

Unlike Fernmail, rnMac's editing environment rewraps entire paragraphs as you type, which is as it should be in a Macintosh application. rnMac can handle messages larger than the 32K limit that plagues so many programs. Roy Wood deserves credit for circumventing that limit.

In its email section, rnMac supports aliases, and, like Fernmail, you can edit a text file that contains them. However, you're more likely to simply enter them from within the program because, as with the settings dialog, Roy provided a simple way of editing aliases.

rnMac can save messages to text files, which in itself isn't all that impressive, but it can also debinhex during the save, if you wish. For files not in rnMac already, it includes Convert From BinHex and Convert To BinHex options in the File menu.

Note

For those who read Chinese, rnMac theoretically can convert back and forth between GB and HZ, two methods of representing Chinese text.

In its Edit menu, rnMac provides commands for pasting certain smileys and acronyms (and you can edit these in ResEdit). You can also paste, with the quoting feature turned on. rnMac can also rot13 messages, change the font and size of the different windows, and—for those who really like to play—change the background color.

Finally, rnMac can act as an external threader application for ToadNews. The utility of this is that rnMac is faster than ToadNews at generating the threading information, and generally as well, since any newsreader that threads its own messages can place them in whatever format it likes, thus speeding up execution later on.

Overall Evaluation

I cannot say that rnMac is the best newsreader I've seen or even the best one on the Mac, but it does have most of the necessary features supported by a good interface.

Roy Wood has done a ton of work enhancing rnMac, and, from the sounds of it, has plans to do even more. In the version that should be available by the time you read this, rnMac should be able to call Eudora as an outgoing mail agent, which is a good thing since Eudora is far more powerful than the email features in rnMac. Roy also plans to add more non-standard shortcut keys that will address my only real complaint with rnMac—the fact that it doesn't have sufficient reading shortcuts. The process of creating the settings should improve in the future, too. We can also expect added features such as uudecoding, enhanced editing, MIME support, and message sorting. I look forward to new versions.

Although it has no balloon help, rnMac has rather good online help, currently located in the Apple menu. If you intend to use the program you should definitely read the help text closely.

Administrative Details

Like ToadNews, rnMac is $25 shareware (money orders or Canadian checks only, Roy asks). It forces you to click on a button labeled "No, I'm a shareware leech..." to get into the program until you register. You can contact Roy by email at **rrwood@io.org**, and you can send shareware payments to:

Roy R. Wood
Silicon Angst Software
7 Heyworth Crescent
Toronto, Ontario, Canada
M4E 1T6

And, at the risk of sounding like a broken record, you can get rnMac on the Internet at:

`ftp://ftp.tidbits.com/pub/tidbits/tisk/uucp/rn-mac-13b2.hqx`

TheNews

The second shareware entrant in the UUCP newsreader field comes from Bill Cramer. Called TheNews, and now in version 2.33, Bill's newsreader also works over a dialup link to a shell account and with MacTCP. Because TheNews doesn't really compare well with the other MacTCP-based newsreaders, I don't talk about it at length in the chapter about MacTCP-based software.

The more I write about newsreaders, the less I can think of to say. TheNews offers several advantages over rnMac, but it also suffers from a few omissions that may outweigh the advantages. I'll let you decide.

Installation and Setup

The previous version of TheNews had the best installation process of any of the UUCP programs I've looked at so far. Unfortunately, in version 2.33, Bill Cramer requires you to set a "transfer media flag" inside the program with ResEdit before you can even start configuring it for use with UUCP. Open the program in ResEdit, double click on the STR resource, and open resource number 1024. Change it to "U" to use TheNews with UUCP. Quit ResEdit, saving your changes.

Note

> *You can also change this resource in the TheNews settings file, which overrides the setting in the program file.*

From the File menu, choose Preferences. TheNews provides a clear dialog (see figure 11.35) for editing your preferences and even goes so far as to read many of the settings from the **UUPC Settings** file. As with rnMac, you must have uupc and ToadNews to use TheNews at all.

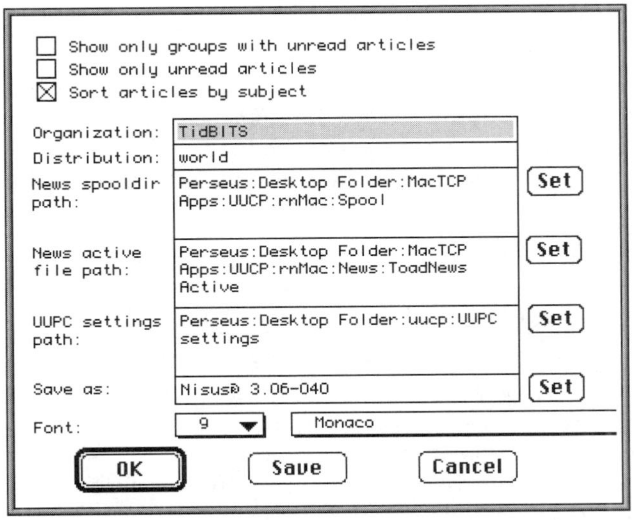

Figure 11.35   *TheNews UUCP configuration*

After you tell TheNews where all of the appropriate files and folders are located, you're almost up and running. Next, you must tell TheNews which groups you want to read. First, from the File menu choose New to create a New Groups file.

You may want to create multiple group files, each containing different groups, so that you don't later mix **rec.aviation** with **comp.unix.wizards**. Second, from the Groups menu choose Edit Group List. TheNews presents you with a dialog listing all the groups available at your site (see figure 11.36). I'm still limited to the two test groups I created in rnMac.

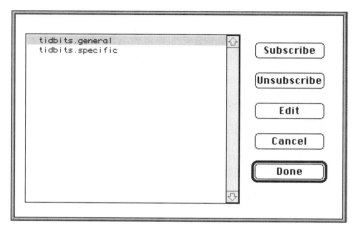

Figure 11.36   *TheNews Edit Group List dialog*

Select the groups you want to read, and click on the Subscribe button. Then click on the Done button to put the dialog away. The groups you subscribed to now appear in your New Groups file, along with the number of unread messages and the number of available messages. Until you start reading, these numbers remain the same.

Basic Usage

Double-clicking on a newsgroup name opens a window listing all of the articles and their subjects. In the process of configuring four different programs that rely on uupc, I've thoroughly screwed up something on my system, so I wasn't able to get any messages to appear in the newsgroup's window, even though it claimed I had one unread. Use your imagination to envision my mouse double-clicking on an article. Another window opens with two scrollable panes: the top one for the header, the bottom one for the article itself.

After you have an article open, you can do the usual things in terms of reply or follow-up, and TheNews actually provides a form that you can fill in when posting a message rather than just giving you a text window that contains text for the header information (see figure 11.37).

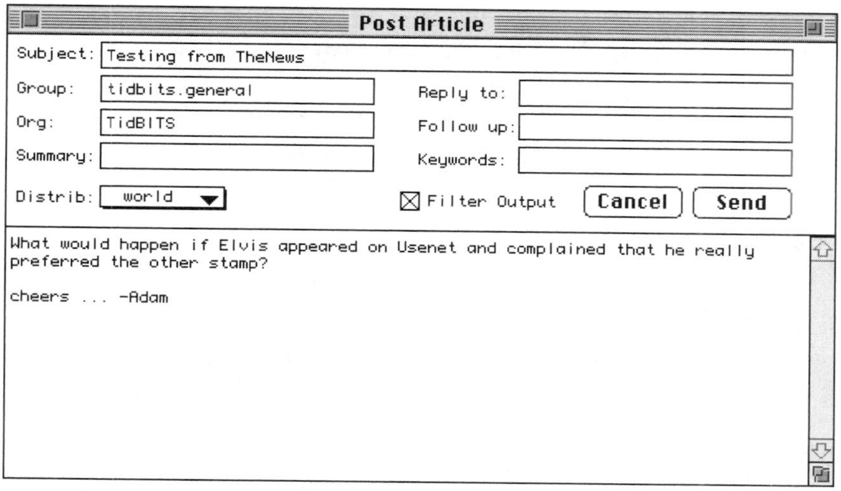

Figure 11.37   *TheNews Post Article window*

In this window you can tab among fields, and TheNews makes sure you fill in at least the required ones. Text entry is handled correctly, with paragraphs rewrapping as you edit, and it's nice to see the Macintosh interface being used as it was intended, with things like the pop-up menu for the distribution options. TheNews fills in what information it knows already, such as your organization and the group you're posting to (you must have a newsgroup window open before you can choose Post New from the Post/Mail hierarchical menu under the Articles menu). Other information it doesn't even bother to display, because you should know your own address, the date, and such details.

Special Features

TheNews can filter your messages so that Macintosh-only 8-bit characters, such as curly quotes and the bullet, are replaced with their 7-bit universal equivalents, the double-prime and an asterisk, for instance. International users can also appreciate this feature, because many characters that are standard in Swedish, for instance, don't exist in the 7-bit character set and must be translated so that they appear even slightly correct.

This feature may seem trivial but is, in fact, quite important. If postings aren't filtered, there's no telling, for instance, what characters end up replacing the smart quotes, and a message can quickly become hard to read fast. I've often seen a capital *R* and capital *S* replace the curly quotes, and the words that were quoted became extremely hard to mentally digest.

In version 2.33, Bill Cramer has added threading, which is a major advance and perhaps makes TheNews the choice for shareware UUCP newsreaders. The threading feature isn't well-supported by navigation features, so there's no shortcut for actions such as skipping to the next thread. However, the threading feature simplifies looking at the subjects in the newsgroup window, because you see only one entry per thread.

Note

If you Shift-select all the articles in a group, then Command-click on the ones you want to read to delesect them, you can choose Mark Read from the Articles menu to mark all the uninteresting ones as read. Choosing the new Read Next Unread command then takes you to just the ones you deselected. It's backward, but it works.

TheNews 2.33 also added the capability to save or append articles to a file directly from the article list window and dynamic sorting and threading of the article list window.

If you don't like the greater-than symbol prefix generally used for quoting on the Internet, you can now change that character in TheNews, although doing so requires ResEdit.

Overall Evaluation

TheNews is a good shareware UUCP newsreader, but it's not perfect. It has various interface problems, such as an unnecessary over-reliance on hierarchical menus and the use of modal dialog boxes where they also aren't necessary. I also have had trouble with its crashing and requiring lots of memory to do anything, but hopefully that's just on my system.

Administrative Details

You can reach Bill Cramer via email at **cramer@world.std.com**, but he doesn't promise to reply to your message immediately. If you want to download TheNews 2.33 from the Internet, it's at:

```
ftp://ftp.tidbits.com/pub/tidbits/tisk/term/the-news-233.hqx
```

The standard shareware price for TheNews-UUCP is $25 (although volume discounts are available), and shareware checks go to:

TheNews
1257 Worcester Road, Suite #196
Framingham, MA 01701

UUCP/Connect

I must admit that I've avoided talking about InterCon's UUCP/Connect so far. Why? Frankly, it scares me. It's a massive program that does almost everything under the UUCP sun, and most of the time it performs admirably. I hoped that by holding off until the end of this chapter, I might become familiar enough with the rest of the programs that I could speak more quickly about how UUCP/Connect outshines all of them. Of course, for the $295 price tag that it carries, it better do a lot of shining. However, for the most full-featured and professional UUCP implementation on the Macintosh, you cannot go wrong with UUCP/Connect.

Installation and Setup

In some ways, UUCP/Connect is harder to configure than the simpler and smaller implementations of UUCP. In part this difficulty has to do with the fact that from UUCP/Connect's massive hierarchical Configuration menu, you can configure the way the email and newsreading works, the UUCP communications process, the background tasks that allow UUCP/Connect to operate unattended, the Call Listener that allows others to call in for UUCP email and news, and a host of other features, including the extensions that add auto-reply and auto-forward features (see figure 11.38).

Most of the necessary UUCP configuration goes on in the Environment Configuration dialog box and its sub-boxes, indicated by the Set Misc, Set Paths, and Compression buttons (see figure 11.39).

There's no way I could walk you through all the possibilities here; luckily, UUCP/Connect comes with a decent manual, although it doesn't answer every question you might have (as if anything ever does!). Perhaps my main complaint with UUCP/Connect's configuration process is that the various different sections are laid out strangely, and they often interact in ways that may not be initially obvious. In the Environment Configuration dialog box, for instance, I have defined **nwnexus** as my mail and news server. If you look at the

Configuration menu, you see entries for Mail Server and News Server. The entries in your Environment Configuration dialog determine which of the potentially many servers show up when you choose Mail Server from the hierarchical Configuration menu (see figure 11.40).

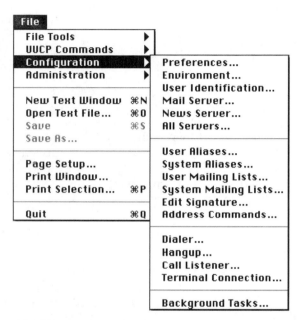

Figure 11.38   *UUCP/Connect Configuration menu*

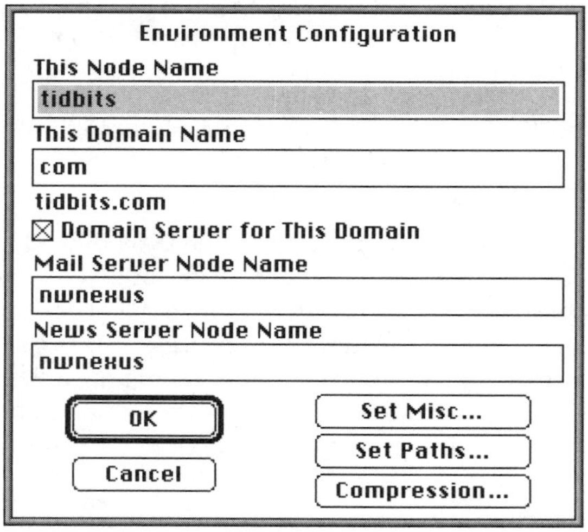

Figure 11.39   *UUCP/Connect Environment Configuration*

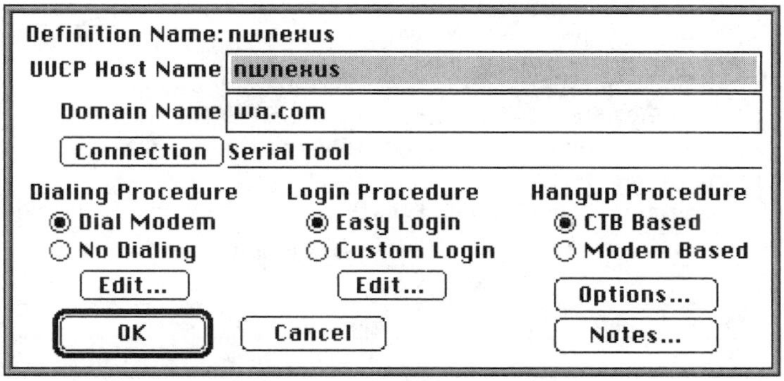

Figure 11.40   UUCP/Connect Server configuration

As you can see, UUCP/Connect does away with all of those nasty text files in specific formats, in favor of a decent, if not perfect, Macintosh interface. Its flexibility is also unparalleled. You can use any of the Mac's Communications Toolbox tools to connect, which means that UUCP/Connect can not only dial a modem, but also can distribute UUCP mail and news over an AppleTalk network with Apple's ADSP tool. This capability makes UUCP/Connect useful for an organization that wants to have one copy call out and then distribute the mail to other copies around a network.

Note

In theory, you could even use a Telnet tool such as TGE TCP Tool (from Tim Endres, who also wrote UUCP/Connect) to connect to a UUCP server over a MacTCP-based connection. There are some low-level technical quirks, so this may not be as simple as it sounds.

I don't want to dwell too much on UUCP/Connect's configuration because it has so many options and preferences that it would take ten pages just to pay lip service to them. But I cannot resist showing you one more dialog that gives an idea of UUCP/Connect's flexibility (see figure 11.41).

You see the Mail and News Preferences dialog, which you reach (confusingly, in my opinion) by selecting Preferences from the hierarchical Configuration menu, and then clicking on the Mail & News button at the top of the resulting dialog box (which has six different buttons, each leading to yet another dialog box of preferences).

I like the way UUCP/Connect lets you toggle your signature separately for mail and news, but I wish it allowed you to add your signature on a piece-by-piece basis. I hate traipsing through all those dialog boxes just to turn off my signature for a single letter. Even with QuicKeys, it's a pain.

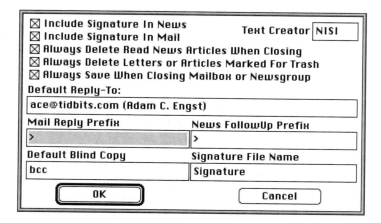

Figure 11.41   UUCP/Connect Mail and News Preferences dialog

Basic Usage

In general, using UUCP/Connect is a dream. Although it certainly has quirks and limitations, it has handled tremendous amounts of mail for me. After you figure out your favorite way of doing something, it's a fast, slick interface.

Sending Messages

Sending a letter or posting an article in UUCP/Connect is simple—you fill in a header form, using a pop-up menu for commonly used aliases (see figure 11.42).

Although the pop-up menu works well for a relatively small number of aliases, it starts to slow down once you have 50 or so. Luckily, you can always simply type the alias manually.

Note

Here's a nice touch: if you hold down the Option key while you're selecting an alias from the pop-up menu, UUCP/Connect puts the address into the Compose Mail dialog rather than the alias name. This capability can be handy when you need to send someone an address of a friend for whom you already have an alias.

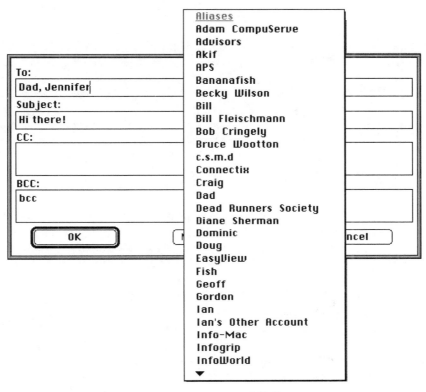

Figure 11.42   *UUCP/Connect Compose Mail dialog*

UUCP/Connect doesn't even force you to fill in the To field until you try to send the letter. This is nice, because there's no telling if you'll want to address the letter before or after you write it. If you click on the OK button, a bare-bones text editing window appears—so barren, in fact, that I'm not going to bother to show you. It looks like almost every other text editing window you've seen. Here's primarily where I think UUCP/Connect falls down. Unlike even some of the shareware programs, it does not rewrap paragraphs as you edit. Although lines wrap as you type them originally, that's only half the battle. Having to select some text and choose the Fit Selection command from the Edit menu is a pain. I cannot imagine this problem not being fixed in the next release, because it's a glaring oversight in an otherwise well-conceived package.

Note

UUCP/Connect's editor has been revamped for the most recent release, 1.8v1, and after using 1.8v1 for a day, I went back the 1.6v2 version that I had been using previously. The problem now is that InterCon added support for WorldScript to sell UUCP/Connect in Japan. In the process, it made the text wrap properly all the time, but also removed a basic feature that moves the cursor to the end of the last line if you press the down arrow while on the last line. This may sound minor, but I do a lot of editing on the last line of messages (not surprisingly) and removing this feature meant that I had to click the mouse button to get back to the end of the line. There weren't other major changes, so I went back without any trouble.

UUCP/Connect has one neat shortcut if you're writing a letter. If you need to address it after the fact or change the subject, instead of going to the Mail menu and choosing Modify Letter Info, you can simply click on the New Letter tag in the lower left of the text editing window. Clicking on the same spot when you're reading a letter displays the entire header, which is often useful if you have abbreviated headers turned on in the preferences.

After you're finished writing a letter, you can send it in a number of ways. You can go to the Mail menu and choose Mail Letter. Or, you can click on the icon in the Functions palette that means the same thing. Or, you can do as I do, closing the window and clicking on the default Send button when UUCP/Connect asks what you want to do with the letter. Because I always want to get the letter off the screen after I'm finished anyway, sending it this way works best for me.

Note

After seeing how Eudora handles reading and sending mail, I recently wrote a series of QuicKeys macros that make it simple to do things such as "send the current message, delete the original, and open the next message." Now, I only hit a single key to do most of my navigation in UUCP/Connect.

Reading Messages

I should talk a bit more about the Functions palette, because it makes a number of actions easier in UUCP/Connect. Because many of the buttons work primarily when reading email, take a look at a UUCP/Connect mailbox at the same time (see figure 11.43).

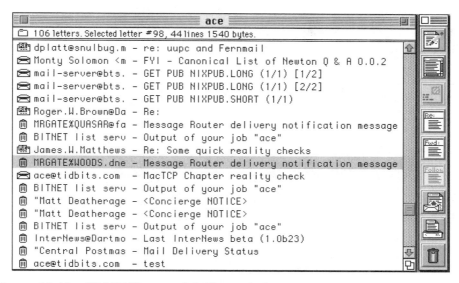

Figure 11.43   *UUCP/Connect Mailbox window*

No smoke and mirrors here; this is my real-life mailbox, complete with the many messages that I plan to reply to in my nonexistent copious spare time. Let's take it from the top. UUCP/Connect puts the name of the mailbox in the window title; mailboxes are in the same Unix mailbox format that other programs use and their names are live, in the sense that if you send a message to **joe@tidbits.com**, UUCP/Connect creates a mailbox called **joe** and tells me that I've got a new mailbox. This feature provides a simple way for multiple people to use the same copy of UUCP/Connect on the same computer.

Note

And, with either the UUCP/Connect client version or Eudora, as I explained previously in this chapter, multiple users don't even have to share the same machine to use the same copy of UUCP/Connect.

In the next line, UUCP/Connect tells me how many messages I have in the mailbox, which one I have selected and how big it is in lines and bytes. If I select multiple messages (contiguous or not), UUCP/Connect informs me how many I have selected. This is helpful when you perform a Find on a mailbox and the Find matches some unknown number of messages.

In the body of the mailbox, which is a completely resizable window, UUCP/ Connect displays a mail status icon, the name or userid of the sender, and the subject of the letter. I rely heavily on UUCP/Connect's icons here because they indicate if I've read a message, replied to it, saved it to disk, or deleted it. It may sound trivial, but eventually I forget whether I've replied to a letter. These icons remind me.

Note

UUCP/Connect doesn't record these icon settings permanently until you close the mailbox. This means that if you crash while a mailbox is open, you lose track of which messages you've replied to or deleted. It's a pain, although certainly better than actually losing the messages.

Functions Palette

UUCP/Connect's Functions palette has nine buttons, of which I use only the last six. The first three are clumsier than using the keyboard and mouse shortcuts; they are, respectively, Create New Letter/Article, Read Message, and Send Message. The next six, though, are extremely important: Reply, Forward, Followup, Save to Disk, Print, and Trash.

Reply, Forward, and Followup all work on the currently selected item or items in a mailbox, or on the front-most message window. If you select a portion of the original message, clicking the Reply or Forward buttons creates a new message with the selected text included as a quote. If you don't select any text, UUCP/ Connect quotes the entire message by default, although a simple Select All selects the message to replace it as soon as you start typing.

Note

In my opinion, all email programs and newsreaders should use this Reply-With-Selected concept by default, to help users to quote more carefully.

The Save to Disk button works in several different ways, depending on where you are and what you have selected. If you're reading a message, clicking on the Save button saves that message to the disk file you specify. However, if you're in the mailbox with one or more messages selected, clicking the Save button gives you the choice of creating a new file or appending to an existing file, with or without headers, and concatenating the files, if you have more than one selected.

The Trash button is handy because, even though you can just press the Delete key when you have one or more messages selected in the mailbox, if you click on the Trash button after you finish reading a message, UUCP/Connect closes the message window and marks the message for deletion, all in one swell foop.

Note

As long as you don't move your Functions palette, you can define a QuicKeys macro to click on that spot. I assigned that macro to Control-Delete, and it's a much faster way of deleting messages.

Messages marked for deletion don't actually disappear until you close the mailbox or newsgroup window (although you can choose an option that lets UUCP/Connect delete all the newsgroup articles that you've read when you close the mailbox). This feature avoids the problem of expiring messages.

News Groups and Mailboxes

As I said earlier in this chapter, UUCP/Connect supports multiple mailboxes (see figure 11.44).

You can add and delete mailboxes and newsgroups, move them around, empty them of messages, get info about them, and check for new ones automatically by using the buttons at the top of the window. At the bottom of the window, you see the number of messages and the number of those that are unread. Like the icons next to the messages in a mailbox window, the icons to the left of the name have several states. At a glance, you can tell whether a mailbox or newsgroup has messages in it and whether any of them are new.

Note

Again, using QuicKeys, you can define a macro that saves a message in a specified mailbox automatically. Once you have as many mailboxes as I do, such shortcuts make life much easier.

I think I've given you a sufficient glimpse at UUCP/Connect's interface so that you should understand the power behind it. Again, despite its few faults, I've used UUCP/Connect for years now to handle the massive quantities of mail that I send and receive every day. I save all of my outgoing messages, and that mailbox often surpasses 1,000 messages by the end of the month.

Chapter 11
UUCP Access

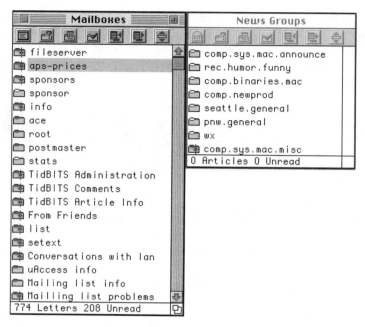

Figure 11.44   *UUCP/Connect Newsgroups and Mailboxes*

Speaking of lots of messages, I forgot to touch on how UUCP/Connect handles large quantities of Usenet news. There's no point in showing you a newsgroup window because it looks exactly the same as a mailbox window, but UUCP/Connect does provide threading in an interesting way. Because reading a message involves opening a window, UUCP/Connect selects all messages in a thread if you hold down the Option key as you click on any article. If you want to read those messages, press Enter to open all of their windows in chronological order. You can also press Delete to delete them all at once, which is the same thing as using the kill function in other newsreaders.

Note

The same Option-click shortcut also works in mailbox windows, which can be handy for selecting all the messages in a discussion that you've had with someone.

There are two drawbacks to this method of reading news. First, UUCP/Connect slows down when it tries to open a mailbox containing hundreds of messages. Second, it can take quite some time to open more than about 15 windows, and it's certainly possible to have a thread with more than 15 articles. So, although

UUCP/Connect works fine for reading a number of newsgroups, you must read them regularly to prevent them from becoming unwieldy. A different interface for news might be appropriate for a future version.

Calling Out

After you've read and replied to your messages, you need to call your host to send them. Remember that because UUCP is by default a non-interactive protocol, UUCP/Connect simply stores your messages in a spool folder until you call out. You have two basic ways of calling out, manually and automatically. For a manual connection, you use the commands in the Comm menu (see figure 11.45).

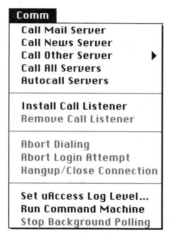

Figure 11.45   *UUCP/Connect Comm menu*

Selecting Call Mail Server from the Comm menu immediately calls your mail server to send and receive all of your mail. I have only one server for both mail and news, but you can select either, depending on what sort of messages you want to send and receive. Alternatively, if you have yet another machine to which you can connect, it appears in the hierarchical Call Other Server menu.

Note

If you press the Option key while you're selecting one of the servers from the Other Servers menu, UUCP/Connect brings up that server's configuration dialog box, rather than calling it.

Along with various calling options and commands that enable you to terminate dialing or a connection, you also can set UUCP/Connect's log level (because I'm still using a differently named version of UUCP/Connect called uAccess, the menu command is called Set uAccess Log Level). Leaving this on the default setting works well in most cases, but you can increase it to higher numbers, such as 20, that record the slightest movement of a packet of information. If you set it to 100, it probably tells you what the electrons are doing as well. You need the detail when troubleshooting a connection; otherwise, stick with the default, or you quickly fill up your hard disk with a massive log file.

I prefer to use UUCP/Connect in unattended mode, in which it calls out at scheduled times. If you go to the hierarchical Configuration menu in the File menu and select Background Tasks from the very bottom, UUCP/Connect displays the Background Tasks Configuration dialog (see figure 11.46).

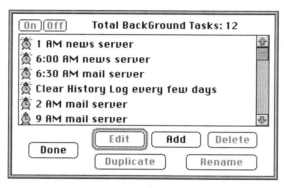

Figure 11.46   *UUCP/Connect Background Tasks configuration dialog*

You can create tasks to call any server at any time, repeating or not, and you can even tell UUCP/Connect to call only if messages are waiting to go out on your machine. You also can clear the logs automatically every few days with a background task, and if you're running UUCP/Connect unattended, it's a good idea to have it restart the machine once a day to periodically clear memory. On the whole, UUCP/Connect is stable, and it always works on a copy of open mailboxes, so even the uncommon crash doesn't damage any data.

Special Features

Perhaps more so than any other area, the area of special features is where UUCP/Connect stands out from the crowd of free UUCP implementations. Tim Endres took a bit of flak on Usenet when he decided to create the then-uAccess as a commercial product, but for the features he added, he made the right move.

Aliases are all fine and nice for distributing email to a group of people, but UUCP/Connect has gone several steps further by providing some *address commands*, which are special additional extensions to the main program. The first one acts as an auto-reply so that any message to an auto-reply address automatically receives a specified message back. The second one automatically forwards messages, so if you send email to one address, the auto-forward address command forwards it to a second address. The auto-forward address command is slightly broken, in that it messes up the sender and subject information in the forwarded message. The most recent address command is auto-kill, and I haven't actually used that yet, but it deletes messages that meet certain criteria.

Last is the fileserver address command, which unfortunately no longer ships with UUCP/Connect. Like the others, it was never meant to be an integral part of the program, only example code, but if you call InterCon and beg and scream, maybe they'll send it to you (see figure 11.47).

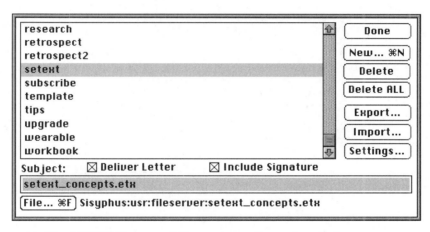

Figure 11.47   *UUCP/Connect Fileserver configuration dialog*

Mail sent to the fileserver address with a specific word in the Subject line elicits a response based on that Subject line. So, for instance, if you send email to **fileserver@tidbits.com** with the single word **setext** in the Subject line, UUCP/Connect sends you a file talking about the setext file format that we use for *TidBITS*. The capabilities offered by these address commands are extremely useful in many types of professional situations, although an individual user may also find uses for them.

Note

I've found that people prefer using auto-reply addresses far more than the fileserver, so if you wish to automatically send out information to people who send email, I recommend using an auto-reply address.

Although you can find utilities to perform all of these translation tasks, take a look at UUCP/Connect's hierarchical File Tools menu under the File menu (see figure 11.48).

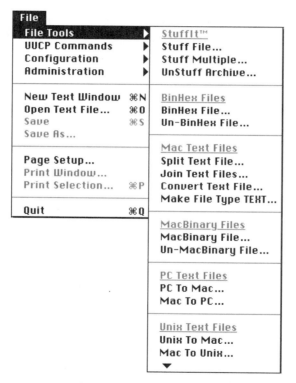

Figure 11.48   UUCP/Connect File Tools menu

The set of utilities is impressive. You may find them easier to use than the various utilities floating around the nets, and although they're not necessarily as powerful or fast, the fact that they're so handy in UUCP/Connect makes up for it.

Whenever you send a message, a UUCP program places it in the spool folder along with two other supporting files that share similar names. If you want to delete these files, finding and deleting all three can be a hassle. UUCP/Connect helps by providing you a Job Queue, which lists all the files waiting to go out or, depending on when you look, the incoming files that haven't yet been processed (see figure 11.49).

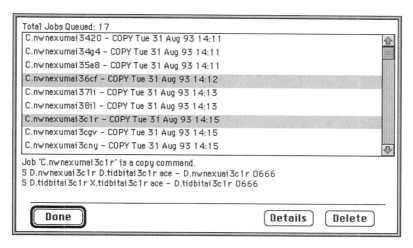

Figure 11.49 *UUCP/Connect Job Queue dialog*

Although the Details button shows you little in the way of useful information (such as the subject of the letter), you can often differentiate messages by the timestamp. I mainly use the Job Queue to see how many messages are waiting in line to go out. This gives me an idea of how much mail I've sent during that session, and also how long the next connection will take if I connect manually.

Note

Since all the files are text files, it's relatively easy to go into the **spool:uucp** *directory with a text editor and look at the contents of each message if you wish to delete a specific one but don't know which it is.*

Finally, UUCP/Connect includes a complete, if simple, Communications Toolbox-based terminal program (see figure 11.50). This feature proves its worth when you're first troubleshooting a new connection, because it's a pain to switch back to a separate terminal emulator to check on how a chat script works.

Because the terminal uses the Comm Toolbox, in theory you can use various different file transfer tools. Because there weren't any others when UUCP/Connect came out, however, the Transfers menu shows only Text and XMODEM protocols.

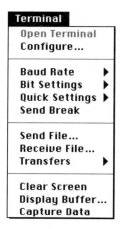

Figure 11.50   UUCP/Connect Terminal menu

The main addition I'd like to see to UUCP/Connect's terminal is the capability to link it more closely to the rest of the program. For instance, it would be nice to be able to select Call Mailserver from the Comm menu and have that host dialed in the terminal. Similarly, it would be nice to have a background-only option for the terminal, so you could see onscreen what the UUCP connection thought was happening at login.

Overall Evaluation

I could go on and on about UUCP/Connect because it's a deep program. A bunch of little touches aren't documented anywhere, such as being able to Option-select a server from the hierarchical Other Servers menu to configure it, or the fact that you can copy the contents of a modal header window with Command-C if you wish. Still, the program suffers from a few interface problems, such as text entry. And, its configuration process could use an overhaul to clarify what's happening and which options affect which other options. Despite its price, I think UUCP/Connect may very well be the most cost-effective method of sending and receiving a lot of mail and news on the Internet today.

Administrative Details

You can purchase UUCP/Connect direct from InterCon Systems for $295. If you want to use UUCP/Connect on a network, you need at least one server copy (which is what I covered in this section), but you also can purchase cheaper client-only versions (which cannot relay news or mail to machines other than the server) for $195. Also, a ton of different pricing tiers exist, based on volume and whether you work at an educational institution (60 percent off) or for the government (15 percent off). UUCP/Connect is also available from some dealers and at a discount from the mail-order firms, Mac's Place and MacZone. For more information, contact InterCon electronically at **sales@intercon.com**, or at:

InterCon Systems Corporation
950 Herndon Pkwy., Ste. 420
Herndon, VA 22070
703-709-5500
703-709-5555 fax

UUCP and You

In this chapter I've attempted to give you a comprehensive overview of all of the UUCP software available for the Macintosh. I won't pretend that UUCP is the wave of the future or the best way to access the Internet, because in fact, UUCP is the wave of the past and is limited to email and news. However, for email and news, you may find that UUCP connections are the most efficient, both in terms of your time and money. In addition, if you want to set up email accounts for a number of people in a single office, the combination of UUCP/Connect and Eudora is pretty hard to beat.

Let's turn now from the UUCP past to the MacTCP present and future. The next chapter looks in gory detail at MacTCP, SLIP, and PPP, which are the underpinnings to today's Internet access method of choice, the MacTCP-based connection.

MacTCP, PPP, and SLIP

"The time has come," the Walrus said,
"To talk of many things:
Of news—and chips—and Gopher hacks,
Of Babbage's—and pings."

Apologies to Lewis Carroll, but the time has come to talk of many things, all of them dependent on Apple's MacTCP. I'm going to start by discussing MacTCP itself, which Hayden licensed from Apple to put on the disk that comes with this book. Then, for those who must use a modem and either PPP (Point to Point Protocol) or SLIP (Serial Line Internet Protocol) to connect to the Internet, I'll look at the different implementations of PPP and SLIP.

Note

PPP and SLIP are communication protocols that fool your MacTCP-equipped Macintosh into thinking that it's attached to a network that connects to the Internet. Instead of that network, SLIP and PPP enable the Mac to communicate over a modem, which is good since most individuals don't have access to networks

continues

continued

connected to the Internet. Whether you use PPP or SLIP depends primarily on if you can get a PPP or SLIP account from your Internet provider. Given a choice, I recommend PPP, but both work fine.

This chapter may seem overly long for discussing the installation and configuration of a couple of programs, but MacTCP and the SLIP and PPP implementations are surprisingly complex, once you look closely at them. In the first edition, I was pleased to realize that I had provided more information on configuring MacTCP than even Apple's official documentation—in this edition, I've expanded the discussion tremendously. In addition to looking closely at MacTCP, I cover InterSLIP and MacPPP in detail, and briefly discuss the other SLIP and PPP implementations. Finally, because this world is not perfect and problems do arise, I have a lengthy section on troubleshooting MacTCP, InterSLIP, and MacPPP, along with some common-sense advice on how to ask for help.

Note

Although I have no experience with it, there's an interesting application called NET/Mac that supports TCP/IP services over packet radio. This means that ham radio operators can run TCP applications over a wireless TCP/IP network. You can find it at:

```
ftp://ftp.ucsd.edu/hamradio/packet/tcpip/mac/NET_Mac2.3.39.sea.hqx
```

With those preliminaries out of the way, let's check out MacTCP 2.0.4.

MacTCP

MacTCP is a translator. It enables the Macintosh to speak the language of the Internet, TCP/IP (*Transmission Control Protocol/Internet Protocol*). Normally, of course, Macs speak AppleTalk to one another, over Macintosh networks. You must have the MacTCP control panel installed and configured properly, in order for the MacTCP-based programs such as Fetch and TurboGopher to work, although MacTCP is not making the connection itself. Think of MacTCP as the Babel Fish from the *Hitchhiker's Guide to the Galaxy*. Pop it in your Mac's ear (the Control Panel folder, actually), and your Mac understands the Internet noise that's flowing in and out. The metaphor of speaking and languages isn't quite accurate, since TCP/IP actually is a transport protocol, but the idea of MacTCP as a Babel Fish that translates Internet gibberish into a language the Mac can understand seems to be the most understandable metaphor. Luckily, everything that MacTCP does happens at such a low level that you never notice. In fact, after you set up MacTCP correctly, you should never notice that it's present.

Once your Mac is connected to the Internet with MacTCP and a network, SLIP, or PPP, it is essentially the same as any other Internet machine and has its own IP number. This means that you can connect to other Internet machines directly, without going through an intermediate machine. You can also, if you want, run server software to turn your Mac into an FTP, Gopher, or Web server.

Note

Because the Internet is based on the TCP/IP protocols, the only way for a Mac to enjoy a full Internet connection is to use MacTCP. If you do not have MacTCP installed and a MacTCP-based connection using PPP, SLIP, ARA (Apple Remote Access), or a Internet-connected network, you cannot use the MacTCP programs. Period.

Apple and other companies have thought in the past that MacTCP is a program that only large organizations want to buy, install, and configure. Accordingly, most of the documentation I've seen makes this assumption, too. It's a poor assumption these days, because individuals using PPP or SLIP can easily gain access to the Internet, and PPP and SLIP require MacTCP. However, if you work at a university or business that provides your Internet connection, it's a good bet that you have a system administrator who knows more about MacTCP than you or I do, and who has probably preconfigured it for your convenience.

Note

If rumors prove true, Apple will bundle MacTCP with System 7.5, due in the latter part of 1994. Let's hope that the MacTCP documentation is improved from what currently ships. Hey, what am I saying? If the documentation stays as incomprehensible as it currently is, everyone will have to buy a copy of this book. Forget I said anything!

In fact, a system administrator can preconfigure and then lock MacTCP so you can't change any of this information. I'm assuming that you want to use the version of MacTCP that I include on the disk, though, and that version enables anyone to configure it.

Because those of you with network administrators can ask them for help, I concentrate on details of interest to the individual who has no local network administrator and must rely solely on this book and the system administrator at a public provider. Therefore, I'm not going to talk about many of the issues specific to dedicated LocalTalk or Ethernet connections. In fact, you wouldn't want me to do so, because I've never been able to work with one of these connections for more than a few hours. Sorry to disappoint, but your local system administrator can be more useful than I can anyway because I have no idea what your specific setup looks like.

Along with the help text that's built into my installer for you to save or print (and I strongly recommend you do one or the other), you may wish to browse through a document about MacTCP written by Eric Behr. It's included with Peter Lewis's MacTCP Watcher program (which is extremely useful if you experience problems). I realize you may not have access to FTP sites yet, but if you do, you can retrieve MacTCP Watcher at:

```
ftp://ftp.tidbits.com/pub/tidbits/tisk/tcp/mactcp-watcher-11.hqx
```

MacTCP Questions

Now, let's go over the questions you need to ask to configure MacTCP on your own. First, of course, comes the connection method—via PPP or SLIP, or network. If you connect via PPP or SLIP, there are a number of other questions you must ask. Before you call your provider, read down through the section, "SLIP and PPP," to find out how to configure MacTCP. If you're connecting via a network, most of the same rules apply, but again, your system administrator knows the details.

Second, find out whether you are supposed to determine your address *Manually*, whether it's assigned dynamically when you call the *Server* each time, or *Dynamically* at random (which is apparently seldom used, dangerous, and worth avoiding). Keep reading, but those three italicized terms are extremely important and confusing because each corresponds to a choice in the MacTCP control panel; the way people talk about the methods doesn't always correspond.

Note

> In talking with system administrators, I find that most call Manually-addressed accounts static (because your IP address is assigned once and never changes) and Server-addressed accounts dynamic (because the server assigns you a different IP address on the fly each time you connect). You see the problem. I've never heard of anyone using a Dynamically-addressed account outside of a controlled laboratory situation, complete with rats, mazes, and spilled ink. (OK, so I exaggerate slightly.)

If you have a Manually-addressed account, you must find out what your IP address number will be. It will be four numbers, separated by periods, and should look something like **192.135.191.128**. If you connect manually, you also need a gateway address number in the same format. You may need this gateway address with a server-addressed account as well, but MacTCP doesn't allow you to enter it—some implementations of SLIP do. Depending on the configuration of your site, you may also need to find out your network class and subnet mask, and your network administrator should know what to tell you here. Most people who use PPP and SLIP do not need to configure the network class and subnet mask part of MacTCP.

No matter what, you need to know the name and number address of one or more *domain name servers*, which are machines that translate between names that you enter, such as **nwnexus.wa.com**, and the number addresses that the machines all speak, such as **192.135.191.1**. Finally, although you don't need them to configure MacTCP, now is a good time to ask your system administrator for the addresses of your SMTP (Simple Mail Transport Protocol) and NNTP (Net News Transport Protocol) servers. Also ask your system administrator what your POP account will be, and whether it's different from your email address. See table 12.1 for examples of each of these data.

Table 12.1
MacTCP Account Information

Item	Example
Connection method	SLIP, LocalTalk, Ethernet
Addressing style	Manually, Server, Dynamically

continues

Table 12.1
continued

Item	Example
IP address (if Manually)	e.g., 192.135.191.128
Gateway address (if necessary)	e.g., 192.135.191.253
Network class (if Manually and necessary)	A, B, or C
Subnet Mask (if Manually and necessary)	Ask
Primary and Secondary Nameservers	e.g., 198.137.231.1
Local domain	e.g., halcyon.com
SMTP mail server	e.g., halcyon.com
NNTP news server	e.g., nwfocus.wa.com
POP account	e.g., tidbits@halcyon.com
Email address	e.g., tidbits@halcyon.com

Note

Every now and then I get a complaint from someone who says that they don't have a system administrator to ask. I hate to tell them, but unless they are in complete charge of the machine that they connect to, there must be someone else who acts as the system administrator. You cannot *set this stuff up entirely on your own—you* must *have the cooperation of the person who runs the machine to which you connect. This person usually works for the organization that provides your Internet access, such as a university information technology department or a commercial provider such as Northwest Nexus, if you connect through them.*

I realize this information is a bit much to swallow at once, but that's why I explain how to configure MacTCP in the following section, so that you can see where each piece of information goes. Also, check out the worksheet at the back of the book—you can fill it in with your information to make it easier to set up MacTCP, and, if you use either, PPP or SLIP.

Note

In the interest of completeness, the examples and screenshots I use in this chapter talk about configuring MacTCP for use with a Manually-addressed account. In chapter 14, "Step-by-Step Internet," I step through the process of configuring MacTCP for Northwest Nexus, which is a Server-addressed account.

Installation and Setup

To start, copy the MacTCP control panel to the Control Panels folder in your System Folder. If you drag it to the System Folder icon, System 7 moves it to the right place. Also drag the Hosts file, which is a small text file, to the System Folder. It shouldn't go into any of the special folders under System 7 and should remain loose in the System Folder.

Note

The ISKM Installer that comes on the disk with this book places MacTCP and the Hosts file in the proper locations for you. However, in the interests of providing you with more general information, I tell you how the installation process would work if you were to ignore the ISKM Installer. Otherwise you would never be able to do anything on your own without using the ISKM Installer.

If you are upgrading from a previous version of MacTCP, open the current MacTCP control panel and write down all of your settings. Then, make sure to delete the old MacTCP control panel, the MacTCP DNR file that lives loose in the System Folder, and the MacTCP Prep file that lives in your Preferences folder. If you fail to delete these items before you install the new version, there's no telling what could go wrong.

Installing SLIP or PPP

If you plan to connect via PPP or SLIP, take a brief break and install MacPPP or InterSLIP. I'm going to crib a few paragraphs from the MacPPP and InterSLIP installation sections, so don't be surprised if this information sounds familiar later.

Note

Again, the ISKM Installer places the various parts of MacPPP and InterSLIP in the proper folders automatically. If you get a new version of either, though, you may need these instructions to know where the different files live.

Installing MacPPP requires placing a control panel called Config PPP in your Control Panels folder, and an extension called PPP in your Extensions folder. If you drop them on your closed System Folder, System 7 automatically places them in the proper folders. After you've installed Config PPP and PPP, restart your Mac.

Installing InterSLIP requires placing a control panel called InterSLIP Control in your Control Panels folder, and an extension called InterSLIP in your Extensions folder. If you drop the pair of them on the System Folder icon, System 7 places them in the correct locations. The application called InterSLIP Setup can live anywhere on your hard disk, but it may be a good idea to put it or an alias to it in your Apple Menu Items folder, for easy access. After you place those three parts in the proper places, restart your Mac.

Configuring the MacTCP Main Window

If you aren't installing MacPPP or InterSLIP, simply restart now. When the Mac comes back up, open the MacTCP control panel from the Control Panels folder (see figure 12.1).

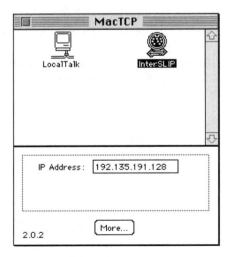

Figure 12.1   *MacTCP control panel*

Note

If you've installed MacPPP rather than InterSLIP, you have an icon labeled PPP instead of InterSLIP in the MacTCP control panel main window.

You must select one of the icons (you may have more, fewer, or different ones) in the upper part of the control panel to tell MacTCP how you plan to connect. If you have a LocalTalk network attached to the Internet through a router, select the LocalTalk icon. If you have an Ethernet connection, I'm jealous, but select that icon anyway. If you use MacPPP, select the PPP icon. And, of course, for a SLIP connection, select the InterSLIP icon.

Note

I don't recommend that you install MacPPP and InterSLIP at the same time— they seem to confuse MacTCP if both are active. Also, if you want to switch between the two, completely reinstall MacTCP before switching.

You can set your IP address in the lower part of the MacTCP control panel. If your provider gives you a Manually-addressed account (or static address) and provides your IP address, type the address into the IP Address field, much as I've done with my address. If your host machine assigns you an address (a Server-addressed account) or, if MacTCP dynamically picks one, leave this box set to **0.0.0.0**. Not too hard yet (I hope).

Configuring the MacTCP Configuration Dialog

Now click on the More button to bring up the configuration dialog box (see figure 12.2).

Remember that I said to ask whether your address was obtained Manually, from your Server, or Dynamically? That's the answer to the Obtain Address set of radio buttons. Select the button that corresponds with what your system administrator tells you.

Time for a brief talk about those Obtain Address buttons. Everything I have read or been told has advised avoiding the Dynamically button like the plague. The problem has something to do with the fact that when you use it, MacTCP makes up an address at random and then looks for duplicate addresses. Apparently, this process tends to fail and can result in duplicate IP addresses on the network at the same time, which is a bad thing.

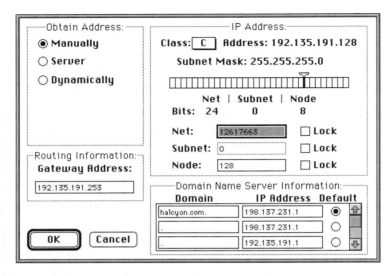

Figure 12.2 *MacTCP configuration dialog*

If you click on the Manually button, you must give MacTCP a permanent IP address that your system administrator has provided for you. Either use the Manually button or the Server button, and remember that if your system administrator talks about dynamic addressing, he probably means what MacTCP calls a Server-addressed account. Don't select MacTCP's Dynamically button unless your system administrator knows how to configure MacTCP and explicitly tells you to do so.

Enough about the Obtain Address buttons. If your system administrator gives you a gateway address, type it into the Routing Information Gateway Address field (it can stay at **0.0.0.0** if it's determined automatically).

Note

If you use Server addressing, you cannot enter anything into the Gateway Address field. However, MacTCP may place an IP number there for you. If you use MacTCP with MacPPP or InterSLIP, there's no way to affect this field, but with VersaTerm SLIP, you can set the Gateway Address.

The large IP Address area in the upper right certainly looks hairy, but for most people, if you use a Manually-addressed account and type your IP address into the first part of the MacTCP control panel, you may be able to ignore this entire section! Similarly, with the standard Server-addressed accounts that Northwest

Nexus users have, there's no need to touch anything in this area. That's the good news.

The bad news is that if you do have to mess with this section of the dialog, you need help from your administrator. From what I've been told by more knowledgeable folks, you may have to set the correct network class (the pop-up menu containing A, B, or C) and the subnet mask (the slider bar beneath the title in the dialog box) manually. I believe that primarily large networked sites must deal with subnet masks because they often use a method called *subnetting* to handle their IP addresses. If you have subnetting at your site, you also have someone who knows something about it and can provide details of how to configure MacTCP for your site. Be sure to ask nicely!

Again, the document from Eric Behr that comes with MacTCP Watcher may be of some help here. Suffice it to say that I don't use subnetting and never have had to mess with anything in that IP Address area to get MacTCP working for anyone I've helped with a personal Internet account. I hope the same proves true for you.

Domain Name Servers

You must fill in Domain Name Server Information section with the name of your domain and the IP numbers of your name servers. As you can see from figure 12.2, I have access to a number of name servers. Unfortunately, the interface for this section of MacTCP is quite confusing. Apple is working on improving it right now, but let me try to explain it as best I can. Warning—this stuff gets pretty technical, so if you're not interested, just skip it.

Note

*I use the **halcyon.com** domain here, but if you don't use Northwest Nexus, you undoubtedly will have a different domain.*

The left-hand fields in the MacTCP Domain Name Server section contain the domain name for which you want the name server whose IP number is in the right-hand field to be used. So, when I put **halcyon.com.** in the first left-hand field, I'm saying that for all domain name server requests within the **halcyon.com** domain, use the name server at **198.137.231.1**, and tack **halcyon.com** on the end of all single word names, such as **coho**. The utility of this is that I could say, telnet to the machine **coho.halcyon.com** by merely telnetting to **coho**. This isn't particularly helpful in normal usage. Also, the domain name server at **198.137.231.1** is used only if the name that you're looking up ends in **halcyon.com**.

Make sure to select the Default button next to this first entry. This has two effects. First, it means the same thing as before—single-word name requests have `halcyon.com` appended to them. Second, it also means that the domain name server at `198.137.231.1` is used if, and only if, no other lines in the domain name server configuration match the request. Reflect on this briefly while I get to the next few lines, since they interact with one another.

Note

You may have noticed the period after the `halcyon.com` domain in the screenshot. That period positively denotes an absolute domain, as opposed to one that's relative to the current domain. However, MacTCP currently treats all names that contain at least one period as absolute names, so it makes no difference at all now. It does on other systems, and it may with MacTCP in future; hence, it's a good idea to get in the habit of appending that last period.

Next, look at the second set of fields. In the left-hand field I have a period, and in the right-hand field, I have exactly the same IP number as the first right-hand field. This second line is necessary because the first line (the primary name server) won't be used for requests outside of the domain listed. By duplicating the IP number, we tell MacTCP to use this name server for all requests outside the `halcyon.com` domain. Keep all this in mind while we look at the third line.

The third set of fields have another period in the left-hand field and a different IP number, `192.135.191.1`, in the right-hand field. This denotes my secondary name server, the name server that MacTCP queries if it doesn't get anything back from the first one.

OK, now we have all the pieces to make sense of this confusing configuration interface.

Note

The domain name server is used every time you use a program to connect an Internet site by name. So, if you use Anarchie to connect to ftp.tidbits.com, the domain name server looks up `ftp.tidbits.com` and sees that its IP number is `192.135.191.2`. Since the computers always use IP numbers and people usually use IP names, the domain name server is an essential part of the MacTCP-based connection.

If you ask for the IP number for a machine in the `halcyon.com` domain, the first line (the primary name server) handles the request. If you ask for the IP number for a machine anywhere outside of the **halcyon.com** domain, the second line does. Finally, if the main name server is down, the secondary name server in the third line handles the request. Although the second line may seem redundant, it's not. If you didn't have it and asked for the IP number of a machine outside of the **halcyon.com** domain, that request would go directly to the secondary name server. If that name server were down, your request would fail.

Note

You can't see it in the screenshot, but I actually have a fourth line with yet another period in the left-hand field and a different IP number in the right-hand field. It handles requests if the first two name servers are down. You can have three or more name servers, but that many aren't generally necessary.

Finishing Up

After you're done with all that domain name server information, click on OK to save your changes, and then close the MacTCP control panel. Depending on what you change, MacTCP may tell you that the changes won't take effect until you restart. Go ahead and restart your Mac if necessary. I cannot figure out why it wants you to restart at some times but not others, so if I'm troubleshooting MacTCP, I restart every time I reconfigure it whether it tells me to or not.

When you use MacTCP, it creates two files; one, called MacTCP DNR, is loose in your System Folder, and the other, called MacTCP Prep, is in your Preferences folder. MacTCP creates both files from scratch if you delete them and doesn't lose any settings in the process, because it stores settings both in its control panel and in the MacTCP Prep file. Deleting these files is a must when you're troubleshooting or upgrading to a new version of MacTCP.

Note

MacTCP DNR *stands for* Domain Name Resolver. *If you want to know more, turn on Balloon Help and point to that file with the arrow.*

The Hosts File

Domain name servers didn't always exist, and before they did, each computer had a Hosts file that contained the IP names and numbers of all the Internet machines you could contact. When a program needed to translate an IP name into an IP number, it looked in the Hosts file for that information (and it failed unless the machine you wanted to connect to was listed). Needless to say, the Hosts file isn't as good a solution as the domain name server, but since there are still instances where people can't contact a domain name server, the Hosts file has remained with us. If you don't have a domain name server (and most people do), you must use the Hosts file. If you do have a domain name server and configure the Domain Name Server Information in MacTCP appropriately, you don't need the Hosts file at all, because your Mac can ask the domain name servers for addresses rather than look them up in the Hosts file.

Note

Theoretically, you can use any Internet machine that is a domain name server as your domain name server, although if it's not local, the domain name server lookups may be quite slow.

One instance when you can't access a domain name server is if you're behind a *firewall* (a security system in which everyone must go through a secure host machine that is the only one in an organization connected to the Internet). If you want to use the Hosts file, you must manually enter all the hosts to which you may want to connect, along with their IP numbers. You can edit the Hosts file with TeachText or SimpleText, but make sure to create the host entries in exactly the same manner as shown in the examples. In any event, here's what a standard host entry looks like:

```
consultant.micro.umn.edu. A 134.84.132.4 ;
```

Note

The Communucations Toolbox Telnet tools like to use the Hosts file as a repository for Internet machines that you have connected to previously. In fact, the VersaTerm Telnet tool adds sites to the Hosts file for you, if you enter them into the tool's configuration dialog.

Phew! That's about it for configuring MacTCP. In most cases, MacTCP is actually easy to configure once you know what information goes into which fields in the Configuration dialog. I provided all of the information even though most people should never need it, because if you do need to figure out what's going on in MacTCP, you need the details. If you use Northwest Nexus and MacPPP, the ISKM Installer configures MacTCP for you entirely. Speaking of MacPPP, let's talk about SLIP and PPP next.

SLIP and PPP

An increasing number of people who don't work at a large business or university want access to the Internet, and an ever-increasing number of Internet providers are springing up to meet that need. Because individuals seldom have the level of connectivity enjoyed by those in business or education, they must make do with slower connections. Until recently, they've had to cope with clumsy shell accounts as well. That has changed with the availability of SLIP (Serial Line Internet Protocol) and PPP (Point to Point Protocol) accounts that are available to anyone. Although distinctly slower than dedicated network connections (because they work with garden-variety modems), SLIP and PPP provide decent performance in normal situations; more importantly, they provide access to some extremely cool software that I talk about in chapter 13, "MacTCP-based Software."

Note

You may also hear about CSLIP accounts. CSLIP stands for Compressed SLIP, and it's generally handled by an option in the SLIP program. You don't need a different SLIP implementation to use a CSLIP account.

SLIP and PPP provide the Internet connection for those of us who connect via modem. If you have a network, either Ethernet or LocalTalk, connected to the Internet, you don't need SLIP or PPP.

Note

Although SLIP and PPP are generally used with normal phone lines and modems, if your provider and telephone company both offer ISDN (Integrated Services Digital Network) service, you can use SLIP or PPP with ISDN to create a very high speed Internet connection, often for not much more than a normal phone line would cost.

The easiest way to think of SLIP and PPP is to assume that you don't have water service inside your house. Every time you want to take a shower, you must run a garden hose out to the water hookup outside, take your shower, and then bring the hose back in. That's exactly what SLIP and PPP do—they establish a temporary, low-speed connection to the Internet. You must create that connection before you can run programs such as Anarchie and TurboGopher that assume the connection exists.

Note

Although most implementations of SLIP and PPP enable you to launch a MacTCP-based program without connecting first (SLIP or PPP see what's up and then establish the connection), I've found that these auto connect features can be flaky. If you can use one, great, but if it doesn't work reliably, always connect manually first.

What's the difference between SLIP and PPP, and should you care? The answer to the first part of the question seems to be that PPP is SLIP done right. Apparently, SLIP was literally designed on the back of an envelope and implemented in an afternoon. PPP, in contrast, was designed more carefully and is far more flexible, so it supports multiple protocols (such as AppleTalk and TCP/IP) at the same time and over the same connection. The capability to support multiple protocols is neat because you can use MacTCP programs at the same time as you are dialed into an AppleTalk server, much as you do with Apple Remote Access now. However, and this fact is probably a testament to its simplicity, SLIP is more prevalent, both in terms of support on the Macintosh side and in terms of available accounts.

Note

SLIP and PPP accounts are not identical. You cannot use a SLIP account with MacPPP, or a PPP account with InterSLIP.

As far as whether or not you should care, my impression is that at the moment it doesn't make much difference. PPP may become the standard because Apple is working on supporting it more fully. Although SLIP is probably still more prevalent than PPP, the release of InterCon's InterPPP (which supports AppleTalk over PPP), and some vague troubles I and other people have had with SLIP in the past nine months, together lead me to believe that PPP is indeed the way to go, if you can. That's why the ISKM Installer installs MacPPP by default, but also enables you to install InterSLIP should you only be able to get a SLIP account.

Now, does that mean that you should run out and switch your existing SLIP account over to PPP? No, definitely not, if everything you want to do with your account works as you expect. PPP and SLIP are functionally identical in that all, or almost all, of the MacTCP-based programs should work the same with either SLIP or PPP accounts. I haven't seen significant performance differences between the two, although PPP occasionally feels a little more responsive in interactive use (as opposed to raw download speed when you're retrieving a file via FTP and nothing else). In addition, I've seen situations in which InterSLIP didn't work worth beans, but MacPPP worked instantly, and also situations in which InterSLIP was working perfectly but MacPPP never quite worked. The same applies to the commercial implementations of SLIP and PPP. Sometimes they can ride in from the hills to save the day (for a small fee); other times, you may as well stick with the freebies.

SLIP for the Macintosh currently has three different implementations (not counting programs that support SLIP internally, because they're of no use if you want to use another program that doesn't support SLIP internally), while PPP has two implementations and a third on the way. Two of the SLIP implementations are commercial, MacSLIP from Hyde Park Software and VersaTerm SLIP from Synergy Software. The third comes from InterCon Systems, a company that has released numerous Internet products, some of which support SLIP internally. InterCon has released this last SLIP, called InterSLIP, as freeware on the Internet, and has graciously allowed me to include it on the disk that comes with this book.

Also included on the disk is the free implementation of PPP for the Mac, called MacPPP, that was written by Larry Blunk of Merit Network, Inc., one of the companies that helped run the NSFNET. Commercial competition for MacPPP comes from the recently released InterPPP, a beefed-up version of PPP, marketed by InterCon. InterPPP's main claim to fame is that it supports AppleTalk over PPP, which is not true of MacPPP.

In this chapter, I concentrate on InterSLIP and MacPPP because the other SLIP and PPP implementations, being commercial, come with printed documentation and support, and because, in many ways, they are all similar. I'll try to point out the few differences that I've encountered.

Getting an Account

When it comes time for you to get a SLIP or PPP account, the details are up to you in terms of what company you work with and the like. You can find a list of companies that provide PPP and SLIP services in Peter Kaminski's PDIAL list in appendix C. However, once you decide on a provider, you need certain information from that provider to configure SLIP or PPP. Some of the necessary information is the same as information you need for configuring MacTCP, which is why some of this may seem redundant. For convenience, I list it all in table 12.2.

Table 12.2
SLIP/PPP Information

Item	Question
Phone number	What number do you call to connect to your server?
Login name	What is the SLIP or PPP account login name? (This name can be different from your userid or machine name.)
Password	What password should you provide when logging in?
MTU/MRU	What is the maximum transmission/receive unit size? (1006 seems to be the standard MTU for SLIP; I've heard of using 296 for CSLIP; PPP defaults to an MRU of 1500.)
Header Compression	Should you use RFC 1144 TCP Header Compression? (This is CSLIP.)
Login Procedure	What should you expect to receive from your host machine and how should your machine respond when logging in?
IP address	What is your IP number (if a Manually-addressed account)?
Gateway Address	What is your gateway IP number?
Domain Name Server	What is the IP number of your primary domain name server?

Again, it's probably easiest to use the worksheet in the back of the book for recording all of this information. I'll cover InterSLIP first, and then look at MacPPP.

InterSLIP

InterCon's InterSLIP is one of the most popular pieces of software among the Macintosh Internet crowd, because it offers functionality equivalent to commercial programs although it is freeware. That's a good way to make friends. InterCon has allowed us to include InterSLIP on the disk that comes with this book.

Note

As with MacTCP, my examples and screenshots in this section apply to configuring my specific modem, a Telebit WorldBlazer, with a Manually-addressed SLIP account. Your settings will be different, I guarantee it. For a step-by-step walkthrough of how to install InterSLIP for the Server-addressed accounts from Northwest Nexus, check out chapter 14, "Step-by-Step Internet."

Installation and Setup

Installing InterSLIP requires placing an extension called InterSLIP in your Extensions folder. If you drag it onto the System Folder icon, System 7 places InterSLIP in the correct location. A control panel called InterSLIP Control is also available (and generally installed by default), but in fact, it's entirely unnecessary for System 7 users; it is only required for use with System 6. An application, called InterSLIP Setup, can live anywhere on your hard disk, but it may be a good idea to put it or an alias to it in your Apple Menu Items folder for easy access. After you place those parts in the proper places, restart your Mac. Make sure InterSLIP is selected in the MacTCP main window, and then proceed with configuring InterSLIP.

Note

The ISKM Installer's custom options for "Generic InterSLIP and Apps" or "InterSLIP Only" install all of the parts of InterSLIP in the proper places. Just as with MacTCP, I provide the detail here in case you install InterSLIP from some other source (like an update), or merely want to know how the manual installation process works.

Although InterSLIP Setup and InterSLIP Control share similar interfaces and functions, you use InterSLIP Setup to configure your connection. InterSLIP Control enables you to select a configuration and connect and disconnect, but you must configure it from InterSLIP Setup (hence the name, I suppose). Frankly, if you use System 7, I'd recommend throwing InterSLIP Control out. I haven't had it installed for months now, and it's made no difference at all (see figure 12.3).

To create a new configuration, launch InterSLIP Setup, and from the File menu choose New. InterSLIP Setup prompts you for a name with a dialog box; name your configuration and click on the OK button. Although InterSLIP Setup provides no way of deleting a configuration from within the program, configuration files are stored in an automatically created InterSLIP Folder within the Preferences folder. If you create a configuration you don't want to keep, throw out its file from this folder.

Figure 12.3   InterSLIP Setup and InterSLIP Control

After you create the configuration, you must configure it for your particular modem and account. You need information from your system administrator to configure InterSLIP, so be prepared to give your provider a call if you didn't get it all when you signed up for the account. Double-click on the configuration you just created to bring up the Configuration dialog (see figure 12.4).

Let's take it from the top left of the dialog. The serial port should generally be set to your Modem port, assuming you're not using a PowerBook Duo with only a Printer port. The baud rate setting is the rate at which your modem and your Mac communicate, which is why there is no setting for 14,400, since that's a speed at which the two modems communicate. The speed that the Mac and the modem communicate can be different from the speed that the modems communicate. Data bits, stop bits, and parity are almost always set as I have them here, to 8 data bits, 1 stop bit, and no parity, although I suppose it's possible that some providers are different. The hardware handshaking checkbox requires that you have a hardware handshaking cable, and if you have a v.32bis modem, you should have one of those. I've heard that if you don't have a hardware handshaking cable, but attempt to use that checkbox, it may cause InterSLIP to hang.

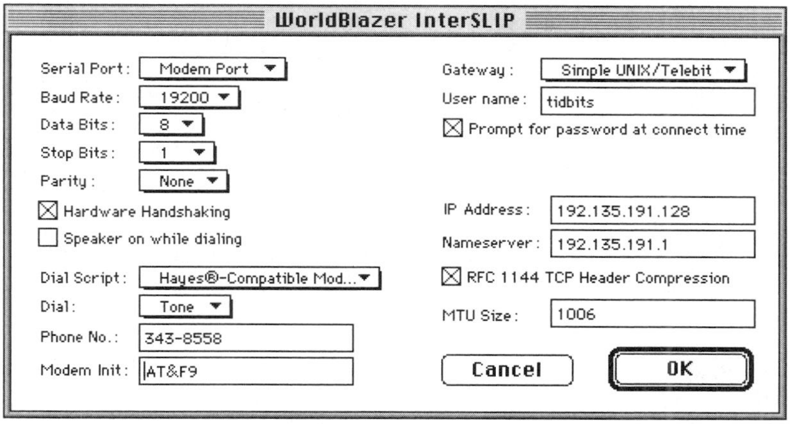

Figure 12.4 *InterSLIP Configuration dialog*

Turning the speaker on or off is up to you, although I generally recommend you leave it on until you have everything working for a few days. Then, when the modem screams start to irritate you, turn it off.

Note

Depending on your modem and your modem initialization string, InterSLIP sometimes seems to ignore the speaker checkbox. You can always override it by adding "M0" to your initialization string to turn off the modem speaker.

The Dial Script pop-up menu defaults to Direct Connection, something I doubt most people have. The other built-in choice is Hayes-Compatible Modem, and I recommend you choose that option to start with. I certainly hope your modem is Hayes-compatible; you're likely to have trouble if it's not. Unfortunately, even if your modem claims it's Hayes-compatible, that doesn't inherently mean that it works with the Hayes-Compatible modem script in InterSLIP. Luckily, InterSLIP supports other modems through the use of *dialing scripts* written in the *CCL* (Connection Control Language). CCL scripts are primarily used with Apple Remote Access (ARA). You can find many dialing scripts (their names start with "scr" and generally include a modem name as well) in:

ftp://ftp.tidbits.com/pub/tidbits/tisk/tcp/

Note

> *Dialing scripts are text files that are very similar to ARA (Apple Remote Access) scripts. The only difference is that ARA turns off file compression and error correction, whereas those two settings should be on for an InterSLIP dialing script. Many modem vendors will send you an ARA script for your modem, if it wasn't included, and you can find many ARA scripts in:*
>
> ```
> ftp://ftp.tidbits.com/pub/tidbits/ara/
> ```

You can add dialing scripts to the Dialing folder inside the InterSLIP Folder inside the Preferences folder. To edit an ARA script, you may have to use Shift-Open in Word, or Nisus's All Files option in its Catalog, to be able to open the ARA script. These scripts are text-only but they tend to come with a type and creator that prevents text editors from reading them. Make sure to save as text when you're done, though, and if you create a new dialing script for your modem, please send it to me so others can use it as well. Dialing scripts can be very important—for some modems, they're even essential.

I've found that many dialing scripts have huge amounts of useless sections; Fred Morris has written a minimal dialing script that works well with many modems, assuming the modem initialization string is correct. I added redial capabilities to the script, and included it on the disk so that the ISKM Installer installs it for InterSLIP by default. It's called Minimal Dialing Script.

Note

> *Normally, I would tell you to call InterCon if you had a problem with InterSLIP, but considering how much technical support costs, they help you with InterSLIP only if you are also a registered user of one of their other programs. I think that arrangement is extremely fair because they've already provided a great service to the Internet community by releasing InterSLIP for free.*

Enough about the Dial Script menu; stick with Hayes-Compatible Modem or my Minimal Dialing Script, if you can. The next three items, that control the dialing method, phone number, and modem initialization string, don't appear until you choose Hayes-Compatible Modem or another dialing script. I hope that when these items appear, it is relatively obvious how to fill them in. Most people have tone dialing these days, and your system administrator should tell you the phone number when you get the account. The modem initialization string is a bit trickier, but most modern modems support something like **AT&F** for setting the factory-default standard options. As you can see, the WorldBlazer goes all out on the **&F** parameters; I must use **AT&F9**, which turns on hardware handshaking for the Macintosh. Look in your modem manual or in another communications program that comes with settings for popular modems, to figure out the most appropriate initialization string.

Note

I've also included a file containing many modem strings on the disk. The ISKM Installer has the information in the installer help text, and the file is installed in the InterSLIP 1.0.1 folder (not the InterSLIP Folder that lives in your Preferences folder). These modem strings are generally untested, but should either work or at least put you on the right track.

The most important thing I know of to watch for here is the hardware handshaking setting. Not only do you want to make sure your initialization string turns on hardware handshaking, but also make sure that software handshaking, more commonly known as XON/XOFF, is turned off. If XON/XOFF is turned on in the modem initialization string or is part of the factory default settings, InterSLIP almost certainly won't work right.

At the top right of the window is another pop-up menu labeled Gateway. It defaults to Direct Connection, but again, I think the other option, Simple Unix/Telebit is more likely to work. Just as with dialing scripts, you can write your own *gateway script* in the Connection Control Language, and place it in the Gateway Scripts folder in the InterSLIP Folder. Unfortunately, if you have a non-standard gateway, you probably will have to write your own, although I've collected a few of them in:

```
ftp://ftp.tidbits.com/pub/tidbits/tisk/tcp/
```

(Look for "scr" in the beginning of the name, and the name of a provider, university, person, or server such as Annex or Cisco in the rest of the name.)

The gateway script is a conversation between your computer and your host computer as your computer tries to log in to the host. There's no telling what sort of prompts your host sends or what it requests, so again, I can't help much with specifics here. I strongly recommend that you work through the process manually, using a terminal emulator to see what the host sends and what it expects back. Once you've done that, you stand a chance of converting that information into a gateway script. Also, ask your system administrator to advise you of any quirks in logging in.

In general, you usually send a return, the host sends a "login:" prompt, you send your login name, the host provides a "Password:" prompt, you send your password, and then you're in. Unless, of course, something else happens at that point. For instance, if you use a Server-addressed account, the gateway script must include some method of finding the IP number that the server assigns to you—it usually appears after you send the password. I've included a gateway script that works with the Northwest Nexus Server-addressed accounts, and I recommend that you use it as an example of how to write your own (not that it's a paragon of scripting virtue, but it does work).

Note

Many people ask where they can find more information on scripting in the CCL language that InterSLIP uses for both dialing and gateway scripts. Unfortunately, the best information available is in InterSLIP's documentation, so you've got it already. Maybe someone will write a CCL tutorial and post it on the nets sometime.

If you have trouble making InterSLIP connect, you might also try a hack that some people have reported success with. Set InterSLIP to Direct Connection in both the dialing script menu and the gateway script menu. Then, using a terminal emulator, dial your host machine, and at the point when SLIP starts on the host, click on InterSLIP's Connect button. It's a hack indeed (ordinarily you'd *never* use a terminal emulator to dial a SLIP account), but it might work while you figure out a gateway script.

On to the User name field in the InterSLIP Configuration dialog. Most of the time, your system administrator assigns this name to you, along with a password, although you may get to pick it. It may or may not be related to your machine name or your email address. It's simply the name you use to log in to your SLIP account. Make sure you enter your username in lowercase—Unix is case-sensitive, so "Adam" is not the same account as "adam," and your password won't work with a mixed-case username if it was created with a lowercase username.

I've checked the Prompt for password at connect time checkbox in the InterSLIP Configuration dialog because publishing a screenshot of my password isn't a terribly clever thing to do in terms of security. However, if that checkbox isn't checked, you get another text field that holds your password. If you don't mind the security risk of having your password visible here, go ahead and enter it.

The next four items—IP Address, Nameserver, checkbox for RFC 1144 TCP Header Compression, MTU (Maximum Transmission Unit) Size—require information from your system administrator. You can see the sorts of things I've put in, but your situation may be entirely different (and your IP Address and Nameserver certainly are). Again, if your provider tells you that you have a CSLIP account, make sure to check the TCP Header Compression checkbox. Even if the term CSLIP isn't mentioned, make sure to check with your administrator, because if the TCP Header Compression setting in InterSLIP doesn't match what your account has set, weird errors will result.

After you're all done, click on the OK button to save your changes. If you have more than one SLIP account on different hosts, you can create additional configuration files and switch between them in InterSLIP Setup by selecting the one you want before you click on the Connect button.

Basic Usage

Clicking on the triangle in the upper left of the InterSLIP Setup window shrinks the window to display only the Connect and Disconnect buttons and the area that displays the connection status (see figure 12.5).

Figure 12.5   *InterSLIP Setup, shrunk*

If you have only one configuration, the only reason to leave the window expanded is if you need to edit your configuration frequently (which shouldn't be the case). InterSLIP Setup also remembers where you put it on the screen, so it's easy to put it out of the way and leave it active most of the time. InterSLIP Setup takes only 128K of RAM, so it's no great liability.

Note

There's a bug in InterSLIP Setup related to the way it remembers where you place the window. If you put InterSLIP Setup's window on a second monitor (assuming you have two attached to your Macintosh, as I do), then move or remove that monitor, InterSLIP Setup will almost certainly crash on launch. To solve the problem, throw away the InterSLIP Preferences file in your InterSLIP Folder. All that's stored there is the window location and the selected configuration file, so it's no loss.

You have two ways to use InterSLIP to connect to your host, manually and automatically. The manual method takes more effort, because you must click on the Connect button in InterSLIP Setup, but works much more reliably. The automatic method is exactly that, automatic, so whenever you launch Fetch or Eudora, or any program that requests MacTCP services, InterSLIP kicks in and connects to your host. Or at least, that's the idea.

The problem with the automatic technique is that it doesn't work all the time. When it doesn't work, you must usually force quit (hold down the Command and Option keys and press Escape) the MacTCP application that couldn't connect and then usually restart the machine, because something at a low level has been hosed. I had trouble using the automatic connection with a number of the applications I discuss later in the next chapter, and everything based on HyperCard caused trouble. Even such usually well-behaved applications as Fetch and WAIS for Macintosh sometimes caused problems, perhaps because the connection takes longer than those applications are prepared to wait. As neat and useful as the automatic connection feature is, therefore, I cannot recommend using it if you use a wide variety of MacTCP software. If you primarily use Eudora and Fetch, you're probably OK—but even then, make sure you have work in other applications saved before you attempt to start an automatic connection.

Either way, manual or automatic, when asked, InterSLIP dials your host, signs in, and then lets you get on with your work. You see various messages (they're stored in the dialing script and the gateway script) in the status area in the upper right of the InterSLIP Setup window that tell you what InterSLIP thinks is happening, most notably the Connected message when you have connected successfully. When you aren't connected, it should say Idle. As soon as you connect, the Connect button becomes disabled and the Disconnect button becomes enabled. There is no automatic disconnection, so you must make sure to click on the Disconnect button when you're finished using your SLIP account.

Note

Many people have asked for a way to have InterSLIP disconnect automatically when they're finished, say, downloading their mail with Eudora, but there's no way this can happen without additional work on your part. Eudora has no way of knowing how the connection has been established, or even that you use InterSLIP. And, InterSLIP can't know when you're done and when you might want to do something else. You could, however, script this behavior with QuicKeys, AppleScript, or Frontier. Using the latter two may be easier with InterSLIP/AE, a little program written by Leonard Rosenthol to control InterSLIP via Apple events. It's at:

```
ftp://gaea.kgs.ukans.edu/applescript/scriptableapps/InterSLIP_AE_1.0b1.sit.hqx
```

Now you know all there is to using InterSLIP, or even one of the other SLIP implementations, but there are a few tricks that I want to mention.

SLIPing

I don't know how common this situation is, but with some SLIP hosts, where you pay for the time you're connected, a timeout is set to hang up the phone line after a certain amount of idle time. If you think about it, this is a feature, not a bug; otherwise, you could get called away from the computer while using your SLIP account, forget about it entirely, and find yourself faced with a much larger usage bill. The timeout generally works well, but it does modify how you work.

If (and only if!) you use manual addressing, and your connection hangs up on you before you are finished, switch back to InterSLIP Setup or InterSLIP Control, click on the Disconnect button, and then click on the Connect button. After you reestablish the connection, you can switch back into your MacTCP application and continue where you left off.

If, however, you use server addressing (where the server assigns an IP address to you each time you log in), you must quit the active MacTCP programs before you reconnect via SLIP! Because you may end up with a different IP address when you call back after being disconnected, MacTCP programs may become extremely flustered at the change, and there's no predicting what could happen (but it probably involves crashing).

You must decide whether the timeout bothers you or not. As long as you can easily see the connection lights on your modem (assuming you're not using an internal PowerBook modem), you can tell when the line has hung up. If you want to keep the line open, you must keep doing things that access the network. One trick is to run Peter Lewis's shareware Talk program whenever you're connected, because it queries the network periodically. There are other tricks that work equally as well, such as having Eudora check your mail every four or five minutes.

More likely, though, you must figure out the proper methods of working. For instance, in a newsreader you can certainly open a bunch of articles or threads at once and then read them all onscreen. Unless you're a very fast reader, though, the connection will almost certainly get bored and hang up on you. Unless you want to treat the newsreader as an off-line newsreader in this way, it might work better to read only one article or thread at a time, making sure that the newsreader periodically has to ask for more articles. In addition, you see that if you ask for a bunch of threads all at once, it takes a long time to get them, whereas if you go for the one-at-a-time approach, you can read constantly. Either approach has pros and cons, and it's up to you to decide which fits your working style best.

The program that can work best in this environment, of course, is one like Eudora, which can log in, transfer mail and send waiting mail, and then log out immediately, letting you do all your work while disconnected from the network. Unfortunately, none of the freeware newsreaders have this feature quite yet, although it does exist in the newsreader built into VersaTerm-Link, one of the commercial applications.

Using System 6

Frankly, I know little about using InterSLIP with System 6, mostly because I haven't used System 6 in almost three years. However, despite the note on the cover about requiring System 7, you may be able to use System 6 for some tasks.

To establish a connection with InterSLIP, you must have InterSLIP Control (a control panel) installed. As long as you have InterSLIP Control installed in the Control Panels folder, InterSLIP should work the same as it does under System 7.

Note

Much of the Internet software released today requires System 7, so you may not be able to use it at all under System 6. That's the price of not upgrading. Eudora 1.4 and later requires System 7, for instance, but Qualcomm keeps Eudora version 1.3.1 around for System 6 users. It's at:

```
ftp://ftp.qualcomm.com/quest/mac/eudora/1.3/eudora131.hqx
```

Overall Evaluation

InterSLIP's primary neat feature, other than the fact that it works well, is its automatic connect feature, which unfortunately I find to be problematic. A feature I'd like to see in InterSLIP is the capability to show a terminal window of the connection and capture a log of what happens during connection, to ease troubleshooting.

One existing feature that I didn't think too much of originally but came to appreciate, is that InterSLIP dials (and redials, if you have a dialing script that redials) in the background. That means you can click on the Connect button in InterSLIP and then go back to whatever you were doing until it finishes connecting. In contrast, MacPPP puts up a modal dialog that prevents you from doing anything else while it dials.

Even if InterSLIP doesn't have every imaginable feature, it's free and it's on the disk, so it's hard to complain too loudly. And, if for some reason you don't like InterSLIP, you can always buy one of the other two SLIP programs, or use PPP.

Administrative Details

As I've said, InterSLIP is free from InterCon Systems, and although it only guarantees support if you own one of its other products, it does a pretty good job of supporting InterSLIP over the Internet. Posting in **comp.sys.mac.comm** often results in help from other users or from Amanda Walker, InterSLIP's author. You can send email to **interslip@intercon.com** if you have problems, comments, suggestions, or possible bugs. Amanda said online that she tries to help people create gateway scripts, but only if she can have an account on the system in question to test with. Writing a gateway script without being able to use the system is almost impossible. InterCon runs its own FTP site at **ftp.intercon.com**, and you can find the latest version of InterSLIP there, or on **ftp.tidbits.com** in either of the following:

```
ftp://ftp.tidbits.com/pub/tidbits/tisk/tcp/inter-slip-installer-101.hqx
```

```
ftp://ftp.intercon.com/intercon/sales/InterSLIP/InterSLIPInstaller1.0.1.hqx
```

MacSLIP

MacSLIP was written by Rick Watson, of Hyde Park Software, and is marketed and supported by TriSoft. MacSLIP 2.0 costs $49.95 and may offer the largest feature set of all three SLIPs. MacSLIP 2.0 has only a control panel (see figure 12.6) and a MacSLIP extension (which, amazingly enough, go in your Control Panels and Extensions folders).

To configure MacSLIP, click on the Configure button, which brings up a dialog that enables you to choose your dialing script (which you must create in a text editor), set your log file, and configure several other options such as speed, compression, and MTU size (see figure 12.7).

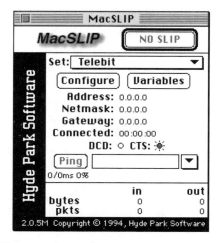

Figure 12.6   *MacSLIP control panel*

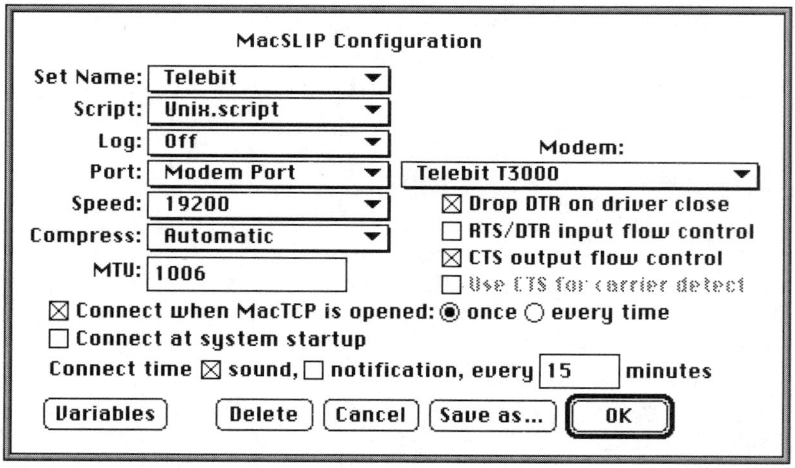

```
                    MacSLIP Configuration
Set Name: [ Telebit              ▼]
   Script: [ Unix.script          ▼]
      Log: [ Off                   ▼]                Modem:
     Port: [ Modem Port            ▼]    [ Telebit T3000              ▼]
    Speed: [ 19200                 ▼]    ☒ Drop DTR on driver close
 Compress: [ Automatic             ▼]    ☐ RTS/DTR input flow control
      MTU: [ 1006                    ]   ☒ CTS output flow control
                                         ☐ Use CTS for carrier detect
  ☒ Connect when MacTCP is opened: ◉ once ○ every time
  ☐ Connect at system startup
  Connect time ☒ sound, ☐ notification, every [ 15    ] minutes
  [ Variables ]    [ Delete ] [ Cancel ] [ Save as... ]  [  OK  ]
```

Figure 12.7   *MacSLIP configuration dialog*

MacSLIP 2.0 sports the same sort of automatic connection feature that InterSLIP has. It also ships with initialization strings for a number of popular modems, can notify you of your connection time to reduce connect charges, and displays statistics about the IP address, connect time, and serial line from within the control panel. In addition, performance has supposedly improved from previous versions. MacSLIP 2.0 also includes an application called Netstat, which displays details about the TCP connection. Although I don't know if its information is useful to the non-expert, those sorts of things are always fun to watch and may be of use in troubleshooting even if you're not sure what's happening. (InterSLIP and VersaTerm SLIP users can accomplish the same thing with the free MacTCP Watcher instead.)

My main complaint about MacSLIP is that the scripting language used to connect to your host—although certainly full-featured—is not the sort of thing a novice wants to mess with. Conversely, of course, for an accomplished scripter, MacSLIP's scripting language may be just what you've always wanted. In normal usage, though, MacSLIP has always worked fine for me. MacSLIP comes with a number of sample scripts and script fragments for you to use as your own, and I've heard positive reports about TriSoft's technical support folks if you have troubles.

Adminstrative Details

MacSLIP 2.0 ships with MicroPhone Pro from Software Ventures (approximately $150). This is a good way to get it if you also want a full-fledged Communications Toolbox-aware terminal emulator such as MicroPhone Pro and a slightly older version of FaxSTF. You can get more information about MacSLIP by sending email to **info@hydepark.com**, and you can order MacSLIP alone, for $49.95, from:

TriSoft
1825 East 38 1/2
Austin, Texas 78722
Sales: 800-531-5170
Support: 512-472-0744
Fax: 512-473-2122

VersaTerm SLIP

Synergy Software claims that VersaTerm SLIP was the first commercially available SLIP for the Macintosh, and in my experience, it's also stable and reliable. Like InterSLIP, VersaTerm SLIP includes an extension, a control panel (which does nothing but allocate memory for the extension), and an application, VersaTerm AdminSLIP, with which you interact (see figure 12.8).

Clicking on the Connect button connects you, as you might expect. When connected, the button changes to Disconnect. Clicking on the Configure button opens a large configuration dialog (see figure 12.9).

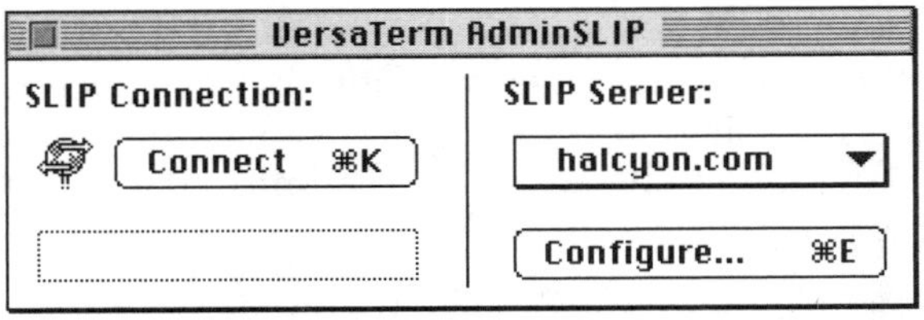

Figure 12.8 *VersaTerm AdminSLIP window*

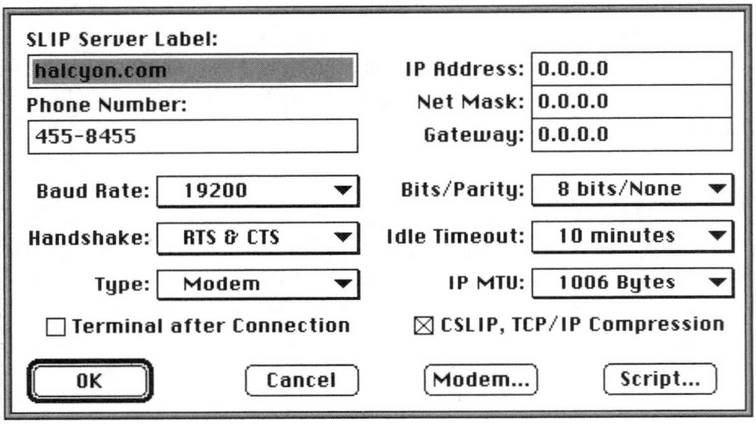

Figure 12.9 *VersaTerm Configuration dialog*

You can name your SLIP configuration, enter the basic modem and SLIP settings, and if you wish, check the Terminal after Connection checkbox to drop into a simple terminal emulator to log in by hand. This manual login feature has helped a number of times when I've been troubleshooting connections with VersaTerm SLIP. If you click on the Modem button, VersaTerm AdminSLIP presents you with a dialog for entering modem initialization strings, and it includes a pop-up menu with a number of common modems. Finally, the feature I like most about VersaTerm AdminSLIP is that clicking on the Scripts button opens a simple script editor in which you enter the text to send and the text to expect (see figure 12.10).

Of all the SLIP implementations, VersaTerm AdminSLIP uses the easiest method of writing a script. Once I entered the necessary information for my username and password, VersaTerm AdminSLIP worked perfectly for me.

In addition, VersaTerm AdminSLIP's File menu offers commands for displaying TCP statistics. It also has an auto-connect feature, and a View Connection command that brings up the simple terminal emulator so you can see what's going on.

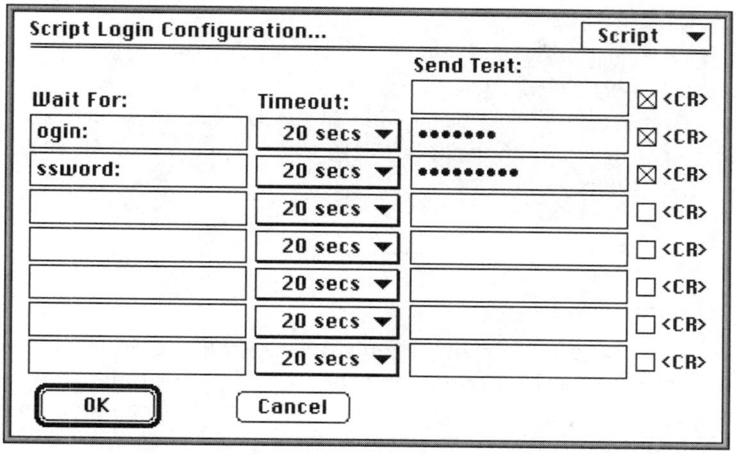

Figure 12.10 *VersaTerm AdminSLIP Script Login Configuration dialog*

Administrative Details

You can't buy VersaTerm SLIP by itself; it comes with Synergy Software's other VersaTerm packages, including the following: VersaTilities (approximately $85), which contains only MacTCP programs; VersaTerm (approximately $120), which provides a terminal emulator in addition to the VersaTilities; and VersaTerm Pro (approximately $170), which provides a graphics terminal emulator along with the VersaTilities. You also get the VersaTerm-Link program with VersaTerm SLIP, whether or not you want it (it is definitely worthwhile). You can contact Synergy to find out more about buying any of its programs via the Internet at **maxwell@sales.synergy.com**, via phone at 215-779-0522, or via fax at 215-370-0548.

MacPPP

The free MacPPP, from Larry Blunk of Merit Network, has recently become my connection method of choice. This is partly because of the simple configuration and setup, and partly because there are a few programs that don't work with the Server-addressed SLIP accounts on Northwest Nexus, but work fine with a Server-addressed PPP account. Because it generally works so well, I've included it on the disk as the default for those who connect to Northwest Nexus.

Note

If you want to switch from SLIP to PPP, you must first switch your account to PPP with your provider. When that's done, throw out MacTCP, MacTCP DNR, MacTCP Prep, InterSLIP, and InterSLIP Control (if installed) and then restart before installing MacPPP.

Installation and Setup

Installing MacPPP requires placing a control panel called Config PPP in your Control Panels folder, and an extension called PPP in your Extensions folder. If you drop them on your closed System Folder, System 7 places them in the proper folders automatically.

Note

Once again, the ISKM Installer installs MacPPP properly for you—I include these instructions so you know what's happened and can duplicate it with original files downloaded from the Internet.

After you've installed Config PPP and PPP, restart your Mac. Make sure that PPP is selected in the main MacTCP window, and that you use Server-addressing as opposed to the other two.

Note

It's possible to use Manually-addressing, but if you do that, you must configure the IPCP dialog (accessible within the Config PPP configuration dialog) with your permanent IP address. The MacPPP documentation doesn't recommend this, and I was unable to test it. Consider yourself forewarned.

Open the Config PPP control panel. As you can see in figure 12.11, Config PPP has a vaguely clunky interface but is almost effortless to configure.

The Port Name pop-up menu enables you to choose the Modem or Printer port (or any other ports registered with the Communications Toolbox), and is usually set to Modem port.

Figure 12.11 *Config PPP control panel*

The Idle Timeout pop-up enables you to set a time from five to 120 minutes after which MacPPP will close the connection. If you do anything during this time, the timer resets and MacPPP starts counting again. If your connection remains idle for the duration specified, MacPPP closes the connection. If you have the Quiet Mode checkbox checked, it does so without warning; if not, then end of the Idle Timeout MacPPP presents you with a dialog that enables you to either ignore the warning and leave the PPP connection active, or close PPP.

I haven't used this feature much, because I simply connect when I want something and disconnect when I'm done. However, I see two tremendous uses for this feature. First, for those people who pay by the minute for their connections, having MacPPP hang up if the line is idle could save you a fair amount of money. Second, if you want to download a large file before you go to bed, simply set MacPPP to a relatively short timeout value and it will hang up when it's done downloading the file. Make sure Quiet Mode is checked if you want it to hang up without confirmation.

Note

Some people have experienced problems with MacPPP connecting seemingly at random. Although most cases are caused by a program like Anarchie or TurboGopher asking for MacTCP services, it seems that on occasion MacTCP simply decides to do something and asks MacPPP to dial out. If you experience this, keeping a short idle time in MacPPP keeps those unwanted connections as short as possible.

It appears that MacPPP does a *soft close* in this situation, which means that a MacTCP-based application can automatically re-open the connection by requesting MacTCP services. If MacPPP did a *hard close*, applications wouldn't be able to re-open the connection automatically; you would have to click on the Open button to do that.

Note

I can't predict how different MacTCP-based applications will behave if their connection disappears due to the line being idle for five or ten minutes. If you anticipate being in a situation where MacPPP might hang up automatically after an idle timeout, make sure to save your work in all other open applications.

The Echo Interval pop-up menu gives the opportunity to configure MacPPP to periodically query the line to see if your connection has dropped. If MacPPP receives no response after three successive requests, MacPPP assumes that the connection has gone dead. I've always left Echo Interval turned off, although if you have trouble with your connection dropping frequently, using it may make life easier. When MacPPP detects a dead connection, it pops up a dialog box with three buttons for Close PPP, Ignore, or Restart, which in this case means restarting the PPP connection, not the Macintosh.

Note

The Echo Interval feature continually sends packets to the server and waits for a response, but these packets don't count as traffic for the Idle Timeout feature.

The Terminal Window checkbox is one of MacPPP's most useful features. If you check it, MacPPP ignores the Phone number and Modem init fields in the Configure Server and Connect Script dialog boxes (I'll get to them in a minute). Instead, it makes you walk through the connection manually, starting with dialing the modem with an ATDT command. You may never need to use MacPPP's terminal emulator, but if you have trouble logging on, it's much easier to have the terminal emulator built into MacPPP rather than be forced to use an external one (see figure 12.12).

If you must use the terminal window, you dial the modem manually, enter your username and password, and once you start seeing some gibberish characters, click on the OK button to start the PPP session.

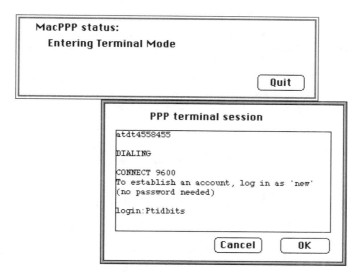

Figure 12.12   *MacPPP terminal window*

The two final checkboxes in the window are Hangup on Close and Quiet Mode. Hangup on Close, if checked, sends the Hayes +++ escape string and then an ATH to hang up the modem. My modem hangs up fine without this checkbox selected, but if yours doesn't, select it. The Quiet Mode checkbox prevents certain actions from requiring confirmation, most notably the Idle Timeout disconnect.

Once you've configured the main part of the Config PPP control panel, click on the New button to create a new configuration. Name it, and it appears in the PPP Server pop-up menu. If you want to delete one, make sure it's showing in the menu and click on the Delete button. After creating a new configuration, click on the Config button to bring up the Configure Server dialog box (see figure 12.13).

If you want to rename your server configuration, you can edit it in the PPP Server Name field, after which you get to configure the basic modem variables. Set the Port Speed pop-up menu as high as it will work with your modem (for some reason my WorldBlazer doesn't like speeds over 19,200 bps). Again, this is the speed at which the Mac and the modem communicate, not the speed at which the two modems communicate (unless it happens to be slower than the fastest speed the modems have in common, at which point it forces the modems to communicate at that speed).

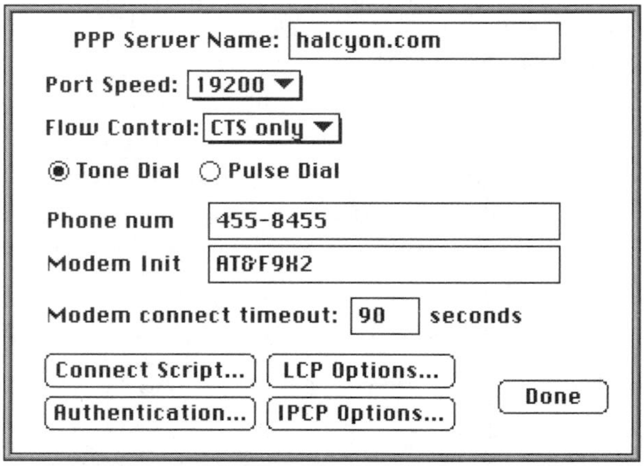

Figure 12.13   *MacPPP Configure Server dialog*

The Flow Control pop-up menu has options for None, CTS only, RTS (DTR) only, and CTS & RTS (DTR). RTS is generally called DTR in the Macintosh world, and I'd recommend that you try setting CTS & RTS (DTR) as the first try. The problem with this setting is that you may experience random hangups when lots of data is coming in. If that's true, try dropping down to CTS only. I ran into some of the hangups, and haven't had any trouble at all since I switched to CTS only.

Note

Modem flow control, also sometimes called handshaking, is one of the most confusing topics in telecommunications on the Macintosh. The basic idea is that the flow of the incoming and outgoing packets must be organized and controlled or else there are the packet equivalent of traffic jams and accidents. It's best if both modems do this in hardware, but that requires a special cable (luckily, one that comes with most fast modems). All of the various options above are forms of hardware flow control or hardware handshaking. Some applications, but not SLIP or PPP, can use software flow control, also called XON/XOFF, which doesn't require a special cable, but as I said, doesn't work with SLIP or PPP at all.

Tone Dial versus Pulse Dial should be obvious based on your telephone. Tone dialing is far more prevalent these days. The phone number field should be self-evident, and then we hit the Modem Init field. Modem initialization strings have been an unending source of headaches for Internet users configuring SLIP and PPP accounts. My recommendation is to start with the factory default configuration for your modem (usually **AT&F**, **AT&F1**, or **AT&F2**, although the numbers change depending on the modem), and then make sure that XON/XOFF, or software flow control, is turned off. I know it messes up InterSLIP badly, and the MacPPP documentation notes that it should be turned off as well, so I'm assuming that XON/XOFF is Public Enemy Number One with these sorts of SLIP and PPP accounts.

Note

You may wonder what the X2 is doing in my initialization string. I discovered that my Telebit WorldBlazer doesn't return the BUSY code in the default X1 setting, and if the modem doesn't return that BUSY code, MacPPP has no way to know that the line is busy and it should redial (which it does automatically).

Finally, the Modem connect timeout field offers you a chance to increase the amount of time MacPPP will wait for the connection to occur. If it takes your modem and the remote modem a long time to negotiate the connection, you may need to increase this value.

As more alert readers will have noticed, I haven't yet mentioned where you enter your userid and password. There are two possibilities here, depending on what the PPP server on your host machine supports. If you're lucky, you can use PPP's Password Authentication Protocol (PAP) to negotiate your connection. If your server doesn't support that (I have no idea how common it is), you instead use a connect script. First, the Authentication dialog (see figure 12.14).

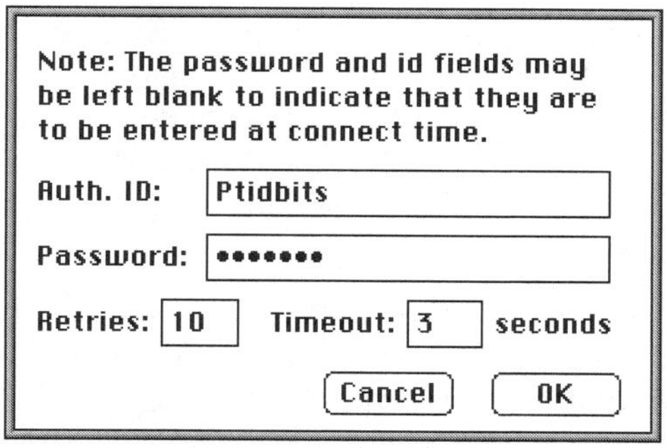

```
┌────────────────────────────────────────┐
│ Note: The password and id fields may   │
│ be left blank to indicate that they are│
│ to be entered at connect time.         │
│                                        │
│ Auth. ID:   │Ptidbits              │   │
│                                        │
│ Password:   │•••••••               │   │
│                                        │
│ Retries: │10│   Timeout: │3│ seconds   │
│                      ┌────────┐ ┌────┐ │
│                      │ Cancel │ │ OK │ │
│                      └────────┘ └────┘ │
└────────────────────────────────────────┘
```

Figure 12.14   *MacPPP Authentication dialog*

As you can see, all you do here is enter your Authentication ID and Password into the appropriate fields. I assumed that the Auth. ID field holds your userid and the Password field holds your normal PPP password, and it worked for me.

The defaults of ten retries and a three-second timeout also seemed to work fine, although you may wish to twiddle them slightly. Click on the OK button to save your changes and return to the Configure Server dialog.

If using the Authentication method of logging in to your PPP server machine doesn't work, you must instead use the Connect Script dialog to script your way in. It's still pretty easy, and in fact a good bit easier than InterSLIP or MacSLIP, and on a par with VersaTerm SLIP (see figure 12.15).

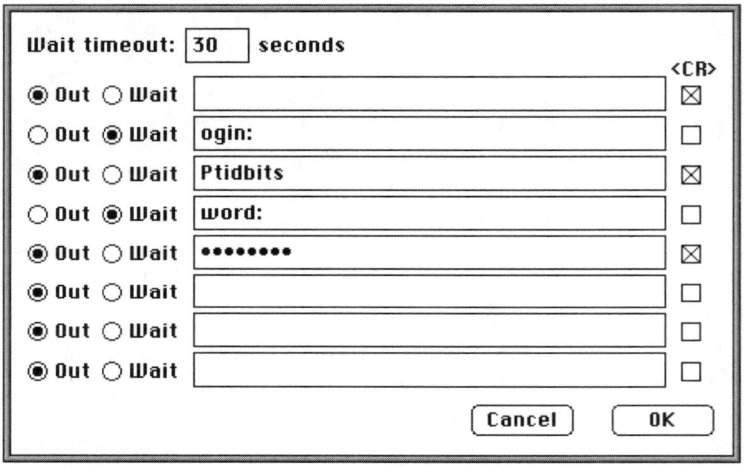

Figure 12.15 *MacPPP Connect Script dialog*

Basically, all you do in the Connect Script dialog is replicate the process of logging in to your host. You click on an Out button to indicate that MacPPP should send the contents of the field to the right (and a carriage return if the checkbox is selected for that line), and you click on a Wait button to indicate that MacPPP should wait for the string specified in the field to appear before moving on to the next line.

My connect script says, when translated: "Send a carriage return as soon as you're connected. Then wait for the string 'ogin:' to appear, and once you've seen it, send the username 'Ptidbits' and a carriage return. Wait for the string 'word:' to appear, and then send the password and a carriage return." Once you're done scripting here, click on the OK button to save your script.

Note

> *The words "login" and "password" often have their first letter or letters removed in scripts like this, because you never know whether or not the first letter will be capitalized.*

If you're unlucky, connecting to your PPP server will require more than the eight fields MacPPP provides here. In that case, if your server doesn't support authenticated logins as discussed previously (which is likely, if it requires more than four send/expect interactions), your only option may be to use the commercial InterPPP.

Meanwhile, back in the Configure Server dialog, you've probably been wondering what's inside the LCP Options dialog and the IPCP Options dialog. You really don't want to know, and I'm not going to show you. Suffice it to say that I'll be very surprised if you know what to do with the options in there. I certainly don't, and the MacPPP documentation says that no normal user should ever have to change any of those settings.

Well, that's it for configuring MacPPP. It's quite easy, and in fact may be the easiest method of connecting to the Internet.

Basic Usage

Once it's configured, using MacPPP is a piece of cake. Like InterSLIP, it works in both manual and automatic modes, so you can either click on the Open button in Config PPP or you can merely open a MacTCP-based program that opens MacTCP, at which point MacPPP connects automatically. Despite my bad luck with InterSLIP's auto-connect feature, I've found MacPPP's auto-connect feature to be more reliable, although not absolutely guaranteed. It seems that some applications don't quite play by the rules, and those applications won't work in auto-connect mode.

Note

> *Be careful of the auto-connect mode—if you do something like put TurboGopher in your Startup Items folder, it will launch on every startup and make MacPPP establish a connection to the Internet. You're unlikely to do that with TurboGopher, but certain control panels or extensions can also activate the auto-connect feature, which can be a pain.*

Once you've established a PPP connection with MacPPP, you can run any of the MacTCP-based applications and do whatever you want. If you click on the Stats button in Config PPP, MacPPP presents you with a relatively meaningless dialog full of technical statistics. I've never bothered with them and I haven't talked to anyone who has, either.

When you're done with your work and want to close your connection, first quit all of your MacTCP-based applications. Some of them dislike having the connection disappear from under their little electronic feet. To pull the plug on the PPP connection, you can do one of two things, depending on how you use MacPPP. First, you can click on the Hard Close button, which hangs up the connection and "locks" MacPPP so that the only way to establish a new connection is to click on the Open button. This prevents any applications from forcing MacPPP to open the connection automatically while, say, you're not present. Second, if it doesn't bother you to possibly have applications dialing your phone behind your back, you can click on the Soft Close button to close a connection. That leaves open the auto-connect feature for the rest of that session, so launching an application makes MacPPP establish a new connection.

Note

If you have AppleScript installed, you can download a MacPPP osax (an extension to AppleScript) and a pair of AppleScript scripts for opening and closing MacPPP, all written by Mark Alldritt. They simplify opening and closing MacPPP connections if you don't want to use the auto-connect feature or don't want to open the Config PPP control panel to open and close connections. You need:

```
ftp://gaea.kgs.ukans.edu/applescript/osaxen/MacPPPControl1.1.sit.hqx
```

Overall Evaluation

My only real quibbles with MacPPP are that I don't think much of the aesthetics of the interface (hey, call me an interface snob—I don't mind), and I wish there were a cleaner way of opening and closing MacPPP for people without AppleScript installed. I can think of any number of ways this could be accomplished, but given that the AppleScript scripts work so well, I see no real need for Larry Blunk to worry about it. Actually, if I wanted to quibble some more, MacPPP could use some updated documentation, and it would be nice if it could dial and redial in the background.

Overall, though, I find MacPPP to be an excellent program and perhaps the simplest way of establishing a connection to the Internet (assuming that the PPP server in question supports authentication).

Administrative Details

Larry Blunk and Merit Network deserve kudos for making such a fine program available to the Macintosh Internet community for free. You can retrieve the latest version of MacPPP on the Internet from either of the following:

```
ftp://ftp.tidbits.com/pub/tidbits/tisk/tcp/mac-ppp-201.hqx
```

```
ftp://merit.edu/pub/ppp/macppp2.0.1.hqx
```

There's also a French version, should that be a more natural language for you.

InterPPP

InterCon's InterPPP is the first of the commercial PPP clients, although more are certainly on the way. I've even heard of another that's based on the same code as used in InterPPP—we'll have to wait and see what the differences will be. The main advantage that InterPPP brings to the PPP world is that it is a full PPP implementation and can carry AppleTalk over the PPP connection.

This may sound thoroughly cool, and it is, but only in certain situations. The problem is that for this feature to be of any use to you at all, your host machine must speak AppleTalk as well as TCP/IP. That may very well may be true in the case of a university campus, where there might be a large Macintosh network that the Unix host is attached to. At most commercial providers, however, there's no reason to run AppleTalk, so they don't. In addition, the simple fact of a machine running the AppleTalk protocols does not make it inherently useful to anyone who dials in. There must be services that are only available via AppleTalk on the host machine's network for it to be of much use for you. Since it's unlikely that a commercial Internet provider will want to provide an AppleShare server or allow users to print on their company LaserWriter, I doubt that most people will have much use for InterPPP's star feature. That said, if you do work at a university or business where you have Unix machines that run the AppleTalk protocol, InterPPP is simply the way to go. There is no competition at the moment.

Configuring InterPPP seems relatively easy, especially if you can use its authentication feature with your provider. If that's true, you can simply select that button in the main configuration window (which you can save using Save in the

File menu, to record your settings) and enter the appropriate username and password information, along with the host's phone number (see figure 12.16).

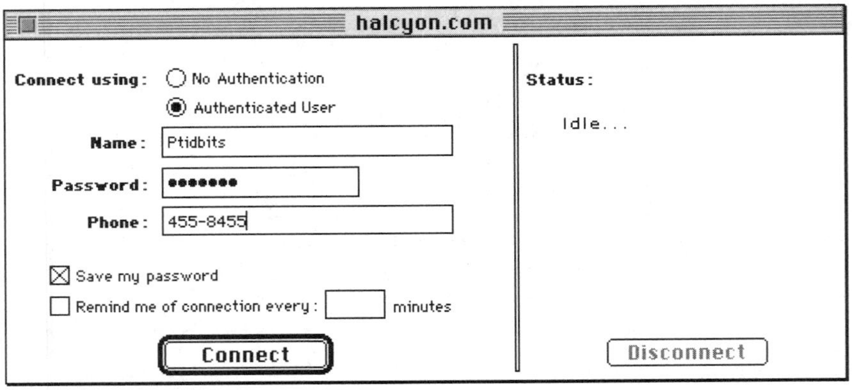

Figure 12.16   *InterPPP Configuration window*

I had trouble getting InterPPP to work with my PPP server, although I was only testing it and not trying to really hammer on it to get it to work. Part of the problem, I think, is that InterPPP relies on CCL scripts (it provides a simple text editor for editing them, which is a nice touch) that live in your Extensions folder for configuring the modem. I far prefer a simple dialog approach to configuring the modem.

In addition, although InterPPP offers an extremely detailed activity log window, I had great difficulty in figuring out what might be causing the problem. Other useful features include a Status window, and in theory, a terminal window for logging in (although it never appeared in my testing, even when I had it selected in the Modem configuration dialog). In a nice touch, InterPPP has a checkbox for using the SLIP protocol instead of PPP—although I cannot imagine most people switching back and forth, it might be helpful during a transition period from a SLIP account to a PPP account.

Administrative Details

You can purchase InterPPP from InterCon Systems for $99. For more information, contact InterCon electronically at **sales@intercon.com**, or at:

InterCon Systems Corporation
950 Herndon Pkwy., Ste. 420
Herndon, VA 22070
800-INTRCON
703-709-5500
703-709-5555 (fax)

MacTCP via ARA

I have no experience using ARA (Apple Remote Access) to access the Internet. ARA is commercial software from Apple that enables you to make a modem connection to another Mac work just like a network connection. Many people have gotten it to work fine using the network at their organization and a Mac at home. The trick, reportedly, is as follows (thanks to George Tempel and Bob Van Valzah for this information):

First, you need a Macintosh, a fast modem, ARA, and MacTCP at home. At work you need a Macintosh running ARA, another fast modem, and most importantly, a network link through a router that connects LocalTalk to Ethernet and then out to the Internet. So, if you can't use the Mac at work with MacTCP applications to access the Internet, you won't be able to do so via ARA, either.

Second, you need a unique IP address assigned to your home Macintosh, either permanently or by the server each time you dial in, because using a Mac via ARA is just like using a Mac on a LocalTalk network at work. If you don't know how or haven't appropriate access to establish an IP number for your home Mac, talk to the person in charge of your router.

Once you have those two things done, choose either a Manually or Server-addressed IP address for the Mac—either should work although Server should be easier, because you might not need to know your Gateway address (which you will need if you use Manually addressed). In addition, if you use Server addressing, your IP address will be in line with the systems at work, simplifying matters if anything changes there. Next bring up the ARA connection to the work Mac. Open MacTCP and select the icon with a pop-up list of zones beneath it. From the list, select the LocalTalk zone containing your IP gateway—a router such as an EtherRoute, GatorBox, FastPath, or whatnot. This ensures that traffic from your Mac must go through the router that handles the encapsulation of packets for Ethernet. Since your Mac isn't really on Ethernet, its packets will be ignored unless you choose one of the zones that goes through the router.

Once you've properly configured MacTCP via ARA, you should be able to establish an ARA connection to work and use the MacTCP-based applications just as though you were directly connected.

Troubleshooting

If you went through the various steps to configure MacTCP and either InterSLIP or MacPPP and everything works, congratulations! Skip this section entirely, since it can get a bit technical in places and if everything works, there's no need to dwell on what might not work. Most people don't have much trouble doing it, but there are some pitfalls to avoid and some tricks and tips I've learned since the first edition of this book came out. I'd like to share some of the problems and solutions with you here, and although I hope you don't need to read this section, if you do, I hope it helps. I've formatted the section along the lines of an Internet FAQ, or Frequently Asked Question, list.

Reporting Problems

Before I even begin to talk about what might go wrong, I want to say a few words about how you can best go about isolating problems and then reporting them on the nets or to tech support. If you ask for help on `comp.sys.mac.comm` by posting a note that says something like, "I'm connecting to the nets via SLIP and it doesn't work. What am I doing wrong?" you won't get any helpful responses. You probably won't get any at all, since people will have no clue what your problem is other than the fact that you don't know how to ask for help. If you follow these steps when working through any problem, not only one with MacTCP, you'll be better off.

When you've determined that you have a problem, do the following: Start over completely from scratch, and then carefully follow each step in the instructions, noting anything that doesn't seem to mesh between your setup and what the instructions say. If you deviate from the instructions, note that, too. In many cases, following this procedure will either solve the problem or reveal where it lies. Don't think of this process as an unpleasant chore, because then you're likely to become careless and miss an important clue. Troubleshooting can be a lot of fun, since you learn a lot more about the topic at hand, and you get to solve a real-life mystery in which no one dies.

Unfortunately, since we're all amateur sleuths, we're not always able to find the solution to a problem and must consult others who are more knowledgeable or who have a different way of looking at the problem. If you are having trouble with a commercial program, the first experts to turn to should be the technical support staff at the company that produced your program. I've heard good things about most of the technical support staffs of companies that make Internet applications, although quality tech support is never a guarantee.

When dealing with telephone tech support people, keep in mind that they probably know a lot more about the program in question than you do, they answer a huge number of calls every day, and the job has a high burnout rate because it's so stressful. You're most likely to get the best help if you're polite and cooperate with what they ask you to do. If you call and announce that you're a power user and why doesn't this stupid program work anyway, you're unlikely to get decent help. If, on the other hand, you call, say that you're having troubles, and give the information the tech support person asks for, she can do a much better job. It never pays to alienate the person whom you're asking for help—whatever is wrong is almost certainly not her fault.

If you are using a freeware or shareware application, it usually says whether or not the author is willing to help via direct email. One way or another, though, there are several places where you can ask for help from other users, many of whom are true experts. Also, the developers of many of the freeware and shareware utilities tend to hang out in these same places and help their users, even if they prefer not to be continually slammed by personal email. The best place to ask for help with Internet stuff is on the Usenet newsgroup **comp.sys.mac.comm**. There also are knowledgeable people who hang out in the Info-Mac Digest at **info-mac@sumex-aim.stanford.edu** (sending email to this address may be easier than sending a newsgroup message if you're having trouble). If you are having trouble with Northwest Nexus specifically, but can post to a newsgroup, the group **halcyon.slip** is the perfect place to ask.

Note

If you don't read these groups regularly, you should specifically ask for replies via email so you don't miss any answers.

No matter what, if you want any of these people to help you, you must help them first by sending a complete report. In that report, you should list the following:

- Exactly what it is that you're trying to accomplish. This should be specific, since telling someone that you want to read Usenet news with NewsWatcher isn't salient to the problem of not being able to get InterSLIP to connect. Take each goal a step at a time.

- The fact that you have carefully followed the directions. This fact tells people that (a) you're not a complete idiot and can read, and (b) that you have gone through a certain set of procedures already. If you haven't followed the directions carefully, don't bother posting until you do so.

- The salient facts of your software and hardware setup. Include things such as what Mac you have, what modem you use, what version of the System software you're running, and any weird stuff that you can't eliminate from the testing (such as, for example, an Outbound user who had additional software from Outbound that was necessary for it to boot properly). Unless asked, don't bother listing out every extension and control panel on your hard disk. You should have already eliminated them in the process of testing by removing everything but MacTCP and either InterSLIP or PPP and Config PPP from your Extensions and Control Panels folders. Also, a too-long report will turn many people off.

■ What you have already tried, whether or not it worked, and whether you noticed anything strange happening at any time during the process. If you encounter error dialogs at any time, report exactly what they say.

Above all, be nice. The last thing you want to do is insult an expert's favorite program, since they're less likely to help you at that point. When you're in trouble, it doesn't help to alienate anyone.

MacTCP Questions

Before anything else, let me emphasize that you may need to reinstall a clean copy of MacTCP at various times to solve problems. Thus, you must keep a clean copy that you have never opened on a locked floppy. The copy that comes on the disk with this book qualifies as a clean copy of MacTCP.

Also, let me recommend that if you have FTP access, you get a copy of Peter Lewis's free MacTCP Watcher. It includes another document on troubleshooting MacTCP connections, written by Eric Behr. It's at:

```
ftp://ftp.tidbits.com/pub/tidbits/tisk/tcp/mactcp-watcher-11.hqx
```

So, here are some questions you may find yourself asking along with answers to them.

Q: I don't see an icon for InterSLIP or PPP in my MacTCP control panel.

A: Install InterSLIP or PPP in your Extensions folder, and try again.

Q: I get a weird -23004 error from MacTCP, and it complains about its drivers not being installed.

A: Make sure that you select InterSLIP or PPP and *not* LocalTalk in the MacTCP control panel.

Q: What about that weird slider bar in the upper right of the MacTCP configuration dialog?

A: Ignore it unless you're on a subnet, which means you'll have a network administrator who can tell you what to do there.

Q: Should I type anything in the IP number box in the MacTCP control panel if I'm using Server addressing?

A: No. Only enter a number there if you use a Manually-addressed account.

Q: Why can't I type anything in the Gateway box in the MacTCP configuration dialog when I'm using Server addressing?

A: As I understand it, you don't need a Gateway address with Server addressing, which is why you can't type in there. InterSLIP fills it in for MacTCP, but it makes no real difference.

However, one reader found that in using VersaTerm SLIP, the first time you log in you must enter a Gateway address and your IP address into VersaTerm SLIP, via either the fields in the upper right of the configuration window or a small pop-up menu in VersaTerm AdminSLIP's terminal window. With Northwest Nexus, the Gateway address in this case is the first of the two IP numbers that the machine provides after you enter your login name and password, something like **198.137.231.150**. Your IP address for that session is the second of the two numbers.

Q: What are the MacTCP DNR and MacTCP Prep files?

A: MacTCP creates them when you restart, to store various settings and preferences. You can throw them out at any time with impunity, since MacTCP will recreate them with the same settings when you restart. Note that you must restart after throwing them out since MacTCP applications require MacTCP DNR to work properly.

If you reinstall MacTCP without throwing them out, MacTCP retains the settings it had before you reinstalled it. This can be useful for moving copies of MacTCP around, but they also tend to retain any corruption.

Q: My Mac crashed the first time I restarted after reinstalling MacTCP. Should I be worried, even though I don't crash now?

A: I would completely reinstall MacTCP (throwing out MacTCP DNR and MacTCP Prep as well) and reconfigure to be safe, but I don't think you should worry too much. Virus software sometimes gets persnickety about MacTCP creating the MacTCP DNR file, and I could see that perhaps causing the problem.

In fact, I hear that if the MacTCP DNR files becomes corrupted, some virus software, such as Gatekeeper, could possibly prevent MacTCP from updating it, which is a bad thing. If you use sensitive antivirus software that tries to prevent unknown actions (Disinfectant is fine), to be very sure it isn't causing problems, turn it off, delete MacTCP, MacTCP DNR, and MacTCP Prep, reinstall a clean copy of MacTCP, restart, turn the virus software back on, and restart again.

Q: I crashed while using Fetch or some other MacTCP-based program. Should I reinstall MacTCP?

A: Possibly. First, connect again to see if Fetch works. If it does, you're OK. If it doesn't, throw out the MacTCP DNR file and restart. Try Fetch again. If it still doesn't work, completely reinstall MacTCP from scratch. This isn't usually necessary, luckily.

After a truly nasty crash, you may find it necessary to reinstall InterSLIP or MacPPP as well. If you use InterSLIP, remove your modem configuration file from the InterSLIP Folder before reinstalling InterSLIP, since it's worth trying with your old configuration file before you toast it as well.

Q: I'm getting the impression that reinstalling MacTCP is a common occurrence. Is that true?

A: Yes and no. I seldom do it any more, but frankly, if anything goes wrong, reinstalling MacTCP is worth trying in every instance. Make sure you throw out MacTCP DNR and MacTCP Prep, too, since they can store the corruption that caused MacTCP to have problems in the first place. Always keep a copy of MacTCP on a locked floppy disk, to facilitate reinstalling.

Q: I'm running MacTCP 2.0.2. Should I update it to 2.0.4?

A: Sure, why not? I personally haven't seen any problems in 2.0.2 that were fixed in 2.0.4, but others have, and it's a free update that's stored on:

---

ftp://ftp.tidbits.com/pub/tidbits/tisk/tcp/mactcp-20x-to-204-updt.hqx

---

Besides, MacTCP 2.0.4 is on the disk that comes with this book, so you can install it from there if you want, first removing the old MacTCP, MacTCP DNR, and MacTCP Prep.

Q: When I went to update MacTCP 2.0.2 to 2.0.4, I got some sort of error about a DRVR 22. What's that all about?

A: You must update *only* a clean copy of MacTCP that has never been opened before. Get a new copy from your master disk, update it, and the updater will work fine. Then, keep a clean copy of 2.0.4 on a locked floppy somewhere for use when reinstalling.

Domain Name Server Errors

I've noticed many people running into a problem where SLIP or PPP (any implementation) connects properly, but trouble arises with the domain name server when they attempt to run TurboGopher or any of the other MacTCP programs. Sometimes they crash or hang instead, but the behavior is usually completely reproducible (although we have seen the occasional exception, where it will work fine once after reinstalling MacTCP but fail on subsequent connections). This problem occurs primarily in Server-addressed situations, but I've also heard sporadic reports from people using Manually addressed accounts.

I haven't absolutely solved this problem yet, I'm sorry to say, but here are some things to try. I find that the easiest way to test this situation is with Peter Lewis's free MacTCP Watcher, which shows an IP number but no Mac name in this instance. It also complains about a "No answer error" or a "Cache fault error" when it is unable to find the domain name server. TurboGopher is the second best test for this, but may crash or hang instead of reporting "Unable to resolve hostname." If you use Fetch, you can tell quickly that you are seeing the problem if when you connect, the dog cursor is frozen. If the dog cursor runs, you're generally better off. If the cursor is frozen, immediately hit command-period to try canceling the connection before Fetch hangs.

Note that the problem is generally not with your account. Each time someone has had this problem and asked me to check their account, it has worked fine if they had a SLIP account. That said, here are some things to try, in this order:

- Check your domain name server configuration in MacTCP carefully to make sure you typed the right numbers. I've made this mistake before.

- If you are using a Manually-addressed account, make sure you have typed the right number into the Gateway address box in MacTCP's configuration dialog. Only your provider can tell you what your Gateway address is— you cannot guess it.

- If you use InterSLIP and Northwest Nexus (this applies to the other providers as well), make sure you're using the Northwest Nexus gateway script (or the appropriate one for your provider). Without this, your Mac won't get an IP number properly. A number of people tried to use the Simple Unix/Telebit script that's built into InterSLIP, and it simply won't work with a Server-addressed account like those that Northwest Nexus provides. This is because that Northwest Nexus gateway script is designed to find your IP number from the login message each time you login. If you use the Simple Unix/Telebit script instead, it will finish successfully after sending your userid and password, and will ignore the IP address that appears next.

- Login with a terminal emulator just to make sure your account is set up for SLIP or PPP. If after providing your user name and password, you don't see garbage or something like "SL/IP session beginning..." and you get to a Unix prompt, then your account has not been set up for SLIP or PPP. Ask your provider to fix it.

- If for some reason you are using InterSLIP 1.0fc3, get version 1.0.1 since that version solved some various problems like this. It's on the disk that comes with this book and at:

```
ftp://ftp.tidbits.com/pub/tidbits/tisk/tcp/inter-slip-installer-101.hqx
```

■ Reinstall MacTCP from scratch. Hey, it's easy, but you'd be surprised how much it helps.

■ Make sure your domain name server setup in the MacTCP configuration dialog looks something like this (it will be different for your domain if you don't use Northwest Nexus):

```
halcyon.com.   198.137.231.1   (•)
      .        198.137.231.1
      .        192.135.191.1
      .        192.135.191.1
```

■ Okay, here's a major realization we've made (thanks to Michael Tardiff of Northwest Nexus for tremendous help in figuring this out). If nothing so far has worked, check to make absolutely sure you are using hardware handshaking with your modem, and more importantly, make sure XON/XOFF is turned off. It seems that if XON/XOFF is turned on, the SLIP or PPP program may appear to log in properly, but will fail to find the Gateway address properly.

Server-addressed accounts aren't supposed to need the Gateway address, which is why you cannot type it into MacTCP. Nonetheless, if, in InterSLIP (and MacPPP, we think) you don't properly use hardware handshaking, then some sort of negotiation that determines the Gateway address fails. When that happens, a necessary line of communication with the host is broken. The upshot of this is that MacTCP Watcher will find no Mac name for your Mac. That Mac name should be supplied by reverse name mapping, but it seems that if that initial negotiation after the login process fails, the Mac receives no Mac name from the host via the gateway. Using exactly the same settings otherwise, we showed that merely toggling a modem setting that turned hardware handshaking on and off could make the difference between a successful connection and a failed one.

■ Make sure that your modem cable is indeed a hardware handshaking cable. Most high-speed modems purchased in "Macintosh kits" within the last year include proper hardware handshaking cables, but if you bought a modem without a cable, or you bought a new cable separately from a computer store, your cable may not be a proper hardware handshaking cable. You may need to call your modem vendor to confirm this. Modern hardware handshaking cables should have the pinouts shown in table 12.3—you can test this if you have the proper electronic testing equipment, or can construct an electric testing device that turns on a light or makes a noise when a circuit is closed by touching leads to the proper pins (I once used an empty battery-powered squirt gun to indicate when a circuit was completed).

Table 12.3

Hardware Handshaking Cable Pin-out

Mac Function	RS-232 Function	Mac Pin	DB-25 Pin
RxD (receive)	Receive Data	5	3
TxD (transmit)	Transmit Data	3	2
Ground	Ground	4 & 8	7
HSKi	CTS	2	5
HSKo	RTS & DTR	1	4 & 20
GPi	CD	7	8

- If you do not have a hardware handshaking cable, you can purchase them from numerous sources, but insist on a hardware handshaking cable, not just a modem cable. Jump up and down, yell, and scream, if necessary, but the two terms are not necessarily interchangeable. I've ordered high-quality, properly wired cables for about $15 from:

Celestin Company

800/835-5514

206/385-3767

206/385-3586 (fax)

celestin@pt.olympus.net

- Once you determine that your modem cable is indeed a hardware handshaking cable, next ensure that hardware handshaking is turned on in your SLIP or PPP program. You may see a checkbox labeled Hardware Handshaking, as in InterSLIP, or a pop-up menu listing choices such as XON/XOFF, CTS, RTS, and CTS/RTS. Choose CTS or CTS/RTS for hardware handshaking. There are other terms for the RS-232 functions that some programs use—if you're confused, ask the program's tech support folks. Hardware handshaking is usually relatively easy to check and set.

- Unfortunately, simply turning on hardware handshaking in your SLIP or PPP program may not be sufficient. It seems that some modems set XON/XOFF, or software handshaking, in their default settings. Thus, when you initialize the modem with the factory default initialization string, you actually turn software handshaking back on. This is bad. I ran into this with a Telebit QBlazer, which defaults to software handshaking with the setting S58=3. By changing that to S58=2 in the initialization string, the domain name server errors disappeared immediately since InterSLIP could then complete the negotiation for the Gateway address and the reverse name mapping that goes on right after the login process.

VersaTerm AdminSLIP may not always suffer from the same problem as InterSLIP. Merely setting hardware handshaking in the configuration window enabled the QBlazer to work, whereas checking the hardware handshaking box in InterSLIP had made no difference. Nonetheless, consult the fine print in your modem's manual for the settings to ensure that hardware handshaking is enabled. Look for settings called DTE Flow Control or DCE Flow Control or anything whose options include CTS/RTS (in full duplex, if it's an option). In Telebit modems, those settings are controlled by the S58 register, although other modems undoubtedly differ.

- Try using another modem. This worked for one user who switched from a Zoom 2,400 bps modem to a QuickTel v.32bis modem. This may well have been related to the hardware handshaking issue.

- Try booting from another hard disk, if you have one.

- Try installing MacTCP and the other software on another Macintosh, if you have one.

- Try rebuilding your desktop. I have no idea why this would make a difference, but it's worth a try. You can rebuild your desktop by holding down Command-Option during startup until the Macintosh asks you if you want to rebuild the desktop.

- Try zapping your PRAM (Parameter RAM—it stores various low level settings). I have no idea whether this makes any difference, but anything is worth a try at this point. To zap your PRAM in System 7, hold down Command-Option-P-R while restarting the Mac. You will lose certain settings such as the time and the mouse speed, but you can reset those later.

- Try reinstalling your System. First, make sure you have a full set of System disks, since you must disable the System on the hard drive before installing, to ensure a completely clean install. Then, drag your System file to your desktop, and restart with the Install disk. Install a System for any Macintosh (you never know what Mac you might want to use with your hard disk) and then restart with your hard disk again. Throw out the System file sitting on your desktop, completely reinstall MacTCP (throwing out MacTCP DNR and MacTCP Prep), and MacPPP (throw out PPP Preferences along with the PPP extension and Config PPP) or InterSLIP (throw out the entire InterSLIP Folder, the InterSLIP extension, and InterSLIP Setup). Then, try again. At least one MacPPP user solved the problem this way.

- Consider switching to the commercial VersaTerm SLIP, MacSLIP, or InterPPP. This may work because of differences in the ways the programs handle Gateway addresses for Server-addressed accounts and the way they specify hardware handshaking for different modems.

- Try a completely different provider.

- If none of these suggestions help, I don't know what to say, except that some problems are never solved. Otherwise we'd have world peace.

InterSLIP Questions

Since its introduction last year, InterSLIP has become popular for its combination of flexibility, utility, and price—it's free. However, InterSLIP isn't always completely simple to use. Following are some of the more common questions and answers relating to InterSLIP.

Q: I can't find InterSLIP Control on my disk.

A: You don't need InterSLIP Control if you use System 7. It is necessary with System 6. More details follow.

Q: I copied the gateway and dialing scripts into the proper folders. Why don't they show up in the pop-up menus in InterSLIP?

A: Two things to check here. Those files should be text files, so if they are any other type, they may not show up, since InterSLIP won't recognize them. If you simply save from Microsoft Word, for instance, those files will be of type WDBN and not of type TEXT. Use Save As and select the Text Only option that should exist in most word processors. Second, if you copy those scripts in while InterSLIP is running, it won't recognize them until you quit and launch InterSLIP Setup again. You don't have to restart; simply quit and relaunch.

Q: If I launch an application without manually connecting with InterSLIP, InterSLIP tries to dial the phone twice, then the Mac hangs. What's going on?

A: In my experience, InterSLIP's auto connect feature doesn't work very well. This may not be InterSLIP's fault, and it does work for some people, so if it does for you, great. If not, make a habit of connecting manually before you launch a MacTCP program such as Fetch. Since Eudora doesn't open MacTCP until you check for mail, you can use it without connecting InterSLIP first. One person said that he had solved his auto connect problems by adding a "pause 30" statement in his Gateway script just before it exits. This may help, although my Mac never even dials the phone before freezing on auto connect.

Q: When I click on the Connect button, nothing happens. Why not?

A: This points directly at an extension conflict with either InterSLIP or MacTCP. I would recommend pulling all of your extensions and control panels out. Or, better yet, use an extension manager such as Apple's free Extension Manager, or the powerful (but commercial) Conflict Catcher from Casady & Greene, which can actually help in your testing process. Leave only MacTCP and InterSLIP, and try again. If the problem disappears, slowly replace the extensions and control panels that you use until the problem reappears, identifying the culprit in the process. We've seen problems possibly related to MacTOPS, DOS Mounter, SuperLaserSpool, and GlobalFax, and a two-way conflict with AutoRemounter and PSI FaxMonitor. In general, be very wary of any extensions that modify a network or a modem, including fax or remote control software. Even if these programs don't specifically conflict with InterSLIP or MacTCP, they may leave the modem in such a state that InterSLIP or MacPPP cannot dial out properly.

Q: I removed all of my extensions and control panels and I still get nothing when I click on the Connect button.

A: Try reinstalling MacTCP from scratch (throwing out MacTCP DNR and MacTCP Prep) and InterSLIP (throw out the entire InterSLIP Folder, the InterSLIP extension, and InterSLIP Setup), and reinstall from clean copies. If you have custom scripts, there's no need to throw them out.

Q: It still doesn't work.

A: Shoot. The next thing to try is reinstalling your System. First, make sure you have a full set of System disks, since you must disable the System on the hard drive before installing, to ensure a completely clean install. Then, drag your System file to your desktop, and restart with the Install disk. Install a System for any Macintosh (you never know what Mac you might want to use with your hard disk), and then restart with your hard disk again. Throw out the System file sitting on your desktop, then completely reinstall MacTCP (throwing out MacTCP DNR and MacTCP Prep) and InterSLIP (throw out the entire InterSLIP Folder, the InterSLIP extension, and InterSLIP Setup), and try again.

Q: Sorry to be a pain, but it still doesn't do anything when I click on the Connect button.

A: Okay, I don't really know what's happening here. Try getting a PPP account and use MacPPP, or purchase VersaTerm SLIP or MacSLIP and see if they work any better. I wish I could give a better answer, but I can't.

Q: My modem doesn't seem to work with the Hayes-Compatible Modem script.

A: You need a dialing script, which is similar to an ARA script. For starters, I recommend the Minimal Dialing Script I provide on the disk. It works with most modems.

Q: I'm using a dialing script, and when I click Connect, it says Dialing, but I don't hear the modem dial or see it do anything else.

A: I've seen this happen a few times. I suspect the script is in some way incorrect—perhaps the error correction and file compression have been turned on improperly. Try the Hayes-Compatible Modem script. If that doesn't work, try the Minimal Dialing Script on the disk. If that doesn't work, ask your modem company for a good ARA script that you can modify (in theory, an ARA script should work without modification, but is best when modified). If that fails, beg for help from others with the same modem on the nets, preferably in **comp.sys.mac.comm** or the Info-Mac Digest at **info-mac@sumex-aim.stanford.edu**.

Q: I can connect on occasion, but not all the time. What could be wrong?

A: Some modems, the US Robotics Sportster and the Global Village TelePort/ Gold in particular, don't seem to like to connect at 19,200 bps, especially without a dialing script. If you set the speed down to 9,600 in InterSLIP, they'll connect better using the Hayes-Compatible Modem script. There is a good one for the TelePort/Gold that solves this problem at:

```
ftp://ftp.tidbits.com/pub/tidbits/tisk/tcp/scr-gv-teleport-gold-bd.hqx
```

Also, I've noticed that sometimes I'll see failed connections on my Northwest Nexus account. They range from receiving tons of data when InterSLIP says "Waiting for prompt," to nothing at all happening when InterSLIP says "Waiting for prompt," "Sending username," or "Sending password." I've even had InterSLIP report "Login incorrect" when I know full well it was fine. Just try again a few times, waiting a bit between tries, if you can. I suspect these problems are related to a bad modem, line noise, or some other situation out of your control, and in my experience they always go away after several tries.

Q: InterSLIP connects fine, but none of the programs seem to quite work, although they try to connect.

A: Try toggling your TCP Header Compression checkbox (also sometimes known as CSLIP). If that checkbox doesn't match the setting for your account, things will fail. Essentially what happens is that small tasks such as looking up a machine name succeed, but anything else fails.

Q: I had InterSLIP working, but now that I've moved my hard drive to another machine, it crashes whenever I launch InterSLIP Setup.

A: Delete your InterSLIP Prefs file. For some reason, this has happened on several machines we've seen.

Q: InterSLIP works fine, except that when I click on the Disconnect button, my modem doesn't hang up. What can I do?

A: First off, consider adding &D2 to the end of your modem initialization string. Doing so will hang up the modem if DTR goes low, which it does when you click the Disconnect button. Unfortunately, DTR can also go low if you have a fast modem and a slow Mac and the modem transfers more data than the Mac can handle at that point. If this is true, you'll see random hang-ups while transferring large files. If you do use &D2, you may be able to set an S-register in the modem init string that lengthens the timeout before DTR goes low, thus preventing the hangups. Only worry about this if you like reading modem manuals.

Second, if you use a dialing script other than the built-in Hayes Compatible Modem script, it usually will have an @hangup section. My Minimal Dialing Script has one, and will hang up the modem just fine if you use it instead of the Hayes Compatible Modem script.

MacPPP Questions

Although its interface can seem a bit more confusing than InterSLIP's, MacPPP is actually quite a bit easier to configure and use. Thus, fewer questions.

Q: I want to switch from InterSLIP to MacPPP. What should I watch out for?

A: First, you need a new account. Second, I don't recommend leaving the InterSLIP extension installed at the same time as the PPP extension. Third, reinstall MacTCP from scratch before trying to connect with MacPPP.

Q: My Open button is grayed out so I can't click on it to connect.

A: Reinstall MacTCP from scratch, making sure to delete MacTCP DNR and MacTCP Prep. This one once threw me for an hour.

Also, be very wary of any fax or remote control software that may have taken over the modem. Even if it doesn't conflict directly with MacTCP or MacPPP, the fax software may leave the modem in such a state that MacPPP is unable to access it.

Q: MacPPP seems to redial the phone randomly on its own.

A: Click on the Hard Close button, rather than on the Soft Close button, to disconnect. The drawback to doing this is that you cannot use MacPPP's auto connect feature after this unless you restart. Also set a short idle timeout in Config PPP so it hangs up relatively quickly if MacPPP does dial on its own.

SLIP-Sliding Away

Well, you should now be as much of an expert on MacTCP, InterSLIP, and MacPPP as I can make you. The length and complexity of this chapter is deceptive because most of the time configuring these programs is almost trivial, especially with the aid of the ISKM Installer. Nonetheless, I believe in providing as much information as I can, which is why I have so much detail on these programs and troubleshooting.

The silly part of this entire chapter is that once you have installed and configure MacTCP and either InterSLIP or MacPPP, if you use a modem, your only interaction with them is opening and closing the connection. The real fun comes in the next chapter, where I talk about all of the programs that rely on the connection that you've established with MacTCP and either InterSLIP or MacPPP. Shall we move on then?

MacTCP-based Software

Finally! You probably never thought you would actually get to read about the MacTCP-based software that I've mentioned throughout the book and included on the disk. I wanted to save this until now mainly because MacTCP software appears so frequently that I wanted to discuss the latest possible versions of these programs. The strategy paid off, since great new programs like MacWeb and Mosaic 2.0 appeared in the last few days of my writing.

Given the amount of the MacTCP software and the speed with which new versions appear, you can be sure that some of the software I talk about here will have been updated at least once by the time you read this book. Because of this, the specific URLs that I give for finding each program may not work (although updates will have similar names to and live in the same directories as the originals).

Don't worry about the discussions being outdated. The programs I'm writing about are relatively mature in most cases, so they're unlikely to change so radically that you cannot get a feel for them here. And, of course, I'll post the latest versions on my FTP site, **ftp.tidbits.com**, in the **/pub/tidbits/tisk** directory.

Note

For those of you with a MacTCP-based connection to the Internet, I've included Anarchie bookmark files on the disk. These bookmark files point to a special directory on **ftp.tidbits.com** *that contains self-extracting archives of the latest version of the twenty-or-so programs that I consider essential for people using MacTCP-based Internet connections. Needless to say, I couldn't include all the programs on the disk itself, so the bookmarks simplify the process of getting new programs and retrieving updates.*

To use these bookmarks, make sure your Internet connection is established and then double-click on the appropriate bookmark. Anarchie launches and retrieves the file. That's all there is to it.

I've collected enough MacTCP-based software that there's no way I can cover it all in detail within the current size of this book. Instead, I'm going to concentrate on the cream of the crop in various categories. Although I don't explore each email program in depth, for instance, I do mention nice features or advantages that might sway you to investigate one of them.

As far as organization goes, let me lay it out right now. We begin with email programs such as Eudora, then discuss Usenet newsreaders such as NewsWatcher, after which we move to FTP clients such as Anarchie and Fetch. Next up are Telnet programs like NCSA Telnet and Comet, WAIS clients such as MacWAIS, Gopher clients such as TurboGopher, and World-Wide Web browsers including MacWeb and NCSA Mosaic. After that, I describe various miscellaneous applications including Timbuktu Pro, MacTCP Watcher, and Finger. Finally, I take a look at several commercial programs that attempt to integrate a number of Internet functions into a single program. These include MicroPhone II from Software Ventures, Synergy Software's VersaTerm-Link, and InterCon's TCP/Connect II.

Note

I tell you where you can find many of the programs discussed here, and in this second edition, I've also added information about any versions of the programs that have been localized for other languages, French, Japanese, Swedish, or whatever. I wasn't able to pin down file locations for all of these foreign-language versions, so I recommend that you do Archie searches if you wish to find them. Searching on the program name alone might work, or if you're looking for French versions, for instance, you might search for "-fr.", which says, "Find me files that have '-fr' right before the filename extension, whatever that might be." Of course, if you cannot find them with Archie, try asking in `comp.sys.mac.comm` *and someone will probably be able to help.*

Email Programs

Considering that email is *the* ubiquitous application on the Internet, you should use the best email program available; otherwise, you will slowly (or quickly, in my case) go stark raving mad. I've looked at many email programs in my time, and although a number of them are becoming more and more impressive, none compete with Steve Dorner's Eudora. Simply put, Eudora does most everything right. Again, I don't want to imply that other programs aren't good, but none I've seen can match the features and capabilities of Eudora.

Eudora

Steve Dorner first wrote Eudora while working at the University of Illinois. Because of its academic heritage, Eudora was made freely available on the Internet, and because of its clean interface and full feature set, it rapidly became the email application of choice. In July of 1992, Steve left the University of Illinois and went to work for a company called QUALCOMM, where he continued to enhance Eudora. Because Steve and QUALCOMM wanted to give something back to the educational community and taxpayers who made Eudora possible, and because free software is the best advertising for commercial software, Eudora has remained freeware (although QUALCOMM has also released a commercial version of Eudora that adds some welcome features).

The freeware version will continue to exist and be developed in parallel with the commercial version, but is unlikely to receive many new features, other than those Steve deems necessary for basic email usage. For example, he has added support for MIME (Multipurpose Internet Mail Extensions), a new Internet standard for transferring non-textual data via email, and support for Apple events, so that Eudora can work more closely with other programs on the Macintosh. In addition, the latest versions of both the freeware and commercial versions now work in Power Mac-native mode, significantly increasing the speed with which they run. The version of Eudora 1.4.3 included on the disk is not the Power Mac-native version since it was too big to fit on the disk. You can find it at:

```
ftp://ftp.qualcomm.com/quest/mac/eudora/1.4/eudora143Fat.hqx
```

Note

There's now a stand-alone MIME utility for the Mac as well, called Mpack, which can pack and unpack MIME files that contain non-textual information (this is primarily useful if you don't use Eudora, of course). It's at:

```
ftp://export.acs.cmu.edu/pub/mpack/mpack-1.4-mac.hqx
```

The commercial Eudora 2.0, which QUALCOMM released in the fall of 1993, is extremely similar to the freeware Eudora 1.4. It looks the same, and for the most part, works the same. Perhaps the most apparent additional feature in Eudora 2.0 is the filtering feature. It lets you annotate the subject of messages, change their priority, or put them in specific mailboxes, based on information in the headers or the bodies of the messages. You can have as many filters as you want, and they can apply to incoming, outgoing, or selected messages. In addition, 2.0 also supports spell checking in messages via the Word Services suite of Apple events. You can even buy Eudora along with Spellswell, an Apple event-aware spelling program.

Note

Many people want to use Eudora to transfer files back and forth between Macs and PCs in email, and this works well if your recipient either uses PC Eudora or another MIME-compatible mail program. If you're sending the files from the Mac, in the Switches dialog, turn on AppleDouble before attaching the file you want to send. If you're sending from PC Eudora, choose MIME before attaching the file. Both versions of Eudora automatically recognize MIME attachments and decode them automatically upon receipt.

Other useful features that exist only in Eudora 2.0 include uuencode support, automatic opening of attachments encoded in MIME, BinHex, or uuencode, multiple nickname files for organizations, support for System 7 drag and drop, stationery mail message for frequently sent messages, menu-sharing for Frontier users, and finally, multiple signatures. In my opinion, if you're a heavy Eudora user, Eudora 2.0 offers an extremely attractive set of features above and beyond the basic set in Eudora 1.4. For those just starting out, try Eudora 1.4 for a while, and if you decide you like it, think about purchasing the full Eudora 2.0 version for $65. (Purchasing details come at the end of this section, if you're interested.)

Note

To answer the question almost everyone always asks, Steve says that he named his Post Office Protocol program "Eudora," after Eudora Welty, the author of a short story he had read called, "Why I Live at the P.O."

Although Apple's Balloon Help is becoming more common, many people never think to use it in current programs because it's flaky and slow. I strongly recommend that you turn it on while exploring Eudora, though, because Steve wrote excellent help balloons that seem to explain every nook and cranny of the program. The balloon help may not supplant the manual, but that's only because the manual is also excellent.

The current versions of Eudora are 1.4.3 and 2.0.3, both of which are primarily bug fix releases over the basic 1.4 and 2.0 versions. They both also make Eudora Power Mac-native for faster execution.

Note

The Power Mac-native versions of Eudora (generally labeled "fat" because they are "fat binary" files that contain both PowerPC and 68000 code to work on both Power Macs and normal Macs) require the ObjectSupportLib extension. This extension comes with AppleScript 1.1, which is distributed with Power Macintosh models sold in the United States. You don't have to install AppleScript, just the ObjectSupportLib extension. To install ObjectSupportLib, dig it out of the AppleScript 1.1 folder (AppleScript Setup:Apple's Scripting System:RISC Support:ObjectSupportLib) and drag it onto your System Folder.

Installation and Setup

Although powerful, Eudora has a surprisingly simple setup that you perform in two large dialog boxes. First, from the Special menu, choose Configuration (see figure 13.1).

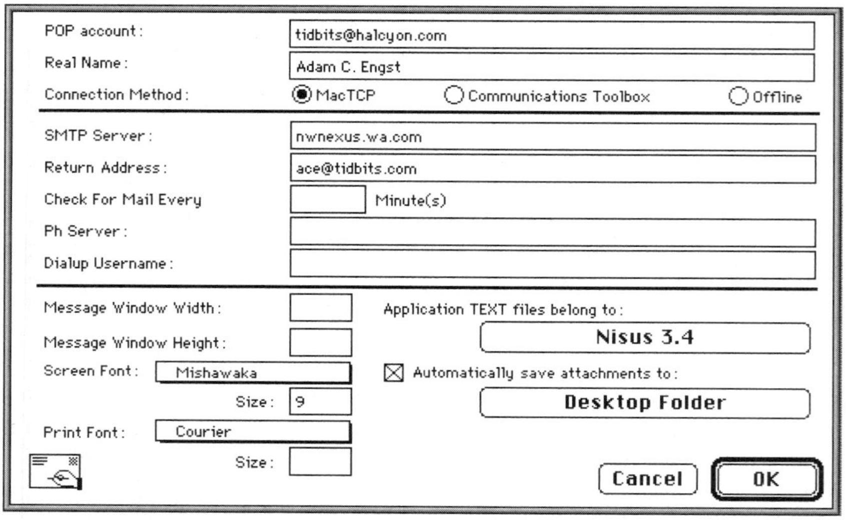

POP account:	tidbits@halcyon.com
Real Name:	Adam C. Engst
Connection Method:	● MacTCP ○ Communications Toolbox ○ Offline
SMTP Server:	nwnexus.wa.com
Return Address:	ace@tidbits.com
Check For Mail Every	[ ] Minute(s)
Ph Server:	[ ]
Dialup Username:	[ ]

Message Window Width: [   ]
Message Window Height: [   ]
Screen Font: Mishawaka   Size: 9
Print Font: Courier   Size: [   ]

Application TEXT files belong to:
Nisus 3.4

☒ Automatically save attachments to:
Desktop Folder

[Cancel] [OK]

Figure 13.1   Eudora Configuration dialog

Despite all the fields you can fill in, only the first few are important. The POP account field holds the full address of your POP account. The best source to find out what to put here is your system administrator. The next field, Real Name, should be obvious. Lastly, click on the MacTCP button located below the Real Name field.

For most people, that's all there is to the setup process. I've filled in the next two fields because my setup is a bit odd, and my POP account is on a different machine from my SMTP (Simple Mail Transport Protocol) server. In addition, because I have my own domain name, **tidbits.com**, I want mail to come back to that address, which is why I put **ace@tidbits.com** in the Return Address field.

Note

If you fill in the Return Address field, be very careful to get it right; otherwise, all your incoming email will go to an incorrect address and you'll never know it.

Click the OK button to close the Configuration dialog. Most of the rest of Eudora's configuration happens in the Special menu as well. You can explore the Nicknames, Signature, and other features later (see figure 13.2).

Figure 13.2   *Eudora Special menu*

For the moment, though, from the Special menu select Switches, so Eudora displays its Switches dialog (see figure 13.3).

Putting this many checkboxes in a single dialog may seem like overkill, but these options enable you to configure Eudora quickly and easily to handle many different situations. I keep copies of all the messages I send, for instance, so I check Keep Copies, but many people don't want to do that.

Similarly, people have different preferences in terms of how they want to be notified of new mail. Eudora's switches cover all the bases, other than perhaps an option to use Apple's PlainTalk technology to read the name of the person who sent the new mail (and I wouldn't be surprised if Steve has that on the list of possible features to add). After you set the switches you want (and remember to explore them with Balloon Help), click the OK button to save your preferences.

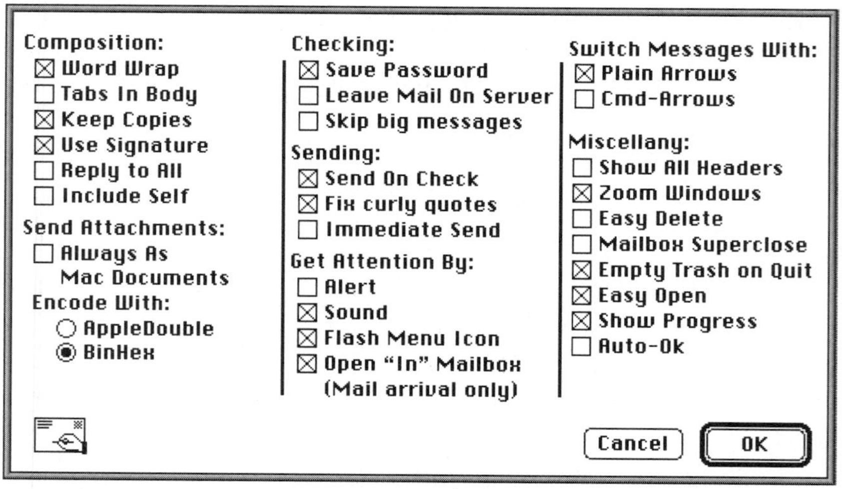

```
Composition:              Checking:                 Switch Messages With:
☒ Word Wrap               ☒ Save Password           ☒ Plain Arrows
☐ Tabs In Body            ☐ Leave Mail On Server     ☐ Cmd-Arrows
☒ Keep Copies             ☐ Skip big messages
☒ Use Signature           Sending:                  Miscellany:
☐ Reply to All            ☒ Send On Check           ☐ Show All Headers
☐ Include Self            ☒ Fix curly quotes        ☒ Zoom Windows
Send Attachments:         ☐ Immediate Send          ☐ Easy Delete
☐ Always As                                         ☐ Mailbox Superclose
   Mac Documents          Get Attention By:         ☒ Empty Trash on Quit
Encode With:              ☐ Alert                   ☒ Easy Open
   ○ AppleDouble          ☒ Sound                   ☒ Show Progress
   ● BinHex               ☒ Flash Menu Icon         ☐ Auto-Ok
                          ☒ Open "In" Mailbox
                          (Mail arrival only)

                                                    [ Cancel ]  [[ OK ]]
```

Figure 13.3   *Eudora Switches dialog*

Basic Usage

You're likely to use Eudora for simple tasks most of the time, creating new messages, reading incoming mail, replying to messages, and the like. Creating a message is the first thing to do. From the Message menu choose New Message, or—to use the shortcut—press Command-N (see figure 13.4).

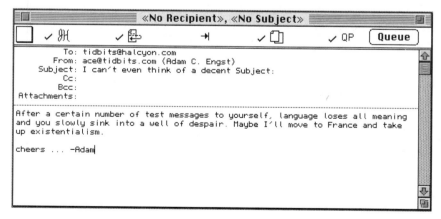

Figure 13.4   *Eudora New Mail window*

Eudora opens a new window with three parts. At the top of the window is a row of switch icons, so you can toggle items such as signatures on a per message basis. Below that is an area for the header. At the bottom of the window is the message area. Tabbing takes you from one header item to another, and finally to the message window.

You can select email addresses in messages or headers, and add them to a Recipients menu (Add as Recipient from the Special menu). The people you add as recipients show up in a hierarchical New Message To menu under the Message menu. If you select someone from that hierarchical menu, Eudora opens a new message with the To line already filled in (the From line is always filled in for you). Similarly, when you create nicknames for people (Nicknames from the Special menu), you're given the option to add that nickname to the recipient list for quick access.

Eudora has a good text entry environment and wraps paragraphs as you write and edit (which is not true of all email programs, so don't laugh). In fact, Eudora can do some neat things with text, as evidenced by the commands in the Edit menu (see figure 13.5).

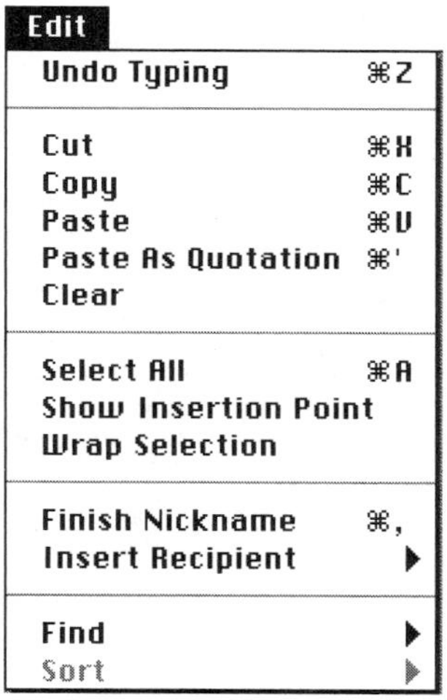

Figure 13.5   *Eudora Edit menu*

I especially like the ability to Insert Recipient and Paste as Quotation. I often want to send an email address to a friend for which I have a recipient defined, and it's nice to be able to just Insert Recipient in the text where I'm typing. Paste as Quotation is also useful when you're pulling several messages together in one reply, although I would like the capability to easily specify the quote character, which is a > sign by default (and without a space between it and the first character of the quoted text, which bothers me a bit).

Note

Actually, you can specify the quote character, but it requires editing Eudora or your Eudora Settings file with ResEdit. In fact, you can change a ton of Eudora defaults with ResEdit. Look in the Eudora Q&A stack for the details:

```
ftp://ftp.qualcomm.com/quest/mac/eudora/documentation/eudora-qa.hqx
```

The only major fault of Eudora's text entry environment is that it doesn't accept more than approximately 32K of text; if you want to send a message longer than that, you must attach a text file to the email message. This particular limitation is in fact the only reason that I don't use Eudora for all of my email. I often want to send messages longer than 32K, and most of the times the information I want to put in those messages doesn't exist by itself in a file that I could easily attach to the message.

In any event, back at the New Mail window, clicking on the Queue button in the New Mail window queues the message for delivery (this is because I unchecked the Immediate Send switch when configuring Eudora). If you work on a network, instead of via PPP as I do, you may want to send all of your mail immediately, at which point that Queue button changes to Send.

Note

I think that even if I were directly connected to the Internet all the time, I'd keep Eudora set to queue messages. While Eudora is sending a message you cannot do anything else in the program (hey, there's a feature request!), and it might be rather distracting to have it continually interrupting other tasks to send the message I just finished typing.

Because I also have the Send on Check switch turned on, if I go to the File menu and choose Check Mail (making sure my PPP connection is active or it will connect automatically when Eudora tries to contact my host machine), Eudora connects to my POP server to receive any waiting mail, and then connects to my SMTP server to send my queued mail.

Note

If Eudora is interrupted while receiving mail, it can sometimes leave your POP mailbox in a locked state, preventing you from receiving any more mail until it's unlocked. You can fix this by telnetting to your account and killing a specific *process, which sounds bad but is quite easy. It's explained well in the Eudora Q&A stack. If you use Northwest Nexus, you can telnet to your account and at the Unix command line, type **pop-lock** to solve this problem.*

If I only want to send mail, I can choose Send Queued Messages, also from the File menu, at which point Eudora only connects to the SMTP server to send messages and ignores any messages that might be waiting to come in.

Note

There are a couple of small utility programs that can notify you when you receive new mail, MacBiff and NotifyMail. I've used neither, since I'm not permanently connected to the Internet, but they may be worth checking out if you don't want to have to tell Eudora to check your mail frequently.

If the In Box isn't open already (another preferences switch makes it open when new mail arrives), open it from the Message menu by choosing In (see figure 13.6).

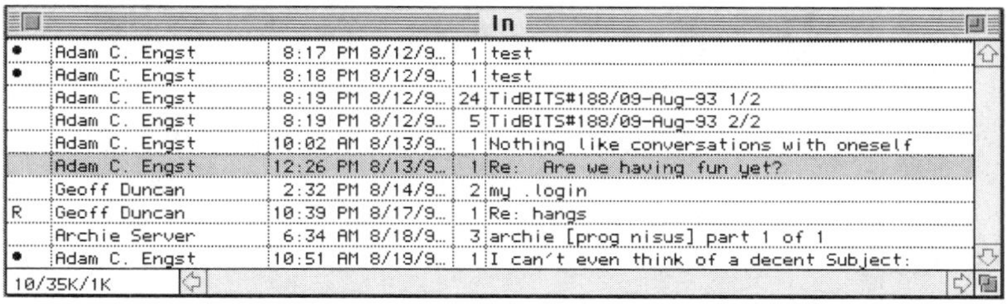

●	Adam C. Engst	8:17 PM 8/12/9...	1	test
●	Adam C. Engst	8:18 PM 8/12/9...	1	test
	Adam C. Engst	8:19 PM 8/12/9...	24	TidBITS#188/09-Aug-93 1/2
	Adam C. Engst	8:19 PM 8/12/9...	5	TidBITS#188/09-Aug-93 2/2
	Adam C. Engst	10:02 AM 8/13/9...	1	Nothing like conversations with oneself
	Adam C. Engst	12:26 PM 8/13/9...	1	Re: Are we having fun yet?
	Geoff Duncan	2:32 PM 8/14/9...	2	my login
R	Geoff Duncan	10:39 PM 8/17/9...	1	Re: hangs
	Archie Server	6:34 AM 8/18/9...	3	archie [prog nisus] part 1 of 1
●	Adam C. Engst	10:51 AM 8/19/9...	1	I can't even think of a decent Subject:

Figure 13.6 Eudora In box window

Eudora's mailboxes, which all look the same, provide a clean display of your mail. A status and priority column at the left edge of the window displays various characters to indicate which messages you haven't read, which you have replied to, which you've forwarded, redirected, and, in your Out Box, which have been sent. Some programs mark deleted messages in this way too, but Eudora instead copies deleted messages to a Trash mailbox available in the Mailbox menu.

The next column is the name of the sender, followed by the time and date, size of the message in kilobytes, and subject of the message. In the lower left corner of the window is an indicator that shows the number of messages in the mailbox, amount of space on disk it takes up, and amount of space that is wasted. You can recover the wasted space by choosing Compact Mailboxes from the Special menu.

Double-clicking on any message opens the message window (see figure 13.7).

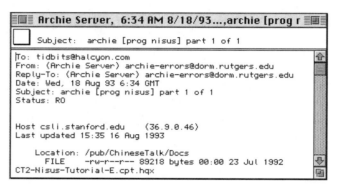

Figure 13.7   *Eudora Message window*

The Eudora Message window is a simple display window with the Subject at the top and a Priority pop-up menu that you can use to mark messages for your own reference, which is a good way to sort them. You can select and find text in the window, but you cannot change it. Again, my only complaint about the way Eudora handles incoming messages is that it cannot display more than approximately 32K of text in a window, so it chops longer messages into two or more pieces, which can be irritating.

Note

Like many other settings in Eudora, you can modify the size at which Eudora splits messages using ResEdit—check the Q&A stack for details on which strings in Eudora or its settings file to modify. I've set Eudora's chunk size higher than normal, to approximately 31K, which ensures that TidBITS always arrives in one piece.

Luckily, Eudora can save multiple selected messages to a single file, removing the header information in the process so that there's no header garbage in the middle of the file. Simply select all the messages you want concatenated into a single file, and choose Save As from the File menu.

With a message open, you can use the items in the Message menu to Reply, Forward, Redirect, or Delete the current message (see figure 13.8).

Message	
New Message	⌘N
Reply	⌘R
Forward	
Redirect	
Send Again	
New Message To	▶
Reply To	▶
Forward To	▶
Redirect To	▶
Queue Message	⌘E
Change Queueing...	
Attach Document...	⌘H
Delete	⌘D

Figure 13.8   Eudora Message menu

Most of the items in the Message menu are self-explanatory, but Redirect is an interesting and useful command. When you forward a message to someone else via Eudora, your address becomes the Reply-To address. However, if you want the original sender's address to remain as the Reply-To address, you use Redirect. That way, when the person you're redirecting to receives the message and replies, that reply goes to the original sender, not back to you.

Special Features

Eudora's clever touches abound. For instance, the program comes set to run in 371K of RAM, which is extremely low these days. In addition, if you choose About Eudora from the Apple menu, Eudora tells you the minimum amount of memory it should have. Should your mailboxes fill up to the point where Eudora needs more memory, it's good about warning you ahead of time and suggesting a size that will support the new requirements.

Steve Dorner must have had fun writing Eudora's dialog boxes. Many of them are, shall I say, less than serious. For instance, I started typing with a mailbox window open in Eudora (I'd forgotten that I hadn't switched over to Nisus on my second monitor), and Eudora beeped at me a couple of times and then opened a dialog saying, "Unfortunately, no one is listening to keystrokes at the moment. You may as well stop typing." I far prefer such human touches like this to dialogs that say, "Text entry not allowed," or some such terse phrase.

Eudora can sort mailboxes on status, priority (which you set), sender, date, and subject. This is a helpful feature for anyone who receives a significant amount of email. And, for those who receive tons of email, definitely get Eudora 2.0 so that you can take advantage of the automatic filtering feature that moves messages into different mailboxes and sorts them according to information gleaned from the headers.

Using Eudora's Transfer menu, you can instantly move one or more messages to any of your mailboxes, and you can create any number of them by simply choosing New from the Transfer menu (you can also create and manage them with the Mailboxes command in the Special menu). Eudora mailboxes can be hierarchical, and are in the same format as the Unix mail mailboxes, so you can download a Unix mailbox and read it with Eudora. InterCon's UUCP/Connect uses the same format. I've switched mailboxes between it and Eudora on numerous occasions as well.

Note

Ken Kirksey wrote a C program called udora that can send a Eudora Out box via Unix mail (if all you have is a Unix terminal access account), because you can manually download your Unix mailbox to read in Eudora with no modifications. You can find udora at:

```
ftp://ftp.tidbits.com/pub/tidbits/tisk/tcp/mail/eudora-offline-reader-unix.shar
```

Eudora supports a number of Apple events, and many people have used Frontier and AppleScript to add functionality to Eudora through scripting. You can peruse some of those scripts in:

```
ftp://ftp.qualcomm.com/quest/mac/eudora/scripts/
```

If you create multiple different settings files, different people can use the same copy of Eudora to send and receive their personal email. This setup is handy if a number of people all share the same computer but don't want to share the same email account ("Hey, no poking about in my email!"). Eudora's ability to launch using different settings files is also the secret to how it's used in large universities. Students get a POP account and a Eudora Settings file that's configured for them on a floppy disk. Whenever they use a public Mac hooked to the campus network, they double-click on their Eudora Settings file, which launches a copy of Eudora over the network (saving the space on the floppy disk). All of their mail comes down to the floppy disk, which they can then read on any other Mac that has Eudora on it.

Finally, although official technical support over the phone only comes with Eudora 2.0, Steve Dorner and other expert Eudora users provide extremely good support online in the newsgroup **comp.sys.mac.comm**. If you have a simple question, ask there before anywhere else (but use the balloon help and the manual before that). Eudora's manual is also excellent. Look in:

```
ftp://ftp.qualcomm.com/quest/mac/eudora/documentation/
```

Overall Evaluation

Although perhaps not perfect, you must have Eudora. That's why I've included it on the disk. Aside from the 32K limitations on messages, I can say almost nothing ill about Eudora. However, any such quibbles are easily outweighed by Eudora's significant capabilities, some of which are relatively unusual, such as the capability to queue up mail and send it all at once, essential for anyone using SLIP or PPP.

In my opinion, Eudora simply is *the* way to go for MacTCP-based email (unless perhaps you are at a university—MIT, for example—which has created its own MacTCP email program, you may want to stick with the homegrown program).

Administrative Details

Eudora has been translated into Swedish and a number of other languages, including French, Finnish (by Risto Virtanen), and Japanese.

Eudora 1.4.3 is free, and comes courtesy of the University of Illinois and QUALCOMM. It is included on the disk that comes with this book, and you can retrieve it from the Internet at:

```
ftp://ftp.tidbits.com/pub/tidbits/tisk/tcp/mail/eudora-143.hqx
```

```
ftp://ftp.qualcomm.com/quest/mac/eudora/1.4/eudora143.hqx
```

Eudora 2.0.3 costs $65 for an individual copy, or $99 for Eudora 2.0.3 and Spellswell. Prices drop quickly from there, depending on how many copies you want to buy, so if you're outfitting a couple of people in an office, check with QUALCOMM for the exact discounts. You can get more information from QUALCOMM via email at **eudora-sales@qualcomm.com**, or at:

QUALCOMM Inc.
c/o Eudora Package
10555 Sorrento Valley Road
San Diego, CA 92121
800-2-EUDORA

Other MacTCP Email Programs

Although I like Eudora, you can try out a number of other email programs. Most of them, including Eudora originally, were created at a university and thus are free. I'm sure I've missed a few, but I discuss the ones I know about and which work without any unusual software on the host (I'm assuming that POP is relatively widespread, because without POP you cannot use even Eudora). I'll try to post most of these programs on `ftp.tidbits.com`, but some of them may have distribution restrictions, and those you'll have to find at the original sites.

Iride

Iride is (or, as the documentation says, will be once it's sufficiently finished) a MIME mailer for the Macintosh. I don't know what its name stands for, but the program transmits multimedia mail via the Internet. Iride was developed as part of an Italian project to integrate multimedia mail with hospital data, primarily the transmission of medical images. Iride supports a number of different MIME data types, including plain text, audio, and GIF images.

Iride feels slow and unfinished, and short of its MIME support, currently has no features to particularly recommend it. Since the first edition, it doesn't appear that Iride has been updated at all, so I cannot recommend that you spend too much time investigating it, especially now that Eudora supports MIME.

LeeMail

Lee Fyock's $10 shareware LeeMail poses one major problem for many people. Because it is primarily only an SMTP mailer and only minimally supports POP for receiving email, LeeMail must be running at all times to receive email (luckily it uses only 300K of RAM by default). In addition, you must be connected to the network at all times, which is fine for people using a network, but for those of us using SLIP or PPP, it's simply not going to work well. The problem is, quite simply, that LeeMail tries to send messages as soon as you're finished creating them, which wreaks havoc if your Mac must connect to the Internet each time you finish a message. I expect that Lee will enhance LeeMail at some point to support message queuing, which would make it significantly more useful for SLIP and PPP users.

Note

The only public access Internet provider that I know of that works in a manner compatible with LeeMail is Demon Systems, a large Internet provider in the U.K., whose machines watch for incoming SLIP connections and then send SMTP mail to the machine.

Those problems aside, LeeMail is a simple program that sports several nice features such as support for multiple users, aliases, automatically decoded attachments, and audio notifications of new mail. LeeMail can hide its windows when you send it to the background, auto-quote text when replying to messages, and also supports multiple mailboxes. The current version of LeeMail, 2.0.4, adds minimal support for POP, although the documentation admits that it's not ideal as of yet. Lee plans to beef up the POP support in the future. LeeMail is available at:

```
ftp://ftp.tidbits.com/pub/tidbits/tisk/tcp/lee-mail-204.hqx
```

There's a version localized for French available at:

```
ftp://chs.cusd.claremont.edu/pub/leemail/lee-mail-204-fr.hqx
```

POPmail

Created by programmers at the University of Minnesota (the Gopher folks) for internal use, POPmail is a free email program that provides much of Eudora's feature set and a few extra features, but without the same clean implementation or the capability to queue messages, which limits its utility when using a SLIP or PPP connection (it tries to connect as soon as you attempt to send a message you've created).

POPmail has many nice touches, though, including a message browser mailbox window with command icons, the capability to create groups of users for simple distribution lists, and support for multiple users on the same program through multiple settings files (see figure 13.9).

POPmail sports compatibility with the older POP2 protocol (most everything else, including Eudora, uses the current POP3 protocol), and with the newer and perhaps more advanced IMAP (Interactive Mail Access Protocol) protocol, which does basically the same thing as POP in terms of storing your incoming email on a host computer until you call in to retrieve it. The utility of working with the older POP2 protocol is that, unlike POP3, a Macintosh POP2 server exists, so you can use a Mac to serve mail out to users. POP3 requires a workstation or Unix machine of some sort, because no one has written a POP3 implementation for the Mac yet, despite many pleas for such a program on Usenet. The Macintosh POP2 server also comes from the University of Minnesota, and is called MailStop.

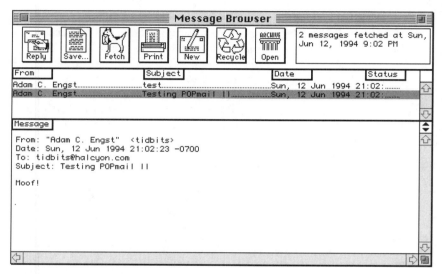

Figure 13.9   *POPmail Message Browser*

POPmail can work with a separate application called HyperSpeller to check the spelling in your message before you send it. You have to purchase HyperSpeller, though, and the documentation doesn't provide details on that. If you need to email files to someone else, POPmail supports enclosures and automatically binhexes files before sending them. Finally, if you are connecting over a slow modem or are expecting a large message, POPmail has a Preview feature that enables you to peruse only the header and first few lines of the file.

Other than the complete lack of a queuing system so that you can write messages while off-line and send them all at once later, POPmail is a decent application. The interface feels clunky, but nothing you cannot get used to. It's certainly miles ahead of many of the other email programs. If you have a bunch of Macs on a network and have MacTCP installed but no POP server available, the combination of MailStop's POP2 implementation and POPmail might become attractive quickly. You can find POPmail II on the Internet at:

```
ftp://ftp.tidbits.com/pub/tidbits/tisk/tcp/mail/pop-mail-2-209.hqx
```

TechMail

Of all the other email programs available, TechMail probably comes the closest to competing with Eudora. Just like POPmail and Eudora, it was developed at a university (MIT, in this instance) and may be freely distributed.

TechMail supports queuing messages, so that you can compose multiple messages off-line and send them later. One neat feature enables you to check your POP mailbox to see how many messages are waiting and how much disk space they take (useful for determining whether you have time to download them). As an added bonus—and like Eudora—TechMail can finger people while you're logged on, a popular feature at a university.

Note

MIT has also released a version of TechMail called TechMail-S that has its own internal SLIP support. If you don't have a SLIP implementation, therefore, TechMail-S can perform that part of the low-level connection on its own. If you have InterSLIP, MacPPP, or one of the other SLIP or PPP programs, the standard version of TechMail works fine.

My main complaints with TechMail are that it feels slow when I'm sending messages, and I think its interface could use some help—especially in the configuration dialog boxes (where it's never clear what OK and Cancel really do), and in some of the menu names (such as Local for all the stuff dealing with email).

Overall, TechMail is a good program, and it has a spiffy startup screen. Also, it's free. What more do you want? You can find the latest version of TechMail at:

```
ftp://net-dist.mit.edu//pub/mac/techmail/techmail-2.2.hqx
```

Maileficus

Continuing on in the field of MacTCP-based email programs that come from universities, we hit Maileficus, from Arizona State University. As do the rest, Maileficus uses SMTP and POP to send and receive mail, and includes many features such as multiple mailboxes, aliases, message notification, signatures, and the like. However, Maileficus cannot queue messages for later sending, without which it has little use for the average SLIP or PPP user. Maileficus requires a system extension for some reason, and it wouldn't load on my Mac, so I couldn't test it any further. You can find Maileficus at:

```
ftp://ftp.tidbits.com/pub/tidbits/tisk/tcp/mail/maileficus-30.hqx
```

MacPost

Although Lund University's MacPost isn't really of interest to the individual looking for email access to the Internet, if you have an AppleTalk network that has access to the Internet already, you may be interested in checking out the MacPost client and server program. The MacPost server runs on a Mac (one of the few that do) and serves mail to the clients using a proprietary protocol. That's not terribly interesting, but what is interesting is that the MacPost server can communicate with an SMTP server as well, thus opening the doors to the Internet for the MacPost clients. I know little about MacPost and haven't tried to hack around it much, but even though the MacPost server uses SMTP, the clients only know how to talk to the server, so you couldn't use a different SMTP client program, such as Eudora. If you're interested, take a look. You can find MacPost on the Internet at either of the following:

```
ftp://ftp.tidbits.com/pub//tidbits/tisk/tcp/mail/mac-post-client-us-10b10.hqx
```

```
ftp://ftp.tidbits.com/pub/tidbits/tisk/tcp/mail/mac-post-server-10b9.hqx
```

Mail*Link Internet for PowerTalk

In the fall of 1993, Apple released System 7 Pro with PowerTalk, which is part of AOCE, or Apple Open Collaboration Environment. The aim of AOCE is to provide mail services to all Macintosh applications (although they must be rewritten to support it) and to bring email to the Macintosh desktop. To that end, PowerTalk creates a single mailbox icon on your desktop, along with various other icons for other network services. Once PowerTalk is installed, you can exchange email with any other PowerTalk users on your network, or, using specially written gateways, to users on any other email service.

Or at least, that's the idea.

In my opinion, PowerTalk suffers from a number of serious problems, the most serious of which is that by integrating it into the Finder, Apple essentially made it as clumsy to use as the Finder. In an email program such as Eudora, it's easy to select several messages at the same time and delete them quickly, or move them to another mailbox with a single menu option. In PowerTalk those actions are tedious and time-consuming. To erase messages from your mailbox, you must drag them to the Trash, which is certainly obvious enough, but becomes tiresome if you receive more than a few messages each day. If you want to file a message in a mailbox, you must instead copy it to a normal Macintosh folder (at which point it loses mail information such as Sender and Date) and then delete it in another step, since messages are only *copied*, not *moved*, out of the PowerTalk mailbox.

I could go on about the problems with PowerTalk for some time, since I depend on email for everything I do, and the prospect of using it for more than a couple of messages each day makes me cringe. However, the other problem that has faced PowerTalk users is that gateways have been slow to arrive. There's one for CompuServe in testing right now, and a few for QuickMail and Microsoft Mail have also appeared (some from StarNine as well), but the main one of interest for this book is StarNine's Mail*Link Internet for PowerTalk gateway, which enables PowerTalk to send email to the Internet using SMTP and receive Internet mail using POP3.

At the moment, you must have a direct connection to the Internet for Mail*Link Internet for PowerTalk to work properly. That's because it attempts to open MacTCP on every reboot unless you tell PowerTalk that you're on the road and away from a connection with the new I'm At command in the Finder's Special menu. With some implementations of SLIP and PPP, that automatic connection may not work or may even crash your Mac, as it did mine. If you can manage to tell PowerTalk that you're on the road quickly enough, Mail*Link Internet for PowerTalk won't attempt to open MacTCP, and all is well. Then, when you want to send and receive mail, you establish your connection using SLIP or PPP, tell PowerTalk that you're at work, and Mail*Link Internet for PowerTalk does its stuff. When you're finished, you tell PowerTalk you're on the road again, and all is well—unless of course, something crashes while you're connected, because then you must go through the whole process of setting your location. That was a massive pain when I tried it. To its credit, StarNine doesn't claim that Mail*Link Internet for PowerTalk works with a dialup SLIP or PPP account.

StarNine has said that it plans to address this limitation in Mail*Link Internet for PowerTalk in version 2.0, due out sometime in the summer of 1994, at which point this program will become a necessity if you use and like both PowerTalk and Internet mail. In the meantime, you can retrieve a time-limited evaluation copy of Mail*Link Internet for PowerTalk from:

```
ftp://ftp.starnine.com/pub/evals/personal-gws/pt-inet/mail_link_ptinet.sea.hqx
```

From what I've heard from people using PowerTalk, those who have just switched from an ugly mainframe email program love it, especially if they don't receive all that much email. People like me who are used to sophisticated Macintosh email programs and who receive tons of mail (I can easily receive 100 messages in a day), wonder what was in the drinking water down in Cupertino at Apple headquarters.

I'm pinning my hopes for PowerTalk on Eudora, in fact, because if Steve Dorner adds PowerTalk support to Eudora, PowerTalk's capability to retrieve all your email from a number of different sources (eventually), will make it useful as a transport agent even if its capabilities as a mail reader range from minimal to painful.

So, although I cannot recommend PowerTalk much at all, it's probably here to stay, and I hope Apple does some serious revamping of its interface soon. If you do use PowerTalk and have a dedicated connection to your SMTP and POP servers, Mail*Link Internet is the way to go. You can buy it from StarNine for $65. For more information, send them email at **info@starnine.com**, or contact:

StarNine Technologies, Inc.
2550 9th Street, Suite 112
Berkeley, CA 94710
510-649-4949
510-548-0393 (fax)

BlitzMail

I didn't intend to talk much about email programs that use non-standard protocols, but given Dartmouth College's outstanding record in developing Macintosh software, I figure I should mention BlitzMail briefly. More than 95 percent of Dartmouth's students use email, in large part because of BlitzMail, which reportedly has an excellent interface. BlitzMail also supports Apple events and AppleScript recording, which is still uncommon. I haven't seen it in action, mostly because it requires that you run the BlitzMail server software, and that, in turn, requires that you run it on a NeXT workstation (you know, the ones that Steve Jobs made for a few years after leaving Apple) or a DEC Alpha workstation.

I thought this limitation was a little ridiculous, until Jim Matthews, a programmer at Dartmouth and creator of Fetch (see later in this chapter), told me that last year Dartmouth supported 11,000 email accounts on only five NeXT machines (since then they've added another DEC Alpha to the mix), which is incredible. So maybe BlitzMail is pretty cool, I don't know. If you're a system administrator-type and you're interested, you can find more information on BlitzMail at:

---

ftp://ftp.dartmouth.edu/pub/mac/BlitzMail/For-Non-Dartmouth-Use/About_BlitzMail

---

Usenet Newsreaders

The sections on email were easy to write because I have a strong opinion about which email program I think is best. In the realm of newsreaders for Usenet, the field is a little smaller, but much stronger. I currently know of eight MacTCP-based newsreading solutions, and three of them are neck and neck. I finally settled on using NewsWatcher, developed by John Norstad of Disinfectant fame, but there's a lot to like about Nuntius, from Peter Speck, and InterNews, from Roger Brown of Dartmouth. In the end, I think you must try all three and decide for yourself because each one brings a different interface philosophy and design to the task of reading news.

Note

> *As this book was going to press, Northwest Nexus added a new news server at* **news.halcyon.com**. *Although the new name makes much more sense (and the new server is faster), I had no time to redo the screenshots for the book. Thus, if you use Northwest Nexus, please use* **news.halcyon.com** *as the news server and don't use* **nwfocus.wa.com**. *Sorry for any confusion this may cause.*

The big question that continues to be asked about Usenet newsreaders relates to the fact that most of them require you to be connected to the Internet while reading news. Many people would prefer an off-line solution that would download all the subject lines in certain specified groups, let you mark some for retrieval, and then log in again and retrieve the actual articles. Never fear, there are two possibilities here: NewsFetcher, which is a HyperCard stack that works with Easy View to display articles (more on it in a bit); and a newsreader that isn't out yet, and whose author doesn't even want it talked about until he considers it acceptable. This other newsreader (I've tested early versions) may become incredibly popular soon after it's released, because it's by far the best off-line newsreader I've seen on the Mac (the other is Synergy's VersaTerm-Link). Keep an eye on the nets, on my World-Wide Web home page, and in *TidBITS*, and I'll be sure to announce the release of this newsreader when it finally happens.

Note

> *Since you can try all the main newsreaders for free, I recommend that you form your own opinion and don't clog the nets with questions asking which newsreaders people like best. Newsreaders are very personal programs, and only you can decide which is right for you.*

NewsWatcher

Although I was wavering when I wrote the first edition of this book, I've since committed to using NewsWatcher to read news. The major challenge that the newsreaders face is presenting a clean and quick method of navigating through gobs of information. Interface is all-important (and a purely personal choice, of course), but raw speed doesn't hurt either, and NewsWatcher feels fast.

Steve Falkenburg, of Apple, first created NewsWatcher, and John Norstad later picked it up to continue development, aided by a team of volunteers from around the net.

Installation and Setup

NewsWatcher requires three pieces of information from you before you can start reading news, and would like five. The first time you launch NewsWatcher, a dialog opens, asking for the addresses of your news server and your mail server (see figure 13.10).

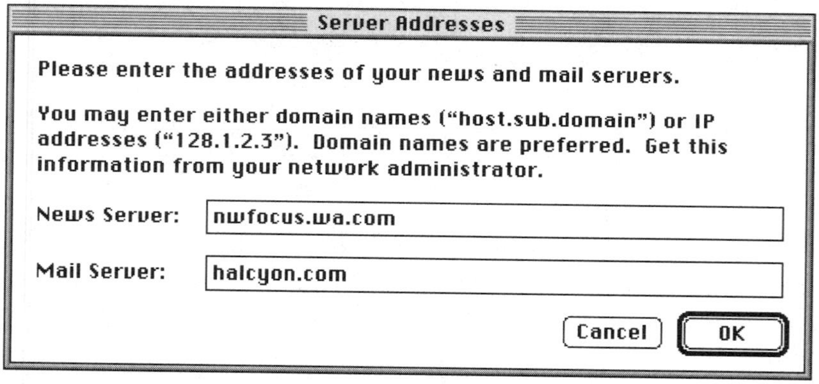

Figure 13.10   NewsWatcher Server configuration dialog

The only way to figure out these addresses is to ask your system administrator. After you fill them in and click the OK button, NewsWatcher presents another, similar dialog that asks for your full name, your organization, and your email address. It only requires the last of the three, but there's no reason not to input the others (see figure 13.11).

After you enter all that information, NewsWatcher goes out to your server and downloads the Full Group List, the big list of all the newsgroups available on your site. Downloading this list takes a long time, possibly as long as 10 or 20 minutes over a 2,400 bps modem! Be prepared to wait, but don't worry. As long as you don't throw out the NewsWatcher Preferences file in your Preferences folder, NewsWatcher never again has to download all the groups.

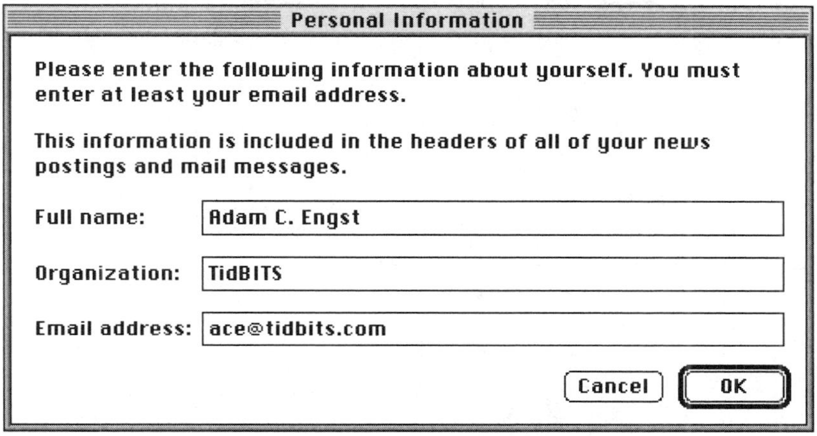

```
╔═══════════════════════════════════════════════════════╗
║              Personal Information                     ║
╠═══════════════════════════════════════════════════════╣
║  Please enter the following information about yourself. You must
║  enter at least your email address.
║
║  This information is included in the headers of all of your news
║  postings and mail messages.
║
║  Full name:      │Adam C. Engst                        │
║
║  Organization:   │TidBITS                              │
║
║  Email address:  │ace@tidbits.com                      │
║
║                              ( Cancel )   ║  OK  ║
╚═══════════════════════════════════════════════════════╝
```

Figure 13.11 *NewsWatcher Personal Information dialog*

After you have the massively long list of all the groups onscreen, from the File menu, choose New Group Window. NewsWatcher then opens a small, empty window. Scroll through the Full Group List (if you accidentally close it or want to add groups again later, look for Show Full Group List under the Windows menu) and drag interesting groups over to the small, empty window. Don't worry about the order; you can drag groups within that window to put them in the right order after you're finished subscribing to groups. Eventually, you have a nice set of groups to read. From the File menu, choose Save and then name your group list whatever you want (see figure 13.12).

That's about it. You're ready to read news, although you may want to configure some more preferences first. If you select Preferences from the File menu, NewsWatcher presents you with a dialog containing some general options. At the top of the dialog is a pop-up menu that lists other types of preferences you can set, such as where to save files, your signature for postings, the font and size for viewing articles and lists, and various other settings.

Note

My favorite preference is the one in General Options that lets you use the keypad keys for single-key navigating of messages.

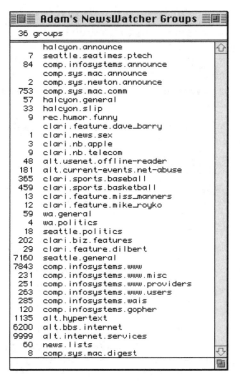

Figure 13.12   NewsWatcher Group List

Basic Usage

To read a newsgroup in your list, double-click on it or use one of the keypad shortcuts (if you have them enabled). NewsWatcher opens another window containing the subjects of all the articles in the group, and alongside each subject is either a dash or a triangle and number (see figure 13.13).

The dash indicates that the article is the only one in the thread, the triangle indicates that there are more than one, and the number indicates how many articles are in that thread. You can click on the triangle to show the other articles, just as you click on a triangle in the System 7 Finder to display a folder's contents. I generally leave the option that displays author names turned off, because NewsWatcher draws windows much faster that way. If you choose not to download author names, there's no reason to expand a thread with the triangle control since all the articles have the same subject and thus look identical.

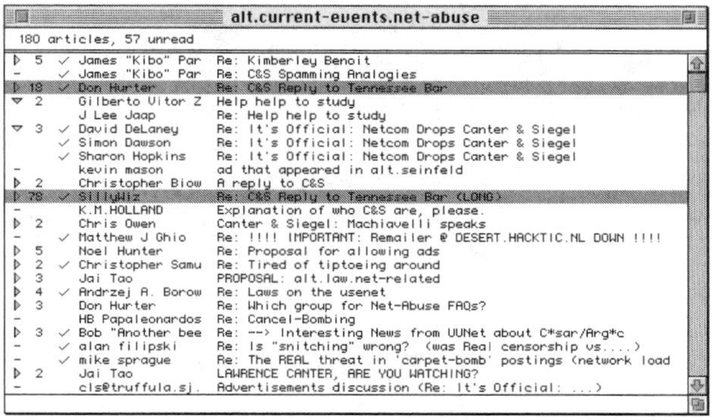

Figure 13.13 *NewsWatcher Newsgroup window*

Double-clicking on an article subject in the Newsgroup window opens a window that NewsWatcher sizes to prevent unnecessary scrolling (see figure 13.14).

Figure 13.14 *NewsWatcher article window*

With an article window open, you can go to the next article, next thread, or next group (marking the current group as read) with keyboard shortcuts or, if you have them turned on in the preferences, a keypad shortcut. I prefer using the keypad shortcuts because reading news should be an easy process, and using a Command key combination is too hard for hundreds of repetitions. That's especially true for those of us with repetitive stress injuries.

In NewsWatcher, you also can reply to an article via email or post a follow-up to the newsgroup using commands in the News menu. In the current version of NewsWatcher, John added useful icons at the top of the reply window that let you specify if the reply should go to the newsgroup, to the poster or another email address that you can enter, or to your email account if you wanted to save a copy yourself (see figure 13.15).

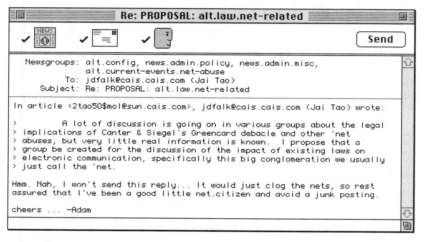

Figure 13.15   NewsWatcher reply window

When you're back in a newsgroup window, you also can quickly mark articles as read or unread, which can be handy for getting through a group quickly.

Note

You might try selecting all the articles in the group with Select All, then holding down the Command key, and clicking on the ones you want to read to deselect them. Then, from the News menu, choose Mark Read, which puts a check mark next to each of the still-selected uninteresting articles. Now you can select the first article in the group and read straight through without being bothered by any of the uninteresting stuff. Pretty slick, although it would be even nicer to do this process forward, that is, select the articles and threads you want to read, and then read them without seeing the rest.

Special Features

NewsWatcher feels fast, clean, and easy to use, which is the result of nice touches at every level. I cannot live without keypad shortcuts or the Spacebar shortcut that moves you to the next screen and then to the next unread message, just as in a Unix newsreader. I also like the ability to move through the massive full group list by typing the first few characters of each part of the newsgroup name.

NewsWatcher has an interesting feature to open referenced articles, which theoretically allows you to go back in a thread, although early articles have expired. All you must do is option click the message-ID if one exists at the top of the article, although many people edit them out. Still, a nice idea.

In the most recent release, John has enhanced this option-click on a message-ID feature, so that option-clicking on an email address opens a new mail window set to send email to that person. Even better, if you option-click on an FTP URL that someone has included in a posting, NewsWatcher calls either Anarchie or Fetch (you set it) and resolves the URL by retrieving the file or directory. In the future, John plans to support the same feature for Gopher (working with TurboGopher) and for the World-Wide Web (working with Mosaic and MacWeb). This is one of the more exciting features in NewsWatcher, and I look forward to seeing how it evolves in the future.

John has recently added automatic extraction code to NewsWatcher, which enables it to automatically download and decode binary files that are posted, usually in BinHex or uuencoded form.

For those of you who read news on a Unix machine using rn or nn at work and perhaps use NewsWatcher at home to read news on the same machine, NewsWatcher has a feature that enables you to use the same **.newsrc** file so that you don't have to duplicate reading effort.

Note

The Remote Host Information preferences controls this feature for retrieving the **.newsrc** *file from a Unix shell account. Don't worry about those preferences if you don't also read news under Unix and wish to share the* **.newsrc** *file.*

Overall Evaluation

The only real complaint I can think of in regard to NewsWatcher is that the text window limits prevents you from posting messages larger than 32K. Chalk up another one for Apple's limited TextEdit routines. You can read messages larger than 32K, though, since NewsWatcher only displays 32K at a time and provides a horizontal slider bar to reach additional 32K chunks of the same message.

Overall, though, what can I say? John Norstad has once again provided the Macintosh community with a great freeware program. John's free Disinfectant is wonderful, but I certainly hope that people have more occasion to read news than to search for viruses.

However, I shouldn't imply that NewsWatcher is perfect or, more accurately, complete. John has big plans for NewsWatcher, but because it's a labor of love, he works at his own pace and implements features that he wants or feels that the program needs in order to be complete. Because of this, I always enjoy reading the To Do document, listing all the wishes and requests for future versions, including my big favorites, off-line reading and message filtering based on the contents of the messages or headers.

Administrative Details

NewsWatcher (an earlier version only, so far) has been translated into French by Jean-Pierre Kuypers, as well as into Japanese and Chinese. NewsWatcher is free, and you can retrieve the latest version from either of the following:

```
ftp://ftp.tidbits.com/pub/tidbits/tisk/tcp/news-watcher-20b1.hqx
```

```
ftp://ftp.acns.nwu.edu/pub/newswatcher/newswatcher2.0b1.sea.hqx
```

InterNews

Continuing with the excellent newsreaders, I come to InterNews, from Dartmouth College. Programmed by Steve Maker and Roger Brown, InterNews is yet another interface for reading news, presenting you with a three-paned window that displays a list of newsgroups at the top (or side, in version 1.0.1), a list of subjects in the selected group in the middle, and the articles in a selected thread at the bottom. In addition, InterNews works on the concept of the subscription, which is a personalized set of newsgroups. You can create any number of subscriptions, so I have, for instance, a subscription for Mac groups, a subscription for ClariNet groups that I read, and so on. Subscriptions work well for organizing your reading, and can make starting to read news less daunting than staring at a long list of all the groups you read.

Installation and Setup

Double-click on InterNews to launch it for the first time. A Site Configuration dialog box immediately opens. You must fill it in before you can read any news (see figure 13.16).

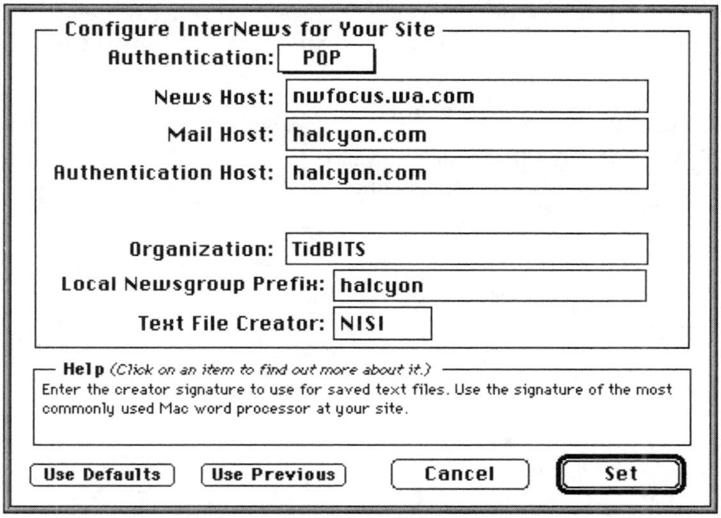

```
┌─ Configure InterNews for Your Site ──────────┐
│         Authentication: [ POP  ]             │
│                                              │
│            News Host: [nwfocus.wa.com      ] │
│                                              │
│            Mail Host: [halcyon.com         ] │
│                                              │
│  Authentication Host: [halcyon.com         ] │
│                                              │
│                                              │
│          Organization: [TidBITS            ] │
│                                              │
│  Local Newsgroup Prefix: [halcyon          ] │
│                                              │
│      Text File Creator: [NISI]               │
│                                              │
│ ┌─ Help (Click on an item to find out more about it.) ─┐ │
│ │ Enter the creator signature to use for saved text files. Use the signature of the most │ │
│ │ commonly used Mac word processor at your site.        │ │
│ └───────────────────────────────────────────┘ │
│                                              │
│ [ Use Defaults ] [ Use Previous ]  [ Cancel ]  (( Set )) │
└──────────────────────────────────────────────┘
```

Figure 13.16   *InterNews Site Configuration dialog*

The Authentication pop-up menu is the most confusing part of this configuration process because you must ask your system administrator what sort of authentication your host provides. You also must find out the name of your news server, of course, so you may as well ask the system administrator that question at the same time, along with the name of the mail server. If you don't use authentication, InterNews doesn't let you send replies via email.

Note

> *Probably the easiest form of authentication is POP (although Unix or FTP might work equally as well), assuming that you have a POP account on a host machine. Simply use that machine and the userid and password that you would use to send email in Eudora, for instance; it should work fine.*

After you finish setting up this dialog with the news server and mail server information (you can always change it later by closing all windows and choosing Configure for Your Site from the Edit menu), InterNews connects to your news server and downloads the full list of groups, then sorts it before presenting you with the Subscriptions window. As you might expect, retrieving the full list of groups takes a long time, and sorting them is also slow.

Once InterNews presents you with the Subscriptions window, the only remaining configuration work comes with your preferences. From the Edit menu, choose Preferences. InterNews displays a large preferences dialog with a pop-up menu to configure different aspects of the program (see figure 13.17).

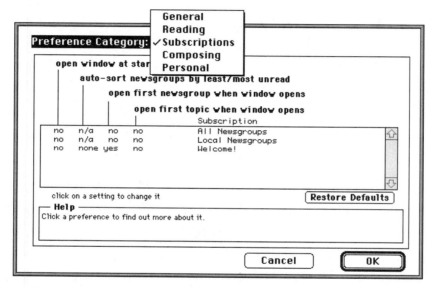

Figure 13.17   *InterNews Preferences dialog*

Although you want to go through each of these screens and fill them in with your preferences and personal information, the most interesting are the Subscriptions preferences shown in the screenshot. By clicking on any of the Yes/No markers in the matrix, you can modify the behavior of any subscription (if I had any personalized ones at this point, they would appear here too). It's a clever interface and a good idea.

After you set your preferences, it's time to subscribe to newsgroups. First, you must create your own subscription, so from the Subscriptions menu, choose New Subscription and then name the icon that InterNews creates. Double-click on it to open its window. Then double-click on the subscription labeled All Newsgroups. You must figure out how to show both windows on the screen at once. You can click on and drag down the double lines under the top pane to make it larger, and I highly recommend doing so, because scrolling through that list is hard enough as it is.

When you see an interesting group, click on it and drag it over to your personal subscription window. Keep clicking and dragging until you've subscribed to all the groups you want to for that subscription, and repeat the process as necessary until you have all the subscriptions you want (see figure 13.18).

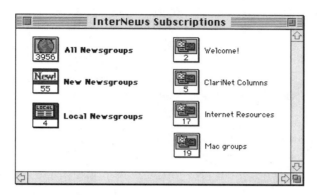

Figure 13.18   *InterNews Subscriptions window*

Double-clicking on any subscription opens the window for that subscription, and you can size the window and its panes so that you feel comfortable working with them. You can switch between two different layouts by clicking on the little icon in the upper right-hand corner of the window—I far prefer the layout that has the newsgroup list parallel to the subject list (see figure 13.19).

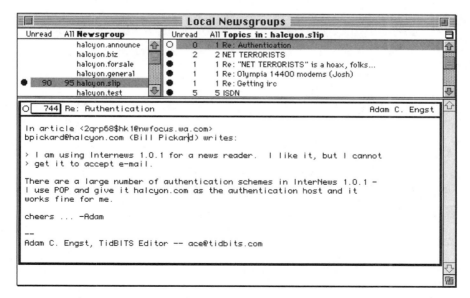

Figure 13.19   *InterNews Article window*

Basic Usage

Double-clicking on any newsgroup in the top, left-hand pane causes InterNews to retrieve the subjects for the articles in that newsgroup and place them in the top, right-hand pane. Then, double-clicking on any subject retrieves all the articles in that thread and places them in the bottom pane. You scroll using either the scroll bars or the Spacebar shortcut, and in the most recent release of InterNews, you can scroll the bottom pane while articles are being received from the NNTP server.

If you're reading a thread, each article that scrolls by in the bottom pane is selectable with the mouse. You must select an article specifically if you want to reply to or save that article. Because InterNews scrolls a bunch of articles through that bottom pane, the concept of selecting a full article in a list of articles is a little odd. With an article selected, though, you can do all the standard replying in mail or to the newsgroup. You also can forward an article to someone else via email, which I approve of, because I often seem to want to do that.

When replying, you can quote selected text and also insert a text file using commands in the Compose menu. On the whole, the message composition window is fairly standard looking, although it does have four radio buttons that enable you to change whether a message is an email or news message, which might help move flames into email rather than clutter newsgroups with them.

Special Features

Like NewsWatcher, InterNews can import and export `.newsrc` files so that you can easily synchronize your news reading between InterNews and a Unix newsreader. InterNews also sports a Windows menu that lists all your subscriptions along with the names of open windows (and a useful Send to Back command).

In the latest version of InterNews, new in the Windows menu, is an FTP Access command that brings up a small window into which you can type a full pathname for a file and a host, and select either Anarchie or Fetch to retrieve the file (see figure 13.20).

Like NewsWatcher, InterNews provides a shortcut for entering information into this box as well, by either selecting the URL and pressing Command-U or Option-clicking on the URL. If you Command-click on the URL, InterNews avoids the FTP Access dialog entirely and simply asks Anarchie or Fetch to retrieve the file. Slick stuff, and I hope to see this sort of feature appear in more programs, as well.

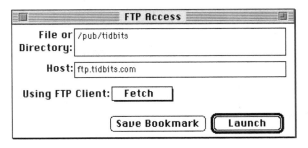

Figure 13.20   *InterNews FTP Access dialog*

Selecting any of your subscriptions from the Windows menu opens it immediately, saving you the trouble of closing all the other windows to get back to your subscriptions window. Finally, a Help item in the Windows menu provides excellent online help and tips for using InterNews, including the keyboard shortcuts that aren't otherwise documented.

Overall Evaluation

InterNews is a fine effort, and much of its interface looks slick and well-done. I continually have trouble with the concept of selecting an article from the bottom reading pane, although I suppose I would get used to it given enough time. Although InterNews has keyboard shortcuts for moving around (the left and right arrow keys move you to the previous and next newsgroup and the up and down arrow keys move you to the previous and next subject), enough different keys are involved that I find the capability somewhat clumsy. Perhaps it would help if you didn't have to press Return or Enter to open each newsgroup or subject after you selected one using the arrow keys.

One relatively serious limitation in InterNews is that because it uses the standard Apple TextEdit routines, you cannot receive (or, I presume, send) an article larger than 32K. Although sending is less of a big deal, there are many articles in Usenet larger than 32K and InterNews can't chunk the articles as can NewsWatcher.

I feel slightly guilty talking about InterNews in this negative fashion because it is a very good program, simply not one that happens to match my preferred method of reading news. It may fit your style better.

Administrative Details

InterNews is distributed under the same system as Fetch, which means that educational and nonprofit users can use it for free, and for commercial and government sites it's $25 shareware (with plenty of discounts for quantity—check the licensing information document that comes with InterNews for more details). You can find InterNews on the Internet at either of the following:

```
ftp://ftp.tidbits.com/pub/tidbits/tisk/tcp/internews-101.hqx
```

```
ftp://ftp.dartmouth.edu//pub/mac/InterNews_1.0.1.sea.hqx
```

Nuntius

The third of the heavy-hitting MacTCP-based newsreaders is Peter Speck's free Nuntius 1.2. Long a favorite of the Usenet crowd, Nuntius combines a Finder-like interface with some clever integration with other programs for mundane tasks such as email and text editing.

Installation and Setup

The first time you launch Nuntius, it quickly asks for your news server's address (which you get, of course, by bribing your system administrator with chocolate), and then proceeds to retrieve the entire list of newsgroups. With a neat twist, it also downloads the descriptions of all the groups, which become useful later on. Again, this long download happens only the first time you start Nuntius; the program is smart enough to keep that information around for later use.

After it has the entire list of groups, Nuntius opens two windows. One, called All Groups, contains a Finder-like outline of all the groups (see figure 13.21).

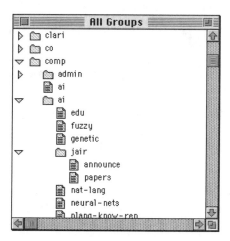

Figure 13.21   Nuntius All Groups window

This method of outlining the hierarchy of new newsgroups works better in some ways than the way NewsWatcher and InterNews list them in one big list, simply because the lists are smaller. However, if you know what newsgroup you want, say **comp.sys.mac.announce**, you must open the **comp** folder by clicking on its triangle and then open the **sys** folder and the **mac** folder before you see the **announce** newsgroup. It takes a while to open each folder and scroll down to the right spot to open the next one. Although typing a key takes you to a newsgroup starting with that letter, I find that feature slow and awkward.

The second window Nuntius opens is empty and is called Untitled group list 1. When you see an interesting group or groups (you can select more than one at a time) in Nuntius, as in NewsWatcher, you click on them and drag them into the Untitled group list 1 window (which you should immediately save with a different name as in figure 13.22).

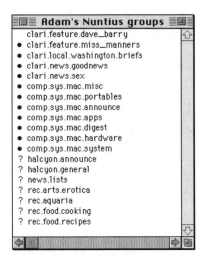

Figure 13.22 *Nuntius Group List window*

In figure 13.22, some of the newsgroups have bullets next to their names, indicating that they have new messages in them. Some newsgroups have question marks next to them because I took this screenshot as Nuntius was querying my news server to see which newsgroups had new articles. Only one group was empty, **clari.feature.dave_barry**, so that group has nothing next to it.

Note

Unfortunately, in the week before this book went to press, **clari.feature.dave_barry** *was removed from ClariNet by Knight-Ridder (the company that syndicates Dave Barry's columns), reportedly because of copyright violations. "...And somewhere men are laughing, and somewhere children shout; But there is no joy in Mudville—Dave Barry has pulled out."*

Although they are not necessary for you to start reading news, you can and should set a number of preferences in the Prefs menu (see figure 13.23).

Figure 13.23 *Nuntius Prefs menu*

Of the several preferences you can set, the most interesting are the Editing Articles and Mail items in the Prefs menu. They let you specify what program you want to use to edit your articles and what program you want to use to mail them out, although Nuntius currently supports only Eudora.

Basic Usage

As you might expect, double-clicking on a newsgroup name causes Nuntius to open the list of articles in that group. In an interesting and useful twist, Nuntius can open multiple groups at the same time. This feature is especially useful, because Nuntius doesn't seem to work as quickly as NewsWatcher. What you can do is start it opening a large group and then open a small group, and have that large group opening in the background as you read the articles in the small group. Even given NewsWatcher's speed, I'd like to see this feature migrate over, because it enables you to work more efficiently.

In any event, opening a newsgroup window displays a window listing the articles in the group (see figure 13.24).

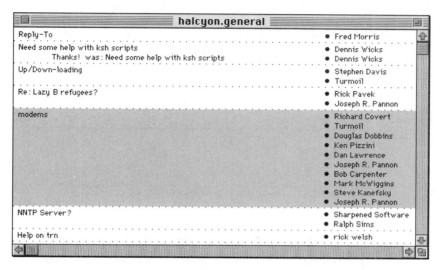

Figure 13.24   *Nuntius Newsgroup window*

The subject of each message appears on the left, unless the message is in the middle of a thread. This use of white space may seem like a waste, but I think it works well to indicate the relative size of threads. The names of the authors of each message appear to the right, preceded by bullets if that article is new. Double-clicking on a thread (and you cannot read just a single article in the middle of a thread) opens the article window (see figure 13.25).

Nuntius uses a custom interface for determining what you do and don't see, and it's another reason why you may prefer one newsreader over another. I have Nuntius set to open only the first article in the thread because there's no point in transferring all that data if the first article proves to be uninteresting. Opening threads of uninteresting articles is especially a problem over a slow link or with a large thread, although you can scroll through the article window as the program fills it. If you have a fast network connection, you probably don't care about this problem as much, and you can set Nuntius to open all articles when opening a thread.

You can select and open multiple threads in the newsgroup window, and you can navigate among them from the article window, either by using the right and left arrow keys or by using the arrows in the lower left of the article window. The down arrow in the article window takes you to the next thread, should you want to switch immediately.

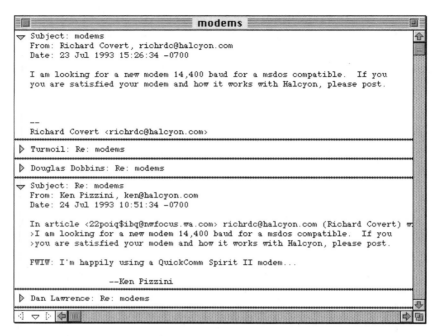

Figure 13.25   *Nuntius Article window*

My biggest problem with Nuntius is that I don't want to spend the time opening all the articles in a thread to begin with, but at the same time I want to open the triangles from the keyboard because clicking on them with the mouse is too much work for such a common action. I may be missing something, but I cannot find any way of opening the triangle this way in the extremely scanty documentation or in the good, but spotty, balloon help.

Perhaps the coolest aspect of using Nuntius comes when you want to reply to a letter or post a follow-up. Nuntius doesn't, in fact, know how to do much in terms of sending email or editing text; instead, it asks other applications to perform those tasks. So, if you want to mail a response, Nuntius launches Eudora (you must locate it in the preferences first) and then fills in the header and quotes the article text in the body of the message. Then you're in Eudora, and you can send the message as you do any normal piece of email. You have to switch back to Nuntius manually when you're finished.

As cool as that setup is, I prefer the way Nuntius calls another program to edit follow-up posts. I live in Nisus, and using any other text editor or word processor, even on the Mac, irritates me to no end because none of them, in my opinion, provides a comparable set of features for writing and editing text. So, whenever I post an article from Nuntius, I get to edit that article in Nisus. (Note that if you use a word processor other than Nisus, you probably must save your files as text if you use a word processor that doesn't use text files as its native format.)

This technique has its drawbacks. You must have enough memory to run both programs at once, and you must use Eudora to send mail. But even with these limitations (which don't bother me at all, since I have enough RAM and I often use Eudora anyway), I'd like to see more programs following this method of working. The trick with editing files isn't even all that fancy. As far as I can tell, Nuntius saves a file with the information to be edited (on the desktop or some other folder you set); then it asks the Finder to open that document with the editor you defined. After you're finished editing, you normally save and close the file. Then you manually switch back to Nuntius, which waits patiently for you to finish and then asks if you want to post that article. To avoid clutter, you can click on a checkbox to trash the temporary file when you're finished. I see no reason why other programs couldn't use this technique, although Nisus is especially well-suited to it because its native file format is straight text.

Special Features

Aside from Nuntius's cool method of sending mail and posting follow-ups, it has several features that set it apart from the crowd. The Spacebar works as it does in Unix newsreaders—as a kind of magic key that performs the most likely next action. Unfortunately, I wanted it to open the next closed triangle in an article window, and it didn't do that, so for me, the magic disappeared at that point.

In Nuntius, you can set the font and size for any of its windows with the Font and Size menus in the Prefs menu, and those settings apply to all newsgroup and article windows. Of all the newsreaders, Nuntius has the most control over which threads it displays, allowing you to show all threads, threads updated today, threads with unread articles, or threads with new articles. You can choose among these threads from the Threads menu. A similar set of commands in the Articles menu enables you to expand all articles, the first article, new articles, unread articles, or no articles. Unfortunately, there aren't keyboard shortcuts for these commands; adding them might be a partial solution to my complaint about not being able to expand articles from the keyboard easily.

Overall Evaluation

In many ways, Nuntius is the most mature of the newsreaders. However, despite my love affair with its method of using other programs for mail and editing, and its clever method of multitasking different actions so that you can work more efficiently, Nuntius simply doesn't make it for me. If there were a better way of just zipping through a set of articles without mucking with the mouse or waiting for Nuntius to transfer the full text of each article, I might use it over NewsWatcher.

You can select only full lines in Nuntius article windows, which makes copying an Internet address a bit of a chore, and documentation is nonexistent. Nuntius comes with a notes document that lists some hidden keyboard shortcuts and lists version changes so that you can see old bugs, but that's it. Its balloon help is useful, especially so when you turn it on while you're pointing at groups in the All Groups window—group descriptions in there. That's a great idea.

Finally, I had more trouble with Nuntius crashing than I did with either InterNews or NewsWatcher (which were both utterly stable). The best way for a program to irritate a writer is to crash while the writing is in progress. Your mileage may vary with a different machine, network connection, and set of extensions.

Administrative Details

If you want to get more information about Nuntius or ask questions about it, a LISTSERV at Cornell University is devoted to discussing the program. Send email to **listserv@cornell.edu** with the following line included in the body: **sub nuntius-l** *your full name*.

You can find Nuntius at:

`ftp://ftp.tidbits.com/pub/tidbits/tisk/tcp/nuntius-12.hqx`

Other News Programs

Despite the power and popularity of the preceding three programs, several other newsreaders might be worth checking out, although I don't feel that they are in the same league. In addition, there are now two programs, MacSlurp and NewsFetcher, that act mostly as news transport programs—they merely download messages for reading in another program.

StackedNews

The first time I started StackedNews, a HyperCard-based newsreader, it asked me for my news server but didn't manage to make InterSLIP dial automatically. I bombed out of HyperCard, started up the SLIP connection, and tried again, but then StackedNews just reported "No such card" when I started it and "Expected True or False" when I quit. It has a basic three-pane interface, with two small upper panes for newsgroups and article subjects, and a large bottom pane for displaying the article.

In my experience, HyperCard-based applications are slower and clumsier than native applications, and although this may not in fact be true of StackedNews, I couldn't get it to work.

TheNews

Bill Cramer's shareware newsreader, TheNews, works by default in MacTCP mode, although it also works with UUCP connections and with Unix shell accounts. For a more detailed discussion of TheNews, check out chapter 11, "UUCP Access," because TheNews compares more favorably there. Unfortunately, I see no real reason why you should bother much with TheNews if you have a MacTCP-based connection, even though the latest version, 2.33, offers support for threads. It's simply not as good as NewsWatcher, InterNews, or Nuntius. You can find it at:

```
ftp://ftp.tidbits.com/pub/tidbits/tisk/tcp/the-news-233.hqx
```

MacSlurp

I wish I could write more about MacSlurp from Tom Davies, but unfortunately it doesn't work with my NNTP server at **nwfocus.wa.com** (it complains about a tcp_open error) and that severely limited my testing. Essentially, though, MacSlurp works by connecting to a specified NNTP server and downloading all the articles in the groups that you specify in your **slurp.sys** file, which is a specially-formatted file that must live in your MacSlurp Files folder in your MacSlurp folder.

In theory, once MacSlurp has downloaded all of all of the messages in a newsgroup, you can set ToadNews to unbatch them (ToadNews is discussed in more detail in chapter 11, "UUCP Access," since it's primarily used with UUCP), and once ToadNews has unbatched the news articles, you can use rnMac or TheNews (again, both discussed in chapter 11) to read the news. If you own UUCP/Connect, MacSlurp can also download the news in a format that UUCP/Connect can read, at which point you don't need the combination of ToadNews and rnMac or TheNews.

Configuration is fairly easy, since the only real options are the name of your NNTP server, the article posting date after which MacSlurp should slurp down articles, and the format of the files once MacSlurp as retrieved them. Even editing the **slurp.sys** file is easy—you simply put the name of your NNTP news server at the beginning of a line, followed by a colon and the name of the newsgroup you want to read. It can get more complex, but that works fine.

Or, at least it does for some people. I wish MacSlurp worked with NNTP server at Northwest Nexus, since many people have been asking for off-line newsreading, but as far as I can tell, it just doesn't. I presume it's related to the version of the NNTP server, but there's no way to tell since MacSlurp's author, Tom Davies, has been on vacation in Africa for a few months. He may be back by the time this book hits the shelves; if so, maybe we can figure out what's wrong. I presume that if MacSlurp doesn't work with Northwest Nexus's NNTP server, there are others that it won't work with as well, but you never know until you try.

Note

*It's possible that MacSlurp will work with Northwest Nexus's new NNTP server at **news.halcyon.com**. I didn't have time to try it before the book went to press.*

The major problem with MacSlurp is that it's indiscriminate. If you ask it to retrieve **comp.sys.mac.comm** it goes out and downloads all the articles in that group, regardless of whether or not it could take two hours because of all the new messages. You must spend the downloading time and have the disk storage space for all the articles, which isn't efficient if you only wanted to read a few in that group. That's why we need a program that enables you to pick the articles you want to download, and for the moment, the only program in that category is the next one, NewsFetcher.

Tom notes that he's happy to receive questions, comments and suggestions at **tomd@horse.demon.co.uk**, and comments that MacSlurp is BullionWare—if you like it, send him a multi-kilogram gold ingot. You can find MacSlurp 1.5 at:

```
ftp://ftp.tidbits.com/pub/tidbits/tisk/tcp/mac-slurp-15.hqx
```

NewsFetcher

A free HyperCard-based news transport agent called NewsFetcher recently appeared from Jörg Shäffer. It's quite limited, and a bit clunky in terms of interface at the moment, but what it does is extremely useful. Instead of providing an interactive interface for reading news, NewsFetcher merely retrieves subject lines in specified groups. Once it's done that, you can select the subjects you wish to read, and it goes out and retrieves those articles. NewsFetcher doesn't attempt to read the articles on its own at all, but instead saves them in a special format that Akif Eyler's Easy View text browser can read. Thus, NewsFetcher, although it does have minimal posting abilities, doesn't work well if you post frequently. If you're more of a lurker, though, NewsFetcher is ideal.

To use NewsFetcher, double-click on the stack to launch HyperCard or HyperCard Player (you need one or the other, and I'm not sure what version is necessary). Click in the splash screen to get to the Subject Fetching card, and then click on the Configure button to get to the Configuration card (see figure 13.26).

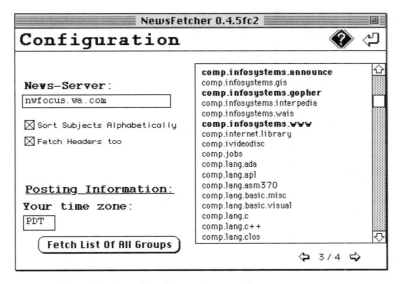

Figure 13.26   *NewsFetcher Configuration card*

Enter your NNTP news server's address and your time zone, and then click on the groups (10 maximum) that you want to read. NewsFetcher comes with a large selection of groups—click on the right or left arrow buttons to move through them—but you can retrieve the list of all the groups by clicking on the Fetch List of All Groups button. When you're finished, click the Return button in the upper right-hand corner to get back to the Subject Fetching card (see figure 13.27).

Here you can post an article or quit, but it's more likely that you'll want to fetch the subjects for the newsgroups that you selected. To do so, connect to the Internet, then click on the Fetch Subjects button. NewsFetcher goes out and gets the subjects for those groups, informs you that you can disconnect if you want, and tells you to click on the right-pointing arrow that has appeared in the upper right-hand corner of the Subject Fetching card. When you do, NewsFetcher takes you to the Article Selection 1 card (see figure 13.28).

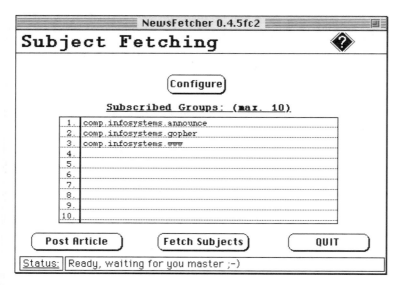

Figure 13.27   *NewsFetcher Subject Fetching card*

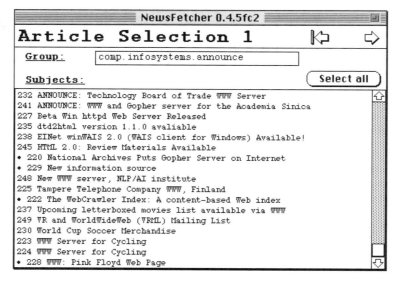

Figure 13.28   *NewsFetcher Article Selection card*

You have one of these cards for each of the newsgroups you told NewsFetcher to browse, and you can scroll through the alphabetically sorted articles, clicking on those that you think might be interesting. NewsFetcher puts a bullet in front of their titles to indicate that they will be downloaded. Select articles in all of your groups, and when you're finished, click on the right-pointing arrow in the last of your Article Selection cards to get to the Article Fetching card (see figure 13.29).

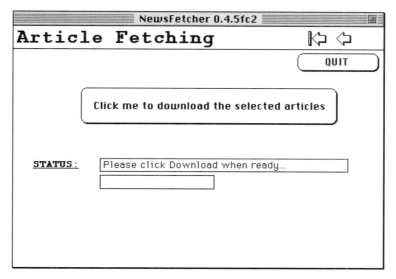

Figure 13.29   *NewsFetcher Article Fetching card*

Click the Click me to download the selected articles button, and NewsFetcher goes off and does just that. When it's finished, it asks whether you'd like to quit or run it again, but it doesn't save the list of subjects, so you'd have to go back through the entire process if you don't quite get what you want. I recommend thinking carefully about what you want, the first time through.

But where did the news go? Into a folder called News that lives in the same folder as the stack. In that folder is a file for each downloaded group, and an Easy View view document. Double-click on the Easy View document to view the news (see figure 13.30).

Easy View is a great program for browsing text, although it would be nice if NewsFetcher had an option for not downloading the complete headers of the messages. I won't get into all of Easy View's features here, but suffice it to say that the arrow keys and the Spacebar will take you around in the file rather quickly.

I won't pretend that NewsFetcher is an ideal off-line newsreading solution, but it's the best freeware solution available at the moment. Others will come, eventually, but until then, the combination of NewsFetcher and Easy View is what I plan to use for some light PowerBook reading on my next airplane flight.

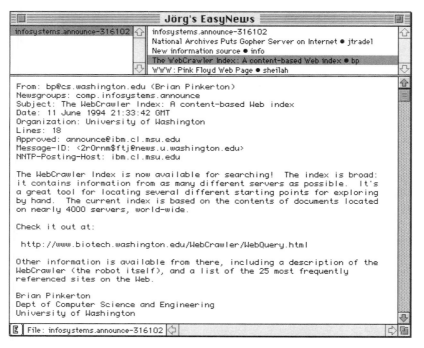

Figure 13.30 *NewsFetcher & Easy View cooperate*

NewsFetcher is free, as is Easy View 2.44. You can find them on the Internet at:

```
ftp://ftp.tidbits.com/pub/tidbits/tisk/tcp/news-fetcher-045-hc.hqx
```

```
ftp://ftp.tidbits.com/pub/tidbits/misc/easy-view-244.hqx
```

FTP Programs

Although more people use email than any other Internet application, more data is transferred via FTP than any other Internet application. FTP is one of the base applications that tie the Internet together. Despite its relative simplicity from a command line, FTP works far better when you can use a graphical application to navigate through remote directories and files.

I'm going to gloss over the programs that let you set your Mac up as an FTP server because although they're neat, they require a direct and constant connection to be significantly useful, and percentage-wise, almost no one sets up a Mac as an FTP server in comparison to the number of people who retrieve files via FTP. If you do want to set up a server, read on for a description of Peter Lewis's FTPd, and check out the FTP Enable feature in NCSA Telnet.

As in the previous sections, there are a number of FTP clients available, ranging from an early HyperCard stack (which I remember as being astonishingly cool at the time) to Anarchie and Fetch, the *de facto* standards in the MacTCP world. I look primarily at Anarchie and Fetch because I think they're the best, but I briefly discuss some of the other FTP programs that I know about. Also, I've included Anarchie 1.2.0 on the disk, complete with all sorts of bookmarks for interesting places and files.

Anarchie

Peter Lewis's Anarchie (see figure 13.31) does something that I've wanted for quite some time. It's an FTP client, as is Fetch, but one that can search Archie servers for files stored on anonymous FTP sites, and once it has found those files, it can retrieve them via FTP. This is a thoroughly simple and powerful idea, but Anarchie is the first Macintosh program to fully implement it (and yes, I know, TurboGopher can do the same thing via Veronica, but it's not as slick as Anarchie for file retrieval).

Figure 13.31 *Anarchie About dialog*

Installation and Setup

You can place Anarchie anywhere on your hard disk, but its folder of bookmarks of popular sites should stay in the same folder as the Anarchie program. I personally make an alias to Anarchie and leave it in my Apple menu, since Anarchie is one of my favorite tools at this point.

If you're using SLIP or PPP, make sure you're connected, and then launch Anarchie. First off, go to the Edit menu and choose Preferences. Most of the defaults here are fine, but make sure to enter your full email address, since Anarchie needs it to give to anonymous FTP servers as your password. You can change things such as the font and destination folder if you like, and unless you know you're behind a firewall (an Internet machine that makes entry into a domain difficult, and unfortunately makes getting out of that machine difficult as well), or you know you have an Alex server (an uncommon method of caching files retrieved via FTP for more efficient use of the Internet), stick with Normal FTP Transfers (see figure 13.32).

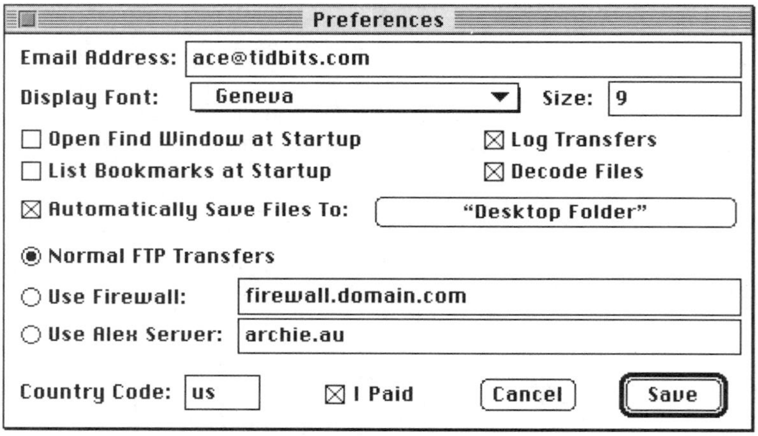

Figure 13.32   *Anarchie Preferences window*

At this point, you can use all of Anarchie's features, save one. If you want to use the File menu's View Selection command to have Anarchie download a file and automatically open it in the text editor of your choice, you must retrieve Dartmouth College's Fetch, run it, and use Suffix Mapping from Fetch's Customize menu to map the `.txt` extension to your word processor of choice.

Note

Although Peter recognizes that using Fetch's suffix mapping is a bit of a pain, it was a pretty good bet when Anarchie came out that everyone who wanted to use it already had Fetch. By sharing Fetch's suffix mappings, Peter was able to eliminate that bit of duplicated interface from Anarchie. In the future, I expect that either Peter will add in some way of configuring the suffix mappings, or another independent solution will appear that a number of Internet programs can share, since they all use essentially the same set of helper applications.

Basic Usage

There are a number of ways to use Anarchie, depending on what you want to accomplish. If you want to browse around in a site that's listed among Anarchie's bookmarks, choose List Bookmarks from the File menu and double-click on one of them. As you can see, Peter included a large list of the most popular FTP sites for various pieces of Macintosh software (see figure 13.33).

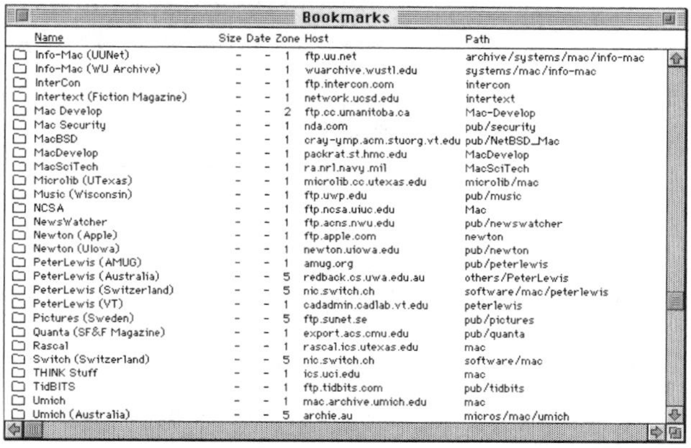

Name	Size	Date	Zone	Host	Path
Info-Mac (UUNet)	–	–	1	ftp.uu.net	archive/systems/mac/info-mac
Info-Mac (WU Archive)	–	–	1	wuarchive.wustl.edu	systems/mac/info-mac
InterCon	–	–	1	ftp.intercon.com	intercon
Intertext (Fiction Magazine)	–	–	1	network.ucsd.edu	intertext
Mac Develop	–	–	2	ftp.cc.umanitoba.ca	Mac-Develop
Mac Security	–	–	1	nda.com	pub/security
MacBSD	–	–	1	cray-ymp.acm.stuorg.vt.edu	pub/NetBSD_Mac
MacDevelop	–	–	1	packrat.st.hmc.edu	MacDevelop
MacSciTech	–	–	1	ra.nrl.navy.mil	MacSciTech
Microlib (UTexas)	–	–	1	microlib.cc.utexas.edu	microlib/mac
Music (Wisconsin)	–	–	1	ftp.uwp.edu	pub/music
NCSA	–	–	1	ftp.ncsa.uiuc.edu	Mac
NewsWatcher	–	–	1	ftp.acns.nwu.edu	pub/newswatcher
Newton (Apple)	–	–	1	ftp.apple.com	newton
Newton (UIowa)	–	–	1	newton.uiowa.edu	pub/newton
PeterLewis (AMUG)	–	–	1	amug.org	pub/peterlewis
PeterLewis (Australia)	–	–	5	redback.cs.uwa.edu.au	others/PeterLewis
PeterLewis (Switzerland)	–	–	5	nic.switch.ch	software/mac/peterlewis
PeterLewis (VT)	–	–	1	cadadmin.cadlab.vt.edu	peterlewis
Pictures (Sweden)	–	–	5	ftp.sunet.se	pub/pictures
Quanta (SF&F Magazine)	–	–	1	export.acs.cmu.edu	pub/quanta
Rascal	–	–	1	rascal.ics.utexas.edu	mac
Switch (Switzerland)	–	–	5	nic.switch.ch	software/mac
THINK Stuff	–	–	1	ics.uci.edu	mac
TidBITS	–	–	1	ftp.tidbits.com	pub/tidbits
Umich	–	–	1	mac.archive.umich.edu	mac
Umich (Australia)	–	–	5	archie.au	micros/mac/umich

Figure 13.33   *Anarchie Bookmarks window*

If you double-click on one of the bookmarks, Anarchie connects to the remote site via FTP and displays the directory listing. Double-clicking on names with folders next to them takes you into that directory, and double-clicking on a file retrieves the file. In this respect, Anarchie resembles the Finder in Name view, whereas Fetch (discussed later) resembles the Standard File dialog box that you use to open and save files within all Macintosh applications. In other words, Anarchie is generally faster and more flexible to use than Fetch.

But what if you want to retrieve a specific file that someone has told you about? Go to the File menu and choose Get. Anarchie opens the Get via FTP window, which provides fields for the name of the FTP host and the pathname of the file. If you don't know the name of the file, but do know the pathname to it, you can click Get Listing instead of Get File, at which point Anarchie connects to the FTP site and displays the directory listing you've asked for. If you provide the full pathname of the file, select Get File, and click the Get button, Anarchie retrieves the file with no fuss (see figure 13.34).

Note

> *Since URLs, such as those in this book, contain the name of the FTP server and the full pathname for a file, you can type that information into Anarchie's Get via FTP window. Be aware that if the file you want has been updated, Anarchie won't be able to retrieve it (since the file name will have changed). At that point, simply remove the file name from the end of the pathname and ask Anarchie to get a listing of the directory that file originally lived in to find the updated program.*

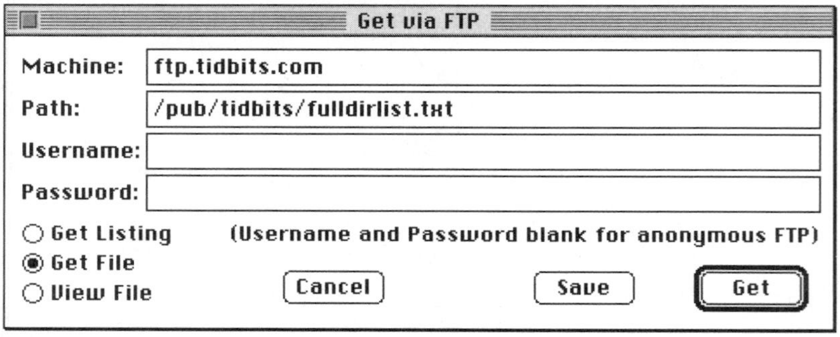

```
████▓                    Get via FTP                    ▓████
  Machine:  ftp.tidbits.com
  Path:     /pub/tidbits/fulldirlist.txt
  Username:
  Password:

  ○ Get Listing    (Username and Password blank for anonymous FTP)
  ● Get File
  ○ View File        ( Cancel )        ( Save )      (( Get ))
```

Figure 13.34   *Anarchie Get via FTP window*

Note

> *If you want to connect to a "nonymous" FTP server—that is, an FTP server that requires a username and password—simply enter them in the appropriate fields in the Get via FTP window.*

If you're retrieving a directory list instead of a file, select the Get Listing button and click the List button in the Get via FTP window. This brings up an Anarchie directory list window, in which you can double-click on files to retrieve them and on folders to open them (see figure 13.35).

You can have multiple listing windows open simultaneously, and can even download multiple files simultaneously, although they don't arrive any faster than if you downloaded them one at a time. If you select several files at once and choose Get from the File menu, Anarchie *pipelines* the files—that is, downloads them all, one after another.

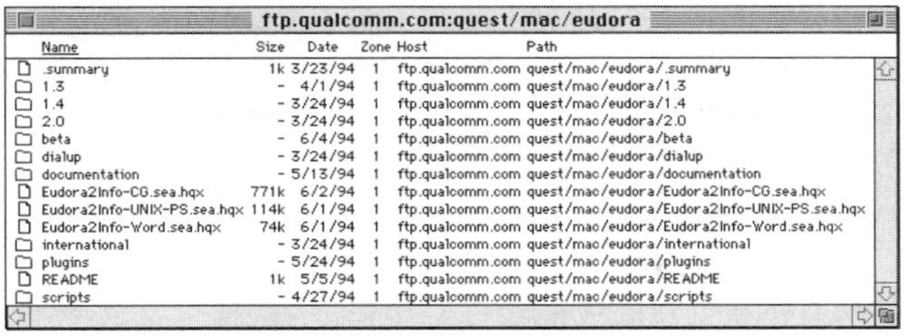
ftp.qualcomm.com:quest/mac/eudora
Name Size Date Zone Host Path
.summary 1k 3/23/94 1 ftp.qualcomm.com quest/mac/eudora/.summary
1.3 - 4/1/94 1 ftp.qualcomm.com quest/mac/eudora/1.3
1.4 - 3/24/94 1 ftp.qualcomm.com quest/mac/eudora/1.4
2.0 - 3/24/94 1 ftp.qualcomm.com quest/mac/eudora/2.0
beta - 6/4/94 1 ftp.qualcomm.com quest/mac/eudora/beta
dialup - 3/24/94 1 ftp.qualcomm.com quest/mac/eudora/dialup
documentation - 5/13/94 1 ftp.qualcomm.com quest/mac/eudora/documentation
Eudora2Info-CG.sea.hqx 771k 6/2/94 1 ftp.qualcomm.com quest/mac/eudora/Eudora2Info-CG.sea.hqx
Eudora2Info-UNIX-PS.sea.hqx 114k 6/1/94 1 ftp.qualcomm.com quest/mac/eudora/Eudora2Info-UNIX-PS.sea.hqx
Eudora2Info-Word.sea.hqx 74k 6/1/94 1 ftp.qualcomm.com quest/mac/eudora/Eudora2Info-Word.sea.hqx
international - 3/24/94 1 ftp.qualcomm.com quest/mac/eudora/international
plugins - 5/24/94 1 ftp.qualcomm.com quest/mac/eudora/plugins
README 1k 5/5/94 1 ftp.qualcomm.com quest/mac/eudora/README
scripts - 4/27/94 1 ftp.qualcomm.com quest/mac/eudora/scripts

Figure 13.35 *Anarchie Listing window*

If you don't know where the file you want lives, but you have an idea what it might be called, you should use an Archie server, and this is where Anarchie shines. Go to the File menu and choose Archie. Anarchie brings up the Find window with fields for the Archie server you want to search (with a pop-up menu of all the known servers), and a field for the search term (see figure 13.36).

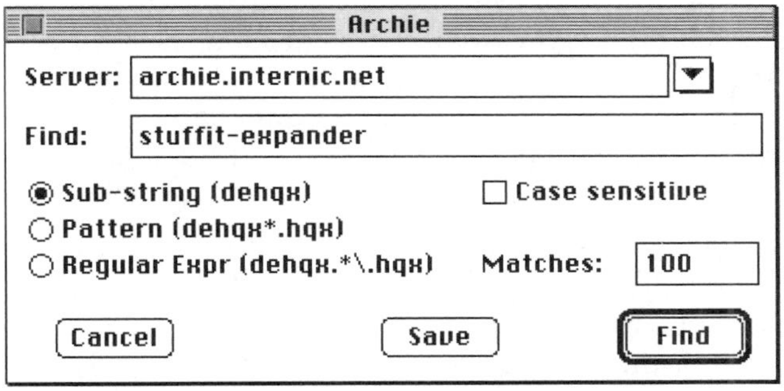
Archie
Server: archie.internic.net
Find: stuffit-expander
Sub-string (dehqx)
Pattern (dehqx*.hqx)
Regular Expr (dehqx.*\.hqx)
Case sensitive
Matches: 100
Cancel
Save
Find

Figure 13.36 *Anarchie Archie window*

You can set how many matches Anarchie asks for, along with a checkbox that forces the search to be case-sensitive. Case-insensitive searches are generally safer than case-sensitive searches, since you never know how the filename might be capitalized on an FTP site. You want to leave the number of matches relatively low, certainly under 100. If you go above that, not only are you stressing the Internet unnecessarily, but the search takes a lot longer to process.

Finally, you have the choice of three types of searches: Sub-string, Pattern, or Regular Expression. *A Sub-string search* is a simple search—if, for instance, you want to find the Macintosh Internet game Bolo, simply type "bolo" into the Find field. However, since there are a lot of files out there with the word "bolo" in their filenames, you'll find far too many files that aren't what you want.

If instead you switch to *Pattern searching*, you can use a wildcard such as *?* (meaning "any character") or * (meaning "any string of characters"). This would enable you to search for **bolo*.hqx**, which would find any BinHex files whose names start with "bolo" and end with ".hqx".

Most people will never need anything more powerful than Pattern searching, but if you're not most people, you can switch to *Regular Expression* searching. Regular expressions are tremendously powerful, but they're also terribly confusing and hard to write. If you want to find out more about them, Peter recommends looking at the man pages for ed, a Unix text editor. For this you must log in to a Unix machine and type **man ed** at the prompt—see chapter 10, "Shell Access," for more details.

Special Features

Although using Anarchie is simple (when in doubt, double-click on something), Peter added lots of neat features that come in handy. When you have a directory listing window showing, you can copy one or more of the entries. This may seem minor, but if you've ever wanted to send someone a list of files in a specific directory, you'll love this feature. As an added bonus, if you hold down the Option key when you choose Copy, or press Command-C, Anarchie copies the selected entries in URL format. Needless to say, I used this feature heavily while writing this book, and I use it every week in preparing *TidBITS*.

Anarchie's knowledge of URLs is even more useful that it seems. If you see a URL for a file in *TidBITS* or anywhere else on the Internet, you can copy that URL and paste it into the Host field in Anarchie's Get via FTP window. Make sure to select Get Listing or Get File appropriately, though. I use this feature all the time, since URLs are becoming the standard way to tell someone where a file lives, and it's so easy to, for example, copy a URL out of an email message and paste it into Anarchie.

Of course, if you use NewsWatcher or InterNews, you can simply Option-click or Command-click on an FTP URL in those programs to have Anarchie (or Fetch) retrieve it automatically.

If you hold down the Option key before selecting the File menu, you see that some of the menu items change. Most notably, Retry changes to Edit Retry, and Open Bookmark changes to Edit Bookmark. This is handy, but what's even handier is that Option-clicking on an item in any Anarchie list window displays a Get via FTP window with the information from that item in it, ready for editing. Anarchie also supports many of the same shortcuts that work in the Finder, so you can move up a level with Command-up arrow, for instance.

I mentioned Anarchie's Bookmarks window already, but didn't note that you can create your own bookmarks. They can point to an FTP site, a specific directory on an FTP site, or a file available via anonymous FTP. So, if you find yourself visiting the same site or directory frequently, simply select the appropriate entry in a directory listing window and choose Save Bookmark from the File menu. If nothing is selected, Anarchie sets the bookmark to the directory referenced by the window itself. Anarchie's bookmarks are extremely useful for providing simple access to files on an FTP site, because double-clicking on the bookmark file to open it automatically retrieves the file that the bookmark references. This is precisely how I created the Essential Bookmarks that I include on the disk.

Note

Bookmark files are also sometimes called AURL files (AURL equals Anarchie URL, *get it?), since that's their Macintosh file type.*

If you visit the same FTP sites over and over again, as I do, you may find Anarchie's Log window useful. Assuming you have the Log Transfer setting checked in Anarchie's Preferences, Anarchie records every directory listing and file retrieval action in a log file. Selecting Show Log from Anarchie's window menu displays the listing of all of these actions, and double-clicking on one works just as double-clicking on any item in an Anarchie window does. So, if you retrieve a file from a certain directory and want to go back there later on for another file, try the Log Window.

Also under the Windows menu is Show Transcript, which shows precisely what you would see had you used a Unix shell account for FTP. The main advantage of this is that Anarchie's normal error messages are terse, so if you want the full error (which usually tells you that the FTP site in question cannot handle any more users at that time), look in the Transcript window (see figure 13.37).

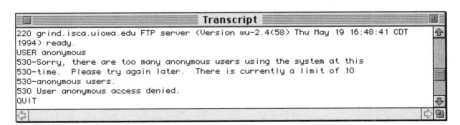

Figure 13.37   Anarchie Transcript window

If you're running a sufficiently new version of the System, which currently is System 7 Pro, and have an extension from Apple installed called Macintosh Drag and Drop, you can use what Apple calls the Drag Manager. Anarchie supports the Drag Manager. This means that if you have the proper system software, you can drag files from an Anarchie window to a Finder window or to your desktop to download them. In addition, you can drag files from the Finder into an Anarchie window that you've opened (you must have upload access to the FTP site reflected in that window) to upload them.

Note

Anarchie does not currently appear to upload binary files in MacBinary format, so if you uploaded a self-extracting archive, for instance, in this fashion, it would be corrupted. If you upload text files in this manner (included binhexed files), it should work fine.

Finally, if you want to delete a file from an FTP site where you have access, simply drag it to the Trash icon on your Finder's desktop. I cannot begin to tell you how unbelievably cool this feature is. The Drag Manager reportedly will be built into Apple's System 7.5, due out sometime in the summer of 1994. Until then, System 7 Pro, or the System that comes with Power Macs, should work with Macintosh Drag and Drop, which is available at:

```
ftp://ftp.apple.com/dts/mac/sys.soft/extensions/macintosh-drag-and-drop-1-1.hqx
```

Anarchie is scriptable and recordable via Apple's AppleScript and UserLand's Frontier, so this should open up Internet file retrieval to some extremely necessary automation. A script might enable you to select a URL in any program and then choose a menu item to automatically retrieve that file. Or, perhaps the script could add the URL to a list of files to retrieve at a later time. Anarchie supports Frontier's Menu Sharing and includes some Frontier stuff from Leonard Rosenthol to get you started if you own Frontier. Also included are some sample AppleScript scripts for automating file downloads and the like.

By clicking on the column names, you can sort any list in Anarchie by name, date, size, host, and so on. Sorting by zone lets you see which hosts are probably closest to you and best to use if a choice exists. Anarchie automatically decodes MacBinary files, and uses a new window for each directory to make browsing back easy. If you select a file and choose Get Selection, and then repeat the process with other files, Anarchie attempts to get all the files at the same time. This often doesn't work very well with overloaded Internet FTP sites, since Anarchie tries to log in once for each file you want and many sites won't allow that. However, you can usually download files from several different FTP sites at the same time with no trouble, although needless to say, it's no faster than downloading them one after another. Only so much data can flow over a connection.

Anarchie works in a *stateless mode*, which means that it doesn't keep the FTP connection open unless it's actually transferring a file or a directory listing. This is an extremely efficient way of using FTP (more like Gopher than FTP, in fact, since Gopher also only keeps the connection open while you're transferring data).

Note

Anarchie's stateless mode means that you may be able to navigate into an FTP site but then be rejected when you try to retrieve a file, because too many other people have logged in while you were navigating around.

One of the problems Archie servers have is that they sometimes appear and disappear. Peter has addressed this problem with the Fetch Server List command in the Edit menu. Simply select it, and Anarchie goes out and gets the current list of Archie servers, which you can then select from the pop-up menu in the Archie window.

Finally, Anarchie's About box displays the number of searches you've made, the number of files you've transferred, and the number of kilobytes you've transferred. Anarchie translates this into a rating. I don't know how many levels there are, but I'm up to Net Terrorist after doing 125 searches and 626 transfers for 34.7M of files.

Overall Evaluation

Anarchie is essential for your Internet tool kit. Despite the slowness and flakiness of Archie servers and the continual problems with finding new files via Archie, Anarchie has proven itself time and time again for me in the months I've used it. Read the documentation, because there are a number of tips and tricks that you won't otherwise discover.

Anarchie isn't quite complete. It would be nice if the windows would update after uploading or deleting a file using the Drag Manager. And, although the way it uses another program to view text files is clever, it results in a lot of files lying around in the destination folder, even if you only wanted to look at the file once.

Administrative Details

Anarchie, from Peter Lewis, is shareware and costs $10. It has been translated into French, by Jean-Pierre Kuypers. You can contact Peter at **peter.lewis@info.curtin.edu.au**. I strongly encourage you to pay for

Anarchie if you find yourself using it. It's an essential Internet tool, and we need to keep Peter happy so that he keeps writing great programs and releasing them as freeware or shareware.

Peter Lewis
10 Earlson Way
Booragoon, WA 6154
AUSTRALIA

Anarchie is included on the disk that comes with this book, and you can retrieve the latest version of Anarchie from:

```
ftp://ftp.tidbits.com/pub/tidbits/tisk/tcp/anarchie-120.hqx
```

Fetch

Fetch comes to the Internet community from Jim Matthews, of Dartmouth College, whose programmers have been notably active in developing and distributing Macintosh software over the years.

Fetch is one of the most elegant and mature MacTCP-based applications, and the latest version, 2.1.2 is Power Mac-native as well. I'm most impressed by the fact that Fetch doesn't do anything fancy—it simply uses standard FTP commands that you could type in by hand if you were so inclined (and have nothing better to do with your time). Fetch intelligently translates your usage of its graphical interface into appropriate FTP commands, sends them off, and then translates the response from the Internet machine back into a form you can easily deal with.

Basic Usage

When you launch the program, Fetch opens an Open Connection dialog box that enables you to pick an FTP site from a list, or type in the necessary information to connect to a new one (see figure 13.38).

Fetch needs to know the same information that the Unix version of FTP does. But, in good Macintosh form, Fetch doesn't require that information at specific times, so you can enter the machine name with which you want to connect, your login name (which usually is **anonymous**), your password (which should be your full email address and doesn't show as you type it), and the directory that you want to start on the remote machine. Of course, if you're using Fetch to connect to a personal account on an Internet host, the userid is your userid and the password is whatever you've set it to. Although many people use Fetch with their own accounts, anonymous FTP is by far the most common usage.

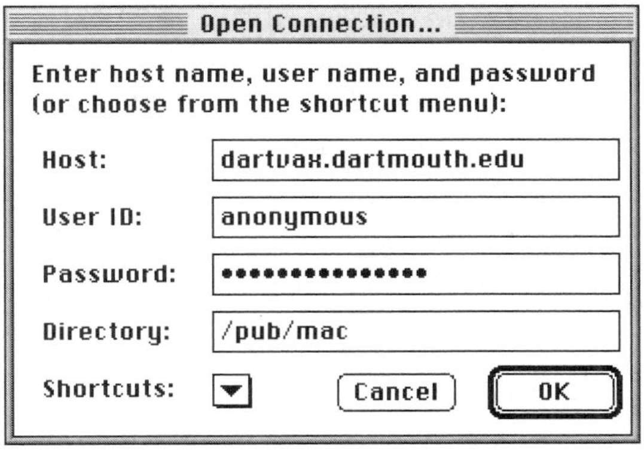

Figure 13.38   *Fetch Open Connection dialog*

You can type in that information each time you connect to an FTP site, but to do so is silly. Fetch enables you to create and modify your own shortcuts via the Edit Shortcuts command in the Customize menu, which brings up a list of existing shortcuts that you can edit (or you can create new ones). The Edit Shortcuts dialog has buttons that enable you to add, remove, and modify shortcuts, along with one you can use to define which shortcut appears by default when Fetch first opens. Set the default shortcut to the FTP site you use most. If you select a shortcut and click the Edit button, or click the New button, Fetch brings up a dialog that looks slightly similar to the Open Connection dialog, with a field for naming the shortcut.

Fetch automatically uses the username and password you set in Preferences (found under the Customize menu), so you don't need to type in that information for each shortcut. Nothing like a shortcut for the shortcuts! Because some FTP sites require your full email address as a password, it's best to use it as your default anonymous password.

Note

*Some sites are finicky about your email address. A workaround might be to use your userid along with the @ sign (for example, **ace@**)—and nothing else. That forces the remote FTP server to figure out the machine name and domain on its own, which sometimes works better.*

In any event, back in the Open Connection dialog, after you either type in the necessary connection information or select a shortcut, click on the Connect button to open a connection to the FTP site. The Open Connection dialog disappears, and you see Fetch's main window (see figure 13.39).

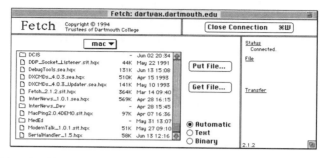

Figure 13.39 *Fetch Main window*

Note

> Keep in mind that a few machines—**ftp.apple.com**, for one—don't allow you to log in if you don't have a valid domain name, such as **tidbits.com**. Just having an IP number isn't good enough; you must have a name associated with your number, or these sites bounce you out for security reasons. Talk to your system administrator if you're bounced out.

The main element in Fetch's window is the list of files and directories on the left side of the window (although that list is, of course, empty until you connect). Next to it are two buttons that enable you to get or send a file. Under that are two radio buttons, Text and Binary, with which you can indicate what sort of files you are transferring, and a third, Automatic, that lets Fetch try to determine the file type for you based on the file extension. I've stuck with Automatic almost entirely and haven't had any trouble, but you might need to switch manually at some point if files are named strangely. You can modify Fetch's defaults if you need to.

To the right of all the buttons is the status area. At the top of the feedback area under Status, Fetch reports precisely what it's doing, such as "Connecting," "Changing dir," "Getting file list," and so on. Then comes the File section, which lists which file Fetch is working on, what format it's in, and how large it is. Below that is the Transfer feedback section, where Fetch reports how many bytes it has transferred along with the rate at which it is transferring the file. You can resize Fetch's main window or place it anywhere on the screen.

If you've used the Mac for any length of time, you'll know how to use Fetch immediately. You double-click on a directory (they have little folder icons) in the list to enter that directory. Double-clicking on a file does the same thing as selecting the file with a single click and then clicking on the Get File button. You can select contiguous multiple files by Shift-clicking on them or multiple discontiguous files by Command-clicking on them, at which point clicking on the Get File button snags the lot of them. After you click on the Get File button, Fetch figures out what sort of file you're getting and either asks you to save it with a standard Save File dialog box, or automatically places it in a folder you've defined in your Preferences.

Fetch is smart, and can decode BinHex and StuffIt 1.5.1 formats. It still has to download all the data, but instead of a BinHex file or a StuffIt 1.5.1 archive, you end up with the file or files that were included in that archive. Fetch doesn't understand StuffIt 3.0 or Compact Pro format archives, but it can launch another program to process a downloaded file (or launch the downloaded file itself, if it's a self-extracting application). You can set up Fetch to work in tandem with other programs, the most useful of which is probably Aladdin's free StuffIt Expander, which you should get as soon as possible if you don't already have it.

Special Features

I especially like the View File command in the Remote menu because it displays text files, which is useful for browsing through the README files that are ubiquitous on FTP sites. I'd far prefer to read a 2K README file than download a 2M file that I cannot use. Using normal FTP, you would have to download the file and then view it in Unix or download to the Mac to look at it in a word processor. That's work. Fetch makes it easy.

In the Directories menu, Fetch lists all of the directories you have visited in that session, which is tremendously useful because you often visit many directories while you're looking for files on a big file site. And, even though Fetch's hierarchical view of directories is easy to navigate, it's even better if you can just jump directly to a directory that you've been in before.

The latest version of Fetch includes support for Anarchie's bookmarks so you can save and open them, which makes for a nice interaction between the two. Fetch comes with a folder of the standard bookmarks as well, so you can use them immediately. Also like Anarchie, Fetch now accepts URLs pasted into its Open Connection dialog. If you select a file and choose Copy from the Edit menu, Fetch places a URL to that file in the clipboard.

Although Fetch keeps the FTP connection open the entire time you are connected to an FTP site, it disconnects after a certain amount of idle time to prevent you from accidentally hogging one of the precious FTP connections.

If you have access to your own account via FTP, you can use Fetch to create and remove directories, rename files, and even issue raw FTP commands. These features won't help the average user of anonymous FTP, but for someone managing their own account, this kind of control is useful. I especially like being able to have Fetch issue a **LIST -R** command that lists the entire contents of a site under the current directory.

Overall Evaluation

How does Fetch compare to Anarchie? I like and use both programs on a regular basis, but at this point I think Fetch is better for maintaining files on your own account via FTP. I've used it exclusively to manage **ftp.tidbits.com** for the last nine months, and it's been a godsend. However, I find that when I'm looking for a file or browsing FTP sites, I prefer to use Anarchie these days, mostly because of its multiple windows and ease of use. You don't use Fetch to explore—you use it to get your work done, and it performs admirably. Of course, the best part about Fetch is its running dog cursor, but you must see that for yourself.

Administrative Details

Jean-Pierre Kuypers has translated Fetch into French, and other translations may exist as well. Educational institutions and nonprofit organizations may use Fetch free of charge, and everyone else can license it from Dartmouth for $25. Read the Fetch Help for more information about licensing. Shareware payments should go to:

Software Sales
Dartmouth College
6028 Kiewit Computation Center
Hanover, NH 03755-3523

If you have any questions or comments about Fetch, send them to **jim.matthews@dartmouth.edu** or **fetch@dartmouth.edu**. You can retrieve the latest version of Fetch via FTP at either of the following:

```
ftp://ftp.dartmouth.edu//pub/mac/Fetch_2.1.2.sit.hqx
```

```
ftp://ftp.tidbits.com/pub/tidbits/tisk/tcp/fetch-212.hqx
```

Other FTP Programs

Although Anarchie and Fetch are the acknowledged standards for FTP clients on the net, several others exist, although I'm not sure how widely they're used.

XferIt

Steve Falkenburg, the programmer who created NewsWatcher, also wrote XferIt 1.4. XferIt was initially shareware, but Steve later made it free when he could no longer support the program or its users. XferIt has essentially the same feature set as Fetch, with an internal scripting capability. XferIt's scripts are straight text files consisting of a slightly limited set of FTP commands. Although not quite as flexible as you might like, you can probably create an XferIt script to transfer files automatically from **sumex-aim.stanford.edu**, for instance, by copying the pathnames for the files from the Info-Mac Digest and pasting them into an appropriate XferIt script.

XferIt's primary problems are its sparse documentation (scripts are never mentioned, for instance) and its bland interface, which isn't nearly as nice or useful as those of Fetch and Anarchie. And as my editor complains, its cursor isn't nearly as cool as Fetch's running dog cursor.

In addition, unless Steve passes the source code along to someone else, XferIt will never be updated, which means it might stop working at some point in the future. Still, considering that the program is free, it's hard to complain. Version 1.5b4 of XferIt apparently added some drag and drop capabilities, such as Anarchie has, but since even that version was created in March of 1992, I don't have high hopes for it still working.

I haven't used XferIt much, because it's simply not as good as Fetch or Anarchie, so I cannot provide much step-by-step guidance. Apparently, at some point you may see a registration dialog, which requests a name and a number. Because Steve decided to release XferIt for free, he, through Jon Pugh, provided a "universal site license." So, if you need to satisfy the registration dialog, the name reportedly is **Anonymous** (it is apparently case-sensitive), and the number is **550035173-2**. You can find the two versions of XferIt on the Internet at:

```
ftp://ftp.tidbits.com/pub/tidbits/tisk/tcp/xferit-14.hqx
```

```
ftp://ftp.tidbits.com/pub/tidbits/tisk/tcp/xferit-15b4.hqx
```

HyperFTP

HyperFTP was probably one of the first graphical clients for FTP. I remember seeing it demonstrated by the programmer, Doug Hornig, at Cornell in 1990. It hasn't changed at all since that time, and as a result, shows its age. It enables you to do many of the same things as Fetch but in a slightly clumsy way, as is common with HyperCard programs. One quirk I've noted with MacTCP programs based in HyperCard is that they don't ask InterSLIP to dial out correctly. If you have InterSLIP connect first manually, it works fine.

If you want to use HyperFTP, it is free, although you cannot sell it or claim you wrote it. You can find it on the Internet at:

```
ftp://ftp.tidbits.com/pub/tidbits/tisk/tcp/tcp/hyper-ftp-13.hqx
```

FTPd

FTPd, a $10 shareware application from Peter Lewis, enables you to make your MacTCP-equipped Macintosh into an FTP and Gopher server. Not surprisingly, it has a relatively complex setup procedure, but to somewhat simplify matters, it uses System 7 File Sharing to create users and groups and assign access privileges. Once it's running as a foreground or background application, anyone on the Internet can use FTP or Gopher to look around on your Mac. If you allow FTP access and don't set your File Sharing privileges correctly, people can also copy and delete files at will, so be careful when you're running FTPd.

To really use FTPd, you need a constant network connection; if you dial in via SLIP or PPP, your FTP site won't be available often. If you have a permanent network connection, FTPd is perfect for setting up a private FTP server for limited use, but if you try to become the next major Info-Mac archive site, your network administrator may stop in for a chat carrying a large blunt instrument. Despite these drawbacks, which have little to do with FTPd and a lot to do with the basic concept of running an FTP site, it's neat that an individual can simply create an FTP site or Gopher server using a $10 shareware application.

I've used FTPd on an SE/30 with a dedicated connection to create a Gopher server, and I'm impressed at how well it works, especially for the price and the age of my hardware. Jean-Pierre Kuypers has translated FTPd into French. You can find the latest English version of FTPd at:

```
ftp://ftp.tidbits.com/pub/tidbits/tisk/tcp/ftpd-22.hqx
```

EasyTransfer

Although EasyTransfer is not exactly an FTP program because it doesn't use the same protocols as FTP and cannot be used as a client, I thought I'd mention it quickly for those who want to transfer files between two Macs, both of which run MacTCP and are on the Internet. This $10 shareware, from Christopher Reid, works as both a server and a client, and enables you to set up specific folders that only certain users can access. There's nothing fancy about EasyTransfer, but I suspect that's the point.

Shareware payments should go to:

Christopher Reid
4/1, 4 Dalcross Pass
Glasgow G11 5RA
Scotland
cr@cs.strath.ac.uk

You can find EasyTransfer at:

```
ftp://ftp.tidbits.com/pub/tidbits/tisk/tcp/easy-transfer-21.hqx
```

Telnet and Friends

I must confess to a certain bias against the next few programs that I talk about. This is not so much because they're bad programs—on the contrary, they're quite good—but because they provide access to standard shell accounts and ugly command-line interfaces, and I have a MacTCP-based connection and lots of great graphical software. Oh well, as Bill Watterson, creator of the Calvin and Hobbes comic strip, has said, "Scientific progress goes 'boink.'"

That's right, I'm talking about NCSA Telnet, Comet, TN3270, and the various Telnet tools, all of which let you travel back in time to the days when you couldn't do the sorts of things that I've talked about so far in this chapter.

NCSA Telnet

NCSA stands for *National Center for Supercomputing Applications*. As a group, NCSA has produced a ton of useful software for the scientific community. A fair amount of that software runs on the Mac. Their best-known application is also their most recent—NCSA Mosaic—but NCSA Telnet comes from the same organization and is equally as much an essential part of your MacTCP toolkit. The latest version of NCSA Telnet is 2.6, and rumor has it that NCSA may not devote any more resources to Telnet, marooning it at this level.

Basic Usage

There isn't any configuration necessary for you to start using NCSA Telnet, but just like the Unix Telnet, there's not much to do with it unless you know where you're going. Telnet doesn't do anything on its own; it's merely a conduit to another program running on a remote machine.

After you launch NCSA Telnet, go to the File menu and choose Open Connection. NCSA Telnet opens a dialog box in which you enter the host to which you want to connect (if you must enter a port number, enter it here to with a space separating it from the host name). There's also a pop-down menu for selecting a predefined host (see figure 13.40).

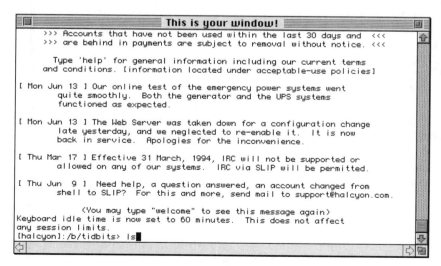

Figure 13.40   *NCSA Telnet Open Connection dialog*

Don't worry about the FTP Session checkbox and the Authenticate and Encrypt options. They are only valid if you get additional software. If you don't want to provide a window name, that's no big deal, either. Click on Connect, and NCSA Telnet opens a terminal window that enables you to log in to the machine you specified, in my case, my account on **halcyon.com** (see figure 13.41).

```
This is your window!
 >>> Accounts that have not been used within the last 30 days and  <<<
 >>> are behind in payments are subject to removal without notice.  <<<

      Type 'help' for general information including our current terms
   and conditions. [information located under acceptable-use policies]

[ Mon Jun 13 ] Our online test of the emergency power systems went
      quite smoothly.  Both the generator and the UPS systems
      functioned as expected.

[ Mon Jun 13 ] The Web Server was taken down for a configuration change
      late yesterday, and we neglected to re-enable it.  It is now
      back in service.  Apologies for the inconvenience.

[ Thu Mar 17 ] Effective 31 March, 1994, IRC will not be supported or
      allowed on any of our systems.  IRC via SLIP will be permitted.

[ Thu Jun  9 ] Need help, a question answered, an account changed from
      shell to SLIP? For this and more, send mail to support@halcyon.com.

            (You may type "welcome" to see this message again)
Keyboard idle time is now set to 60 minutes.  This does not affect
any session limits.
[halcyon]:/b/tidbits> ls
```

Figure 13.41   *NCSA Telnet Terminal window*

Once you get to this point, you must play by the rules of the remote machine, which in this case involves using the basic Unix shell account on **halcyon.com**. I could also have connected to an Archie server, to a MUD, to a library catalog, or any other resource that's available via Telnet.

Although NCSA Telnet certainly has plenty of other commands in its menus, on the whole, you shouldn't have to mess with them regularly. A number of them control how NCSA Telnet reacts to certain types of host machines; with others you can query the network; and various options enable you to determine how your terminal windows look and act. But at the base level, NCSA Telnet enables you, from your Mac, to access services that are limited to the command line.

I like the new shortcut for accessing commonly used sites from the Open Connection dialog (you define those sites in the Session submenu from the Preferences menu in the Edit menu). Version 2.6 of NCSA Telnet added an hierarchical Open Special menu to the File menu—it provides even quicker access to the shortcuts that you've defined. What I'd really like, though, is to have NCSA Telnet remember the last ten or so sites I've visited and provide instant access to them as well.

Special Features

I may have sounded terse in the preceding section, but NCSA Telnet provides some extra neat features. I'm impressed by the ability to open multiple sessions to different sites or even to the same site. For instance, I can telnet to an Archie server, start a long search, and then open a different window telnetting to a Gopher server. Switching between sites is as simple as clicking another window.

If you regularly use one or more Telnet sessions, you can save Set documents, that record the open sessions. Opening that document later automatically connects you to all of those sites.

One feature I often find myself using is the Delete/Backspace toggle under the Session menu. Some sites interpret the Mac's Delete key differently, so if pressing the Delete key doesn't delete a character, try switching to Backspace (or vice versa, if the Backspace key is the problem) from the Session menu.

If you have a large screen, you can use the Set Screen Size command under the Session menu to increase the size of the terminal window. The default is a paltry 24 rows by 80 columns, and it's often much nicer to work with 50 rows.

Although simple, NCSA Telnet does provide a macro feature for commonly used commands. This feature would never replace something such as QuicKeys, but it's a nice touch.

When you run NCSA Telnet, if you go the File menu and select FTP Enable, NCSA Telnet turns your Mac into a simple FTP server. As with Peter Lewis's FTPd, be careful of this capability because it constitutes a possible security risk. Check your settings in the Preferences submenus carefully. As you can see in figure 13.42, I've turned on FTP for my machine and connected to it.

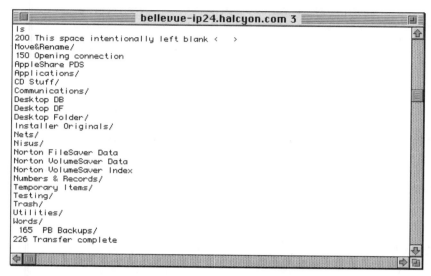

Figure 13.42   *NCSA Telnet FTP session window*

Overall Evaluation

NCSA Telnet is an essential part of your MacTCP software collection. For instance, there are some services which provide excellent information that you must access via Telnet. If you don't have a Unix account but can use MacTCP, with or without PPP or SLIP, you can use NCSA Telnet. You also should keep it around because TurboGopher, the main Macintosh Gopher client, calls NCSA Telnet whenever you access a Telnet-based service accessible in Gopherspace. Without NCSA Telnet around, those services, which are commonly library catalogs and campus-wide information systems, become completely inaccessible.

In addition, there are times when it's handy to be able to go in and use Unix. As long as the SLIP and PPP accounts generally available are based on Unix, there will always be some reasons why you might want to log in via Telnet and use Unix. Perhaps you need to unlock a POP mailbox or want move a file from one Unix host to another without bringing to the Mac in between. Those tasks and various others require access to the Unix command-line, and Telnet provides that access.

Administrative Details

NCSA Telnet has been translated into a number of different languages, including French, Japanese, Chinese, and Swedish, although character conversion apparently is still a major nuisance. NCSA Telnet is a public domain program, which means you can use it for free in any manner you want. You can even get the source code if you want to use it. You can retrieve NCSA Telnet from either of the following:

```
ftp://ftp.tidbits.com/pub/tidbits/tisk/tcp/ncsa-telnet-26.hqx
```

```
ftp://ftp.ncsa.uiuc.edu/Mac/Telnet/Telnet2.6/Telnet2.6.sit.hqx
```

Comet

Although not in as widespread use as NCSA Telnet, Cornell's Comet seems to have many of the same features as NCSA Telnet, with a few added in. Comet offers a number of emulation modes, most notably 3270 (full-screen IBM mode) that NCSA Telnet doesn't have, and it provides access to various special keys that you might not have on your keyboard via buttons on the screen. This is especially handy with 3270 sessions, since they require special keyboard mapping (see figure 13.43).

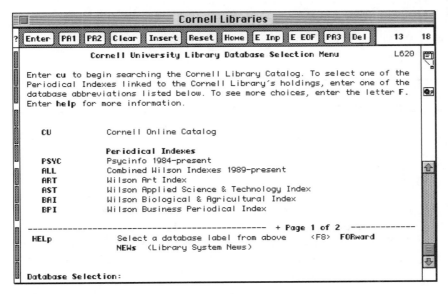

Figure 13.43   *Comet 3270 Session window*

I'm not going to explore all of Comet's many settings and options, since I don't use enough command-line services to have any sense of why they might be useful. However, here are a few neat features that you won't want to miss.

Special Features

If you click on the zoom box, rather than zooming the window, Comet minimizes it into an icon on your desktop, much the way Microsoft Windows applications behave. Although less useful for those of us using SLIP or PPP accounts, for people who must be logged in to a terminal session all day long, this is a great feature for getting Comet out of the way while keeping it easily accessible.

In its File menu, Comet has a command called Type file name at cursor. Although an unwieldy name for a menu item, this command displays a standard file dialog box and types the name of the file that you select at the cursor, just as you'd expect. If, for instance, you need to type a filename for an upload, this might be a nice aid.

Like NCSA Telnet, Comet has a macro facility, but you can also record macros within the program, rather than just creating them manually.

Finally, if you want to copy text from a terminal window, Comet has a Table Mode for Copy and Save command in the Edit menu. When Table Mode selected, Comet copies ASCII tables with tabs rather than spaces between the rows, which can save a lot of work if you must for some reason transfer information from a terminal window to a Macintosh word processor.

Comet 3.0.8 is free from Cornell University, and you can retrieve the latest version of it from either of the following:

```
ftp://ftp.cit.cornell.edu//pub/mac/comm/comet308.sit
```

```
ftp://ftp.tidbits.com/pub/tidbits/tisk/tcp/comet-308.hqx
```

TN3270

NCSA Telnet cannot handle all the mainframe sites that you may want to explore. Some IBM mainframes use 3270 terminals, and without delving into the ugly details, let me say that if you want to telnet to one of these machines, you must use either Cornell's Comet or Brown University's TN3270 rather than NCSA Telnet.

TN3270 looks as though it were based on NCSA Telnet, and it does almost exactly the same thing, only with IBM mainframes rather than with machines running more common operating systems.

There's not much to show you and no real configuration to speak of with TN3270 because, like NCSA Telnet, it merely provides a window to a text-based machine. Unfortunately, it doesn't appear that you can have multiple windows open with TN3270.

You need both the main file for version 2.3d26 and the updated files from 2.4a4 for a complete package. They are freely available and you can retrieve them from:

```
ftp://ftp.tidbits.com/pub/tidbits/tisk/tcp/tn3270-23d26.hqx
```

```
ftp://ftp.tidbits.com/pub/tidbits/tisk/tcp/tn3270-24a4.hqx
```

Telnet CTB Tools

Although NCSA Telnet and Comet are the main full implementations of Telnet that are freely available, several Communications Toolbox (CTB) tools for Telnet also exist. These tools should work with any CTB-aware communications application, such as the free Termy from Tim Endres, MicroPhone II from Software Ventures, Aladdin's SITcomm, or Communicate from Mark/Space Softworks. Unfortunately, the popular ZTerm does not use the CTB.

I'm aware of three main Telnet tools at the moment. MicroPhone Pro ships with one called the MP Telnet Tool; VersaTerm includes the VersaTerm Telnet Tool; and Tim Endres has written a free one called TGE TCP Tool. There's not much to differentiate the three of these tools because, in essence, all they do is allow a CTB-aware terminal emulator to pretend to be a Telnet application. All three provide methods of listing commonly accessed hosts (the most important option in each enables you to define hosts), and TGE TCP Tool also provides a transparent feature that is useful in certain complex setups where you want one protocol such as UUCP to communicate over a TCP link. Don't ask; I don't understand it fully, and it's not a common thing to do.

Just for fun, I tested VersaTerm, MicroPhone II, and Termy with all three tools and had fairly good success. Neither VersaTerm nor MicroPhone liked Tim's TGE TCP Tool (needless to say, Tim's Termy liked it just fine), but all three emulators worked fine with the VersaTerm Telnet Tool and the MP Telnet Tool. The main difference that I noted among the three was that Termy offered the best interface for working with multiple simultaneous sessions to different hosts. The moral of the story is that if you don't like NCSA Telnet, the freeware combination of Termy and the TGE TCP Tool provides much of the same functionality. You can get Termy and the TGE TCP Tool at:

```
ftp://ftp.tidbits.com/pub/tidbits/tisk/term/termy-23.hqx
```

```
ftp://ftp.tidbits.com/pub/tidbits/tisk/ctb/tge-tcp-tool-20.hqx
```

WAIS

Thinking Machines' WAIS has recently spawned at least three client applications for the Macintosh. Of them, the oldest is the WAIS for Macintosh 1.2a application, from WAIS, Inc., written by Harry Morris. The most recent, MacWAIS, is shareware from MCC, and the third, written in HyperCard by Francois Schiettecatte, is HyperWAIS. WAIS for Macintosh hasn't been updated since the first edition of this book came out, and in fact Harry Morris tells me that WAIS currently recommends that people use MacWAIS 1.29 instead. Both WAIS for Mac 1.2a and MacWAIS 1.29 are described below.

MacWAIS

With continual updates and a simple interface, MacWAIS, from the EINet group of MCC, has become the WAIS interface of choice for most Macintosh users who use WAIS. In the most recent version, 1.29, programmer John Hardin of EINet has integrated MacWAIS with EINet's new World-Wide Web browser, MacWeb, making MacWAIS an even more essential utility.

Basic Usage

Make sure you're connected to the Internet, launch MacWAIS, and from the File menu select New Question. MacWAIS brings up a new question window, and presents you with a dialog showing the contents of your wais-sources folder, which lives in the MacWAIS folder. (If for some reason it doesn't show you this folder, navigate to it in the Standard File dialog that you can see in figure 13.44).

Double-click on the **Directory of Servers** source in the left-hand list, to copy it over to the right-hand list of selected sources, and then click on the Done button to close the Select Sources dialog. The problem is that MacWAIS only ships with one useful source, the **Directory of Servers**, so you must use it to find additional sources that you can then use in specific searches. Let's look for information about the Macintosh.

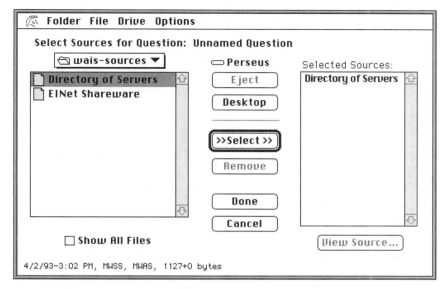

Figure 13.44 *MacWAIS Select Source dialog*

In the Unnamed Question window's Tell Me About field, type **Macintosh**. You've already selected the **Directory of Servers**, so that's where your search for Macintosh things takes place. Click the Ask button to send the search to the WAIS server (see figure 13.45).

MacWAIS asks the WAIS server which sources might contain Macintosh information. When the search comes back, the Information Found field lists nine items that might have something to do with the Mac. As you can see in figure 13.45, some of them may be pushing it a bit, but the top two items, **macintosh-news.src** and **macintosh-tidbits.src**, are pretty likely to be what you want, since they have the highest scores (the numbers to the left of the result list items).

Note

The "score" in MacWAIS is merely its method of displaying ranking information about which results are most likely to answer your question.

If you select one of the sources in the Information Found field, you can click on the Save button to save it to your wais-sources folder, or you can click on the View button to see what its description says (see figure 13.46).

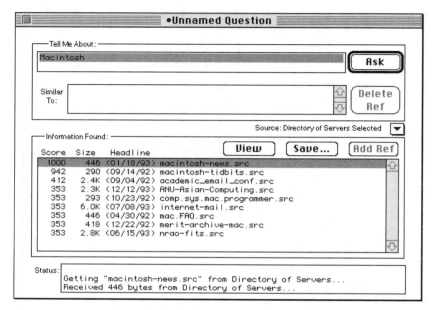

Figure 13.45   *MacWAIS Unnamed Question window*

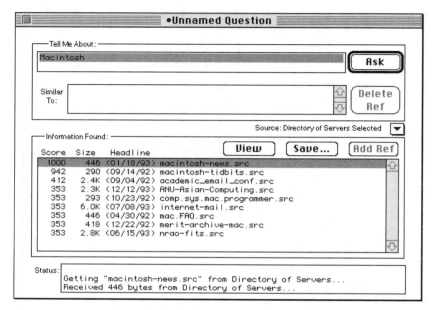

Figure 13.46   *MacWAIS Edit Source dialog*

Clicking on the OK button in the Edit Source dialog also saves the source; clicking on the Cancel button merely dismisses the dialog if you don't want to save it. If you want to go immediately to a specific question, select the Use with current question checkbox in the Edit Source dialog, and MacWAIS replaces the current source with the one you just saved. You can repeat the process with the rest of the sources listed here, and perform other searches on the **Directory of Servers** to find other searches.

In fact, the process of searching for a specific piece of information in a source is exactly the same as that of searching for a source. Instead of the **Directory of Servers** source, you select whichever one is appropriate, and enter a different search phrase in the Tell Me About field. For instance, I want to find out what's been said about MacWeb, so I ask MacWAIS to tell me about the latest version of MacWeb (see figure 13.47).

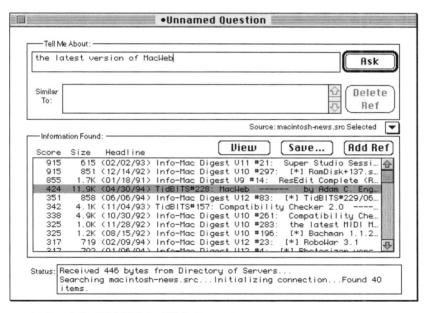

Figure 13.47   MacWAIS MacWeb Question

The results are mixed, probably because the phrase "the latest version of" is fairly common. However, MacWAIS did find the article I wrote about MacWeb for *TidBITS*, and if you select that item you can either View it, Save it, or Add it as a reference with the Add Ref button. If you click on the Add Ref button, that document title appears in the Similar To field. Clicking on the Ask button results in somewhat different information, because MacWAIS now realizes that I'm more interested in MacWeb and other Web-related information than in "the latest version of" different programs (see figure 13.48).

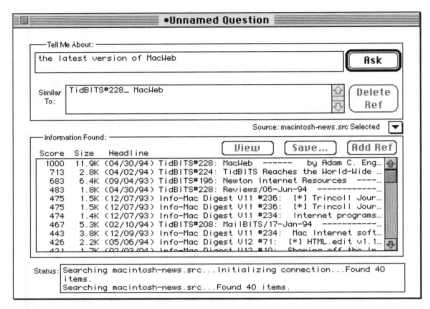

Figure 13.48   *MacWAIS MacWeb Question II*

That about covers using MacWAIS's basic features. You can save questions, which is a good way of avoiding the Select Source dialog (which I find rather clumsy). Also, if you want to create a new question that's similar to an existing one, you can select Clone Question from the File menu.

Special Features

Like many of the other Internet applications, MacWAIS knows only how to handle straight text. Although unusual, it's possible for a WAIS search to return documents of other types, images, sounds, or whatever. If you find such documents, you should configure MacWAIS to launch appropriate helper documents, using the Launchers command in the Edit menu.

One problem with WAIS applications is that sometimes the document that you find is quite large, which can make scrolling through it to find the actual piece of information you wanted a bit tedious. To help, MacWAIS has Find and Find Again commands in the Edit menu.

MacWAIS 1.29 adds support for the OURL (Open URL) Apple event. Although only MacWeb currently supports this event as well, the idea is that MacWAIS can accept OURL events from other programs (such as MacWeb) and pass the results back after performing the requested WAIS search. The utility of this design is that MacWeb and Web browsers in general don't provide particularly good interfaces to WAIS, so by working with MacWAIS, you reap the benefit of each program doing what it does best.

Although it's not currently all that useful, MacWAIS can search local WAIS sources. This means that if you had a program to create a WAIS source of information on your hard disk (John Hardin is working on just such a program now), you could use MacWAIS to search through it. I want to be able to do this badly, since I store a lot of text and have trouble finding specific pieces of information quickly.

Finally, although there's no need to mess with them, MacWAIS provides a few preferences that make life easier. Most notable are the capability to default to using a specific source in new questions, and the capability to save sources in a specific folder—so you don't have to collect them manually when you accidentally save them somewhere else on your hard disk (see figure 13.49).

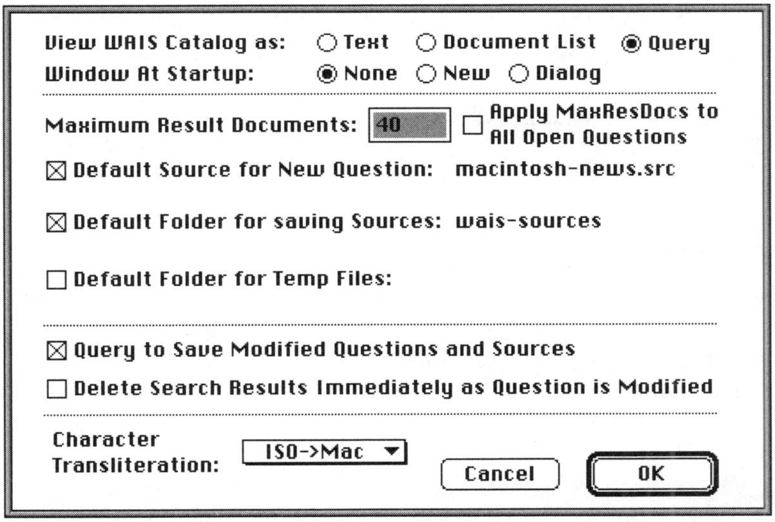

Figure 13.49 *MacWAIS Preferences dialog*

Overall Evaluation

MacWAIS is a good, simple program that does its job well, but there are some areas that could stand improvement. I'd like to see a better way of selecting sources, since the old Font/DA Mover interface lost its appeal years ago. Perhaps a scrolling list attached to each question window would work well. In my experience, you frequently want to change sources and it shouldn't be a difficult process. In addition, it would be nice if the MacWAIS window was resizable. John Hardin has already said that he plans to fix that problem and to devote some more energy to MacWAIS's interface once the hullabaloo surrounding MacWeb dies down a bit. In any event, I like and use MacWAIS regularly, which is one reason I decided to include it on the disk that comes with this book. You can also retrieve MacWAIS from either of the following:

```
ftp://ftp.einet.net/einet/mac/macwais1.29.sea.hqx
```

```
ftp://ftp.tidbits.com/pub/tidbits/tisk/tcp/mac-wais-129.hqx
```

You can contact the MacWAIS folks at **mac-shareware@einet.net**. MacWAIS is $35 shareware from the Microelectronics and Computer Technology Corporation (MCC), which is an industry consortium formed by several computer companies a few years ago. If you use MacWAIS for more than 30 days, MCC requests that you pay your shareware fee. Send checks payable to MCC to:

EINet Mac Shareware
MCC
3500 West Balcones Center Drive
Austin, TX 78759-5398

WAIS for Macintosh

You may feel concerned about the 1.2a version number on WAIS for Macintosh, but in fact, version 1.1 had some problems that prompted the release of the alpha version of 1.2. I've found 1.2a to be stable and usable, which is more than I can say for version 1.1.

Note

You normally must download both WAIS for Macintosh 1.1 and 1.2a for a complete program—the 1.2a file on the nets isn't complete on its own. However, the bookmark that I've included for it on the disk provides a complete copy of 1.2a.

Harry Morris based WAIS 1.2a on his public domain application called WAIStation, and this heritage shows up in the About menu, which says About WAIStation instead of About WAIS for Macintosh. Oops.

Installation and Setup

Installing WAIS is fairly easy. You can put the WAIS application anywhere on your hard disk, but the folder called WAIS, which holds several other folders—Types, Sources, and Documents—must live in your System Folder. This setup is a big step up from WAIStation, which had to live on your boot disk or wouldn't work, irritating those of us with partitioned hard disks.

Basic Usage

After you have everything in the right places and are sure MacTCP is installed, double-click on the WAIS icon to launch the program. WAIS opens two windows on startup, the Sources window and the Questions window (see figure 13.50).

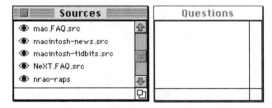

Figure 13.50   *WAIS Sources and Questions*

As you can see in figure 13.50, I have several sources in my Sources window already, whereas you probably have only the **Directory-of-Servers** and the **Connection-Machine Server** (which runs on a supercomputer at Thinking Machines). I haven't saved questions to appear in my Questions window yet, mostly because I always ask different questions. I sometimes save empty questions containing sources, to avoid the step of dragging sources over.

To accomplish anything, then, you must ask a question. From the Questions menu, choose New Question. WAIS opens a Question-1 window (see figure 13.51).

From the Sources window, select the **Connection-Machine Server** and drag it into the "In these sources" box in the Question window. Then type a question into the "Look for documents about" box, as I've done. You can phrase your question in any way you want, but think about adding different forms of the same word if you don't have many words in your question. The rule of thumb is, type as many words as you think are unique to the document you want to find.

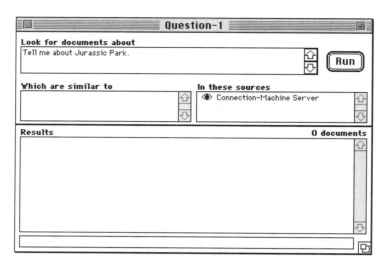

Figure 13.51   *WAIS New Question window*

Now, click the Run button, and watch the messages at the bottom of the window. The WAIS initializes the connection to the **Connection-Machine Server**, searches it, and returns a response in the form of a list in the Results box (see figure 13.52).

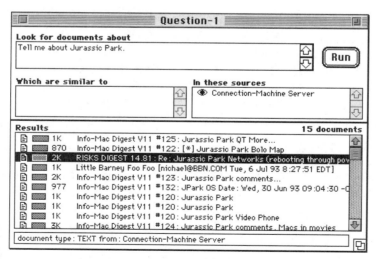

Figure 13.52   *WAIS question answered*

In the Results box, the first icon at the left of each entry shows that the document is a text document, although other document types show here as well. The bar next to it shows how closely the document matches your question, and it's followed by the size of the document and the document's name. Double-clicking on any document retrieves it from the server and displays it in a rather normal-looking text window for you to read (see figure 13.53).

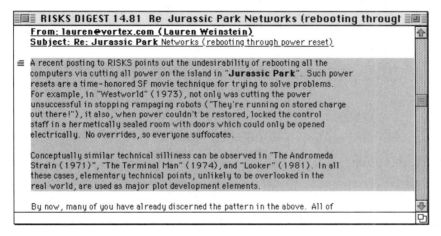

Figure 13.53   WAIS Document window

Because the WAIS program cannot display any other file types, if it finds a picture or some other type of data, it asks you to save it on your hard disk for viewing with some other program when you double-click on the document within WAIS for Mac. A folder called Displayers comes with WAIS for Macintosh and contains various freeware programs for displaying different types of data.

Figure 13.53 shows some text selected in the document window because I want to show you relevance feedback. I could have dragged one or more documents from the Results list into the "Which are similar to" box in the Question window, but I also can drag the little icon that appears to the left of the selected text. When I rerun the search, it changes the list to reflect the text that I used for relevance feedback, refining my search and eliminating bogus matches.

But what if I want to find new sources? I replaced the **Connection-Machine Server** with the **Directory-of-Servers** and asked WAIS for Mac to tell me about music and literature. The trick here is that the documents returned also are servers, just as the **Connection-Machine Server** is. Most of the time, you must find the appropriate server before you can ask your question. Think of this task as going to the right guru (see figure 13.54).

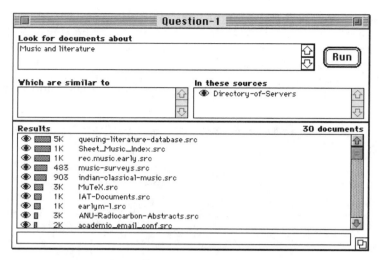

Figure 13.54   WAIS searching for sources

When you find an interesting server, double-clicking on it opens a window with various different settings, along with a description of its data. If you want to keep this window around, you can save it (the WAIS asks you when you close the window) to your Sources folder. Alternately, without opening the source, simply drag it to your Sources window and acknowledge the Save dialog box that WAIS presents.

Now you should know enough to get started searching in WAIS. Remember to use relevance feedback and to modify your question if your search turns up strange stuff. For instance, in my search the word *literature* matched the **queuing-literature-database** source best, but I was looking for items like Hemingway, not for technical documentation. Using *fiction* might have been more effective.

Special Features

Those of you who are experienced in searching are undoubtedly clamoring for Boolean operators (to be distinguished from bowling lane operators) such as AND, OR, and NOT. Well, clamor no more, because the WAIS does support them, along with a fourth operator called ADJacent. Although I don't want to explain the intricacies of Boolean logic, suffice it to say that if you want to find only documents that contain both the words *TidBITS* and *PowerBook*, you phrase the question as "Tell me about TidBITS AND PowerBooks." The AND must be in capital letters. Similarly, OR enables you to find documents that contain either *rainforest* or *rainforests*, and NOT enables you to eliminate documents that contain a certain word, such as "Tell me about music NOT jazz." Finally, using the ADJ operator, you can specify phrases, so you can find documents that contain *Apple Computer* by searching for *Apple ADJ Computer*. Otherwise, the WAIS would find documents that have *Apple* and *Computer* in them in them but may not have the two words together.

Unfortunately, not all WAIS servers support Boolean searches, and there isn't any good way to find out which do.

Overall Evaluation

WAIS 1.2 for Macintosh has a way to go. It slows down a bit and accesses the disk often when I have more than several sources stored. There also are other quirks, such as the download status bar (when you retrieve a non-text document) starting at 15 percent or so. Finally, I still think WAIS for Macintosh should provide an easier way to find sources. Unfortunately, it seems that this program is on Harry Morris's back burner at the moment, and until he gets some free time to clean up the code a bit, WAIS for Macintosh is going to stay right where it is. Still, WAIS itself is impressive, and the WAIS for Macintosh client is a solid performer. If you don't like MacWAIS for one reason or another, check out WAIS for Macintosh.

Administrative Details

WAIS for Macintosh is a free application from WAIS, Inc., although this fact is hard to tell from their documentation. You can retrieve WAIS for the Macintosh from the following two URLs:

```
ftp://ftp.tidbits.com/pub/tidbits/tisk/tcp/wais-for-mac-11.hqx
```

```
ftp://ftp.tidbits.com/pub/tidbits/tisk/tcp/wais-for-mac-12a.hqx
```

Other WAIS Clients

I've run across three other specialized WAIS clients that run on the Macintosh— HyperWAIS, JFIFBrowser, and WAIS Picture Browser.

HyperWAIS

Based on HyperCard, HyperWAIS from Francois Schiettecatte, then of Johns Hopkins University and now a developer at WAIS Inc., is an example of good stack interface design. Unfortunately, it requires that a separate background application called WAIS Listener be running, and its interface doesn't add much over that of MacWAIS (see figure 13.55).

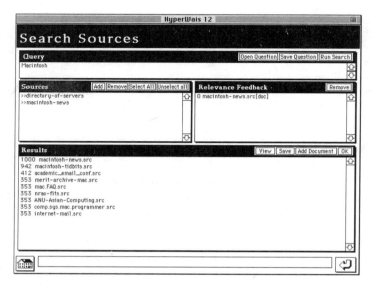

Figure 13.55   *HyperWAIS Search Sources card*

By the time you run HyperCard and the background application, HyperWAIS has chewed up quite a bit of your available memory, and for no real apparent advantage, except as an example of what can be accomplished in HyperCard. You can get source code to HyperWAIS, if you like; if you're an enterprising programmer, it might be an interesting place to look at some MacTCP code.

You can reach Francois at **francois@wais.com**, and you can get HyperWAIS from either of the following:

```
ftp://wais.com/pub/freeware/mac/HyperWAIS/HyperWais.sea.hqx
```

```
ftp://ftp.tidbits.com/pub/tidbits/tisk/tcp/hyper-wais-hc.hqx
```

JFIFBrowser

I suspect that Francois Schiettecatte also wrote JFIFBrowser, since it's a HyperCard stack that looks almost exactly like HyperWAIS. It even comes with what looks like the same WAIS Listener application. Unfortunately, when I used it, it seemed to want to search a specific jfif source, and when it couldn't find that source it merely complained at me.

JFIF Browser can be found at either of the following:

```
ftp://wais.com/pub/freeware/mac/JFIFBrowser.sea.hqx
```

```
ftp://ftp.tidbits.com/pub/tidbits/tisk/tcp/jfif-browser.hqx
```

WAIS Picture Browser

Once again programmed by the intrepid Francois Schiettecatte, WAIS Picture Browser is an example of a dedicated WAIS client. It only knows how to search a single source, in this case one containing images from the Smithsonian Institute. Nonetheless, it might be fun to play around with, to see what images you can find. I found a neat one of a Black Opal (see figure 13.56).

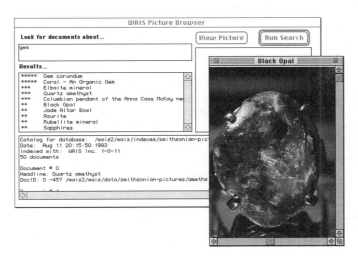

Figure 13.56   *WAIS Picture Browser and picture*

As far as I can tell, WAIS Picture Browser is free, and you can find it at either of the following:

```
ftp://wais.com//pub/freeware/mac/WAISBrowser.sea.hqx
```

```
ftp://ftp.tidbits.com/pub/tidbits/tisk/tcp/wais-picture-browser-14.hqx
```

Gopher

The University of Minnesota's Gopher system lends itself to graphical interfaces, perhaps more so than the WAIS. Because Gopher is inherently a list-based system, it maps perfectly to separate windows of lists, between which you can switch back and forth, clicking on interesting items to explore deeper in Gopherspace.

The most commonly used Gopher client is TurboGopher, which was written by the same folks who created the entire Gopher system. However, in true "we can do that, too" fashion, several other Gopher clients have appeared, and although I'm not going to focus on them as closely, they're both worth a look. GopherApp comes from Don Gilbert, of Indiana University. Rhett "Jonzy" Jones, of the University of Utah, wrote MacGopher, which uses a different metaphor for burrowing through Gopherspace.

TurboGopher

I presume that the primary reasons for TurboGopher's popularity are that it comes from the developers of Gopher at the University of Minnesota (and they must know more about Gopher than anyone else) and that it has the fastest perceived speed (especially over slow links such as PPP or SLIP) of any Gopher client available, supposedly for any platform. TurboGopher is indeed well constructed, and has some useful features that make it one of the necessary components of your MacTCP software collection. The latest version of TurboGopher, as of this writing, is 1.08b4. It supports the Gopher+ extensions that are starting to propagate throughout Gopherspace. The extensions add new features, such as letting the server tell you the size of a file.

Basic Usage

TurboGopher comes configured out of the box, so to speak, to point at one of two identical Gopher servers at the University of Minnesota. Incidentally, each runs on a Macintosh IIci running A/UX, I believe. Unlike some other protocols, the Gopher system runs well on even relatively small machines, although they must have fast network connections for true responsiveness.

Double-clicking on the TurboGopher icon launches the program, at which point it connects to the home Gopher server and displays the main menu in the Home Gopher Server window (see figure 13.57).

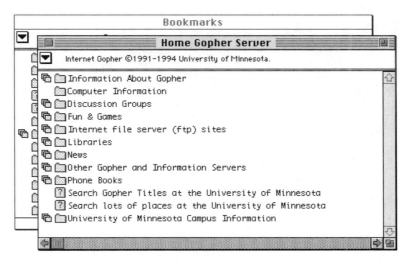

Figure 13.57   *TurboGopher Home and Bookmarks windows*

Behind the Home Gopher Server window is the Bookmarks window, which holds customized pointers. You can create your own bookmarks by selecting an item and then choosing Set Bookmark from the Gopher menu.

Note

You can save a Bookmarks window as a Bookmark file (use the Save as Bookmark File command in the File menu), and if you then double-click on that file to launch TurboGopher rather than double-clicking on the program itself, TurboGopher won't automatically connect to the Home Gopher Server.

Let's browse around a bit so you can get a feel for navigation in Gopherspace. Double-click the "Information About Gopher" item, to open that window. Next, double-click on "Gopher Software Distribution," to move into that area. Finally, click on the "Macintosh-TurboGopher" item, and in there, double-click on "ReadMe-Versions-Bugs," to open that document for reading (see figure 13.58).

If you wanted another copy of TurboGopher, you could double-click on the "TurboGopher1.0.8b4.hqx" item, and TurboGopher would download it for you. Since you've already got that version from the disk, though, I wouldn't bother until a new version came out.

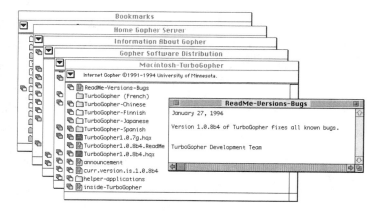

Figure 13.58   *Browsing through Gopherspace*

If you download a file, TurboGopher can download the file while you continue to explore Gopherspace, although it takes longer for windows to open and text files to display. When a download is complete, you can click on the Open button to open the file just as though you had double-clicked on it in the Finder. TurboGopher automatically debinhexes files, as Fetch does, but it doesn't automatically expand them. Instead, it provides an Open button that opens the document when it's finished downloading, so TurboGopher can call StuffIt to expand StuffIt files.

TurboGopher can connect to any FTP site, whether or not it also runs the Gopher server software, and you can use it to search Archie, double-clicking on the results to download them. Both FTP sites and Archie access are available in the main Home Gopher Server window. In addition, TurboGopher can download several files at once, which Fetch cannot do, although Anarchie can. However, TurboGopher fails to compete with Anarchie and Fetch in one major regard. Unless an item resides on a Gopher+ server, you have no way of checking how large the file is or when it was uploaded. Even if the item resides on a Gopher+ server, you must use the Get Attribute Info command from the Gopher menu to find out about it. The Gopher team made a conscious trade-off here, because displaying the size of each file would significantly slow down operations, and people generally spend more time browsing than downloading.

Other than the disk that indicates a downloadable file, TurboGopher may display a number of little icons next to the items in the lists. Most common, of course, is the folder, followed by the text file icon. Double-clicking on a text file displays it immediately. Then comes the question-mark icon. This brings up a simple search dialog that lets you, for example, enter one or more words to search for in an Archie database. The book icon opens a simple dialog for searching, and if you click on the More Choices button, you get a more complex dialog for phone directory-type searches (see figure 13.59).

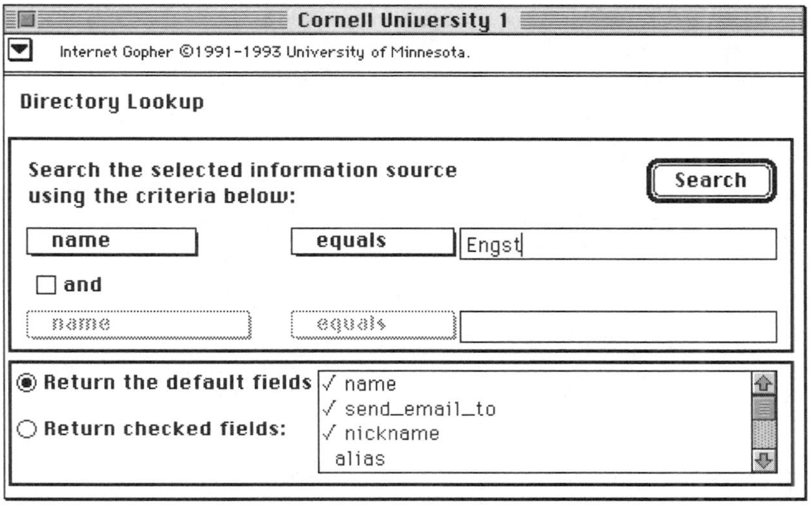

Figure 13.59   *TurboGopher Directory Lookup (more choices)*

Also, some special icons indicate file types. There's one that looks like a starburst and identifies a GIF image, a speaker that marks sampled sounds, another that denotes QuickTime movies, and one that indicates a DOS program. You also see an icon that looks like a Mac Plus; it indicates that the service is terminal-based and launches NCSA Telnet for you if you double-click on it. I'm not sure how many of these special icon types TurboGopher supports, but the number undoubtedly will continue to grow with future revisions.

As you may realize, Gopherspace is huge, and the tool that makes navigating it possible is Veronica, which allows searches of either only Gopher Directories or of all items in Gopherspace (see figure 13.60).

You can generally find Veronica under Other Gopher and Information Servers, or perhaps under a folder called World, but whatever you do, make sure that you have a bookmark to both types of Veronica searches. I generally do a directory search first, when I'm just trying to get a handle on what might be available. Using that information, I can then determine whether I'm using a good search term that works for all items in Gopherspace.

Note

If you read the FAQ in the Veronica folder, it tells you about a number of useful features in Veronica that you'd never know otherwise, such as using the -t7 switch in a search string to only find searchable items.

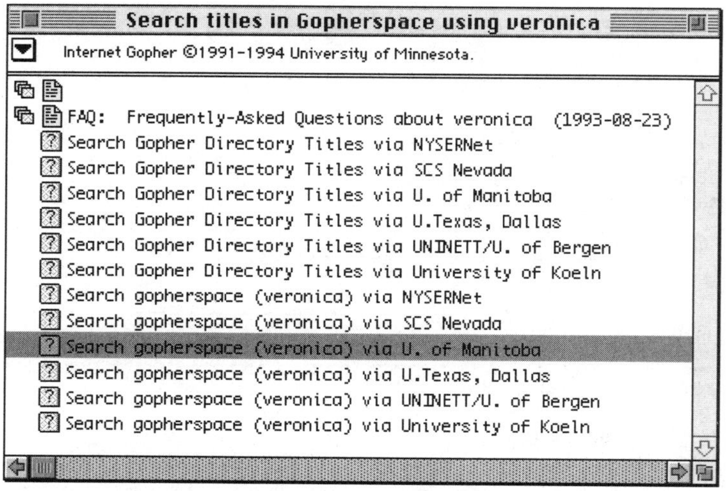

Figure 13.60   *TurboGopher and Veronica*

If someone tells you to check something on a specific Gopher site, you can jump directly to it. From the File menu select Another Gopher, and in the Server field type the Internet address of the Gopher site to which you want to connect. Don't worry about entering anything in the Title or Selector fields (see figure 13.61).

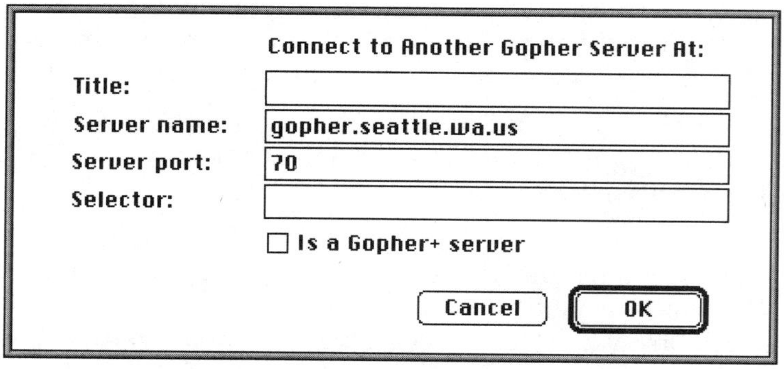

Figure 13.61   *TurboGopher Another Gopher dialog*

Unfortunately, unlike Anarchie and Fetch, TurboGopher knows nothing about URLs, so even if you have one, you cannot paste it directly into the Another Gopher dialog box's Server field. Instead, extract only the Internet address of the server—the bit, for instance, that comes after `gopher://` in `gopher://gopher.seattle.wa.us`.

If the Gopher server to which you connect proves interesting, make a bookmark of it by going to the Gopher menu and choosing Set Bookmark. That way, you don't have to retype the address manually if you want to visit that site again.

Special Features

Like Fetch, TurboGopher enables you to set up a number of helper applications to process types of data, such as GIF images, that it doesn't handle internally. Helpfully, a folder of these applications is available in the same area as TurboGopher itself on the Home Gopher Server. These applications also are generally available on the Internet as well. Check in:

```
ftp://ftp.tidbits.com/pub/tidbits/tisk/utilities/
```

I'm perhaps most impressed by TurboGopher's capability to download several files at once, not so much because it's faster than downloading them one after another, but because it makes more efficient use of my time.

If you hold down the Option key and double-click on a word, TurboGopher places it in the text field of a search dialog. This capability simplifies searching for new terms while you're reading about something in a text window.

More than anything else, TurboGopher is fast and, at the same time, cooperates extremely well when placed in the background (during a long download, for instance). One of the major speed increases comes from TurboGopher's capability to let you start reading a document while it's being retrieved. Although this capability doesn't actually speed up execution, it reduces the time you wait for the program, which is all-important.

TurboGopher is *stateless* (as is the Gopher protocol in general), which means that it opens a connection each time you request a new file or open a new folder, and as soon as the information has come over the network, Gopher closes the connection. Although this process may slightly slow performance (certainly not by any noticeable amount), it significantly reduces the load on the servers because you aren't taxing the remote system unnecessarily, especially when you're just reading a text document onscreen.

To aid in navigation, you can optionally have TurboGopher reuse the same window rather than open a new one each time. This capability prevents window clutter, although it may make moving around more confusing. Also, a Recent menu lists all the places you've visited, in reverse chronological order; selecting any item from this menu takes you there instantly. If you end up in a window with a large number of items, such as a directory listing on an FTP site, you can type the first few letters of a name to move directly to it, or you can use TurboGopher's Find feature, available from the Edit menu. Arrow keys work fine for navigation, along with the Return or Enter key for moving into an item. Finally, TurboGopher, although it comes with no documentation separate from the program, has extensive online help, although for some reason it's in the Gopher menu, rather than in the standard locations of the Apple menu or Balloon Help menu.

Overall Evaluation

TurboGopher is definitely a must for your collection, which is why I include it on the disk. It's fast, it's easy to use, and most importantly, in conjunction with Veronica, it enables you to find useful information in Gopherspace. Overall, I find the TurboGopher/Veronica combination to be the most useful of any method for finding answers to questions I have. I almost always start with Veronica unless I know that what I'm looking for is a file, at which point I usually try Archie via Anarchie instead.

Perhaps the biggest problem with TurboGohper is that you may have a hard time figuring out where you really are with it, although Shift-clicking on an item (to Get Attribute Info on it) tells you a fair amount of information, especially if the machine is a Gopher+ server.

Administrative Details

TurboGopher has been localized for Spanish, Japanese, Chinese, and Finnish (translated by Sami-Jaakko Tikka), and copies of all of those versions are available at:

```
ftp://boombox.micro.umn.edu/pub/gopher/Macintosh-TurboGopher/
```

I also hear there is a French version and a Swedish version (translated by Lennart Jareteg), although they're not located in the same place. TurboGopher is free for noncommercial use (commercial use requires permission—ask at **gopher@boombox.micro.umn.edu**), and the most recent release of TurboGopher is always available from the University of Minnesota Gopher server, and at either of the following:

```
ftp://ftp.tidbits.com/pub/tidbits/tisk/tcp/turbo-gopher-108b4.hqx
```

```
ftp://boombox.micro.umn.edu/pub/gopher/Macintosh-TurboGopher/TurboGopher1.0.8b4.hqx
```

Blue Skies

Although actually a Gopher client, Blue Skies, from the University of Michigan's Weather Underground (written by Alan Steremberg) is primarily a neat application for, well, interacting with the weather. You need not go outside or travel to other parts of the world, though. All you need to do is launch Blue Skies and select GroundHog Server from the GroundHog menu.

Note

Apparently they call 'em groundhogs *in Michigan instead of* gophers.

Blue Skies opens a window that looks suspiciously similar to the Finder in Name view, complete with the little triangles that you can click on to reveal the contents of their folders (see figure 13.62).

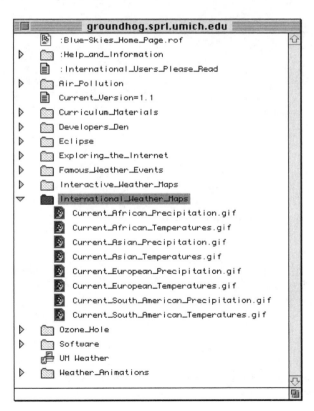

Figure 13.62 *Blue Skies main window*

I especially like the interactive weather maps, which bring up a map of the United States. Moving your mouse over different locations on the map displays the weather conditions for that city, such as in Billings, Montana, to pick an example out of a geographic hat. You can even zoom in and out to a few different magnifications, and in doing so gain access to more detailed weather data (see figure 13.63).

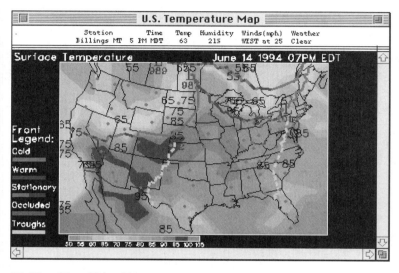

Figure 13.63   *Blue Skies Temperature Map—it's better in color*

There are also plenty of other weather-related pieces of information available on the GroundHog server, ranging from climactic data to forecasts to famous weather events to weather animations. Now the Internet can enable you to be just as inaccurate as the weather forecasters on TV!

Note

The Weather Underground is seeking schools outside of the United States to become partners for the purpose of exchanging weather information via the nets.

Although you could retrieve this stuff with TurboGopher, the Blue Skies application makes it a lot more fun. What I'd really like to see via Blue Skies is some historical weather data for the recent past. Remember that really hard winter when you were a kid? Or was it really all that bad?

The Finder metaphor actually works pretty well in Blue Skies, although I suspect it would become unwieldy if you tried to use it with long lists of information.

Currently, no restrictions are being placed on Blue Skies, although since its primary audience is K-12 schools, if they start having trouble using it because of the load, some restrictions may be added later. You can contact the Blue Skies folks at **blueskies@umich.edu**, and you can retrieve the latest version of Blue Skies from the GroundHog server itself, or from:

```
ftp://ftp.tidbits.com/pub/tidbits/tisk/tcp/blue-skies-11.hqx
```

MacPanda

I'm not really sure quite what MacPanda is, but it seems to be able to access Gopher servers (although not all of them—I encountered a number of errors while testing it). It comes from the University of Iowa, and beyond that, I can't really tell you too much more about it (see figure 13.64).

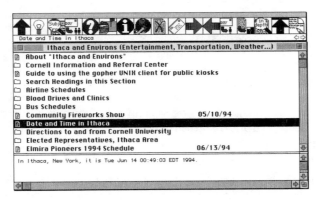

Figure 13.64   *MacPanda Main window*

If you're the curious type, you can retrieve MacPanda from:

```
ftp://PANDA.UIOWA.EDU/pub/Panda/MacPanda.4-26.sea.hqx
```

Sextant

I've only glanced at Brown University's Sextant, which is yet another simple Gopher client without the power or flexibility of TurboGopher (it only does one thing at a time and cannot retrieve non-textual items). It has a decent interface, though, and might be worth checking out if you like playing with different programs (see figure 13.65).

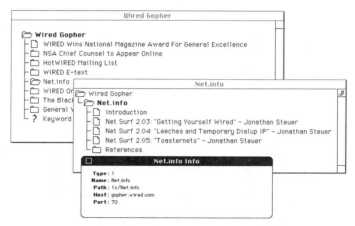

Figure 13.65   *Sextant windows*

Sextant offers a small Info window that tells you where the item you're looking at actually resides, which is a handy feature at times, especially when sorting through long Veronica lists of seemingly identical resources. Unlike TurboGopher, Sextant supports multiple (even discontiguous) selections, so you can open multiple documents in a Gopher list at once, or get more information about more than one document at a time. You can also save a window to a file. Double-clicking on that file opens that window again, although there's no integrated bookmarks feature.

I cannot tell from the documentation whether or not Sextant is freeware, but I doubt you'd want to use it in favor of TurboGopher, anyway. It's at:

```
ftp://ftp.tidbits.com/pub/tidbits/tisk/tcp/sextant-10.hqx
```

GopherApp

GopherApp's interface resembles that of TurboGopher in that it uses the same window-with-iconic-lists metaphor. It does boast a neat feature—the capability to display attribute information in the list, as does the Finder (see figure 13.66).

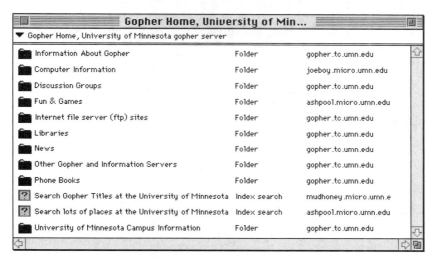

Figure 13.66   *GopherApp Home window*

Although the preferences allow you to ask for attributes such as date and size, I never saw them listed, because only Gopher+ servers provide such information.

The other feature that sets GopherApp apart from the rest is that it includes an email feature that enables you to send and receive email from within GopherApp. This part of GopherApp has the most interface problems, with buttons overlapping text fields and the like.

Although a little unstable in my testing (Okay, it crashed fairly quickly), GopherApp has a great About GopherApp picture—and because it isn't animated like TurboGopher's cute gopher cursor, I can show it to you (see figure 13.67).

GopherApp is free, and you cannot charge for redistribution or modify it, although the source code is available for noncommercial use. If you have comments or questions, send them to **software@bio.indiana.edu**. You can find the latest version of GopherApp at:

```
ftp://ftp.bio.indiana.edu//util/gopher/gopherapp/gopherapp++2.2b43.hqx
```

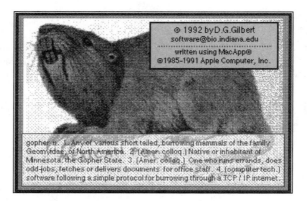

Figure 13.67   GopherApp About box

MacGopher

Although not nearly as fast as TurboGopher, and lacking in the same type of multitasking features, the free MacGopher from the University of Utah has an interesting interface (see figure 13.68).

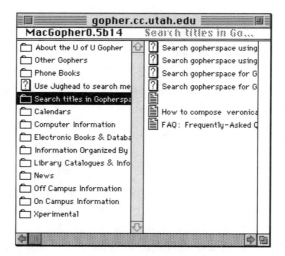

Figure 13.68   MacGopher Browser window

You can see only two panes at a time, but you can use the scroll bar on the bottom of the window to move back and forth between the different panes.

Although more structured, this interface method suffers when you want to keep two paths open. You must open a New Gopher from the File menu to traverse two separate paths at the same time. When you open a text document, it opens in its own window, though, and the pane concept falls down at that point.

MacGopher has one feature that I especially like (although I'm not sure why it's important—I just like it). It's an Item Inspector window, which displays information about the currently selected item (see figure 13.69).

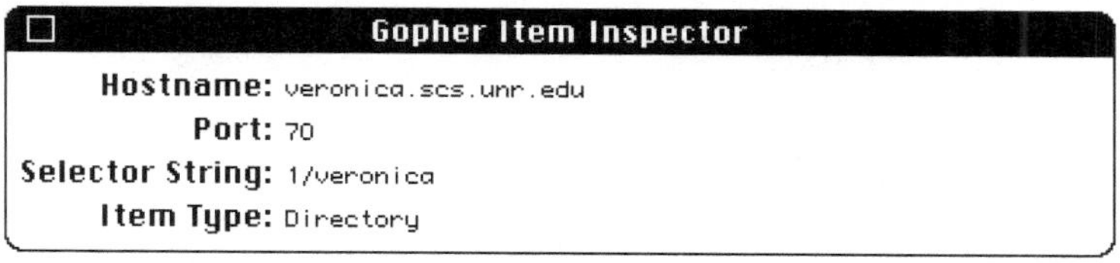

Figure 13.69 *MacGopher Item Inspector*

Along with the normal Gopher functions, MacGopher also provides a simple Finger client. FTP and Mail items in the same Services menu both are disabled, perhaps indicating future features.

The main problems from which MacGopher suffers are a lack of speed and an inability to do more than one thing at a time. Given that the version number of the current MacGopher is 0.5b14, though, I think MacGopher may improve significantly by the time it hits 1.0, should it ever reach that plateau.

You can distribute MacGopher freely as long as there is no monetary gain for anyone involved in the transaction. Comments, questions, and bug reports should go to Rhett Jones at **jonzy@cc.utah.edu**. You can find MacGopher at either of the following:

```
ftp://ftp.cc.utah.edu//pub/gopher/Macintosh/MacGopher.sit.hqx
```

```
ftp://ftp.tidbits.com/pub/tidbits/tisk/tcp/mac-gopher.hqx
```

GopherSurfer

Although the point of this book is to help an individual gain access to the Internet, not to help someone set up a server on the Internet, you have two options if you want to set up a Gopher server on a Mac. I mentioned Peter Lewis's FTPd previously, and the University of Minnesota also has a Gopher server called GopherSurfer.

I haven't played with GopherSurfer much, but I gather that the most recent releases can work with AppleSearch, Apple's heavy-duty (it requires a 68040-based Macintosh) searching engine that is based on WAIS technology. So, if you were serious about setting up a useful Gopher server on a Mac, I'd check out the combination of GopherSurfer and AppleSearch. It's at:

```
ftp://boombox.micro.umn.edu/pub/gopher/Mac_server/
```

There's also a French version, translated by Jean-Pierre Kuypers.

World-Wide Web

When I wrote the first edition of this book, the World-Wide Web was just starting to explode and the Macintosh was being left out. Then, along came NCSA Mosaic for the Macintosh and all was well in the world again. That went on for a while, until it became clear that the neatest services available on the Web used forms, and Mosaic didn't support forms. This too went on for a few months, and then, as I was heading into the home stretch on this second edition, the EINet group of MCC released the free MacWeb, complete with forms support. Never being one to miss out on a good thing, I immediately got permission to include MacWeb on the disk with this book, so you can try out the Web as soon as you have a MacTCP-based Internet connection.

NCSA wasn't exactly sitting around twiddling its thumbs. It matched EINet's MacWeb with the alpha release of NCSA Mosaic for Macintosh 2.0. Kind of ironic—I wrote about the alpha version of 1.0 for the first edition and I'm going to write about the alpha version of 2.0 for this edition.

NCSA Mosaic for the Mac

The beauty of writing about World-Wide Web browsers is that there are almost no instructions you need to follow. The basic idea is that you connect to the Internet, run Mosaic or MacWeb, then click on the underlined words (they can also be in a color, but that doesn't show up in a black and white book well) to traverse the links between Web pages.

Installation and Setup

Although you don't need to configure anything to use Mosaic, it's a good idea to visit the Preferences dialog and adjust some of the settings to match your personal information and preferences. Launch Mosaic, and from the Options menu choose Preferences, to bring up the Preferences dialog (see figure 13.70).

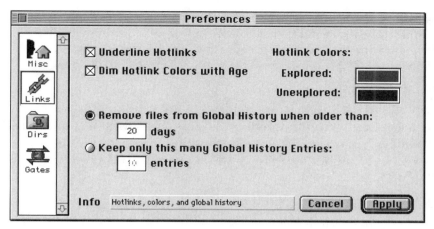

Figure 13.70   *Mosaic Preferences dialog*

In the Misc part of the Preferences dialog you set the URL for your home page (if you want it to be something other than the default NCSA Home Page), your name, and your email address. The Links section enables you to modify how the links look and work; the Dirs section lets you specify directories for various Mosaic files; and the Gates part lets you configure various bits of technical gateway information.

Below the Preferences command in the Options menu is the Styles command, which brings up the Styles dialog, where you specify which fonts you want to use for the different HTML styles that exist on the Web (see figure 13.71).

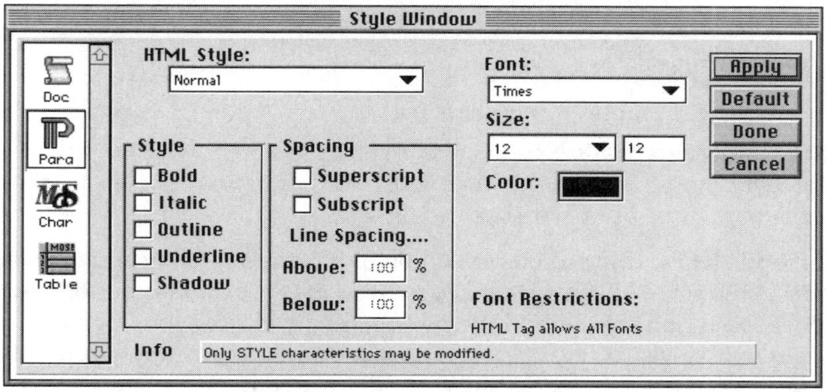

Figure 13.71   *Mosaic Styles dialog*

The basic idea is that you can choose an HTML style and then modify the font, size, and style characteristics that go with it. I strongly recommend that you experiment with these settings, because the defaults aren't all that readable, at least on my system, and I suspect you're going to read a lot on the Web.

Basic Usage

Other than a healthy curiosity, it doesn't take much to use a Web browser. The main window shows you the text and inline graphics on the Web page you are connected to. Clicking on any underlined word takes you to another place on the Web (see figure 13.72).

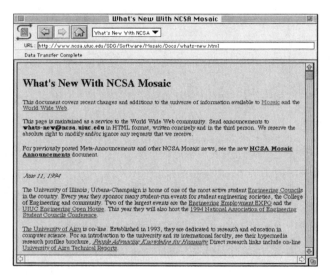

Figure 13.72   *Mosaic Main Window*

The NCSA Mosaic What's New page is a great place to browse for new Web servers that have arrived on the Internet in the recent past. Sometimes they seem to appear at the rate of five or six per day.

The left and right arrow buttons at the top of the screen enable you to go back or forward in the set of Web pages that you've visited. The house button jumps directly to your home page, and the pop-up menu enables you to go to any of the pages you've visited previously. The Mosaic icon in the upper-left of the window indicates what Mosaic thinks it's doing at any given time, and clicking on it acts as an interrupt, or at least it did in the previous version.

Chapter 13
MacTCP-based
Software

Note

Interrupting Mosaic 1.0.3 was generally a bad idea, since it was prone to crashing when interrupted. Mosaic 2.0 hasn't been out long enough, nor is it sufficiently complete, to determine if it suffers from the same problem.

I have Mosaic set to display URLs in the URL field, which not only shows you the current URL, but enables you to select it and copy it for sending to someone else, for instance, or modify it for visiting a slightly different URL. Simply change the text of the URL and press the Return key. I also have Mosaic set to show me status messages (both of these options are in the Options menu, as you might suspect) so that I can tell what it's doing and how long it might take.

If you find a Web site in your travels that you want to return to later, you add it to your Hotlist. NCSA seriously revamped the interface to the Hotlist in Mosaic 2.0—it was a menu and is now a separate window with buttons for editing hotlist entries, deleting them, adding them, and so on. Overall, I think the new Hotlist interface is a good thing, since the old menu become overloaded quickly, but I haven't used Mosaic 2.0 long enough to tell for sure (see figure 13.73).

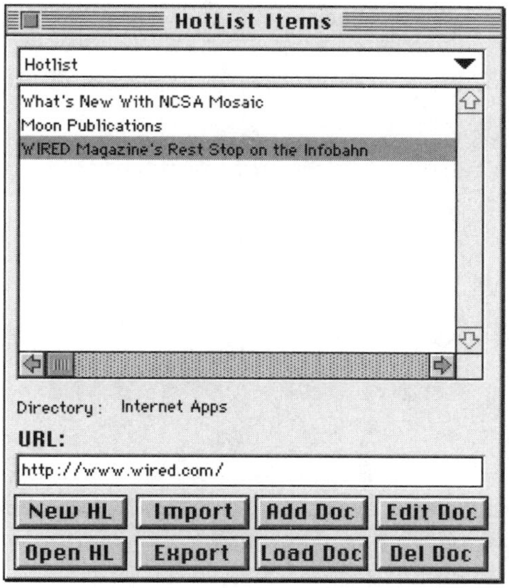

Figure 13.73   *Mosaic Hotlist window*

That's about all there is to using Mosaic's basic features. Although the Web is a vast and quickly-growing place, it's surprisingly easy to use.

Special Features

It's difficult to talk about the special features in Mosaic 2.0 since it's only been out for about three days, as of this writing, and hasn't even reached beta phase. Nonetheless, since it supports forms, I suspect that many people will switch over almost instantly. The forms support seems to work well, although the formatting of the results from this server currently leaves a little to be desired (see figure 13.74).

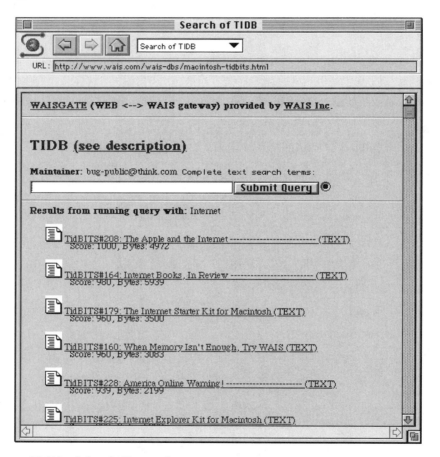

Figure 13.74   Mosaic Forms Support

Mosaic has good online (and I do mean online, as in on the Internet) help, but in a neat twist of interfaces, it's available from the Balloon Help menu. Selecting any of MacMosaic Documentation, HTML Help, URL Help, or FAQ connects to a Web server and brings the help information down from the Internet. This is a great system assuming that the user isn't having trouble getting Mosaic to work.

Although the feature doesn't appear to be working completely in the current alpha release, you can make personal annotations to any document on the Web, either in text-only or using the audio-input features of your Mac. These annotations are added to the bottom of the documents as links; clicking on the links brings up your annotation later on. Since annotations are merely HTML documents stored locally, you can even annotate your annotations.

In a clever move (or perhaps a really dumb one, depending on how much mail they can handle), the Mosaic developers added a Mail Developers command to the File menu, making it easy to send them comments and bug reports (see figure 13.75).

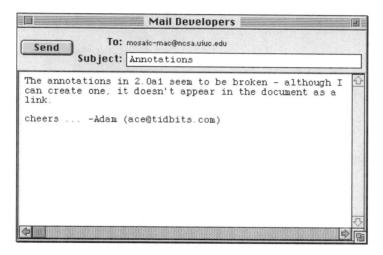

Figure 13.75   *Mosaic Mail Developers window*

Since we are discussing standard items, you can always open a new URL with the Open URL command in the File menu, and the Open Local menu item enables you to open an HTML document that resides on your hard disk.

New in Mosaic 2.0 is the capability to modify the menu structure almost completely. I would have settled for the capability to modify the Navigate menu, and I hope that people don't go around removing standard Macintosh menu items, such as New and Quit.

Although I don't have a firewall to test with, Mosaic reportedly can work from behind one, unlike many other Internet applications. A firewall is a system that sits between you and the Internet, theoretically to keep intruders out. However, firewalls also make getting out to the Internet difficult, and something called *proxy service* makes this possible by routing the Internet requests appropriately through the firewall.

Overall Evaluation

When it was the only game in town, NCSA Mosaic was an absolutely essential program to have for accessing the Internet. However, now that MacWeb is out, you have a choice. I recommend that you spend some time with both programs to see which you prefer.

Despite MacWeb's forms support, Mosaic is a step ahead in other ways, which makes a certain amount of sense, given the chronology. Whether that will remain true in the future, I cannot say.

Note

One interesting comment on the entire Mosaic discussion is that at least five or six companies have licensed (for big bucks) the Mosaic source code for use in commercial Web browsers. In the near future you should have commercial Mosaics to consider as well, although I do wonder if they'll be sufficiently better to be worth the money.

Administrative Details

NCSA Mosaic is free to users (although I couldn't have put it on the disk even if I'd had the space—NCSA guards Mosaic pretty closely). You can find it on the Internet at either of the following:

```
ftp://ftp.tidbits.com/pub/tidbits/tisk/tcp/ncsa-mosaic-200a2.hqx
```

```
ftp://ftp.ncsa.uiuc.edu/Mac/Mosaic/NCSAMosaicMac.200A2.sit.hqx
```

MacWeb

Recently, while browsing through **comp.sys.mac.comm**, what should I see but an announcement for a new World-Wide Web browser called MacWeb, written by John Hardin, for MCC's EINet group (see figure 13.76).

Figure 13.76   *MacWeb About box*

The simple fact that previously there had been only one stable Web browser available made this announcement interesting enough; but the feature set, including the lusted-after forms support that Mosaic 1.0.3 doesn't have, made talking about it a necessity. And, from first glance, it looks as if MacWeb will be solid competition for even Mosaic 2.0, with its added forms support.

Installation and Setup

There's no installation or setup worth mentioning for MacWeb; essentially, you make sure you're connected to the Internet, and then you launch MacWeb.

MacWeb has only a few preferences, which you get to by going to the File menu and choosing Preferences. You can change the home page that MacWeb automatically accesses on launch to any valid URL (or even an HTML document on your disk; there's one in the MacWeb Documents folder that works well); you can have MacWeb automatically open a specific hotlist of stored URLs at startup; and you can set little things such as Autoload Images (turn this option off for faster performance over a SLIP or PPP connection) and the window background color (see figure 13.77).

Note

I'd prefer that MacWeb kept the option for autoloading images out in the menus because I find that I often want to toggle that setting in Mosaic, depending on what I'm doing and what kind of performance I want.

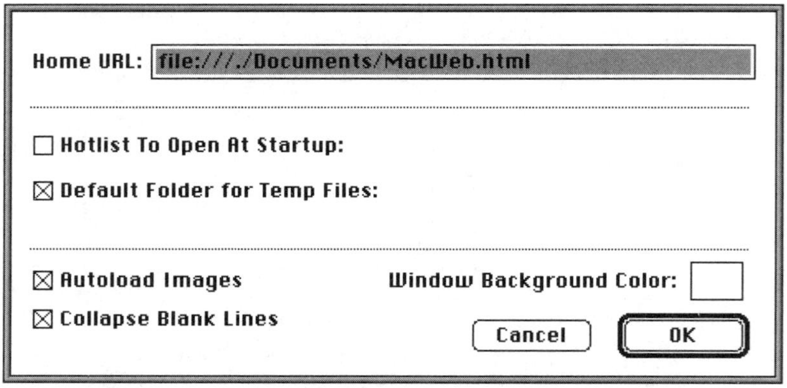

Figure 13.77   *MacWeb Preferences dialog*

If you don't like the way MacWeb assigns fonts to the HTML styles, you can change those fonts. From the Edit menu choose Styles, to display the Styles dialog (see figure 13.78).

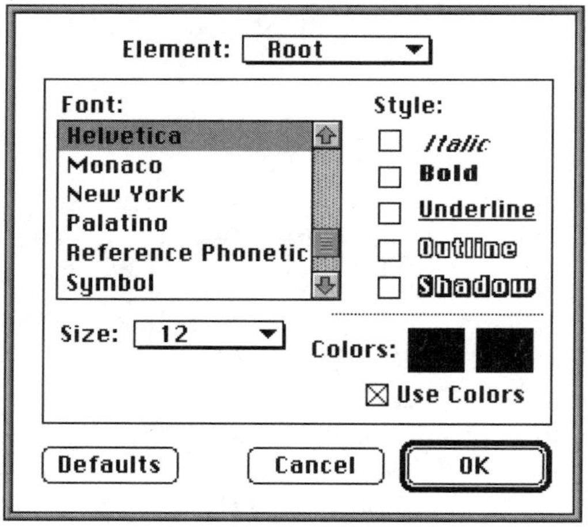

Figure 13.78   *MacWeb Styles dialog*

The Element pop-up menu and its sub-menus enable to you pick what style you're editing. Since the styles are hierarchical, it's easy to set all the heading styles to, say, Helvetica, and then vary the font size for the different heading sizes. You can also modify colors as well, but I'd recommend restraint here. Colored text (and too many colors in text, especially) can be difficult to read.

Basic Usage

I always feel funny telling people how to use a Web browser, because it seems so obvious. MacWeb is no exception, and in fact the basic window design looks a lot like Mosaic 1.0.3, as do the menu layout and features, such as the Hotlist interface. Anyway, when you first launch MacWeb, it accesses its local home page (see figure 13.79).

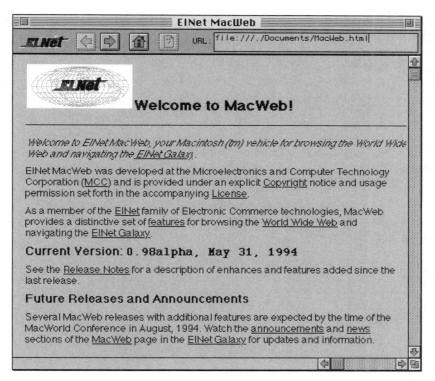

Figure 13.79   *MacWeb home page*

The basic parts of the MacWeb window are self-explanatory. MacWeb offers forward and back buttons for moving back and forth between the places you've visited, a home button for bouncing back to your home page, a question mark button for Web search items, an editable but somewhat small URL field for copying URLs, and, at the bottom of the screen, a status field that indicates what MacWeb is doing, along with a preview of what URL goes with any given link. My favorite part of the status line is that it often tells you the size of the file MacWeb is accessing, and counts up as it retrieves the file. That kind of feedback is truly pleasant when you're on a slow connection and waiting for a graphic to transfer.

When you click on an underlined link, MacWeb promptly takes you to the appropriate page, and as it fills the page, you can scroll down. However, if MacWeb must also bring in a graphic, it forces you back to the top of the page when it draws the graphic, which can make for some confusing jumps in the text if you've started reading. Reading text in the MacWeb window works exactly as you'd expect it to, and the Find feature available in the Edit menu is a big help if you hit a large page and want to jump directly to a certain part.

If you find a Web resource that you like and wish to visit again, you can add it to your Hotlist with the Add This Document item under the Hotlist menu. The Hotlist menu also has a hierarchical Hotlist Interface menu that provides options for creating new hotlists, opening old ones, editing them, saving them, and so on. If you edit the hotlist, MacWeb brings up a list of all of your hotlist entries, and clicking on the Edit button enables you to modify the name and URL (see figure 13.80).

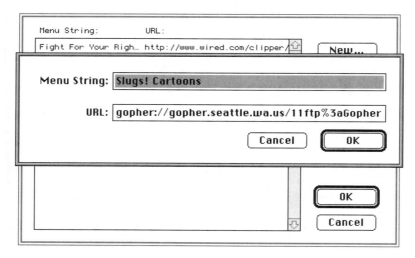

Figure 13.80   MacWeb Hotlist Editor

Of course, if you have a URL from a newsgroup posting or a *TidBITS* article, you can always enter it manually into MacWeb. From the File menu choose Open URL and type or paste the URL in before pressing Return to activate the link. MacWeb can also open local documents and can reload the page if for some reason it isn't up to date.

Problems

There is one major problem with the current version of MacWeb. You cannot select text in the main window, which means that you cannot copy it for use anywhere else. I need to do this all the time, when I want to tell someone about a neat Web site, for instance, or want to send email to an address I see on a Web site. A simple copy & paste operation is essential for these tasks, and any Macintosh application should allow you to copy text from a text display window. This is apparently the most-requested feature so far, and John has promised to fix it soon.

Other minor irritations exist. Although MacWeb allows you to resize its window to any size you like, it doesn't remember the size, so you must resize it each time if you don't like the default.

MacWeb doesn't always like being interrupted (although it's much better than Mosaic 1.0.3 in this regard). If you press Command-Period to stop the transfer of data, the data transfer will stop, but so might your Mac.

Finally, there are many different types of data on the Web, and Mosaic handles them through a set of helper applications. It seems that MacWeb wants to do the same, but it currently provides no interface for choosing which applications will help with which data types. If you don't have the proper helper applications, MacWeb claims that it cannot find the viewing application and asks if you'd like to launch one manually. Nice idea, but opening one in the Standard File dialog box currently doesn't work. I'm sure John will fix the bug, but I'd like more control over which applications MacWeb uses.

Note

If MacWeb cannot launch your helper applications properly, try rebuilding your desktop—if the desktop database is out of date, MacWeb may not be able to find the proper helper application.

Special Features

Although relatively simple, MacWeb has a number of special features that complement its sparse interface. Although it has a hierarchical History menu under its Navigate menu, MacWeb also provides a shortcut for navigating to the sites you've previously visited. Simply click and hold on either the Forward or Back buttons. After a second or two, a pop-up menu appears, listing the history.

When you choose Open URL to type or paste in a new URL, MacWeb provides a pop-up menu of your hotlist items; selecting an item from that list pastes its URL into the URL field for you to edit if you so choose. You can also type, paste, or edit a URL in the editable URL field in the main window. Once you do that, pressing Return or Enter will open that URL.

In a nod to NCSA Mosaic, MacWeb can import hotlists generated by Mosaic. This simplifies switching to MacWeb if you have a large hotlist in Mosaic.

If you decide to run with images turned off by default, you can load selected ones by clicking them, as you would expect. If, however, you just want to get all of the images on a page, the Options menu contains Load Images This Page, which does just that.

MacWeb enables you to save a document as either straight text (which is often strikingly ugly without the formatting you see onscreen) or as HTML, which is useful for seeing how a certain effect has been achieved. If you want to view the HTML quickly, though, from the Options menu choose View Source, and MacWeb opens the HTML source file in TeachText or SimpleText.

Note

Holding down the Shift key when you select View Source retrieves the page again and displays the original HTML rather than the generated HTML that you otherwise get (a subtle difference). Holding down the Shift and Control keys while selecting View Source retrieves the original HTML file and also retains any MIME headers sent from the server. These modifiers apply to all document retrieval actions, so you can load a document to disk, merely by Shift-clicking on a link or Shift-entering a URL.

In its Navigate menu, MacWeb lists a few common places you might want to visit, including the EINet Galaxy, which I find to be an extremely useful launch point for finding information on the Internet. EINet has done some interesting things, such as building a search into many of the navigational links, so when you see the results, not only do you have the few hard-coded links, but also many dynamic links created from the search. EINet searches a Veronica database, the HYTELNET database, and many places on the Web itself, so it does pretty well.

Note

I'd still like a hard-coded link to the NCSA What's New page. You can hack this one in for yourself. Edit MacWeb with ResEdit, and in the STR# resource, add two new fields at the end of the NavigateM resource. Call the first "NCSA What's New Page" and for the other, enter:

```
http://www.ncsa.uiuc.edu/SDG/Software/Mosaic/Docs/whats-new.html
```

MacWeb supports two Apple events, one of which is Open URL (OURL). In theory, AppleScript or another application (such as Eudora or NewsWatcher— plans are already in the making) could send MacWeb an OURL event to have it access a particular URL, or could respond to an OURL event sent from MacWeb from a **mailto** or **news** URL (which are URLs corresponding to email addresses and news articles). EINet's shareware MacWAIS client supports the OURL event too, and thus can take special advantage of this, by handling direct WAIS connections for MacWeb, with the documents being sent back to MacWeb for viewing. You can get the necessary version of MacWAIS at either of the following:

```
ftp://ftp.einet.net/einet/mac/macwais1.29.sea.hqx
```

```
ftp://ftp.tidbits.com/pub/tidbits/tisk/tcp/mac-wais-129.hqx
```

Last, and perhaps most important at this point in time, is MacWeb's forms support. Mosaic also has forms support in version 2.0, currently in alpha testing, but you simply must get MacWeb and try it out. Once you run into a site with forms, you get fields and buttons and menus on-screen, and you can work with them just as though they were part of, say, a Macintosh dialog box (see figure 13.81).

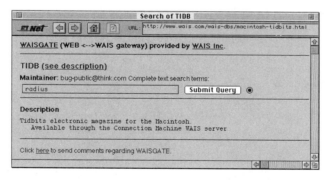

Figure 13.81   *MacWeb forms*

Overall Evaluation

MacWeb is a excellent program in its early releases, and I fully anticipate that most of the rough edges will be worked out in the near future. I would like to see it stray a little from the Mosaic model. The two look and feel extremely similar, and simply because Mosaic is currently the most popular Web browser doesn't mean it has a lock on how a Web browser should look and act. In particular, the Hotlist feature could be improved and differentiated. But these are quibbles. As a first effort, MacWeb does fine.

Given that Mosaic 2.0 is only in alpha testing, I expect MacWeb to garner a significant mindshare of the Macintosh Internet community. All too often, I've arrived at an interesting-sounding Web site and then had to leave without trying it due to the lack of forms support in Mosaic.

At 374K on disk, MacWeb has a surprisingly small footprint, which is welcome, especially given some of today's bloated applications. It requires less memory than many as well, and can run in a 700K memory partition (don't believe the 2048K number in the Get Info dialog box for the current version). Perhaps because of its small size, it feels faster and more responsive than Mosaic.

Administrative Details

MacWeb was written by John Hardin, of the EINet group of MCC (Microelectronics and Computer Technology Corporation—and no, I don't know how they get the acronym to work). MCC has released MacWeb as freeware for academic, research, or personal use; companies should contact MCC for licensing information. To report problems with or make suggestions about MacWeb, send email to **macweb@einet.net**. You can retrieve the current version of MacWeb on the Internet at either of the following:

```
ftp://ftp.einet.net/einet/mac/macweb/macweb0.98alpha.sea.hqx
```

```
ftp://ftp.tidbits.com/pub/tidbits/tisk/tcp/mac-web-098a.hqx
```

MacWWW

The first and most rudimentary browser for the World-Wide Web is called MacWWW or Samba, depending on what you read online. MacWWW is not of the caliber of MacWeb or Mosaic, and the versions I've used have had some problems. Confusing installation is not one of them, because there's no installation at all. You simply launch the program, and it displays a page of text with some words in bold (or in a different color, your choice). Double-click on a word, and you're taken to another window with the text of a different documents (see figure 13.82).

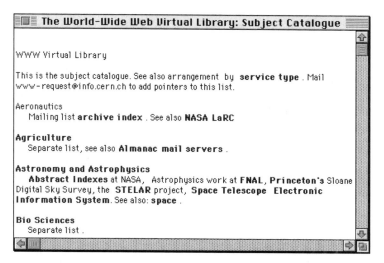

Figure 13.82   *MacWWW sample window*

Now you know literally all the program does, other than provide simple controls for navigating (Home, Back, Next, and Previous) and Font, Size, Style, and Color controls.

MacWWW was the first Web browser for the Mac, written by Robert Cailliau and others at CERN, and to be fair, CERN didn't have nearly the resources to devote to programming that NCSA did, which accounts for MacWWW's minimalist approach.

Administrative Details

It turns out that MacWWW is not freeware or even shareware. It's commercial software from CERN. I don't know how many people use and have paid for MacWWW, but it costs 50 ECU (European Currency Units). The source code is also available, for quite a lot more. Check the information at CERN for the details:

---

http://info.cern.ch/hypertext/WWW/Clients.html

You can find MacWWW at:

---

ftp://info.cern.ch/pub/www/bin/mac/MacWWW_V1_03.sea

MacHTTP

MacHTTP is a World-Wide Web server currently being written by Chuck Shotton, from the University of Texas Houston Health Science Center's Office of Academic Computing. It allows your Mac, presumably connected permanently to the Internet, to serve World-Wide Web documents to other WWW browsers. Basically, you create HTML (HyperText Markup Language) documents and store them along with binary files, such as GIF images, in the MacHTTP folder. Then, whenever anyone browses into your Mac from the Web, MacHTTP makes those documents and files available. Unlike the FTPd and NCSA Telnet FTP servers, MacHTTP makes sure that no one can see any files on your hard disk that aren't in the same folder as the MacHTTP application, thus limiting any security risk.

Note

If you do wish to serve HTML documents via the Web, check out the various utilities available for aiding in their creation. Look for programs called WYSIWYG, and Simple HTML Editor, and for conversion programs for hotlists to HTML, for RTF to HTML, and for some extensions to the popular programmer's editor BBEdit.

Although I haven't yet tried to set up a Web server with MacHTTP, reports on the nets indicate that you can do some impressive things with it. The main feature that provides MacHTTP with an unusual amount of power is that it supports Apple events and can link AppleScript scripts to URLs. Thus, when a browser such as MacWeb accesses that URL, the MacHTTP server runs the AppleScript script. Since many of the most powerful applications on the Mac are compatible with AppleScript as well, this feature opens up FileMaker Pro and Microsoft Excel, among many others, to the Web.

If you have any questions or comments about MacHTTP, you can contact Chuck at **cshotton@oac.hsc.uth.tmc.edu**. The latest version of MacHTTP, version 1.3, lives at both of the following:

```
ftp://oac.hsc.uth.tmc.edu/public/mac/MacHTTP/machttp.sit.hqx
```

```
ftp://ftp.tidbits.com/pub/tidbits/tisk/tcp/mac-http-13.hqx
```

Utilities and Miscellany

Okay, I admit it; I've run into a completely ambiguous group of software that isn't really related in any way. I'm talking about programs such as Bolo, CU-SeeMe, Maven, Archie, Finger, Talk, ircle, Homer, MacTCP Watcher and a number of others. They do a variety of things, but most are one-trick ponies, so I've decided to lump them all together here.

Bolo

I wish I could say more about Stuart Cheshire's shareware Bolo, but for a couple of good reasons I'm not particularly familiar with it. First, Bolo is an addictive multi-player tank game that supports robot opponents as well. Since I suffer from carpal tunnel syndrome, I don't allow myself to play games—it's just too hard on my hands, and I prefer to write. Second, Bolo, chews bandwidth and doesn't work particularly well over a modem-based SLIP or PPP connection. Although it might be possible for a Bolo game to have one person connected via SLIP or PPP, if two people attempt to connect to each other over SLIP or PPP, Bolo complains about the network's not being fast enough.

Note

Bolo also works over AppleTalk networks, so if you have a LocalTalk or Ethernet network between Macs, you can play Bolo with friends locally.

That said, Bolo is extremely cool. If you enjoy strategy tank games, definitely check it out. Although it's not arcade-level action, Bolo is graphical and quite good looking (see figure 13.83).

As I said, strategy is all-important, and Bolo makes possible all sorts of alliances and rivalries. Numerous "brains" (specially programmed robot tanks) have been distributed on the nets, so even if you don't have anyone to play with you may be able to have a good time playing against a brain or two. Note, however, that running a brain requires making and launching a second copy of Bolo, so you need a fairly fast Mac and a fair amount of RAM. Along with the brains, people have written all sorts of utilities for Bolo, including map generators that create the terrain maps that you play on, and utilities for finding Bolo games in progress on the Internet. There's even a `rec.games.bolo` newsgroup for discussing Bolo. The FAQ for that group is a good place to get started learning about Bolo, since there are a number of basic rules of etiquette that you should know about.

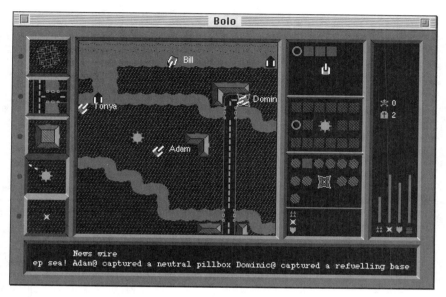

Figure 13.83   *Bolo standoff*

Copies of Bolo can be found in all sorts of places on the Internet if you do an Archie or Veronica search. There's also an entire Bolo folder in the Info-Mac archives devoted to Bolo and its brains, maps, and utilities. Try this, or any other Info-Mac mirror site in the Anarchie Bookmarks list:

---

ftp://mrcnext.cso.uiuc.edu/pub/info-mac/game/Bolo/

You can contact Stuart Cheshire at **cheshire@cs.stanford.edu**. Shareware payments of $25 or £15 (if you're in the U.K.) should be sent to either of the following:

Stuart Cheshire
P.O. Box 8323
Stanford, CA 94309, USA

Stuart Cheshire
290 Clarence Road,
Four Oaks, Sutton Coldfield
West Midlands, B74 4LT, England

CU-SeeMe

Cornell University's CU-SeeMe provides videoconferencing over the Internet. Nothing more, nothing less, but if you've seen the prices for some of the videoconferencing software available, you realize what an incredible accomplishment this program is.

To use CU-SeeMe to receive video, all you need is a MacTCP-based Internet connection, the faster the better. If you want to send video as well, you must have a video-capable Mac, such as a 660AV, or a video-input card. And, of course, you must have a video camera.

When you launch CU-SeeMe, it asks for some preferences. Fill in your name and check the appropriate settings boxes. Since I use a 660AV, I can send video (or at least I could if I had a camera attached to the Mac), but for just viewing with CU-SeeMe there's no need (see figure 13.84).

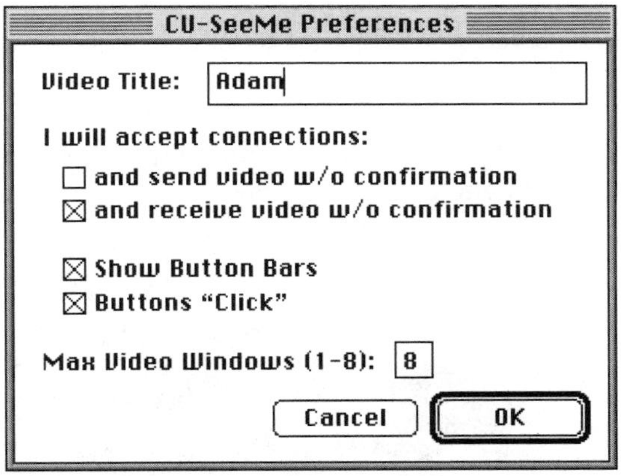

Figure 13.84   *CU-SeeMe Preferences window*

Once in CU-SeeMe, go to the Conference menu and choose Connect. You must know the address to type in the Connection dialog. You can use CU-SeeMe in either point-to-point mode with another person (at which point you type in their address) or broadcast mode with a CU-SeeMe reflector.

A *reflector* takes incoming streams from CU-SeeMe and reflects them back out to people who connect. Using a reflector, you can view up to eight windows onscreen at the same time. I entered **192.35.82.96**, which is one of Cornell's reflectors. Along with my window, which is black because I don't have a camera and am not sending to the reflector, seven other video windows appeared on my screen, along with the audio controls (which do not work at all if you connect over a modem). Take a look at figure 13.85 to see what it looked like on my setup.

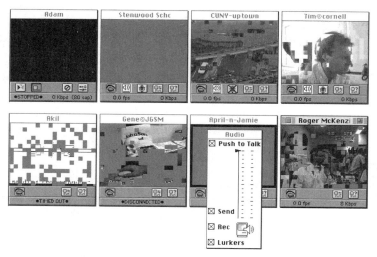

Figure 13.85   *CU-SeeMe windows*

As you can see, the windows are fairly broken up, and most haven't updated very well. That's partly a result of my poor modem trying to constantly bring in seven streams of video. If I close all of the unnecessary windows, the pictures in the remaining two get significantly better (see figure 13.86).

Figure 13.86   *More CU-SeeMe windows*

That's about all there is to using CU-SeeMe, although if you can send video, you can also type scrolling messages along the bottom or top of the screen. I used CU-SeeMe on a number of occasions with my sister, Jennifer, and her boyfriend, Jeff, back when they were at Cornell, since Jeff had a 660AV and a video camera. When we were both using SLIP connections to the Internet, the quality of the CU-SeeMe images was good, but there was essentially no motion to them—they were just screenshots separated in time by a few seconds. Even still, it was impressive that CU-SeeMe worked at all over a modem, especially since Cornell hadn't gotten around to optimizing it for modem usage, last I checked.

Note

CU-SeeMe works its magic by only transmitting information that has changed in the image—that significantly reduces the amount of data it must pump over the Internet.

The most recent version of CU-SeeMe added a neat feature that tells you whether someone else has your video stream open on their screen. The eye-con (sorry, not my fault) is open if they can see you and closed if they cannot.

CU-SeeMe (which was primarily written by Tim Dorcey) is freely available for both the Macintosh and the PC, although in terms of development, the Mac version is well ahead of the PC one. You can retrieve the latest version of CU-SeeMe from either of the following:

```
ftp://gated.cornell.edu//pub/video/Mac.CU-SeeMe0.70b1/
```

```
ftp://ftp.tidbits.com/pub/tidbits/tisk/tcp/cu-see-me-07b1.hqx
```

Maven

Along with Cornell's CU-SeeMe, Maven, from the University of Illinois, goes a long way toward turning the Internet into a general-purpose communication medium. Where CU-SeeMe provides video (and has audio support using Maven's code in the works), Maven provides only audio. In some respects this seems silly, since a telephone does exactly the same thing, and generally for less money. But with the costs of international phone calls, I could see programs such as Maven becoming all too popular (in fact, they might seriously overload the networks).

I tried to use Maven a while back, when it was in version 2.0a16. I was unsuccessful because it required a fast Internet connection. Over my SLIP connection back then, my friend Geoff and I couldn't get anything more than what sounded like chirps and warbles, and occasionally a fragment of a word. So while I don't recommend even trying Maven over a modem-based connection, give it a spin if you've got a real network connection to the Internet.

There's not all that much to show, since Maven only has a configuration dialog and a single bar feedback window, but if you do have the proper connections for it, play with Encoding and Quantization sub-menus under the Audio menu, to see what effect they have on sound quality.

Maven was written by Charley Kline, and may be freely redistributed. You can find it via Veronica (that was how I located the latest release, anyway), or at:

```
ftp://ftp.tidbits.com/pub/tidbits/tisk/tcp/maven-20a16.hqx
```

MacWeather

The Blue Skies application that I mentioned in the Gopher section is extremely neat, but I'm also fond of Christopher Kidwell's shareware program, MacWeather. You tell MacWeather what city you want to see the weather for, and it retrieves the current data for you, displaying it in either digital or analog form (see figure 13.87).

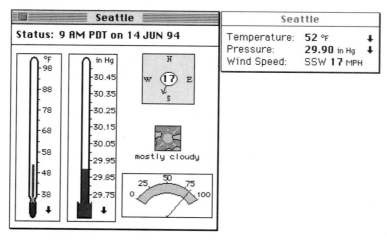

Figure 13.87   *MacWeather window*

MacWeather has preferences for each of the weather items it reports on, so you can have the temperature display in Fahrenheit or Celsius, the barometer display in inches of Hg, millimeters of Hg, or millibars, and the wind speed display in miles per hour, knots, or meters per second. You can also get the forecast in a separate window and have MacWeather update automatically every so often, say you're constantly connected to the Internet from a room with no windows to the outside world.

What I like most about MacWeather is that it's completely focused. It doesn't try to do anything fancy—it simply displays weather data for a selected city. I'd like to see a few minor enhancements, such as the capability to have more than one city onscreen at the same time (for comparison purposes), and an easier way to switch between cities. But these are quibbles, and MacWeather is a neat program. I highly recommend that you get a copy.

If you like MacWeather, send Christopher $10 for the shareware fee. You can reach him at **kidwell@wam.umd.edu**, and shareware payments should go to:

Christopher Kidwell
3405 Tulane Drive, Apt. 2
Hyattsville, MD 20783

You can find MacWeather at:

```
ftp://ftp.tidbits.com/pub/tidbits/tisk/tcp/mac-weather-111.hqx
```

Network Time and NTP for Macintosh

I used to be truly retentive about always being on time and knowing exactly what time it was. I remember, as a child, being thoroughly pleased when I got my first digital watch. (I also remember becoming slightly ashamed when I read Douglas Adams's gentle put-down of people who thought that digital watches were pretty cool things.) And, of course, I grew up in the highly regimented world of high school and college, where a few minutes one way or another was important, for some unknown reason. Moving to Seattle cured me of much of my concern about time, but still, it's nice to know whether your VCR is accurate—otherwise, you'll miss the first few minutes of a TV show, or even worse, the last few minutes.

That's why I thoroughly enjoy Network Time, a shareware control panel from Pete Resnick, one of the MacTCP gurus on the Internet. Network Time is a perfect example of a simple utility dedicated to performing a task in an elegant fashion. All it does is synchronize the clock in your Macintosh with what's called a *network time server*, which is a special program on an Internet host that speaks the *Network Time Protocol* (NTP). Internet machines use multiple network time servers on other Internet machines to keep their clocks in synch, and, a number of hops on down the Internet, one of the machines gets its time from an atomic clock. Needless to say, an Internet machine that gets its time from a source several hops away from the atomic clock won't be perfectly accurate, due to variables in network traffic, the load on the machine, and so on. However, it will be easily close enough for normal use—perhaps within a second or two.

NTP itself can supposedly provide accuracy to 232 picoseconds, although I seldom believe any numbers that are that accurate.

Another shareware control panel, NTP for Macintosh, from John Dundas, works in a similar fashion. John designed NTP for Macintosh, however, as a more complete solution. NTP for Macintosh works over both AppleTalk networks and the Internet, and John sells server software for the Macintosh operating system, A/UX, and DEC's VAX/VMS operating system. In other words, if all you want to do is make sure the time on your Mac is right, you don't need the server software. However, if you want to ensure that every Macintosh on your network is synchronized with the time on the company's VMS machine, you should buy a copy of the server software.

Installation and Setup

Pete's Network Time control panel is simple to set up. Although you can drag it into your Control Panels folder and restart, there's not really any need to do so, unless you want Network Time to check your Mac's clock periodically and synchronize it with the network time server. All that you really need to do is open the control panel, enter the name or IP number of your network time server (ask your system administrator or provider, or try guessing at one of the machines you use for your NNTP server or SMTP server), and customize the other options (see figure 13.88).

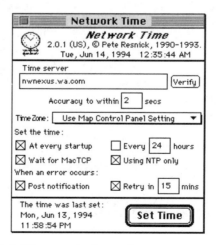

Figure 13.88   *Network Time control panel*

The options are quite clever—you can set Network Time to check at every startup or every few hours. If you connect via SLIP or PPP, you can ask Network

Time to wait to check until you've used another MacTCP-based program, indicating that the SLIP connection is active. You want to be a bit careful with Network Time if you don't ask it to wait for another program to open MacTCP, because otherwise it could decide to synchronize the time when you weren't connected, forcing your SLIP or PPP program to auto connect, a process fraught with danger. You can set Network Time to post notifications if an error occurs, and it can also retry automatically if something goes wrong. Finally, you can have Network Time figure out what time zone you're in from the Map control panel.

NTP for Macintosh is decidedly more complicated to set up than Network Time. Although you can configure it before placing it in your Control Panels folder and restarting, it must load at startup to work properly. To be honest, I couldn't really figure out how to configure NTP for Macintosh—it seemed to assume that something would be broadcasting times at me, which didn't appear to be the case. I selected TCP/IP (rather than AppleTalk), checked Accept Broadcasts, and checked Enable at StartUp (see figure 13.89).

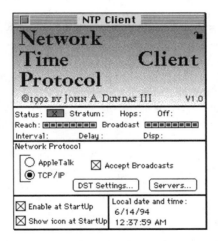

Figure 13.89 *NTP for Macintosh control panel*

NTP for Macintosh is a bit weird about how it handles your network time server. Rather than look up a name you give it, as most MacTCP programs do, it requires that you add your network time server to the Hosts file that may or may not live in your System Folder. I know of no other program that requires the Hosts file, and thus didn't even have it installed myself when I started playing with NTP for Macintosh. Once I added **nwnexus.wa.com** to the Hosts file, I was able to select it, Get Info on it, and Poll it, using the appropriate buttons, but I never managed to get NTP for Macintosh to set the time properly.

NTP for Macintosh has the best method of setting a Macintosh for Daylight Savings Time that I've seen—not only does it enable you to set whether your area observes Daylight Savings Time, but it even lets you configure when Daylight Savings Time starts and ends in your area.

Basic Usage

Using Network Time is simplicity itself. If you never want to see it working, configure it to set the time at every startup, making sure to wait for MacTCP if you aren't directly connected to the Internet. I've tried this and it works like a charm. However, many people prefer not to run unnecessary control panels, and unless you're really picky about your times—or your Mac's clock is seriously fast or slow—you may just want to leave Network Time with the rest of your Internet programs, open it every now and then when you're connected, and click on its Set Time button. *Poof*, it updates the time for you.

As I said previously, I never managed to get NTP for Macintosh to work for me with my network time server. That may be due to a number of reasons, but as far as I can tell, there is no real usage to NTP for Macintosh. In theory, once it's configured properly and knows about a compatible network time server, it simply works. The more serious problem is that NTP for Macintosh must load at startup, but if you use something such as InterSLIP, NTP for Macintosh forces InterSLIP to auto connect. This actually worked (one of the few times I've seen it work with InterSLIP) when NTP for Macintosh hadn't loaded properly. However, when it did load properly, it attempted to dial out before all of the other extensions and control panels had finished loading, and was unable to find the domain name resolver (at least, it reported some such error message). After it warned me that it wasn't going to work, it thoroughly confused QuicKeys, and when the Finder appeared, I had garbage characters filling my entire menu bar. Moral of the story: don't expect NTP for Macintosh to work well with a SLIP or PPP account.

Overall Evaluation

Pete Resnick's Network Time is definitely the way to go for individuals wanting to synchronize clocks, especially if you don't have a dedicated connection to the Internet. It's clean, simple to use, and has elegant touches, such as an area that tells you the last time Network Time set your clock for you. As do a number of other Macintosh Internet programs, Network Time has excellent balloon help that not only tells you what a button or control does, but explains why you might want to use it.

NTP for Macintosh, on the other hand, may be a fine program, but seems far more suited to an AppleTalk network or to an organization that would also buy the NTP server software from John Dundas. It certainly has plenty of features, and nice little readouts that tell you things such as the delay between your Mac and the server, the number of hops between your Mac and the primary time server, and the status of the synchronization state.

Administrative Details

Network Time has been translated into French and Dutch, Chinese and Russian are in the works, according to Pete Resnick. Network Time 2.0.1 is $5 shareware from Pete Resnick, at **resnick@cogsci.uiuc.edu**. I encourage you to remember Pete if you start using Network Time. It's often easy to forget about shareware programs that work so transparently in the background.

Pete Resnick
1009 North Busey Avenue
Urbana, IL 61801

You can retrieve the latest version of Network Time from:

```
ftp://ftp.tidbits.com/pub/tidbits/tisk/tcp/network-time.hqx
```

NTP for Macintosh 1.0 is $25 shareware from John Dundas, and registering gets you a 60-page manual that might explain it a bit better than I've been able to do. Send your payment to:

John Dundas
P.O. Box 50784
Pasadena, CA 91115

You can retrieve the latest version of NTP for Macintosh from:

```
ftp://ftp.tidbits.com/pub/tidbits/tisk/tcp/macntp-10.hqx
```

TCP/IP Scripting Addition

I've muttered about AppleScript here and there in this book, but always in the context of being able to script a program. With the release of the TCP/IP Scripting Addition from Atul Butte, however, those of you who are fluent in AppleScript can create entire Internet applications without leaving AppleScript. Since, for most people, AppleScript is an easier programming environment than something such as C or Pascal, I'm very curious to see to what purposes people put the TCP/IP Scripting Addition.

When I first heard about the TCP/IP Scripting Addition, I couldn't imagine quite what might be possible with it. Atul anticipated my questions by distributing a number of sample programs along with the scripting addition itself (which goes in the Scripting Additions folder inside your Extensions folder, and requires AppleScript).

The sample applications sound as though they might be plenty useful in their own right, not just as sample code. There's an application on which you can drop a file to have it uploaded via FTP, a simple Finger implementation, a script that displays the weather in Washington, DC (in case you're concerned about the political climate), a script that can send email, and finally a full Gopher server. I'll admit it, I'm impressed. If you create a unique Internet program using the TCP/IP Scripting Addition, make sure to check with Atul about distribution, and then send me a copy. I'll upload it to the nets and mention it in the next edition of this book.

Atul has a reasonable set of licensing fees, depending on the use to which you put the TCP/IP Scripting Addition, so be sure to read the licensing information that comes with it. The important clauses are that it's free for personal use, and if you plan to distribute a free program based on it, it's probably also free. For anything written to support an organization or for sale purposes, there are various charges. You can reach Atul at **atul_butte@brown.edu**, and any payments should go to:

Atul Butte
Box G—Brown University School of Medicine
Providence, Rhode Island 02912

You can find the TCP/IP Scripting Addition on the Internet at either of the following:

```
ftp://gaea.kgs.ukans.edu/applescript/osaxen/tcpip.osax.hqx
```

```
ftp://ftp.tidbits.com/pub/tidbits/tisk/tcp/tcp-scripting-addition-as.hqx
```

Hytelnet

Hytelnet, which stands for *Hypertelnet*, isn't a communications application at all. Instead, it's what you'd expect from a HyperCard stack—a database. The information in the database is rather interesting: Telnet sites that are accessible by NCSA Telnet or TN3270.

Hytelnet 6.7 was written by Peter Scott; Charles Burchill created the HyperCard front end, which requires HyperCard 2.1 or later. The HyperCard front end uses a large database of cryptically named text files to present a menu interface that closely resembles the one you see if you use Hytelnet on the command line from a Unix machine (see figure 13.90).

Figure 13.90   *Hytelnet Main card*

The text files are in fact the same ones used by the Unix version of Hytelnet, but the Hytelnet stack adds some functionality not present in the Unix version.

You can use the same arrow keys as you would in the online version, but Charles improved the interface so that you can click on any of the words in <> brackets, to delve a level deeper in that area. The databases are extensive, being composed of more than 1,700 files, and they take up 1.3M of disk space.

Note

Do not *use the option-click on a triangle shortcut in the Finder to open all of these folders in outline view, or you will spend an hour trying to recover from it, as I did. The Finder cannot handle that many files in outline view.*

So, what's neat about Hytelnet? I haven't been all that impressed with it online. In my experience, it doesn't do as much as Gopher, and I don't like the interface as much. Even so, I love the possibilities of searching a massive database of Internet resources off-line. After you click your way through various menus and arrive at a specific resource, Hytelnet often provides a help screen or piece of information about that resource, so it's a good way to find out what's available before connecting.

If you want to connect to a listed resource, Hytelnet has a Go for it! button, which launches either NCSA Telnet or TN3270 (whichever is appropriate; the database lists that information, too) and connects you to the appropriate machine. It works well, and in the most recent version (6.7.1) Charles added support for TurboGopher, so you no longer must put up with a mediocre Telnet interface to Gopher when you have a MacTCP-based connection. In the future, I hope to see support for the Web and WAIS as well, perhaps through the Open URL event that has appeared in MacWeb and MacWAIS.

Hytelnet requires a bit of configuration, available by clicking on the Configure button (see figure 13.91).

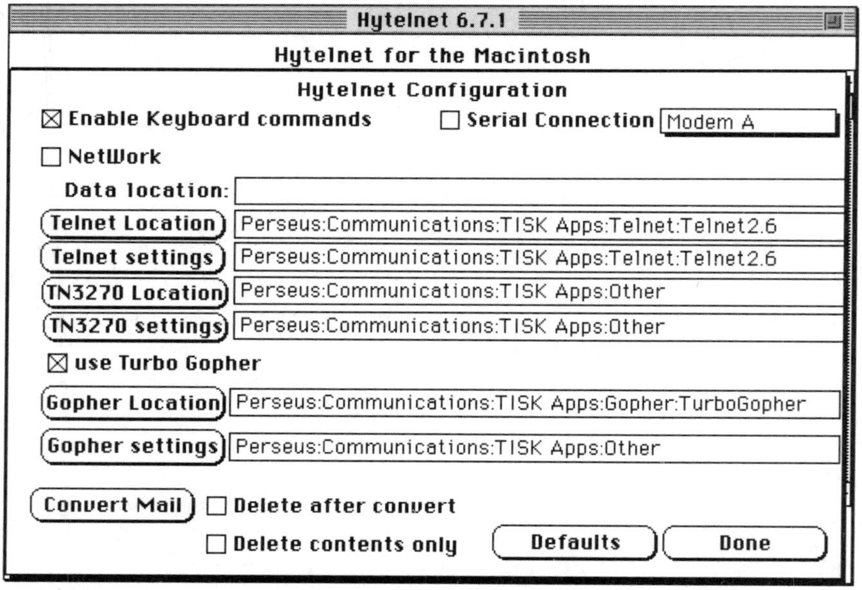

Figure 13.91   Hytelnet Configuration card

Notice the Serial Connection button at the top of the card. If you're using a terminal to access a Unix machine, you can have Hytelnet send the appropriate text command out the serial port to your online session. It may or may not work, according to the documentation.

More important for those using MacTCP are the locations of Telnet, TN3270, TurboGopher, and their settings files. You must locate each of those files by clicking on the respective button, but be aware that the settings files are included for you in the Hytelnet Data folder, as is another file that Hytelnet asks for if you click on the NetWork Data location button.

I cannot pretend that Hytelnet for Macintosh is a slick, useful piece of communications software, because it only launches other programs. Hytelnet in general isn't that impressive, in my personal opinion. However, as a resource guide to tremendous numbers of Internet resources, Hytelnet for Macintosh is incredibly useful. Charles continues to enhance the stack with all the features I suggested in the first edition of this book. He has included a list of favorite places, much like TurboGopher's bookmarks, and a Find feature for searching the entire database. The one feature I'd like to see next time may be too much to ask for. Hytelnet plays havoc with my hard drive, since 1,700 small files is a massive waste of space on a large hard drive (where a file can take up 11K even if it's one byte large, as on my main hard drive partition). If there were some way of retaining the import feature that can bring in new Hytelnet files and add them to a single large file rather than the many small files, that would make it easier to deal with on disk.

You can retrieve Hytelnet for Macintosh from either of the following:

```
ftp://ftp.usask.ca//pub/hytelnet/mac/Hytelnet6.7.sea.bin
```

```
ftp://ftp.tidbits.com/pub/tidbits/tisk/tcp/hytelnet-67.hqx
```

Archie

Before the appearance of Anarchie, the only Archie client on the Mac was Archie 0.9, and it had been released for some time. Although Chris McNeil hasn't added many features to Archie in bringing it up to 1.0, he has made it compatible with the Archie servers out there again, which had ceased to be true of 0.9.

Basic Usage

Using Archie is simplicity itself. The first time you use it, go to the Prefs menu and select Archie Server. In the dialog box that appears, make sure an Archie server is listed; use `archie.rutgers.edu`, if nothing else is present. After you define your Archie server, simply type in the word you want to find in the Search String field, and click on the Search button (see figure 13.92).

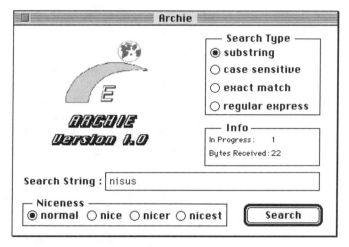

Figure 13.92   Archie main window

If you want, you can click on one of the radio buttons at the top of the main window to change the type of search. *Substring searches* are simply normal, case-insensitive, inexact-match searches (ones that match both *apple* and *Apple*, and find *tidbits-189* when you search for *tidbits*). *Case-sensitive searches* differentiate between upper- and lowercase letters in your search string. *Exact match searches* find only exact matches (searching for *tidbits* does not find *tidbits-189*). *Regular-express searches* use Unix-style *regular expressions*, which are ways of defining patterns in text. Don't worry about regular expressions if you don't already know about them, because they're pretty hairy to use.

The Niceness buttons enable the Archie server to reduce the priority of your query, so if you don't particularly want a reply back soon, check the Nicest button.

It may not seem as though Archie is doing anything. However, after you click on the Search button, you should see In Progress: (in the Info area) become 1; the Bytes Received: should read 11, to indicate that the Archie server has received the request and is processing it. When the results come back—which can take minutes or even hours, depending on how busy the server is—Archie displays the results in a normal scrollable text window.

Archie has a couple of nice options that enable you to set the creator of any files you save (you can save the text window that lists your search results), and that optionally notify you with a sound if a search finishes when Archie is in the background.

Overall Evaluation

Had Anarchie not appeared on the scene, doing everything that Archie does and far more, Archie might have stood a chance at becoming an essential Macintosh Internet application. As it is, though, I cannot really recommend you mess with it much—Anarchie is simply better.

Administrative Details

Archie 1.0 is $10 shareware from Chris McNeil, whom you can reach at **cmcneil@mta.ca**. You can send payments to:

Chris McNeil
Box 153
Middle Sackville NB Canada
E0A 2E0

You can find Archie in all the usual spots, including:

```
ftp://ftp.tidbits.com/pub/tidbits/tisk/tcp/archie-10.hqx
```

Finger

I mentioned the Unix Finger program in the section on using Unix, but those people with MacTCP-based access can use an elegant program from Peter Lewis, called Finger 1.3.7 (and its companion, Fingerd 1.3.7). Finger, an implementation of the Unix Finger program, allows you to be fingered or enables you to finger other people to see if they are logged on, or to read information they have put in their Plan files. If you don't want to leave Finger running on your Mac all day long, Fingerd is a background-only application (background-only applications are called *daemons*, in the murky depths of the Unix world) which enables others to finger you with a minimum of fuss. Talking about Finger always sounds so kinky!

If you use SLIP or PPP to dial-up your account, there's little point in running Fingerd or telling people they can finger you, because Finger can respond to such a request only when you are connected, and few people pay for a dedicated PPP or SLIP connection (some do, but not many in comparison with the number that dial in periodically). Therefore, if you want to create a Plan file (the file that holds the information someone would see if he fingered you) and use Fingerd, I'm going to let you read the documentation that Peter Lewis provides. It's not difficult; you simply create a straight text file that holds the information you want to show people, including *tokens*, which essentially are variables corresponding to the date, time, and various bits of system information.

Note

As an aside to the system administrators in the reading audience, think about using Finger and Fingerd to check the status of a Mac that's at a remote site but still on your network. As long as the site is running MacTCP and Fingerd, you can set up a Plan file that tells you details about the sort of Mac it is, when it was last restarted, how long it has been running, and so on.

More interesting to most people is the Finger program itself, which enables you to finger other people. I find Finger useful for accessing certain types of information over the Internet. People put all sorts of neat things in their Plan files, ranging from the latest reports of earthquake activity to current baseball scores.

Basic Usage

After launching Finger, simply select Finger from the File menu (see figure 13.93).

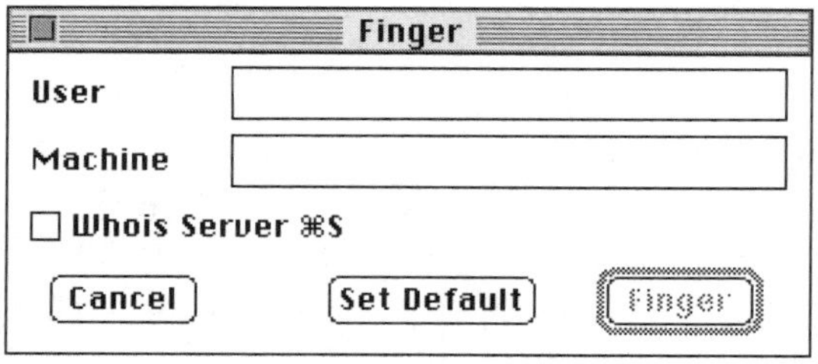

Figure 13.93   Finger dialog

Type the username you want to finger in the User text entry box, and below that type the machine name in the Machine entry box.

Note

You can simply type the entire address in either one of the boxes, and it works just fine.

If you want to access a Whois server (a different Unix program that looks up information about machines), check that box, enter the name of the machine you want learn about in the User field, and **rs.internic.net** in the Machine field. Then click on the Finger button to have Finger go out and execute your request.

Finger saves requests in a hierarchical Finger menu, and you can select an item such as **yanoff@csd4.csd.uwm.edu** to finger that address immediately (see figure 13.94).

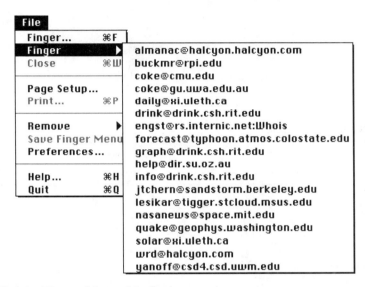

Figure 13.94   *Finger hierarchical menu*

Now, assuming that the remote machine is up and running, you should see the results of the Finger search appear on your screen (see figure 13.95).

You can print the results window or copy information from it, if you so choose. After you finger someone, you can save that entry in your Finger Preferences file by selecting Save Finger Menu from the File menu. That's how I created the list you see in figure 13.94, and it makes it easy to finger the same person or service at a later time.

Finger has only three options. If you choose Preferences from the File menu, you can locate your predefined Plan file; decide whether you want to see the IP number (which is the number corresponding to the machine name) in the title bar of the Finger results window; or decide whether you want the Finger window to open on startup (using the Set Default button in the Finger window, you can choose which service or person should appear by default).

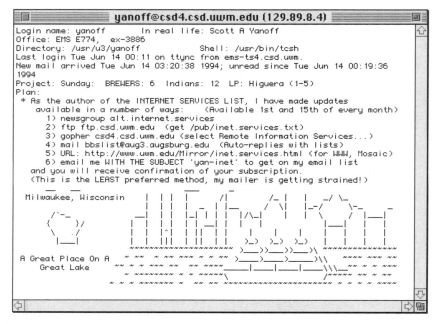

Figure 13.95   *Finger Results window*

Overall Evaluation

I like Finger a lot. It's small, sweet, and to the point. As long as people continue to store useful bits of information in Plan files, Finger will remain an essential part of your MacTCP software kit. One last plug for Peter Lewis—if you use Finger, send him some money, because he's created a number of the useful MacTCP programs mentioned in this book, and without his programming skills, the Mac view on the Internet would be much narrower.

Note

There's another implementation of Finger on the nets that I just found, called HyperFinger Pro. Although HyperCard-based, it seems to work fine and has a nice interface.

```
ftp://ftp.tidbits.com/pub/tidbits/tisk/tcp/hyper-finger-pro-hc.hqx
```

I haven't run into any problems with Finger, other than some sites not responding, but that's not Finger's fault. Sometimes a machine may be down, or the person updating the information may have gone on vacation.

Administrative Details

Finger is $5 shareware, payable in either U.S. or Australian dollars. One way or another, drop Peter a note via email at **peter.lewis@info.curtin.edu.au** and let him know how you like Finger. Contact him at:

Peter N. Lewis
10 Earlston Way
Booragoon, WA, 6154
AUSTRALIA

Finger is available at:

```
ftp://ftp.tidbits.com/pub/tidbits/tisk/tcp/finger-137.hqx
```

Daemon

Peter Lewis's Daemon program is a generalized server program that can provide services to the appropriate clients. Hm, that doesn't make a lot of sense, does it? Basically, if you want to provide a Finger server, you could use Peter's Fingerd, but if you also want to provide a Whois server (a variant of Finger that is generally less personal), an Ident server (fairly useless on a single-user Macintosh), and an NTP (Network Time Protocol) server, Daemon is the program for you.

Of course, any program such as Daemon, that is designed to provide information about you to others on the Internet all the time, is of dubious use if you have a SLIP or PPP account that isn't active all day long. That's not to say that you cannot use Daemon if you have a SLIP or PPP account, merely that it's more trouble and less useful.

The only hard part of configuring Daemon is that like Finger, you must create a Plan file. You can also create a Whois file for Whois queries, if you like. In creating the Plan and Whois files, you can include straight text that tells people your userid and so on, but you can also include tokens (variables that change with time). Possible tokens include ones that provide the current time and date, the startup time and date, the idle time, and various information about your Macintosh; some particularly clever tokens can return information based on the username that was fingered.

Daemon is free, and you can retrieve the latest version from:

```
ftp://ftp.tidbits.com/pub/tidbits/tisk/tcp/daemon-10.hqx
```

Script Daemon

Script Daemon is yet another tiny background application from Peter Lewis. It enables you to telnet to your Macintosh from another machine and enter AppleScript commands. Needless to say, it requires MacTCP, System 7 or later, AppleScript, and only allows the owner (using the Owner name and password) to log in (mostly for security reasons, I suspect).

Peter states up front in the documentation that Script Daemon is rather rough, which is one reason he released it for free and without many features. He's waiting to see how people attempt to use it and what questions and suggestions they have, before he spends any more time on it. Script Daemon only makes much sense if you have a permanent connection to the Internet. Still, being able to telnet to a Macintosh and then enter AppleScript commands and run AppleScript scripts is a neat idea, so if you can imagine how you would use this, check out Script Daemon at:

```
ftp://ftp.tidbits.com/pub/tidbits/tisk/tcp/script-daemon-10.hqx
```

Talk

Talk, yet another elegant program from Peter Lewis, implements the Unix talk protocol on the Mac, providing a decent Macintosh interface in the process. I almost never use Talk, not because there's anything wrong with it, but merely because I find email to be a much more efficient use of my time. Even though I type pretty quickly, I dislike typing under pressure and that's always what it feels like when I use Talk.

After you launch it, choose Talk from the File menu. Talk presents you with a small dialog box that looks almost exactly like Finger's dialog box. You can type a username and a machine in the two fields provided. When you click on the Talk button, Talk adds that person to your Status window, which lists all of your current connections and their status (see figure 13.96).

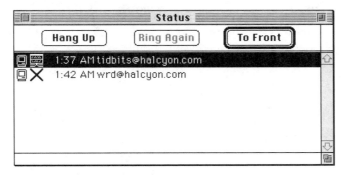

Figure 13.96 *Talk Status window*

At this point, Talk notifies your friend to alert him to your talk request. After your party makes the connection, Talk opens a two-paned window for you to type in and be typed at (see figure 13.97).

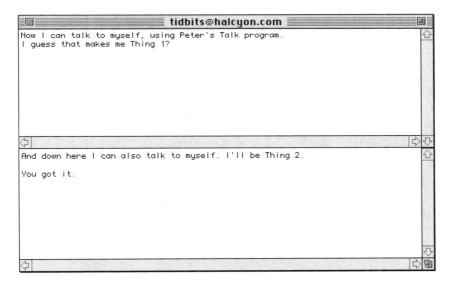

Figure 13.97 *Talk window*

You type in the bottom pane and your friend types in the top pane. (Since I had to fake figure 13.97, I'm actually talking to myself on my Unix shell account.)

If you have a use for Talk, it's worth getting. Like Finger, it enables you to save a hierarchical menu of the people you commonly talk to, and the interface is uncluttered and simple.

Like Finger, Talk comes with a background application called Talkd, which simply receives requests to talk from others. Talk is $5 shareware, and you can send checks (either U.S. or Australian dollars) to:

Peter N. Lewis
10 Earlston Way
Booragoon, WA, 6154
AUSTRALIA
peter.lewis@info.curtin.edu.au

You can retrieve Talk from:

```
ftp://ftp.tidbits.com/pub/tidbits/tisk/tcp/talk-111.hqx
```

Chat

Whereas Talk enables you to talk directly with another person, and Homer (discussed later) enables you to talk with multiple people on Internet Relay Chat, Chat 2.0.3 acts as a Chat Server, much like IRC itself. It's limited in comparison to IRC, so unless you have a specific use in mind, it probably makes more sense to use Homer and a private channel on IRC than it does to attempt to run your own Chat Server.

Since I only have a Server-addressed PPP account, I've never tried to set up Chat, but there's no reason it couldn't be done. It's just a bit of a pain to provide everyone with your IP number if it's not the same all the time.

Chat was originally created by the ubiquitous Peter Lewis, and was significantly updated by Nathan Neulinger, whom you can contact at **nneul@umr.edu**. Nathan's version of Chat is shareware. He doesn't give an amount or an address, however, so if you find Chat 2.0.3 useful, drop Nathan a line and see what you can do for him.

You can find the latest version of Chat at:

```
ftp://ftp.tidbits.com/pub/tidbits/tisk/tcp/chat-203.hqx
```

Homer

Homer is the killer app for Internet Relay Chat (IRC). It enables you to participate in worldwide Internet chats from the comfort of your Mac. My problem is that as I pushed toward finishing this book, the last thing I felt like doing was joining a massive chat on anything, undoubtedly making some incredible social gaffe in the first thirty seconds and trying to get off before I was flamed. As a result, I'm going to wimp out and settle for telling you that Homer is a great program if you're interested in IRC.

Homer has a colorful and unique interface that significantly eases using IRC, since it simplifies switching channels, keeping multiple discussions going, giving and taking operator privileges, and much more. In recent releases of Homer, creator Toby Smith added support for Apple's PlainTalk technology, so Homer can speak all or some of what goes on in your IRC discussion. With the addition of Face resources, it can even display a picture of the people with whom you're typing. It's hard for me to say much more about Homer, but I'm thoroughly impressed at all the effort that has gone into it. I can think of many commercial programs that could do with an equal level of interface design and thought (see figure 13.98).

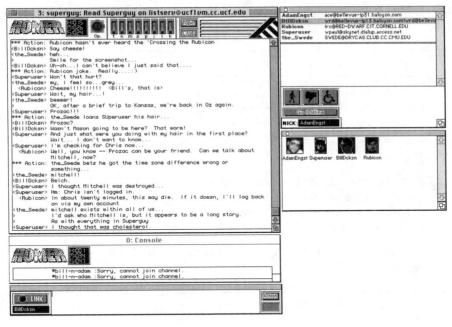

Figure 13.98   *Homer windows*

Note

I originally found a little program called HomerPaint in the same folder as Homer; apparently a simple painting program written by Steve Mariotti, HomerPaint uses Homer and IRC to enable people to collaborate on a graphic document. Although the concept of just talking in real time to others over IRC doesn't excite me, the possibilities suggested by a program such as HomerPaint are far more interesting. Steve Mariotti is at **stevem@cs.utexas.edu**. *I don't know whether HomerPaint works with the current version of Homer, since it has become hard to find, but it's at:*

```
ftp://ftp.tidbits.com/pub/tidbits/tisk/tcp/homer-clients.hqx
```

Homer is $25 shareware from Toby Smith, whom you can reach via email at **tob@zaphod.ee.pitt.edu**. You can find Homer on the Internet at either of the following:

```
ftp://zaphod.ee.pitt.edu/pub/
```

```
ftp://ftp.tidbits.com/pub/tidbits/tisk/term/homer-0934.hqx
```

ircle

Olaf Titz's free ircle 1.5.1 takes a more traditional approach to IRC than does Homer, although I'm certainly not qualified to say much more about it. It has some nice features such as user-definable shortcuts for common phrases, the capability of capturing a conversation to a file, and font and size control.

You can reach Olaf Titz at **s_titz@ira.uka.de**. If you want to see how ircle compares to Homer, it's at:

```
ftp://ftp.tidbits.com/pub/tidbits/tisk/tcp/ircle-151.hqx
```

MacMud and MUDDweller

I'm lumping MacMud and MUDDweller together because I don't have a lot to say about either, and they can work together. MacMud is a Macintosh implementation of a MUD (which, as you may remember, stands for *Multi-User Dungeon* or *Multi-User Dimension*). From what I can see, MacMud is a definite instance of "If you have to ask, you won't understand it." I didn't understand it, even after reading the minimal documentation, but I gather that if you want to run your own MUD on a Macintosh that is permanently connected to the Internet, you can use MacMud, which is a port of the Unix LPMud program. One of the pieces of documentation is a description of MacMud's scripting language, but it too is fairly minimal.

MacMud is free and was written by Mimir Reynisson. You can contact Mimir at **skelmir@uvapsy.psy.uva.nl**. MacMud is available from this or any of the Info-Mac mirror sites:

```
ftp://mrcnext.cso.uiuc.edu/pub/info-mac/game/mac-mud-32.hqx
```

The public domain MUDDweller 1.2, from O. Maquelin, is a dedicated MUD client program, something that you can use to access a MUD instead of NCSA Telnet. MUDDweller enables you to connect either via the Communications Toolbox or via MacTCP. It has a few features that make it more useful than Telnet, such as being line-oriented (so you have an edit line to compose on before sending your command), a command history that you can use to avoid retyping commands, and a simple file transfer tool. Other than that, it doesn't do much you cannot do from the command line, other than open multiple sessions. The latest version of MUDDweller is available from either of the following:

```
ftp://rudolf.ethz.ch/pub/mud/muddweller-12.hqx
```

```
ftp://mrcnext.cso.uiuc.edu/pub/info-mac/game/mud-dweller-12.hqx
```

Meeting Space

I've said little about MUDs throughout the book, mostly talking about the concepts and the concerns behind them. Nonetheless, the idea of an online virtual environment is a powerful one, and a small company called World Benders has brought it to the Macintosh business and educational world.

Stop thinking of MUDs as games for a moment, and think of them as online spaces—places where you can do things and interact with other people who happen to be in the same place. As you might imagine, those spaces can carry with them the trappings of any situation you'd like. If you work with a company that frequently does business over great distances, or in an educational institution that brings students together from all over the world, consider the possibility of creating a meeting space online. For a business it might be a virtual conference center; for a school, a virtual classroom. The virtual conference center could facilitate communication among employees at different locations without the high costs of travel; the virtual classroom could enable a world-renowned professor to teach a class of students from many different colleges and universities around the world.

That's the idea behind Meeting Space, and it's one that becomes especially attractive when paired with a simple Macintosh interface. There's no need to type cryptic commands or to know how to program in a MUD scripting language—in Meeting Space almost everything is in plain view. Although World Benders could have tried to support QuickTime and sound and all that, they decided instead to stick to more or less straight text to reduce the network traffic (Meeting Space works well over both AppleTalk and TCP/IP connections, even slow PPP or SLIP connections) and hardware requirements. Thus, Meeting Space can run happily on a 4M Classic II, although a large screen and color make it nicer (see figure 13.99).

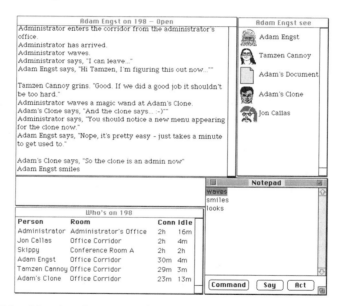

Figure 13.99   Meeting Space windows

As you can see, Meeting Space enables you to see the log (you can also save it to a file, and each room can keep minutes of what was said in it) of the text that everyone has typed, and provides a small text entry area at the bottom of that window. There's no need to issue commands to see what and who might be around you. The window with icons shows you exactly what's present, just as the Finder always shows you the files in open folders. You can pick your own icon, and, as you can see from my clone, you can be in more than one place at the same time. The Who's On window tells you who is logged in currently (you cannot see them if they're in a different room), and the Notepad window serves as a place to jot down thoughts, frequently used commands, and the like. You can change the font and text size for all the text in a set of windows—distinct fonts make it easier to keep track of multiple conversations at once.

Creating new places and objects is simple, and moving among places and working with objects is equally simple (it's all controlled through options in the menus). After a brief learning curve, Meeting Space is easy to use. I picked up the basics in about ten minutes of talking with Jon Callas, one of Meeting Space's programmers at World Benders.

Unfortunately, there are no public Meeting Space servers available on the Internet, although World Benders is interested in making one available when it gets a permanent Internet connection. At that point, the freely-distributable Meeting Space client should appear on the Internet, too. Meeting Space is designed for use by groups of people, rather than individuals, but if that's what you're looking for, check it out. For pricing details and more information, you can contact World Benders via email at **wb-info@worldbenders.com**, or at:

World Benders, Inc.
1 Chestnut Street, Suite 333
Nashua, NH 03060
603/881-5432 (voice & fax)

Timbuktu Pro

Not surprisingly, as time goes by in the Internet world, software that once ran solely on local area networks such as LocalTalk or Ethernet is migrating to the Internet. Often, it's not all that much of a chore to support the Internet—simply another network protocol, after all. However, with so many people accessing the Internet via SLIP or PPP and a relatively slow modem, the challenge to network programmers becomes more serious. How can they provide adequate performance with a program that was designed to work over a network many times faster than the average modem?

The network wizards at Farallon faced this problem with Timbuktu Pro, a recent release of their long-standing Timbuktu application for controlling Macs and PCs remotely. Let me explain the idea behind Timbuktu a little more before I get into the version that now works over the Internet, because once you see what Timbuktu is doing, you'll better understand why supporting Internet connections was such a coup.

Networking the Macintosh has always been easy, thanks to Apple's foresight in including all the network hardware in every Mac, and (since System 7) including all the software necessary to create a small network complete with servers and clients. Because of this, relatively wide-flung Macintosh networks sprang up quickly, making it difficult for a network administrator to physically visit each Mac that might be having a problem or simply need to be checked on. Farallon solved this problem with Timbuktu, an application that enabled the network administrator (or anyone else running the program, for that matter) to work on a host Mac somewhere else on the network, just as though it were on that person's desk. Timbuktu became especially popular in large corporations because Sam on the 15th floor could call down to the help desk when he had a problem, and the help desk could not only watch onscreen what Sam was doing, but could even perform the task correctly—so he could see how to do it next time. All without some peon dashing up 18 flights of stairs (my hypothetical help desk is buried in the sub-basement, since corporations often like to stick the people who know things out of the public eye).

This was all fine and nice, and Timbuktu became popular. Farallon added the capability for Timbuktu to control PC-compatibles running Windows as well, and continually increased Timbuktu's speed, since transferring all that data over a network was poky, to say the least. Then, in late 1993, Farallon released Timbuktu Pro (only for the Macintosh, as of this writing, although I suspect the Windows version will be along shortly). Timbuktu Pro increased the speed of execution, added support for Apple Remote Access (ARA) and probably fixed a few bugs, but most importantly for this book, it added support for TCP/IP networks—in other words, the Internet.

All of a sudden, not only can you observe or control a Mac on your network, but you can observe or control a Macintosh running Timbuktu anywhere in the world. Before you start shaking in your shoes about the security implications of this, let me assure you that Timbuktu has strong security features, and unless you allow another person to control your Mac, no one is able to do so. Same goes for observation; it's completely under the user's control, so there are no security or privacy implications that you cannot control yourself. One last thing—you must have two copies of Timbuktu to use it. When you buy it, you get both the client and the server, and I currently know of only one public Macintosh running Timbuktu, a demo machine at Farallon. But enough discussion; let's take a look.

Installation and Setup

Installation of Timbuktu is handled by the Apple Installer and is thus relatively straightforward, although it's best to restart with the Shift key held down before running the installer, to make sure that all anti-virus software is disabled. After you finish and restart, you should see a Timbuktu icon appear as the Mac starts up. This icon comes from Timbuktu Extension in your Extensions folder. Also in your Extensions folder will be Timbuktu Help and Timbuktu Help.note. The Timbuktu application appears in your Apple Menu Items folder, and the Timbuktu Sender application shows up on your desktop. If you use System 7 Pro, a Timbuktu Catalogs Extension goes in your Extensions folder as well.

The first time you launch Timbuktu Pro, either from the menu that the extension creates in your menu bar, or by double-clicking on the application, it asks you to personalize it—the trick here is getting the serial number from your disk or master list entered properly without any spaces.

Basic Usage

You use the Timbuktu application for one of four tasks: observing a host Mac, controlling a host Mac, sending files to a host Mac, or exchanging files both ways with a host Mac. When you launch Timbuktu Pro, it presents a New Connection window and a User Access window, the latter of which enables you to easily see and control what sort of access others have to your Mac. More on that in a bit (see figure 13.100).

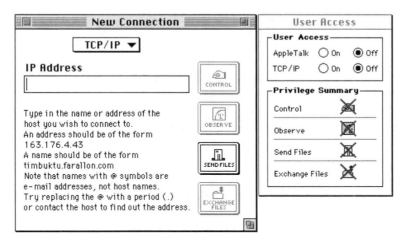

Figure 13.100   Timbuktu New Connection and User Access windows

The New Connection window has a pop-up menu with two choices, AppleTalk and TCP/IP. I'll ignore the AppleTalk setting here, since this is a book about the Internet, and there's a perfectly good manual that comes with Timbuktu that explains all about that as well. Anyway, if AppleTalk is showing in the pop-up menu, switch it to TCP/IP.

Farallon graciously has made a Macintosh-running Timbuktu available as a demo machine, and Farallon cleverly placed that demo machine's name and IP number into the New Connection window when the TCP/IP option is selected. So, type **timbuktu.farallon.com** into the IP address field, and click on the Control button to the right (see figure 13.101).

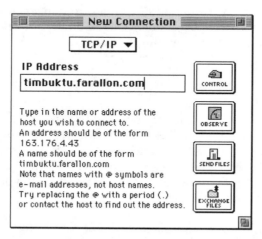

Figure 13.101   *Connecting to Farallon*

Once you're connected to **timbuktu.farallon.com**, a window appears on your screen representing the host Mac. In fact, it looks just like a normal Macintosh screen. When your mouse cursor is in that window, your keyboard works for the host Mac, and you can do anything there that you can do on any other Mac, except touch it (see figure 13.102).

Needless to say, the screen redraws slowly, since Timbuktu must transfer all the screen redraw information over your Internet connection, and if that's a modem, it takes time. However, I've used Timbuktu over LocalTalk and over a SLIP connection to the Internet, and although it's certainly faster over LocalTalk, it's not as slow over the modem as you might expect. You won't work on a machine like that all day long, but it's fine for basic troubleshooting and server control.

Note

*Because **timbuktu.farallon.com** is a public Mac that Farallon wants you to use, the program doesn't ask for a username or password. Most Macs would have security features in place to prevent unsavory characters from riffling through files on your machine.*

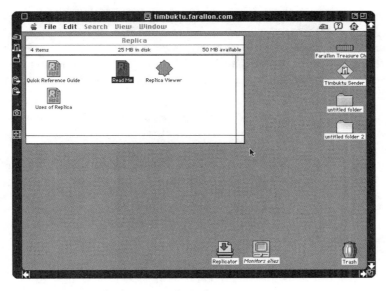

Figure 13.102 *Using the host Macintosh*

Speaking of file riffling, let's go riffle a few on Farallon's demo machine. They cleverly set it up to encourage you to do so, including tech support files about Timbuktu, Disinfectant (only slightly out of date), a demo version of Replica (another of their programs), and a folder titled "Leave your comments here!" To exchange files, click on the small icon of a folder with a double-headed arrow on the left-hand side of the Timbuktu window. Timbuktu asks for your username and password (I told it I was a guest) and brings up the Exchange Files window (see figure 13.103).

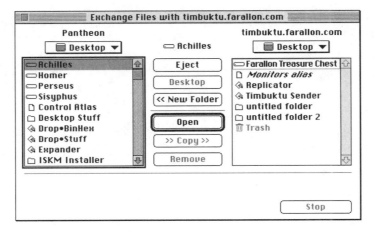

Figure 13.103 *Timbuktu Exchange Files dialog*

The Exchange Files window works much like the old Font/DA Mover did (not that many of you necessarily remember the old Font/DA Mover, which hasn't been used since System 6 days). You can navigate through the hierarchy on either the guest or the host Mac, and by Shift- or Command-clicking on items, select files to transfer. Clicking on the Copy button copies the files in the direction of the arrows.

That's about it for basic usage in Timbuktu Pro as a guest. If you want to be a host, your Mac must be connected to the Internet via MacTCP and either SLIP or PPP or a network. You should use Define Users from the Setup menu to create users with specific privileges before turning on access, because if you provide full access to your Mac, nothing prevents someone from wreaking havoc on your system. After you've defined some users and properly set up Guest access if you wish to use it all, selecting TCP/IP User Access from the Timbuktu Extension's menu in the menu bar, or clicking the On radio button for TCP/IP User Access in the User Access window of the Timbuktu application makes your Mac available as a host.

Needless to say, for someone to connect to you, they must know either your Mac's IP name or IP number, so if you use a Server-addressed account, you must somehow communicate the proper IP number to the guest.

Special Features

In many ways, Timbuktu sports no special features. After all, what it does is astonishing enough—the concept of using another Macintosh over the Internet is extremely cool. However, the attention to detail is high, and little things such as screen sharing in color without a major speed hit is impressive.

Note

Speaking of color, 8-bit color, *also known as* 256 colors, *requires eight times as much information to render as* 1-bit color, *also known as* Black and White. *That's why a color screenshot is so much larger than a black and white screenshot, and also why Timbuktu's capability to transfer color screens without slowing is so impressive.*

Timbuktu has a number of other buttons along the side of the Timbuktu main window, for useful functions that often come in handy (see table 13.1).

Table 13.1
Timbuktu Buttons

Button	Function
Control/Observe	Toggles between controlling and observing
Send Files	Sends files to the host Mac
Exchange Files	Exchanges files both ways
Send Clipboard	Transfers clipboard to host Mac
Get Clipboard	Transfers clipboard from host Mac
Snapshot	Takes a PICT of host screen
Autoscroll	Toggles autoscrolling on a large host screen
Switch Monitors	Switches to host Mac's second monitor, if present
Color/Grayscale	Toggles between color and grayscale when host Mac's monitor is set to more colors than the guest Mac

The Timbuktu Sender application that resides on your desktop (unless you move it) is a clever feature that simplifies sending files to host Macs—you can even send multiple files to multiple hosts at the same time. Just drag one or more files onto Timbuktu Sender and, when it asks, provide the IP address of each of your intended recipients. Timbuktu then sends the files to each of the hosts in turn, placing the files in a folder with your name on it inside another folder called (by default) Files Received. It's a bit like broadcasting.

After you create a new connection, you can save it as a connection document. Launching that document connects you to the specified host Mac automatically. It's actually kind of eerie—launch a document and suddenly you're using or watching another Mac in a window on your screen.

Finally, Timbuktu keeps an activity log that tracks what everyone does on your Mac, which can be handy for seeing who has been peeking in. It also tracks when Timbuktu itself loads or shuts down, which corresponds closely with when your Mac restarts. It's interesting to see how often you restart, if nothing else.

Overall Evaluation
As you may have gathered, I'm rather impressed with Timbuktu Pro. I'd never used it until the Internet version, but a friend of mine swears by it for using his Windows machine on his local area network. Most of my experience has come in

administrating a Gopher server on a Macintosh SE/30 running Peter Lewis's FTPd. The Macintosh lives elsewhere, but it's directly connected to the Internet, and I can check in at any time by simply connecting with InterSLIP and launching my Timbuktu Pro connection document.

Timbuktu Pro's worst problem is simply that using it is not as fast as using a Mac normally, especially when connecting over the Internet via modem. The mouse is jerky and the menus drop slowly, and highlighting a menu item can take forever. You wouldn't use a host Mac via Timbuktu Pro for daily work over a modem connection to the Internet. Nonetheless, most actions are fast enough to be worth the trade-off, and keep in mind that just because the screen draws slowly doesn't mean the host Mac is operating slowly. Programs run at full speed on the host Mac—the only slowdown is in how fast you see the screen draw. You get used to this after a while and learn to do things such as let up on a menu option when your cursor is in the right place but before the highlight has caught up with you.

The second limitation from which Timbuktu Pro suffers is that you cannot reach out and touch the host Mac, if you're controlling it over the Internet. This may not seem like a major liability until the Mac crashes or needs to be turned off. You can do a fair amount with software, but there's no guaranteed way to recover from a serious freeze.

Note

The shareware control panel AutoBoot from Karl Pottie looks for system errors, then freezes and attempts to restart the Macintosh if it catches a crash. The latest version is 1.3. Do an Archie search for "auto-boot" or "autoboot," and you'll find it for downloading via anonymous FTP.

Although Timbuktu Pro would seem to be a fairly focused tool mainly for use in situations where both people know each other, a little creative thinking reveals some interesting uses. For instance, everyone complains about not being able to try software before buying it, except in crippled demo versions. A Mac running Timbuktu Pro could easily act as a demonstration Mac for someone connecting over the Internet—it shouldn't be difficult to use security software to prevent people from copying the programs. Farallon even provides demo versions of some of their programs on their public Timbuktu server, most notably Replica and Timbuktu Pro itself.

Administrative Details

If you want to get more information about Timbuktu or other Farallon products, what better way to do it than via the Internet? Farallon runs an anonymous FTP site at **ftp.farallon.com** and a World-Wide Web server accessible at:

```
http://www.farallon.com
```

Both sites seem to offer much the same information, ranging from technical notes about all of Farallon's products to press releases to free trial versions of Timbuktu Pro for the Macintosh. It's easy to navigate the Web site, but if you're connecting via FTP, look in the directory:

```
ftp://ftp.farallon.com/pub/farallon.products/timbuktu.products/freeversions/
```

The free trial version works for up to seven days and on three Macs. During that time it works just like the full version, except that it won't connect to regular versions of Timbuktu Pro. You must use Apple's DiskCopy utility to create the installer disk for the free trial version.

Timbuktu Pro requires System 6.0.5 or later (it works best with System 7), a minimum of 4M of RAM, a network, and, if you're using the Internet, MacTCP 1.1.1 or later. (Of course, if you're reading this book, you have MacTCP 2.0.4 so there's no need to use any earlier buggy versions of MacTCP.)

Farallon sells Timbuktu Pro through various distribution channels. Mail order prices seem to run at approximately $140 for one user, up to $1,400 for 30 users.

You can contact Farallon in many different ways, and Amy Roberts and the other folks working on the Web server at Farallon earn major brownie points for putting all of Farallon's contact information on the Web server. The standard contact information is **info@farallon.com** for Customer Service and the following address:

Farallon Computing, Inc.
2470 Mariner Square Loop
Alameda, CA 94501
510-814-5000
510-814-5023 (fax)

MacTCP Watcher

Continuing on in the Peter Lewis archives is MacTCP Watcher, a free program Peter wrote to look at the internals of MacTCP. You must be an expert to decipher most of this information, and Peter claims that even he doesn't know what most of it means.

However, if you're having troubles with MacTCP, MacTCP Watcher proves to be one of the best tools available for troubleshooting a bad connection. I still don't understand what it complains about, but it tends to react in specific ways to specific problems. Those reactions are usually more useful than the generic error messages that come back from other programs.

The Ping button performs a *ping test*, which is a bit like sonar over a network. It's useful for determining whether a remote machine is up, and if so, about how far away it is (or how slow the network to it is). The UDP and TCP tests mean even less to me, but I use the DNS button fairly frequently, because, like Query It! (discussed later), MacTCP Watcher's DNS button enables me to figure out what IP name goes with what IP number and vice versa (see figure 13.104).

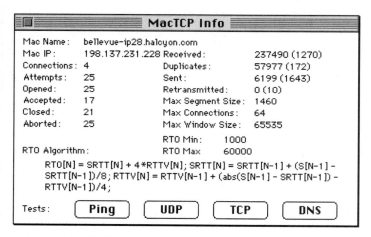

Figure 13.104   MacTCP Watcher window

MacTCP Watcher can also list your current TCP connections if you choose Show Connection List from the File menu. If you click on a connection in the Connections window, you can choose Show Connection from the File menu, to display even more incomprehensible statistics about that specific connection.

So, definitely pick up MacTCP Watcher next time you think of it, and poke at the buttons every now and then to see if anything that comes back looks useful. I always have a smashing good time looking at stuff I don't understand. It's at:

```
ftp://ftp.tidbits.com/pub/tidbits/tisk/tcp/mactcp-watcher-11.hqx
```

There's also a French version from Jean-Pierre Kuypers, if you really want to have trouble understanding what's going on.

MacPing

Along with their shareware software, Dartmouth College has some commercial quality applications that it sells as well. Included in this category are the $99 MacPing 3.0 and the $399 MacPing 3.0 Pro, ping utilities that work with both AppleTalk and TCP/IP networks such as the Internet. MacPing 3.0 is limited to testing five AppleTalk zones, whereas MacPing 3.0 Pro can test an unlimited number of AppleTalk zones. They're otherwise identical.

Not being a network administrator, I'm not really sure what MacPing tells me, but I gather that by watching the way the pings come back from all the machines, you can tell where there might be a network problems. Check out its help text for more information about what all the parts of the window do (see figure 13.105).

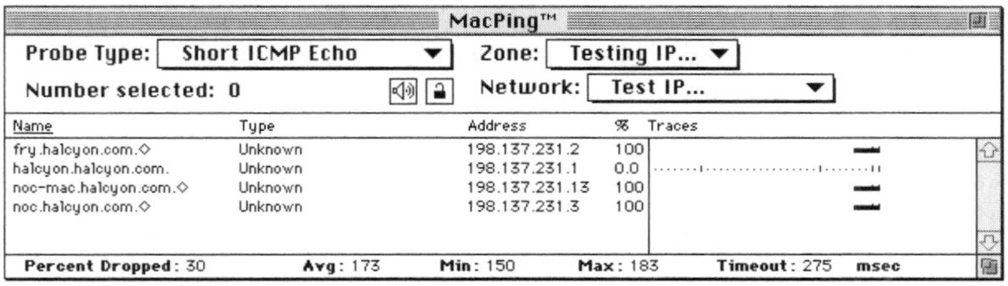

Figure 13.105 *MacPing window*

For ordering information contact the MacPing distributors at:

True BASIC, Inc.
12 Commerce Road
West Lebanon, NH 03784-1669
800/436-2111

MacTCP Switcher and MacTCP Netswitch

A problem that many people who have MacTCP-based access both at home and at work face is that MacTCP itself can only be configured in one way at one time. This may sound redundant, but if you use an Ethernet network at work and a PPP dialup account at home, you must modify MacTCP each time you switch from one to the other. If you own a PowerBook, this process becomes tedious extremely quickly.

Two free solutions have sprung up, although I haven't had the opportunity to test them (since I only have one sort of connection). They are MacTCP Switcher, from John Norstad, and MacTCP Netswitch, written by David Walton, of the University of Notre Dame. From what I can tell, MacTCP Netswitch is the more sophisticated of the two utilities, since it works by sensing at startup whether you're connected to an AppleTalk network, and if so, what zone you're in. After it's sensed whether you're in a network or not, it swaps in an appropriate MacTCP Prep file from a group of preconfigured ones. The major advantage of the way MacTCP Netswitch senses the environment at startup is that theoretically you don't have to restart, since it has forced MacTCP to load the proper MacTCP Prep file at startup.

MacTCP Switcher requires a bit more interaction from the user. After you have MacTCP set up properly, you run MacTCP Switcher and save a configuration file that records the current MacTCP settings. Do the same for your other configurations. To restore a saved configuration, double-click on it in the Finder, and when it asks you, click on the Set MacTCP button to set MacTCP to use the saved configuration. Another alert then appears telling you that MacTCP has been set; it may also tell you to restart your Mac, and if so provides a Restart button to do so instantly. MacTCP Switcher doesn't work with whole MacTCP Prep files, as MacTCP Netswitch does, but instead copies the relevant resources from the MacTCP Prep file to the configuration file and back again. It never touches the MacTCP control panel itself.

Although many of you will have no use for these programs, if you do, they may save a huge amount of work in switching MacTCP back and forth manually. You can find them on the Internet at:

```
ftp://ftp.tidbits.com/pub/tidbits/tisk/tcp/mactcp-switcher-10.hqx
```

```
ftp://ftp.tidbits.com/pub/tidbits/tisk/tcp/mactcp-netswitch-10b2.hqx
```

There's also a French version of MacTCP Switcher from Jean-Pierre Kuypers, should you want that.

Query it!

Chris McNeil, author of Archie, has another available MacTCP program that's worth snagging because it's free, easy to use, and potentially useful. Query it! enables you to query your local nameserver to find out more information about various Internet hosts. The most useful piece of information you can get from Query it! is the IP address for a host, the number that goes with the name. For instance, I asked Query it! to tell me the address of **halcyon.com** (see figure 13.106).

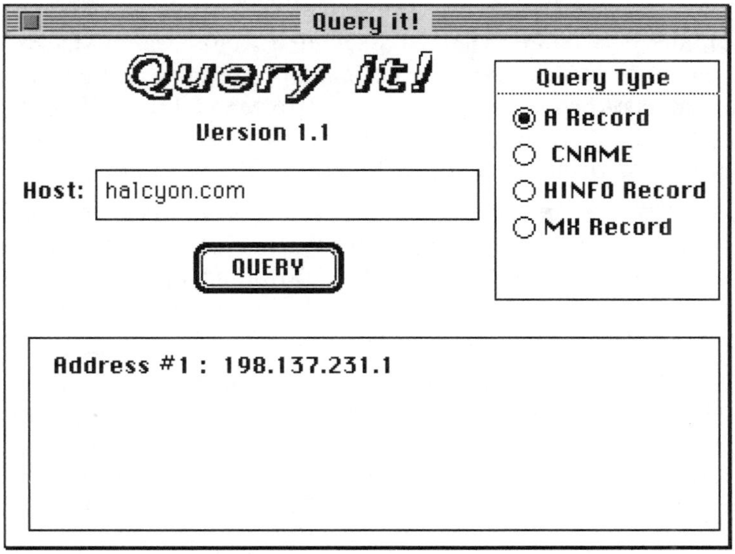

Figure 13.106 *Query it! window*

That's all there is to Query it!, although you can see if the CNAME, HINFO Record, or MX Record results are of interest to you. For instance, since my domain **tidbits.com** isn't real (I get all my mail via UUCP) you can see which machine handles my MX record by entering **tidbits.com** in the Host field and selecting the MX Record button before clicking on Query. You can find Query It! at:

```
ftp://ftp.tidbits.com/pub/tidbits/tisk/tcp/query-it-11.hqx
```

Integrated Internet Programs

Perhaps one of the most requested programs during the last year or so has been an integrated program for accessing all of the Internet services. In fact, two integrated programs on the Mac already provide access to the basic Internet services (although not the more recent ones like WAIS, Gopher, and the World-Wide Web). Synergy's VersaTerm-Link and InterCon's TCP/Connect II both do a good job in this area, and that's my first answer to those seeking an integrated Internet program. There's also MicroPhone Pro 2.0 from Software Ventures, which sort of fits into this category, based not so much on what it can do as on what's bundled with it. More on these programs in a bit.

My second answer to the question is itself a question. Why would you want an integrated Internet program? That's like wanting an integrated Macintosh program that subsumes all the functions of the programs you have on your Mac. A program that could concurrently play Maelstrom (a fabulous Asteroids-like shareware game available on the nets), edit word-processing documents, and check your disk for viruses sounds a little ludicrous, doesn't it?

Similarly, there are simply too many Internet services that have nothing in common—just as it makes no sense to combine Maelstrom with Disinfectant, neither does it make sense to combine CU-SeeMe and Gopher. They're simply different programs, and an interface that works for video does nothing for navigating a menu-based Gopher interface.

Integrated programs are always notable by what features they don't support. Internet integrated programs, both those that exist and those that people ask for, are no exception. VersaTerm-Link cannot connect to World-Wide Web servers and TCP/Connect II cannot navigate Gopherspace. Even if the next version of VersaTerm-Link adds Web support, there will always be something it doesn't do.

Finally, we're entering the age of software components. With Apple's OpenDoc and Microsoft's OLE, it will become possible to write tightly focused components that do one thing and do it well. In an ideal world, you'll be able to assemble modules from different vendors (the small programmer will theoretically once again be able to compete with the software monoliths currently dominating the market) to create a customized Internet tool that does exactly what you want and no more. Adding features will be as simple as adding a new module, and you won't pay for features you will never use.

Enough pontificating—the commercial integrated Internet applications do a good job and are ideal for some people. The following discussion should help you decide if you're one of those people.

MicroPhone Pro 2.0

At some point, Software Ventures decided that its MicroPhone terminal emulation software made a good base for Internet access, and thus came up with the MicroPhone Pro 2.0 package. MicroPhone Pro doesn't exactly provide integrated Internet access, but it does provide many of the tools you need for Internet access in a single package. I don't know whether or not that's the same thing as an integrated Internet package.

First off, MicroPhone Pro includes the MP Telnet tool, for use with MicroPhone itself along with other Communications Toolbox-aware programs. Then,

Software Ventures licensed MacTCP from Apple and made some sort of a deal with Hyde Park Software and TriSoft to include MacSLIP 2.0. The tools I've mentioned so far constitute a good start, since they get you a connection and a terminal session once you're connected, either via a normal shell account or a PPP or SLIP account.

Next, Software Ventures added support for email and news by writing a set of scripts, call it a module, for each feature. The Internet Mail and Internet News modules offer the basics of mail and news, and do so over a normal modem connection or a MacTCP-based SLIP connection. Check out the discussions of Internet Mail and Internet News back in chapter 10, "Shell Access," if you're interested.

Still missing from the Internet package were support for FTP, Gopher, the World-Wide Web, and all of the less-common protocols. Rather than attempt to reinvent the wheel once again, Software Ventures went out and licensed Fetch from Dartmouth (which means that if you buy MicroPhone Pro, you do not have to pay the shareware fee for Fetch) and TurboGopher from the University of Minnesota.

So that's the package, although to be complete I should mention that it also includes a slightly older version of the FaxSTF fax software, and MicroPhone's graphical environment for various different commercial services, called Loran.

But is it actually an integrated Internet package? No, I don't think so. If you need a Telnet tool, a powerful terminal emulator, a good implementation of SLIP and fax software for your modem, MicroPhone Pro 2.0 is a good deal and a good way to get on the Internet. But it isn't really the same as the next two programs I talk about, VersaTerm-Link and TCP/Connect II. No shame in that; there's a lot of power and utility in the MicroPhone Pro package.

You can purchase MicroPhone Pro 2.0 mail order for approximately $150, and if you have questions or comments about it, you can contact Software Ventures at `microphone@svcdudes.com`, or at:

Software Ventures
2907 Claremont Ave.
Berkeley, CA 94075
510-644-3232
510-644-1325

VersaTerm-Link

Synergy Software's VersaTerm has been one of the preeminent terminal emulation programs for years. Developed by Lonnie Abelbeck, of Abelbeck Software,

VersaTerm always seemed to support more terminal types than other terminal emulators, which made it a favorite in academia, where strange terminal types are more common. In more recent years, Lonnie updated VersaTerm to work with the Communications Toolbox, in the process opening it up to MacTCP connections. I don't know the history for sure, but it seems as though that introduction created additional interest in MacTCP utilities. Lonnie then came out with VersaTilities, a package that included numerous Communications Toolbox tools, including a Telnet tool, an FTP Client tool, a Terminal Server tool, and others designed for Ethernet networks. Also included were a SLIP implementation, an FTP server, a time server, and a simple application for using the FTP Client tool without firing up a full-fledged terminal emulator.

All that stuff still exists in VersaTilities. Until the introduction of InterSLIP, it was an excellent way to purchase SLIP. However, Lonnie recently added a new application, called VersaTerm-Link, to the VersaTilities package, and that's what I'm going to concentrate on, because it is of most interest to the individual wanting to access the Internet.

VersaTerm-Link is an integrated client application for email, news, Finger, FTP, and Telnet. I look quickly at each part of the program in turn, but in summary, none of the parts quite compete with the best of the freeware or shareware applications I talked about previously. The synergy created by the links between the different clients, however, makes for some interesting capabilities. More on those links as I go.

First, VersaTerm-Link provides a toolbar that enables you to access all of its parts with a double-click or keystroke (see figure 13.107).

Figure 13.107   *VersaTerm-Link toolbar*

I find the need for a double-click odd, because most toolbars require only a single-click, but the shortcut of being able to type a single key without even using the Command key makes up for it.

Email

Although I'm not as fond of VersaTerm-Link's interface as Eudora's, there's a lot to like here. You can have multiple mailboxes, and the program provides icons for indicating mail status (see figure 13.108).

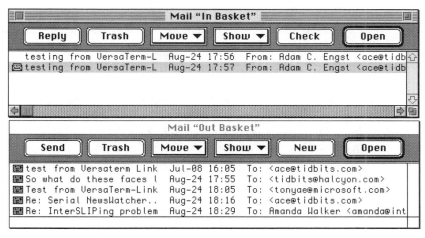

Figure 13.108 *VersaTerm-Link In and Out Baskets*

You can sort the messages, move them to another mailbox, trash them (and as in Eudora, they are then moved to a special Trash mailbox), reply to them (and the text is quoted automatically), and forward them. I don't see any command corresponding to Eudora's Redirect command; and when you reply to a message, even if it includes only one person in the header, VersaTerm-Link asks whether you want to reply to all or only the recipient.

VersaTerm-Link works off-line in the sense that you can queue messages and send them later. If you use VersaTerm SLIP, VersaTerm-Link automatically connects (asking whether it's OK first), transfers your mail, and then disconnects. If you aren't using VersaTerm SLIP, you must select the messages in your Out Basket to send, which is a minor pain.

In messages that you cannot edit, such as incoming mail and news, you are limited to selecting entire lines, much like Nuntius. This interface decision is extremely odd because many people want to copy an address or directory path from a message without getting everything else on the line. One nice touch, though, is that with a message open (and this applies to news articles as well) you can select Add to Address Book from the Edit menu, and VersaTerm-Link adds the person to your address book.

The address book is generally well done, enabling you to add people and groups, along with notes about who they are. It's available whenever you create a new mail message or news posting. You can enter an address into a message manually if you like, but unfortunately there's no way to import that address into your address book with a single click. It's a minor point, but a tad annoying.

VersaTerm-Link supports one or more enclosures to messages. If you so choose, it even compresses them in the StuffIt format before binhexing them and sending them out as an attachment to the message.

The worst problem suffered by the email portion of VersaTerm-Link, in my opinion, is its limitation on message sizes. Incoming messages larger than 20K turn into files that you must view separately (although you can use the View Text File command in the Tools menu), and you cannot put more than approximately 30K of text in an outgoing message. I didn't check this figure exactly, but it was easy to get VersaTerm-Link to complain that the clipboard was too large to paste. I may be coming down hard on these file size limitations, but I regularly get files, such as the Info-Mac Digest, that are well over 20K or even 80K, and it would be a major pain to have to read them outside of my email program.

Enough about the email portion of VersaTerm-Link. Let's look at the newsreader.

News

VersaTerm-Link's newsreader is the first implementation of a non-threaded newsreader that I like. I didn't think it was possible because I'm utterly addicted to reading and killing threads while scanning Usenet. When you double-click on the toolbar's Read News icon, VersaTerm-Link opens your Subscribed News Groups window (see figure 13.109).

Figure 13.109   VersaTerm-Link Subscribed Groups window

If you want to subscribe to more groups, clicking on the Groups button enables you to view a list of either all groups or only the new ones that have appeared since you last checked. When you open a group (groups that have new articles have a little folder icon next to their name) from the Subscribed Groups window, VersaTerm-Link displays the newsgroup window (see figure 13.110).

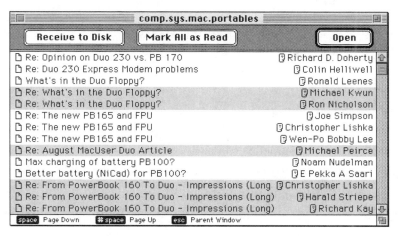

Figure 13.110   *VersaTerm-Link Newsgroup window*

The trick here is, even though VersaTerm-Link doesn't understand threads (although it can group articles with the same subjects), you scan through the list of new articles and select the ones you want by Command-clicking them. After you have selected articles, you can read through them relatively easily by using the Spacebar to page down through an article and the Return key to move to the next selected article.

The steps I described above are just what you do if you connect via SLIP or PPP and want to stay online. Most interesting, and VersaTerm-Link is unique in this regard right now, is that you can alternately click the Receive to Disk button and VersaTerm-Link downloads all of your selected articles as fast as it can, which is much faster than you can read. Later on, you can check Local via Disk in the News menu (it's normally set to Remote via Network) and read the news you saved just as though you were logged on. You can reply to messages, and forward them (this feature is sorely lacking in other newsreaders)—and you can do all that off-line as well, because VersaTerm-Link knows how to queue both mail and news.

This feature alone almost makes buying VersaTerm-Link worth it. Just think how much fun it would be to spend a long airplane trip reading news, which is, as we all know, one of the absolute best ways to waste time in a semi-productive manner. I would like to see a kill feature because if you get into a long set of articles about something you don't want to read, you must switch out of the article window and deselect those articles in the newsgroup window.

It's not a major problem, but VersaTerm-Link allows you to have only one newsgroup window and one article window open at a time. I don't do it often, but every now and then I want to have multiple windows open. If you choose to read news online with VersaTerm-Link, I think you'll find that it's not as snappy to use as, say NewsWatcher, although its speed is certainly acceptable.

FTP

When it comes to FTP, unfortunately, VersaTerm doesn't hold a candle to Fetch. Double-clicking on the FTP Files button on the toolbar opens the FTP Client List (see figure 13.111).

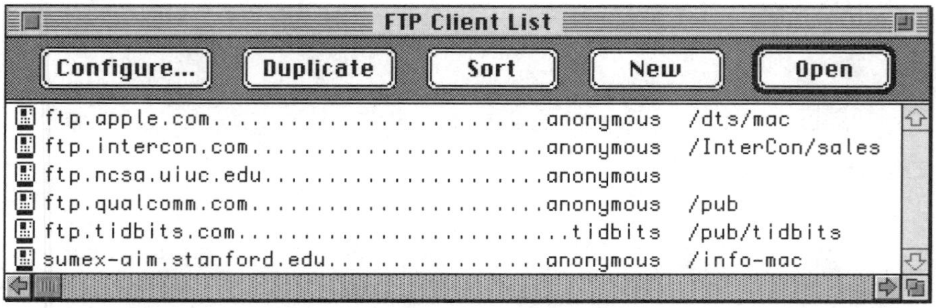

Figure 13.111   *VersaTerm-Link FTP Client List*

You can define shortcuts with the New button, and they appear in the list, as shown in figure 13.111. However, there is no way to connect to an FTP site without creating a shortcut for it in your list, and once you create one, it may take a bit of searching to realize that the only way to delete it is by choosing Clear from the Edit menu (a fact that is buried in the manual). All too often I want to connect to a site once, without creating a shortcut; so even though the shortcut asks for the same information that I'm using in logging at once, it feels slightly clumsier. Okay, maybe it's not that big of a deal.

When you double-click on an entry in your list to connect, though, you see the problem (see figure 13.112).

VersaTerm-Link doesn't display a large window, so some filenames extend past the window, making it impossible to see their extensions. Even though you can use the Get Info command to view a straight Unix directory listing for the file, VersaTerm-Link doesn't show the file size as a matter of course. In addition, when you're downloading a file, the program gives you a running count of the bytes transferred but never tells you what kind of throughput you're getting. I often abort a file transfer if I'm getting poor throughput; poor throughput tells me that something is wrong with the remote site, and they don't need to handle my download just now. VersaTerm-Link doesn't try to determine the transfer type automatically by looking at the file extension, as Fetch and Anarchie do, and it has no facility for calling another program to decompress or debinhex the downloaded files after the fact.

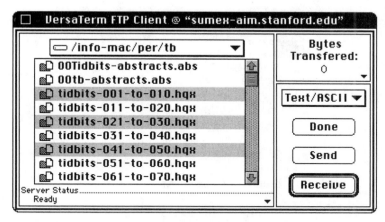

Figure 13.112   *VersaTerm-Link FTP window*

The primary good thing about the FTP client in VersaTerm-Link is that you can have it download in the background as you read news or email, although the same thing works with Anarchie and Fetch and one of the free newsreaders.

Telnet

VersaTerm-Link's Telnet client resembles all other Telnet programs, with the exception of being able to define a login script when you create the shortcut for a site. Like the FTP client, with Telnet you must create the shortcut; there's no provision for a one-time connect without saving that information.

If the Telnet client in VersaTerm-Link isn't powerful enough for you, you can open another one, such as VersaTerm itself (because the entire VersaTilities package comes with both VersaTerm and VersaTerm Pro) or presumably NCSA Telnet. The Telnet client isn't sufficient in two major areas. First, it supports only the "dumb" terminal type, which prevents you from using Gopher via Telnet, for instance, because it requires a VT100 terminal type. Second, you can have only one Telnet session open at a time, unlike either VersaTerm or NCSA Telnet.

Finger and Friends

VersaTerm-Link can query Finger, Whois, and Ph servers (which are used to store phone books of users, usually at universities), although using them is often an exercise in frustration when you're looking for someone. Unlike Peter Lewis's

Finger, with VersaTerm-Link you must make sure to type the userid and the machine name in the appropriate fields. Other utilities exist too, so you can find out the IP numbers that go with domain name by using the Resolve Domain Name command in the Network menu. And you can do all sorts of stuff using the Tools menu (see figure 13.113).

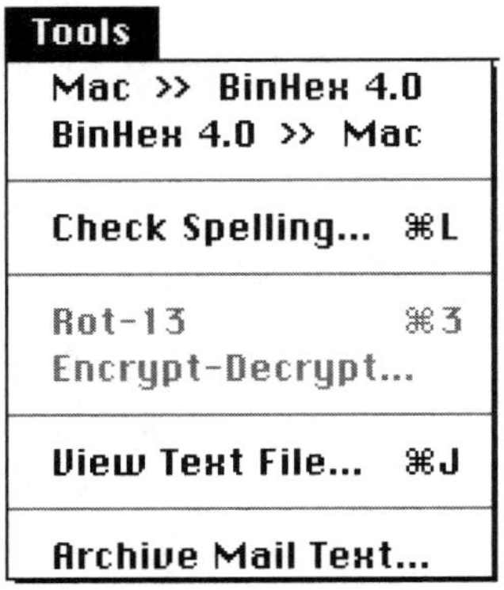

```
┌─────────────────────────────┐
│ Tools                       │
├─────────────────────────────┤
│ Mac >> BinHex 4.0           │
│ BinHex 4.0 >> Mac           │
├─────────────────────────────┤
│ Check Spelling...    ⌘L     │
├─────────────────────────────┤
│ Rot-13               ⌘3     │
│ Encrypt-Decrypt...          │
├─────────────────────────────┤
│ View Text File...    ⌘J     │
├─────────────────────────────┤
│ Archive Mail Text...        │
└─────────────────────────────┘
```

Figure 13.113   VersaTerm-Link Tools menu

You can encode and decode BinHex files, check spelling with the included dictionary (a nice touch, especially considering the abysmal spelling habits of many people on the Internet), use rot13 to encode or decode a news message, encrypt or decrypt a message with a password that someone has given you, view a text file, or archive your mail to a text file. Interestingly, VersaTerm-Link includes the code used for the encryption and decryption in the manual, and encourages others to implement it as a method of keeping messages private. The encryption is not secure, in the sense that any good cryptographer could crack it quickly, but it does discourage prying eyes.

VersaTerm-Link doesn't contain a WAIS or Gopher client, but the Open Special Client command in the Network menu enables you to link a single MacTCP application into VersaTerm-Link. I'd like it even more if you could add one or more applications to your toolbar, but I'm glad to see the VersaTerm-Link folks acknowledging that you might want to use other software. They even give TurboGopher as the example.

As a clever touch, VersaTerm-Link has a hierarchical Paste Face menu in the Edit menu that lists and describes a number of the common smileys used on the Internet (see figure 13.114).

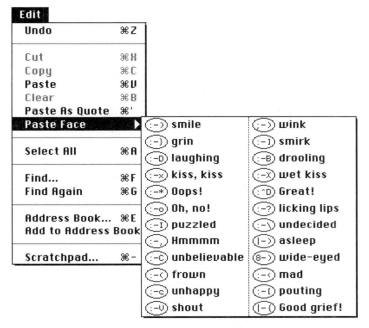

Figure 13.114   *VersaTerm-Link Paste Face menu*

Hidden in the back of the manual, I noticed one really neat feature. If you double-click on a word in any display text window (even though you can select only an entire line, you can still double-click on a word), VersaTerm-Link searches for the next occurrence of that word. You can continue searching forward for that same word by pressing the Tab key, and Shift-Tab searches backwards. That's elegant.

Speaking of the manual, although it's not inspired or particularly fun to read, it covers all of VersaTerm-Link quite thoroughly. A separate manual talks about using all the connection and transfer tools included with the VersaTilities. With commercial software, a lot of what you're paying for is the documentation and support (which I had no need to call), so it's nice to see adequate manuals.

Overall Evaluation

Despite its many nice features, I cannot necessarily recommend that you spend $85 for VersaTilities when you can buy this book (to get MacTCP 2.0.4, which is bundled with VersaTilities) and use some excellent programs that provide the same features. If programs such as InterSLIP, Eudora, NewsWatcher, Fetch, and NCSA Telnet didn't exist, it would be a no-brainer to buy VersaTilities, and I must give Synergy credit for pricing the package where you can easily consider it. You may decide that the excellent off-line news reading feature for SLIP and PPP users, and some nice integration between the different parts of the program with items such as the Address Book and the spell checking, make the cost worthwhile. And remember, even if you decide that Fetch is the best FTP client, you can still use the rest of the VersaTerm-Link package quite happily. There's no shame in not using one of a number of bundled features. Now, if only you could reconfigure that toolbar with your favorites...

If, however, you are the sort of person who doesn't mind spending some money and wants a set of utilities in a single package complete with full documentation and support, VersaTilities is definitely the way to go. I usually assume that people want to make this choice on their own and spend the least amount of money possible because that's how I am, but I realize that many people prefer to spend some money and avoid the hassles.

Administrative Details

You can buy VersaTerm-Link in the VersaTilities package for a list price of $145, in the VersaTerm package for $195, or in the VersaTerm-Pro package for $295. All of these prices are at least 30 to 40 percent lower if you buy through a mail-order vendor such as MacWarehouse or MacConnection, or direct from Synergy. You can contact Synergy to find out more about buying any of their programs via the Internet at **maxwell@sales.synergy.com**, via phone at 215-779-0522, or via fax at 215-370-0548.

TCP/Connect II

The second commercial application comes from InterCon, the company that made InterSLIP freely available to the Internet community. TCP/Connect II can best be compared to either VersaTerm or VersaTerm-Pro, in the sense that it is a package of TCP-based programs that work equally well on various dedicated networks or via SLIP, although not as a dial-up terminal emulator. TCP/Connect II comes in four flavors: Basic, 3270, VT, and Extended. Each offers different set features and different list prices, ranging from $195 to $495. Unfortunately, only the most expensive Extended edition includes the mail and news features that I discuss in the following paragraphs.

TCP/Connect II doesn't come with a separate implementation of SLIP or PPP but includes SLIP support internally. This means that if you only have TCP/Connect II and you connect via its SLIP, you cannot use TurboGopher or WAIS or any other separate program. However, TCP/Connect II works fine with InterSLIP and PPP, and that's how I used it primarily, because the internal SLIP implementation isn't as automated as InterSLIP or MacPPP. It is worth noting that TCP/Connect II 1.2.1 is Power Mac-native, which should significantly improve its speed on a Power Macintosh.

Email

In terms of email, TCP/Connect provides all the basic features with a few interesting twists that those who receive a lot of email can especially appreciate. You can modify the order and size of each of the panels at the top of each mailbox window, so the From, Date, and Subject fields can all be customized to your taste. An icon to the left of each message indicates its status, and the icons at the top of the windows provide access to common commands (see figure 13.115).

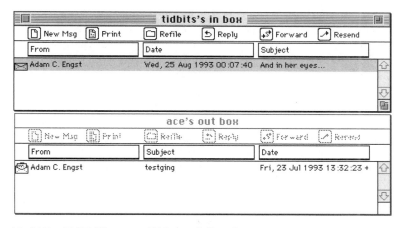

Figure 13.115   *TCP/Connect II In and Out boxes*

Like Eudora and VersaTerm-Link, TCP/Connect II can operate in off-line mode, so messages you send don't go out until you do connect. However, you must make sure to change the Network options from MacTCP to None in the Configuration panel; otherwise, TCP/Connect II assumes it is connected to a network. There is no Send Mail command for messages that you've queued—TCP/Connect II sends them sometime after you've reconnected to your network and reconfigured it from within TCP/Connect II.

You can have multiple mailboxes and move mail among them, and TCP/Connect II provides a Mailboxes window that lists all of your mailboxes along with the number of total and unread messages in each.

TCP/Connect II's most impressive mail feature is its Mail Actions feature. It enables you to filter mail based on specific items in the headers or bodies of messages. People who get a lot of mail need a feature like this one, and except for QUALCOMM's Eudora 2.0, TCP/Connect II is the only program that features filtering. You can use this feature to put mail from a certain mailing list in a specific mailbox to read at your leisure, or you can have mail from your boss highlighted so that you see it instantly each morning (see figure 13.116).

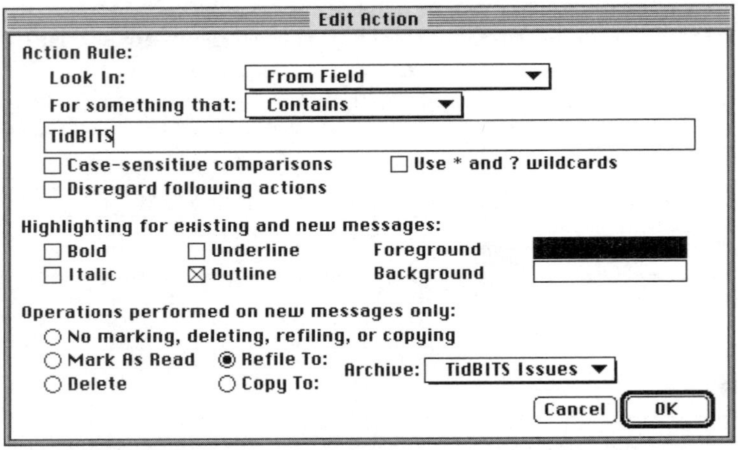

Figure 13.116   *TCP/Connect II Mail Actions*

A variant of this feature, called Select Messages, enables you to use some of the same filtering techniques on already existing messages in a mailbox. After you select them, you can then refile or delete them. In addition, if you only want to find a single message in a mailbox or find some text within a message, TCP/Connect II's Edit menu contains several Find commands that should help out.

Unlike most other email programs, when you delete a message by selecting it and pressing Delete, the message is gone (although you can use Undo to recover it immediately afterward).

Note

Even though there's no intermediate Trash mailbox in TCP/Connect II, you can certainly create your own Trash mailbox and use it as your own personal email purgatory.

On the good side, though, TCP/Connect II has absolutely no trouble sending and receiving messages larger than 32K, which is a surprisingly uncommon feature. In my testing of large messages, it transferred them faster than I was expecting—another bonus.

News

TCP/Connect's newsreader has one of the nicest interfaces for reading news I've seen. It's a three-pane interface that shows you the newsgroups to which you're subscribed (although that process takes some time), the subjects of the messages in the selected group, and the text of the selected article (see figure 13.117).

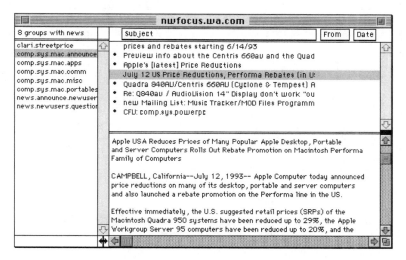

Figure 13.117   *TCP/Connect II News window*

You can drag the Subject, From, and Date panels at the top of the subjects pane to determine which piece of information shows up where. You also can resize each of these fields to fit your tastes and the font you've chosen (I have somehow chosen an ugly one).

Unfortunately, TCP/Connect II downloads the full group of lists each time you connect, which is a major pain if you have a slow SLIP or PPP connection. Once you're into the TCP/Connect II newsreader it feels responsive, and the most recent version, currently 1.2.1, is faster than previous versions.

Note

If you come from the Unix world, you will appreciate the feature that enables you to use the same keys for navigation as you use in the Unix rn newsreader.

Equally unfortunately, TCP/Connect II's newsreader isn't threaded. It can sort messages by subject, but that never quite solves the problem, especially because, unlike VersaTerm-Link, there's no way to select multiple messages and then read them all at once. However, TCP/Connect II's unique filtering system helps significantly with the lack of threads. If you're the sort of person who reads most of a newsgroup, you won't care too much about filtering, or threads, for that matter. However, if you are interested only in certain subjects, you can use filters to highlight them in some way so that it's easy to find them during your reading session. You also can use filters to mark articles as read or to delete them (see figure 13.118).

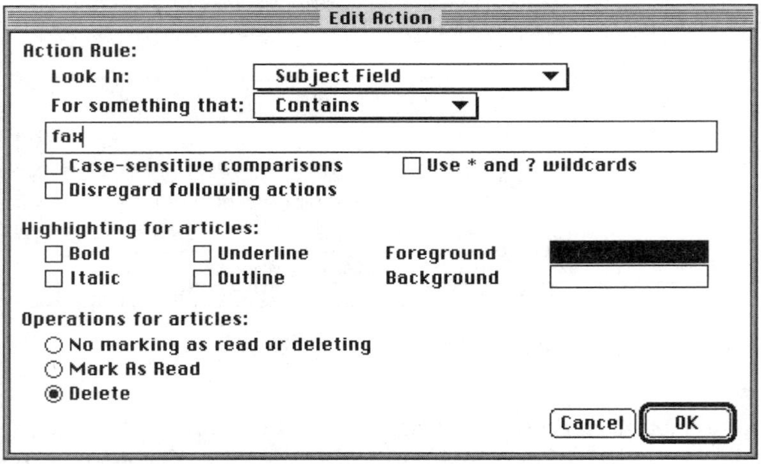

Figure 13.118   TCP/Connect II Edit Actions

By marking uninteresting articles as read, or deleting them, you can significantly reduce the amount of news that you see in the newsgroup. It may take a while, but you should gradually figure out a set of actions that display only interesting articles, ignoring the rest.

You can, of course, do all the expected things, such as reply to messages, reply via email, and the like. None of that's very surprising, and after the filters, there's nothing all that special about TCP/Connect II's newsreader other than the clean interface. If InterCon could add threading features and reduce the amount of time it takes to start up by remembering the full newsgroup list, the newsreader could be one of the best around.

FTP

The FTP client in TCP/Connect II is mediocre and doesn't even begin to compete with Anarchie or Fetch. First, you must define commonly accessed sites in the Configuration window, not when you are working with FTP. For security reasons, you have no way to save a user name or a password, although if you hold down the Option key and select Anonymous Connect from the FTP menu, TCP/Connect II fills in the standard userid and password for you. Once you connect, the window looks similar to Apple's old Font/DA Mover (see figure 13.119).

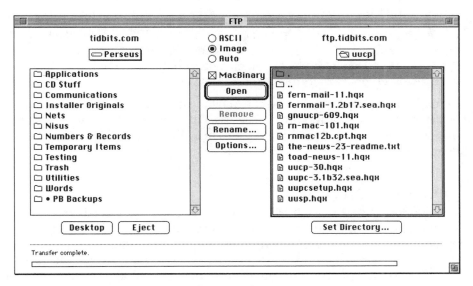

Figure 13.119   *TCP/Connect II FTP window*

The list on the left shows the folder on your Mac where files are placed when you retrieve them (you also can move them from that or any other folder onto the FTP site if uploading is allowed). The right-hand window shows the files on the remote host. Although you can now resize the window so that you can see the end of the filenames, you still have no way of finding out how large these files are from TCP/Connect II.

TCP/Connect II provides feedback while it's downloading files, but unlike Fetch and Anarchie, is unable to process BinHex files or call other programs to expand files after it has downloaded them.

I cannot recommend that you use the TCP/Connect II FTP client; it has too many problems that Fetch and Anarchie don't share. The folks at InterCon know about these interface troubles and have indicated that some may be fixed in future versions of TCP/Connect II.

Telnet

TCP/Connect II provides a good environment for using Telnet-based services. You can have multiple windows open at once, and in the Extended version that supports mail and news, you also have access to a slew of various different terminal types, most importantly VT100, because it's the most commonly used on the Internet.

For frequently used commands, you can define up to 10 macros that are attached to Command-0, Command-1, and so on. TCP/Connect II can use Finger if you append ", finger" to the hostname when connecting via Telnet. It also supports the Ph protocol for phone book lookups.

There isn't much else to say about the Telnet features in TCP/Connect II mostly because they work fine and provide access to other services. I cannot imagine what sort of features you could really add to a Telnet client that haven't been added already.

Overall Evaluation

The problem TCP/Connect II faces is that it's not really designed for a single user trying to access the Internet, and that's primarily the sort of person at whom I've aimed this book. As a result, TCP/Connect II seems to compare poorly with the free and shareware programs on the net. However, the fact is that TCP/Connect provides several features that aren't really interesting to the single user, such as being able to set up your own FTP server, use local PostScript printers for DEC pass-through printing, and act as a Finger server. In addition, TCP/Connect II comes with a manual packed with useful information, although the organization and layout of the manual (there are as many appendixes as chapters) make finding that information tough.

I very much get the impression that TCP/Connect II is aimed at large organizations that want a single solution to a lot of problems, and they want to have someone to call when they're confused. I've had occasion to call InterCon on a couple of occasions, and their tech support people have always been friendly and helpful. In the end, I cannot recommend that you as an individual spend $495 on a package that doesn't meet your needs as well as the standard free and shareware utilities readily available.

Administrative Details

TCP/Connect II has been translated into French, German, and Japanese so far. You can purchase TCP/Connect II direct from InterCon Systems for $495. There also are many different pricing tiers based on volume and whether you work at an educational institution (60 percent off) or for the government (15 percent off). TCP/Connect II also should be available from some dealers and at a discount from two large mail-order firms, Mac's Place and MacZone. For more information, contact InterCon electronically at **sales@intercon.com**, or at:

InterCon Systems Corporation
950 Herndon Pkwy., Ste. 420
Herndon, VA 22070
703-709-5500
703-709-5555 (fax)

Summarizing Proust

My apologies to those who aren't familiar with the Monty Python "Summarizing Proust" skit, but attempting to summarize this chapter in a few sentences feels much like trying to summarize Marcel Proust's seven-volume *Remembrance of Things Past* in 30 seconds. That said, here goes.

I began by discussing the email programs with a distinct focus on Eudora, since nothing really competes with it. MacTCP-based Usenet newsreaders are more competitive with one another, and I looked mainly NewsWatcher, InterNews, and Nuntius, although the others may be worth some investigation as well. FTP was easy, with Fetch and Anarchie providing more features that most people will ever need, and NCSA Telnet and Comet ably filled out the Telnet category. TurboGopher claimed the crown in the Gopher world, as did MacWAIS among the WAIS clients. MacWeb and Mosaic vied equally among the World-Wide Web browsers. After that, things got messy, with hard-to-classify programs like Bolo, MacWeather, CU-SeeMe, Meeting Space, and Timbuktu Pro each fitting into the discussion. Finally, I looked in depth at the commercial programs that attempt to provide the solutions to all your Internet needs, MicroPhone Pro 2.0, VersaTerm-Link, and TCP/Connect II.

Perhaps the lesson that I'd like you to take away from this chapter, and from this book, is that the Internet is a vast and multi-faceted place. Although there may be a single great program like Eudora that everyone uses, there are undoubtedly many lesser programs that have their devotees. And, because new stuff appears all the time, you should always keep an eye out or you might miss fabulous new programs like Anarchie and MacWeb, both of which were released since the first edition of this book was published. Luckily, most of these tools are either freeware or shareware, which enables you to try them out to your heart's content, although I do encourage you to support the shareware programmers who do such good work.

That said, for those of you who are feeling somewhat overwhelmed with using the main programs, let's move next to a simple, step-by-step discussion of how to use the main programs in each category.

Step-by-Step Internet

By now, you've probably noticed that I tend to avoid giving detailed, blow-by-blow directions for using Internet programs. You may be wondering why, since such specifics are so common in technical books. Don't worry, there is a method to my madness.

On the Internet, things change rapidly. Something that is available one day may disappear the next. Or, in some cases, something may be available at random times during the day, but not at others. Herein lies my concern with rigid instructions that people will attempt to follow closely. What if I give instructions for performing some task, and it simply doesn't work? The fault may lie not with my instructions, it may instead lie with the Internet resource I explain—but that makes no difference to the person following the directions.

So, my strategy in the previous chapter is to provide the basic information necessary to use the MacTCP programs in a variety of situations, hopefully giving you the background you need to work around any difficulties you may encounter. However, several of the responses I received to the first edition of the book indicated that some step-by-step instruction would be welcome, and far be it from me to ignore such suggestions from readers. After all, I'm writing the book for you, not for me.

Note

> *You must have a PPP or SLIP account set up to be able to work through the following instructions, although you're welcome to read through them before you have the account.*

Unlike any other book, I cover literally all the Internet software for the Mac that I know about, so providing step-by-step instructions for every program in this book would fill thousands of pages—and be as boring as all get out. Instead, then, I provide the steps necessary to perform several basic tasks in the applications I consider to be the most important. All of these applications require MacTCP and either a network or a SLIP or PPP connection. I start by covering MacTCP, MacPPP, and InterSLIP first, and then follow with the essential applications. All of the specific settings are for Northwest Nexus—your settings undoubtedly will vary if you use a different provider.

Note

> *In each case, I assume that you have the program available on your hard disk. You may need to copy it from a floppy disk or download it from the Internet, debinhex, and expand the file. In the case of many of these programs, you may be able to install them from the disk that comes with this book. You can always install a clean copy of each of these programs that has never been configured, but the ISKM Installer can install copies that are pre-configured for your convenience. So, some of these instructions may be redundant. For instance, there's no reason to configure MacTCP for Northwest Nexus since the ISKM Installer does it for you. Nonetheless, I wanted to be complete, and without instructions that start from a clean copy, you might not be able to duplicate these configurations on your own.*

MacTCP 2.0.4

Quick Reminder: MacTCP is a control panel that makes it possible for Macs to connect to TCP/IP-based networks such as the Internet.

Tasks:

1. Install MacTCP
2. Configure MacTCP for use with Northwest Nexus and MacPPP

Install MacTCP

1. Drop the MacTCP control panel on your closed System Folder.

   The Mac asks if you would like to put MacTCP in the Control Panels folder (see figure 14.1).

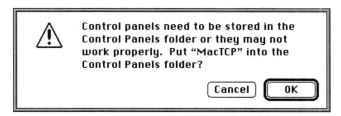

   > ⚠ **Control panels need to be stored in the Control Panels folder or they may not work properly. Put "MacTCP" into the Control Panels folder?**
   >
   > [Cancel] [OK]

Figure 14.1   *Placing MacTCP*

2. Click the OK button to confirm that MacTCP should go in the Control Panels folder.

Configure MacTCP for Use with Northwest Nexus and MacPPP

1. Jump ahead and install MacPPP as set out in the "Install MacPPP" section that follows.

2. Open the Control Panels folder and double-click on MacTCP. Select the PPP icon in the upper part of the MacTCP window (see figure 14.2).

3. Click on the More button.

   MacTCP presents you with its configuration dialog (see figure 14.3).

4. Select the Server button in the Obtain Address area, in the upper left of the dialog.

5. In the Domain Name Server Information area, click the first field under the Domain column. Type **halcyon.com.**, making sure to include the trailing period. Press Tab, or click the first field under IP address. Type **198.137.231.1**, and turn on the Default button.

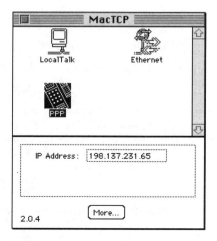

Figure 14.2 *Selecting PPP*

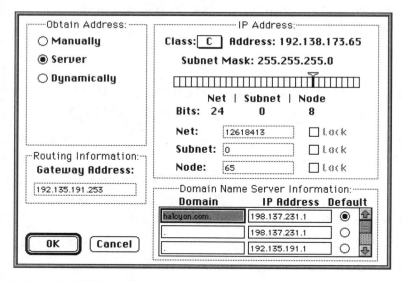

Figure 14.3 *MacTCP configuration dialog*

6. Press Tab, or click the second field under Domain. Type a period. Press Tab, or click the second field under IP Address. Type **198.137.231.1** again.

7. Press Tab, or click the third field under Domain. Type a period. Press Tab, or click the third field under IP address. Type **192.135.191.1** this time.

8. Press Tab, or click the fourth field under Domain (you must scroll to see it). Type a period. Press Tab, or click the fourth field under IP Address. Type **192.135.191.3** this time.

Your configuration dialog should now look similar to my screenshot (figure 14.3), although yours probably will have **0.0.0.0** in the Gateway Address field and something different in the IP Address area at the top. Don't worry about those differences as long as the Server radio button is selected and the Domain Name Server Information area is the same.

9. Click the OK button to save your changes and close the configuration dialog.

10. Close MacTCP by clicking its close box in the upper left-hand corner.

   MacTCP may or may not tell you that you must restart for your changes to take effect.

11. Restart your Macintosh.

You've now configured MacTCP for use with MacPPP and Northwest Nexus. If you use a different provider, you'll have different domain name server information, and you may have to select the Manually button instead of the Server button. Also, if you use InterSLIP instead of MacPPP, in the main MacTCP window you select the InterSLIP icon instead of the PPP icon.

MacPPP 2.0.1

Quick Reminder: MacPPP consists of a control panel called Config PPP and an extension called PPP. MacPPP uses your modem to establish a connection to a PPP account over which MacTCP-based programs can work.

Tasks:

1. Install MacPPP

2. Configure MacPPP for Northwest Nexus

3. Establish an Internet connection

4. Close the Internet connection

Install MacPPP

1. Select both the Config PPP and PPP icons and drop them on your closed System Folder.

   The Mac tells you that they need to be stored in special places within the System Folder, and asks if you would like to put them where they belong (see figure 14.4).

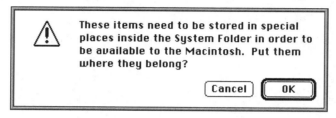

Figure 14.4   Placing MacPPP

2. Click the OK button to confirm that the Config PPP control panel should go in the Control Panels folder and that the PPP extension should go in the Extensions folder.

   The Mac then tells you where it has placed them.

Configure MacPPP for Northwest Nexus

1. Open the Control Panels folder and double-click on Config PPP (see figure 14.5).

2. Click on the Config button to bring up the Server Configuration dialog (see figure 14.6).

Note

If the PPP Server pop-up menu doesn't have Untitled selected, you may wish to create a new server definition by clicking on the New button, typing a name in the dialog box, and clicking the OK button.

3. Click the PPP Server Name field. Type **halcyon.com**.

4. From the Port Speed pop-up menu, choose 19200.

Config PPP
PPP DOWN
Open
Soft Close
Stats...
Hard Close
Port Name: Modem Port
Idle Timeout (minutes): None
Echo Interval (seconds): Off
Terminal Window
Hangup on Close
Quiet Mode
PPP Server: Untitled
Config...
New...
Delete...
v2.0.1

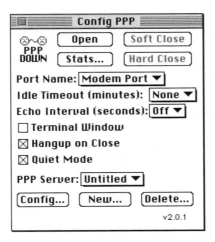

Figure 14.5 *Config PPP window*

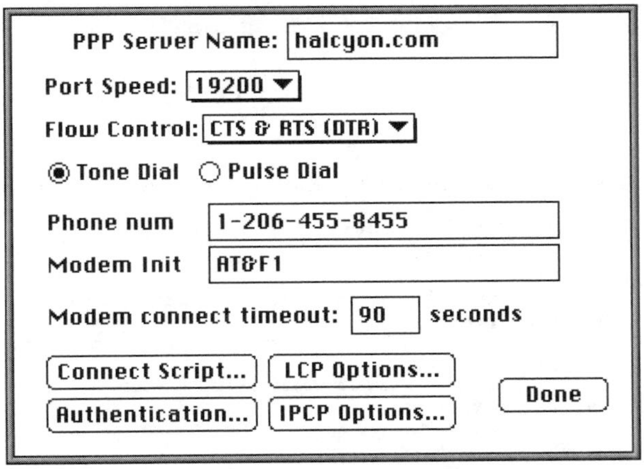

PPP Server Name: halcyon.com
Port Speed: 19200
Flow Control: CTS & RTS (DTR)
Tone Dial
Pulse Dial
Phone num 1-206-455-8455
Modem Init AT&F1
Modem connect timeout: 90 seconds
Connect Script...
LCP Options...
Authentication...
IPCP Options...
Done

Figure 14.6 *Configuring the Server Configuration dialog*

5. From the Flow Control pop-up menu, choose CTS only. (Yes, I know that I have chosen CTR & RTS(DTR). Don't worry about it.)
6. If you have touch-tone phone service, select the Tone Dial button. Otherwise, select the Pulse Dial button.
7. In the Phone Number field, type **1-206-455-8455**. If you are within the local calling area for Bellevue, Washington, enter **455-8455**. If you cannot call Bellevue locally, but can call Seattle locally, enter **382-6245**. If you must use any specific prefixes, like 9, to dial out, add them here, such as **9,1-206-455-8455**.

Note

The comma in the phone number above tells the modem to pause for two seconds before dialing the rest of the number. You can insert multiple commas to use additional two-second pauses.

8. In the Modem Init field, enter **AT&F1** if you use a SupraFAXmodem or Global Village TelePort or PowerPort modem. For other modem types, check your modem manual for the appropriate factory default init string. Make sure that string turns off XON/XOFF flow control.

Note

If you installed MacPPP using the ISKM Installer, look in the MacPPP 2.0.1 folder that is in the ISKM Folder on your hard disk for a text file called Modem Strings. It contains a number of untested modem init strings that might work.

9. Click the Connect Script button to bring up the Script Login dialog (see figure 14.7).

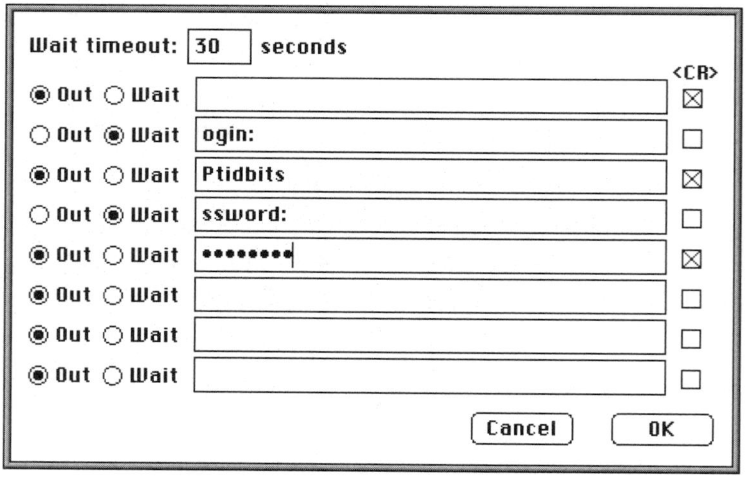

Figure 14.7   Configuring the login script

10. In the first set of fields, select the Out button and check the checkbox to send a carriage return.

11. In the second set of fields, select the Wait button and enter **ogin:** in the field to wait for the login prompt.

12. In the third set of fields, select the Out button and enter your userid in the field. Check the checkbox so that MacPPP sends your userid and then a carriage return.

13. In the fourth set of fields, select the Wait button and enter **ssword:** in the field to wait for the password prompt.

14. In the fifth set of fields, select the Out button and enter your password in the field. Check the checkbox so that MacPPP sends your password, followed by a carriage return. Ignore the rest of the fields.

15. Finally, click the OK button to save your changes.

16. Back in the Server Configuration dialog, click the Done button to save your server configuration.

17. Back in the Config PPP main window, click the close box in the upper left-hand corner to close the Config PPP window.

Establish an Internet Connection

1. Open the Control Panels folder and double-click on the Config PPP control panel to open it.

   Note the frowning faces and the PPP DOWN label in the upper left-hand corner (see figure 14.8).

Figure 14.8   *Disconnected*

2. Click the Open button.

MacPPP configures your modem according to the string you entered in the Server Configuration dialog, and dials the number you provided (see figure 14.9).

Figure 14.9   *MacPPP dialing dialog*

After the modems connect, MacPPP sends your userid and password to log you in, and then establishes the connection (see figure 14.10).

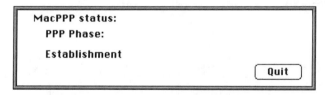

Figure 14.10   *PPP Establishment phase*

Notice that the faces are smiling and the label now says PPP UP (see figure 14.11).

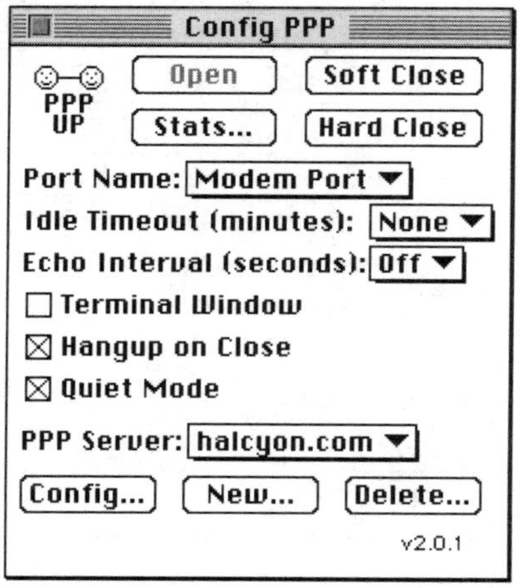

Figure 14.11   *Connected*

You should now be able to run MacTCP-based applications such as Fetch and MacWAIS.

Close the Internet Connection

1. Quit any MacTCP-based applications other than Eudora that you may have launched.

2. Open the Control Panels folder and double-click on the Config PPP control panel, if it isn't already open.

3. Click on the Hard Close button.

   MacPPP disconnects from the Internet and hangs up your modem.

Congratulations! You've successfully configured MacPPP, established a connection to the Internet, and closed that connection. If anything went wrong during this process, reread the section on MacPPP in chapter 12, "MacTCP, PPP, and SLIP."

InterSLIP 1.0.1

Quick Reminder: InterSLIP consists of an application called InterSLIP Setup and an extension called InterSLIP (a control panel called InterSLIP Control is necessary only for System 6 users). InterSLIP uses your modem to establish a connection to a SLIP account over which MacTCP-based programs can work.

Tasks:

1. Install InterSLIP

2. Configure InterSLIP for Northwest Nexus

3. Establish an Internet connection

4. Close the Internet connection

Install InterSLIP

1. Select the InterSLIP icon and drag it onto your System Folder.

   The Mac tells you that extensions need to be stored in the Extensions folder, and asks if you would like to put InterSLIP in the Extensions folder (see figure 14.12).

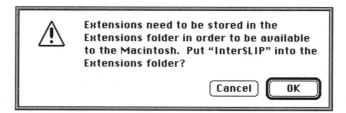

Figure 14.12   *Placing InterSLIP*

2. Click the OK button to confirm that the InterSLIP extension should be placed in the Extensions folder.

Configure InterSLIP for Northwest Nexus

1. Double-click on the InterSLIP Setup icon to launch the program. From the File menu, choose Quit.

   This forces InterSLIP Setup to create an InterSLIP Folder in the Preferences folder.

2. Open the System Folder, then the Preferences folder and, inside it, open the InterSLIP Folder. Drag the Minimal Dialing Script icon into the Dialing Scripts folder.

3. Drag the Northwest Nexus icon into the Gateway Scripts folder that is also in the InterSLIP Folder. Close the InterSLIP Folder and the Preferences folder.

Note

The ISKM Installer places these files for you, so they may already be in the right folders if you used the ISKM Installer to install InterSLIP.

4. Launch InterSLIP Setup, again (see figure 14.13).

5. From the File menu, choose New. In the dialog box that appears, enter **halcyon.com SLIP config**, and click the OK button (see figure 14.14).

Figure 14.13   *InterSLIP Setup*

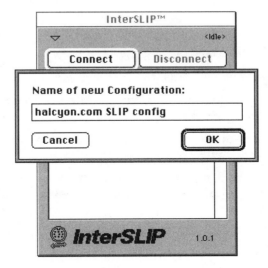

Figure 14.14   *Naming your configuration*

6. Double-click the configuration you just created in the InterSLIP Setup window.

   InterSLIP brings up the Configuration dialog (see figure 14.15).

7. From the Serial Port pop-up menu, choose Modem Port.

8. From the Baud Rate pop-up menu, choose 19200.

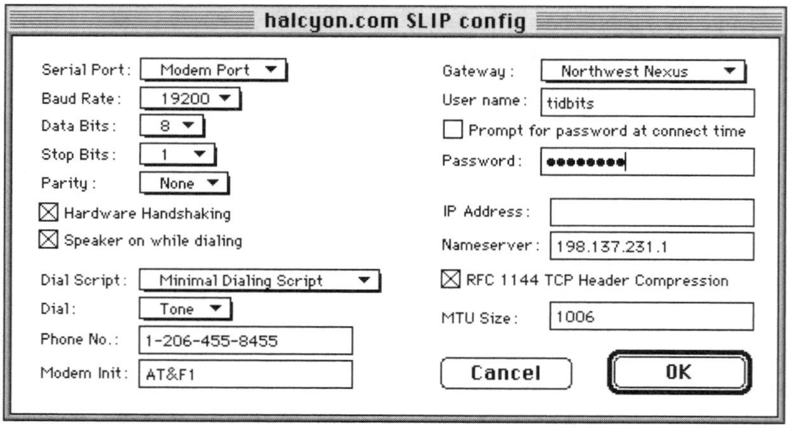

Figure 14.15   Configuring InterSLIP

9. From the Data Bits pop-up menu, choose 8.

10. From the Stop Bits pop-up menu, choose 1.

11. From the Parity pop-up menu, choose None.

12. Select the Hardware Handshaking checkbox.

13. Select the Speaker on while dialing checkbox.

14. From the Dial Script pop-up menu, choose Minimal Dialing Script (if you failed to install it above, choose Hayes-Compatible Modem).

15. From the Dial pop-up menu, choose Tone (if you have touch-tone phone service—if you have pulse service, choose Pulse).

16. In the Phone No. field, type **1-206-455-8455**. If you are within the local calling area for Bellevue, Washington, enter **455-8455**. If you cannot call Bellevue locally, but you can call Seattle locally, enter **382-6245**. If you must use any specific prefixes, like 9, to dial out, add them here, such as **9,1-206-455-8455**.

Note

The comma in the phone number above tells the modem to pause for two seconds before dialing the rest of the number. You can insert multiple commas to use additional two-second pauses.

17. In the Modem Init field, enter **AT&F1** if you use a SupraFAXmodem or Global Village TelePort or PowerPort modem. For other modem types,

check your modem manual for the appropriate factory default string. Make sure that string turns off XON/XOFF flow control.

18. From the Gateway pop-up menu, choose Northwest Nexus.

19. In the User name field, enter your username, making sure to enter it entirely in lowercase.

20. Deselect the Prompt for password at connect time checkbox, and enter your password into the Password field.

21. Leave the IP address field blank.

22. In the Nameserver field, enter **198.137.231.1**

23. Select the RFC 1144 TCP Header Compression checkbox.

24. In the MTU Size field, enter 1006.

25. When you're finished, your configuration dialog should resemble the one in figure 14.15. Click the OK button to save your changes.

Establish an Internet Connection

1. Double-click on InterSLIP Setup to launch it, if it's not still running.

2. Click the Connect button.

   InterSLIP Setup dials the modem and sends your username and password. Eventually, the status message in the upper right should say, "<Connected>" (see figure 14.16).

Figure 14.16   *Connected*

You should now be able to run MacTCP-based applications such as TurboGopher and Anarchie.

Close the Internet Connection

1. Quit any MacTCP-based applications other than Eudora that are running.

2. Double-click on InterSLIP Setup to launch it or, if it's still running, bring it to the front.

3. Click the Disconnect button.

   InterSLIP disconnects you from the Internet and hangs up your modem.

Congratulations! You've successfully installed and configured InterSLIP, established a connection to the Internet, and closed that connection. If anything went wrong during this process, reread the sections about InterSLIP and Troubleshooting in chapter 12, "MacTCP, PPP, and SLIP."

Eudora 1.4.3

Quick Reminder: Eudora is an email client program. Although it can work with both a shell account and a UUCP transport agent, it is most commonly used with MacTCP, and that's how we configure it here.

Tasks:

1. Launch and configure Eudora

2. Compose and send an email message to President Clinton

3. Subscribe to the *TidBITS* mailing list

4. Read, reply to, and delete an email message

Launch and Configure Eudora

1. Double-click on the Eudora icon.

   Eudora launches.

2. From the Special menu, choose Configuration.

   Eudora presents you with the Configuration dialog box.

3. In the first field, labeled POP account, enter your POP account, which you should have received from your provider. In most cases, this will be the same as or similar to your email address. If you use Northwest Nexus, enter your userid and **halcyon.com** with no spaces. For example, I would enter **tidbits@halcyon.com**. Make sure to enter this in lowercase only!

4. Press Tab, or click the next field down, labeled Real Name. Enter your real name here as you would like it to appear in your email messages.

5. Make sure that the MacTCP radio button, directly below the Real Name field, is selected (see figure 14.17).

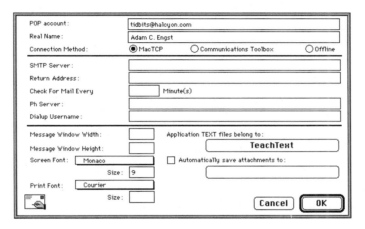

Figure 14.17   *Eudora Configuration dialog*

6. If your provider has explicitly given you an SMTP server that is different from the machine name in your POP account, enter its name in the SMTP Server field. If you use Northwest Nexus, leave this field blank, since your SMTP server is on the **halcyon.com** machine, and by default Eudora checks the machine name from your POP account for an SMTP server.

7. Click the OK button to close the Configuration dialog and save your changes.

8. From the Special menu, choose Switches.

Eudora brings up the Switches dialog. Turn off the Immediate Send checkbox, in the Sending category of options. This ensures that you can compose mail and queue it for sending without being connected to the Internet the entire time (see figure 14.18).

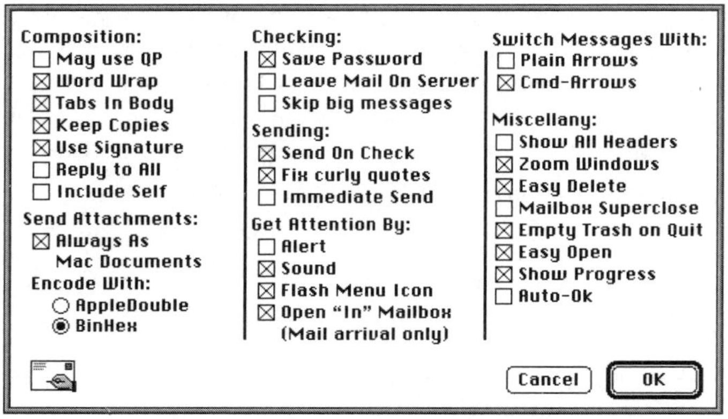

Figure 14.18   *Eudora Switches dialog*

9. Click the OK button to dismiss the Switches dialog and save your changes.

You have now performed the minimum configuration to use Eudora. There are many other options in the Configuration and Switches dialogs that you may wish to explore further. I recommend that you turn on balloon help from the Balloon Help menu and point at all of the fields and checkboxes in the Congiuration and Switches dialogs, for a quick explanation of what each does.

Compose and Send an Email Message to President Clinton

1. Make sure Eudora is running. From the Message menu, choose New Message.

    Eudora presents you with a new message window, with the From field already filled in with your email address and name.

2. Make sure your insertion point is in the To field (it should be unless you've clicked elsewhere in the window) and type your recipient's email address. In this case, enter **president@whitehouse.gov**.

3. Press Tab, or click to the right of the Subject field label to move your insertion point to the Subject field. Enter your subject, something like *Communicating with the President*.

4. Click in the large area of the window for typing the body of your message, or press Tab three times to move the insertion point. Type your message.

Since this example sends email to an address that replies automatically, the body of the message isn't that important for the time being, although you can use this method to express your opinions to President Clinton. At minimum, type something like *I strongly support the concept of a National Information Infrastructure.* It's considered polite to sign your name at the bottom (see figure 14.19).

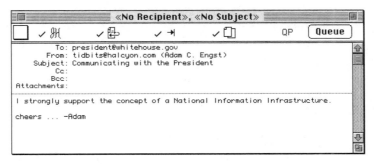

Figure 14.19   *Sending email to the President*

5. When you are finished, click on the Queue button in the upper right-hand corner of the window. If that button is labeled Send instead, go back to the previous task, make sure that the Immediate Send checkbox is empty in the Switches dialog, and try again with another message.

6. Now connect to the Internet. Connect with MacPPP or InterSLIP if necessary. Do not quit Eudora at this point; simply switch out to the Finder to launch InterSLIP Setup or open Config PPP to connect.

7. Switch back to Eudora, if necessary.

8. From the File menu choose Check Mail.

Eudora immediately presents you with a dialog box asking for your password. Enter it, making sure to capitalize it as you did when you originally created it (or as it was when it was given to you). The characters will not be displayed.

9. Click OK to enter the password you just typed.

Eudora then contacts your POP server and looks for new mail, transferring it back to your Macintosh if you have any. After retrieving new mail, Eudora contacts the SMTP server and sends the mail that you just queued for delivery. After it finishes sending, Eudora displays a dialog telling you whether or not you have new mail.

10. If you're paying for your Internet connection by the hour, or if you're paying for a long distance call, switch to Config PPP or InterSLIP Setup and disconnect to save money. Otherwise, go ahead and stay connected as we work through the next few tasks.

Assuming everything was set up correctly on your Macintosh and on your host machine, you've just sent an email message via Eudora.

Subscribe to the *TidBITS* Mailing List

1. Make sure Eudora is open, and from the Message menu choose New Message.

   Eudora presents you with a new message window, with the From field already filled in with your email address and name and with the cursor in the To field.

2. In the To field, type **listserv@ricevm1.rice.edu**.

3. Press Tab four times, or click in the message section of the window. Type **SUBSCRIBE TIDBITS** *your full name* (replace *your full name* with your real name, not your email address) and nothing else (see figure 14.20).

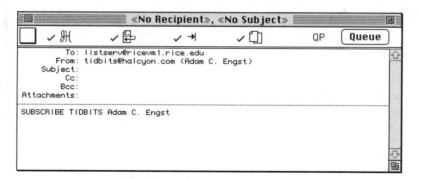

Figure 14.20   Subscribing to TidBITS

4. Click on the Queue button in the upper right-hand corner of the window to queue the message to be sent.

5. Make sure you are connected to the Internet.

6. From the File menu, choose Check Mail.

7. As before, Eudora first connects to your POP server and checks for new mail. Depending on how long it has taken you to create this message, you may have received mail back from the White House. Either way, after checking for new mail, Eudora contacts your SMTP server and sends your subscription message to the LISTSERV program.

8. If you are paying for your connection, feel free close the connection now to save money.

You've just subscribed to a mailing list! Although other mailing lists may be slightly different, mostly in terms of the mailing list manager's address and the listname, the basics are the same.

Read, Reply to, and Delete an Email Message

1. Make sure Eudora is running.

   If you received a reply from the White House when you sent the subscription message to the *TidBITS* list, Eudora automatically opened your In Box for you.

   If you have not yet received the reply from the White House or the confirmation of your subscription to the *TidBITS* list, wait for a while (there's no way to know how long it could take, although when I wrote these instructions the responses came back within minutes).

2. Make sure you're connected to the Internet, and from the File menu, choose Check Mail.

3. Eudora opens your In Box after receiving new mail; if you have closed it while waiting, go to the Mailbox menu and choose In. Eudora then displays the In Box again and marks unread messages with a bullet (•) character (see figure 14.21).

4. Double-click on the reply from the White House, which probably looks as though it came from **autoresponder@WhiteHouse.Gov**, which is the program that automatically replies to email sent to President Clinton.

   Eudora opens the message and displays it, along with the first four lines of the header (see figure 14.22).

5. Read through the message, scrolling with the scroll bar or the Page Up/Page Down keys.

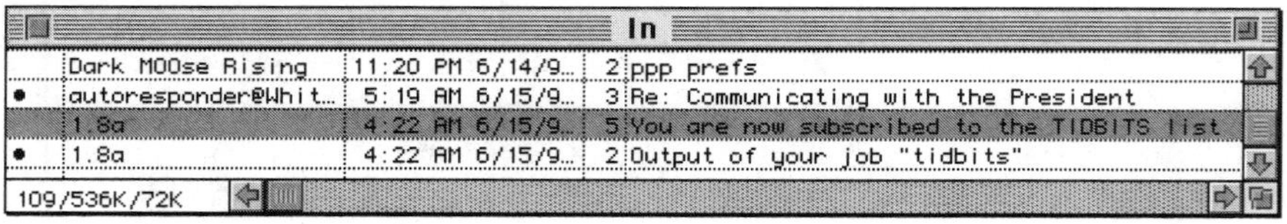

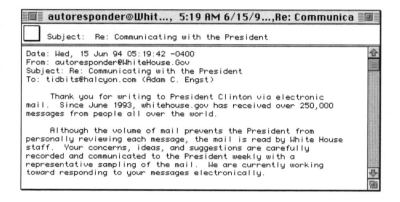

	In				
	Dark M00se Rising	11:20 PM 6/14/9...	2	ppp prefs	
●	autoresponder@Whit...	5:19 AM 6/15/9...	3	Re: Communicating with the President	
	1.8a	4:22 AM 6/15/9...	5	You are now subscribed to the TIDBITS list	
●	1.8a	4:22 AM 6/15/9...	2	Output of your job "tidbits"	

109/536K/72K

Figure 14.21   *Eudora In Box*

Figure 14.22   *Email from the White House*

6. After reading the message, go to the Message menu and choose Reply.

   Eudora creates a new message window for you, entering the original sender's address in the To field and the subject of your original message, prefixed with "Re:" in the Subject field. The entire body of the original message is quoted in the body of the message, and Eudora automatically selects the quoted text. You can edit this text, or delete it entirely (see figure 14.23).

7. When your reply is ready, you could click the Queue button to queue it for delivery again, but please don't, since it's a waste of Internet resources to send meaningless test messages back and forth.

   When replying to personal email, you would queue the message, perhaps along with others that you have queued and ready to send out, and then choose either Check Mail or Send Queued Messages from the File menu.

8. Once you're finished sending any messages, go ahead and disconnect from the Internet, especially if you're being charged.

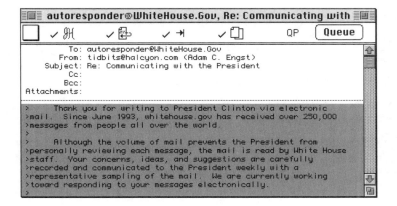

Figure 14.23 *Replying to a message*

9. To delete the message from the White House, make sure its window is open or make sure it is selected in the In Box; then, from the Message menu choose Delete. Eudora then moves that message to the Trash mailbox.

That's about all you need to know to get started reading and writing email with Eudora, although, as I've said, there are many other options and shortcuts to make the process of using Eudora even easier.

NewsWatcher 2.0b1

Quick Reminder: NewsWatcher is what's called a newsreader, or a client program for Usenet news. It requires access to an NNTP news server on an Internet host.

Tasks:

1. Launch and configure NewsWatcher

2. Create a personalized subscription list and subscribe to several newsgroups

3. Read articles in the subscribed newsgroups

4. Post a message

Launch and Configure NewsWatcher

1. Make sure you are connected to the Internet—connect with MacPPP or InterSLIP, if necessary.

2. Double-click on the NewsWatcher icon.

   NewsWatcher launches, and presents you with two dialogs (assuming that you haven't previously configured it).

3. The first dialog asks for the names of your news server and your mail server. Enter the appropriate names, which you have obtained from your provider. If you use Northwest Nexus, enter **news.halcyon.com** for your news server, and **halcyon.com** for your mail server (see figure 14.24).

Note

As this book was going to press, Northwest Nexus added a new news server at **news.halcyon.com**. *Although the new name makes much more sense (and the new server is faster), I had no time to redo the screenshots for the book. Thus, if you use Northwest Nexus, please use* **news.halcyon.com** *as the news server and don't use* **nwfocus.wa.com**. *Sorry for any confusion this may cause.*

Click the OK button to dismiss the dialog.

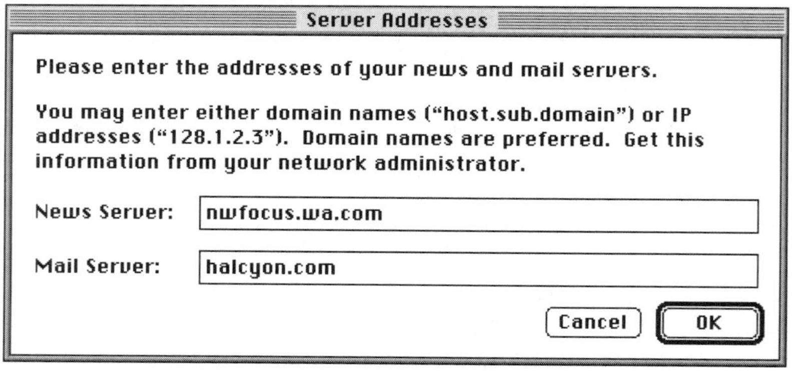

Figure 14.24   Configuring server addresses

4. The second dialog asks for your full name, organization, and email address. Fill in the appropriate information, making sure to enter your email address in all lowercase letters (see figure 14.25).

Click the OK button to dismiss the dialog.

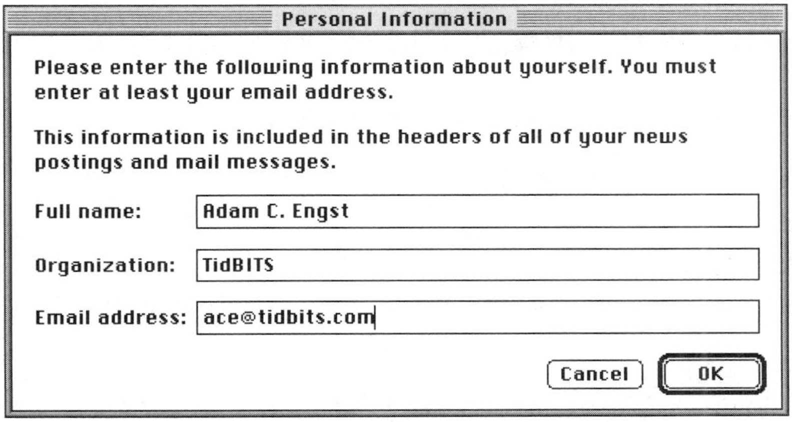

Figure 14.25 *Configuring your personal information*

5. NewsWatcher then connects to your news server and retrieves the full group list from the server. This can take some time, especially over a slow modem. Once NewsWatcher sorts the list, it displays it in a scrollable window.

Do not quit NewsWatcher now, but go on to the next task in which you learn how to create a personalized subscription list and subscribe to newsgroups that might interest you.

You've now successfully completed the minimum of steps necessary to configure and use NewsWatcher. I strongly recommend that you read my discussion of NewsWatcher in chapter 13, "MacTCP-based Software," and the user documentation that comes with NewsWatcher. Most of the additional configuration options live in the Preferences dialog available in the File menu (see figure 14.26).

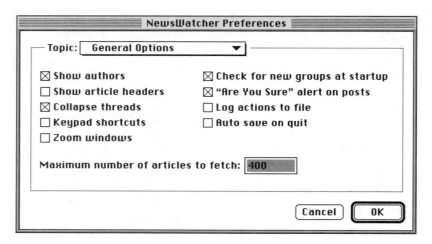

Figure 14.26   *NewsWatcher Preferences dialog*

Create a Personalized Subscription List and Subscribe to Several Newsgroups

1. From the File menu, choose New Group Window.

   NewsWatcher creates a small window labeled "untitled." Move it so that you can see both it and the Full Group List window on your screen at the same time.

2. Making sure that "untitled" is the frontmost window, go to the File menu and choose Save. Give the file an appropriate name, such as "My Newsgroups," and save it on your desktop (see figure 14.27).

   You may wish to move the file later, perhaps to your Apple Menu Items folder so that it shows up in your Apple menu.

3. Scroll down in the Full Group List window until you find the newsgroup called **news.announce.newusers**. Groups are sorted alphabetically, so it should be about halfway down. As a shortcut, you could press the N key to immediately jump to the newsgroups whose names start with the letter N.

4. Click the **news.announce.newusers** item in the list and drag it over the subscription window that you just created. You should see a dark black line appear in that window, indicating where the newsgroup will appear once you drop it. Let go of the mouse button to drop the group in your subscription window. NewsWatcher may show the spinning beach ball cursor briefly; then, **news.announce.newusers** appears in your subscription window. The number next to its name indicates the number of unread articles in that group.

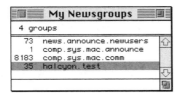

Figure 14.27 *My Newsgroups window*

5. Repeat the process with **comp.sys.mac.announce** and **comp.sys.mac.comm**, and, if you use Northwest Nexus, with a group called **halcyon.test**.

   Announcements important to the entire Mac community appear in **comp.sys.mac.announce**. Discussions about Macintosh communications software appear in **comp.sys.mac.comm**, which is also a good place to ask about things that you cannot otherwise figure out. I use **halcyon.test** later, when providing instructions on posting. Add any other groups that you think might be interesting—check out the newsgroup list in Appendix B, "Newsgroup List," for brief descriptions of many of the newsgroups.

6. Making sure your subscription list's window is frontmost, choose Save from the File menu to save the list of the newsgroups that you've subscribed to.

7. Close the Full Group List window. (You can open it again at any time from the Windows menu with Show Full Group List.)

8. Quit NewsWatcher by choosing Quit from the File menu.

   This isn't absolutely necessary, but bear with me. I want you to start on the next task, reading articles, as you would normally, and that includes launching NewsWatcher.

You've now successfully created your own personalized subscription list and saved it for future use. You can add newsgroups to this list at any time, and remove newsgroups that no longer interest you. NewsWatcher starts up slightly faster with a small subscription list, so it may be a good idea to only subscribe to newsgroups that you actually read.

Read Articles in the Subscribed Newsgroups

1. Launch NewsWatcher, not by double-clicking on the application, but by double-clicking on the subscription list that you created in the previous task.

NewsWatcher launches, connects to the news server, checks for new groups and new articles, and then displays your subscription list window.

2. Double-click on **news.announce.newusers**.

NewsWatcher retrieves the subjects and authors of the articles contained in that newsgroup, and presents you with a window displaying the list of those articles (see figure 14.28).

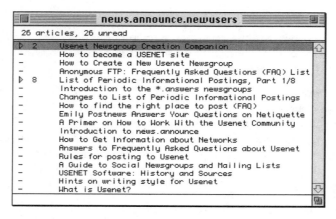

Figure 14.28   *Articles in* **news.announce.newusers**

3. Double-click on the first article in the newsgroup.

Since articles in **news.announce.newusers** are relatively large, it may take a minute or so to download them if you're using a modem. NewsWatcher then displays the article itself.

4. Read through the article, if you wish. I recommend that you browse through the articles in this group early on, since they're designed to answer many questions that new users have.

5. To read the next article, you can close the article window and double-click on the next article in the newsgroup. An easier method is to go to the News menu and choose Read Next Article, or to press Command-I.

You've now successfully opened a newsgroup and read several articles. You can close the window listing articles in **news.announce.newusers**, and double-click on **comp.sys.mac.announce** to see the list of articles in that group and read them if you wish.

Post a Message

Before I get into the steps for posting a message from NewsWatcher, we need to find a proper place for you to post it. If you have no special question to ask in an appropriate newsgroup, but still wish to post a test article to see whether it works, you must find a test newsgroup. Scroll down in the Full Group List window looking for a newsgroup name, preferably a local one that might be named after your machine, ending in **test**. Add it to your subscription list, just as we did the other group. I'm using the newsgroup **halcyon.test** in this example, and it should be available for anyone using Northwest Nexus.

1. In your subscription window, double-click on the newsgroup into which you wish to post.

2. From the News menu choose New Message.

   NewsWatcher brings up the New Message window, with the Newsgroups line already filled in, and the cursor on the Subject line.

3. Type your article, then click on the Send button, at which point NewsWatcher posts your article to the newsgroup (see figure 14.29).

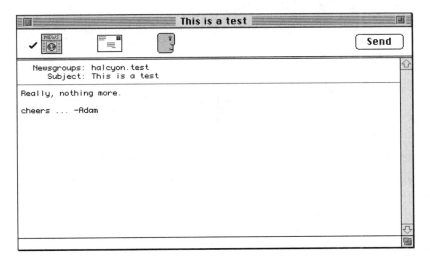

Figure 14.29   NewsWatcher New Message window

4. After posting your article, feel free to read other articles, post more questions (but remember, it's a good idea to lurk for a while before becoming a prolific poster), and subscribe to additional newsgroups. (You won't see your post show up unless you quit NewsWatcher and relaunch it.)

When you're finished, choose Quit from the File menu and save your subscription list when NewsWatcher prompts you about it.

Congratulations! You've successfully performed all the basic tasks you do with NewsWatcher. I won't pretend that there aren't many more subtleties in using this program, but you can learn about those from reading the previous chapter and NewsWatcher's documentation files.

Anarchie 1.2.0

Quick Reminder: Anarchie is a shareware FTP and Archie client program that you use to search for and retrieve files available via anonymous FTP.

Tasks:

1. Launch and configure Anarchie

2. Connect to a site and retrieve a file

3. Use a bookmark to retrieve a file

4. Search an Archie server and retrieve the results

Launch and Configure Anarchie

1. Make sure you are connected to the Internet—connect with MacPPP or InterSLIP, if necessary.

2. Double-click on the Anarchie icon in the Finder to launch it.

   Anarchie launches and displays its About box and its Bookmarks window.

3. From the Edit menu choose Preferences.

   Anarchie displays its Preferences dialog (see figure 14.30).

4. Type your email address into the Email Address field.

5. Click the Save button to save your changes.

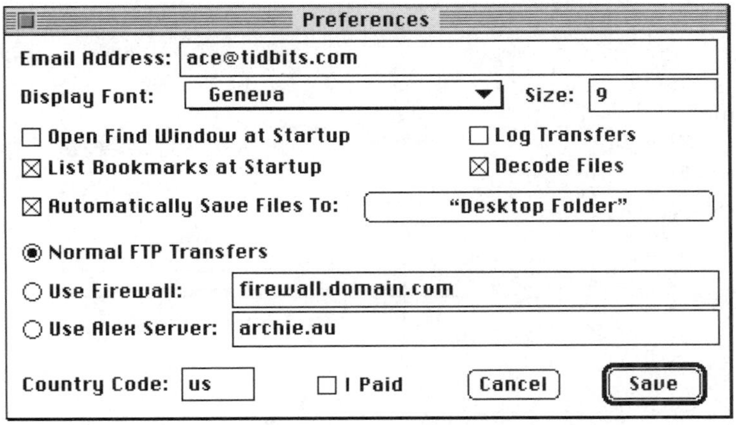

Figure 14.30 *Anarchie Preferences dialog*

Connect to a Site and Retrieve a File

1. Make sure Anarchie is still running, and from the File menu choose Get.

   Anarchie brings up the Get via FTP window.

2. In the Machine field, enter **ftp.tidbits.com**, and in the Path field, enter **/pub/tidbits/select/stuffit-expander.sea**.

3. Select the Get File radio button (see figure 14.31).

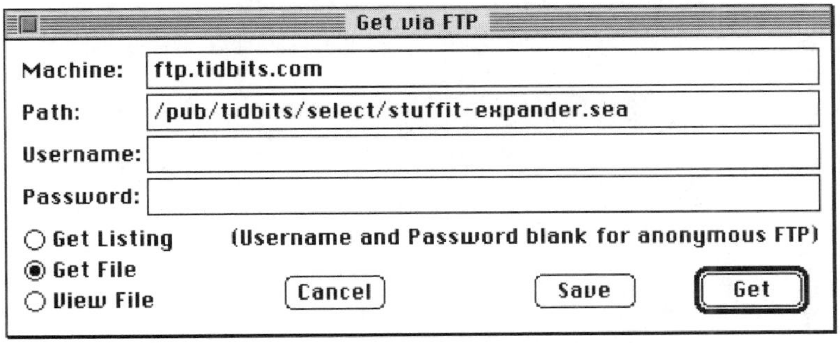

Figure 14.31 *Anarchie Get via FTP window*

4. Click the Get button to retrieve the file.

   Anarchie displays a progress dialog, and the file appears on your desktop when the download is complete (see figure 14.32).

stuffit-expander.sea
Host: ftp.tidbits.com
Status: Getting
State: Transferring
Transfered: 37248
Bytes/Sec: 1552
Time Left: 0:36
200 PORT command successful.

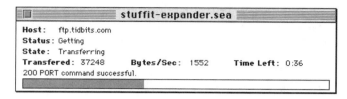

Figure 14.32 *Anarchie Progress dialog*

5. Since this is a self-extracting archive, double-click on it to expand Aladdin's free StuffIt Expander. Anarchie works with StuffIt Expander to debinhex and expand other files that you download.

Use a Bookmark to Retrieve a File

1. Make sure Anarchie is running. If the Bookmarks window is not showing, choose List Bookmarks from the File menu (see figure 14.33).

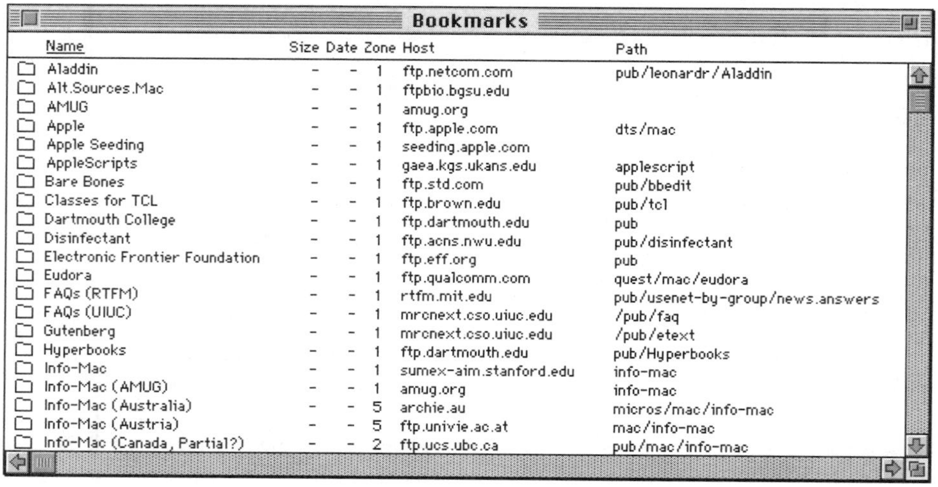

Bookmarks
Name Size Date Zone Host Path
Aladdin - - 1 ftp.netcom.com pub/leonardr/Aladdin
Alt.Sources.Mac - - 1 ftpbio.bgsu.edu
AMUG - - 1 amug.org
Apple - - 1 ftp.apple.com dts/mac
Apple Seeding - - 1 seeding.apple.com
AppleScripts - - 1 gaea.kgs.ukans.edu applescript
Bare Bones - - 1 ftp.std.com pub/bbedit
Classes for TCL - - 1 ftp.brown.edu pub/tcl
Dartmouth College - - 1 ftp.dartmouth.edu pub
Disinfectant - - 1 ftp.acns.nwu.edu pub/disinfectant
Electronic Frontier Foundation - - 1 ftp.eff.org pub
Eudora - - 1 ftp.qualcomm.com quest/mac/eudora
FAQs (RTFM) - - 1 rtfm.mit.edu pub/usenet-by-group/news.answers
FAQs (UIUC) - - 1 mrcnext.cso.uiuc.edu /pub/faq
Gutenberg - - 1 mrcnext.cso.uiuc.edu /pub/etext
Hyperbooks - - 1 ftp.dartmouth.edu pub/Hyperbooks
Info-Mac - - 1 sumex-aim.stanford.edu info-mac
Info-Mac (AMUG) - - 1 amug.org info-mac
Info-Mac (Australia) - - 5 archie.au micros/mac/info-mac
Info-Mac (Austria) - - 5 ftp.univie.ac.at mac/info-mac
Info-Mac (Canada, Partial?) - - 2 ftp.ucs.ubc.ca pub/mac/info-mac

Figure 14.33 *Anarchie Bookmarks window*

2. Double-click on the Disinfectant item in the Name field (you may have to scroll down).

Anarchie connects to **ftp.acns.nwu.edu** and puts in you the **/pub/ disinfectant** directory (see figure 14.34).

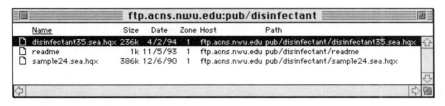

Figure 14.34 *Anarchie at* **ftp.acns.nwu.edu**

3. Double-click on the **disinfectant35.sea.hqx** item in the Name field.

Anarchie starts downloading Disinfectant, and places it on your desktop when it's finished (see figure 14.35).

Figure 14.35 *Anarchie Progress dialog II*

4. When the download finishes, Anarchie launches StuffIt Expander to debinhex and expand the file.

Search an Archie Server and Retrieve the Results

1. Make sure Anarchie is running, and from the File menu, choose Archie.

Anarchie displays the Archie dialog.

2. In the Find field, type **internews** (see figure 14.36).

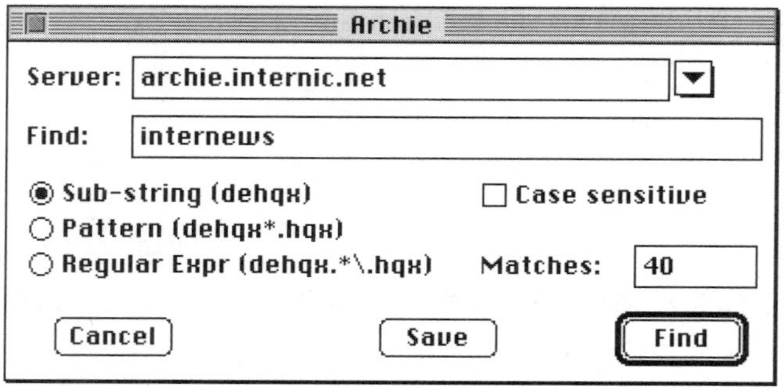

Figure 14.36   Anarchie Archie dialog

3. Click the Find button to submit the search to the Archie server.

Note

Unfortunately, I cannot guarantee this search will work when you try it. If it doesn't, try a different search term, or select another Archie server from the pop-up menu in the Archie dialog box.

4. If all goes well, Anarchie displays a window containing the results of the search. To retrieve any one of these files, merely double-click on it (see figure 14.37).

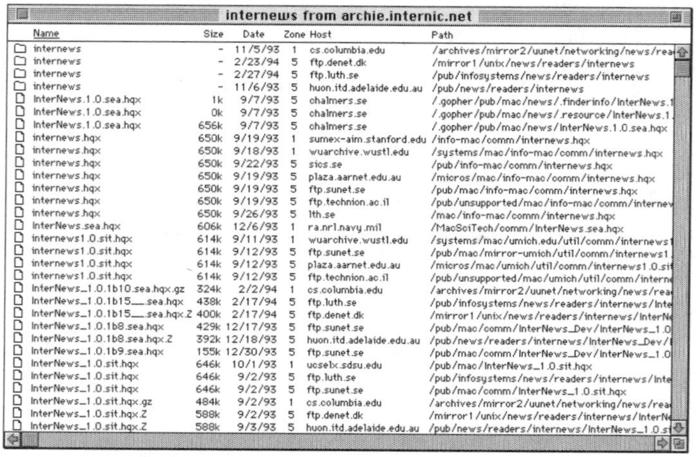

Figure 14.37   Anarchie search results window

5. When Anarchie has finished, it calls StuffIt Expander to debinhex and expand the file. Once you're finished downloading, you can quit Anarchie and disconnect from the Internet.

Congratulations! You've just performed all the basic tasks in Anarchie you're likely to do in real life. Extrapolate from these instructions to retrieve other files using Anarchie's Bookmarks and Archie searching.

Fetch 2.1.2

Quick Reminder: Fetch is a shareware FTP client program that you use to retrieve files available via anonymous FTP.

Tasks:

1. Launch Fetch

2. Connect to a site and retrieve a file

Launch Fetch

1. Make sure you are connected to the Internet—connect with MacPPP or InterSLIP, if necessary.

2. Double-click on the Fetch icon in the Finder to launch it.

   Fetch launches, and displays its main window and Open Connection dialog.

Connect to a Site and Retrieve a File

1. In the Password field, type your email address.

   Bullets appear instead of the characters you type (see figure 14.38).

2. Click the OK button to connect to the FTP site at **ftp.dartmouth.edu**.

3. Double-click on the item in the list called Hyperbooks (see figure 14.39).

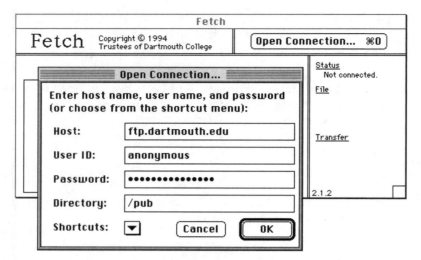

Figure 14.38   Fetch Open Connection dialog

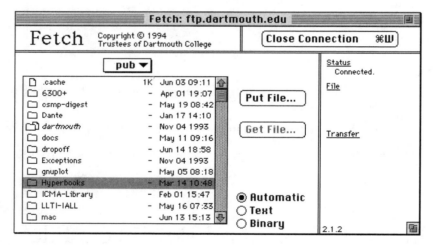

Figure 14.39   Fetch main window

4. Scroll down until you see a book that interests you. Double-click on its name to retrieve it. Fetch presents a Standard File dialog box for you to save the file.

   Click on the Desktop button and then on the Save button to save it on your desktop (see figure 14.40).

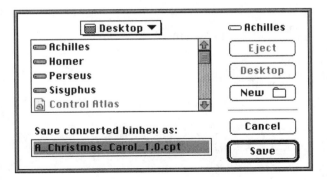

Figure 14.40   *Fetch saving file*

5. Fetch downloads the file and debinhexes it (see figure 14.41).

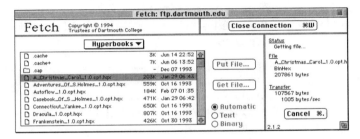

Figure 14.41   *Fetch downloading file*

6. Since these files are all compressed as well as binhexed, you must drop the file on StuffIt Expander to expand the file after Fetch finishes.

7. When Fetch is finished, click the Close Connection button to sever your connection to the FTP server. Now you can quit Fetch and disconnect from the Internet, if you wish.

Congratulations! You've downloaded a file using Fetch. With other FTP sites to type into the Host dialog box in the Open Connection dialog, you can download many more.

MacWAIS 1.29

Quick Reminder: MacWAIS is a shareware WAIS client program that you use to search massive databases of information.

Tasks:

1. Launch and configure MacWAIS

2. Find a source

3. Ask a specific question

Launch and Configure MacWAIS

1. Make sure you are connected to the Internet—connect with MacPPP or InterSLIP, if necessary.

2. Double-click on the MacWAIS icon.

   MacWAIS launches and displays its shareware dialog. You can find out the details of the shareware agreement by clicking on the Shareware Info button, or you can click on the Not Yet button to actually use the program. Do not click on the Register button unless you've paid your shareware fee and need to register your copy.

3. Select New Question from the File Menu and MacWAIS opens an Unnamed Question and brings up the source selection dialog. Navigate to the wais-sources folder that is in the same folder as MacWAIS, and open it. You should see at least two sources, **Directory of Servers** and **EINet Shareware**. Double-click on **Directory of Servers** so that it appears in the right-hand scrolling list (see figure 14.42).

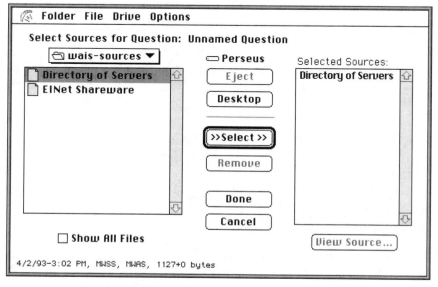

Figure 14.42   *MacWAIS Source Selection dialog*

4. Click the Done button to dismiss the source selection dialog.

You can now see the Unnamed Question window with the Directory of Servers source selected (see figure 14.43).

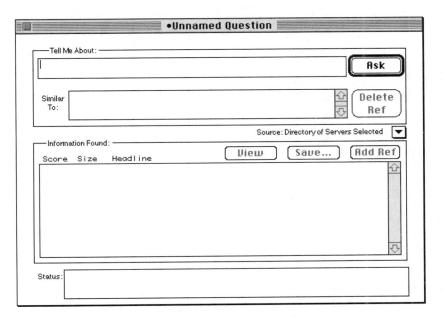

Figure 14.43   *MacWAIS Unnamed Question window*

5. From the File menu, choose Preferences (see figure 14.44). Click the checkbox labeled Default Source for New Question, and in the source selection dialog that appears, double-click on the Directory of Servers source to move it to the right-hand list. Click the Done button to dismiss the dialog.

You may need to navigate to the wais-sources folder to find it again. (You may wish to change this default later on, after you've become more comfortable with WAIS.)

6. Click the checkbox labeled Default Folder for saving Sources, and in the Standard File dialog that appears, navigate to the wais-sources folder that you visited before. Once there, click the Select: wais-sources button.

7. Click the OK button to save your changes and dismiss the Preferences dialog.

Although you may wish to experiment with some of the other options in the Preferences dialog, that's about all there is to setting up MacWAIS.

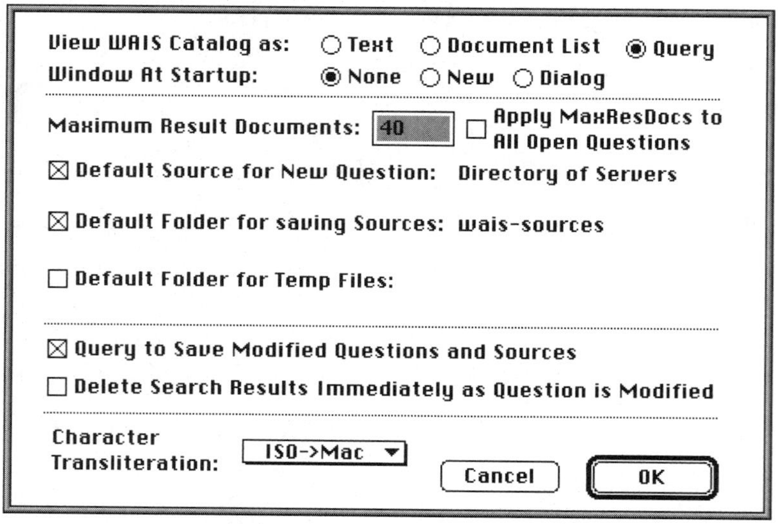

Figure 14.44   *MacWAIS Preferences dialog*

Find a Source

1. Back at the Unnamed Question window, type **Macintosh** in the Tell Me About field. Click the Ask button to send your question to the WAIS Directory of Servers.

2. MacWAIS reports in its Status field that it is searching the Directory of Servers and initializing the connection. Then, it tells you how many sources it found for you (see figure 14.45).

Note

If you installed MacWAIS with the ISKM Installer, you already have some of these sources available.

3. Double-click on `macintosh-news.src`, which should be the first entry in the list.

   MacWAIS brings up the description of the source, that tells you that `macintosh-news.src` contains compilations of the Info-Mac Digest, the `comp.sys.mac.programmer` digest, and *TidBITS*. Click the OK button to save the file in your wais-sources folder (see figure 14.46).

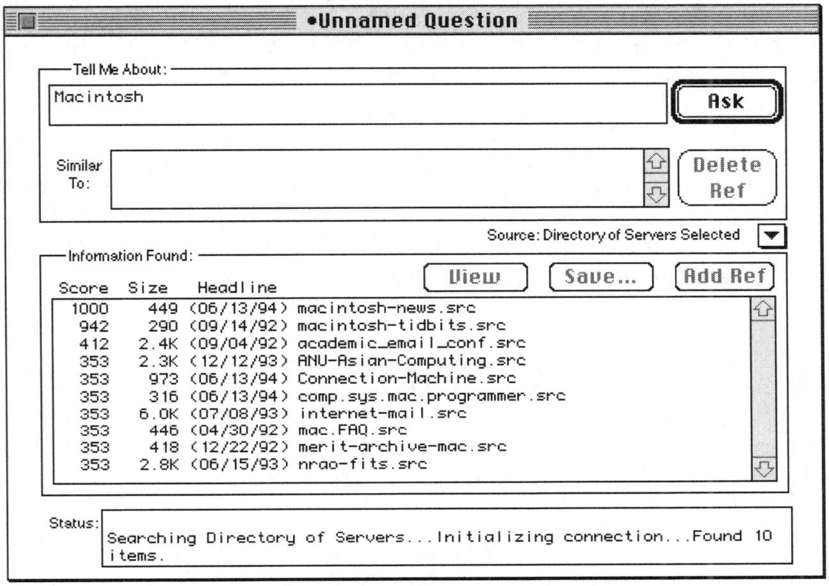

Figure 14.45 *Finding Macintosh sources*

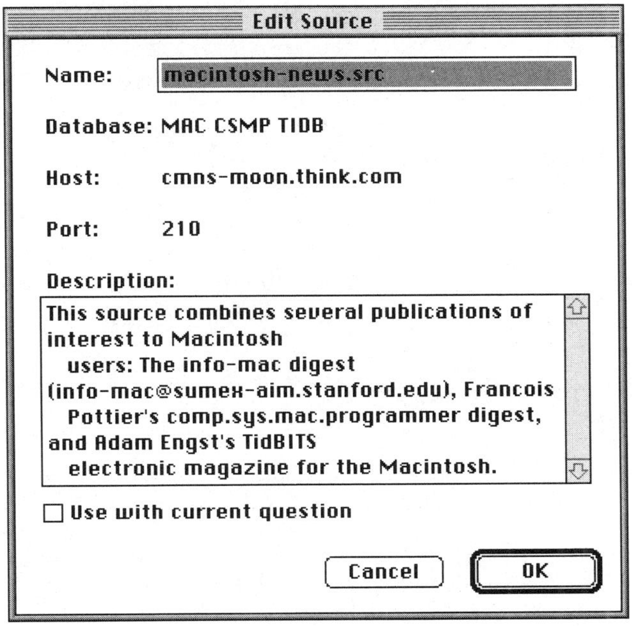

Figure 14.46 *MacWAIS Edit Source dialog*

4. If you wish, repeat the process described previously with `macintosh-tidbits.src`, `merit-archive-mac.src`, and `mac.FAQ.src`. Clicking the Cancel button in the source description dialog closes the dialog without saving the source in your wais-sources folder.

You've now found several sources of information about the Macintosh that you could search if you had a question about some piece of Macintosh hardware or software. Obviously, if you changed the entry in the Tell Me About field, you could find many other sources for different topics.

Ask a Specific Question

1. From the File menu, choose New Question.

   MacWAIS opens another window, called Unnamed Question. Notice that **Directory of Servers** is the selected source.

2. From the Sources menu, choose Select. MacWAIS presents you with a source selection dialog, with **Directory of Servers** already selected on the right-hand side.

3. Double-click the `macintosh-news.src` to move it to the right-hand list. Click the Directory of Servers entry in the right-hand list, and click the Remove button to remove it. Click the Done button to dismiss the dialog.

4. In the Tell Me About field, type **the IIsi sound problem**.

   MacWAIS searches the `macintosh-news.src` source and finds 40 items, which is the maximum default setting (see figure 14.47).

5. Double-click on the first item in the list to view it in a text window.

   You can save the text in the window, copy it and paste it into another application, perform a Find within it (if it's a lot of text, that's often a useful feature), or use it as relevance feedback (see figure 14.48).

6. For the time being, close the Unnamed Question window, and, when prompted, click the Save button to save the question in the MacWAIS folder.

   The next time you want to ask a question of the `macintosh-news.src` source, you can simply double-click on this question to launch MacWAIS and open the question with the proper source already selected.

7. From the File menu, choose Quit to quit MacWAIS. If you wish, disconnect from the Internet.

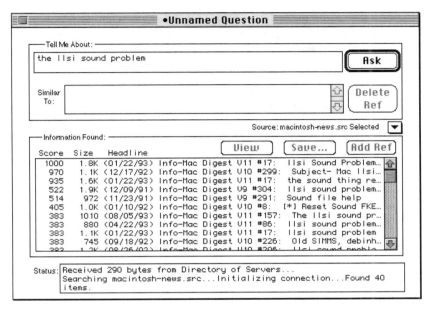

Figure 14.47 *Asking the IIsi question*

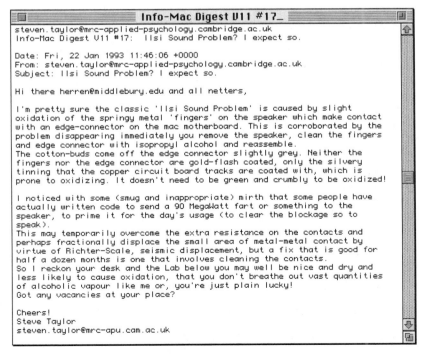

Figure 14.48 *The answer to the question*

That's all there is to asking a basic question of WAIS, although in practice you may find it a bit more difficult to properly phrase a question to get the results you want. It may also take some work to find the proper source in which to search.

TurboGopher 1.0.8b4

Quick Reminder: TurboGopher is a free Gopher client program that you use to retrieve information available on Gopher servers.

Tasks:

1. Launch TurboGopher

2. Navigate to and view a file on a Gopher server

3. Search a Veronica server and retrieve the results

Launch TurboGopher

1. Make sure you are connected to the Internet—connect with MacPPP or InterSLIP if necessary.

2. Double-click on the TurboGopher icon in the Finder to launch it.

   TurboGopher launches and displays your Bookmarks window and the window for the Home Gopher Server (see figure 14.49).

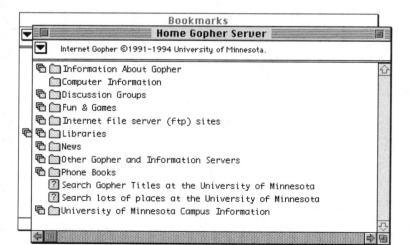

Figure 14.49   *TurboGopher Home Gopher Server*

Navigate to and View a File on a Gopher Server

1. Double-click on the "Other Gopher and Information Servers" item in the Home Gopher Server window.

   TurboGopher opens that window (see figure 14.50).

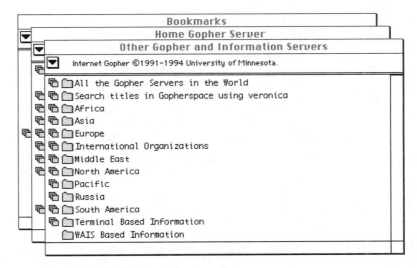

Figure 14.50   *TurboGopher opening a window*

2. Double-click on "Search all titles in Gopherspace using veronica."

   TurboGopher opens that window (see figure 14.51).

3. Double-click on "FAQ: Frequently-Asked Questions about veronica" to display its document window (see figure 14.52).

4. Click the close box to close that document window. Do not close any other windows.

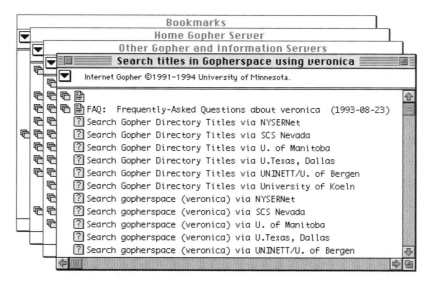

Figure 14.51   *TurboGopher opening another window*

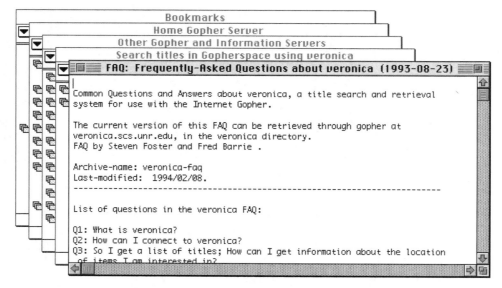

Figure 14.52   *TurboGopher opening a document window*

Search a Veronica Server and Retrieve the Results

1. Double-click on the "Search gopherspace (veronica) via NYSERNET" item in the Search titles in Gopherspace using veronica window.

   TurboGopher displays a search dialog (see figure 14.53).

2. In the search field, type **Apple** to retrieve information about Apple. Click on OK.

   TurboGopher connects to the Veronica server and displays a window with the search results.

Note

I cannot guarantee what will come back, or even that the Veronica server will work, since they are often overloaded. If you don't get anything, simply try again later, or try a different Veronica server.

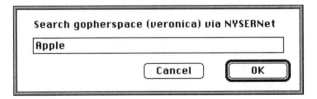

Figure 14.53 *TurboGopher search dialog*

3. Double-click on one of the items in the results window with a little page icon next to it to display that document window (see figure 14.54).

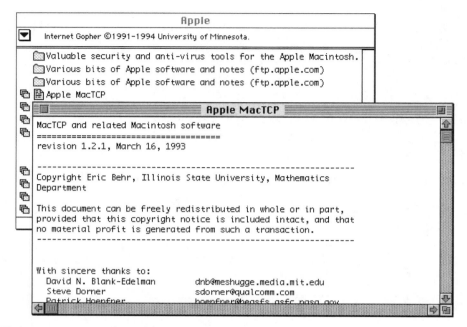

Figure 14.54   *TurboGopher result document*

Congratulations! You've just navigated through Gopherspace, searched a
Veronica server, and retrieved a document. That's basically about all there is to
using TurboGopher.

NCSA Mosaic 2.0a1

Quick Reminder: Mosaic is a client application for the World-Wide Web, the
most graphical and flexible of the Internet services.

Tasks:

1. Launch and configure Mosaic

2. Browse the Web

3. Visit the *Wired* Web server

4. Use the hotlist

Launch and Configure Mosaic

1. Make sure you are connected to the Internet—connect with MacPPP or InterSLIP, if necessary.

2. Double-click on the NCSA Mosaic icon to launch the program. (Mosiac isn't on the ISKM Disk. If you don't have it already, just double-click on the Get NCSA Mosaic bookmark to automatically retrieve it.)

   Mosaic immediately begins to load its home page, which by default is the NCSA Home Page.

   The NCSA Home Page looks like figure 14.55.

3. From the Options menu, choose Auto-Load Images (if it already checked, leave as is).

   You may wish to turn this off again later, for better performance.

4. From the Options menu, choose Preferences. Mosaic brings up the Preferences dialog box. Click the Misc button at the upper left of the dialog box to reveal the miscellaneous preferences (see figure 14.56). Depending on what version you are using, the screens you see may look different from what we have here. Remember, on the net you have to be flexible.

5. In the Home Page field, type **http://www.tidbits.com/tidbits/index.html** to ensure that you go to the *Internet Starter Kit for Macintosh* home page when you launch Mosaic.

6. In the User Name field, enter your real name.

7. In the EMail Address field, enter your email address.

8. Click the Apply button to save your changes.

There are many other optional settings in the Mosaic Preferences dialog—feel free to explore them later on.

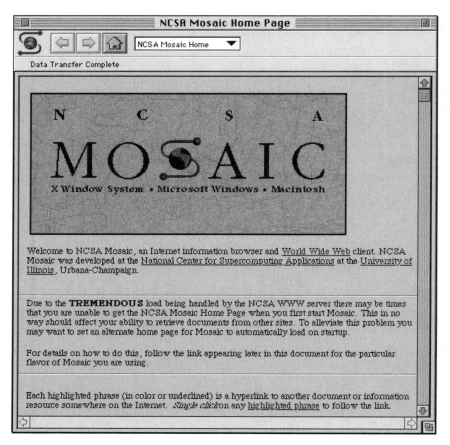

Figure 14.55   *Mosaic Home Page*

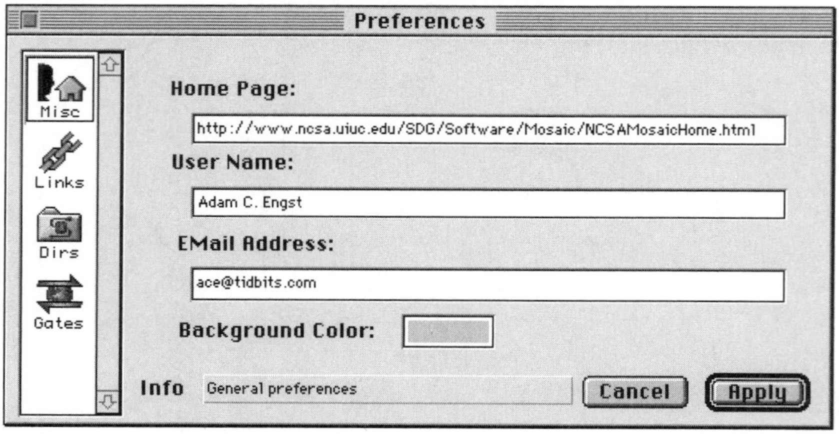

Figure 14.56   *Mosaic Preferences window*

Browse the Web

1. From the Navigate menu, select NCSA What's New Page.

   Mosaic displays the contents of the What's New Page (see figure 14.57).

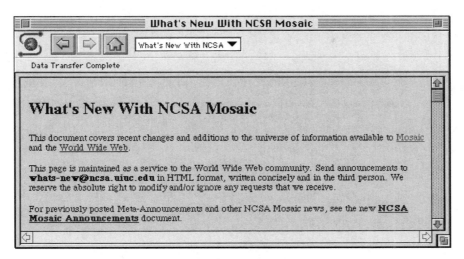

Figure 14.57   *Mosaic What's New Page*

Note

Depending on how late in the month you connect, the What's New Page may be quite large and thus take some time to retrieve fully.

2. Click the underlined words **World Wide Web** to follow that link to the home of the World-Wide Web, at CERN in Switzerland (see figure 14.58).

3. Feel free to continue clicking on underlined link words to move to other parts of the Web—it's too large and fast-moving for me to give you any further explicit browsing directions. But what if you want to go to a specific site?

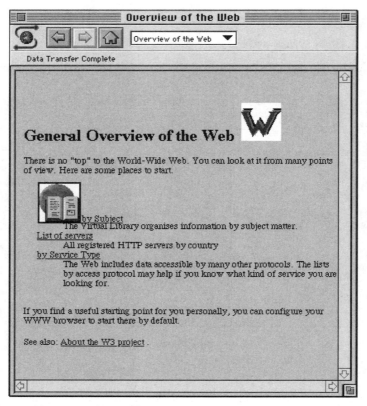

Figure 14.58   *Mosaic Overview of the Web*

Visit the *Wired* Web Server

1. From the File menu, choose Open URL.

   Mosaic displays a dialog into which you can type a URL (Uniform Resource Locator).

Note

I have listed various URLs throughout the book, so you might try some of the "http" URLs here in Mosaic.

2. In the field, type **http://www.wired.com** (see figure 14.59).

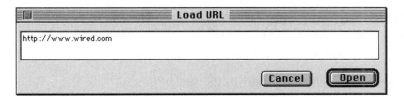

Figure 14.59   *Mosaic Open URL dialog*

3. Click the Open button to connect to the Web server run by *Wired* magazine (see figure 14.60).

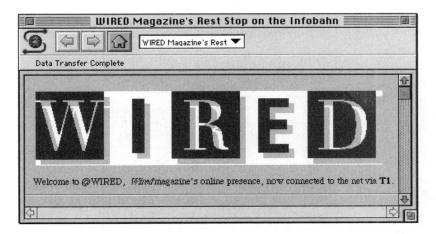

Figure 14.60   *Mosaic at the Wired Server*

Use the Hotlist

Note

A hotlist is a list of places to which you have saved pointers in case you might want to revisit them later.

1. With the window to the *Wired* Web server still open, from the Navigate menu select Add This Document.

   Mosaic adds the *Wired* Web server to your hotlist.

2. From the Navigate menu again, choose Hotlist.

   Mosaic brings up the Hotlist window with the *Wired* Web server in the list (see figure 14.61).

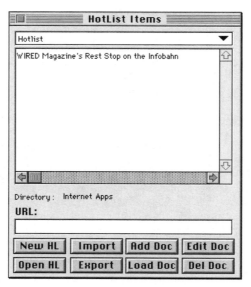

Figure 14.61   Mosaic Hotlist window

3. To see the hotlist in action, click the Home button at the top of your main Mosaic window to return to your home page.

4. Click back in the Hotlist window, and double-click on the *Wired* Web server item. Mosaic takes you directly the *Wired* Web server again.

That's basically about all there is to using Mosaic. Explore the Web to see the wide variety of servers that have appeared. You also may want to explore Mosaic's online help, available under the Balloon Help menu.

MacWeb 0.98a

Quick Reminder: MacWeb is a client application for the World-Wide Web, the most graphical and flexible of the Internet services.

Tasks:

1. Launch and configure MacWeb

2. Browse the Web

3. Visit the *TidBITS* Web Server

4. Use the hotlist

Launch and Configure MacWeb

1. Make sure you are connected to the Internet—connect with MacPPP or InterSLIP, if necessary.

2. Double-click on the MacWeb icon to launch the program.

   MacWeb immediately begins to load its home page, which by default is the MacWeb Home Page. (If you used the ISKM Installer to install MacWeb, it installs a customized version that points to the *Internet Starter Kit for Macintosh* home page, but it doesn't matter for these instructions.) To see what the MacWeb Home Page looks like, see figure 14.62.

Note

Your home page may look different. That's fine.

3. From the File menu choose Preferences. MacWeb brings up the Preferences dialog box. Turn on the Autoload Images checkbox (see figure 14.63).

5. Click the OK button to save your changes.

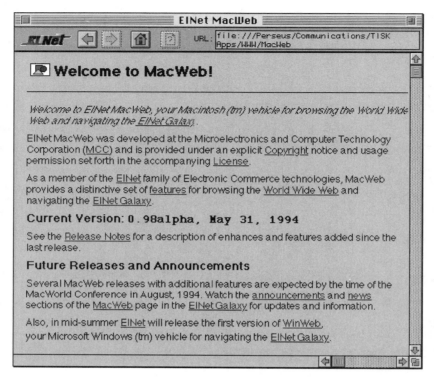

Figure 14.62   *MacWeb Home Page*

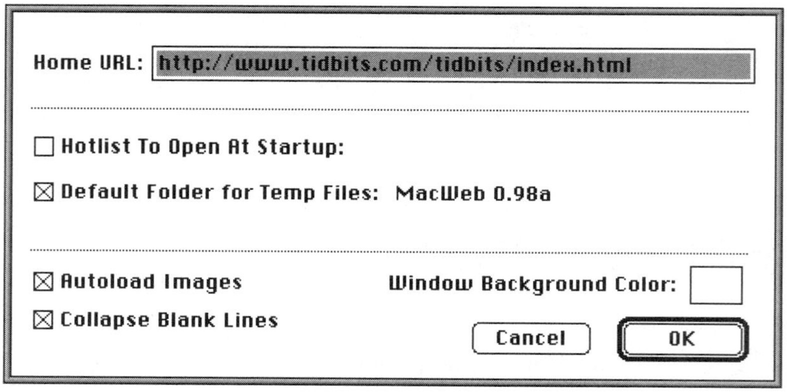

Figure 14.63   *MacWeb Preferences dialog*

Browse the Web

1. From the Navigate menu, select EINet Galaxy.

   MacWeb displays the contents of the EINet Galaxy page (see figure 14.64).

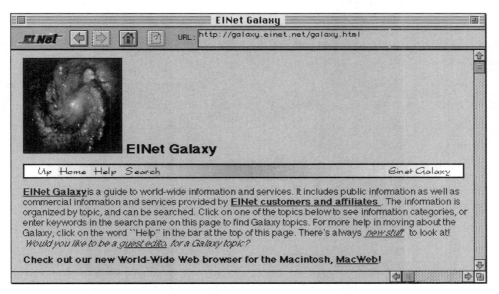

Figure 14.64   *MacWeb EINet Galaxy*

2. Scroll down until you get to the Arts and Humanities topic. Click the underlined words, **Visual Arts**.

   MacWeb takes you to the Visual Arts page on the EINet Galaxy (see figure 14.65).

3. Feel free to continue clicking on underlined link words to move to other parts of the Web—it's too large and fast-moving for me to give you any further explicit browsing directions. But, what if you want to go to a specific site?

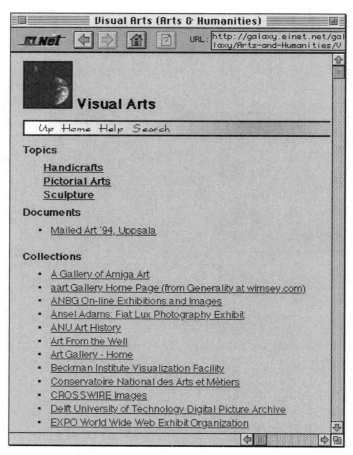

Figure 14.65   *MacWeb Visual Arts page*

Visit the *TidBITS* Web Server

1. From the File menu, choose Open URL. MacWeb displays a dialog into which you can type a URL (Uniform Resource Locator).

2. In the field, type **http://mmm.dartmouth.edu/Pages /TidBITS/TidBITS.html** (see figure 14.66).

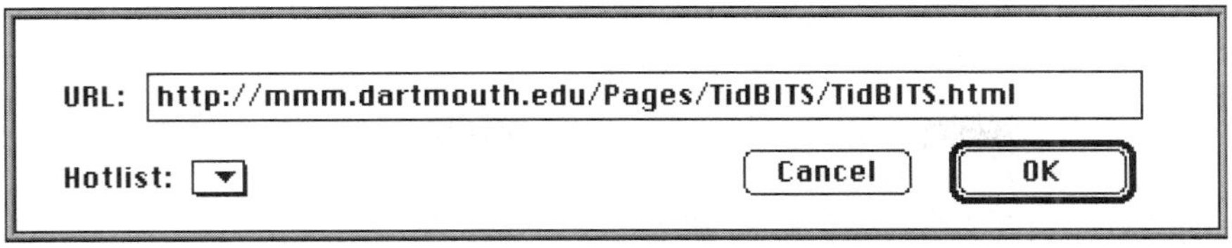

URL: `http://mmm.dartmouth.edu/Pages/TidBITS/TidBITS.html`

Hotlist: [▼]   (Cancel)   (**OK**)

Figure 14.66   *MacWeb Open URL dialog*

3. Click the OK button to connect to the Web server that stores issues of *TidBITS* in HTML format (see figure 14.67).

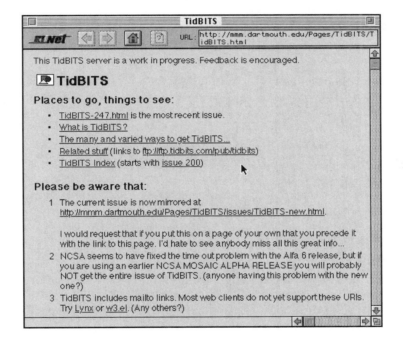

Figure 14.67   *MacWeb at the* TidBITS *server*

Use the Hotlist

1. With the window to the *TidBITS* Web server still open, select Add This Document from the Hotlist menu.

   MacWeb adds the *TidBITS* Web server to the bottom of the Hotlist menu.

2. To see the hotlist in action, click the Home button at the top of your main MacWeb window to return to your home page.

3. From the Hotlist menu, select the *TidBITS* item.

   MacWeb takes you directly the *TidBITS* Web server again.

4. To save your hotlist, go to the Hotlist menu and from the hierarchical Hotlist Operations menu, choose Save. MacWeb brings up a Standard File Dialog, and you can save the hotlist anywhere you wish.

That's basically about all there is to using MacWeb. Explore the Web to see the wide variety of servers that have appeared in the past few months. You can now quit MacWeb and disconnect from the Internet.

This is Only the Beginning

If you've followed some or all of the previous tasks, you've done quite a bit on the Internet. Here are the tasks I described:

1. Learned to configure MacTCP

2. Learned to configure MacPPP or InterSLIP

3. Learned to read, write, and send email with Eudora

4. Learned to read, write, and post articles with NewsWatcher

5. Learned to find and download files via FTP with Anarchie

6. Learned to download files via FTP with Fetch

7. Learned to search WAIS databases with MacWAIS

8. Learned to browse Gopherspace and search with Veronica using TurboGopher

9. Learned to browse the World-Wide Web with NCSA Mosaic

10. Learned to browse the World-Wide Web with MacWeb

My apologies if you found this section a bit stilted and boring to read, but I hope it conveyed just the information you need to get over the hump of using these programs. If something has changed such that the instructions didn't quite work right, my apologies, but don't lose heart. The Internet changes rapidly and you must be flexible enough to deal with that change. Just keep trying and you're bound to get the hang of it soon.

This chapter also brings us to the end of *Internet Starter Kit for Macintosh*. It may seem as though there are lots of pages left, but they're all appendixes, some of which you may want to browse through. If you're like many people, you've probably already flipped through them and seen the lists of Internet resources and Usenet newsgroups and Internet providers. I especially recommend you check out appendix F, "Special Internet Access Offer," if you don't already have Internet access, and if you plan on installing the software that comes with this book, please read appendix G, "The Internet Starter Kit Disk." You won't regret it.

I hope you've enjoyed this book, and I hope you enjoy the Internet.

P a r t
IV

Appendixes

I certainly hope you have enough of a life that you don't pore through the following appendixes in great detail, absorbing every molecule of information. I don't intend you to do that; instead, I recommend that you flip through them more or less at random until you see a section that looks interesting. The appendixes are mostly straight lists of information. Although you may want to explore certain sections in detail, I included them as pointers, or launch pads, to get you started.

Appendix A, Internet Resources

Perhaps the most troubling thing for an Internet novice is finding interesting mailing lists, Gopher sites, and Web servers. It's not actually difficult, but it can take some effort to achieve the proper mindset. This resource list, although making no pretensions to completeness, should help you get started. After you have explored some of the resources mentioned here, you undoubtedly will happen upon others that either didn't exist at the time of publication or simply didn't get mentioned here. That's good.

The bulk of this list was ably compiled by Ken Stuart, and thanks are due to him for his efforts.

Appendix B, Newsgroup List

Appendix B is a long list of many of the thousands of newsgroups that currently exist on Usenet. It comes by way of the list's editors, Gene Spafford and David Lawrence, and is regularly posted in various groups on Usenet. So many newsgroups are available that it can be overwhelming. I hope this list helps you figure out a few newsgroups you want to read.

Appendix C, PDIAL List

Peter Kaminski's PDIAL list, although not guaranteed to be up to date or fully accurate, is the best source in which to find a local provider with full Internet access. I recommend obtaining the latest information from the provider, by sending email to the information address (if you already have email access in some fashion), or by giving them a call.

Appendix D, Supplementary PDIAL List

This appendix contains some additional providers that are not listed in Peter's PDIAL list. Look here to find a provider that can help you get full Internet access.

Appendix E, Glossary

Appendix E provides you with a list of common Internet terms and their definitions. If you're ever troubled by a vocabulary question—at least, one regarding the Internet—check here.

Appendix F, Special Internet Access Offer

Appendix F provides details about our special Internet access offer. Brief descriptions of Northwest Nexus (the access provider) and of the connecting procedure are included. Note that as an *Internet Starter Kit for Macintosh* reader, you get a substantial discount off Northwest Nexus' regular price.

Appendix G, The Internet Starter Kit Disk

Last, but certainly not least, Appendix G describes what I've included on the disk that comes with this book. Also, it explains how the ISKM Installer places everything on your hard disk, sometimes with configuration already done for you.

Internet Resources

Foreword to Appendix A, by Ken Stuart

If you ask me, the Internet is about sharing, meeting people, talking, listening, and communicating. It's not about computers or programs, though you need those to use it. There are plenty of opportunities to take advantage of the Internet for your own needs, but there are even more ways to use it constructively to help others. I hope that this book will get you started doing just that.

In case you wonder about the potential of the Internet, I can offer you a personal anecdote to sway your opinion: Adam and I have never met. I've met Adam's mother and sister in person, but not him. We may have an opportunity to do so when he passes through Ithaca later this year, but time will tell. Thanks to the Internet we've learned what others wanted to see in this book, pulled it together for the first time, and revised it the second. I hope that, by using the Internet, you will also have the opportunity to meet, work, and communicate with people that you otherwise would not have met, and that you all benefit from the experience.

Drop me a line if you wish, or visit my Archaeological Fieldwork World-Wide Web server if you're looking for a way to pass a summer.

-Ken Stuart, **kps1@cornell.edu**

June 15, 1994

Ithaca, NY

Discovering New Internet Resources

The collection of programs accompanying this book can be a wonderful vehicle for cruising the so-called information superhighway, but like having a new car and nowhere to go, they are not useful unless you have some Internet resources to explore. Keeping up with all of the information and files can be a full-time job because so much is already there, and more appears every day. This section points you to a few places that you can use to learn of new Internet resources such as mailing lists, Usenet news groups, and Gopher and World-Wide Web servers. By watching for announcements, you can learn of resources useful to your job, resources that will educate you or your children, and resources that let you develop your personal interests.

With these signposts directing you to new and interesting places to visit, exploring the Internet should be as exciting as taking a new car out for a drive. To learn of Internet resources, you can use the Internet itself in a number of ways. You can subscribe to mailing lists, watch for messages in Usenet news, or use Gopher or World-Wide Web to look around on your own. If you are not familiar with the programs on your disk, you might find it easier to ask co-workers about resources they have found.

It is important to keep in mind that announcements of Internet resources sometimes contain errors or are published prematurely. In either case, don't be discouraged if you cannot connect to a particular resource immediately. Because the Internet continues to rapidly increase in size and scope, it occasionally suffers growing pains. If you try a service and cannot get through, try again in a few days. If you still cannot get through, try writing to the person who made the announcement. You can also check to see if they indicated that the service was available only during certain hours, just in case there are limits to when connections are allowed.

Learning About Internet Resources Through Email

If you wish to receive notices about new Internet resources via email, there are a number of mailing lists you can join. Many of these are high-volume, which means you will receive scores of mail messages every day. Some of these announce events happening off the Internet (though related to its operation or use), so you may not be interested if you only want to learn about things you can access.

To remain on top of everything going on in the Internet world, consider subscribing to a mailing list called Net-Happenings. This list is quite active, but it is one of the best ways of learning about new resources. To subscribe, use your email program to send a note to **majordomo@is.internic.net** with the following command in the body of the message: **subscribe net-happenings** *your full name* (use your first and last names here).

If you have an email program that filters (automatically sorts) incoming messages, you can set it up to discard notices of conferences (or other topics) if you are not interested in them. Gleason Sackman, the person who runs the Net-Happenings mailing list, adds a code in the subject line of every message indicating the category of each resource. With this bit of information, you can quickly go through the messages by the type of resource to which they refer, such as mailing lists, Gopher, World-Wide Web, and so on.

You can also arrange for Net-Happenings email to be delivered to you in digest format, which means the mail files will come less frequently, but in larger files. To subscribe to Net-Happenings in digest format, use your email program to send a note to **majordomo@is.internic.net** with the following command in the body of the message: **subscribe net-happenings-digest** *your full name* (use your first and last names here).

The InterNIC Scout Report is another excellent electronic mailing list to join because it's interesting and relatively brief. It's a weekly publication offered by InterNIC Information Services to the Internet community. It includes a wide range of topics, and is provided in multiple formats including email, Gopher, and World-Wide Web. The Gopher and World-Wide Web versions of the Scout Report include links to all of the listed resources.

To receive the email version of the Scout Report each Friday, join the Scout-Report mailing list. This mailing list is used only to distribute the Scout Report once a week. Send email to: **majordomo@is.internic.net** and in the body of the message, type: **subscribe scout-report** *your full name* (use your first and last names here).

You can also search a subset of LISTSERV-based mailing lists by sending email to **listserv@bitnic.educom.com** with a line in the body of the message similar to this: **list global** */baseball*. Obviously, replace *baseball* with whatever topic interests you. The message you receive back provides the list name and instructions for subscribing.

Learning About Internet Resources Through Usenet News

You can also monitor Usenet news to keep abreast of new Internet resources. Monitoring Usenet can make it easier to manage announcements because it does not innundate your personal mailbox with the large number of messages that a mailing list does. Since many people employ Usenet news to ask for help about using various programs to access services, you must sort through a number of questions and answers when looking for announcements of services.

In Usenet News, the groups **comp.infosystems.announce** and **alt.internet.services** are the best places to watch for announcements of new things to access. Some other groups that carry useful information include **comp.infosystems.www**, **comp.infosystems.gopher**, **bit.listserv.new-list**, and **bit.listserv.hytel-l**.

Subscribe to any of these groups if you want to read their articles frequently (add the group's name to your list of personal groups in whatever program you use for reading news, such as NewsWatcher). Otherwise, just select them from the complete list of all groups when you wish to see what's been announced most recently.

Learning About Internet Resources Through Gopher And the World-Wide Web

The "Internet Meta-Resources" described below offers excellent collections of starting points for network exploration. Use a Gopher or World-Wide Web client program to access numerous services and documents with more listings. Then follow links to servers that look interesting to you, and you're sure to come upon invaluable resources.

The InterNIC Scout Report (described above) can be accessed directly from Gopher and the World-Wide Web. Gopher users can connect to **is.internic.net** and choose "Information Services" from the top directory. From there go directly to "Scout Report." To access the hypertext version of the Report, use the World-Wide Web service to connect to:

```
http://www.internic.net/scout-report/
```

If you want to check this resource frequently, set a bookmark in TurboGopher (or whatever you use for a Gopher client), or add the address to your hotlist in MacWeb or Mosaic.

When you're using MacWeb or Mosaic, look in the Navigate menu (they both have one) for links to some interesting collections of resources. The NCSA What's New Page, the Internet Meta-Resources Index, and the EINet Galaxy in particular are useful places to start your explorations. All are accessible via the Navigate menus of either MacWeb or Mosaic.

Browsing with Gopher is another way to find interesting stuff, though it can be time-consuming. To look around on your own, open folders, double-click on files or links to other resources. Don't be afraid to see where a path leads you—if you get lost, simply back up to your previous menu or quit and start over. You can't break anything by playing around on the Internet. Exploring through Gopherspace or the World-Wide Web can be most enjoyable when you come upon something that you did not know existed, and then have the opportunity to share your discovery with others.

Learning About Internet Resources Through Books And Co-Workers

Many new books have appeared that cover Internet resources, though such paper publications become out-of-date quickly (and you have to pay for them, whereas all the methods discussed above are free). Most of these books first describe the Internet, then discuss the tools needed to make use of it, often using Unix. After this they provide an appendix or list of resources that you might like to explore. Some books, though, contain nothing but lists of interesting places to visit in the course of your Internet travels, and assume that you already know how to use the correct tools. If you intend to purchase a book other than this one, be sure to flip through it to make sure it covers both the technical information you want to know and the sort of resources that interest you.

If you have co-workers who are interested in exploring the Internet, you might spend some time during a lunch break together exploring or discussing the Internet. You can also connect to and explore the Internet from home if you have an appropriate Internet connection via modem, and then share your discoveries the next day in person.

Internet Resources

The resources listed in this appendix fall into several major categories: mailing lists, FTP sites, Telnet-based resources, WAIS servers you can search using MacWAIS, Gopher servers you access via TurboGopher, and finally, World-Wide Web servers you access via MacWeb or NCSA Mosaic.

Note

Be forewarned that Internet resources come and go, and we cannot guarantee that the resources here will all be accessible when you try to access them. The problem might be temporary, or the resource may simply have moved or disappeared. Try again later, or use Internet searching tools like Veronica to see if you can find the new or correct information.

Mailing Lists

When you see an announcement for a mailing list, use an email program such as Eudora to subscribe. In most cases, you'll find instructions for signing on to a new mailing list when you find a reference to the list itself. If an announcement does not indicate how to subscribe to a mailing list, try writing to the person who sent the announcement for details.

We've included a number of interesting mailing lists. We chose a specific format to convey a great deal of information in a small space, so pay attention. The item in the first column is the list name. That's also the userid to which you send submissions. The second column is the userid of the address to which you send subscription requests and other administrative requests. The item in the third column is the machine name for the previous two columns. The fourth column, if present, is a brief description of the list if it's not apparent from the list name. Here's an example:

```
tidbits    listserv  ricevm1.rice.edu    Weekly electronic
                                          newsletter
```

To subscribe to the *TidBITS* list, you combine column two and column three and send email to **listserv@ricevm1.rice.edu** (and follow the rules laid out in chapter 6 for subscribing to LISTSERV-based lists—namely, type **SUBSCRIBE TIDBITS** *your full name* on the first line of the message). To submit a posting, combine column one and column three and send it to **tidbits@ricevm1.rice.edu**.

Here's a slightly different example:

```
ultralight-flight   ultralight-flight-request  ms.uky.edu
```

Here the userid to which you send subscription requests is a Unix mailing list, as indicated by the **-request** at the end. There are no special rules for Unix mailing lists, so just combine column two and three and send email to **ultralight-flight-request@ms.uky.edu** with a request for subscription to sign up. Then submit postings to the combination of column one and column three, or **ultralight-flight@ms.uky.edu**.

By now you are certainly asking, "How can I tell what sorts of things are discussed on any given list?" Aside from the descriptions in this appendix, the best way to find out that information is to subscribe and watch the postings for a day or so. If the postings don't meet your expectations, sign off from the list (to sign off, type the **SIGNOFF** *listname* command for lists that use LISTSERV or ListProcessor or Majordomo, or send email to the **-request** address for other lists).

Usenet Newsgroups

We decided not to include newsgroups in this resource section specifically because Gene Spafford and David Lawrence gave us permission to reprint their massive list of newsgroups, complete with short descriptions. You'll find that information in appendix B, Newsgroups List.

Use a newsreader like NewsWatcher or Nuntius to subscribe. If the newsgroup does not appear in the full group list, it may not be available on your machine, or it may have to be added by the system administrator who operates the news server.

FAQs and FTP Sites

Many newsgroups on Usenet have created Frequently Asked Question (FAQ) lists. These FAQs are extremely useful. Although you can read the newsgroup in question for a month or so and wait until the FAQ list goes by (they're usually posted on a regular basis), it's probably more efficient for you to retrieve a specific file via FTP from either:

Appendix A
Internet
Resources

```
ftp://rtfm.mit.edu/pub/usenet-by-group/
```

```
ftp://rtfm.mit.edu/pub/usenet-by-group/news.answers/
```

The /pub/usenet directory on **rtfm.mit.edu** is so large that even Fetch slows down considerably when you're retrieving it for the first time. Anarchie is a better choice for this purpose because you can leave the main window open while you switch into subdirectories.

We have included a few FTP sites that have interesting files. For them, just use Anarchie or Fetch to connect and retrieve files. Of course, the best ways to find additional FTP sites that contain interesting files are either to use Anarchie or search the Archie servers.

Telnet-based Resources

You access Telnet-based services via NCSA Telnet or another Telnet program. From the File menu, choose Open Connection and enter the address of the service to which you wish to connect in the dialog box. You must play by the rules of the service to which you're connecting. We haven't provided too many of these resources, in part because they are the ugliest to use and the least Mac-like. However, a great deal of interesting information is available via Telnet, and one of the best ways to browse through it is to use the Hytelnet HyperCard stack you read about in chapter 13. Although not a communications tool in its own right, the Hytelnet stack works well as a database that you can flip through to find different resources along with brief descriptions.

For the services mentioned, we provide a description of the site, the name of the site you telnet to, the login name, and password (if necessary).

WAIS Sources

To retrieve a specific WAIS source mentioned in this appendix, create a new question with MacWAIS, select the Directory of Servers source in the Select Sources dialog, and type the name of the source into the question. While you're at it, consider typing some related words to see whether the search finds anything along the same topics. After you click on the Ask button, MacWAIS should return a list of sources, one of which should be the one you want. If not, make sure you spelled everything correctly.

After you have this new source, select it and save it by clicking on the Save button in MacWAIS. Once you've saved it, you can ask a new question using the new source you just found.

Gopher Servers

Gopher servers are a bit more problematic than the other resources listed here. You can access Gopher servers in three ways: directly by entering the name into the Server name field in the Another Gopher dialog box (access it from the File menu) in TurboGopher, by searching with Veronica, or by browsing manually through Gopherspace. The last technique is the least efficient, and not recommended when you want to find anything specific. Veronica searches are accurate and useful, but may return more than you want to peruse. Entering the Gopher name manually is the most trouble, but it is the most accurate. We recommend a combination of direct access and Veronica.

In most cases we've provided the address of the Gopher server (and the port number, unless it is the default, 70) in question so you can travel there directly. On occasion we left the address worded in terms of a Veronica search. After all, you must do some of this exploration on your own, and Veronica leads you down the most interesting paths.

If you want to revisit a Gopher server later, make a bookmark to the site in TurboGopher.

Web Servers

For the Web sites that we've listed below, we provide a URL that you can type directly into MacWeb's or Mosaic's Open URL dialog box, and in most cases we've also provide a short description of the site. If you want to revisit the site later, add it to your hotlist in either MacWeb or Mosaic.

Now, on to the resources!

Air & Space, Astronomy, & Astrophysics

World-Wide Web Sites

```
http://nearnet.gnn.com/wic/tech.toc.html
```

The Technology section of the Global Network Navigator offers links to archives of discussion groups covering NASA, aeronautics, satellites and images they produce, and so on. Also included here is a link to access shuttle and satellite images for viewing on your own computer screen.

```
http://nearnet.gnn.com/wic/sci.toc.html
```

The Science section of the Global Network Navigator offers links to other resources based on particular disciplines (there's quite a variety). If you are interested in one or more of these, you can link to whatever is available in your area through this route.

```
http://aviation.jsc.nasa.gov/
```

Items on this server relate to aviation. They include links to all types of resources, and offer labels such as "Civil Air Patrol," "FAA Information," and "Piloting Tips." This is a simple yet useful site to visit if you're interested in flying or learning about aviation.

```
http://stsci.edu/top.html
```

Images from the Hubble Space Telescope are easily accessible through the Space Telescope Science Institute's Web server. (See figure on following page.) It's also possible to find out a lot about the space telescope and to visit various related data archives at this site. The images are available in multiple formats, and may take a few minutes to come across a slow modem connection due to their size.

WAIS Sources

`aeronautics.src:`	information about aircraft, flying, and aeronautics
`astro-images-gif.src:`	images of astronomical objects

Mailing Lists

`aircraft`	`listserv`	`iubvm.bitnet`	covers all aspects of aircraft
`airline`	`listserv`	`cunyvm.cuny.edu`	discussion of issues relating to airlines
`airplane-clubs`	`airplane-clubs-request`	`dg-rtp.dg.com`	covers topics of interest to groups which manage and operate aircraft
`aviation`	`listserv`	`brufpb.bitnet`	a general aviation discussion group
`isss`	`listserv`	`jhuvm.hcf.jhu.edu`	International Student Space Simulations issues and concerns
`space`	`space-request`	`andrew.cmu.edu`	discussion of topics relating to space
`ultralight-flight`	`ultralight-flight-request`	`ms.uky.edu`	discussion and advice about flying and maintaining ultralight aircraft

Anthropology & Archaeology

World-Wide Web Sites

```
http://durendal.cit.cornell.edu/TestPit.html
```

Want to go on a 'dig' this summer? Check out this server that lists fieldwork opportunities available at archaeological sites throughout the world. Please keep in mind that many project leaders try to fill their open positions during the winter and spring, so that's the best time to watch for postings. This server is maintained by the author of this appendix. **:-)**

```
http://rome.classics.lsa.umich.edu/welcome.html
```

This is the mother of all archaeological Internet resources. It holds links to information about various projects, programs, exhibits, images, and so on, that are directly accessible through the Web. It also provides easy access to related mailing lists and newsgroups, Gopher and FTP servers, and Telnet-based services.

```
http://nearnet.gnn.com/wic/hum.toc.html
```

At the top of the Arts & Humanities section of the Global Network Navigator, there are links to anthropological studies, the Dead Sea Scrolls exhibition, the Oriental Institute, and other related items.

WAIS Sources

archaeological_computing.src	covers articles related to computing in archaeology

Mailing Lists

aia-l	listserv	cc.brynmawr.edu	the American Institute of Archaeology (AIA) provides this forum for discussing any aspect of archaeology, especially those related to computing

ancien-l	listserv	ulkyvm.louisville.edu	covers scholarly topics relating to the ancient Mediterranean
ane	majordomo	oi.uchicago.edu	covers topics pertaining to the ancient Near East
anthro-l	listserv	ubvm.cc.buffalo.edu	general discussions of anthropology are carried here
arch-l	listserv	tamvm1.tamu.edu	discussions related to a broad range of archaeological issues
contex-l	listserv	acadvm1.uottawa.ca	discussions relating to cross-disciplinary studies of ancient texts
heritage	listserv	massey.ac.nz	covers topics related to interpretation and presentation of heritage sites
papy	listserv	igl.ku.dk	forum for discussing papyrology, epigraphy and archaeology of Graeco-Roman Egypt

Gopher Servers

Anthropology and Archaeology links here	cwis.usc.edu	Other Gophers and Information Resources/ Gophers by Subject/ Gopher Jewels

Biology, Agriculture & Environment

(see also "Sciences, Math, & Engineering")

World-Wide Web Sites

http://ecosys.drdr.virginia.edu/EcoWeb.html

EcoWeb provides quite a number of links to information and servers related to the environment and recycling. Various bodies and institutions such as NOAA, the USGS, and Woods Hole have machines that can be accessed here too.

http://nearnet.gnn.com/wic/newrescat.toc.html

The Business section of the Global Network Navigator offers connections to information about forestry and trees in one section, and resources relating to the U.S. Dept. of Agriculture in another. Also in the latter are reports on the commodity market, and links to 'Not Just Cows' and 'PEN Pages,' two valuable resources which contain loads of information about agricultural and rural-life resources on the Internet.

```
http://nearnet.gnn.com/wic/sci.toc.html
```

The Science section of the Global Network Navigator offers links to other resources based on particular disciplines (there's quite a variety). If you are interested in one or more of these, you can link to whatever is available in your area through this route.

```
http://info.er.usgs.gov/network/science/biology/index.html
```

This is the mother of all biological resources on the Internet. No matter what field interests you, this is the place to explore first. From here you can access many, many biologically related Internet resources. Before accessing this server, you may wish to turn off your image loading capabilities because many of the links here have a small image associated with it. The sheer number of these will take a few minutes to come across the net if you are using a phone line, though they are interesting to see as a portion of them show in the figure on the following page.

WAIS Sources

alt.drugs.src	archived information from the drugs newsgroup
biology-journal-contents.src	covers molecular biology
bionic-directory-of-servers.src	covers Finnish bionic sources
bionic-genbank-software.src	a list of relevant software titles
DOE_Climate_Data.src	covers topics relating to U.S. Dept. of Energy studies on many subjects
environment-newsgroups.src	accesses archives of multiple discussion groups concerned with environmental issues
Global_Change_Data_Directory.src	searches reports dealing with climatic issues
great-Lakes-factsheets.src	covers environmental issues and other subjects
IUBio-fly-clones.src	resources related to Drosophila genetics
IUBio-INFO.src	multiple resources covering biological topics
livestock.src	covers livestock management and production

continues

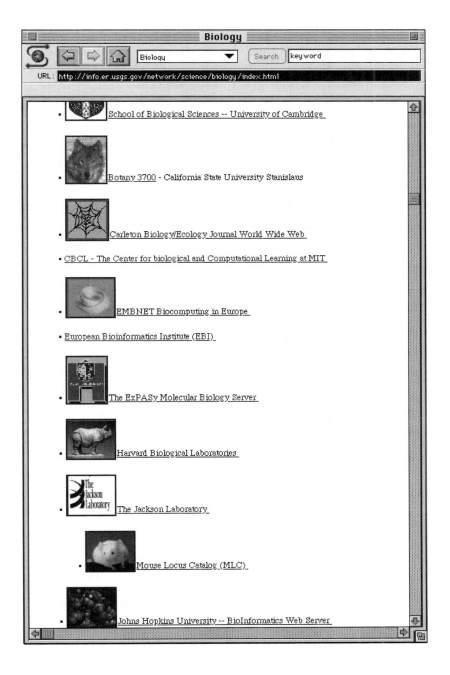

`NIH-Guide.src`	information about U.S. National Institutes of Health grants and programs of interest to biomedical researchers
`NOAA_National_Environmental` `_Referral_Service.src`	data concerning environmental tests and information about the sun, earth, oceans, atmosphere, etc.
`online-mendelian-inheritance-` `in-man.src`	catalogues of various phenotypes
`prosite.src`	database covering protein sites and patterns
`sustainable-agriculture.src`	deals with issues related to organic farming, the environment, technology, etc.
`usda-rrdb.src`	covers agricultural and economic research issues for the U.S. Dept. of Agriculture
`USGS_Earth_Science_Data_` `Directory.src`	information about earth sciences and related natural resources

FTP Sites

The Electronic Zoo is an extensive list of animal-related computer resources of all types. It can be obtained via FTP from `wuarchive.wustl.edu` in the directory `/doc/techreports/wustl.edu/compmed/elec_zoo.x_x` (where `x_x` refers to the most current version).

Internet Resources

`sci.bio` (includes "A Biologist's Guide to Internet Resources")

`sci.environment`

Mailing Lists

`agmodels-1`	`listserv`	`unl.edu`	agricultural simulation models of all types are discussed here
`alife`	`alife-request`	`cognet.ucla.edu`	multi-disciplinary discussions of artificial life
`bee-1`	`listserv`	`albnyvm1.bitnet`	covers all aspects of bee biology
`biodiv-1`	`listserv`	`bdt.ftpt.ansp.br`	discussion of technical, economic, practical, and other considerations relating to biodiversity issues
`biosph-1`	`listserv`	`ubvm.bitnet`	discussion list related to the biosphere and ecology

biotech	listserv	umdc.bitnet	for discussing biotechnology
cacti_etc	listserv	hpl-opus.hpl.hp.com	topics relating to all kinds of cacti, their growth, and cultivation
camel-l	listserv	sakfu00.bitnet	forum for discussing camel research
deepsea	listserv	uvvm.uvic.ca	news about the deep sea and its vents
dinosaur	listproc	lepomis.psych.upenn.edu	discussions relating to dinosaurs of all types
envbeh-l	listserv	graf.poly.edu	covers the environment and human behavior
envst-l	listserv	brownvm.bitnet	discusses environmental studies programs
ethology	saarikko	cc.helsinki.fi	discussion of animal behavior and behavioral ecology, including theories, conferences, research, etc.
forest management	listserv	pnfi.forestry.ca	about topics of concern to people involved with forest management in any aspect
lactacid	listserv	searn.sunet.se	topics include uses of lactic acid bacteria
marine-facilities	mailserv	ac.dal.ca	for managers and technical staff who work at marine research facilities to discuss relevant business and technical topics
nplc	listproc	genesys.cps.msu.edu	facilitates communication between researchers investigating plant lipids
park rangers	60157903	wsuvm1.csc.wsu.edu	discussion of topics of interest to current and future U.S. National Park Service employees as well as related services
socinsct	listserv	albany.bitnet	covers research on social insect biology
vetinfo	listserv	ucdcvdls.bitnet	discussion group for veterinary informatics

Appendix A
Internet Resources

Gopher Servers

Agriculture and Forestry resources	`cwis.usc.edu`	Other Gophers and Information Resources/ Gophers by Subject/ Gopher Jewels
Environment-related resources are numerous (see illustration below)	`cwis.usc.edu`	Other Gophers and Information Resources/ Gophers by Subject/ Gopher Jewels
Not Just Cows		use Veronica via Gopher to search for the term "cows" — from the returned choices, choose "Not Just Cows" for extensive information on agricultural resources
EcoGopher at the University of Virginia	`ecosys.drdr.virginia.edu`	EcoGopher provides a central location for environmental agencies and organizations to store data to be distributed
Bedford Institute Of Oceanography (Canada)	`biome.bio.dfo.ca`	primarily designed to assist the exchange of information with colleagues and clients of the Canadian Department of Fisheries and Oceans
Global Biological Information Servers	`weeds.mgh.harvard.edu`	as shown, there are links to all kinds of biologically oriented Gopher servers here

Business, Economics & Jobs

World-Wide Web Sites

`http://nearnet.gnn.com/wic/newrescat.toc.html`

The Business section of the Global Network Navigator provides links to various commercial services as well as information about economics, the stock market, and government agencies related to business interests. Economics resources have their own section here, and each connects to different sorts of data and archives, many of which are provided by universities.

`http://sashimi.wwa.com/~notime/eotw/EOTW.html`

Entrepreneurs on the Web have a couple of main areas that will interest those looking for business and commercial information and services on the Internet. These include a link to business information resources and another to goods and services. Much of the information here is about using the Internet for business and commercial operations. Before offering such a service, it would be best to go through the information stored and linked here.

```
http://www.gems.com/realestate/
```

Want to buy or sell a house? How about a piece of commercial property? This is the Internet service that allows you to shop for real estate from the comfort of your own living room (or wherever your computer is). Real estate agents from across the world (and private individuals) advertise properties they wish to sell. All you need to do is connect, choose the type of property you wish to investigate, then select the location where you wish to buy. If there are real estate agents with the appropriate offerings in that area, then you can view images of the properties, read about them, check out the asking price, and obtain contact information so you can proceed with taking the place off of the market if you want it.

```
http://www.secapl.com/cgi-bin/qs
```

Stock quotes are available via the Web if you have a Web client program that accepts forms. At this time of this writing, MacWeb allows one to take advantage of this service, though NCSA Mosaic does not. Version 2 of Mosaic supports forms as well, however, and it should be out by the time you read this. This site offers general trading information and graphs of stock markets along with current quotes. If you don't know the symbol of the stock you want to check, grab a newspaper that lists this information because you cannot look up quotes by entering a company's name—you must know the ticker symbol.

WAIS Sources

`agricultural-market-news.src`	U.S. Dept. of Agriculture commodity market reports
`EIA-Petroleum-Supply-Monthly.src`	covers various documents concerning petroleum products
`wall-street-journal-sample.src`	database of several months' worth of issues of the Wall Street Journal

Mailing Lists

bpr-l	listserv	is.twi.tudelft.nl	about business process redesign concerns
commercial real estate	commercial. realestate	data-base.com	send and receive information about commercial real estate
e-europe	listserv	pucc.princeton.edu	the Eastern Europe business network
econ-dev	majordomo	csn.org	a place to share information with economic development professionals
economy	listserv	tecmtyvm.mty. itesm.mx	discussion of the economy and economic problems of less-developed countries
fedjobs	listserv	dartcms1. dartmouth.edu	the U.S. federal jobs mail list
international trade & commerce	info-request	tradent.wimsey.bc.ca	all about trade and commerce on an international scale and within a global economy
ioob-l	listserv	uga.bitnet	discussion of industrial and organizational psychology and organization behavior
market-l	listserv	ucf1vm.cc.ucf.edu	covers marketing related issues
mba-l	listserv	marist.bitnet	for the discussion of MBA programs
quality	listserv	pucc.princeton.edu	covers Total Quality Management (TQM) in the manufacturing and service industries
stock market secrets	smi-request	world.std.com	daily comments on the stock market reports and answers to questions about investment and financial topics
trdev-l	listserv	psuvm.psu.edu	information and discussion about the training and development of human resources

Gopher Servers

Numerous Economics and Business resources are linked here	`cwis.usc.edu`	Other Gophers and Information Resources/ Gophers by Subject/ Gopher Jewels
Employment Opportunities and Resume Postings are available via Gopher	`cwis.usc.edu`	Other Gophers and Information Resources/ Gophers by Subject/ Gopher Jewels

Cultures, Social Groups & Lifestyles

World-Wide Web Sites

`http://nearnet.gnn.com/wic/curraffs.toc.html`

The Current Affairs section of the Global Network Navigator contains links to issues related to gender and sexuality and to items of regional and cultural interest. Many of these latter resources are archives of discussion groups dedicated to particular topic and are arranged by country.

WAIS Sources

`india-info.src`	covers topics concerning the Indian community
`israel-info.src`	indexes information about Israel
`kidsnet.src`	covers archives of a mailing list dedicated to the use of the Internet by kids and their school teachers

Mailing Lists

adoptees	listserv	ucsd.edu	adult adoptees discuss topics related to adoption
africa-n	listserv	utoronto.bitnet	for the exchange of information and news about Africa

continues

alternates	alternates-request	ns1.rutgers.edu	forum for those who are interested in open sexual lifestyles
amazons	amazons-request	math.uio.no	discussion and support by and for strong and assertive women
argentina	argentina-request	ois.db.toronto.edu	general information and discussion about Argentina and its problems
auglbc-l	listserv	american.edu	support forum for Lesbian, Gay, Bisexual, and Transgender students
balt-l	listserv	ubvm.cc.buffalo.edu	forum for discussing the Baltic Republics
bears	bears-request	spdcc.com	forum for gay and bisexual men
bisexu-l	listserv	brownvm.brown.edu	discussions about ideas, opinions, and experiences relating to bisexuality
e-hug	listserv	dartcms1.bitnet	Electronic Hebrew users newsletter
gaynet	gaynet-request	queernet.org	concerns gay, lesbian, and bisexual issues especially as they relate to colleges and universities
hungary	listserv	gwuvm.bitnet	Hungarian discussion list
india-l	india-l-request	utarlvm1.uta.edu	the India News Network
info-russ	info-russ	smarty.ece.jhu.edu	discussion of issues relating to the Russian-speaking community
j-food-l	listserv	jpnknu01.bitnet	discussion of Japanese food and culture
masonic digest	ptrei	mitre.org	items relating to Free Masonry and affiliated groups
men	mail-men-request	summit.novell.com	about men's issues of all types
mexico	listserv	itesmvf1.bitnet	Mexican news and culture, in Spanish
misg-l	listserv	psuvm.psu.edu	Malaysian Islamic Study Group discussion list
nativenet	gst	gnosys.svle.ma.us	discussion of issues concerning any or all indigenous peoples

pacific	listserv	brufpb.bitnet	forum for the discussion of the peoples of the Pacific Ocean and its islands
pakistan	listserv	asuvm.inre.asu.edu	the Pakistan news service list
pcorps-l	listserv	cmuvm.csv.cmich.edu	discussion list for Peace Corps volunteers
pen-pals	pen-pals-request	mainstream.com	forum for children to develop writing skills and meet others through email
poland-l	listserv	ubvm.bitnet	forum for discussing items relating to Polish culture
scouts-l	listserv	tcubvm.bitnet	discussions relating to various youth groups
wisenet	listserv	uicvm.uic.edu	Women in science, mathematics, or engineering
wmst-l	listserv	umdd.umd.edu	Women's studies issues

Gopher Servers

Country-Specific Information links abound here	gopher.ora.com	Other Gophers and Information Resources/ Gophers by Subject/ Gopher Jewels

Government, Politics & Activism

World-Wide Web Sites

http://nearnet.gnn.com/wic/govt.toc.html

The Government & Politics section of the Global Network Navigator connects to many resources relating to the U.S. Federal and State Governments and their agencies, bureaus, boards, and so on. One can access the full text of many documents produced by the Congress, Supreme Court, and other bodies.

Budgets, health plans, census information, copyright information, and legislation can all be found here. Additionally, a number of connections to resources made available by various law schools is accessible, as are items from the United Nations. Several archives of forums dedicated to political activism are linked here, and contact information for congressional representatives is available too.

```
http://debra.dgbt.doc.ca/opengov
```

```
http://debra.dgbt.doc.ca/isc/isc.html
```

These two URLs connect to Web servers operated by the Canadian government. If you're a Canadian citizen you'll probably find them extremely useful. If you're not, then you might wish to pay a visit to them so that you can see an example of what sorts of information a government can make available if it wants to. Both French and English resources are available by choosing the link you want. There are also links to Web servers run by other national governments, including Australia, France, Israel, Italy, and the U.S.

```
http://www.ssa.gov/SSA_Home.html
```

The U.S. Social Security Administration has established a Web server "to provide easy access to a large variety of information about our programs and activities via one simple interface." While at this site, you can read SSA news concerning recent legislation, programs of all sorts, and access a number of links to servers with related information. It's also possible to take a peek at the SSA's budget and get to statistical databases.

WAIS Sources

clinton-speeches.src	indexes speeches given by Bill Clinton
congress.src	makes it easy to find the names, addresses, and phone numbers for your elected officials in the U.S. Congress
eff-documents.src	Electronic Frontier Foundation documents related to computers, communications, the law, privacy, policies, the government, etc.
eff-talk.src	archives of a discussion group covering the same issues as eff-documents.src
Omni-Cultural-Academic-Resource.src	information about a wide range of cultures, including their food, language, politics, religion, and much more
ota.src	Office of Technology Assessment policies
supreme-court.src	indexes the full text of U.S. Supreme Court documents

US-Gov-Programs.src	covers various research programs
world91a.src	the 1991 edition of the CIA's World Factbook

FTP Sites

Addresses and phone numbers of members of Congress	nifty.andrew.cmu.edu	/pub/QRD/qrd/info/GOVT/congress-103
Resumes of cabinet members	nifty.andrew.cmu.edu	/pub/QRD/qrd/info/GOVT/cabinet
Government Accounting	cu.nih.gov	/GAO-REPORTS Office reports

Mailing Lists

activ-l	listserv	mizzou1.missouri.edu	issues relating to environmental issues, empowerment, justice, etc.
ar-news	ar-news-request	cygnus.com	news items related to animal rights and welfare
ar-talk	ar-talk-request	cygnus.com	discussion related to animal rights and welfare
bosnet	listproc	cu23.crl.aecl.ca	carries information pertaining to events in and around Bosnia
canada-l	listserv	vm1.mcgill.ca	forum for the discussion of Canadian issues
dont-tell	dont-tell-request	choice.princeton.edu	deals with "don't ask, don't tell" ROTC policy
ec	listserv	vm.cc.metu.edu.tr	European Community topics are covered here
govdoc-l	listserv	psuvm.bitnet	covers issues related to government documents
mideur-l	listserv	ubvm.bitnet	discussion of Middle European politics
politics	listserv	ucf1vm.cc.ucf.edu	serious discussion of politics
the frog farm	frog-farm-request	blizzard.lcs.mit.edu	about defending, claiming, and exercising American rights
y-rights	listserv	sjuvm.bitnet	discussion of rights of kids and teenagers, especially individual liberty

Gopher Servers

Lots of U.S. government documents	`sunsite.unc.edu`	Worlds of SunSITE—by Subject/ U.S. and World Politics
The Freedom of Information Act for the U.S.	`eryx.syr.edu`	Citizen's Guide to FOIA
A huge number of U.S. Federal Agencies can be accessed here	`cwis.usc.edu`	Other Gophers and Information Resources/ Gophers by Subject/ Gopher Jewels

Telnet Sites

FedWorld Government BBS	`fedworld.doc.gov`

Miscellaneous

President Clinton's email address	`president@whitehouse.gov`
Vice President Gore's email address	`vice.president@whitehouse.gov`

Health Issues

World-Wide Web Sites

`http://nearnet.gnn.com/wic/curraffs.toc.html`

The Current Affairs section of the Global Network Navigator provides access to servers which contain various resources useful to those with disabilities of various types.

`http://nearnet.gnn.com/wic/sci.toc.html`

`http://nearnet.gnn.com/wic/med.toc.html`

The Science and Medicine & Health sections (listed respectively) of the Global Network Navigator offer many links to other resources based on particular disciplines (there's quite a variety). If you are interested in one or more of these, you can link to whatever is available in your area through this route. Information about AIDS, cholesterol, alcoholism, cancer, and other topics is easily accessible here.

```
http://www.who.ch/
```

The World Health Organization (WHO) operates a Web server on an experimental basis. At the time of this writing there were links to WHO press releases and newsletters as well as information about vaccination requirements and health advice. You can also read descriptions of WHO's major programs relating to AIDS, various diseases, and food and nutrition.

WAIS Sources

```
water-quality.src        covers water quality assessment topics
```

Mailing Lists

12step	muller	camp.rutgers.edu	discussion of 12-step programs such as Alcoholics and Overeaters Anonymous
ada-law	listserv	vm1.nodak.edu	covers the Americans with Disabilities Act and other related legislation in the U.S. and other countries
add-parents	add-parents-request	mv.mv.com	support forum with parents of children with Attention Deficit/ Hyperactivity Disorder
addict-l	listserv	kentvm.kent.edu	discussion of issues related to drinking and driving
aids	aids-request	cs.ucla.edu	mostly carries items relating to medical issues and AIDS, but also covers political and social issues
alcohol	listserv	lmuacad.bitnet	studies of alcohol and drugs
autism	listserv	sjuvm.bitnet	issues related to autism and developmental disabilities
blindnws	listserv	vm1.nodak.edu	issues concerning the blind and visually impaired
deafblnd	listserv	ukcc.uky.edu	mailing list for the deaf-blind
diabetic	listserv	pccvm.bitnet	support and information list for diabetics
drugabus	listserv	umab.bitnet	research and information related to drug abuse education
fit-l	listserv	etsuadmn.bitnet	discussion of issues related to wellness, exercise, and diet
healthre	listserv	ukcc.uky.edu	U.S. health care reform discussion
l-hcap	listserv	ndsuvm1.bitnet	covers aspects of technology for the handicapped
lymenet-l	listserv	lehigh.edu	carries news of all kinds relating to Lyme disease
recovery	recovery	wvnvm.wvnet.edu	support group for those who have suffered sexual abuse during childhood

rsi-east	listserv	sjuvm.stjohns.edu	Carpal Tunnel Syndrome and other typing-related injuries
safety	listserv	uvmvm.bitnet	covers environmental, health, and safety issues
smoke-free	listserv	ra.msstate.edu	support list for people recovering from addiction to cigarettes
stroke-l	listserv	ukcc.uky.edu	discussion of issues related to strokes
tbi-sprt	listserv	sjuvm.stjohns.edu	support forum for people directly and indirectly affected by traumatic brain injury
wmn-hlth	listserv	uwavm.u.washington.edu	covers women's health issues

Gopher Servers

CAMIS (Center for Advanced Medical Informatics at Stanford)	camis.stanford.edu	
The On-line Grief and Loss Network holds links to a variety of resources related to death, dying, bereavement, and major emotional and physical losses.	garnet.msen.com	Good Causes/Rivendell Resources
AIDS and HIV information	cwis.usc.edu	Other Gophers and Information Resources/ Gophers by Subject/ Gopher Jewels

Hobbies, House & Home

World-Wide Web Sites

http://nearnet.gnn.com/wic/rec.toc.html

The Recreation section of the Global Network Navigator contains links in categories such as cooking, gardening, genealogy, hobbies & crafts, and pets. The last of these has a link dedicated to llamas, where you can find pictures of them if you want one. In the other sections, there are links to various guides and resource files, which will likely be useful to someone interested in these areas. An archive of recipes is also linked here so you can use your computer to assist in the preparation of meals.

```
http://www.cis.ufl.edu/~thoth/library/recreation.html
```

This "Games and Recreation" file contains numerous links that relate to hobbies of all sorts. This is a nice site to visit if you're seeking information, pictures, or discussion about your favorite recreational activities. There are separate links to other files which hold information specifically about gardening, pets, and cooking (to name a few).

```
http://www.actwin.com/fish/index.html
```

Aquarium keepers will be glad they visited this server! It offers access to FAQ files and a full-color catalog of marine fish and invertebrates. There are archives of related discussions about all aspects of aquarium keeping. Furthermore, there are pictures and movies of various sorts of attractive tanks. These can be used as goals to set for your own system.

```
http://www-cse.ucsd.edu/users/bowdidge/railroad/rail-home.html
```

Railroad enthusiasts will find archives of related discussion groups, train schedules, railroad maps, and many other items of interest here. According to the introduction, there is model-railroading information along with links to other sites. A link to a site dedicated to steam locomotives can also be accessed.

```
http://www.latrobe.edu.au/Glenn/KiteSite/Kites.html
```

If you're a fan of kite flying, you'll certainly want to check out this site. It seems to be a kite-lovers paradise; there are many pictures of all kinds of kites as well as discussions of and information pertaining to kite flying.

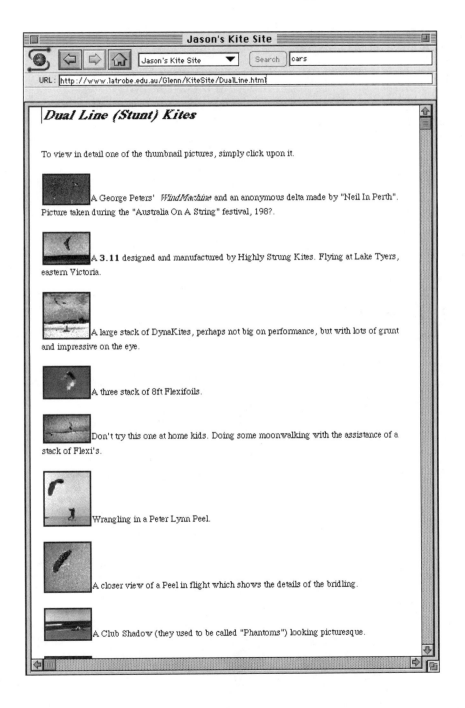

WAIS Sources

`homebrew.src`	information to help you brew your own drinks
`rec.gardens.src`	covers archives of gardening discussion groups
`rec.pets.src`	recent archives from discussion groups talking about pets
`recipes.src`	thousands of recipes for when you grow tired of your usual fare

FTP Sites

The Electronic Zoo is an extensive list of animal-related computer resources. It can be obtained via FTP from `wuarchive.wustl.edu` in the directory `/doc/techreports/wustl.edu/compmed/elec_zoo.x_x` (where `x_x` refers to the most current version).

Recipes via FTP	`gatekeeper.dec.com`	`/pub/recipes`

Mailing Lists

`aquarium`	`listserv`	`emuvm1.cc.emory.edu`	for talking about fish and aquaria
`balloon`	`balloon-request`	`lut.ac.uk`	discussion of topics relating to hot air and gas ballooning
`biblio`	`biblio-request`	`iris.claremont.edu`	aspects of fine book collecting, including want lists
`bicycle`	`listserv`	`bitnic.bitnet`	discussion forum for cycling enthusiasts
`birdchat`	`listserv`	`arizvm1.bitnet`	the chat line for the National Birding Hotline Cooperative
`bonsai`	`listserv`	`cms.cc.wayne.edu`	covers the art and craft of Bonsai at all levels
`bpm`	`bpm-request`	`andrew.cmu.edu`	forum for novice DJs that covers techniques and music releases, etc.
`bread`	`bread-digest-request`	`cykick.infores.com`	discussions related to making bread
`canine-l`	`listserv`	`psuvm.bitnet`	discussions of interest to dog fanciers
`cards`	`cards-request`	`tanstaafl.uchicago.edu`	discussion of all types of trading cards as well as a marketplace for these
`cavers-digest`	`listproc`	`speleology.cs.yale.edu`	covers topics relating to exploring caves

clocks	listserv	suvm.syr.edu	for discussing clock collection, repair, and construction
coins	coins-request	iscsvax.uni.edu	for coin and paper money collectors to discuss their related interests
comics-l	listserv	unlvm.unl.edu	discussions of all sorts of comics
comix	comix-request	world.std.com	discussion of independent and non-mainstream comic books
equestrians	equestrians-request	world.std.com	covers horses and equestrianism for people of all levels of experience
equine-l	listserv	psuvm.bitnet	discussions of interest to horse fanciers
f-costume	f-costume-request	lunch.asd.sgi.com	discussion forum for those interested in the design and creation of fantasy costumes
ferrets	ferret-request	ferret.ocunix.on.ca	for those who want to discuss ferrets, their care, experiences, etc.
firearms	listserv	utarlvm1.bitnet	covers topics related to firearms
flags	bottasini	cesi.it	discussion of various flags' symbols, colors, and meanings and the creation of a relevant database
gardens	listserv	ukcc.uky.edu	for those interested in gardens and gardening
glass	glass-request	dixie.com	covers topics related to stained and hot glass art
golden	golden-request	hobbes.ucsd.edu	for those who want to discuss golden retrievers, their care, experiences, etc.
h-costume	h-costume-request	andrew.cmu.edu	discussion forum for those interested in the design and creation of historical costumes of all ages
homebrew	homebrew-request%hpfcmr	hplabs.hp.com	covers all aspects of the making of beer, cider, mead, wine, and similar beverages
jewelry	listproc	mishima.mn.org	for the discussion of metalworking, lapidary, work-shops, materials, and many other aspects of jewelry making

continues

Appendix A
Internet Resources

jugglen	listserv	indycms.iupui.edu	juggling enthusiasts discuss their interests here
kites	kites-request	harvard.harvard.edu	discussion of making and flying all kinds of kites
magic	magic-request	maillist.crd.ge.com	for those seriously interested in sleight-of-hand and magic tricks
martial-arts	martial-arts-request	dragon.cso.uiuc.edu	covers many kinds of martial arts such as training, philosophy and techniques
origami-l	origami-l-request	nstn.ns.ca	those who like to practice origami can find others who share the interest here
photo-l	listserv	buacca.bitnet	forum for the discussion of photography
pinhole	pinhole-request	mintir.fidonet.org	covers topics related to pin-hole cameras
postcard	listserv	idbsu.bitnet	postcard collectors and traders discuss their interests here
quilt	listserv	cornell.edu	for those interested in quilts and quilting
railroad	listserv	cunyvm.cuny.edu	discussion of railroads and railroading
roots-l	listserv	vm1.nodak.edu	covers genealogical research
sca	sca-request	mc.lcs.mit.edu	discussions pertaining to the Society for Creative Anachronism, a medievalist organization
scouts-l	listserv	tcubvm.bitnet	discussions relating to various youth groups
scuba-l	listserv	browvm.bitnet	covers issues of concern to scuba divers
stamps	listserv	cunyvm.cuny.edu	discussions related to philately
tandem	listserv	hobbes.ucsd.edu	for tandem bicycle enthusiasts to discuss cycles, riding techniques, etc.
woodwork	listserv	ipfwvm.bitnet	discussions covering all aspects of woodworking

Gopher Servers

The Fun Stuff & Multimedia section here contains numerous links to resources likely to be interesting to a large number of people	cwis.usc.edu	Other Gophers and Information Resources/ Gophers by Subject/ Gopher Jewels

Literature, Fiction & Writing

World-Wide Web Sites

http://nearnet.gnn.com/wic/hum.toc.html

The Arts & Humanities section of the Global Network Navigator lists quite a few useful links to items such as the Dante Project, collections of poetry, many on-line books made available by Project Gutenberg and others, and information relating to writers such as Lewis Carroll and characters like Dracula. There are many reviews accessible here too, especially about science fiction. Shakespeare's works are all available for easy access, and projects dealing with French, Chinese, and Scandinavian literature are easy to reach as well.

ftp://gandalf.rutgers.edu/pub/sfl/sf-resource.guide.html

The Science Fiction Resource Guide is a must-visit for any fan of the genre. Links to information about movies, books, TV shows, and magazines will point science fiction fans to days worth of Internet explorations. Additional connections to files containing information about science fiction authors, awards, fandom, bookstores, reviews, criticism, games, and so on are included. "Now, there's more information on sf available than any one person can comfortably keep track of," the introduction says. Thankfully, this site provides tremendous help for those interested in the subjects with which it deals.

http://dewey.lib.ncsu.edu/reference.html

If you need to check your facts or grammar before you write, as you write, or after you write, connect to this site for a nice collection of dictionaries, thesauri, and almanacs. There are links to resources that define jargon, access a dictionary of acronyms, and connect to services that offer maps. If you're writing about the Internet, you'll find almost every standard network reference linked here too.

WAIS Sources

Aesop-Fables.src	covers more than 300 stories
poetry.src	lots and lots of complete poems can be searched; includes all of the works of Shakespeare and Yeats
proj-gutenberg.src	full-text versions of documents put into electronic format by Project Gutenberg
Science-Fiction-Series-Guide.src	reviews of various SF writers' works
sf-reviews.src	reviews related to works of science fiction
thesaurus.src	look up entries in Roget's Thesaurus, courtesy of Project Gutenberg

Mailing Lists

a.word.a.day	wordsmith	viper.elp.cwru.edu	receive one English word and its definition each day
amlit-l	listserv	umcvmb.missouri.edu	American literature discussion forum
blister	majordomo	world.std.com	a place to read and post lists of favorite or least favorite books
chaucer	listserv	siucvmb.siu.edu	covers topics related to Chaucer's works
copyediting-l	listserv	cornell.edu	mailing list which covers issues related to copy-editing
crewrt-l	listserv	umcvmb.missouri.edu	covers creative writing in education
deryni-l	mail-server	mintir.new-orleans.la.us	readers and fans of Kurtz's novels and other works discuss them here
dorothyl	listserv	kentvm.kent.edu	covers the mystery genre
e-poetry	listserv	ubvm.cc.buffalo.edu	distribution list for those interested in poetry
fiction	listserv	psuvm.psu.edu	this is the Fiction Writers Workshop list
fwake-l	listserv	irlearn.bitnet	discussions of James Joyce's work *Finnegan's Wake*
journet	listserv	qucdn.queensu.ca	discussion list concerning journalism education
literary	listserv	bitnic.bitnet	covers literature and related topics
mendele	listserv	yalevm.ycc.yale.edu	covers Yiddish literature and language

modbrits	listserv	kentvm.kent.edu	discussion of modern British and Irish literature
rra-1	listserv	kentvm.kent.edu	Romance Readers Anonymous email list
sflovers	listserv	rutgers.edu	discussion forum for science fiction enthusiasts
shaksper	listserv	utoronto.bitnet	discussion list for fans for William Shakespeare
sharp-1	listserv	iubvm.ucs.indiana.edu	Society for the History of Authorship, Reading, and Publishing
tolkien	listserv	jhuvm.bitnet	discussion list for fans of J.R.R. Tolkien's works
twain-1	listserv	vm1.yorku.ca	forum covering Mark Twain's works
vampyres	listserv	guvm.bitnet	covers Vampiric fiction and lore

Macintosh

World-Wide Web Sites

http://ici.proper.com/1/mac

This site claims "you will find all of the information on the Internet that relates to the Macintosh" when you connect to it. Indeed, this boast may be correct. There are numerous links to FAQ files, anonymous FTP sites, news groups, mailing lists, and Gopher and WWW servers. Additionally, there are connections to on-line Macintosh publications, indices of Macintosh-related reviews, and more. A nice, one-stop site for all your Macintosh needs.

http://www.dartmouth.edu/Pages/TidBITS/TidBITS.html

Adam Engst's weekly Macintosh-related electronic newsletter can be accessed via the World-Wide Web if you prefer to read it this way, or if you want to search or obtain back issues (starting with #200).

http://www.apple.com/

Apple itself has put a World-Wide Web server on the Internet. It offers information about Apple products, connections to resources useful to Mac programmers, and Apple press releases. Additional links describe new products and provide access to Apple-oriented resources and the Apple Library of Tomorrow. Be sure to pay a visit to this site and let Apple know how you feel about their server.

WAIS Sources

`mac.FAQ.src`	compilation of frequently asked questions (and answers) related to Macintosh computers
`macintosh-news.src`	archive of discussions related to Macs
`macintosh-tidbits.src`	includes all of the issues of Adam Engst's weekly electronic newsletter dedicated to Macintosh systems
`merit-archive-mac.src`	index of thousands of Mac programs available via FTP from mac.archive.umich.edu
`risks-digests.src`	information pertaining to risks associated with computers of all types
`tcl-talk.src`	covers discussion of Think compilers for Mac

FTP Sites

QuicKeys FTP site	`gaea.kgs.ukans.edu`	`/quickeys`
Frontier FTP site	`gaea.kgs.ukans.edu`	`/frontier`
Applescript FTP site	`gaea.kgs.ukans.edu`	`/applescript`
Nisus FTP site	`gaea.kgs.ukans.edu`	`/nisus`
Info-Mac Archive Site	`sumex-aim.stanford.edu`	`/info-mac`
Mac.Archive	`mac.archive.umich.edu`	
Macintosh Mirror Site	`wuarchive.wustl.edu`	`/mirrors`
Apple's FTP Site	`ftp.apple.com`	`/dts`
Macintosh FTP Site List	`sumex-aim.stanford.edu`	`/info-mac/comm/info/mac-ftp-List-###.txt`

Mailing Lists

`hypercrd`	`listserv`	`msu.bitnet`	covers HyperCard programming issues
`info-mac`	`listserv`	`ricevm1.rice.edu`	carries general information about Macintosh computers

mac-l	listserv	yalevm.ycc.yale.edu	Macintosh news and information
mac-mgrs	majordomo	world.std.com	discussion forum for those involved with Mac systems and networks of Mac computers
mac-security mac-security-request		world.std.com	covers issues pertaining to security of Mac computers on a network
macappli	listserv	dartmouth.edu	carries news and usage tips about applications
machrdwr	listserv	dartmouth.edu	covers Macintosh hardware and peripheral devices
macmulti	listserv	fccj.bitnet	covers items related to multimedia on Macintosh computers
macnet-l	listserv	yalevm.bitnet	carries items concerning Macintosh networking issues
macpb-l	listserv	yalevm.ycc.yale.edu	discussion list relating to PowerBook topics
macprog	listserv	wuvmd.wustl.edu	discussions of Macintosh programming
macscrpt	listserv	dartmouth.edu	covers Macintosh scripting systems
macsystm	listserv	dartmouth.edu	offers advice about the Macintosh operating system
mae-announce, mae-bugs, mae-users	listproc	medraut.apple.com	three lists for the discussion of Apple's Macintosh Application Environment: announcements, bugs, and use
nisus	listserv	gaea.kgs.ukans.edu	for those interested in the Nisus Macintosh program
qm-l	listserv	yalevm.bitnet	discussion forum for QuickMail (CE software) users
quickeys	listserv	gaea.kgs.ukans.edu	covers the QuicKeys program
sys7-l	listserv	uafsysb.uark.edu	discussion list related to Mac System 7 issues
tidbits	listserv	ricevm1.rice.edu	Adam Engst's weekly electronic newsletter which covers many sorts of issues of interest to Macintosh users
tincan-l	listserv	yalevm.bitnet	discussions relating to Macintosh terminal emulator issues
word-mac	listproc	scu.edu.au	discussion of the Microsoft Word program and its use on Macintosh computers

Appendix A
Internet Resources

Gopher Servers

Apple Computer Higher Education Gopher server　　info.hed.apple.com

Music & Dance

World-Wide Web Sites

http://nearnet.gnn.com/wic/hum.toc.html

The Arts & Humanities section of the Global Network Navigator also has a section with this name. In it you find links that access Billboard's Top 10 lists, archives of discussions related to playing a variety of instruments, music libraries, scholarly discussions of music, and the Internet Underground Music Archive. This last site contains lots of digitized music that you can transfer to your computer so that you can hear what various musicians have to offer. You might find that some of the people distributing music here become stars in their own right in the not too distant future.

http://sunsite.unc.edu/ianc/

The Internet Underground Music Archive "...intends to apply the principles of free software to music distribution. Going beyond the limits of what's defined as commercially viable, the Archive seeks to promote obscure and unavailable bands..." via the World-Wide Web. After connecting to this site, you can obtain songs, music, interview transcripts, and submit your own music for distribution. Other links lead to information about bands.

http://sunsite.unc.edu/ianc/IUMA/pages/links.html

The IUMA, described previously, not only offers on-line sounds, music, and information related to bands and musical personalities, but also provides connections to Internet resources of interest to their staff, including a complete collection of Schoolhouse Rock lyrics.

WAIS Sources

BGRASS-L.src	archives of Blue Grass music discussion list
cdbase.src	database of information about CDs, including titles, stock numbers, and producing companies
indian-classical-music.src	covers Indian musicians and their work
lyrics.src	look up the words when you can't quite understand what the musician sang or when you forget the whole song and just can't rest until you get all the words right
music-surveys.src	material related to musicians and their productions
MuTeX.src	covers music typesetting for TeX
rec.music.early.src	archives of discussions related to Medieval, Renaissance and Baroque music

Mailing Lists

78-1	listserv	cornell.edu	for discussing music and recordings of the pre-LP era
accordion	accordion-request	cs.cmu.edu	accordion enthusiasts talk about all aspects of the instrument
allmusic	listserv	auvm.bitnet	a discussion of all types of music
analogue	analogue-request	magnus.acs.ohio-state.edu	vintage analogue musical devices are discussed in this forum
bagpipe	bagpipe-request	cs.dartmouth.edu	piping enthusiasts talk about all aspects of bagpiping
ballroom	ballroom-request	athena.mit.edu	covers all aspects of ballroom dancing, including places to dance and competitions
barbershop	bbshop-request	cray.com	discussion of barbershop quartet singing and activities
bgrass-l	listserv	ukcc.uky.edu	Bluegrass music is discussed in this forum
blues-l	listserv	brownvm.brown.edu	carries talk about the blues for those who cannot get enough of it

continues

bolton	ai411	yfn.ysu.edu	Michael Bolton fans discuss his music and work here
brass	brass-request	geomag.gly.fsu.edu	covers brass musical performances and ensembles
classm-l	listserv	brownvm.brown.edu	forum for discussing classical music
dance-l	listserv	hearn.bitnet	covers international folkdance and traditional dance
dire-straits	dire-straits-request	merrimack.edu	devoted to discussing the group Dire Straits
dj-l	listserv	ndsuvm1.bitnet	a list for campus DJs to discuss their activities
earlym-l	listserv	aearn.bitnet	covers topics related to early music
emusic-l	listserv	auvm.bitnet	discussion covering electronic music
filmus-l	listserv	ubvm.ucs.indiana.edu	those interested in film music discuss it here
folk-dancing	tjw+	pitt.edu	for the discussion of all aspects of folk dancing
folk_music	listserv	nysernet.org	covers the music, tours, reviews, etc., of American singers and songwriters
funky-music	funky-music-request	mit.edu	forum for discussing funk, rap, soul, r & b, and related types of music
morris	listserv	suvm.acs.syr.edu	for discussing all aspects of Morris dancing
music	music	pulse.com	all aspects of classical music are discussed here
musicals	musicals-request	world.std.com	general coverage of musical theatre topics
piporg-l	listserv	albany.edu	covers pipe organs and related topics
rmusic-l	listserv	gitvm1.bitnet	devoted to discussing the music industry

savoynet	savoynet-request	cescc.bridgewater.edu	for discussing the works of Gilbert and/ or Sullivan
strathspey	strathspey-request	math.uni-frankfurt.de	covers Scottish Country Dancing including technique, descriptions, teaching, etc.
tuning	listproc	varese.mills.edu	discussion of ideas relating to alternate tunings and experimental instruments

Pictures, Graphics & Visual Arts

World-Wide Web Sites

http://nearnet.gnn.com/wic/hum.toc.html

The Arts & Humanities section of the Global Network Navigator provides easy access to nice collections of art that you can view right on your computer screen. In the Art section, one can walk the virtual galleries of several institutions and view many paintings, photographs, and other forms of visual expression. If you're seeking a cute or clever text-based rendition of something, check out the ASCII clip art Collection—there are hundreds of little files (and some big ones too!) that you could use to embellish a simple email message.

http://nearnet.gnn.com/wic/rec.toc.html

The Recreation section of the Global Network Navigator has a link or two to items that might be of interest to photographers.

gopher://cs4sun.cs.ttu.edu/11/Art%20and%20Images

If you want some images, visit this site! There are some 69 categories of pictures, images, and movies on the top-level menu alone, giving you access to thousands of files. Quality and file size vary tremendously, as the collections linked here come from a number of sources and were created for different reasons. The pictures range from simple character-based creations to superb, high-resolution photographs. Keep in mind that many of these files may take several minutes to transmit over a phone line.

```
Art and Images

 1. ASCII Clipart Collection/
 2. DOS and Mac viewing software/
 3. TAEX Clip Art Collection (TIFF)/
 4. U.S. Weather Map <Picture>
 5. Entertainment Images from Texas A&M (GIF)/
 6. Entertainment Images from U Michigan (GIF)/
 7. WUARCHIVE Collection (GIF)/
 8. WUARCHIVE Collection (JPEG)/
 9. - - - - - - - - - - - - - - - - -.
10. Search for Pictures/Images in all of GopherSpace <?>
11. - - - - - - - - - - - - - - - - -.
12. Animals, Plants, Scenic Beauty from U of Indiana/
13. ArchiGopher: Images from U of Michigan/
14. Architectural Projects from Johns Hopkins U/
15. Art Gallery (from University of Vermont)/
16. Astronomical Images (from U of Arizona)/
17. Astronomical Images (from U of California at Irvine)/
18. Bicycling Pictures (from U of California, Irvine)/
19. Birds from U.S. Army/
20. Birds from U.S. Army (Individual descriptions)/
21. Bodleian Libraries Images (from Radcliffe Science Library)/
22. California Museum of Photography/
23. Campus Images from Michigan State University/
24. Campus Images from Texas A&M/
25. Campus Images from U of Texas at Austin/
26. Central American Images/
27. Centre for Innovative Computer Applications (Indiana Univ.)/
28. Craigdarroch Castle Images (from Victoria Freenet)/
29. Dallas Museum of Art - Information & Images/
30. Doctor Fun: The first daily cartoon of the Internet/
31. Endoscopic Test Images/
32. Global Satellite Images from NOAA and AMRC (collected by SSEC)/
33. Hubble Telescope Images/
34. Image Archives from NASA/
35. Imagenes Antiguas Culturas (Mexico)/
```

36. Imagenes Arquitectonicas (Mexico)/
37. Images from the LBJ Library Photo Collection/
38. Images of Hurricane Emily/
39. Images of Mars/
40. Images of the Earth/
41. Impressionist Art from U of Vermont/
42. Jackets and Photos Images (from MIT Univ. Press)/
43. Jewish Graphics (from Jerusalem One Network)/
44. Kandinsky Image Archive (from U.Mich Library)/
45. Kodak PhotoCD Images (via Johns Hopkins Univ.)/
46. Lunar Architecture (from U.Mich Library)/
47. MPEG Movies (from Texas A&M)/
48. MPEG Movies (from U of Texas)/
49. Maps and Images from Ann Arbor (from U.Mich Library)/
50. Music Images from U Wisconsin-Parkside/
51. NASA Ames GMS vis/IR images/
52. Nature and Science Pictures from Smithsonian/
53. PET Centre Medical Image Library (from Austin Hospital)/
54. Picasso in Mexico/
55. Pictures from Victoria Freenet/
56. Plant Species Images from Harvard U/
57. Postcard Collection from U of Vermont/
58. Russian Far East, Maps/
59. Soviet Archive Exhibit at Library of Congress/
60. Strange Interactions: Art Work by John E. Jacobsen/
61. Train Pictures (from plaza.aarnet.edu.au)/
62. U.S. Color Relief Maps/
63. Vatican Library Exhibit at Library of Congress/
64. Weather Images (University of Illinois)/
65. Weather Maps and Images (from Unidata)/
66. White House Pictures from Univ. of N. Carolina SUNsite/
67. White Shark Images from UC Berkeley/
68. Wolf Images and Sounds/
69. World Maps (DOS)/

Appendix A
Internet Resources

FTP Site

Smithsonian Institute photo archives   photo1.si.edu or sunsite.unc.edu   /pub/multimedia/
                                                                               pictures/
                                                                               smithsonian

Mailing Lists

3d	jhbercovitz	lbl.gov	discussion of 3-D photography, including equipment, techniques and experiences
alt-photo-process	listproc	vast.unsw.edu.au	for discussing photographic processes that are not based on silver chemistry
artcrit	listserv	yorkvm1.bitnet	forum for the discussion of art criticism
clayart	listserv	ukcc.bitnet	ceramics are the topic of discussion here
image-l	listserv	trearn.bitnet	covers image processing and related issues

Gopher Servers

| See listing in World-Wide Web section | cs4sun.cs.ttu.edu | Art and Images |
| A number of links to Photography and Pictures resources are listed here Gopher Multimedia | cwis.usc.edu | Other Gophers and Information Resources/Gophers by Subject/ Jewels/Fun Stuff & |

Publications and Journalism

World-Wide Web Sites

http://nearnet.gnn.com/wic/curraffs.toc.html

The Current Affairs section of the Global Network Navigator links an index of journalism periodicals. Some electronic magazines, and lists of others, can also be accessed.

ftp://netcom5.netcom.com//pub/spj/html/spj.html

The Society of Professional Journalists Online offers this site that provides access to electronic mailings lists, archives of various sorts, and many other links to Internet resources likely to be of interest to journalists.

`http://www.jou.ufl.edu/home.html`

Journalists and communications scholars will find this site interesting for its version of The Journalism List and links to prototypical Web news services. Several others links to related topics can also be accessed here.

`http://ftp.etext.org/Zines/InterText/intertext.html`

If you enjoy fiction of various genres, you owe it to yourself to check out *InterText*, a long-standing Internet fiction magazine. *InterText* is published every other month, and is available via email, FTP, and the World-Wide Web.

WAIS Sources

`factsheet-five.src`	covers underground and small 'zines
`London-Free-Press-Regional-Index.src`	story index for this Canadian paper

FTP Sites

Books in HyperCard format	`sumex-aim.stanford.edu`	`/info-mac/info/nms`
InterText (fiction)	`ftp.etext.org`	`/Zines/InterText/`
For over 120 other electronic publications	`ftp.etext.org`	`/Zines`

Mailing Lists

`cdpub`	`mail-server`	`knex.mind.org`	covers all topics relating to publishing on CD-ROM media
`sharp-l`	`listserv`	`iubvm.ucs.indiana.edu`	forum for the Society for the History of Authorship, Reading, and Publishing
`vidpro-l`	`listserv`	`uxa.ecn.bgu.edu`	discussion of professional video production and operations at all levels of experience

Telnet Sites

LOCIS: Library of Congress Information System	`locis.loc.gov`

Gopher Sites

Books Online via the Internet Wiretap	`wiretap.spies.com`	Wiretap Online Library
OCF Online Library	`ocf.berkeley.edu`	
O'Reilly & Associates Online Catalog	`gopher.ora.com`	
Books, Journals, Magazines, Newsletters, and Publications are linked here	`cwis.usc.edu`	Other Gophers and Information Resources/Gophers by Subject/ Gopher Jewels

Sciences, Math, & Engineering

(see also "Biology, Agriculture & Environment")

World-Wide Web Sites

`http://nearnet.gnn.com/wic/tech.toc.html`

The Technology section of the Global Network Navigator provides connections to the U.S. National Institute of Standards & Technology and the Cornell Theory Center. There's also easy access to many resources related to computing, computer science, and multimedia.

`http://nearnet.gnn.com/wic/sci.toc.html`

The Science section of the Global Network Navigator offers links to other resources based on particular disciplines (there's quite a variety). If you are interested in one or more of these, you can link to whatever is available in your area through this route.

`http://www.cchem.berkeley.edu/Table/index.html`

This Web version of the periodic table of elements allows you to select a given table entry with your mouse. Once you click on an element's symbol, you are linked to information about it. This resource should be useful to those just learning chemistry and can serve as a refresher course on specific data to those who are well-versed in it.

`http://info.er.usgs.gov/`

The U.S. Geological Survey runs this server to provide general information about the organization. This site also offers contact data, and informs the public of various issues and educational efforts related to them. Publications, geographic information systems, and environmental research as well as data and network resources are all linked too.

`http://ucmp1.berkeley.edu/welcome.html`

Geologists, paleontologists, ecologists, climatologists, and anyone else with an interest in dinosaurs and the earth's past will love this full-color exhibit! With a World-Wide Web program, you can point and click your way through an extensive, educational, and virtual museum. The University of California Museum of Paleontology says "the purpose of this server is to explore the possibilities of an interactive natural history museum through the Internet. Although we cannot possibly emulate the feel of a real life museum, we hope this adventure can be just as fun and interactive." And they have succeeded. (See figure on following page.)

WAIS Sources

`chem-eng-current-contents.src`	indexes bibliographies related to chemical engineering
`nsf-awards.src`	searches abstracts of U.S. National Science Foundation awards
`nsf-pubs.src`	covers U.S. National Science Foundation publications

Mailing Lists

ae	listserv	sjsuvm1.sjsu.edu	discussion of current and future alternate energy technologies that are renewable and sustainable

continues

anneal	anneal-request	cs.ucla.edu	simulated annealing techniques are discussed here
chminf-l	listserv	iubvm.bitnet	discussions list concerning chemical information sources
cryonics	kqb	whscad1.att.com	relates to all topics relevant to the use of cryonic suspension
cybsys-l	listserv	bingvaxu.cc.binghamton.edu	covers cybernetics and related systems
earthandsky	majordomo	lists.utexas.edu	transcripts of the U.S. National Public Radio broadcasts of Earth & Sky which discuss topics relating to earth science and astronomy
ectl	ectl-request	snowhite.cis.uoguelph.ca	discussion of computer speech interface research
fusion	fusion-request	zorch.sf-bay.org	covers topics relating to fusion
geograph	listserv	searn.bitnet	forum for the discussion of geography
geology	listserv	ptearn.bitnet	forum for the discussion of geology
iams	iams-request	hh.sbay.org	the Internet Amateur Mathematics Society's forum for discussing math puzzles and problems
idforum	listserv	yorkvm1.bitnet	forum that covers industrial design issues
ilas-net	listserv	technion.technion.ac.il	the International Linear Algebra Society's forum
mech-l	listserv	utarlvm1.bitnet	covers topics related to mechanical engineering
opt-proc	listserv	taunivm.bitnet	covers topics related to optical computing and holography
optics	listserv	taunivm.bitnet	newsletter related to optics
physics	physics-request	qedqcd.rye.ny.us	covers developments in both theoretical and experimental physics of all types
polymerp	listserv	rutvm1.bitnet	polymer physics discussions take place on this list
quake-l	listserv	vm1.nodak.edu	discussion of earthquakes

continues

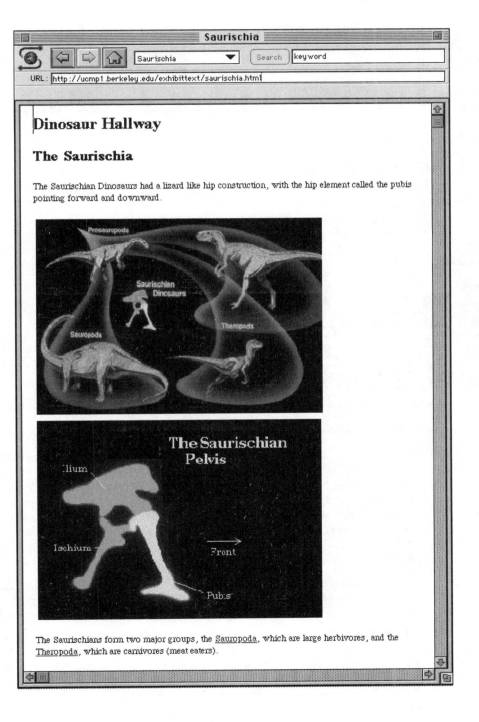

| seism-l | listserv | bingvmb.bitnet | mailing list for distribution of seismological data |
| textiles | listserv | trearn.bitnet | discussion area for those interested in studying textiles and clothing |

Gopher Servers

| GeoGopher (geological and earth sciences information and links to related servers) | dillon.geo.ep.utexas.edu | |
| Math Sciences, Physics, and Chemistry all have their own collections of links here | cwis.usc.edu | Other Gophers and Information Resources/ Gophers by Subject/ Gopher Jewels |

Shopping

World-Wide Web Sites

`http://nearnet.gnn.com/wic/newrescat.toc.html`

The Business section of the Global Network Navigator provides links to various commercial services that you can use to purchase goods and services via the Internet. Some of these simply allow you to view catalogs, while others actually permit you to order items while connected. Since no standard exists to ensure privacy of information such as credit card numbers, details of transactions, etc., Internet shopper should be aware that these services are not risk-free. Those services that offer only catalogs usually require an order via traditional methods such as phone, fax, or paper mail.

`http://branch.com:1080/index.html`

The Branch Mall provides access to several commercial services that allow you to order flowers, gift baskets, and magazines. You can also buy videos and purchase a CD-ROM. InfoVID, the on-line video store, "is your complete guide to the best educational, instructional, and informative videos from around the world." They offer thousands of films that cover scores of subjects. The Internet Flower Shop offers pictures of various arrangements, which you can order for yourself or have sent to someone else anywhere in the U.S. or Canada.

`http://www.gems.com/realestate/`

Want to buy or sell a house? How about a piece of commercial property? This is the Internet service that allows you to shop for real estate from the comfort of your own living room (or wherever your computer is). Real estate agents from across the world (and private individuals) advertise properties they wish to sell. All you need to do is connect, choose the type of property you wish to investigate, then select the location where you wish to buy. If there are real estate agents with the appropriate offerings in that area, then you can view images of the properties, read about them, check out the asking price, and obtain contact information so you can proceed with taking the place off the market if you want it.

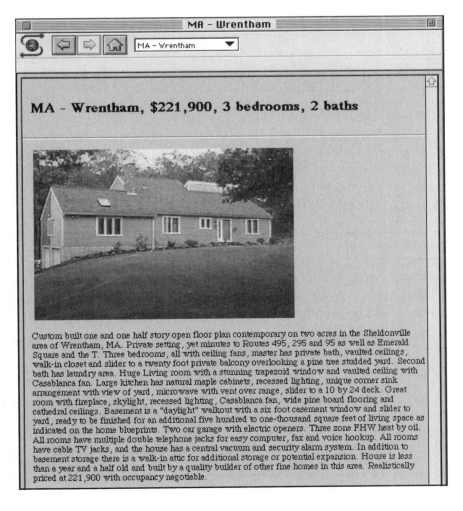

Telnet Sites

A very large on-line bookstore	books.com	enter real name and create a password when you connect
MarketBase online catalog of goods and services	mb.com	login: mb

Gopher Servers

Wordsworth Books, complete with email orders and title, author, or ISBN searches	gopher.wordsworth.com	
A menu item called "Products and Services - Store Fronts" provides access to a number of commercial offerings here	cwis.usc.edu	Other Gophers and Information Resources/ Gophers by Subject/ Gopher Jewels
On-line bookstore	nstn.ns.ca	/NSTN's CyberMall/ Roswell Electronic Computer Bookstore

Sports & Exercise

World-Wide Web Sites

http://nearnet.gnn.com/wic/rec.toc.html

The Recreation section of the Global Network Navigator has an area dedicated to links pertaining to Sports & Games. Various information files and archives of discussion groups are stored here for ease of access.

http://www.inslab.uky.edu/People/stevem/horses/KyDerbyInfo/kyderby.html

If you enjoy horse racing and follow the Kentucky Derby then you'll certainly be interested in visiting this server. Pictures of the contenders are available along with statistics and other information about them. Each of the probable starters' backgrounds are described along with their results for the past 15 years. You can also read daily training updates in case you want to follow them closely.

http://www.explore.com/Explorer_forums.html

Divers, skiers, and snowboarders will find many good items here, including guides to various diving sites and lists of snow conditions at various places (including Australia). The many links here provide useful information on destinations in which divers, skiers, and snowboarders would likely be interested. This site also provides links to archives of discussions groups for these topics, and to lists of frequently asked questions concerning the sports.

`http://www.mit.edu:8001/services/sis/sports.html`

The WWW Sports Information Server currently provides information about professional basketball and football teams in the U.S. In the future, this site may carry items related to other sports as well, so check back later if you're interested in different games.

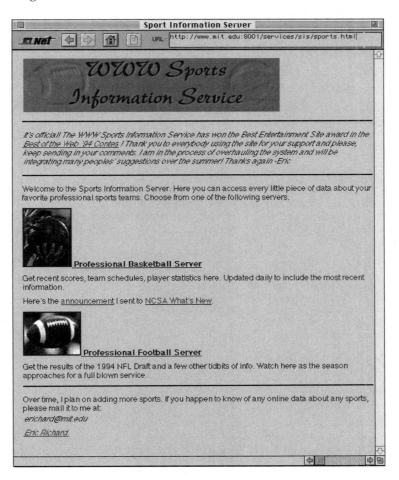

Mailing Lists

ahl-news	ahl-news-request	andrew.cmu.edu	for those wishing to discuss and follow the American Hockey League
aikido-l	listserv	psuvm.psu.edu	covers topics relevant to the Japanese martial art of Aikido
base-jumping	base-request	lunatix.lex.ky.us	skydiving discussions and information for those who have already jumped
dead-runners	dead-runners-request	unx.sas.com	Dead Runners Society forum for talking about personal aspects of running
derby	derby-request	ekrl.com	discussion forum relating to horse racing
dragnet	dragnet-request	chiller.compaq.com	covers drag racing from a participant's perspective
golf-l	listserv	ubvm.cc.buffalo.edu	covers golf and golfing
gymn	owner-gymn	mit.edu	discusses all aspects of the sport of gymnastics
hang-gliding	hang-gliding-request	virginia.edu	hang-gliding enthusiasts discuss their interests here
hockey-l	listserv	maine.maine.edu	covers college hockey teams, their scores, schedules, etc.
lacrosse	listserv	suvm.bitnet	discussion of lacrosse
pbp-l	listserv	etsuadmn.etsu.edu	a list for play-by-play sportscasters for all sports
sportpsy	listserv	templevm.bitnet	discussions of exercise and sport psychology
statlg-l	listserv	sbccvm.bitnet	covers statistics related to baseball and other sports
swim-l	listserv	uafsysb.uark.edu	covers all aspects of swimming
waterski	waterski-request	nda.com	all levels of water-skiers can join this discussion of equipment, technique, safety, sites, etc.
weights	weights-request	mickey.disney.com	discussion of exercising with weights and also covers bodybuilding
wheel-to-wheel	wheeltowheel-request	abingdon.eng.sun.com	drivers and crews of race cars discuss their sport here

whitewater	whitewater-request	gynko.circ.upenn.edu	concerned with experiences and information about whitewater sports such as kayaking and canoeing
windsurfing	windsurfing-request	fly.com	all levels of windsurfers can join this discussion of equipment, technique, safety, sites, etc.
yacht-l	listserv	grearn.bitnet	forum dedicated to sailing and amateur boat building topics

Gopher Servers

Sports from archery to volleyball are covered here	cwis.usc.edu	Other Gophers and Information Resources/ Gophers by Subject/ Gopher Jewels/Fun Stuff & Multimedia

Telnet Sites

NBA schedules	culine.colorado.edu 859
NHL schedules	culine.colorado.edu 860
MLB schedules	culine.colorado.edu 862
NFL schedules	culine.colorado.edu 863

TV, Movies & Theatre

World-Wide Web Sites

http://nearnet.gnn.com/wic/hum.toc.html

The Arts & Humanities section of the Global Network Navigator contains links to Monty Python sketches, a guide to the hottest science fiction program on TV these days, Babylon-5, an archive of material relating to The Simpsons and information about satellite TV. There's also a film database and a collection of film reviews that you can browse before you head out to the theatre for a show.

```
ftp://gandalf.rutgers.edu/pub/sfl/sf-resource.guide.html
```

The Science Fiction Resource Guide is a must-visit for any fan of the genre. Links to information about movies, books, TV shows, and magazines will point science fiction fans to days worth of Internet explorations. Additional connections to files containing information about science fiction authors, awards, fandom, bookstores, reviews, criticism, games, etc. are included. "Now, there's more information on sf available than any one person can comfortably keep track of," the introduction says. Thankfully, this site provides tremendous help for those interested in the subjects with which it deals.

WAIS Sources

`movie-lists.src`	database of references to movie and TV credits
`movie-reviews.src`	check here before you decide what show you're going to see
`simpsons.src`	keep up with Bart and family in case you miss an episode

Mailing Lists

`30something`	`30something-request`	`fuggles.acc.virginia.edu`	discussion of 30 Something's episodes, characters, etc.
`90210`	`90210-request`	`ferkel.ucsb.edu`	covers the Beverly Hills 90210 show
`b5-review-l`	`listserv`	`cornell.edu`	reviews of Babylon 5 material of all types
`clarissa`	`clarissa-request`	`tcp.com`	discussion of Clarissa Explains It All, a Nickelodeon TV show
`film-l`	`listserv`	`vmtecmex.bitnet`	discussions pertaining to film-making and film reviews
`late-show-news`	`listserv`	`mcs.net`	a weekly digest carrying opinions and facts about late-night talk shows
`melrose-place`	`melrose-place-request`	`ferkel.ucsb.edu`	discussion of Melrose Place's episodes, characters, etc.
`sf-lovers`	`sf-lovers-request`	`rutgers.edu`	discussions of all aspects of science fiction, not just TV and movies

space-1999	space-1999-request	quack.kfu.com	fans of this 70s show discuss it here
strek-l	listserv	pccvm.bitnet	discussions pertaining to the Star Trek Fan Club
trek-review-l	listserv	cornell.edu	reviews of Star Trek material of all types
tv-l	listserv	trearn.bitnet	covers all aspects of TV

Gopher Servers

| Vanderbilt Television News Archive | tvnews.vanderbilt.edu | copies of TV news broadcasts, regular and special, going back to 1968 can be borrowed from this archive |
| Lots of television and movie resources are linked here | cwis.usc.edu | Other Gophers and Information Resources/ Gophers by Subject/ Gopher Jewels/Fun Stuff & Multimedia |

Hard to Classify

World-Wide Web Sites

http://sunsite.unc.edu/expo/restaurant/restaurant.html

Explore a week's worth of recipes available at a place of fine dining, Restaurant Le Cordon Bleu. Once you connect, you can check out a number of meals, and get the recipes to make them. Some of the recipes include photographs showing how to prepare the food in case it's not clear from the directions provided. Bon appétite!

http://www.englib.cornell.edu/humor/engr_jokes.html

http://www.law.cornell.edu/Humor/lawyer_jokes

These two servers hold collections of engineer(ing) and lawyer jokes, respectively. If you're looking for a good laugh, connect to one of these and read a few entries.

WAIS Sources

`acronyms.src`	find out what those letters stand for with this database
`college-email.src`	look up how to send email to someone at a given college or university
`jargon.src`	database of terms used by computer 'hackers' and their ilk
`usenet-addresses.src`	look up the address of someone who has posted a message through USENET (network news)
`weather.src`	covers various information related to weather systems and their analysis
`zipcodes.src`	no more trips to the Post Office—find the ZIP code for the town, or the town for the ZIP code

FTP Sites

Navy News Service	`nctamslant.navy.mil`	
High Weirdness By Email	`nexus.yorku.ca`	`/pub/Internet-info/high-weirdness`

Mailing Lists

`dot`	`dot`	`t3ew.dot.ca.gov` `(put 'subscribe' in the subject line)`	covers issues of concern to public and private transportation organizations and vendors who provide solutions for them
`giggles`	`listserv`	`vtvm1.cc.vt.edu`	forum for jokes, stories, and anecdotes
`janitor`	`listserv`	`ukanvm.cc.ukans.edu`	discussion of any topic of interest to those engaged in the cleaning of public buildings
`meh2o-l`	`listserv`	`taunivm.tau.ac.il`	information and research related to water in the Middle East
`nerdnosh@ scruz.ucsc.edufelton.ca.us`		`tcbowden@clovis.`	virtual campfire gathering of storytellers
`oracle`	`oracle-request`	`iuvax.cs.indiana.edu`	the Usenet Oracle is available to answer all your questions; for assistance, send mail to `oracle@iuvax.cs.indiana.edu` with the word "help" in the Subject line
`psi-l`	`listserv`	`rpiecs.bitnet`	ESP, out-of-body experiences, dream experiments, and altered states of consciousness are discussed here
`skeptic`	`listserv`	`jhuvm.bitnet`	skeptics discuss various phenomena here

tftd-l	listserv	tamvm1.bitnet	thought for the day
transit	listserv	gitvm1.bitnet	discussion of issues related to public transit
weird-l	listserv	brownvm.bitnet	all manner of weirdness
wx-talk	listserv	uiucvmd.bitnet	discussion of weather-related phenomena

Gopher Servers

Museums, Exhibits, and Special Collections that fall within several categories are all accessible here	cwis.usc.edu	Other Gophers and Information Resources/ Gophers by Subject/ Gopher Jewels
ASCII Cows: use Veronica to search on the terms "cows" and you'll find this amusing collection of cows drawn with standard keyboard characters		
ERIC educational gopher	ericir.syr.edu	ERIC is the Educational Resources Information Center (ERIC), a federally funded national information system that provides access to an extensive body of education-related resources
Armadillo, the Texas Studies Gopher	chico.rice.edu 1170	a service designed with the middle school teacher and student in mind; it presents information about Texas natural and cultural history to support an interdisciplinary course of study around themes of interest to students involved in their surroundings
Whole Earth 'Lectronic Magazine — The WELL's Gopherspace	gopher.well.sf.ca.us	this gopher is "an experiment in publishing in Cyberspace" that resembles a magazine since it has "editors, editorial control and comments, and a clear 'point of view'"
Electronic Frontier Foundation (EFF)	gopher.eff.org	includes a collection of electronic magazines and files relating to the EFF's efforts to protect rights

Internet Meta-Resources

World-Wide Web Sites

```
http://nearnet.gnn.com/wic/internet.toc.html
```

The Internet section of the Global Network Navigator makes it extremely easy to access Internet services of all kinds including Archie, HYTELNET, WAIS, and others discussed in this book. There are many links to various other lists of resources available via the nets, such as the Yanoff List, Zen and the Art of the Internet, the Internet Business Journal, and others. Basically, this is where you can truly go wild looking for things on the Internet, either by browsing around, or reading a number of files that tell you where to start and how to get there. You can also access a number of Free-Nets through links here, in case you want to see what these look like and see the ways different communities are experimenting with Internet. Additionally, if you want to try to locate someone on the Internet, you can try using the items in the White Pages category to find an email address for them.

```
http://www.ii.uib.no/cgi-bin/paml
```

Mailing list references abound here, and this resource is dedicated to listing them and providing links to their descriptions. If you want to explore for lists about a certain topic, then you should connect to this site and check out its huge list. The mailing lists are arranged alphabetically; if the name of a list does not give a clue about its purpose, simply click on it for more information. You must open up the list's description to determine how to subscribe to it.

```
http://www.internic.net/scout-report/
```

This resource can assist you in keeping up with some of the best new resources available on the Internet; it is updated once a week. "Its purpose is to combine, in one place, the highlights of new resource announcements, newly discovered resources, and other news that occurred on the Internet during the previous week."

```
ftp://csd4.csd.uwm.edu/pub/inet.services.html
```

Scott Yanoff maintains a compilation entitled "Special Internet Connections," which provides the access methods and addresses for all sorts of resources. The URL above will connect you to the hypermedia version of this document and allow you to easily try the various services he describes. There are links to everything from files of specialized information to Internet name look-up services to online games. This document offers you the chance to gain plenty of practice with a variety of Internet tools.

```
http://ds.internic.net/
```

After you connect to this site and select Information Services from the initial screen, you'll have a good idea of what's available here: "The InterNIC is a collaborative project of three organizations which work together to offer the Internet community a full scope of network information services. These services include providing information about accessing and using the Internet, assistance in locating resources on the network, and registering network components for Internet connectivity. The overall goal of the InterNIC is to make networking and networked information more easily accessible to researchers, educators, and the general public. The term 'InterNIC' signifies cooperation between Network Information Centers, or NICs." You can access a wide variety of directory services at this site.

WAIS Sources

`Directory-of-Servers.src`	database of servers at quake.think.com
`finding-sources.src`	database useful for discovering information stored on the network
`internet_info.src`	indexes documents concerning proper use of the Internet
`internet_services.src`	covers files detailing the availability of various Internet services
`mailing-lists.src`	descriptions and access details for many electronic mailings lists, serials, newsgroups, etc.
`network-bibliography.src`	find network-related documents so that you can read more about it
`news.answers-faqs.src`	search all those FAQ files in one fell swoop!

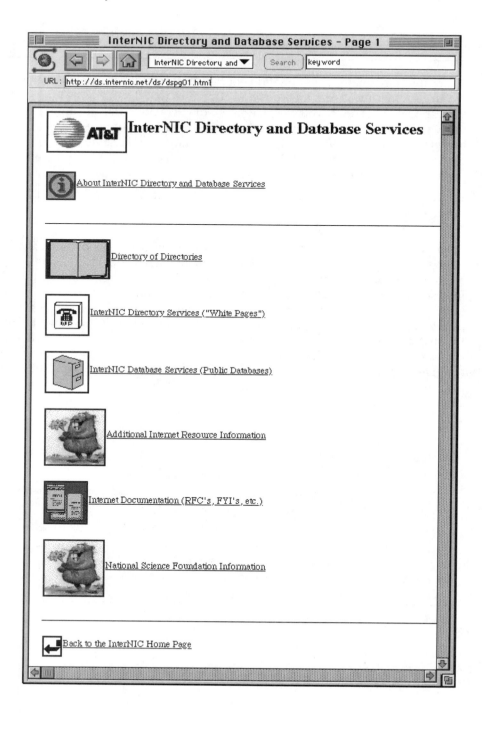

FTP Sites

Scott Yanoff's List of Special Internet Services	`csd4.csd.uwm.edu`	`/pub/inet.services.txt`
Internet and Computer Mediated Communication	`ftp.rpi.edu`	`/pub/communications`
Campus-Wide Information Systems	`ftp.oit.unc.edu`	`pub/docs/about-the-net/cwis/cwis-L`
The Incomplete Guide to the Internet	`ftp.ncsa.uiuc.edu`	`/Education/Education_Resources`
A guide to the Internet from the Electronic Frontier Foundation	`sumex-aim.stanford.edu`	`/info-mac/comm/big-dummys-guide-to-intenet.hqx`
A Cruise of the Internet (requires color)	`nic.merit.edu`	`/resources/cruise.mac`

Mailing Lists

`bits & bytes online`	`jmachado`	`pacs.pha.pa.us`	miscellaneous electronic news; put SUBSCRIBE in the Subject line and your email address in the body of the message
`edupage`	`listserv`	`bitnic.educom.edu`	informative twice-weekly newsletter on information technology
`net-happenings`	`majordomo`	`is.internic.net`	if it happens on the Internet, you'll learn about it here
`nettrain`	`listserv`	`ubvm.cc.buffalo.edu`	discussion of issues related to training people to use the network
`scout-report`	`majordomo`	`is.internic.net`	weekly reports of new and exciting Internet resources
`tow`	`listserv`	`vm1.nodak.edu`	The Online World

Gopher Servers

The Clearinghouse for Subject-Oriented Internet Resource Guides	`una.hh.lib.umich.edu`	"Its goal is to collect and make widely available guides to Internet resources which are subject-oriented. These guides are produced by members of the Internet community, and by SILS students who participate in the Internet Resource Discovery project."

continues

The Gopher Jewels collection is a very nice place to start browsing when looking for information about a certain topic.	`cwis.usc.edu`	Other Gophers and Information Resources/ Gophers by Subject/ Gopher Jewels
InterNIC Information Services	`is.internic.net`	this is an official site for Internet information, so there are documents relating to the Internet and to directory and database services.
Merit/NSFNET Information Services	`nic.merit.edu`	this site also contains many files relating to the Internet itself

Newsgroup List

The following list of newsgroups was taken from several periodic postings to the **news.lists** newsgroup on Usenet. Gene Spafford first created the list and acted as the original editor until May, 1993, and David Lawrence now edits the list. Keep in mind that this list is not exhaustive, and it was probably out of date the day after I pulled it off Usenet. Nevertheless, browsing through this list can give you a good idea of what newsgroups you might want to read. When you're forced to choose from thousands of possibilities, this list can be a big help.

For a list of alternative newsgroups (and I do mean alternative!), see the list of alternative hierarchies in **news.lists**.

Currently Active Usenet Newsgroups

The following is a list of currently active USENET newsgroups as of June 2, 1994. This list does not include the gatewayed Internet newsgroups (discussed later). The groups distributed worldwide are divided into seven broad classifications: **news**, **soc**, **talk**, **misc**, **sci**, **comp**, and **rec**. Each of these classifications is organized into groups and subgroups according to topic. See table B.1 for a list of these hierarchies.

Table B.1
Main Hierarchies

Abbreviation	Description
comp	Topics of interest to both computer professionals and hobbyists, including topics in computer science, software source, and information on hardware and software systems.
sci	Discussions marked by special and usually practical knowledge, relating to research in or application of the established sciences.
misc	Groups addressing themes not easily classified under any of the other headings or which incorporate themes from multiple categories.
soc	Groups primarily addressing social issues and socializing.
talk	Groups largely debate-oriented and tending to feature long discussions without resolution and without appreciable amounts of generally useful information.
news	Groups concerned with the news network and software themselves.
rec	Groups oriented towards the arts, hobbies, and recreational activities.

These "world" newsgroups are (usually) circulated around the entire USENET—this implies world-wide distribution. Not all groups actually enjoy such wide distribution, however. Some sites take only a selected subset of the more "technical" groups, and controversial "noise" groups are often not carried by many sites (these groups are often under the **talk** and **soc** classifications). Many sites do not carry some or all of the **comp.binaries** groups.

There are groups in other subcategories, but they are local: to institutions, to geographic regions, and so forth, and they are not listed here. Note that these distribution categories can be used to restrict the propagation of news articles. Currently, distributions include those shown in table B.2.

Table B.2
Main Distributions

Abbreviation	Distribution
world	worldwide distribution (default)
can	limited (mostly) to Canada
eunet	limited (mostly) to European sites in EUNet
na	limited (mostly) to North America
usa	limited (mostly) to the United States

There may be other regional and local distribution categories available at your site. Most U.S. states have distribution categories named after the two-letter abbreviation for that state or category (e.g., "ga" for Georgia, "nj" for New Jersey). Please use an appropriate distribution category if your article is not likely to be of interest to USENET readers worldwide.

Table B.3 is a list of newsgroups along with a brief description of what topics they cover. Use this to find some groups in which you would like to participate.

Table B.3
Newsgroup List

Newsgroup	Description
comp.admin.policy	Discussions of site administration policies.
comp.ai	Artificial intelligence discussions.
comp.ai.fuzzy	Fuzzy set theory, aka fuzzy logic.
comp.ai.genetic	Genetic algorithms in computing.
comp.ai.jair.announce	Announcements & abstracts of the Journal of AI Research. (Moderated)
comp.ai.jair.papers	Papers published by the Journal of AI Research. (Moderated)
comp.ai.nat-lang	Natural language processing by computers.
comp.ai.neural-nets	All aspects of neural networks.
comp.ai.nlang-know-rep	Natural Language and Knowledge Representation. (Moderated)
comp.ai.philosophy	Philosophical aspects of Artificial Intelligence.
comp.ai.shells	Artificial intelligence applied to shells.
comp.answers	Repository for periodic USENET articles. (Moderated)
comp.apps.spreadsheets	Spreadsheets on various platforms.
comp.arch	Computer architecture.
comp.arch.arithmetic	Implementing arithmetic on computers/digital systems.
comp.arch.bus.vmebus	Hardware and software for VMEbus Systems.
comp.arch.storage	Storage system issues, both hardware and software.
comp.archives	Descriptions of public access archives. (Moderated)
comp.archives.admin	Issues relating to computer archive administration.
comp.archives.msdos.announce	Announcements about MS-DOS archives. (Moderated)
comp.archives.msdos.d	Discussion of materials available in MS-DOS archives.

continues

Table B.3
Continued

Newsgroup	Description
comp.bbs.misc	All aspects of computer bulletin board systems.
comp.bbs.tbbs	The Bread Board System bulletin board software.
comp.bbs.waffle	The Waffle BBS and USENET system on all platforms.
comp.benchmarks	Discussion of benchmarking techniques and results.
comp.binaries.acorn	Binary-only postings for Acorn machines. (Moderated)
comp.binaries.amiga	Encoded public domain programs in binary. (Moderated)
comp.binaries.apple2	Binary-only postings for the Apple II computer.
comp.binaries.atari.st	Binary-only postings for the Atari ST. (Moderated)
comp.binaries.cbm	For the transfer of 8bit Commodore binaries. (Moderated)
comp.binaries.geos	Binaries for the GEOS operating system. (Moderated)
comp.binaries.ibm.pc	Binary-only postings for IBM PC/MS-DOS. (Moderated)
comp.binaries.ibm.pc.d	Discussions about IBM/PC binary postings.
comp.binaries.ibm.pc.wanted	Requests for IBM PC and compatible programs.
comp.binaries.mac	Encoded Macintosh programs in binary. (Moderated)
comp.binaries.ms-windows	Binary programs for Microsoft Windows. (Moderated)
comp.binaries.newton	Apple Newton binaries, sources, books, etc. (Moderated)
comp.binaries.os2	Binaries for use under the OS/2 ABI. (Moderated)
comp.bugs.2bsd	Reports of UNIX* version 2BSD related bugs.
comp.bugs.4bsd	Reports of UNIX version 4BSD related bugs.
comp.bugs.4bsd.ucb-fixes	Bug reports/fixes for BSD Unix. (Moderated)
comp.bugs.misc	General UNIX bug reports and fixes (incl V7, uucp).
comp.bugs.sys5	Reports of USG (System III, V, etc.) bugs.
comp.cad.cadence	Users of Cadence Design Systems products.
comp.cad.compass	Compass Design Automation EDA tools.
comp.cad.pro-engineer	Parametric Technology's Pro/Engineer design package.
comp.cad.synthesis	Research and production in the field of logic synthesis.
comp.client-server	Topics relating to client/server technology.
comp.cog-eng	Cognitive engineering.
comp.compilers	Compiler construction, theory, etc. (Moderated)
comp.compression	Data compression algorithms and theory.
comp.compression.research	Discussions about data compression research. (Moderated)
comp.constraints	Constraint processing and related topics.
comp.databases	Database and data management issues and theory.

Newsgroup	Description
comp.databases.informix	Informix database management software discussions.
comp.databases.ingres	Issues relating to INGRES products.
comp.databases.ms-access	MS Windows' relational database system, Access.
comp.databases.object	Object-oriented paradigms in database systems.
comp.databases.oracle	The SQL database products of the Oracle Corporation.
comp.databases.paradox	Borland's database for DOS & MS Windows.
comp.databases.pick	Pick-like, post-relational, database systems.
comp.databases.rdb	The relational database engine RDB from DEC.
comp.databases.sybase	Implementations of the SQL Server.
comp.databases.theory	Discussing advances in database technology.
comp.databases.xbase.fox	Fox Software's xBase system and compatibles.
comp.databases.xbase.misc	Discussion of xBase (dBASE-like) products.
comp.dcom.cell-relay	Forum for discussion of Cell Relay-based products.
comp.dcom.fax	Fax hardware, software, and protocols.
comp.dcom.isdn	The Integrated Services Digital Network (ISDN).
comp.dcom.lans.ethernet	Discussions of the Ethernet/IEEE 802.3 protocols.
comp.dcom.lans.fddi	Discussions of the FDDI protocol suite.
comp.dcom.lans.misc	Local area network hardware and software.
comp.dcom.lans.token-ring	Installing and using token ring networks.
comp.dcom.modems	Data communications hardware and software.
comp.dcom.servers	Selecting and operating data communications servers.
comp.dcom.sys.cisco	Info on Cisco routers and bridges.
comp.dcom.sys.wellfleet	Wellfleet bridge & router systems hardware & software.
comp.dcom.telecom	Telecommunications digest. (Moderated)
comp.dcom.telecom.tech	Discussion of technical aspects of telephony.
comp.doc	Archived public-domain documentation. (Moderated)
comp.doc.techreports	Lists of technical reports. (Moderated)
comp.dsp	Digital Signal Processing using computers.
comp.edu	Computer science education.
comp.emacs	EMACS editors of different flavors.
comp.emulators.announce	Emulator news, FAQs, announcements. (Moderated)
comp.emulators.apple2	Emulators of Apple II systems.
comp.emulators.cbm	Emulators of C-64, C-128, PET, and VIC-20 systems.
comp.emulators.misc	Emulators of miscellaneous computer systems.
comp.fonts	Typefonts—design, conversion, use, etc.

continues

Table B.3
Continued

Newsgroup	Description
comp.graphics	Computer graphics, art, animation, and image processing.
comp.graphics.algorithms	Algorithms used in producing computer graphics.
comp.graphics.animation	Technical aspects of computer animation.
comp.graphics.avs	The Application Visualization System.
comp.graphics.data-explorer	IBM's Visualization Data Explorer, aka DX.
comp.graphics.explorer	The Explorer Modular Visualisation Environment (MVE).
comp.graphics.gnuplot	The GNUPLOT interactive function plotter.
comp.graphics.opengl	The OpenGL 3D application programming interface.
comp.graphics.raytracing	Ray tracing software, tools, and methods.
comp.graphics.research	Highly technical computer graphics discussion. (Moderated)
comp.graphics.visualization	Info on scientific visualization.
comp.groupware	Software and hardware for shared interactive environments.
comp.groupware.lotus-notes.misc	Lotus Notes related discussions.
comp.home.automation	Home automation devices, setup, sources, etc.
comp.home.misc	Media, technology, and information in domestic spaces. (Moderated)
comp.human-factors	Issues related to human-computer interaction (HCI).
comp.infosystems	Any discussion about information systems.
comp.infosystems.announce	Announcements of Internet information services. (Moderated)
comp.infosystems.gis	All aspects of Geographic Information Systems.
comp.infosystems.gopher	Discussion of the Gopher information service.
comp.infosystems.interpedia	The Internet Encyclopedia.
comp.infosystems.wais	The Z39.50-based WAIS full-text search system.
comp.infosystems.www	The World-Wide Web information system.
comp.internet.library	Discussing electronic libraries. (Moderated)
comp.ivideodisc	Interactive videodiscs—uses, potential, etc.
comp.lang.ada	Discussion about Ada*.
comp.lang.apl	Discussion about APL.
comp.lang.basic.misc	Other dialects and aspects of BASIC.
comp.lang.basic.visual	Microsoft Visual Basic & App Basic; Windows & DOS.
comp.lang.c	Discussion about C.
comp.lang.c++	The object-oriented C++ language.
comp.lang.clos	Common Lisp Object System discussions.

Newsgroup	*Description*
comp.lang.dylan	For discussion of the Dylan language.
comp.lang.eiffel	The object-oriented Eiffel language.
comp.lang.forth	Discussion about Forth.
comp.lang.fortran	Discussion about FORTRAN.
comp.lang.functional	Discussion about functional languages.
comp.lang.hermes	The Hermes language for distributed applications.
comp.lang.idl-pvwave	IDL and PV-Wave language discussions.
comp.lang.lisp	Discussion about LISP.
comp.lang.lisp.mcl	Discussing Apple's Macintosh Common Lisp.
comp.lang.logo	The Logo teaching and learning language.
comp.lang.misc	Different computer languages not specifically listed.
comp.lang.ml	ML languages including Standard ML, CAML, Lazy ML, etc. (Moderated)
comp.lang.modula2	Discussion about Modula-2.
comp.lang.modula3	Discussion about the Modula-3 language.
comp.lang.oberon	The Oberon language and system.
comp.lang.objective-c	The Objective-C language and environment.
comp.lang.pascal	Discussion about Pascal.
comp.lang.perl	Discussion of Larry Wall's Perl system.
comp.lang.pop	Pop11 and the Plug user group.
comp.lang.postscript	The PostScript Page Description Language.
comp.lang.prograph	Prograph, a visual object-oriented dataflow language.
comp.lang.prolog	Discussion about PROLOG.
comp.lang.python	The Python computer language.
comp.lang.sather	The object-oriented computer language Sather.
comp.lang.scheme	The Scheme Programming language.
comp.lang.sigplan	Info & announcements from ACM SIGPLAN. (Moderated)
comp.lang.smalltalk	Discussion about Smalltalk 80.
comp.lang.tcl	The Tcl programming language and related tools.
comp.lang.verilog	Discussing Verilog and PLI.
comp.lang.vhdl	VHSIC Hardware Description Language, IEEE 1076/87.
comp.laser-printers	Laser printers, hardware, and software. (Moderated)
comp.lsi	Large scale integrated circuits.
comp.lsi.testing	Testing of electronic circuits.
comp.mail.elm	Discussion and fixes for the ELM mail system.

continues

Table B.3
Continued

Newsgroup	Description
comp.mail.headers	Gatewayed from the Internet header-people list.
comp.mail.maps	Various maps, including UUCP maps. (Moderated)
comp.mail.mh	The UCI version of the Rand Message Handling system.
comp.mail.mime	Multipurpose Internet Mail Extensions of RFC 1341.
comp.mail.misc	General discussions about computer mail.
comp.mail.mush	The Mail User's Shell (MUSH).
comp.mail.pine	The PINE mail user agent.
comp.mail.sendmail	Configuring and using the BSD sendmail agent.
comp.mail.smail	Administering & using the smail email transport system.
comp.mail.uucp	Mail in the uucp network environment.
comp.misc	General topics about computers not covered elsewhere.
comp.multimedia	Interactive multimedia technologies of all kinds.
comp.newprod	Announcements of new products of interest. (Moderated)
comp.object	Object-oriented programming and languages.
comp.object.logic	Integrating object-oriented and logic programming.
comp.org.acm	Topics about the Association for Computing Machinery.
comp.org.cpsr.announce	Computer Professionals for Social Responsibility. (Moderated)
comp.org.cpsr.talk	Issues of computing and social responsibility.
comp.org.decus	Digital Equipment Computer Users' Society newsgroup.
comp.org.eff.news	News from the Electronic Frontier Foundation. (Moderated)
comp.org.eff.talk	Discussion of EFF goals, strategies, etc.
comp.org.fidonet	FidoNews digest, official news of FidoNet Assoc. (Moderated)
comp.org.ieee	Issues and announcements about the IEEE & its members.
comp.org.issnnet	The International Student Society for Neural Networks.
comp.org.lisp-users	Association of Lisp Users related discussions.
comp.org.sug	Talk about/for the The Sun User's Group.
comp.org.usenix	Usenix Association events and announcements.
comp.org.usenix.roomshare	Finding lodging during Usenix conferences.
comp.os.386bsd.announce	Announcements relating to the 386bsd operating system. (Moderated)
comp.os.386bsd.apps	Applications which run under 386bsd.
comp.os.386bsd.bugs	Bugs and fixes for the 386bsd OS and its clients.
comp.os.386bsd.development	Working on 386bsd internals.
comp.os.386bsd.misc	General aspects of 386bsd not covered by other groups.
comp.os.386bsd.questions	General questions about 386bsd.

Newsgroup	Description
comp.os.coherent	Discussion and support of the Coherent operating system.
comp.os.cpm	Discussion about the CP/M operating system.
comp.os.geos	The GEOS operating system by GeoWorks for PC clones.
comp.os.linux.admin	Installing and administering Linux systems.
comp.os.linux.announce	Announcements important to the Linux community. (Moderated)
comp.os.linux.development	Ongoing work on the Linux operating system.
comp.os.linux.help	Questions and advice about Linux.
comp.os.linux.misc	Linux-specific topics not covered by other groups.
comp.os.lynx	Discussion of LynxOS and Lynx Real-Time Systems.
comp.os.mach	The MACH OS from CMU & other places.
comp.os.minix	Discussion of Tanenbaum's MINIX system.
comp.os.misc	General OS-oriented discussion not carried elsewhere.
comp.os.ms-windows.advocacy	Speculation and debate about Microsoft Windows.
comp.os.ms-windows.announce	Announcements relating to Windows. (Moderated)
comp.os.ms-windows.apps	Applications in the Windows environment.
comp.os.ms-windows.apps.comm	MS-Windows communication applications.
comp.os.ms-windows.apps.financial	MS-Windows financial & tax software.
comp.os.ms-windows.apps.misc	MS-Windows applications.
comp.os.ms-windows.apps.utilities	MS-Windows utilities.
comp.os.ms-windows.apps.word-proc	MS-Windows word-processing applications.
comp.os.ms-windows.misc	General discussions about Windows issues.
comp.os.ms-windows.networking.misc	Windows and other networks.
comp.os.ms-windows.networking.tcp-ip	Windows and TCP/IP networking.
comp.os.ms-windows.networking.windows	Windows' built-in networking.
comp.os.ms-windows.nt.misc	General discussion about Windows NT.
comp.os.ms-windows.nt.setup	Configuring Windows NT systems.
comp.os.ms-windows.programmer.controls	Controls, dialogs, and VBXs.
comp.os.ms-windows.programmer.drivers	Win16/Win32 drivers and VxDs.
comp.os.ms-windows.programmer.graphics	GDI, graphics, and printing.
comp.os.ms-windows.programmer.memory	Memory management issues.
comp.os.ms-windows.programmer.misc	Programming Microsoft Windows.
comp.os.ms-windows.programmer.multimedia	Multimedia programming.
comp.os.ms-windows.programmer.networks	Network programming.

continues

Table B.3
Continued

Newsgroup	Description
comp.os.ms-windows.programmer.ole	OLE2, COM, and DDE programming.
comp.os.ms-windows.programmer.tools	Development tools in Windows.
comp.os.ms-windows.programmer.win32	32-bit Windows programming interfaces.
comp.os.ms-windows.programmer.winhelp	WinHelp/Multimedia Viewer development.
comp.os.ms-windows.setup	Installing and configuring Microsoft Windows.
comp.os.ms-windows.video	Video adapters and drivers for Windows.
comp.os.msdos.apps	Discussion of applications that run under MS-DOS.
comp.os.msdos.desqview	QuarterDeck's Desqview and related products.
comp.os.msdos.mail-news	Administering mail & network news systems under MS-DOS.
comp.os.msdos.misc	Miscellaneous topics about MS-DOS machines.
comp.os.msdos.pcgeos	GeoWorks PC/GEOS and PC/GEOS-based packages.
comp.os.msdos.programmer.	Programming MS-DOS machines.
comp.os.msdos	
programmer.turbovision	Borland's text application libraries.
comp.os.os2.advocacy	Supporting and flaming OS/2.
comp.os.os2.announce	Notable news and announcements related to OS/2. (Moderated)
comp.os.os2.apps	Discussions of applications under OS/2.
comp.os.os2.beta	All aspects of beta releases of OS/2 systems software.
comp.os.os2.bugs	OS/2 system bug reports, fixes, and work-arounds.
comp.os.os2.games	Running games under OS/2.
comp.os.os2.misc	Miscellaneous topics about the OS/2 system.
comp.os.os2.multimedia	Multimedia on OS/2 systems.
comp.os.os2.networking	Networking in OS/2 environments.
comp.os.os2.networking.misc	Miscellaneous networking issues of OS/2.
comp.os.os2.networking.tcp-ip	TCP/IP under OS/2.
comp.os.os2.programmer.misc	Programming OS/2 machines.
comp.os.os2.programmer.oop	Programming system objects (SOM, WPS, etc).
comp.os.os2.programmer.porting	Porting software to OS/2 machines.
comp.os.os2.programmer.tools	Compilers, assemblers, interpreters under OS/2.
comp.os.os2.setup	Installing and configuring OS/2 systems.
comp.os.os2.ver1x	All aspects of OS/2 versions 1.0 through 1.3.
comp.os.os9	Discussions about the OS/9 operating system.
comp.os.qnx	Using and developing under the QNX operating system.

Newsgroup	*Description*
comp.os.research	Operating systems and related areas. (Moderated)
comp.os.vms	DEC's VAX* line of computers & VMS.
comp.os.vxworks	The VxWorks real-time operating system.
comp.os.xinu	The XINU operating system from Purdue (D. Comer).
comp.parallel	Massively parallel hardware/software. (Moderated)
comp.parallel.pvm	The PVM system of multi-computer parallelization.
comp.patents	Discussing patents of computer technology. (Moderated)
comp.periphs	Peripheral devices.
comp.periphs.scsi	Discussion of SCSI-based peripheral devices.
comp.programming	Programming issues that transcend languages and OSs.
comp.programming.literate	Literate programs and programming tools.
comp.protocols.appletalk	Applebus hardware & software.
comp.protocols.dicom	Digital Imaging and Communications in Medicine.
comp.protocols.ibm	Networking with IBM mainframes.
comp.protocols.iso	The ISO protocol stack.
comp.protocols.kerberos	The Kerberos authentication server.
comp.protocols.kermit	Info about the Kermit package. (Moderated)
comp.protocols.misc	Various forms and types of protocol.
comp.protocols.nfs	Discussion about the Network File System protocol.
comp.protocols.ppp	Discussion of the Internet Point to Point Protocol.
comp.protocols.tcp-ip	TCP and IP network protocols.
comp.protocols.tcp-ip.ibmpc	TCP/IP for IBM(-like) personal computers.
comp.publish.cdrom.hardware	Hardware used in publishing with CD-ROM.
comp.publish.cdrom.multimedia	Software for multimedia authoring & publishing.
comp.publish.cdrom.software	Software used in publishing with CD-ROM.
comp.publish.prepress	Electronic prepress.
comp.realtime	Issues related to real-time computing.
comp.research.japan	The nature of research in Japan. (Moderated)
comp.risks	Risks to the public from computers & users. (Moderated)
comp.robotics	All aspects of robots and their applications.
comp.security.misc	Security issues of computers and networks.
comp.security.unix	Discussion of Unix security.
comp.simulation	Simulation methods, problems, uses. (Moderated)
comp.society	The impact of technology on society. (Moderated)
comp.society.cu-digest	The Computer Underground Digest. (Moderated)
comp.society.development	Computer technology in developing countries.

continues

Table B.3
Continued

Newsgroup	Description
comp.society.folklore	Computer folklore & culture, past, & present. (Moderated)
comp.society.futures	Events in technology affecting future computing.
comp.society.privacy	Effects of technology on privacy. (Moderated)
comp.soft-sys.khoros	The Khoros X11 visualization system.
comp.soft-sys.matlab	The MathWorks calculation and visualization package.
comp.soft-sys.powerbuilder	Application development tools from PowerSoft.
comp.soft-sys.ptolemy	The Ptolemy simulation/code generation environment.
comp.soft-sys.sas	The SAS statistics package.
comp.soft-sys.shazam	The SHAZAM econometrics computer program.
comp.soft-sys.spss	The SPSS statistics package.
comp.soft-sys.wavefront	Wavefront software products, problems, etc.
comp.software-eng	Software Engineering and related topics.
comp.software.config-mgmt	Configuration management, tools, and procedures.
comp.software.international	Finding, using, & writing non-English software.
comp.software.licensing	Software licensing technology.
comp.software.testing	All aspects of testing computer systems.
comp.sources.3b1	Source code-only postings for the AT&T 3b1. (Moderated)
comp.sources.acorn	Source code-only postings for the Acorn. (Moderated)
comp.sources.amiga	Source code-only postings for the Amiga. (Moderated)
comp.sources.apple2	Source code and discussion for the Apple2. (Moderated)
comp.sources.atari.st	Source code-only postings for the Atari ST. (Moderated)
comp.sources.bugs	Bug reports, fixes, discussion for posted sources.
comp.sources.d	For any discussion of source postings.
comp.sources.games	Postings of recreational software. (Moderated)
comp.sources.games.bugs	Bug reports and fixes for posted game software.
comp.sources.hp48	Programs for the HP48 and HP28 calculators. (Moderated)
comp.sources.mac	Software for the Apple Macintosh. (Moderated)
comp.sources.misc	Posting of software. (Moderated)
comp.sources.postscript	Source code for programs written in PostScript. (Moderated)
comp.sources.reviewed	Source code evaluated by peer review. (Moderated)
comp.sources.sun	Software for Sun workstations. (Moderated)
comp.sources.testers	Finding people to test software.
comp.sources.unix	Postings of complete, UNIX-oriented sources. (Moderated)
comp.sources.wanted	Requests for software and fixes.
comp.sources.x	Software for the X windows system. (Moderated)

Newsgroup	Description
comp.specification	Languages and methodologies for formal specification.
comp.specification.z	Discussion about the formal specification notation Z.
comp.speech	Research & applications in speech science & technology.
comp.std.c	Discussion about C language standards.
comp.std.c++	Discussion about C++ language, library, standards.
comp.std.internat	Discussion about international standards.
comp.std.lisp	User group (ALU) supported standards. (Moderated)
comp.std.misc	Discussion about various standards.
comp.std.mumps	Discussion for the X11.1 committee on Mumps. (Moderated)
comp.std.unix	Discussion for the P1003 committee on UNIX. (Moderated)
comp.std.wireless	Examining standards for wireless network technology. (Moderated)
comp.sw.components	Software components and related technology.
comp.sys.3b1	Discussion and support of AT&T 7300/3B1/UnixPC.
comp.sys.acorn	Discussion on Acorn and ARM-based computers.
comp.sys.acorn.advocacy	Why Acorn computers and programs are better.
comp.sys.acorn.announce	Announcements for Acorn and ARM users. (Moderated)
comp.sys.acorn.games	Discussion of games for Acorn machines.
comp.sys.acorn.tech	Software and hardware aspects of Acorn and ARM products.
comp.sys.alliant	Info and discussion about Alliant computers.
comp.sys.amiga.advocacy	Why an Amiga is better than XYZ.
comp.sys.amiga.announce	Announcements about the Amiga. (Moderated)
comp.sys.amiga.applications	Miscellaneous applications.
comp.sys.amiga.audio	Music, MIDI, speech synthesis, other sounds.
comp.sys.amiga.cd32	Technical and computing talk for Commodore Amiga CD32.
comp.sys.amiga.datacomm	Methods of getting bytes in and out.
comp.sys.amiga.emulations	Various hardware & software emulators.
comp.sys.amiga.games	Discussion of games for the Commodore Amiga.
comp.sys.amiga.graphics	Charts, graphs, pictures, etc.
comp.sys.amiga.hardware	Amiga computer hardware, Q&A, reviews, etc.
comp.sys.amiga.introduction	Group for newcomers to Amigas.
comp.sys.amiga.marketplace	Where to find it, prices, etc.
comp.sys.amiga.misc	Discussions not falling in another Amiga group.
comp.sys.amiga.multimedia	Animations, video, and multimedia.
comp.sys.amiga.programmer	Developers & hobbyists discuss code.
comp.sys.amiga.reviews	Reviews of Amiga software, hardware. (Moderated)

continues

Table B.3
Continued

Newsgroup	Description
comp.sys.apollo	Apollo computer systems.
comp.sys.apple2	Discussion about Apple II micros.
comp.sys.apple2.comm	Apple II data communications.
comp.sys.apple2.gno	The AppleIIgs GNO multitasking environment.
comp.sys.apple2.marketplace	Buying, selling, and trading Apple II equipment.
comp.sys.apple2.programmer	Programming on the Apple II.
comp.sys.apple2.usergroups	All about Apple II user groups.
comp.sys.atari.8bit	Discussion about 8 bit Atari micros.
comp.sys.atari.advocacy	Attacking and defending Atari computers.
comp.sys.atari.st	Discussion about 16 bit Atari micros.
comp.sys.atari.st.tech	Technical discussions of Atari ST hard/software.
comp.sys.att	Discussions about AT&T microcomputers.
comp.sys.cbm	Discussion about Commodore micros.
comp.sys.concurrent	The Concurrent/Masscomp line of computers. (Moderated)
comp.sys.convex	Convex computer systems hardware and software.
comp.sys.dec	Discussions about DEC computer systems.
comp.sys.dec.micro	DEC Micros (Rainbow, Professional 350/380).
comp.sys.encore	Encore's MultiMax computers.
comp.sys.harris	Harris computer systems, especially real-time systems.
comp.sys.hp.apps	Discussion of software and apps on all HP platforms.
comp.sys.hp.hardware	Discussion of Hewlett Packard system hardware.
comp.sys.hp.hpux	Issues pertaining to HP-UX & 9000 series computers.
comp.sys.hp.misc	Issues not covered in any other comp.sys.hp.* group.
comp.sys.hp.mpe	Issues pertaining to MPE & 3000 series computers.
comp.sys.hp48	Hewlett-Packard's HP48 and HP28 calculators.
comp.sys.ibm.pc.demos	Demonstration programs which showcase programmer skill.
comp.sys.ibm.pc.digest	The IBM PC, PC-XT, and PC-AT. (Moderated)
comp.sys.ibm.pc.games.action	Arcade-style games on PCs.
comp.sys.ibm.pc.games.adventure	Adventure (non-rpg) games on PCs.
comp.sys.ibm.pc.games.announce	Announcements for all PC gamers. (Moderated)
comp.sys.ibm.pc.games.flight-sim	Flight simulators on PCs.
comp.sys.ibm.pc.games.misc	Games not covered by other PC groups.
comp.sys.ibm.pc.games.rpg	Role-playing games on the PC.
comp.sys.ibm.pc.games.strategic	Strategy/planning games on PCs.
comp.sys.ibm.pc.hardware.cd-rom	CD-ROM drives and interfaces for the PC.

Newsgroup	Description
comp.sys.ibm.pc.hardware.chips	Processor, cache, memory chips, etc.
comp.sys.ibm.pc.hardware.comm	Modems & communication cards for the PC.
comp.sys.ibm.pc.hardware.misc	Miscellaneous PC hardware topics.
comp.sys.ibm.pc.hardware.networking	Network hardware & equipment for the PC.
comp.sys.ibm.pc.hardware.storage	Hard drives & other PC storage devices.
comp.sys.ibm.pc.hardware.systems	Whole IBM PC computer & clone systems.
comp.sys.ibm.pc.hardware.video	Video cards & monitors for the PC.
comp.sys.ibm.pc.misc	Discussion about IBM personal computers.
comp.sys.ibm.pc.rt	Topics related to IBM's RT computer.
comp.sys.ibm.pc.soundcard	Hardware and software aspects of PC sound cards.
comp.sys.ibm.ps2.hardware	Microchannel hardware, any vendor.
comp.sys.intel	Discussions about Intel systems and parts.
comp.sys.isis	The ISIS distributed system from Cornell.
comp.sys.laptops	Laptop (portable) computers.
comp.sys.m6809	Discussion about 6809s.
comp.sys.m68k	Discussion about 68ks.
comp.sys.m68k.pc	Discussion about 68k-based PCs. (Moderated)
comp.sys.m88k	Discussion about 88k-based computers.
comp.sys.mac.advocacy	The Macintosh computer family compared to others.
comp.sys.mac.announce	Important notices for Macintosh users. (Moderated)
comp.sys.mac.apps	Discussions of Macintosh applications.
comp.sys.mac.comm	Discussion of Macintosh communications.
comp.sys.mac.databases	Database systems for the Apple Macintosh.
comp.sys.mac.digest	Apple Macintosh: info & uses, but no programs. (Moderated)
comp.sys.mac.games	Discussions of games on the Macintosh.
comp.sys.mac.graphics	Macintosh graphics: paint, draw, 3D, CAD, animation.
comp.sys.mac.hardware	Macintosh hardware issues & discussions.
comp.sys.mac.hypercard	The Macintosh Hypercard: info & uses.
comp.sys.mac.misc	General discussions about the Apple Macintosh.
comp.sys.mac.oop.macapp3	Version 3 of the MacApp object-oriented system.
comp.sys.mac.oop.misc	Object-oriented programming issues on the Mac.
comp.sys.mac.oop.tcl	Symantec's THINK Class Library for object programming.
comp.sys.mac.portables	Discussion particular to laptop Macintoshes.
comp.sys.mac.programmer	Discussion by people programming the Apple Macintosh.
comp.sys.mac.scitech	Using the Macintosh in scientific & technological work.
comp.sys.mac.system	Discussions of Macintosh system software.

continues

Appendix B
Newsgroup
List

Table B.3
Continued

Newsgroup	Description
comp.sys.mac.wanted	Postings of "I want XYZ for my Mac."
comp.sys.mentor	Mentor Graphics products & the Silicon Compiler System.
comp.sys.mips	Systems based on MIPS chips.
comp.sys.misc	Discussion about computers of all kinds.
comp.sys.ncr	Discussion about NCR computers.
comp.sys.newton.announce	Newton information posts. (Moderated)
comp.sys.newton.misc	Miscellaneous discussion about Newton systems.
comp.sys.newton.programmer	Discussion of Newton software development.
comp.sys.next.advocacy	The NeXT religion.
comp.sys.next.announce	Announcements related to the NeXT computer system. (Moderated)
comp.sys.next.bugs	Discussion and solutions for known NeXT bugs.
comp.sys.next.hardware	Discussing the physical aspects of NeXT computers.
comp.sys.next.marketplace	NeXT hardware, software, and jobs.
comp.sys.next.misc	General discussion about the NeXT computer system.
comp.sys.next.programmer	NeXT related programming issues.
comp.sys.next.software	Function, use, and availability of NeXT programs.
comp.sys.next.sysadmin	Discussions related to NeXT system administration.
comp.sys.novell	Discussion of Novell Netware products.
comp.sys.nsc.32k	National Semiconductor 32000 series chips.
comp.sys.palmtops	Super-powered calculators in the palm of your hand.
comp.sys.pen	Interacting with computers through pen gestures.
comp.sys.powerpc	General PowerPC Discussion.
comp.sys.prime	Prime Computer products.
comp.sys.proteon	Proteon gateway products.
comp.sys.psion	Discussion about PSION Personal Computers & Organizers.
comp.sys.pyramid	Pyramid 90x computers.
comp.sys.ridge	Ridge 32 computers and ROS.
comp.sys.sequent	Sequent systems, (Balance and Symmetry).
comp.sys.sgi.admin	System administration on Silicon Graphics' Irises.
comp.sys.sgi.announce	Announcements for the SGI community. (Moderated)
comp.sys.sgi.apps	Applications which run on the Iris.
comp.sys.sgi.bugs	Bugs found in the IRIX operating system.
comp.sys.sgi.graphics	Graphics packages and issues on SGI machines.
comp.sys.sgi.hardware	Base systems and peripherals for Iris computers.

Newsgroup	Description
comp.sys.sgi.misc	General discussion about Silicon Graphics's machines.
comp.sys.sinclair	Sinclair computers, eg. the ZX81, Spectrum, and QL.
comp.sys.stratus	Stratus products, incl. System/88, CPS-32, VOS, and FTX.
comp.sys.sun.admin	Sun system administration issues and questions.
comp.sys.sun.announce	Sun announcements and Sunergy mailings. (Moderated)
comp.sys.sun.apps	Software applications for Sun computer systems.
comp.sys.sun.hardware	Sun Microsystems hardware.
comp.sys.sun.misc	Miscellaneous discussions about Sun products.
comp.sys.sun.wanted	People looking for Sun products and support.
comp.sys.tahoe	CCI 6/32, Harris HCX/7, & Sperry 7000 computers.
comp.sys.tandy	Discussion about Tandy computers: new & old.
comp.sys.ti	Discussion about Texas Instruments.
comp.sys.transputer	The Transputer computer and OCCAM language.
comp.sys.unisys	Sperry, Burroughs, Convergent and Unisys* systems.
comp.sys.xerox	Xerox 1100 workstations and protocols.
comp.sys.zenith.z100	The Zenith Z-100 (Heath H-100) family of computers.
comp.terminals	All sorts of terminals.
comp.text	Text processing issues and methods.
comp.text.desktop	Technology & techniques of desktop publishing.
comp.text.frame	Desktop publishing with FrameMaker.
comp.text.interleaf	Applications and use of Interleaf software.
comp.text.sgml	ISO 8879 SGML, structured documents, markup languages.
comp.text.tex	Discussion about the TeX and LaTeX systems & macros.
comp.theory.info-retrieval	Information Retrieval topics. (Moderated)
comp.unix.admin	Administering a UNIX-based system.
comp.unix.advocacy	Arguments for and against UNIX and UNIX versions.
comp.unix.aix	IBM's version of UNIX.
comp.unix.amiga	Minix, SYSV4 and other *nix on an Amiga.
comp.unix.aux	The version of UNIX for Apple Macintosh II computers.
comp.unix.bsd	Discussion of Berkeley Software Distribution UNIX.
comp.unix.dos-under-unix	MS-DOS running under UNIX by whatever means.
comp.unix.internals	Discussions on hacking UNIX internals.
comp.unix.large	UNIX on mainframes and in large networks.
comp.unix.misc	Various topics that don't fit other groups.
comp.unix.osf.misc	Various aspects of Open Software Foundation products.
comp.unix.osf.osf1	The Open Software Foundation's OSF/1.

Appendix B
Newsgroup
List

continues

Table B.3
Continued

Newsgroup	Description
comp.unix.pc-clone.16bit	UNIX on 286 architectures.
comp.unix.pc-clone.32bit	UNIX on 386 and 486 architectures.
comp.unix.programmer	Q&A for people programming under UNIX.
comp.unix.questions	UNIX neophytes group.
comp.unix.shell	Using and programming the UNIX shell.
comp.unix.sys3	System III UNIX discussions.
comp.unix.sys5.misc	Versions of System V which predate Release 3.
comp.unix.sys5.r3	Discussing System V Release 3.
comp.unix.sys5.r4	Discussing System V Release 4.
comp.unix.ultrix	Discussions about DEC's UNIX.
comp.unix.unixware	Discussion about Novell's UnixWare products.
comp.unix.user-friendly	Discussion of UNIX user-friendliness.
comp.unix.wizards	For only true Unix wizards. (Moderated)
comp.unix.xenix.misc	General discussions regarding XENIX (except SCO).
comp.unix.xenix.sco	XENIX versions from the Santa Cruz Operation.
comp.virus	Computer viruses & security. (Moderated)
comp.windows.garnet	The Garnet user interface development environment.
comp.windows.interviews	The InterViews object-oriented windowing system.
comp.windows.misc	Various issues about windowing systems.
comp.windows.news	Sun Microsystems' NeWS window system.
comp.windows.open-look	Discussion about the Open Look GUI.
comp.windows.suit	The SUIT user-interface toolkit.
comp.windows.x	Discussion about the X Window System.
comp.windows.x.apps	Getting and using, not programming, applications for X.
comp.windows.x.i386unix	The XFree86 window system and others.
comp.windows.x.intrinsics	Discussion of the X toolkit.
comp.windows.x.pex	The PHIGS extension of the X Window System.
misc.activism.progressive	Information for Progressive activists. (Moderated)
misc.answers	Repository for periodic USENET articles. (Moderated)
misc.books.technical	Discussion of books about technical topics.
misc.consumers	Consumer interests, product reviews, etc.
misc.consumers.house	Discussion about owning and maintaining a house.
misc.creativity	Promoting the use of creativity in all human endeavors.
misc.education	Discussion of the educational system.
misc.education.adult	Adult education and adult literacy practice/research.

Newsgroup	Description
misc.education.language.english	Teaching English to speakers of other languages.
misc.education.multimedia	Multimedia for education. (Moderated)
misc.education.science	Issues related to science education.
misc.emerg-services	Forum for paramedics & other first responders.
misc.entrepreneurs	Discussion on operating a business.
misc.fitness	Physical fitness, exercise, bodybuilding, etc.
misc.forsale	Short, tasteful postings about items for sale.
misc.forsale.computers.d	Discussion of misc.forsale.computers.*
misc.forsale.computers.mac	Apple Macintosh-related computer items.
misc.forsale.computers.other	Selling miscellaneous computer stuff.
misc.forsale.computers.pc-clone	IBM PC related computer items.
misc.forsale.computers.workstation	Workstation related computer items.
misc.handicap	Items of interest for/about the handicapped. (Moderated)
misc.headlines	Current interest: drug testing, terrorism, etc.
misc.health.alternative	Alternative, complementary, and holistic health care.
misc.health.diabetes	Discussion of diabetes management in day to day life.
misc.int-property	Discussion of intellectual property rights.
misc.invest	Investments and the handling of money.
misc.invest.canada	Investing in Canadian financial markets.
misc.invest.funds	Sharing info about bond, stock, real estate funds.
misc.invest.real-estate	Property investments.
misc.invest.stocks	Forum for sharing info about stocks and options.
misc.invest.technical	Analyzing market trends with technical methods.
misc.jobs.contract	Discussions about contract labor.
misc.jobs.misc	Discussion about employment, workplaces, careers.
misc.jobs.offered	Announcements of positions available.
misc.jobs.offered.entry	Job listings only for entry-level positions.
misc.jobs.resumes	Postings of resumes and "situation wanted" articles.
misc.kids	Children, their behavior and activities.
misc.kids.computer	The use of computers by children.
misc.kids.vacation	Discussion on all forms of family-oriented vacationing.
misc.legal	Legalities and the ethics of law.
misc.legal.computing	Discussing the legal climate of the computing world.
misc.legal.moderated	All aspects of law. (Moderated)
misc.misc	Various discussions not fitting in any other group.
misc.newmisc.s.east-europe.rferl	Radio Free Europe/Radio Liberty Daily Report. (Moderated)

continues

Table B.3
Continued

Newsgroup	Description
misc.news.southasia	News from Bangladesh, India, Nepal, etc. (Moderated)
misc.rural	Devoted to issues concerning rural living.
misc.taxes	Tax laws and advice.
misc.test	For testing of network software. Very boring.
misc.test.moderated	Testing of posting to moderated groups. (Moderated)
misc.wanted	Requests for things that are needed (NOT software).
misc.writing	Discussion of writing in all of its forms.
news.admin.misc	General topics of network news administration.
news.admin.policy	Policy issues of USENET.
news.admin.technical	Technical aspects of maintaining network news. (Moderated)
news.announce.conferences	Calls for papers and conference announcements. (Moderated)
news.announce.important	General announcements of interest to all. (Moderated)
news.announce.newgroups	Calls for newgroups & announcements of same. (Moderated)
news.announce.newusers	Explanatory postings for new users. (Moderated)
news.answers	Repository for periodic USENET articles. (Moderated)
news.config	Postings of system down times and interruptions.
news.future	The future technology of network news systems.
news.groups	Discussions and lists of newsgroups.
news.groups.questions	Where can I find talk about topic X?
news.groups.reviews	What is going on in group or mailing list named X? (Moderated)
news.lists	News-related statistics and lists. (Moderated)
news.lists.ps-maps	Maps relating to USENET traffic flows. (Moderated)
news.misc	Discussions of USENET itself.
news.newsites	Postings of new site announcements.
news.newusers.questions	Q & A for users new to the Usenet.
news.software.anu-news	VMS B-news software from Australian National Univ.
news.software.b	Discussion about B-news-compatible software.
news.software.nn	Discussion about the "nn" news reader package.
news.software.notes	Notesfile software from the Univ. of Illinois.
news.software.readers	Discussion of software used to read network news.
rec.answers	Repository for periodic USENET articles. (Moderated)
rec.antiques	Discussing antiques and vintage items.
rec.aquaria	Keeping fish and aquaria as a hobby.
rec.arts.animation	Discussion of various kinds of animation.

Newsgroup	Description
rec.arts.anime	Japanese animation fen discussion.
rec.arts.anime.info	Announcements about Japanese animation. (Moderated)
rec.arts.anime.marketplace	Things for sale in the Japanese animation world.
rec.arts.anime.stories	All about Japanese comic fanzines. (Moderated)
rec.arts.bodyart	Tattoos and body decoration discussions.
rec.arts.bonsai	Dwarfish trees and shrubbery.
rec.arts.books	Books of all genres, and the publishing industry.
rec.arts.books.marketplace	Buying and selling of books.
rec.arts.books.tolkien	The works of J.R.R. Tolkien.
rec.arts.cinema	Discussion of the art of cinema. (Moderated)
rec.arts.comics.info	Reviews, convention information and other comics news. (Moderated)
rec.arts.comics.marketplace	The exchange of comics and comic related items.
rec.arts.comics.misc	Comic books, graphic novels, sequential art.
rec.arts.comics.strips	Discussion of short-form comics.
rec.arts.comics.xbooks	The Mutant Universe of Marvel Comics.
rec.arts.dance	Any aspects of dance not covered in another newsgroup.
rec.arts.disney	Discussion of any Disney-related subjects.
rec.arts.drwho	Discussion about Dr. Who.
rec.arts.erotica	Erotic fiction and verse. (Moderated)
rec.arts.fine	Fine arts & artists.
rec.arts.int-fiction	Discussions about interactive fiction.
rec.arts.manga	All aspects of the Japanese storytelling art form.
rec.arts.marching.drumcorps	Drum and bugle corps.
rec.arts.marching.misc	Marching-related performance activities.
rec.arts.misc	Discussions about the arts not in other groups.
rec.arts.movies	Discussions of movies and movie making.
rec.arts.movies.reviews	Reviews of movies. (Moderated)
rec.arts.poems	For the posting of poems.
rec.arts.prose	Short works of prose fiction and followup discussion.
rec.arts.sf.announce	Major announcements of the SF world. (Moderated)
rec.arts.sf.fandom	Discussions of SF fan activities.
rec.arts.sf.marketplace	Personal forsale notices of SF materials.
rec.arts.sf.misc	Science fiction lovers' newsgroup.
rec.arts.sf.movies	Discussing SF motion pictures.
rec.arts.sf.reviews	Reviews of science fiction/fantasy/horror works. (Moderated)

Appendix B
Newsgroup
List

continues

Table B.3
Continued

Newsgroup	Description
rec.arts.sf.science	Real and speculative aspects of SF science.
rec.arts.sf.starwars	Discussion of the Star Wars universe.
rec.arts.sf.tv	Discussing general television SF.
rec.arts.sf.tv.babylon5	Babylon 5 creators meet Babylon 5 fans.
rec.arts.sf.tv.quantum-leap	Quantum Leap TV, comics, cons, etc.
rec.arts.sf.written	Discussion of written science fiction and fantasy.
rec.arts.startrek.current	New Star Trek shows, movies, and books.
rec.arts.startrek.fandom	Star Trek conventions and memorabilia.
rec.arts.startrek.info	Information about the universe of Star Trek. (Moderated)
rec.arts.startrek.misc	General discussions of Star Trek.
rec.arts.startrek.reviews	Reviews of Star Trek books, episodes, films. (Moderated)
rec.arts.startrek.tech	Star Trek's depiction of future technologies.
rec.arts.theatre	Discussion of all aspects of stage work & theatre.
rec.arts.theatre.misc	Miscellaneous topics and issues in theatre.
rec.arts.theatre.musicals	Musical theatre around the world.
rec.arts.theatre.plays	Dramaturgy and discussion of plays.
rec.arts.theatre.stagecraft	Issues in stagecraft and production.
rec.arts.tv	The boob tube, its history, and past and current shows.
rec.arts.tv.mst3k	For fans of Mystery Science Theater 3000.
rec.arts.tv.soaps	Postings about soap operas.
rec.arts.tv.uk	Discussions of telly shows from the UK.
rec.arts.wobegon	"A Prairie Home Companion" radio show discussion.
rec.audio	High fidelity audio.
rec.audio.car	Discussions of automobile audio systems.
rec.audio.high-end	High-end audio systems. (Moderated)
rec.audio.marketplace	Buying and selling of home audio equipment.
rec.audio.misc	Post about audio here if you can't post anywhere else.
rec.audio.opinion	Everybody's two bits on audio in your home.
rec.audio.pro	Professional audio recording and studio engineering.
rec.audio.tech	Theoretical, factual, and DIY topics in home audio.
rec.autos.antique	Discussing all aspects of automobiles over 25 years old.
rec.autos.driving	Driving automobiles.
rec.autos.marketplace	Buy/Sell/Trade automobiles, parts, tools, accessories.
rec.autos.misc	Miscellaneous discussion about automobiles.
rec.autos.rod-n-custom	High performance automobiles.

Newsgroup	Description
rec.autos.simulators	Discussion of automotive simulators.
rec.autos.sport	Discussion of organized, legal auto competitions.
rec.autos.sport.info	Auto racing news, results, announcements. (Moderated)
rec.autos.sport.nascar	NASCAR and other professional stock car racing.
rec.autos.sport.tech	Technical aspects & technology of auto racing.
rec.autos.tech	Technical aspects of automobiles, et. al.
rec.autos.vw	Issues pertaining to Volkswagen products.
rec.aviation.announce	Events of interest to the aviation community. (Moderated)
rec.aviation.answers	Frequently asked questions about aviation. (Moderated)
rec.aviation.homebuilt	Selecting, designing, building, and restoring aircraft.
rec.aviation.ifr	Flying under Instrument Flight Rules.
rec.aviation.military	Military aircraft of the past, present, and future.
rec.aviation.misc	Miscellaneous topics in aviation.
rec.aviation.owning	Information on owning airplanes.
rec.aviation.piloting	General discussion for aviators.
rec.aviation.products	Reviews and discussion of products useful to pilots.
rec.aviation.questions	Aviation questions and answers. (Moderated)
rec.aviation.simulators	Flight simulation on all levels.
rec.aviation.soaring	All aspects of sailplanes and hang-gliders.
rec.aviation.stories	Anecdotes of flight experiences. (Moderated)
rec.aviation.student	Learning to fly.
rec.backcountry	Activities in the Great Outdoors.
rec.bicycles.marketplace	Buying, selling, and reviewing items for cycling.
rec.bicycles.misc	General discussion of bicycling.
rec.bicycles.racing	Bicycle racing techniques, rules and results.
rec.bicycles.rides	Discussions of tours and training or commuting routes.
rec.bicycles.soc	Societal issues of bicycling.
rec.bicycles.tech	Cycling product design, construction, maintenance, etc.
rec.birds	Hobbyists interested in bird watching.
rec.boats	Hobbyists interested in boating.
rec.boats.paddle	Talk about any boats with oars, paddles, etc.
rec.climbing	Climbing techniques, competition announcements, etc.
rec.collecting	Discussion among collectors of many things.
rec.collecting.cards	Collecting all sorts of sport and non-sport cards.
rec.collecting.stamps	Discussion of all things related to philately.
rec.crafts.brewing	The art of making beers and meads.

continues

Table B.3
Continued

Newsgroup	Description
rec.crafts.jewelry	All aspects of jewelry making and lapidary work.
rec.crafts.metalworking	All aspects of working with metal.
rec.crafts.misc	Handiwork arts not covered elsewhere.
rec.crafts.quilting	All about quilts and other quilted items.
rec.crafts.textiles	Sewing, weaving, knitting, and other fiber arts.
rec.crafts.winemaking	The tasteful art of making wine.
rec.equestrian	Discussion of things equestrian.
rec.folk-dancing	Folk dances, dancers, and dancing.
rec.food.cooking	Food, cooking, cookbooks, and recipes.
rec.food.drink	Wines and spirits.
rec.food.drink.beer	All things beer.
rec.food.drink.coffee	The making and drinking of coffee.
rec.food.historic	The history of food making arts.
rec.food.recipes	Recipes for interesting food and drink. (Moderated)
rec.food.restaurants	Discussion of dining out.
rec.food.sourdough	Making and baking with sourdough.
rec.food.veg	Vegetarians.
rec.food.veg.cooking	Vegetarian recipes, cooking, nutrition. (Moderated)
rec.gambling	Articles on games of chance & betting.
rec.games.abstract	Perfect information, pure strategy games.
rec.games.backgammon	Discussion of the game of backgammon.
rec.games.board	Discussion and hints on board games.
rec.games.board.ce	The Cosmic Encounter board game.
rec.games.board.marketplace	Trading and selling of board games.
rec.games.bolo	The networked strategy war game Bolo.
rec.games.bridge	Hobbyists interested in bridge.
rec.games.chess	Chess & computer chess.
rec.games.chinese-chess	Discussion of the game of Chinese chess, Xiangqi.
rec.games.corewar	The Core War computer challenge.
rec.games.deckmaster	The Deckmaster line of games.
rec.games.design	Discussion of game design related issues.
rec.games.diplomacy	The conquest game Diplomacy.
rec.games.empire	Discussion and hints about Empire.
rec.games.frp.advocacy	Flames and rebuttals about various role-playing systems.

Newsgroup	Description
rec.games.frp.announce	Announcements of happenings in the role-playing world. (Moderated)
rec.games.frp.archives	Archivable fantasy stories and other projects. (Moderated)
rec.games.frp.cyber	Discussions of cyberpunk related roleplaying games.
rec.games.frp.dnd	Fantasy role-playing with TSR's Dungeons and Dragons.
rec.games.frp.live-action	Live-action roleplaying games.
rec.games.frp.marketplace	Role-playing game materials wanted and for sale.
rec.games.frp.misc	General discussions of role-playing games.
rec.games.go	Discussion about Go.
rec.games.hack	Discussion, hints, etc. about the Hack game.
rec.games.int-fiction	All aspects of interactive fiction games.
rec.games.mecha	Giant robot games.
rec.games.miniatures	Tabletop wargaming.
rec.games.misc	Games and computer games.
rec.games.moria	Comments, hints, and info about the Moria game.
rec.games.mud.admin	Administrative issues of multiuser dungeons.
rec.games.mud.announce	Informational articles about multiuser dungeons. (Moderated)
rec.games.mud.diku	All about DikuMuds.
rec.games.mud.lp	Discussions of the LPMUD computer role-playing game.
rec.games.mud.misc	Various aspects of multiuser computer games.
rec.games.mud.tiny	Discussion about Tiny muds, like MUSH, MUSE, and MOO.
rec.games.netrek	Discussion of the X window system game Netrek (XtrekII).
rec.games.pbm	Discussion about Play by Mail games.
rec.games.pinball	Discussing pinball-related issues.
rec.games.programmer	Discussion of adventure game programming.
rec.games.rogue	Discussion and hints about Rogue.
rec.games.roguelike.angband	The computer game Angband.
rec.games.roguelike.announce	Major info about rogue-styled games. (Moderated)
rec.games.roguelike.misc	Rogue-style dungeon games without other groups.
rec.games.trivia	Discussion about trivia.
rec.games.video.3do	Discussion of 3DO video game systems.
rec.games.video.advocacy	Debate on merits of various video game systems.
rec.games.video.arcade	Discussions about coin-operated video games.
rec.games.video.arcade.collecting	Collecting, converting, repairing etc.
rec.games.video.atari	Discussion of Atari's video game systems.
rec.games.video.cd32	Gaming talk, info and help for the Amiga CD32.

continues

Appendix B
Newsgroup
List

Table B.3
Continued

Newsgroup	Description
rec.games.video.classic	Older home video entertainment systems.
rec.games.video.marketplace	Home video game stuff for sale or trade.
rec.games.video.misc	General discussion about home video games.
rec.games.video.nintendo	All Nintendo video game systems and software.
rec.games.video.sega	All Sega video game systems and software.
rec.games.xtank.play	Strategy and tactics for the distributed game Xtank.
rec.games.xtank.programmer	Coding the Xtank game and its robots.
rec.gardens	Gardening, methods, and results.
rec.guns	Discussions about firearms. (Moderated)
rec.heraldry	Discussion of coats of arms.
rec.humor	Jokes and the like. May be somewhat offensive.
rec.humor.d	Discussions on the content of rec.humor articles.
rec.humor.funny	Jokes that are funny (in the moderator's opinion). (Moderated)
rec.humor.oracle	Sagacious advice from the USENET Oracle. (Moderated)
rec.humor.oracle.d	Comments about the USENET Oracle's comments.
rec.hunting	Discussions about hunting. (Moderated)
rec.juggling	Juggling techniques, equipment, and events.
rec.kites	Talk about kites and kiting.
rec.mag	Magazine summaries, tables of contents, etc.
rec.martial-arts	Discussion of the various martial art forms.
rec.misc	General topics about recreational/participant sports.
rec.models.railroad	Model railroads of all scales.
rec.models.rc	Radio-controlled models for hobbyists.
rec.models.rockets	Model rockets for hobbyists.
rec.models.scale	Construction of models.
rec.motorcycles	Motorcycles and related products and laws.
rec.motorcycles.dirt	Riding motorcycles and ATVs off-road.
rec.motorcycles.harley	All aspects of Harley-Davidson motorcycles.
rec.motorcycles.racing	Discussion of all aspects of racing motorcycles.
rec.music.a-cappella	Vocal music without instrumental accompaniment.
rec.music.afro-latin	Music with Afro-Latin, African, and Latin influences.
rec.music.beatles	Postings about the Fab Four & their music.
rec.music.bluenote	Discussion of jazz, blues, and related types of music.
rec.music.cd	CDs—availability and other discussions.
rec.music.celtic	Traditional and modern music with a Celtic flavor.

Newsgroup	Description
rec.music.christian	Christian music, both contemporary and traditional.
rec.music.classical	Discussion about classical music.
rec.music.classical.guitar	Classical music performed on guitar.
rec.music.classical.performing	Performing classical (including early) music.
rec.music.compose	Creating musical and lyrical works.
rec.music.country.western	C&W music, performers, performances, etc.
rec.music.dementia	Discussion of comedy and novelty music.
rec.music.dylan	Discussion of Bob's works & music.
rec.music.early	Discussion of pre-classical European music.
rec.music.folk	Folks discussing folk music of various sorts.
rec.music.funky	Funk, rap, hip-hop, house, soul, r&b, and related.
rec.music.gaffa	Discussion of Kate Bush & other alternative music. (Moderated)
rec.music.gdead	A group for (Grateful) Dead-heads.
rec.music.indian.classical	Hindustani and Carnatic Indian classical music.
rec.music.indian.misc	Discussing Indian music in general.
rec.music.industrial	Discussion of all industrial-related music styles.
rec.music.info	News and announcements on musical topics. (Moderated)
rec.music.makers	For performers and their discussions.
rec.music.makers.bass	Upright bass and bass guitar techniques and equipment.
rec.music.makers.builders	Design, building, repair of musical instruments.
rec.music.makers.guitar	Electric and acoustic guitar techniques and equipment.
rec.music.makers.guitar.acoustic	Discussion of acoustic guitar playing.
rec.music.makers.guitar.tablature	Guitar tablature/chords.
rec.music.makers.marketplace	Buying & selling used music-making equipment.
rec.music.makers.percussion	Drum & other percussion techniques & equipment.
rec.music.makers.piano	Piano music, performing, composing, learning, styles.
rec.music.makers.synth	Synthesizers and computer music.
rec.music.marketplace	Records, tapes, and CDs: wanted, for sale, etc.
rec.music.misc	Music lovers' group.
rec.music.movies	Music for movies and television.
rec.music.newage	"New Age" music discussions.
rec.music.phish	Discussing the musical group Phish.
rec.music.reggae	Roots, Rockers, Dancehall Reggae.
rec.music.rem	The musical group R.E.M.

continues

Table B.3

Continued

Newsgroup	Description
rec.music.reviews	Reviews of music of all genres and mediums. (Moderated)
rec.music.video	Discussion of music videos and music video software.
rec.nude	Hobbyists interested in naturist/nudist activities.
rec.org.mensa	Talking with members of the high IQ society Mensa.
rec.org.sca	Society for Creative Anachronism.
rec.outdoors.fishing	All aspects of sport and commercial fishing.
rec.outdoors.fishing.fly	Fly fishing in general.
rec.parks.theme	Entertainment theme parks.
rec.pets	Pets, pet care, and household animals in general.
rec.pets.birds	The culture and care of indoor birds.
rec.pets.cats	Discussion about domestic cats.
rec.pets.dogs	Any and all subjects relating to dogs as pets.
rec.pets.herp	Reptiles, amphibians and other exotic vivarium pets.
rec.photo	Hobbyists interested in photography.
rec.puzzles	Puzzles, problems, and quizzes.
rec.puzzles.crosswords	Making and playing gridded word puzzles.
rec.pyrotechnics	Fireworks, rocketry, safety, and other topics.
rec.radio.amateur.antenna	Antennas: theory, techniques, and construction.
rec.radio.amateur.digital.misc	Packet radio and other digital radio modes.
rec.radio.amateur.equipment	All about production amateur radio hardware.
rec.radio.amateur.homebrew	Amateur radio construction and experimentation.
rec.radio.amateur.misc	Amateur radio practices, contests, events, rules, etc.
rec.radio.amateur.policy	Radio use & regulation policy.
rec.radio.amateur.space	Amateur radio transmissions through space.
rec.radio.broadcasting	Discussion of global domestic broadcast radio. (Moderated)
rec.radio.cb	Citizen-band radio.
rec.radio.info	Informational postings related to radio. (Moderated)
rec.radio.noncomm	Topics relating to noncommercial radio.
rec.radio.scanner	"Utility" broadcasting traffic above 30 MHz.
rec.radio.shortwave	Shortwave radio enthusiasts.
rec.radio.swap	Offers to trade and swap radio equipment.
rec.railroad	For fans of real trains, ferroequinologists.
rec.roller-coaster	Roller coasters and other amusement park rides.
rec.running	Running for enjoyment, sport, exercise, etc.
rec.scouting	Scouting youth organizations worldwide.

Newsgroup	Description
rec.scuba	Hobbyists interested in SCUBA diving.
rec.skate	Ice skating and roller skating.
rec.skiing	Hobbyists interested in snow skiing.
rec.skiing.alpine	Downhill skiing technique, equipment, etc.
rec.skiing.announce	FAQ, competition results, automated snow reports. (Moderated)
rec.skiing.nordic	Cross-country skiing technique, equipment, etc.
rec.skiing.snowboard	Snowboarding technique, equipment, etc.
rec.skydiving	Hobbyists interested in skydiving.
rec.sport.baseball	Discussion about baseball.
rec.sport.baseball.college	Baseball on the collegiate level.
rec.sport.baseball.fantasy	Rotisserie (fantasy) baseball play.
rec.sport.basketball.college	Hoops on the collegiate level.
rec.sport.basketball.misc	Discussion about basketball.
rec.sport.basketball.pro	Talk of professional basketball.
rec.sport.basketball.women	Women's basketball at all levels.
rec.sport.boxing	Boxing in all its pugilistic facets and forms.
rec.sport.cricket	Discussion about the sport of cricket.
rec.sport.cricket.scores	Scores from cricket matches around the globe. (Moderated)
rec.sport.disc	Discussion of flying disc based sports.
rec.sport.fencing	All aspects of swordplay.
rec.sport.football.australian	Discussion of Australian (Rules) Football.
rec.sport.football.canadian	All about Canadian rules football.
rec.sport.football.college	U.S.-style college football.
rec.sport.football.fantasy	Rotisserie (fantasy) football play.
rec.sport.football.misc	Discussion about American-style football.
rec.sport.football.pro	U.S.-style professional football.
rec.sport.golf	Discussion about all aspects of golfing.
rec.sport.hockey	Discussion about ice hockey.
rec.sport.hockey.field	Discussion of the sport of field hockey.
rec.sport.misc	Spectator sports.
rec.sport.olympics	All aspects of the Olympic Games.
rec.sport.paintball	Discussing all aspects of the survival game paintball.
rec.sport.pro-wrestling	Discussion about professional wrestling.
rec.sport.rowing	Crew for competition or fitness.
rec.sport.rugby	Discussion about the game of rugby.

continues

Table B.3
Continued

Newsgroup	Description
rec.sport.soccer	Discussion about soccer (Association Football).
rec.sport.swimming	Training for and competing in swimming events.
rec.sport.table-tennis	Things related to table tennis (aka Ping Pong).
rec.sport.tennis	Things related to the sport of tennis.
rec.sport.triathlon	Discussing all aspects of multi-event sports.
rec.sport.volleyball	Discussion about volleyball.
rec.sport.water-polo	Discussion of water polo.
rec.sport.waterski	Waterskiing and other boat-towed activities.
rec.toys.lego	Discussion of Lego, Duplo (and compatible) toys.
rec.toys.misc	Discussion of toys that lack a specific newsgroup.
rec.travel	Traveling all over the world.
rec.travel.air	Airline travel around the world.
rec.travel.cruises	Travel by cruise ship.
rec.travel.marketplace	Tickets and accomodations wanted and for sale.
rec.video	Video and video components.
rec.video.cable-tv	Technical and regulatory issues of cable television.
rec.video.desktop	Amateur, computer-based video editing and production.
rec.video.production	Making professional quality video productions.
rec.video.releases	Pre-recorded video releases on laserdisc and videotape.
rec.video.satellite	Getting shows via satellite.
rec.windsurfing	Riding the waves as a hobby.
rec.woodworking	Hobbyists interested in woodworking.
sci.aeronautics	The science of aeronautics & related technology. (Moderated)
sci.aeronautics.airliners	Airliner technology. (Moderated)
sci.agriculture	Farming, agriculture, and related topics.
sci.agriculture.beekeeping	Beekeeping, bee-culture, and hive products.
sci.answers	Repository for periodic USENET articles. (Moderated)
sci.anthropology	All aspects of studying humankind.
sci.anthropology.paleo	Evolution of man and other primates.
sci.aquaria	Only scientifically-oriented postings about aquaria.
sci.archaeology	Studying antiquities of the world.
sci.archaeology.mesoamerican	The field of mesoamerican archaeology.
sci.astro	Astronomy discussions and information.
sci.astro.fits	Issues related to the Flexible Image Transport System.
sci.astro.hubble	Processing Hubble Space Telescope data. (Moderated)

Newsgroup	Description
sci.astro.planetarium	Discussion of planetariums.
sci.astro.research	Forum in astronomy/astrophysics research. (Moderated)
sci.bio	Biology and related sciences.
sci.bio.ecology	Ecological research.
sci.bio.ethology	Animal behavior and behavioral ecology.
sci.bio.evolution	Discussions of evolutionary biology. (Moderated)
sci.bio.herp	Biology of amphibians and reptiles.
sci.chem	Chemistry and related sciences.
sci.chem.electrochem	The field of electrochemistry.
sci.chem.organomet	Organometallic chemistry.
sci.classics	Studying classical history, languages, art, and more.
sci.cognitive	Perception, memory, judgement, and reasoning.
sci.comp-aided	The use of computers as tools in scientific research.
sci.cryonics	Theory and practice of biostasis, suspended animation.
sci.crypt	Different methods of data en/decryption.
sci.data.formats	Modelling, storage and retrieval of scientific data.
sci.econ	The science of economics.
sci.econ.research	Research in all fields of economics. (Moderated)
sci.edu	The science of education.
sci.electronics	Circuits, theory, electrons, and discussions.
sci.energy	Discussions about energy, science, and technology.
sci.energy.hydrogen	All about hydrogen as an alternative fuel.
sci.engr	Technical discussions about engineering tasks.
sci.engr.advanced-tv	HDTV/DATV standards, formats, equipment, practices.
sci.engr.biomed	Discussing the field of biomedical engineering.
sci.engr.chem	All aspects of chemical engineering.
sci.engr.civil	Topics related to civil engineering.
sci.engr.control	The engineering of control systems.
sci.engr.lighting	Light, vision, and color in architecture, media, etc.
sci.engr.manufacturing	Manufacturing technology.
sci.engr.mech	The field of mechanical engineering.
sci.engr.semiconductors	Semiconductor devices, processes, materials, physics.
sci.environment	Discussions about the environment and ecology.
sci.fractals	Objects of non-integral dimension and other chaos.
sci.geo.eos	NASA's Earth Observation System (EOS).
sci.geo.fluids	Discussion of geophysical fluid dynamics.

continues

Table B.3
Continued

Newsgroup	Description
sci.geo.geology	Discussion of solid earth sciences.
sci.geo.hydrology	Surface and groundwater hydrology.
sci.geo.meteorology	Discussion of meteorology and related topics.
sci.geo.satellite-nav	Satellite navigation systems, especially GPS.
sci.image.processing	Scientific image processing and analysis.
sci.lang	Natural languages, communication, etc.
sci.lang.japan	The Japanese language, both spoken and written.
sci.life-extension	Slowing, stopping, or reversing the ageing process.
sci.logic	Logic—math, philosophy, and computational aspects.
sci.materials	All aspects of materials engineering.
sci.math	Mathematical discussions and pursuits.
sci.math.research	Discussion of current mathematical research. (Moderated)
sci.math.symbolic	Symbolic algebra discussion.
sci.mech.fluids	All aspects of fluid mechanics.
sci.med	Medicine and its related products and regulations.
sci.med.aids	AIDS: treatment, pathology/biology of HIV, prevention. (Moderated)
sci.med.dentistry	Dentally related topics; all about teeth.
sci.med.nursing	Nursing questions and discussion.
sci.med.nutrition	Physiological impacts of diet.
sci.med.occupational	Preventing, detecting, and treating occupational injuries.
sci.med.pharmacy	The teaching and practice of pharmacy.
sci.med.physics	Issues of physics in medical testing/care.
sci.med.psychobiology	Dialog and news in psychiatry and psychobiology.
sci.med.radiology	All aspects of radiology.
sci.med.telemedicine	Clinical consulting through computer networks.
sci.military	Discussion about science and the military. (Moderated)
sci.misc	Short-lived discussions on subjects in the sciences.
sci.nanotech	Self-reproducing molecular-scale machines. (Moderated)
sci.nonlinear	Chaotic systems and other nonlinear scientific study.
sci.op-research	Research, teaching, and application of operations research.
sci.optics	Discussion relating to the science of optics.
sci.philosophy.tech	Technical philosophy: math, science, logic, etc.
sci.physics	Physical laws, properties, etc.
sci.physics.accelerators	Particle accelerators and the physics of beams.

Newsgroup	Description
sci.physics.computational.fluid-dynamics	Computational fluid dynamics.
sci.physics.electromag	Electromagnetic theory and applications.
sci.physics.fusion	Info on fusion, esp. "cold" fusion.
sci.physics.particle	Particle physics discussions.
sci.physics.plasma	Plasma Science & Technology community exchange. (Moderated)
sci.physics.research	Current physics research. (Moderated)
sci.polymers	All aspects of polymer science.
sci.psychology	Topics related to psychology.
sci.psychology.digest	PSYCOLOQUY: Refereed Psychology Journal and Newsletter. (Moderated)
sci.psychology.research	Research issues in psychology. (Moderated)
sci.research	Research methods, funding, ethics, and whatever.
sci.research.careers	Issues relevant to careers in scientific research.
sci.research.postdoc	Anything about postdoctoral studies, including offers.
sci.skeptic	Skeptics discussing pseudo-science.
sci.space.news	Announcements of space-related news items. (Moderated)
sci.space.policy	Discussions about space policy.
sci.space.science	Space and planetary science and related technical work. (Moderated)
sci.space.shuttle	The space shuttle and the STS program.
sci.space.tech	Technical and general issues related to space flight. (Moderated)
sci.stat.consult	Statistical consulting.
sci.stat.edu	Statistics education.
sci.stat.math	Statistics from a strictly mathematical viewpoint.
sci.systems	The theory and application of systems science.
sci.techniques.mag-resonance	Magnetic resonance imaging and spectroscopy.
sci.techniques.microscopy	The field of microscopy.
sci.techniques.spectroscopy	Spectrum analysis.
sci.techniques.xtallography	The field of crystallography.
sci.virtual-worlds	Virtual Reality—technology and culture. (Moderated)
sci.virtual-worlds.apps	Current and future uses of virtual-worlds technology. (Moderated)
soc.answers	Repository for periodic USENET articles. (Moderated)
soc.bi	Discussions of bisexuality.
soc.college	College, college activities, campus life, etc.
soc.college.grad	General issues related to graduate schools.

continues

Table B.3
Continued

Newsgroup	Description
soc.college.gradinfo	Information about graduate schools.
soc.college.org.aiesec	The Int'l Assoc. of Business and Commerce Students.
soc.college.teaching-asst	Issues affecting collegiate teaching assistants.
soc.couples	Discussions for couples (cf. **soc.singles**).
soc.couples.intercultural	Inter-cultural and inter-racial relationships.
soc.culture.afghanistan	Discussion of the Afghan society.
soc.culture.african	Discussions about Africa & things African.
soc.culture.african.american	Discussions about Afro-American issues.
soc.culture.arabic	Technological & cultural issues, *not* politics.
soc.culture.argentina	All about life in Argentina.
soc.culture.asean	Countries of the Assoc. of SE Asian Nations.
soc.culture.asian.american	Issues & discussion about Asian-Americans.
soc.culture.australian	Australian culture and society.
soc.culture.austria	Austria and its people.
soc.culture.baltics	People of the Baltic states.
soc.culture.bangladesh	Issues & discussion about Bangladesh.
soc.culture.belgium	Belgian society, culture(s), and people.
soc.culture.bosna-herzgvna	The independent state of Bosnia and Herzegovina.
soc.culture.brazil	Talking about the people and country of Brazil.
soc.culture.british	Issues about Britain & those of British descent.
soc.culture.bulgaria	Discussing Bulgarian society.
soc.culture.burma	Politics, culture, news, discussion about Burma.
soc.culture.canada	Discussions of Canada and its people.
soc.culture.caribbean	Life in the Caribbean.
soc.culture.celtic	Irish, Scottish, Breton, Cornish, Manx & Welsh.
soc.culture.chile	All about Chile and its people.
soc.culture.china	About China and Chinese culture.
soc.culture.colombia	Colombian talk, social, politics, science.
soc.culture.croatia	The lives of people of Croatia.
soc.culture.czecho-slovak	Bohemian, Slovak, Moravian and Silesian life.
soc.culture.europe	Discussing all aspects of all-European society.
soc.culture.filipino	Group about the Filipino culture.
soc.culture.french	French culture, history, and related discussions.
soc.culture.german	Discussions about German culture and history.
soc.culture.greek	Group about Greeks.

Newsgroup	Description
soc.culture.hongkong	Discussions pertaining to Hong Kong.
soc.culture.hongkong. entertainment	Entertainment in Hong Kong.
soc.culture.indian	Group for discussion about India & things Indian.
soc.culture.indian.info	Info group for **soc.culture.indian**, etc. (Moderated)
soc.culture.indian.telugu	The culture of the Telugu people of India.
soc.culture.indonesia	All about the Indonesian nation.
soc.culture.iranian	Discussions about Iran and things Iranian/Persian.
soc.culture.israel	Israel and Israelis.
soc.culture.italian	The Italian people and their culture.
soc.culture.japan	Everything Japanese, except the Japanese language.
soc.culture.jewish	Jewish culture & religion. (cf. **talk.politics.mideast**)
soc.culture.jewish.holocaust	The Shoah. (Moderated)
soc.culture.korean	Discussions about Korea & things Korean.
soc.culture.laos	Cultural and Social Aspects of Laos.
soc.culture.latin-america	Topics about Latin-America.
soc.culture.lebanon	Discussion about things Lebanese.
soc.culture.maghreb	North African society and culture.
soc.culture.magyar	The Hungarian people & their culture.
soc.culture.malaysia	All about Malaysian society.
soc.culture.mexican	Discussion of Mexico's society.
soc.culture.mexican.american	Mexican-American/Chicano culture and issues.
soc.culture.misc	Group for discussion about other cultures.
soc.culture.mongolian	Everything related to Mongols and Mongolia.
soc.culture.native	Aboriginal people around the world.
soc.culture.nepal	Discussion of people and things in & from Nepal.
soc.culture.netherlands	People from the Netherlands and Belgium.
soc.culture.new-zealand	Discussion of topics related to New Zealand.
soc.culture.nordic	Discussion about culture up north.
soc.culture.pakistan	Topics of discussion about Pakistan.
soc.culture.palestine	Palestinian people, culture, and politics.
soc.culture.peru	All about the people of Peru.
soc.culture.polish	Polish culture, Polish past, and Polish politics.
soc.culture.portuguese	Discussion of the people of Portugal.
soc.culture.puerto-rico	Puerto Rican culture, society, and politics.
soc.culture.romanian	Discussion of Romanian and Moldavian people.

continues

Table B.3
Continued

Newsgroup	Description
soc.culture.scientists	Cultural issues about scientists & scientific projects.
soc.culture.singapore	The past, present, and future of Singapore.
soc.culture.slovenia	Slovenia and Slovenian people.
soc.culture.somalia	Somalian affairs, society, and culture.
soc.culture.soviet	Topics relating to Russian or Soviet culture.
soc.culture.spain	Spain and the Spanish.
soc.culture.sri-lanka	Things & people from Sri Lanka.
soc.culture.swiss	Swiss culture.
soc.culture.taiwan	Discussion about things Taiwanese.
soc.culture.tamil	Tamil language, history, and culture.
soc.culture.thai	Thai people and their culture.
soc.culture.turkish	Discussion about things Turkish.
soc.culture.ukrainian	The lives and times of the Ukrainian people.
soc.culture.uruguay	Discussions of Uruguay for those at home and abroad.
soc.culture.usa	The culture of the United States of America.
soc.culture.venezuela	Discussion of topics related to Venezuela.
soc.culture.vietnamese	Issues and discussions of Vietnamese culture.
soc.culture.yugoslavia	Discussions of Yugoslavia and its people.
soc.feminism	Discussion of feminism & feminist issues. (Moderated)
soc.history	Discussions of things historical.
soc.history.moderated	All aspects of history. (Moderated)
soc.history.war.misc	History & events of wars in general.
soc.history.war.world-war-ii	History & events of World War II. (Moderated)
soc.libraries.talk	Discussing all aspects of libraries.
soc.men	Issues related to men, their problems, and relationships.
soc.misc	Socially-oriented topics not in other groups.
soc.motss	Issues pertaining to homosexuality.
soc.net-people	Announcements, requests, etc. about people on the net.
soc.penpals	In search of net.friendships.
soc.politics	Political problems, systems, solutions. (Moderated)
soc.politics.arms-d	Arms discussion digest. (Moderated)
soc.religion.bahai	Discussion of the Baha'i Faith. (Moderated)
soc.religion.christian	Christianity and related topics. (Moderated)
soc.religion.christian. bible-study	Examining the Holy Bible. (Moderated)

Newsgroup	Description
soc.religion.eastern	Discussions of Eastern religions. (Moderated)
soc.religion.islam	Discussions of the Islamic faith. (Moderated)
soc.religion.quaker	The Religious Society of Friends.
soc.religion.shamanism	Discussion of the full range of shamanic experience. (Moderated)
soc.rights.human	Human rights & activism (e.g., Amnesty International).
soc.roots	Discussing genealogy and genealogical matters.
soc.singles	Newsgroup for single people, their activities, etc.
soc.veterans	Social issues relating to military veterans.
soc.women	Issues related to women, their problems, and relationships.
talk.abortion	All sorts of discussions and arguments on abortion.
talk.answers	Repository for periodic USENET articles. (Moderated)
talk.bizarre	The unusual, bizarre, curious, and often stupid.
talk.environment	Discussion the state of the environment & what to do.
talk.origins	Evolution versus creationism (sometimes hot!).
talk.philosophy.misc	Philosophical musings on all topics.
talk.politics.animals	The use and/or abuse of animals.
talk.politics.china	Discussion of political issues related to China.
talk.politics.crypto	The relation between cryptography and government.
talk.politics.drugs	The politics of drug issues.
talk.politics.guns	The politics of firearm ownership and (mis)use.
talk.politics.medicine	The politics and ethics involved with health care.
talk.politics.mideast	Discussion & debate over Middle Eastern events.
talk.politics.misc	Political discussions and ravings of all kinds.
talk.politics.soviet	Discussion of Soviet politics, domestic and foreign.
talk.politics.theory	Theory of politics and political systems.
talk.politics.tibet	The politics of Tibet and the Tibetan people.
talk.rape	Discussions on stopping rape; not to be crossposted.
talk.religion.misc	Religious, ethical, and moral implications.
talk.religion.newage	Esoteric and minority religions & philosophies.
talk.rumors	For the posting of rumors.

UNIX might be a Trademark of Novell. Or Beatrice.
DEC and Ultrix are Trademarks of the Digital Equipment Corporation.
VAX is a Trademark of the Digital Equipment Corporation.
Ada is a registered Trademark of the Ada Joint Program Office of the United States Department of Defense.
Unisys is a registered trademark of Unisys Corporation.

Appendix B
Newsgroup List

PDIAL List

This appendix contains the text of Peter Kaminski's PDIAL List, a large but certainly not complete list of organizations that provide full Internet access, usually for a fee. I include Peter's list for you because it's an invaluable resource for locating Internet providers near you. Neither Peter nor I make any claims about the completeness or accuracy of this list, however; I provide it merely as an aid.

Public Dialup Internet Access List

```
The Public Dialup Internet Access List (PDIAL)
================================================
      File PDIAL015.TXT — 09 December 1993


Copyright 1992-1993 Peter Kaminski.  Do not modify.  Freely distributable
for non-commercial purposes. Please contact me if you wish to distribute
commercially or in modified form.

I make no representations about the suitability or accuracy of this document
for any purpose. It is provided "as is" without express or implied warranty.
All information contained herein is subject to change.
```

```
Contents:

-00- Quick Start!
-01- Area Code Summary: Providers With Many Local Dialins (1-800, PDN)
-02- Area Code Summary: US/Canada Metro and Regional Dialins
-03- Area Code Summary: International Dialins
-04- Alphabetical List of Providers
-05- What *Is* The Internet?
-06- What The PDIAL Is
-07- How People Can Get The PDIAL (This List)
-08- Appendix A: Other Valuable Resources
-09- Appendix B: Finding Public Data Network (PDN) Access Numbers
-10- Providers: Get Listed in PDIAL!
```

Subject headers below are formatted so this list may be read as a
digest by USENET newsreaders that support digests. Example commands:
rn, "control-G" skips to next section; nn, "G%" presents as a digest.

Or, just skip to desired section by searching for the desired section
number string (e.g. "-01-") from the list above.

PDIAL Quick Start

From: PDIAL -00-
Subject: Quick Start!

THE INTERNET is a global cooperative information network which can give
you instant access to millions of people and terabytes of data. Providers
listed in the PDIAL provide inexpensive public access to the Internet
using your regular modem and computer.

[Special note: the PDIAL currently lists only providers directly connected
to the Internet. Much of the Internet can still be explored through
systems with only Internet email and USENET netnews connections, but you
need to check other BBS lists to find them.]

GET A GUIDE: I highly recommend obtaining one of the many good starter or
guide books to the Internet. Think of them as travel guides to a new and
different country, and you wouldn't be far off. See section -08- below
for more details.

CHOOSING A PROVIDER: Phone charges can dominate the cost of your access to
the Internet. Check first for providers with metro or regional dialins
that are a local call for you (no per-minute phone charges). If there
aren't any, move on to comparing prices for PDN, 800, and direct-dial long
distance charges. Make sure to compare all your options. Calling long
distance out-of-state or across the country is often cheaper than calling
30 miles away.

If you're not in North America and have no local provider, you may still
be able to use one of the providers listed as having PDN access. Contact
the individual providers with PDN access (see listings below) to find out.

INFORMATION CHANGES: The information listed in the PDIAL changes and
expands rapidly. If this edition is more than 2 months old, consider
obtaining a new one. You can use the Info Deli email server, which
will provide you with updates and other information. Choose from the
commands below and just email them to <info-deli-server@netcom.com>.

   "Send PDIAL" — receive the current PDIAL
   "Subscribe PDIAL" — receive new editions of the PDIAL automatically
   "Subscribe Info-Deli-News" — news of Info Deli changes and additions

See section -07- below for more details and other ways to obtain the
PDIAL.

CHECK IT OUT: Remember, the PDIAL is only a summary listing of the
resources and environment delivered by each of the various providers.
Contact the providers that interest you by email or voice phone and make
sure you find out if they have what you need.

Then GO FOR IT! Happy 'netting!

Area Code Summary: Providers With Many Local Dialins

From: PDIAL -01-
Subject: Area Code Summary: Providers With Many Local Dialins (1-800, PDN)

     800 class cns crl csn dial-n-cerf-usa hookup.net IGC jvnc OARnet
     PDN delphi holonet hookup.net IGC michnet millennium novalink portal
     PDN psi-world-dial psilink tmn well world

"PDN" means the provider is accessible through a public data network
(check the listings below for which network); note that many PDNs
listed offer access outside North America as well as within North
America. Check with the provider or the PDN for more details.

"800" means the provider is accessible via a "toll-free" US phone
number. The phone company will not charge for the call, but the
service provider will add a surcharge to cover the cost of the 800
service. This may be more expensive than other long-distance options.

Area Code Summary: U.S./Canada Metro and Regional Dialins

From: PDIAL -02-
Subject: Area Code Summary: US/Canada Metro and Regional Dialins

If you are not local to any of these providers, it's still likely you
are able to access those providers available through a public data
network (PDN). Check the section above for providers with wide area
access.

```
201 jvnc-tiger
202 CAPCON clarknet express michnet tmn
203 jvnc-tiger
205 nuance
206 eskimo GLAIDS halcyon netcom nwnexus olympus
212 echonyc maestro mindvox panix pipeline
213 crl dial-n-cerf kaiwan netcom
214 metronet netcom
215 jvnc-tiger PREPnet
216 OARnet wariat
217 prairienet
301 CAPCON clarknet express michnet tmn
302 ssnet
303 cns csn netcom nyx
305 gate.net
310 class crl dial-n-cerf kaiwan netcom
312 InterAccess mcsnet netcom xnet
313 michnet MSen
401 anomaly ids jvnc-tiger
403 PUCnet UUNET-Canada
404 crl netcom
407 gate.net
408 a2i netcom portal
410 CAPCON clarknet express
412 PREPnet telerama
415 a2i class crl dial-n-cerf IGC netcom portal well
416 hookup.net UUNET-Canada uunorth
419 OARnet
503 agora.rain.com netcom teleport
504 sugar
508 anomaly nearnet northshore novalink
510 class crl dial-n-cerf holonet netcom
512 realtime
513 fsp OARnet
514 CAM.ORG UUNET-Canada
516 jvnc-tiger
517 michnet
519 hookup.net UUNET-Canada uunorth
602 crl Data.Basix evergreen indirect
603 MV nearnet
604 UUNET-Canada
609 jvnc-tiger
613 UUNET-Canada uunorth
614 OARnet
616 michnet
```

```
617 delphi nearnet netcom northshore novalink world
619 cg57 class crash.cts.com cyber dial-n-cerf netcom
703 CAPCON clarknet express michnet netcom tmn
704 concert Vnet
707 crl
708 InterAccess mcsnet xnet
713 blkbox nuchat sugar
714 class dial-n-cerf express kaiwan netcom
717 PREPnet
718 maestro mindvox netcom panix pipeline
719 cns csn oldcolo
804 wyvern
810 michnet MSen
814 PREPnet
815 InterAccess mcsnet xnet
817 metronet
818 class dial-n-cerf netcom
905 UUNET-Canada
906 michnet
907 alaska.edu
908 express jvnc-tiger
910 concert
916 netcom
919 concert Vnet
```

These are area codes local to the dialups, although some prefixes in the area codes listed may not be local to the dialups. Check your phone book or with your phone company.

Area Code Summary: International Dialins

From: PDIAL -03-
Subject: Area Code Summary: International Dialins

If you are not local to any of these providers, there is still a chance you are able to access those providers available through a public data network (PDN). Check section -01- above for providers with wide area access, and send email to them to ask about availability.

```
+44 (0)81 Demon dircon ibmpcug
      +49 Individual.NET
   +49 23 ins
  +49 069 in-rhein-main
  +49 089 mucev
    +61 2 connect.com.au
    +61 3 connect.com.au
     +301 Ariadne
  +353 1 IEunet
```

Alphabetical List of Providers

```
From: PDIAL -04-
Subject: Alphabetical List of Providers


Fees are for personal dialup accounts with outgoing Internet access;
most sites have other classes of service with other rate structures as
well.  Most support email and netnews along with the listed services.


"Long distance: provided by user" means you need to use direct dial
long distance or other long distance services to connect to the provider.
```

```
a2i

name — — — — —> a2i communications
dialup — — — —> 408-293-9010 (v.32bis), 415-364-5652 (v.32bis), 408-293-9020
               (PEP); login 'guest'
area codes — —> 408, 415
local access —> CA: West and South SF Bay Area
long distance -> provided by user
services — — —> shell (SunOS UNIX and MS-DOS), ftp, telnet, irc, feeds,
               domains and host-less domains, virtual ttys, gopher
fees — — — — —> $20/month or $45/3 months or $72/6 months
email — — — —> info@rahul.net
voice — — — —> 408-293-8078 voicemail
ftp more info -> ftp.rahul.net:/pub/BLURB
```

```
agora.rain.com

name — — — — —> RainDrop Laboratories
dialup — — — —> 503-293-1772 (2400) 503-293-2059 (v.32, v.32 bis) 'apply'
area codes — —> 503
local access —> OR: Portland, Beaverton, Hillsboro, Forest Grove, Gresham,
               Tigard, Lake Oswego, Oregon City, Tualatin, Wilsonville
long distance -> provided by user
services — — —> shell, ftp, telnet, gopher, usenet
fees — — — — —> $6/month (1 hr/day limit)
email — — — —> info@agora.rain.com
voice — — — —> n/a
ftp more info -> agora.rain.com:/pub/gopher-data/agora/agora
```

```
alaska.edu

name — — — — —> University Of Alaska Southeast, Tundra Services
dialup — — — —> 907-789-1314
area codes — —> 907
local access —> All Alaskan sites with local UACN access — Anchorage,
               Barrow, Fairbanks, Homer, Juneau, Keni, Ketchikan, Kodiak,
               Kotzebue, Nome, Palmer, Sitka, Valdez
long distance -> provided by user
```

```
services  — — —> Statewide UACN Mail, Internet, USENET, gopher, Telnet, FTP
fees  — — — — —> $20/month for individual accounts, discounts for 25+ and 50+
                 to public, gov't and non-profit organizations.
email  — — — —> JNJMB@acad1.alaska.edu
voice  — — — —> 907-465-6453
fax  — — — — —> 907-465-6295
ftp more info -> n/a
```

---

anomaly

```
name  — — — — —> Anomaly - Rhode Island's Gateway To The Internet
dialup  — — — —> 401-331-3706 (v.32) or 401-455-0347 (PEP)
area codes  — —> 401, 508
local access  —> RI: Providence/Seekonk Zone
long distance -> provided by user
services  — — —> shell, ftp, telnet, SLIP
fees  — — — — —> Commercial: $125/6 months or $200/year; Educational: $75/6
                 months or $125/year
email  — — — —> info@anomaly.sbs.risc.net
voice  — — — —> 401-273-4669
ftp more info -> anomaly.sbs.risc.net:/anomaly.info/access.zip
```

Ariadne

```
name  — — — — —> Ariadne - Greek Academic and Research Network
dialup  — — — —> +301 65-48-800 (1200 - 9600 bps)
area codes  — —> +301
local access  —> Athens, Greece
long distance -> provided by user
services  — — —> e-mail, ftp, telnet, gopher, talk, pad(EuropaNet)
fees  — — — — —> 5900 drachmas per calendar quarter, 1 hr/day limit.
email — — — — >  dialup@leon.nrcps.ariadne-t.gr
voice   — — — —> +301 65-13-392
fax  — — — — —> +301 6532910
ftp more info -> n/a
```

---

blkbox

```
name  — — — — —> The Black Box
dialup  — — — —> (713) 480-2686 (V32bis/V42bis)
area codes  — —> 713
local access  —> TX: Houston
long distance -> provided by user
services  — — —> shell, ftp, telnet, SLIP, PPP, UUCP
fees  — — — — —> $21.65 per month or $108.25 for 6 months
email   — — — —> info@blkbox.com
voice   — — — —> (713) 480-2684
ftp more info -> n/a
```

CAM.ORG

```
name  — — — —> Communications Accessibles Montreal
dialup — — — —> 514-931-7178 (v.32 bis), 514-931-2333 (2400bps)
area codes — —> 514
local access —> QC: Montreal, Laval, South-Shore, West-Island
long distance -> provided by user
services — — —> shell, ftp, telnet, gopher, wais, WWW, irc, feeds, SLIP,
                PPP, AppleTalk, FAX gateway
fees  — — — —> $25/month Cdn.
email  — — — —> info@CAM.ORG
voice  — — — —> 514-931-0749
ftp more info -> ftp.CAM.ORG
```

CAPCON

```
name  — — — —> CAPCON Library Network
dialup — — — —> contact for number
area codes — —> 202, 301, 410, 703
local access —> District of Columbia, Suburban Maryland & Northern Virginia
long distance -> various plans available/recommended; contact for details
services — — —> menu, archie, ftp, gopher, listservs, telnet, wais, whois,
                full day training and 'CAPCON Connect User Manual'
fees  — — — —> $35 start-up + $150/yr + $24/mo for first account from an
                institution; $35 start-up + $90/yr + $15/mo for additional
                users (member rates lower); 20 hours/month included,
                additional hours $2/hr
email  — — — —> capcon@capcon.net
voice  — — — —> 202-331-5771
fax  — — — — —> 202-797-7719
ftp more info -> n/a
```

---

cg57

```
name  — — — — —> E & S Systems Public Access *Nix
dialup — — — —> 619-278-8267 (V.32bis, TurboPEP), 619-278-8267 (V32)
                619-278-9837 (PEP)
area codes — —> 619
local access —> CA: San Diego
long distance -> provided by user
services — — —> shell, ftp, irc, telnet, gopher, archie, bbs (UniBoard)
fees  — — — —> bbs (FREE), shell - $30/3 months, $50/6 months, $80/9
                months, $100/year
email  — — — —> steve@cg57.esnet.com
voice  — — — —> 619-278-4641
ftp more info -> n/a
```

```
clarknet

name  — — — —>  Clark Internet Services, Inc. (ClarkNet)
dialup  — — — —>  410-730-9786, 410-995-0271, 301-596-1626, 301-854-0446,
                  301-621-5216 'guest'
area codes  — —>  202, 301, 410, 703
local access  —>  MD: Baltimore; DC: Washington; VA: Northern VA
long distance ->  provided by user
services  — — —>  shell, menu, ftp, telnet, irc, gopher, hytelnet, www, WAIS,
                  SLIP/PPP, ftp space, feeds (UUCP & uMDSS), dns, Clarinet
fees  — — — —>  $23/month or $66/3 months or $126/6 months or $228/year
email  — — — —>  info@clark.net
voice  — — — —>  Call 800-735-2258 then give 410-730-9764 (MD Relay Svc)
fax  — — — —>  410-730-9765
ftp more info ->  ftp.clark.net:/pub/clarknet/fullinfo.txt
```

```
class

name  — — — —>  Cooperative Library Agency for Systems and Services
dialup  — — — —>  contact for number; NOTE: CLASS serves libraries and
                  information distributors only
area codes  — —>  310, 415, 510, 619, 714, 818, 800
local access  —>  Northern and Southern California or anywhere (800) service
                  is available
long distance ->  800 service available at $6/hour surcharge
services  — — —>  menus, mail, telnet, ftp, gopher, wais, hytelnet, archie,
                  WWW, IRC, Unix shells, SLIP, etc.  Training is available.
fees  — — — —>  $4.50/hour + $150/year for first account + $50/year each
                  additional account + $135/year CLASS membership.  Discounts
                  available for multiple memberships.
email  — — — —>  class@class.org
voice  — — — —>  800-488-4559
fax  — — — —>  408-453-5379
ftp more info ->  n/a
```

```
cns

name  — — — —>  Community News Service
dialup  — — — —>  719-520-1700 id 'new', passwd 'newuser'
area codes  — —>  303, 719, 800
local access  —>  CO: Colorado Springs, Denver; continental US/800
long distance ->  800 or provided by user
services  — — —>  UNIX shell, email, ftp, telnet, irc, USENET, Clarinet,
                  gopher, Commerce Business Daily
fees  — — — —>  $2.75/hour; $10/month minimum + $35 signup
```

```
email   — — — —> service@cscns.com
voice   — — — —> 719-592-1240
ftp more info -> cscns.com
```

```
concert

name   — — — — —> CONCERT-CONNECT
dialup — — — —> contact for number
area codes — —> 704, 910, 919
local access —> NC: Asheville, Chapel Hill, Charlotte, Durham, Greensboro,
                Greenville, Raleigh, Winston-Salem, Research Triangle Park
long distance -> provided by user
services — — —> UUCP, SLIP
fees — — — — —> SLIP: $150 educational/research or $180 commercial for first
                60 hours/month + $300 signup
email   — — — —> info@concert.net
voice   — — — —> 919-248-1999
ftp more info -> ftp.concert.net
```

```
connect.com.au

name   — — — — —> connect.com.au pty ltd
dialup — — — —> contact for number
area codes — —> +61 3, +61 2
local access —> Australia: Melbourne, Sydney
long distance -> provided by user
services — — —> SLIP, PPP, ISDN, UUCP, ftp, telnet, NTP, FTPmail
fees — — — — —> AUS$2000/year (1 hour/day), 10% discount for AUUG members;
                other billing negotiable
email   — — — —> connect@connect.com.au
voice   — — — —> +61 3 5282239
fax    — — — — —> +61 3 5285887
ftp more info -> ftp.connect.com.au
```

```
crash.cts.com

name   — — — — —> CTS Network Services (CTSNET)
dialup — — — —> 619-637-3640 HST, 619-637-3660 V.32bis, 619-637-3680 PEP
                'help'
area codes — —> 619
local access —> CA: San Diego, Pt. Loma, La Jolla, La Mesa, El Cajon, Poway,
                Ramona, Chula Vista, National City, Mira Mesa, Alpine, East
                County, new North County numbers, Escondido, Oceanside, Vista
long distance -> provided by user
services — — —> Unix shell, UUCP, Usenet newsfeeds, NNTP, Clarinet, Reuters,
                FTP, Telnet, SLIP, PPP, IRC, Gopher, Archie, WAIS, POPmail,
                UMDSS, domains, nameservice, DNS
```

```
fees  — — — —> $10-$23/month flat depending on features, $15 startup,
                personal $20-> /month flat depending on features, $25
                startup, commercial
email  — — —> info@crash.cts.com (server), support@crash.cts.com (human)
voice  — — — —> 619-637-3637
fax    — — — — —> 619-637-3630
ftp more info -> n/a
```

---

crl

```
name  — — — — —> CR Laboratories Dialup Internet Access
dialup — — — —> 415-389-UNIX
area codes — —> 213, 310, 404, 415, 510, 602, 707, 800
local access —> CA: San Francisco Bay area + San Rafael, Santa Rosa, Los
                Angeles, Orange County; AZ: Phoenix, Scottsdale, Tempe, and
                Glendale; GA: Atlanta metro area; continental US/800
long distance -> 800 or provided by user
services — — —> shell, ftp, telnet, feeds, SLIP, WAIS
fees   — — — — —> $17.50/month + $19.50 signup
email  — — — —> info@crl.com
voice  — — — —> 415-381-2800
ftp more info -> n/a
```

---

csn

```
name  — — — — —> Colorado SuperNet, Inc.
dialup — — — —> contact for number
area codes — —> 303, 719, 800
local access —> CO: Alamosa, Boulder/Denver, Colorado Springs, Durango, Fort
                Collins, Frisco, Glenwood Springs/Aspen, Grand Junction,
                Greeley, Gunnison, Pueblo, Telluride; anywhere 800 service
                is available
long distance -> provided by user or 800
services — — —> shell or menu, UUCP, SLIP, 56K, ISDN, T1; ftp, telnet, irc,
                gopher, WAIS, domains, anonymous ftp space, email-to-fax
fees   — — — — —> $1/hour off-peak, $3/hour peak ($250 max/month) + $20
                signup, $5/hr surcharge for 800 use
email  — — — —> info@csn.org
voice  — — — —> 303-273-3471
fax    — — — —> 303-273-3475
ftp more info -> csn.org:/CSN/reports/DialinInfo.txt
off-peak — — —> midnight to 6am
```

---

cyber

```
name  — — — — —> The Cyberspace Station
dialup — — — —> 619-634-1376 'guest'
area codes — —> 619
```

```
local access —> CA: San Diego
long distance -> provided by user
services — — —> shell, ftp, telnet, irc
fees — — — — —> $15/month + $10 startup or $60 for six months
email   — — — —> help@cyber.net
voice   — — — —> n/a
ftp more info -> n/a
```

Data.Basix

```
name — — — — —> Data Basix
dialup — — — —> 602-721-5887
area codes — —> 602
local access —> AZ: Tucson
long distance -> provided by user
services — — —> Telnet, FTP, NEWS, UUCP; on-site assistance
fees — — — — —> $25 monthly, $180 yearly; group rates available
email   — — — —> info@Data.Basix.com (automated); sales@Data.Basix.com (human)
voice   — — — —> 602-721-1988
ftp more info -> Data.Basix.COM:/services/dial-up.txt
```

Demon

```
name — — — — —> Demon Internet Systems (DIS)
dialup — — — —> +44 (0)81 343 4848
area codes — —> +44 (0)81
local access —> London, England
long distance -> provided by user
services — — —> ftp, telnet, SLIP/PPP
fees — — — — —> GBPounds 10.00/month; 132.50/year (inc 12.50 startup
                charge).  No on-line time charges.
email   — — — —> internet@demon.co.uk
voice   — — — —> +44 (0)81 349 0063
ftp more info -> n/a
```

---

delphi

```
name — — — — —> DELPHI
dialup — — — —> 800-365-4636 'JOINDELPHI password:INTERNETSIG'
area codes — —> 617, PDN
local access —> MA: Boston; KS: Kansas City
long distance -> Sprintnet or Tymnet: $9/hour weekday business hours, no
                charge nights and weekends
services — — —> ftp, telnet, feeds, user groups, wire services, member
                conferencing
```

```
fees  — — — — —> $10/month for 4 hours or $20/month for 20 hours + $3/month
                 for Internet services
email   — — — —> walthowe@delphi.com
voice   — — — —> 800-544-4005
ftp more info -> n/a
```

```
dial-n-cerf
```

```
name  — — — — —> DIAL n' CERF or DIAL n' CERF AYC
dialup  — — — —> contact for number
area codes  — —> 213, 310, 415, 510, 619, 714, 818
local access  —> CA: Los Angeles, Oakland, San Diego, Irvine, Pasadena, Palo
                 Alto
long distance -> provided by user
services  — — —> shell, menu, irc, ftp, hytelnet, gopher, WAIS, WWW, terminal
                 service, SLIP
fees  — — — — —> $5/hour ($3/hour on weekend) + $20/month + $50 startup OR
                 $250/month flat for AYC
email   — — — —> help@cerf.net
voice   — — — —> 800-876-2373 or 619-455-3900
ftp more info -> nic.cerf.net:/cerfnet/dial-n-cerf/
off-peak  — — —> Weekend: 5pm Friday to 5pm Sunday
```

```
dial-n-cerf-usa
```

```
name  — — — — —> DIAL n' CERF USA
dialup  — — — —> contact for number
area codes  — —> 800
local access  —> anywhere (800) service is available
long distance -> included
services  — — —> shell, menu, irc, ftp, hytelnet, gopher, WAIS, WWW, terminal
                 service, SLIP
fees  — — — — —> $10/hour ($8/hour on weekend) + $20/month
email   — — — —> help@cerf.net
voice   — — — —> 800-876-2373 or 619-455-3900
ftp more info -> nic.cerf.net:/cerfnet/dial-n-cerf/
off-peak  — — —> Weekend: 5pm Friday to 5pm Sunday
```

```
dircon
```

```
name  — — — — —> The Direct Connection
dialup  — — — —> +44 (0)81 317 2222
area codes  — —> +44 (0)81
local access  —> London, England
```

```
long distance -> provided by user
services ———> shell or menu, UUCP feeds, SLIP/PPP, ftp, telnet, gopher,
              WAIS, Archie, personal ftp/file space, email-to-fax
fees ————> Subscriptions from GBPounds 10 per month, no on-line
              charges. GBPounds 7.50 signup fee.
email  ———> helpdesk@dircon.co.uk
voice  ————> +44 (0)81 317 0100
fax  —————> +44 (0)81 317 0100
ftp more info -> n/a
```

```
echonyc

name ————> Echo Communications
dialup ———> (212) 989-8411 (v.32, v.32 bis) 'newuser'
area codes ——> 212
local access —> NY: Manhattan
long distance -> provided by user
services ———> shell, ftp, telnet, gopher, archie, wais, SLIP/PPP
fees ————> Commercial: $19.95/month; students/seniors: $13.75/month
email  ———> horn@echonyc.com
voice  ————> 212-255-3839
ftp more info -> n/a
```

```
eskimo

name ————> Eskimo North
dialup ———> 206-367-3837 300-14.4k, 206-362-6731 for 9600/14.4k,
              206-742-1150 World Blazer
area codes ——> 206
local access —> WA: Seattle, Everett
long distance -> provided by user
services ———> shell, ftp, telnet
fees ————> $10/month or $96/year
email  ———> nanook@eskimo.com
voice  ————> 206-367-7457
ftp more info -> n/a
```

```
evergreen

name ————> Evergreen Communications
dialup ———> (602) 955-8444
area codes ——> 602
local access —> AZ
long distance -> provided by user or call for additional information
services ———> ftp, telnet, gopher, archie, wais, www, uucp, PPP
```

```
fees — — — — —> individual: $239/yr; commercial: $479/yr; special
                 educational rates
email  — — — —> evergreen@libre.com
voice  — — — —> 602-955-8315
fax   — — — — —> 602-955-5948
ftp more info -> n/a
```

---

express

```
name — — — — —> Express Access - A service of Digital Express Group
dialup — — — —> 301-220-0462, 410-766-1855, 703-281-7997, 714-377-9784,
                 908-937-9481 'new'
area codes — —> 202, 301, 410, 703, 714, 908
local access —> Northern VA, Baltimore MD, Washington DC, New Brunswick NJ,
                 Orange County CA
long distance -> provided by user
services — — —> shell, ftp, telnet, irc, gopher, hytelnet, www, Clarinet,
                 SLIP/PPP, archie, mailing lists, autoresponders, anonymous
                 FTP archives
fees — — — — —> $25/month or $250/year
email  — — — —> info@digex.net
voice  — — — —> 800-969-9090, 301-220-2020
ftp more info -> n/a
```

---

fsp

```
name — — — — —> Freelance Systems Programming
dialup — — — —> (513) 258-7745 to 14.4 Kbps
area codes — —> 513
local access —> OH: Dayton
long distance -> provided by user
services — — —> shell, ftp, telnet, feeds, email, gopher, archie, SLIP, etc.
fees — — — — —> $20 startup and $1 per hour
email  — — — —> fsp@dayton.fsp.com
voice  — — — —> (513) 254-7246
ftp more info -> n/a
```

---

gate.net

```
name — — — — —> CyberGate, Inc
dialup — — — —> 305-425-0200
area codes — —> 305, 407
local access —> South Florida, expanding in FL
long distance -> provided by user
services — — —> shell, UUCP, SLIP/PPP, leased, telnet, FTP, IRC, archie,
                 gopher, etc.
```

```
fees  — — — —> $17.50/mo on credit card; group discounts; SLIP/PPP:
                $17.50/mo + $2/hr
email  — — — —> info@gate.net or sales@gate.net
voice  — — — —> 305-428-GATE
fax   — — — — —> 305-428-7977
ftp more info -> n/a
```

```
GLAIDS

name  — — — — —> GLAIDS NET (Homosexual Network)
dialup — — — —> 206-322-0621
area codes  — —> 206
local access —> WA: Seattle
long distance -> provided by user
services  — — —> BBS, Gopher, ftp, telnet
fees  — — — — —> $10/month.  Scholarships available. Free 7 day trial.
                Visitors are welcome.
email  — — — —> tomh@glaids.wa.com
voice  — — — —> 206-323-7483
ftp more info -> GLAIDS.wa.com
```

```
halcyon

name  — — — — —> Halcyon
dialup — — — —> 206-382-6245 'new', 8N1
area codes  — —> 206
local access —> Seattle, WA
long distance -> provided by user
services  — — —> shell, telnet, ftp, bbs, irc, gopher, hytelnet
fees  — — — — —> $200/year, or $60/quarter + $10 start-up
email  — — — —> info@halcyon.com
voice  — — — —> 206-955-1050
ftp more info -> halcyon.com:/pub/waffle/info
```

```
holonet

name  — — — — —> HoloNet
dialup — — — —> 510-704-1058
area codes  — —> 510, PDN
local access —> Berkeley, CA
long distance -> [per hour, off-peak/peak] Bay Area: $0.50/$0.95; PSINet A:
                $0.95/$1.95; PSINet B: $2.50/$6.00; Tymnet: $3.75/$7.50
services  — — —> ftp, telnet, irc, games
fees  — — — — —> $2/hour off-peak, $4/hour peak; $6/month or $60/year minimum
email  — — — —> info@holonet.net
```

```
voice  — — — —> 510-704-0160
ftp more info -> holonet.net:/info/
off-peak  — — —> 5pm to 8am + weekends and holidays
```

```
hookup.net

name  — — — — —> HookUp Communication Corporation
dialup  — — — —> contact for number
area codes  — —> 800, PDN, 416, 519
local access  —> Ontario, Canada
long distance -> 800 access across Canada, or discounted rates by HookUp
services  — — —> shell or menu, UUCP, SLIP, PPP, ftp, telnet, irc, gopher,
                 domains, anonymous ftp space
fees  — — — — —> Cdn$14.95/mo for 5 hours; Cdn$34.95/mo for 15 hrs;
                 Cdn$59.95/mo for 30 hrs; Cdn$300.00/yr for 50 hrs/mo;
                 Cdn$299.00/mo for unlimited usage
email  — — — —> info@hookup.net
voice  — — — —> 519-747-4110
fax  — — — — —> 519-746-3521
ftp more info -> n/a
```

```
ibmpcug

name  — — — — —> UK PC User Group
dialup  — — — —> +44 (0)81 863 6646
area codes  — —> +44 (0)81
local access  —> London, England
long distance -> provided by user
services  — — —> ftp, telnet, bbs, irc, feeds
fees  — — — — —> GBPounds 15.50/month or 160/year + 10 startup (no time
                 charges)
email  — — — —> info@ibmpcug.co.uk
voice  — — — —> +44 (0)81 863 6646
ftp more info -> n/a
```

```
ids

name  — — — — —> The IDS World Network
dialup  — — — —> 401-884-9002, 401-785-1067
area codes  — —> 401
local access  —> East Greenwich, RI; northern RI
long distance -> provided by user
services  — — —> ftp, telnet, SLIP, feeds, bbs
fees  — — — — —> $10/month or $50/half year or $100/year
```

```
email    ————> sysadmin@ids.net
voice    ————> 401-884-7856
ftp more info -> ids.net:/ids.net
```

IEunet

```
name  —————> IEunet Ltd., Ireland's Internet Services Supplier
dialup ————> +353 1 6790830, +353 1 6798600
area codes  ——> +353 1
local access —> Dublin, Ireland
long distance -> provided by user, or supplied by IEunet
services  ———> DialIP, IPGold, EUnet Traveller, X400, X500, Gopher, WWW,
               FTP, FTPmail,SLIP/PPP, FTP archives
fees  —————> IEP25/month Basic
email    ————> info@ieunet.ie, info@Ireland.eu.net
voice    ————> +353 1 6790832
ftp more info -> ftp.ieunet.ie:/pub
```

IGC

```
name  —————> Institute for Global Communications/IGC Networks (PeaceNet,
               EcoNet, ConflictNet, LaborNet, HomeoNet)
dialup ————> 415-322-0284 (N-8-1), 'new'
area codes  ——> 415, 800, PDN
local access —> CA: Palo Alto, San Francisco
long distance -> [per hour, off-peak/peak] SprintNet: $2/$7; 800: $11/$11
services  ———> telnet, local newsgroups for environmental, peace/social
               justice issues; NO ftp
fees  —————> $10/month + $3/hr after first hour
email    ————> support@igc.apc.org
voice    ————> 415-442-0220
ftp more info -> igc.apc.org:/pub
```

---

indirect

```
name  —————> Internet Direct, Inc.
dialup ————> 602-274-9600 (Phoenix); 602-321-9600 (Tucson); 'guest'
area codes  ——> 602
local access —> AZ: Phoenix, Tucson
long distance -> provided by user
services  ———> Shell/menu, UUCP, Usenet, NNTP, FTP, Telnet, SLIP, PPP, IRC,
               Gopher, WAIS, WWW, POP, DNS, nameservice, QWK (offline
               readers)
```

```
fees  — — — —> $20/month (personal); $30/month (business)
email  — — —> info@indirect.com (automated); support@indirect.com (human)
voice  — — —> 602-274-0100 (Phoenix), 602-324-0100 (Tucson)
ftp more info -> n/a
```

Individual.NET

```
name  — — — —> Individual Network e.V. (IN)
dialup — — — —> contact for number
area codes  — —> +49
local access  —> Germany: Berlin, Oldenburg, Bremen, Hamburg, Krefeld, Kiel,
                 Duisburg, Darmstadt, Dortmund, Hannover, Ruhrgebiet, Bonn,
                 Magdeburg, Duesseldorf, Essen, Koeln, Paderborn, Bielefeld,
                 Aachen, Saarbruecken, Frankfurt, Braunschweig, Dresden, Ulm,
                 Erlangen, Nuernberg, Wuerzburg, Chemnitz, Muenchen,
                 Muenster, Goettingen, Wuppertal, Schleswig, Giessen,
                 Rostock, Leipzig and other
long distance -> provided by user
services  — — —> e-mail, usenet feeds, UUCP, SLIP, ISDN, shell, ftp, telnet,
                 gopher, irc, bbs
fees  — — — — —> 15-30 DM/month (differs from region to region)
email  — — — —> in-info@individual.net
voice  — — — —> +49 2131 64190 (Andreas Baess)
fax  — — — —> +49 2131 605652
ftp more info -> ftp.fu-berlin.de:/pub/doc/IN/
```

---

in-rhein-main

```
name  — — — — —> Individual Network - Rhein-Main
dialup — — — —> +49-69-39048414, +49-69-6312934 (+ others)
area codes  — —> +49 069
local access  —> Frankfurt/Offenbach, Germany
long distance -> provided by user
services  — — —> shell (Unix), ftp, telnet, irc, gopher, uucp feeds
fees  — — — — —> SLIP/PPP/ISDN: 40 DM, 4 DM / Megabyte
email  — — — —> info@rhein-main.de
voice  — — — —> +49-69-39048413
ftp more info -> n/a
```

---

ins

```
name  — — — — —> INS - Inter Networking Systems
dialup — — — —> contact for number
area codes  — —> +49 23
```

```
local access —> Ruhr-Area, Germany
long distance -> provided by user
services — — —> e-mail,uucp,usenet,slip,ppp,ISDN-TCP/IP
fees — — — —> fees for commercial institutions and any others:
                uucp/e-mail,uucp/usenet:$60/month; ip:$290/month minimum
email  — — — —> info@ins.net
voice  — — — —> +49 2305 356505
fax   — — — — —> +49 2305 25411
ftp more info -> n/a
```

InterAccess

```
name — — — — —> InterAccess
dialup — — — —> 708-671-0237
area codes — —> 708, 312, 815
local access —> Chicagoland metropolitan area
long distance -> provided by user
services — — —> ftp, telnet, SLIP/PPP, feeds, shell, UUCP, DNS, ftp space
fees — — — — —> $23/mo shell, $26/mo SLIP/PPP, or $5/mo +$2.30/hr
email  — — — —> info@interaccess.com
voice  — — — —> (800) 967-1580
fax   — — — — —> 708-671-0113
ftp more info -> interaccess.com:/pub/interaccess.info
```

jvnc

```
name — — — — —> The John von Neumann Computer Network - Tiger Mail & Dialin'
                Terminal
dialup — — — —> contact for number
area codes — —> 800
local access —> anywhere (800) service is available
long distance -> included
services — — —> email and newsfeed or terminal access only
fees — — — — —> $19/month + $10/hour + $36 startup (PC or Mac SLIP software
                included)
email  — — — —> info@jvnc.net
voice  — — — —> 800-35-TIGER, 609-897-7300
fax   — — — — —> 609-897-7310
ftp more info -> n/a
```

jvnc-tiger

```
name — — — — —> The John von Neumann Computer Network - Dialin' Tiger
dialup — — — —> contact for number
area codes — —> 201, 203, 215, 401, 516, 609, 908
local access —> Princeton & Newark, NJ; Philadelphia, PA; Garden City, NY;
                Bridgeport, New Haven, & Storrs, CT; Providence, RI
```

```
long distance -> provided by user
services — — —> ftp, telnet, SLIP, feeds, optional shell
fees — — — — —> $99/month + $99 startup (PC or Mac SLIP software included —
                shell is additional $21/month)
email   — — — —> info@jvnc.net
voice   — — — —> 800-35-TIGER, 609-897-7300
fax    — — — — —> 609-897-7310
ftp more info -> n/a
```

```
kaiwan

name — — — — —> KAIWAN Public Access Internet Online Services
dialup — — — —> 714-539-5726, 310-527-7358
area codes — —> 213, 310, 714
local access —> CA: Los Angeles, Orange County
long distance -> provided by user
services — — —> shell, ftp, telnet, irc, WAIS, gopher, SLIP/PPP, ftp space,
                feeds, dns, 56K leasd line
fees — — — — —> $15.00/signup + $15.00/month or $30.00/quarter (3 month) or
                $11.00/month by credit card
email   — — — —> info@kaiwan.com
voice   — — — —> 714-638-2139
ftp more info -> kaiwan.com:/pub/KAIWAN
```

```
maestro

name — — — — —> Maestro
dialup — — — —> (212) 240-9700 'newuser'
area codes — —> 212, 718
local access —> NY: New York City
long distance -> provided by user
services — — —> shell, ftp, telnet, gopher, wais, irc, feeds, etc.
fees — — — — —> $15/month or $150/year
email   — — — —> info@maestro.com (autoreply); staff@maestro.com,
                rkelly@maestro.com, ksingh@maestro.com
voice   — — — —> 212-240-9600
ftp more info -> n/a
```

```
mcsnet

name — — — — —> MCSNet
dialup — — — —> (312) 248-0900 V.32, 0970 V.32bis, 6295 (PEP), follow prompts
area codes — —> 312, 708, 815
local access —> IL: Chicago
long distance -> provided by user
```

```
services  — —-> shell, ftp, telnet, feeds, email, irc, gopher, hytelnet, etc.
fees  — — — —-> $25/month or $65/3 months untimed, $30/3 months for 15
                hours/month
email  — — —-> info@genesis.mcs.com
voice  — — —-> (312) 248-UNIX
ftp more info -> genesis.mcs.com:/mcsnet.info/
```

---

metronet

```
name  — — — —-> Texas Metronet
dialup — — — —-> 214-705-2901/817-261-1127 (V.32bis),214-705-2929(PEP),'info'
                or 214-705-2917/817-261-7687 (2400) 'signup'
area codes — —-> 214, 817
local access —-> TX: Dallas, Fort Worth
long distance -> provided by user
services  — —-> shell, ftp, telnet, SLIP, PPP, uucp feeds
fees  — — — —-> $5-$45/month + $10-$30 startup
email  — — —->  info@metronet.com
voice  — — —->  214-705-2900, 817-543-8756
fax  — — — —->  214-401-2802 (8am-5pm CST weekdays)
ftp more info -> ftp.metronet.com:/pub/metronetinfo/
```

---

michnet

```
name  — — — —-> Merit Network, Inc. — MichNet project
dialup — — — —-> contact for number or telnet hermes.merit.edu and type
                'help' at 'Which host?' prompt
area codes — —-> 202, 301, 313, 517, 616, 703, 810, 906, PDN
local access —-> Michigan; Boston, MA; Wash. DC
long distance -> SprintNet, Autonet, Michigan Bell packet-switch network
services  — —-> telnet, SLIP, PPP, outbound SprintNet, Autonet and Ann Arbor
                dialout
fees  — — — —-> $35/month + $40 signup ($10/month for K-12 & libraries in
                Michigan)
email  — — —-> info@merit.edu
voice  — — —-> 313-764-9430
ftp more info -> nic.merit.edu:/
```

---

millennium

```
name  — — — —-> Millennium Online
dialup — — — —-> contact for numbers
area codes — —-> PDN
local access —-> PDN private numbers available
long distance -> PDN
```

```
services  — — —> shell, ftp, telnet, irc, feeds, gopher, graphical bbs
                 (interface required)
fees  — — — — —> $10 monthly/.10 per minute domestic .30 internationally
email  — — — —> jjablow@mill.com
voice  — — — —> 800-736-0122
ftp more info -> n/a
```

---

mindvox

```
name  — — — — —> MindVOX
dialup  — — — —> 212-989-4141 'mindvox' 'guest'
area codes  — —> 212, 718
local access  —> NY: New York City
long distance -> provided by user
services  — — —> conferencing system ftp, telnet, irc, gopher, hytelnet,
                 Archives, BBS
fees  — — — — —> $15-$20/month.   No startup.
email  — — — —> info@phantom.com
voice  — — — —> 212-989-2418
ftp more info -> n/a
```

MSen

```
name  — — — — —> MSen
dialup  — — — —> contact for number
area codes  — —> 313, 810
local access  —> All of SE Michigan (313, 810)
long distance -> provided by user
services  — — —> shell, WAIS, gopher, telnet, ftp, SLIP, PPP, IRC, WWW,
                 Picospan BBS, ftp space
fees  — — — — —> $20/month; $20 startup
email  — — — —> info@msen.com
voice  — — — —> 313-998-4562
fax  — — — — —> 313-998-4563
ftp more info -> ftp.msen.com:/pub/vendor/msen
```

---

mucev

```
name  — — — — —> muc.de e.V.
dialup  — — — —> contact for numbers
area codes  — —> +49 089
local access  —> Munich/Bavaria, Germany
long distance -> provided by user
services  — — —> mail, news, ftp, telnet, irc, gopher, SLIP/PPP/UUCP
```

```
fees  — — — —> From DM 20.— (Mail only) up to DM 65.— (Full Account with
                PPP)
email  — — —> postmaster@muc.de
voice  — — —>
ftp more info -> ftp.muc.de:public/info/muc-info.*
```

```
MV

name  — — — —> MV Communications, Inc.
dialup — — —> contact for numbers
area codes — —> 603
local access —> Many NH communities
long distance -> provided by user
services — — —> shell, ftp, telnet, gopher, SLIP, email, feeds, dns,
                archives, etc.
fees  — — — —> $5.00/mo minimum + variable hourly rates.  See schedule.
email  — — — —> info@mv.com
voice  — — — —> 603-429-2223
ftp more info -> ftp.mv.com:/pub/mv
```

```
nearnet

name  — — — —> NEARnet
dialup — — —> contact for numbers
area codes — —> 508, 603, 617
local access —> Boston, MA; Nashua, NH
long distance -> provided by user
services — — —> SLIP, email, feeds, dns
fees  — — — —> $250/month
email  — — — —> nearnet-join@nic.near.net
voice  — — — —> 617-873-8730
ftp more info -> nic.near.net:/docs
```

```
netcom

name — — — —> Netcom Online Communication Services
dialup — — —> 206-547-5992, 214-753-0045, 303-758-0101, 310-842-8835,
              312-380-0340, 404-303-9765, 408-241-9760, 408-459-9851,
              415-328-9940, 415-985-5650, 503-626-6833, 510-274-2900,
              510-426-6610, 510-865-9004, 617-237-8600, 619-234-0524,
              703-255-5951, 714-708-3800, 818-585-3400, 916-965-1371
area codes — —> 206, 213, 214, 303, 310, 312, 404, 408, 415, 503, 510,
              617, 619, 703, 714, 718, 818, 916
```

```
local access —> CA: Alameda, Irvine, Los Angeles, Palo Alto, Pasadena,
                    Sacramento, San Diego, San Francisco, San Jose, Santa Cruz,
                    Walnut Creek; CO: Denver; DC: Washington; GA: Atlanta; IL:
                    Chicago; MA: Boston; OR: Portland; TX: Dallas; WA: Seattle
long distance -> provided by user
services ———> shell, ftp, telnet, irc, WAIS, gopher, SLIP/PPP, ftp space,
                    feeds, dns
fees —————> $19.50/month + $20.00 signup
email ————> info@netcom.com
voice ————> 408-554-8649, 800-501-8649
fax ————> 408-241-9145
ftp more info -> ftp.netcom.com:/pub/netcom/
```

```
northshore

name —————> North Shore Access
dialup ————> 617-593-4557 (v.32bis, v.32, PEP) 'new'
area codes —> 617, 508
local access —> MA: Wakefield, Lynnfield, Lynn, Saugus, Revere, Peabody,
                    Salem, Marblehead, Swampscott
long distance -> provided by user
services ———> shell (SunOS UNIX), ftp, telnet, archie, gopher, wais, www,
                    UUCP feeds
fees —————> $9/month includes 10 hours connect, $1/hr thereafter, higher
                    volume discount plans also available
email ————> info@northshore.ecosoft.com
voice ————> 617-593-3110 voicemail
ftp more info -> northshore.ecosoft.com:/pub/flyer
```

```
novalink

name —————> NovaLink
dialup ————> (800) 937-7644 'new' or 'info', 508-754-4009 2400, 14400
area codes —> 508, 617, PDN
local access —> MA: Worcester, Cambridge, Marlboro, Boston
long distance -> CPS: $1.80/hour 2400, 9600; SprintNet $1.80/hour nights and
                    weekends
services ———> ftp, telnet, gopher, shell, irc, XWindows, feeds, adult,
                    user groups, FAX, Legends of Future Past
fees —————> $12.95 sign-up (refundable and includes 2 hours), + $9.95/mo
                    (includes 5 daytime hours) + $1.80/hr
email ————> info@novalink.com
voice ————> 800-274-2814
ftp more info -> ftp.novalink.com:/info
```

```
nuance

name  — — — — —>  Nuance Network Services
dialup  — — — —>  contact for number
area codes  — —>  205
local access  —>  AL: Huntsville
long distance ->  provided by user
services  — — —>  shell (Unix SVR4.2), ftp, telnet, gopher, SLIP, PPP, ISDN
fees  — — — — —>  personal $25/mo + $35 start-up, corporate: call for options
email   — — — —>  staff@nuance.com
voice   — — — —>  205-533-4296 voice/recording
ftp more info ->  ftp.nuance.com:/pub/NNS-INFO
```

```
nuchat

name  — — — — —>  South Coast Computing Services, Inc.
dialup  — — — —>  (713) 661-8593 (v.32) - (713) 661-8595 (v.32bis)
area codes  — —>  713
local access  —>  TX: Houston metro area
long distance ->  provided by user
services  — — —>  shell, ftp, telnet, gopher, Usenet, UUCP feeds, SLIP,
                  dedicated lines, domain name service, FULL time tech support
fees  — — — — —>  dialup - $3/hour, UUCP - $1.50/hour or $100/month unlimited,
                  dedicated - $120, unlimited access
email   — — — —>  info@sccsi.com
voice   — — — —>  713-661-3301
ftp more info ->  sccsi.com:/pub/communications/*
```

```
nwnexus

name  — — — — —>  Northwest Nexus Inc.
dialup  — — — —>  contact for numbers
area codes  — —>  206
local access  —>  WA: Seattle
long distance ->  provided by user
services  — — —>  UUCP, SLIP, PPP, feeds, dns
fees  — — — — —>  $10/month for first 10 hours + $3/hr; $20 start-up
email   — — — —>  info@nwnexus.wa.com
voice   — — — —>  206-455-3505
ftp more info ->  nwnexus.wa.com:/NWNEXUS.info.txt
```

```
nyx

name  — — — — —>  Nyx, the Spirit of the Night; Free public internet access
                  provided by the University of Denver's Math & Computer
                  Science Department
dialup  — — — —>  303-871-3324
area codes  — —>  303
```

```
local access  —> CO: Boulder/Denver
long distance -> provided by user
services  — — —> shell or menu; semi-anonymous accounts; ftp, news, mail
fees  — — — — —> none; donations are accepted but not requested
email   — — — — —> aburt@nyx.cs.du.edu
voice   — — — — —> login to find current list of volunteer 'voice' helpers
ftp more info -> n/a
```

OARnet

```
name  — — — — —> OARnet
dialup  — — — —> send e-mail to nic@oar.net
area codes  — —> 614, 513, 419, 216, 800
local access  —> OH: Columbus, Cincinnati, Cleveland, Dayton
long distance -> 800 service
services  — — —> email, ftp, telnet, newsfeed
fees  — — — — —> $4.00/hr to $330.00/month; call for code or send email
email   — — — —> nic@oar.net
voice   — — — —> 614-292-8100
fax   — — — — —> 614-292-7168
ftp more info -> n/a
```

---

oldcolo

```
name  — — — — —> Old Colorado City Communications
dialup  — — — —> 719-632-4111 'newuser'
area codes  — —> 719
local access  —> CO: Colorado Springs
long distance -> provided by user
services  — — —> shell, ftp, telnet, AKCS, home of the NAPLPS conference
fees  — — — — —> $25/month
email   — — — —> dave@oldcolo.com / thefox@oldcolo.com
voice   — — — —> 719-632-4848, 719-593-7575 or 719-636-2040
fax   — — — — —> 719-593-7521
ftp more info -> n/a
```

---

olympus

```
name  — — — — —> Olympus - The Olympic Peninsula's Gateway To The Internet
dialup  — — — —> contact voice number below
area codes  — —> 206
local access  —> WA:Olympic Peninsula/Eastern Jefferson County
long distance -> provided by user
services  — — —> shell, ftp, telnet, pine, hytelnet
fees  — — — — —> $25/month + $10 startup
email   — — — —> info@pt.olympus.net
voice   — — — —> 206-385-0464
ftp more info -> n/a
```

```
panix

name  — — — —> PANIX Public Access Unix
dialup  — — — —> 212-787-3100 'newuser'
area codes  — —> 212, 718
local access  —> New York City, NY
long distance -> provided by user
services  — — —> shell, ftp, telnet, gopher, wais, irc, feeds
fees  — — — — —> $19/month or $208/year + $40 signup
email   — — — —> alexis@panix.com, jsb@panix.com
voice   — — — —> 212-877-4854 [Alexis Rosen], 212-691-1526 [Jim Baumbach]
ftp more info -> n/a
```

```
pipeline

name  — — — — —> The Pipeline
dialup  — — — —> 212-267-8606 'guest'
area codes  — —> 212, 718
local access  —> NY: New York City
long distance -> provided by user
services  — — —> Windows interface or shell/menu; all IP services
fees  — — — — —> $15/mo. (inc. 5 hrs) or $20/20 hrs or $35 unlimited
email   — — — —> info@pipeline.com, staff@pipeline.com
voice   — — — —> 212-267-3636
ftp more info -> n/a
```

```
portal

name  — — — — —> The Portal System
dialup  — — — —> 408-973-8091 high-speed, 408-725-0561 2400bps; 'info'
area codes  — —> 408, 415, PDN
local access  —> CA: Cupertino, Mountain View, San Jose
long distance -> SprintNet: $2.50/hour off-peak, $7-$10/hour peak; Tymnet:
                 $2.50/hour off-peak, $13/hour peak
services  — — —> shell, ftp, telnet, IRC, UUCP, feeds, bbs
fees  — — — — —> $19.95/month + $19.95 signup
email   — — — —> cs@cup.portal.com, info@portal.com
voice   — — — —> 408-973-9111
ftp more info -> n/a
off-peak  — — —> 6pm to 7am + weekends and holidays
```

```
prairienet

name  — — — — —> Prairienet Freenet
dialup  — — — —> (217) 255-9000 'visitor'
area codes  — —> 217
```

```
local access —> IL: Champaign-Urbana
long distance -> provided by user
services — — —> telnet, ftp, gopher, IRC, etc.
fees — — — — —> Free for Illinois residents, $25/year for non-residents
email  — — — —> jayg@uiuc.edu
voice  — — — —> 217-244-1962
ftp more info -> n/a
```

PREPnet

```
name — — — — —> PREPnet
dialup — — — —> contact for numbers
area codes — —> 215, 412, 717, 814
local access —> PA: Philadelphia, Pittsburgh, Harrisburg
long distance -> provided by user
services — — —> SLIP, terminal service, telnet, ftp
fees — — — — —> $1,000/year membership.  Equipment-$325 onetime fee plus
                $40/month
email  — — — —> prepnet@cmu.edu
voice  — — — —> 412-268-7870
fax  — — — — —> 412-268-7875
ftp more info -> ftp.prepnet.com:/prepnet/general/
```

---

psilink

```
name — — — — —> PSILink -  Personal Internet Access
dialup — — — —> North America: send email to classa-na-numbers@psi.com and
                classb-na-numbers@psi.com; Rest of World: send email to
                classb-row-numbers@psi.com
area codes — —> PDN
local access —>
long distance -> [per hour, off-peak/peak] PSINet A: included; PSINet B:
                $6/$2.50; PSINet B international: $18/$18
services — — —> email and newsfeed, ftp
fees — — — — —> 2400: $19/month; 9600: $29/month (PSILink software included)
email  — — — —> all-info@psi.com, psilink-info@psi.com
voice  — — — —> 703-620-6651
fax  — — — — —> 703-620-4586
ftp more info -> ftp.psi.com:/
```

---

psi-world-dial

```
name — — — — —> PSI's World-Dial Service
dialup — — — —> send email to numbers-info@psi.com
area codes — —> PDN
local access —>
```

```
long distance -> [per hour, off-peak/peak] V.22bis: $1.25/$2.75; V.32:
                 $3.00/$4.50; 14.4K: $4.00/$6.50
services — — —> telnet, rlogin, tn3270, XRemote
fees — — — — —> $9/month minimum + $19 startup
email  — — — —> all-info@psi.com, world-dial-info@psi.com
voice  — — — —> 703-620-6651
fax  — — — — —> 703-620-4586
ftp more info -> ftp.psi.com:/
off-peak — — —> 8pm to 8am + weekends and holidays
```

PUCnet

```
name — — — — —> PUCnet Computer Connections
dialup — — — —> 403-484-5640 (v.32 bis) 'guest'
area codes — —> 403
local access —> AB: Edmonton and surrounding communities in the Extended
                Flat Rate Calling Area
long distance -> provided by user
services — — —> shell, menu, ftp, telnet, archie, gopher, feeds, USENET
fees — — — — —> Cdn$25/month (20 hours connect time) + Cdn$6.25/hr (ftp &
                telnet only) + $10 signup
email  — — — —> info@PUCnet.com (Mail responder) or pwilson@PUCnet.com
voice  — — — —> 403-448-1901
fax  — — — — —> 403-484-7103
ftp more info -> n/a
```

realtime

```
name — — — — —> RealTime Communications (wixer)
dialup — — — —> 512-459-4391 'new'
area codes — —> 512
local access —> TX: Austin
long distance -> provided by user
services — — —> shell, ftp, telnet, irc, gopher, feeds, SLIP, UUCP
fees — — — — —> $75/year.  Monthly and quarterly rates available.
email  — — — —> hosts@wixer.bga.com
voice  — — — —> 512-451-0046 (11am-6pm Central Time, weekdays)
fax  — — — — —> 512-459-3858
ftp more info -> n/a
```

ssnet

```
name — — — — —> Systems Solutions
dialup — — — —> contact for info
area codes — —> 302
local access —> Wilminton, Delaware
```

```
long distance -> provided by user
services — — —> shell, UUCP, SLIP, PPP, ftp, telnet, irc, gopher, archie,
                mud, etc.
fees — — — — —> full service  $25/month $20/startup; personal slip/ppp
                $25/month + $2/hour, $20/startup; dedicated slip/ppp
                $150/month, $450/startup
email  — — — —> sharris@marlin.ssnet.com
voice  — — — —> (302) 378-1386, (800) 331-1386
ftp more info -> n/a
```

```
sugar

name  — — — — —> NeoSoft's Sugar Land Unix
dialup — — — —> 713-684-5900
area codes — —> 504, 713
local access —> TX: Houston metro area; LA: New Orleans
long distance -> provided by user
services — — —> bbs, shell, ftp, telnet, irc, feeds, UUCP
fees — — — — —> $29.95/month
email  — — — —> info@NeoSoft.com
voice  — — — —> 713-438-4964
ftp more info -> n/a
```

```
teleport

name  — — — — —> Teleport
dialup — — — —> 503-220-0636 (2400) 503-220-1016 (v.32, v.32 bis) 'new'
area codes — —> 503
local access —> OR: Portland, Beaverton, Hillsboro, Forest Grove, Gresham,
                Tigard, Lake Oswego, Oregon City, Tualatin, Wilsonville
long distance -> provided by user
services — — —> shell, ftp, telnet, gopher, usenet, ppp, WAIS, irc, feeds,
                dns
fees — — — — —> $10/month (1 hr/day limit)
email  — — — —> info@teleport.com
voice  — — — —> 503-223-4245
ftp more info -> teleport.com:/about
```

```
telerama

name  — — — — —> Telerama Public Access Internet
dialup — — — —> 412-481-5302 'new' (2400)
area codes — —> 412
local access —> PA: Pittsburgh
long distance -> provided by user
services — — —> telnet, ftp, irc, gopher, ClariNet/Usenet, shell/menu, uucp
```

```
fees  — — — —> 66 cents/hour 2400bps; $1.32/hour 14.4K bps; $6 min/month
email  — — —> info@telerama.pgh.pa.us
voice  — — —> 412-481-3505
ftp more info -> telerama.pgh.pa.us:/info/general.info
```

```
tmn
```

```
name  — — — —> The Meta Network
dialup — — — —> contact for numbers
area codes  — —> 703, 202, 301, PDN
local access  —> Washington, DC metro area
long distance -> SprintNet: $6.75/hr; FTS-2000; Acunet
services  — — —> Caucus conferencing, email, shell, ftp, telnet, bbs, feeds
fees  — — — — —> $20/month + $15 signup/first month
email  — — — —> info@tmn.com
voice  — — — —> 703-243-6622
ftp more info -> n/a
```

```
UUNET-Canada
```

```
name  — — — — —> UUNET Canada, Inc.
dialup — — — —> contact for numbers
area codes  — —> 416, 905, 519, 613, 514, 604, 403
local access  —> ON: Toronto, Ottawa, Kitchener/Waterloo, London, Hamilton,
                 QC: Montreal,   AB: Calgary,   BC: Vancouver
long distance -> provided by user
services  — — —> terminal access to telnet only, UUCP (e-mail/news),
                 SLIP/PPP, shared or dedicated basis, from v.32bis to 56k+
fees  — — — — —> (All Cdn$ + GST) TAC: $6/hr, UUCP: $20/mo + $6/hr, IP/UUCP:
                 $50/mo + $6/hr, ask for prices on other services
email  — — — —> info@uunet.ca
voice  — — — —> 416-368-6621
fax  — — — — —> 416-368-1350
ftp more info -> ftp.uunet.ca
```

```
uunorth
```

```
name  — — — — —> UUnorth
dialup — — — —> contact for numbers
area codes  — —> 416, 519, 613
local access  —> ON: Toronto
long distance -> provided by user
services  — — —> shell, ftp, telnet, gopher, feeds, IRC, feeds, SLIP, PPP
fees  — — — — —> (All Cdn$ + GST) $20 startup + $25 for 20 hours off-peak +
                 $1.25/hr OR $40 for 40 hours up to 5/day + $2/hr OR $3/hr
```

```
email   — — — —> uunorth@uunorth.north.net
voice   — — — —> 416-225-8649
fax     — — — — —> 416-225-0525
ftp more info -> n/a
```

Vnet

```
name   — — — — —> Vnet Internet Access, Inc.
dialup — — — —> 704-347-8839, 919-406-1544, 919-851-1526 'new'
area codes — —> 704, 919
local access —> NC: Charlotte, RTP, Raleigh, Durham, Chappel Hill. Winston
                Salem/Greensboro
long distance -> Available for $3.95 per hour through Global Access. Contact
                Vnet offices for more information.
services — —> shell, ftp, telnet, hytelnet, irc, gopher, WWW, wais,
                usenet, clarinet, NNTP, DNS, SLIP/PPP, UUCP, POPmail
fees   — — — — —> $25/month individual. $12.50 a month for telnet-in-only.
                SLIP/PPP/UUCP starting at $25/month.
email  — — — —> info@char.vnet.net
voice  — — — —> 704-374-0779
ftp more info -> n/a
```

---

well

```
name   — — — — —> The Whole Earth 'Lectronic Link
dialup — — — —> 415-332-6106 'newuser'
area codes — —> 415, PDN
local access —> Sausalito, CA
long distance -> Compuserve Packet Network: $4/hour
services — —> shell, ftp, telnet, bbs
fees   — — — — —> $15.00/month + $2.00/hr
email  — — — —> info@well.sf.ca.us
voice  — — — —> 415-332-4335
ftp more info -> n/a
```

---

wariat

```
name   — — — — —> APK- Public Access UNI* Site
dialup — — — —> 216-481-9436  (V.32bis, SuperPEP on separate rotary)
area codes — —> 216
local access —> OH: Cleveland
long distance -> provided by user
services — —> shell, ftp, telnet, archie, irc, gopher, feeds,
                BBS(Uniboard1.10)
```

```
fees  — — — —> $15/20 hours, $35/monthly, $20 signup
email  — — —> zbig@wariat.org
voice  — — —> 216-481-9428
ftp more info -> n/a
```

```
world

name  — — — —> The World
dialup  — — — —> 617-739-9753 'new'
area codes  — —> 617, PDN
local access  —> Boston, MA
long distance -> Compuserve Packet Network: $5.60/hour
services  — — —> shell, ftp, telnet, irc
fees  — — — —> $5.00/month + $2.00/hr or $20/month for 20 hours
email  — — — —> office@world.std.com
voice  — — — —> 617-739-0202
ftp more info -> world.std.com:/world-info/description
```

```
wyvern

name  — — — —> Wyvern Technologies, Inc.
dialup  — — — —> (804) 627-1828 Norfolk, (804) 886-0662 (Peninsula)
area codes  — —> 804
local access  —> VA: Norfolk, Virginia Beach, Portsmouth, Chesapeake, Newport
                 News, Hampton, Williamsburg
long distance -> provided by user
services  — — —> shell, menu, ftp, telnet, uucp feeds, irc, archie, gopher,
                 UPI news, email, dns, archives
fees  — — — —> $15/month or $144/year, $10 startup
email  — — — —> system@wyvern.com
voice  — — — —> 804-622-4289
fax  — — — —> 804-622-7158
ftp more info -> n/a
```

```
xnet

name  — — — —> XNet Information Systems
dialup  — — — —> (708) 983-6435 V.32bis and TurboPEP
area codes  — —> 312, 708, 815
local access  —> IL: Chicago, Naperville, Hoffman Estates
long distance -> provided by user
```

```
services ———> shell, telnet, hytelnet, ftp, irc, gopher, www, wais,
               SLIP/PPP, dns, uucp feeds, bbs
fees ————-> $45/3 months or $75/6 months
email ———-> info@xnet.com
voice ———-> (708) 983-6064
ftp more info -> ftp.xnet.com:/xnet.info/
```

What Is The Internet?

From: PDIAL -05-
Subject: What *Is* The Internet?

The Internet is a global cooperative network of university, corporate,
government, and private computers, all communicating with each other by
means of something called TCP/IP (Transmission Control Protocol/Internet
Protocol). Computers directly on the Internet can exchange data quickly
and easily with any other computer on the Internet to download files, send
email, provide remote logins, etc.

Users can download files from publicly accessible archive sites ("anonymous
FTP"); login into remote computers (telnet or rlogin); chat in real-time
with other users around the world (Internet Relay Chat); or use the newest
information retrieval tools to find a staggering variety of information
(Wide Area Information Servers, Gopher, World-Wide Web).

Computers directly on the Internet also exchange email directly and very
quickly; email is usually delivered in seconds between Internet sites.

Sometimes the Internet is confused with other related networks or types of
networking.

First, there are other ways to be "connected to the Internet" without being
directly connected as a TCP/IP node. Some computers connect via UUCP or
other means at regular intervals to an Internet site to exchange email and
USENET newsgroups, for instance. Such a site can provide email (though not
as quickly as a directly connected systems) and USENET access, but not
Internet downloads, remote logins, etc.

"Email" (or "Internet email", "netmail") can be exchanged with a wide
variety of systems connected directly and indirectly to the Internet. The
email may travel solely over the Internet, or it may traverse other
networks and systems.

"USENET" is the collection of computers all over the world that exchange
USENET news — thousands of "newsgroups" (like forums, or echoes) on a wide
range of topics. The newsgroup articles are distributed all over the world
to USENET sites that wish to carry them (sometimes over the Internet,
sometimes not), where people read and respond to them.

The "NSFNET" is one of the backbones of the Internet in the U.S. It is
funded by the NSF, which restricts traffic over the NSFNET to "open
research and education in and among U.S. research and instructional
institutions, plus research arms of for-profit firms when engaged in
open scholarly communication and research." Your Internet provider
can give you more details about acceptable use, and alternatives
should you need to use the Internet in other ways.

What The PDIAL Is

From: PDIAL -06-
Subject: What The PDIAL Is

This is the PDIAL, the Public Dialup Internet Access List.

It is a list of Internet service providers offering public access dialins
and outgoing Internet access (ftp, telnet, etc.). Most of them provide
email and USENET news and other services as well.

If one of these systems is not accessible to you and you need email or
USENET access, but *don't* need ftp or telnet, you have many more public
access systems from which to choose. Public access systems without ftp or
telnet are *not* listed in this list, however. See the nixpub (alt.bbs,
comp.misc) list and other BBS lists.

Some of these providers offer time-shared access to a shell or BBS program
on a computer connected directly to the Internet, through which you can
FTP or telnet to other systems on the Internet. Usually other services
are provided as well. Generally, you need only a modem and terminal or
terminal emulator to access these systems. Check for "shell", "bbs", or
"menu" on the "services" line.

Other providers connect you directly to the Internet via SLIP or PPP when
you dial in. For these you need a computer system capable of running the
software to interface with the Internet, e.g., a Unix machine, PC, or Mac.
Check for "SLIP", or "PPP" on the services line.

While I have included all sites for which I have complete information, this
list is surely incomplete. If you have any additions or corrections please
send them to me at one of the addresses listed in section -10-.

How People Can Get The PDIAL (This List)

From: PDIAL -07-
Subject: How People Can Get The PDIAL (This List)

EMAIL:

From the Information Deli archive server (most up-to-date):
To receive the current edition of the PDIAL, send email containing
the phrase "Send PDIAL" to "info-deli-server@netcom.com".

To be put on a list of people who receive future editions as they
are published, send email containing the phrase "Subscribe PDIAL"
to "info-deli-server@netcom.com".

To receive both the most recent and future editions, send both
messages.

From time to time, I'll also be sending out news and happenings
that relate to the PDIAL or The Information Deli. To receive
the Info Deli News automatically, send email containing the
phrase "Subscribe Info-Deli-News" to "info-deli-server@netcom.com".

From the news.answers FAQ archive:
Send email with the message "send usenet/news.answers/pdial" to
"mail-server@rtfm.mit.edu". For help, send the message "help" to
"mail-server@rtfm.mit.edu".

USENET:

The PDIAL list is posted semi-regularly to alt.internet.access.wanted,
alt.bbs.lists, alt.online-service, ba.internet, and news.answers.

FTP ARCHIVE SITES (PDIAL and other useful information):

Information Deli FTP site:
ftp.netcom.com:/pub/info-deli/public-access/pdial [192.100.81.100]

As part of a collection of public access lists:
VFL.Paramax.COM:/pub/pubnet/pdial [128.126.220.104]
(used to be GVL.Unisys.COM)

From the Merit Network Information Center Internet information archive:
nic.merit.edu:/internet/providers/pdial [35.1.1.48]

As part of an Internet access compilation file:
   liberty.uc.wlu.edu:/pub/lawlib/internet.access [137.113.10.35]

As part of the news.answers FAQ archive:
   rtfm.mit.edu:/pub/usenet/news.answers/pdial [18.70.0.209]

Other Valuable Resources

From: PDIAL -08-
Subject: Appendix A: Other Valuable Resources

InterNIC Internet Help Desk

   The U.S. National Science Foundation has funded Information, Registration,
   and Directory services for the Internet, and they are available to all
   Internet users. The most useful branch for PDIAL readers is Information
   Services, which provides all sorts of information to help Internet users.
   Contact Information Services by:

   voice: 800-444-4345 (US)
   voice: +1 (619) 455-4600
   fax: +1 (619) 455-4640
   email: mailserv@is.internic.net, put "SEND HELP" in body
   email: info@internic.net
   gopher: gopher gopher.internic.net / telnet gopher.internic.net
   ftp: is.internic.net
   postal: InterNIC Information Services
            General Atomics
            PO Box 85608
            San Diego, CA 92186-9784 USA

Internet Guide Books

   Connecting To The Internet; Susan Estrada; O'Reilly & Associates; ISBN
   1-56592-061-9 (A how-to on selecting the right IP provider, from dialup
   to dedicated.)

   A DOS User's Guide to the Internet — E-mail, Netnews and File Transfer
   with UUCP; James Gardner; MKS; ISBN 0-13-106873-3 ("Internet" in the
   title is misleading — covers UUCP connections only.)

   The Electronic Traveller — Exploring Alternative Online Systems;
   Elizabeth Powell Crowe; Windcrest/McGraw-Hill; ISBN 0-8306-4498-9. (A
   good tour of various personal IP and other types of providers, but some
   data is seriously out of date.)

Internet Basics; Steve Lambert, Walt How; Random House; ISBN
0-679-75023-1

The Internet Companion; Tracy LaQuey, Jeanne C. Ryer; Addison-Wesley;
ISBN 0-201-62224-6

The Internet Companion Plus; Tracy LaQuey, Jeanne C. Ryer;
Addison-Wesley; ISBN 0-201-62719-1

The Internet Complete Reference; Harley Hahn, Rick Stout; Osborne;
ISBN 0-07-881980-6

The Internet Directory; Eric Brawn; Fawcett Columbine; ISBN
0-449-90898-4 (Phone book style listing of resources.)

The Internet for Dummies; John R. Levine, Carol Baroudi; IDG Books
Worldwide; ISBN 1-56884-024-1 (Lots of useful information, but much
of it is intermediate level, not "dummy".)

Internet: Getting Started; April Marine, Susan Kirkpatrick, Vivian
Neou, Carol Ward; PTR Prentice Hall; ISBN 0-13-289596-X

The Internet Guide for New Users; Daniel P. Dern; McGraw-Hill; ISBN
0-07-016511-4 (Good, very thorough guide for new users.)

The Internet Navigator; Paul Glister; John Wiley & Sons; ISBN
0-471-59782-1 (Good, comprehensive guide for new users.)

The Internet Roadmap; Bennet Falk; Sybex; ISBN 0-7821-1365-6

**Internet Starter Kit for the Macintosh With Disk; Adam C. Engst; Hayden
Books; ISBN 1-56830-111-1**

The Mac Internet Tour Guide; Michael Fraase; Ventana Press; ISBN
1-56604-062-0

Navigating the Internet; Richard J. Smith, Mark Gibbs; SAMS
Publishing; ISBN 0-672-30362-0

Welcome to... Internet — From Mystery to Mastery; Tom Badgett, Corey
Sandler; MIS:Press; ISBN 1-55828-308-0

The Whole Internet User's Guide & Catalog; Ed Krol; O'Reilly & Associates;
ISBN 1-56592-025-2 (Good all around guide.)

Zen & the Art of the Internet: A Beginner's Guide; Brendan P. Kehoe;
PTR Prentice Hall; ISBN 0-13-010778-6

```
Other BBS/Internet Provider Lists

  FSLIST — The Forgotten Site List.  USENET: alt.internet.access.wanted;
  ftp: freedom.nmsu.edu:/pub/docs/fslist/ or login.qc.ca:/pub/fslist/

  nixpub — public access Unixes. USENET: comp.bbs.mis, alt.bbs;
  email: to <mail-server@bts.com>, body containing "get PUB nixpub.long";
  ftp: VFL.Paramax.COM:/pub/pubnetc/nixpub.long
```

Finding Public Data Network (PDN) Access Numbers

```
From: PDIAL -09-
Subject: Appendix B: Finding Public Data Network (PDN) Access Numbers

Here's how to get local access numbers or information for the various
PDNs. Generally, you can contact the site you're calling for help, too.

IMPORTANT NOTE: Unless noted otherwise, set your modem to 7E1 (7 data
bits, even parity, 1 stop bit) when dialing to look up access numbers
by modem as instructed below.


BT Tymnet
— — — —


For information and local access numbers, call 800-937-2862 (voice) or
215-666-1770 (voice).

To look up access numbers by modem, dial a local access number, hit
<cr> and 'a', and enter "information" at the "please log in:" prompt.


Compuserve Packet Network
— — — — — — — — — — — —

You do NOT have to be a Compuserve member to use the CPN to dial other
services.

For information and local access numbers, call 800-848-8199 (voice).

To look up access numbers by modem, dial a local access number, hit
<cr> and enter "PHONES" at the "Host Name:" prompt.
```

PSINet

— — —

For information, call 800-82PSI82 (voice) or 703-620-6651 (voice), or
send email to all-info@psi.com. For a list of local access numbers
send email to numbers-info@psi.com.

— — — — — — — — — — — — — —

From: PDIAL -10-
Subject: Providers: Get Listed in PDIAL!

NEW SUBMISSION/CORRECTION PROCEDURES:

The PDIAL will be undergoing expansion in both breadth (how many and what
kinds of public access providers) and depth (how much information is
carried for each provider). To collect the data, I will be emailing a
questionnaire to providers already on the PDIAL, and to any providers who
wish to be added. Corrections can also be submitted via update
questionnaires.

To be listed in the PDIAL, retrieve the PDIAL questionnaire by sending email
to <info-deli-server@netcom.com> containing the command "Send PDIAL-Q". The
questionnaire will not be available until 15 Dec 1993, but requests received
before then will be queued and honored when it is available.

—

Peter Kaminski / The Information Deli

kaminski@netcom.com (preferred)
71053.2155@compuserve.com

— — — — — — — — — — — — — —

End of PDIAL
****

Appendix D

Supplementary PDIAL List

Useful as the PDIAL list is, it's not completely up to date (either in providers listed or fees), and I wanted to provide pointers to as many Internet providers as I could. I asked on Usenet for people to send me their provider information if that provider was not listed in the PDIAL list, and here are the results. If you have email access via America Online or CompuServe, for instance, I recommend sending email to their information address. If you have no email access at all, call the voice number; see tables D.1 (U.S.), D.2 (Canada), D.3 (Europe), D.4 (Australia), and D.5 (Far East).

Table D.1
U.S. Internet Providers Not in PDIAL List

Name	Info Address	Phone	Area Codes Covered
CCnet Communications	info@ccnet.com	510-988-0680	510
Colmik's Connection	mps@colmiks.com	203-230-4848	203
Community Internet Connect	info@cici.com	205-722-0199	205

continues

Connected	info@connected.com	206-562-4224	206
Digital Express Group	info@digex.net	800-969-9090, 301-220-2020	201, 301, 410, 609, 703, 714, 908, 909
EarthLink Network	info@earthlink.net	213-644-9500	213, 310, 818
FXnet	info@fx.net	704-338-4670	704, 803
GlobalCom	ealbrigo @globalcom.net	703-205-2723	703, 202, 301
Great Basin Internet Services	info@greatbasin.com	702-829-2244	702
Internet On-Ramp	info@on-ramp.ior.com	509-927-8553	509
InterNex Information Services	info@internex.net	415-473-3060	415, 510, 408
Interpath	info@interpath.net	800-849-6305	919, 704, 910
Lightside	info@lightside.com	818-858-9261	818, 909, 310, 714
LineX Communications	info@linex.com	415-491-7900	415, 510
NetDepot	info@netdepot.com	404-434-5595	404, 910, 407
North Bay Network	info@nbn.com	415-472-1600	415
Olympus	info@pt.olympus.net	206-385-0464	206
Opus One	info@opus1.com	602-324-0494	602
RAIN	picard@rain.org	805-564-1871	805
Silicon Valley Public Access Link	gopher://svpal.org	415-961-1681	408, 415
South Valley Internet	info@garlic.com	408-683-4533	Exchanges 683, 778, 779, 842, 847, 848 in area code 408
Tech Com USA	info@wizard.com	702-871-4461	702
TIAC— The Internet Access Company	info@tiac.net	617-275-2221	617, some 508
US Net	info@us.net	301-572-5926	301
Winternet	info@winternet.com	612-941-9177	612

Table D.2
Canadian Internet Providers Not in PDIAL List

Name	Info Address	Phone	Area Codes Covered
HookUp Communications	info@hookup.net	905-847-8000	(Canada)
Inter-Accès	sales@interax.net	514-934-5017	514, 800 (Canada)
InterLog Internet Services	internet@interlog.com	416-537-7435	416 (Canada)
Mind Link	tracy@mindlink.bc.ca	604-534-5663	604 (Vancouver, Canada)
NB*Net	newmanb@nbnet.nb.ca	506-450-2780	506 (Canada)

Table D.3
European Internet Providers Not in PDIAL List

Name	Info Address	Phone	Area Codes Covered
Agora' telematica	s.agora@agora.stm.it	39-6-6991742	(Italy)
CityScape	sales@cityscape.co.uk	0223-566950	071/081, 021, 0272, 0223, 031, 061 (UK)
EUnet	sales@britain.eu.net	0227-475497	(UK)
EUnet Belgium N.V.	info@belgium.eu.net	32-0-16-236099	016, 02, 03 (Belgium)
EUNet France/FNet	info@france.eu.net	33-1-53-81-60-60	Paris (France)
ExNet	helpex@exnet.com	081-244-0077	081, 031 (UK)
FDN (French Data Network)	info@fdn.org	33-1-44-62-90-64	Paris (France)
FranceNet	info@francenet.fr	36-70-75-25	Paris (France)
Infoboard Telematics	info@infoboard.be	32-0-2-4752531	02 (Belgium)
INFONET		32-0-2-6466000	02 (Belgium, Sep-94)
INnet	info@inbe.net	32-0-14-319937	014 (Belgium)
Ireland On-Line	info@iol.ie	353-91-92727	(Ireland)
Oleane	info@oleane.net	33-1-43-28-32-32	Paris (France)
Pipex	pipex@pipex.net	0223-250120	071/081, 0223, 031 (UK)
RCI/Calvacom/CalvaNet	rci1@calvacom.fr	33-1-41-08-11-00	Paris & Lyon (France)
Research And Academic Network In Poland	hostmaster@nask.org.pl	48-22-268000	(Poland)
SCT/World-Net	info@world-net.sct.fr	33-1-60-20-85-14	Paris (France)
SpaceNet GmbH	info@space.net	49-89-324683-0	08 (Bavaria, Germany)
Telecom Finland	info@tfi.be	32-2-726-8655	02 (Belgium)

Table D.4
Australian Internet Providers Not in PDIAL List

Name	Info Address	Phone	Area Codes Covered
APANA	info@apana.org.au		02, 03, 05, 06, 07, 08, & parts of 085 for SLIP, as well as 002, 049, 042 for UUCP (Australia)
DIALix Internet Services	info@dialix.com	61-9-244-2433	02, 03, 08, 09, 1-800 (Australia)
iiNet Technologies	iinet@iinet.com.au	61-09-307-1183	09 (Australia)

Table D.5
Far Eastern Internet Providers Not in PDIAL List

Name	Info Address	Phone	Area Codes Covered
Hong Kong SuperNet	cjparker@hk.super.net	852-6585515	(Hong Kong)
Typhoon	n.fung@genie.geis.com	81-3-3757-4640 (fax)	03, 0990 (Tokyo, Japan)

Hayden Books has worked out a deal with one of the providers, Northwest Nexus, for two weeks free access time and a reduced flat rate of $22.50 per month for PPP or SLIP accounts. This deal is certainly worth comparing with other providers (and be aware that the listings don't always carry complete or updated data), but I think you'll find that the Northwest Nexus offer is extremely attractive for Internet access (see appendix F for the details, and note that using Northwest Nexus requires a long distance call if you live outside of the Puget Sound/Seattle area).

I also recommend that you briefly look at the rates for the commercial services such as AppleLink ($37.00 per hour at 9,600 bps) and CompuServe ($22.50 per hour at 9,600 bps) in chapter 9 because they help bring home what a good deal some of these Internet providers give you.

Glossary

A

address commands   Small extensions for UUCP/Connect that give it additional capabilities, much as XMCDs and XFCNs give HyperCard additional capabilities.

addressing   A method of identifying a resource (such as a program) or piece of information (such as a file) on a network. Methods of addressing vary considerably from network-to-network.

ADJ   The Boolean ADJACENT operator, used by WAIS to indicate that the two terms on either side of an ADJ tag should sit next to each other in found documents.

Adventure   One of the earliest text adventure games written for computers. It is the forerunner of the popular Zork series from Infocom.

alias   In System 7, a file that "points to" another file, folder, or disk, and may generally be used in place of the original item. In network usage, alias usually refers to a simple name, location, or command that you can use in place of a more complex name, location, or command. Aliases are commonly used for email addresses, directories, or commands.

America Online A popular commercial information service with a graphical interface.

AND The Boolean AND operator, used by WAIS to indicate that found documents must contain both terms that appear in the question.

AOL Shorthand for **America Online**. Each letter is pronounced separately.

AppleLink Apple's commercial online information service. Expensive, but graphical.

AppleLink packages The archiving and compression format used solely by AppleLink. The program, StuffIt Expander, can decompress AppleLink packages.

AppleTalk A local area network protocol Apple developed to connect computers and peripherals over various different types of wiring.

ARA *Apple Remote Access.* A software program from Apple Computer that allows one Mac to dial another Mac via a modem and, through AppleShare and/or Personal File Sharing, access local or network resources available to the "answering" Mac. (Common resources include shared directories, servers, and printers.) Although I don't cover the issue in this book, you can do some neat things with ARA and MacTCP.

.ARC An older DOS archiving format.

Archie An invaluable Internet service that maintains, and allows users to search, a large database of materials stored on anonymous FTP sites.

archive site A site that archives files for users to retrieve, via either FTP or email.

ARPA *Advanced Research Projects Agency.* The governmental organization responsible for creating the beginnings of the Internet.

ARPAnet The proto-Internet network created by ARPA.

ASCII *American Standard Code for Information Interchange.* In the context of a file, an ASCII file is one that contains only "text" characters—numbers, letters, and standard punctuation. Although ASCII text can contain international characters available on the Mac ("upper-ASCII"), these characters are not commonly supported by Internet services such as email, Gopher, and FTP. In FTP, it's a command that tells FTP that you will be transferring text files (which is the default).

atob (pronounced "a to b") A Unix program that turns ASCII files into binary files. The **btoa** program does the reverse.

attachments Files that are linked to a specific email message, just as you might paperclip a clipping to a **snail mail** letter.

B

bandwidth   Information theory used to express the amount of information that can flow through a given point at any given time. Some points have narrow bandwidth (indicating not much information can flow through at one time), and others have high bandwidth (indicating a great deal of information can flow through at one time). This term is commonly used in reference to "wasted bandwidth," indicating that some (or most) of the information flowing by a point is of no use to a user. This term can include overloading a site's network connection (thus curtailing other users' use of the lines) or including lengthy signature files in Usenet postings or discussion groups. "Wasted bandwidth" is often relative: What one person views as wasteful might be essential to someone else.

bang   The exclamation point (!) used to separate machine names in UUCP bang-style addressing, which isn't all that common anymore.

BART   Short for *Brode's Archive Retrieval Thang*. A mailserver that provides email access to the FTP archives at `mac.archive.umich.edu`. See also **mailserver**.

baud   A measure of modem speed equal to one signal per second. 300 baud equals 300 bits per second (bps), but at higher speeds one signal can contain more than one bit, so a 9,600 baud modem is not a 9,600 bps modem. (The terms often are incorrectly used interchangeably). See also **bps**.

BBS   *Bulletin Board System*. A computer system that provides its users files for downloading and areas for electronic discussions. Bulletin board systems usually are run by and for local users, although many now provide Internet, UUCP, or FidoNet mail.

Binary   In the context of a file, any file that contains non-textual data. (Images and applications are examples of binary files.) In FTP, a command that tells FTP to transfer information as an arbitrary stream of bits rather than as a series of textual characters.

BinHex   The standard Macintosh format for converting a binary file into an ASCII file that can pass through email programs. (For those of you wondering how to pronounce it, "Bin" rhymes with "tin," and "hex" rhymes with "sex," and the accent is on the first syllable.) See also **uucode**.

BITFTP   A program that provides email access to FTP sites for BITNET users. See also **mailserver**.

BITNET   An academic large-scale computer network, primarily connecting academic institutions. BITNET is often expanded as the "Because It's Time" Network. A friend notes, "Actually, it seems that the definitive answer to what the BIT stands for is 'It has varied, and depends on who you asked and when.'"

BIX   The online commercial information service called the *BYTE Information Exchange*, although I have never heard anyone use the full name in favor of BIX.

body   The part of an email message where you type your message, as opposed to the **header** or the **signature**.

bounce   What email does when it doesn't go through.

bps   *Bits per second*. The measurement of modem transmission speed. Not comparable to baud after 300 bps.

Brownian motion   With apologies to Douglas Adams, the best example is indeed a really hot cup of tea. It has something to do with internal movement within a hot liquid.

browser   A client program that enables one to search, often somewhat randomly, through the information provided by a specific type of server. Generally used in relation to the World-Wide Web.

btoa   (pronounced "b to a") A Unix program that turns binary files into ASCII files for transmission via email. The **atob** program decodes such files.

BTW   Abbreviation for the expression, *"By the way."*

C

Call For Votes   What you do after discussing whether a new newsgroup should be created.

CCL   *Connection Control Language*. Used in Apple Remote Access, InterSLIP, and other communications programs, CCL is a scripting language that lets you control your modem.

CEO   *Chief Executive Officer*. The head honcho of a company, who has little time to learn computer systems. CEOs generally earn a lot more money than you or I.

CERN   The birthplace of the **World-Wide Web**, although in real life they do high energy physics research. Located in Geneva, Switzerland. CERN doesn't stand for anything any more, although it once was an acronym for a French name.

CFV   See **Call For Votes**.

channel   In IRC, an area that theoretically has a specific discussion topic. See **IRC**.

charter   The document that lays out what topics a newsgroup will cover, what its name will be, and other relevant details.

chat script   A simple (you hope) conversation between your Mac and your host machine that allows your Mac to log in automatically. Chat scripts usually involve a series of send and expect strings. Your host sends a login prompt; your Mac responds with your username. Your host sends a password prompt; your Mac responds with your password.

chiasmus   A term from classical rhetoric that describes a situation in which you introduce subjects in the order A, B, and C, and then talk about them in the order C, B, and A.

CIM   See **CompuServe Information Manager**.

CIS   Stands for *CompuServe Information Service*, or simply *CompuServe*. Wags often replace the *S* with a *$*. See **CompuServe**.

ClariNet   An alternate hierarchy of newsgroups that uses the same transmission routes as Usenet, but carries commercial information from UPI and others. You, or your provider, must pay to read ClariNet news.

client   The program or computer that requests information from a server computer or program. Used in terms of client/server computing. See also **server**.

clone   A DOS-based computer that imitates computers made by IBM. Referred to as clones because they don't distinguish themselves enough for us to bother referring to them any other way.

CMS   Short for *Conversational Monitor System*. The part of the operating system on certain IBM mainframes with which you interact. Not at all conversational.

command line   Where you type commands to an operating system such as DOS or Unix. Command-line operating systems can be powerful, but are often a pain to work with, especially for Macintosh users accustomed to a graphical interface.

Compact Pro   A popular shareware compression program on the Macintosh. Its filenames generally have the `.cpt` extension.

Compress   Generically, to make a file smaller by removing redundant information. Specifically, the Unix Compress program that does just that. Files compressed with the Unix compress command end with a `.Z` suffix (always a capital Z). Compressed files may be expanded with the Unix command uncompress.

comp.sys.mac.digest   A Usenet newsgroup useful for keeping tabs on what's happening in the Macintosh world, and for getting help with obscure problems. Carries the same information as the **Info-Mac Digest**.

CompuServe   One of the oldest and largest commercial online services. Sometimes abbreviated as **CIS**.

CompuServe Information Manager   A decent graphical program for the Mac (and Windows) that puts a nice face on CompuServe. Generally abbreviated **CIM**.

connect time   The amount of time you are actually connected to and using a computer. Because connect or telephone charges are based on this amount of time, you want to keep it as low as possible.

.cpt   The filename extension used by Compact Pro.

CREN   *Corporation for Research and Educational Networking.*

cross-posted   What happens to a Usenet posting when you put several newsgroup names in the Newsgroups line. More efficient than posting multiple individual copies.

CSLIP   Compressed SLIP. A type of SLIP account that uses compression to increase performance.

D

daemons   Small programs in Unix that run frequently to see whether something has happened: if so, they act as they were programmed; if not, they go back to sleep.

DARPA   *Defense Advanced Research Projects Agency.* Replaced ARPA and had a more military bent. Has since been renamed ARPA again. See also **ARPA**.

.dd   The filename extension used by DiskDoubler for its combined files.

DEC   *Digital Equipment Corporation.* Also known as *Digital*, this company produces the popular VAX line of computers and the VMS operating system.

dialing scripts   In InterSLIP, the scripts that control modem dialog. See also **CCL**.

dial up   To call another computer via modem. The term is often lumped together as one word except when used as a verb.

dialup   A connection or line reached by modem, as in "a dialup line."

digest   A single message that contains multiple individual postings to a mailing list or newsgroup.

domain   A level of hierarchy in a machine's full nodename. For instance, `tidbits.com` is in the `com` domain, as are many other machines.

domain name server   A computer that keeps track of names of other machines and their numeric IP addresses. When you refer to a machine by name, your domain name server translates that information appropriately into the numeric IP address necessary to make the connection.

domain name system   The system that makes it possible for you to think in terms of names such as `tidbits.com`, whereas computers think in terms of `192.135.191.128`.

DOS   An elderly operating system that is frequently helped across the street by Microsoft Windows.

download   To retrieve a file from another machine, usually a host machine, to your machine.

downstream   Usenet neighbors that are downstream from you get most of their news from your machine, in contrast to machines that are **upstream** from you.

Dynamically   The evil button in the MacTCP control panel. Don't use it unless you know what you're doing.

E

electronic mail or **email**   Messages that travel through the networks rather than being committed to paper and making the arduous journey through the U.S. Postal Service.

emoticons   A rather silly name for **smileys**.

Ethernet   A type of local area network that is much faster than LocalTalk. Most Macs can use Ethernet by adding an Ethernet expansion card; some recent Macs come with Ethernet built in.

.etx   The filename extension for **setext** files, which are straight text files in a specific format that's easy to read online and can be decoded for even better display.

expire   After a certain amount of time, Usenet postings can be set to expire, which means that they will be deleted even if they haven't been read, so they don't waste space.

F

FAQ   *Frequently Asked Question.* Lists of commonly asked questions and their answers, often posted in newsgroups to reduce the number of novice questions. Read a FAQ list before asking a question, to make sure yours isn't a frequently asked one.

Fax   Slang for *facsimile.* A technology that takes paper from the sender and produces more paper that looks just like it at the recipient's end. You can use fax modems to eliminate the paper step at one end or both, but they may be less reliable than stand-alone fax machines. Email is cleaner, often cheaper, and more environmentally friendly, and the results are more useful in other programs. However, you can't easily send signatures or existing paper documents via email.

Federal Express   A company that can transport paper mail overnight for a hefty sum of money. Email is far faster and cheaper.

feed   Shorthand for a connection to another machine that sends you mail and news. I might say, "I have a mail feed from Ed's machine."

Fidonet   A network of cooperating bulletin board systems that has some links to the Internet.

filename extension   A three-letter (usually) code at the end of a filename that indicates what type of file it is. Essential in non-Macintosh environments that lack icons or other methods of identifying files. Common extensions include **.txt** for text files, **.hqx** for BinHexed files, and **.sit** for StuffIt files.

fileserver or **file server**   A machine that provides files via a network. Perhaps because of time spent working on BITNET, I tend to use it as a synonym for **mailserver**, or a machine that returns files that are requested via email.

file site   Another name for archive site or FTP site. A computer on which files are stored for anyone on the Internet to retrieve.

Finger   A Unix program that helps you find out information about someone else on the Internet. A Macintosh program of the same name does the same thing with a nicer interface.

firewall   A security system that not only prevents intruders from entering, but also often prevents legitimate users from getting out to the Internet from the local network. A firewall usually has a single machine that's connected to the Internet and all Internet traffic must pass through that machine.

flame war   A conflagration in which lots of people jump in on different sides of an argument and start insulting each other. Fun to watch briefly, but a major waste of **bandwidth**.

flaming   The act of calling into question someone's thoughts, beliefs, and parentage simply because you don't agree with them. Don't do it.

followup   An article on Usenet posted in reply to another article. The subject should stay the same so readers can tell the two articles are related.

forms   In the World-Wide Web, online electronic forms that you can fill in if you have a forms-capable Web browser such as MacWeb or NCSA Mosaic 2.0.

Freenet   An organization whose goal is to provide free Internet access in a specific area, often by working with local schools and libraries. Ask around to see if a Freenet has sprung up in your area. The first and preeminent example is the Cleveland Freenet. Freenet also refers to the specific Freenet software, and the information services that use it.

freeware   Software that you can distribute freely and use for free, but for which the author often retains the copyright, which means that you can't modify it.

FTP   *File Transfer Protocol.* One of the main ways in which you retrieve, umm, well, files from other machines on the Internet.

FTPmail   A method of retrieving files stored on FTP sites via email.

FYI   Abbreviation for the expression, *"For your information."*

G

gateway   A machine that exists on two networks, such as the Internet and BITNET, and that can transfer mail between them.

gateway script   In InterSLIP, a script that controls the login process. See also **CCL**.

GIF   *Graphics Interchange Format.* A platform-independent file format developed by CompuServe, the GIF format is commonly used to distribute graphics on the Internet. Mighty battles have been waged over the pronunciation of this term, and although Robin Williams notes that it's pronounced "jiff" in her book, *Jargon*, both of my glossary proofreaders flagged it as being pronounced with a hard *g*, as in "graphics." I surrender; pronounce it as you like.

`.gif`   The filename extension generally given to GIF files.

GNU   With apologies for the circular reference, GNU stands for *GNU's Not Unix*. Developed by Richard Stallman and the Free Software Foundation, GNU is (or will be, when finished) a high-quality version of the Unix operating system that is free of charge and freely modifiable by its users. GNU software is distributed at no cost with source code. Many GNU applications and utilities are mainstays of the Unix community.

Gopher   An information retrieval system created by the University of Minnesota. In wide acceptance on the Internet, Gopher is one of the most useful resources available.

Gopherspace   The collection of all available Gopher servers.

.gz   An extension used by GNU's version of **ZIP**, called gzip.

H

hard close   In MacPPP, a process that disconnects you from the Internet and prevents any programs from automatically redialing until you reboot.

header   The part of an email message or Usenet posting that contains information about the message, such as who it's from, when it was sent, and so on. Headers are mainly interesting when something doesn't work.

home page   In the World-Wide Web, the document that you access first after launching a Web **browser**.

host   The large computer you connect to for your Internet access.

.hqx   The filename extension used for BinHex files.

HTML   *HyperText Markup Language*. The language used to mark up text files with styles and links for use with World-Wide Web browsers.

HTTP   *HyperText Transport Protocol*. The protocol used by the World-Wide Web.

hypertext   A term created by visionary Ted Nelson to describe non-linear writing in which you follow associative paths through a world of textual documents.

HYTELNET   Stands for *HyperTelnet*. Essentially a database of Telnet sites and other Internet resources that can link to other programs when you want to connect to a site you've found. Interesting, but not as useful as Gopher.

I

IAB   See **Internet Architecture Board.**

IBM   *International Business Machines.* Many flip expansions for the acronym exist, but IBM remains one of the most powerful companies in the computer industry despite numerous problems in recent years. Developer of numerous mainframes and obtuse operating systems, some of which are still in use today. Co-developer (with Apple and Motorola) of the PowerPC chip, used in the Power Macintoshes.

IETF   See **Internet Engineering Task Force.**

IMAP   *Interactive Mail Access Protocol.* A new protocol for the storage and retrieval of email (much like **POP**, the Post Office Protocol). It's not in wide use yet.

IMHO   Abbreviation for the expression, *"In my humble opinion."*

Info-Mac Digest   A daily digest of questions, answers, and discussions about all things Macintosh. The same information comes through in the Usenet newsgroup, `comp.sys.mac.digest`.

information agent   A software program (currently only an interface to frequently updated databases) that can search numerous databases for information that interests you without your having to know what it is searching. Archie and Veronica are current examples of information agents.

internet   With a lowercase *i*, it's a group of connected networks.

Internet   The collection of all the connected networks in the world, although it is sometimes better called WorldNet or just the Net. More specifically, the Internet is the set of networks that communicate via TCP/IP. If you're still confused, go back and read chapters 1 through 8.

Internet Architecture Board   A group of invited volunteers that manages certain aspects of the Internet, such as standards and address allocation.

Internet Engineering Task Force   A volunteer organization that meets regularly to discuss problems facing the Internet.

IP   *Internet Protocol.* The main protocol used on the Internet.

IP number   A four-part number that uniquely identifies a machine on the Internet. For instance, my IP number for `tidbits.com` is `192.135.191.128`. People generally use the name, instead.

IRC   *Internet Relay Chat.* A world-wide network of people talking to each other in real time over the Internet rather than in person.

IRS   *Internal Revenue Service.* If you live in the United States and are not aware of them, you might want to watch out.

ISOC   *The Internet Society.* A membership organization that supports the Internet and is the governing body to which the **IAB** reports.

J

JANET   *Joint Academic Network.* Great Britain's national network. In true British fashion, JANET addresses work backwards from normal Internet addresses. They work from largest domain to the smallest, as in `joe@uk.ac.canterbury.cc.trumble`. Luckily, most gateways to JANET perform the necessary translations automatically.

jargon   The sometimes incomprehensible language used to talk about specialized topics. If you need help with computer jargon, check out *Jargon*, by Robin Williams, a light-hearted and detailed trip through this industry.

Jolt cola   All the sugar and twice the caffeine of normal colas. First suggested as a joke by comedian George Carlin, later developed and marketed by Carlin and a food industry entrepreneur.

JPEG   *Joint Photographic Experts Group.* A group that has defined a compression scheme that reduces the size of image files by up to 20 times at the cost of slightly reduced image quality.

.jpeg   A filename extension used to mark **JPEG**-compressed images.

Jughead   A searching agent for Gopher, much like Veronica, but more focused.

K

Kermit   A file transfer protocol actually named after the popular Kermit the Frog. Kermit is generally slower than **XMODEM, YMODEM,** and the top-of-the-line **ZMODEM**.

Knowledge Navigator   A video of John Sculley's anthropomorphic vision of an information agent. Information agents probably will be more successful if they don't look like people, because computers cannot currently meet the high expectations we have of people.

L

LAN   See **local area network**.

leaf site   A machine on Usenet that talks to only one other machine instead of passing news onto other machines.

line noise   Static on a telephone line that causes trouble for modem connections.

LISTSERV   A powerful program for automating mailing lists. It currently requires an IBM mainframe, but that requirement may change in the near future.

local area network   Often abbreviated *LAN*. Two or more computers connected together via network cables. If you have a Macintosh connected to a LaserWriter printer (which contains a CPU), you have a rudimentary local area network.

LocalTalk   The form of local area networking hardware that Apple builds into every Macintosh.

login   The process by which you identify yourself to a host computer. Usually involves a userid and a password.

lurkers   Not a derogatory term. People who merely read discussions online without contributing to them.

M

MacBinary   A file format that combines the three parts of a Macintosh file: the data fork, resource fork, and Finder information block. No other computers understand the normal Macintosh file format, but they can transmit the MacBinary format without losing data. When you download a binary Macintosh file from another computer using the MacBinary format, your communications program automatically reassembles the file into a normal Macintosh file.

MacTCP   A control panel from Apple that implements TCP on the Macintosh. MacTCP is required to use programs such as Fetch and TurboGopher.

mail bombing   The act of sending hundreds or thousands of messages to someone you think deserves the punishment for transgressions against the Internet. Highly discouraged.

mailing list   A list of people who all receive postings sent to the group. Mailing lists exist on all sorts of topics.

mailserver   A program that provides access to files via email. See also **fileserver**.

man pages   The Unix *manual pages*. You must go to the man pages to find out more about a Unix command. Accessed through use of the **man** command followed by the command whose description you want to view.

Manually   A button in the MacTCP control panel. Use it if your system administrator gives you a specific IP address.

MCC   *Microelectronics and Computer Technology Corporation.* No, I don't know where the *T* went, either. An industry consortium that developed MacWAIS and MacWeb.

MCI   A large telecommunications company that provides an email system called MCI Mail. It's not Macintosh-friendly, but can be used efficiently to receive Internet email.

MIME   *Multipurpose Internet Mail Extensions.* A new Internet standard for transferring non-textual data, such as audio messages or pictures, via email.

mirror site   An FTP site that contains exactly the same contents as another site. Mirror sites help distribute the load from a single popular site.

modem   Stands for *modulator-demodulator*, because that's what it does, technically. In reality, a modem allows your computer to talk to another computer via the phone lines.

moderator   An overworked volunteer who reads all of the submissions to a mailing list or newsgroup, to make sure they are appropriate, before posting them.

monospaced font   A font whose characters are all the same width. Courier and Monaco are common monospaced fonts on the Macintosh. You generally want to use a monospaced font for documents on the Internet.

MPEG   *Motion Picture Experts Group.* More commonly, a compression format for video. Files compressed with MPEG generally have the extension `.mpeg`.

MTU   *Maximum Transmission Unit.* A number that your system administrator must give you so that you can configure SLIP.

MUD   *Multi-User Dungeon*, or sometimes *Multi-User Dimension*. A text-based alternate reality where you can progress to a level at which you can modify the environment. Mostly used for games, and extremely addictive.

MX record   *Mail Exchange record.* An entry in a database that tells domain name servers where they should route mail so it gets to you.

N

NCSA   *National Center for Supercomputing Applications*. A group that has produced a great deal of public domain software for the scientific community. They wrote NCSA Telnet and NCSA Mosaic for the Macintosh.

net heavies   Those system administrators who run large sites on the Internet. Although they don't necessarily have official posts, they wield more power than most people on the nets.

Network Information Center   An organization that provides information about a network.

Network Time Protocol   A protocol for transmitting the correct time around the Internet.

network time server   The machine from which you set your clock using **Network Time Protocol**.

news   Synonymous with *Usenet news*, or sometimes just *Usenet*.

newsgroup   A discussion group on Usenet devoted to talking about a specific topic. Currently, approximately 5,000 newsgroups exist.

.newsrc   The file that Unix newsreaders use to keep track of which messages in which newsgroups you've read.

newsreader   A program that helps you read news and provides capabilities for following or deleting threads.

NIC   See **Network Information Center**.

nickname   An easy-to-remember shortcut for an email address. Sometimes also called an **alias**.

nn   A popular Unix newsreader.

NNTP   *Net News Transport Protocol*. A transmission protocol for the transfer of Usenet news.

nodename   The name of a machine, like `tidbits.com`.

NOT   The Boolean operator NOT, which WAIS uses to limit the found documents to ones that contain one term but not another.

NREN   *National Research and Education Network*. The successor to the NSFNET.

NSF   *National Science Foundation*. The creators of the NSFNET.

NSFNET   *National Science Foundation Network.* The current high-speed network that links users with supercomputer sites around the country. Also called the interim NREN.

O

offline   Actions performed when you aren't actually connected to another computer.

online   Actions performed when you are connected to another computer.

P

page   In the World-Wide Web, the name for the basic document type.

PDIAL list   Peter Kaminski's list of public providers that offer full Internet access.

PEP   *Packetized Ensemble Protocol.* Telebit's proprietary method of increasing throughput when two of Telebit's modems connect to each other.

.pit   The filename extension used by the long-dead PackIt format on the Macintosh.

POP   *Post Office Protocol.* A protocol for the storage and retrieval of email. Eudora uses POP.

port   In software, the act of converting code so that a program runs on more than one type of computer. In networking, a number that identifies a specific "channel" used by network services. For instance, Gopher generally uses port 70, but occasionally is set to use other ports on various machines.

post   To send a message to a discussion group or list.

PPP   *Point to Point Protocol.* A protocol functionally similar to **SLIP** that enables your Mac to pretend it is a full Internet machine, using only a modem and a normal telephone line.

proportionally spaced font   A font whose characters vary in width, so that, for example, a *W* is wider than an *i*. Proportionally spaced fonts often work poorly when you're reading text on the Internet.

protocol   A language that computers use when talking to each other.

public access provider   An organization that provides Internet access for individuals or other organizations, often for a fee.

public domain   Software that you can use freely, distribute freely, and modify in any way you wish. See also **freeware** and **shareware**.

Q

QuickTime   An Apple technology for time-based multiple media data. QuickTime files can include text, sound, animation, and video, among other formats. Despite being internally compressed, QuickTime movies are often huge and hard to work with on the Internet.

quoting   The act of including parts of an original message in a reply. The standard character used to set off a quote from the rest of the text is a column of > (greater-than) characters along the left margin.

R

ranking   The method by which WAIS displays found documents in order of possible utility.

rec.humor.funny   A popular moderated newsgroup devoted to jokes judged funny by the group's moderator. Set up by ClariNet creator Brad Templeton because the **rec.humor** group became overrun with jokes that no one found funny, and discussions about how unfunny they all were.

relevance feedback   A method WAIS uses to "find me more documents like this one."

Request for Comments   Documents containing the standards, proposed standards, and other necessary details regarding the operation of the Internet.

Request for Discussion   The part of the newsgroup creation process where you propose a group and discussion begins.

RFC   See **Request for Comments**.

RFD   See **Request for Discussion**.

rn   A popular, if aging, Unix newsreader. Perhaps the most common newsreader available under Unix—if a Unix machine has a newsfeed, it almost certainly will have rn.

root directory   The topmost directory that you can see. On the Mac, you see the root directory when you double-click on your hard disk icon.

rot13   A method of encoding possibly offensive postings on Usenet so that those who don't want to be offended can avoid accidentally seeing the posting. Works by converting each letter to a number (*a = 1, b = 2,* and so forth), adding 13 to the number, and then converting back into letters, rendering the file unreadable without deciphering.

S

.sea   The filename extension used by almost all self-extracting archives on the Mac.

self-extracting archive   A compressed file or files encapsulated in a decompression program, so you don't need any other programs to expand the archive.

server   A machine that makes services available on a network to **client** programs. A file server makes files available. A WAIS server makes full-text information available through the WAIS protocol (although WAIS uses the term source interchangeably with server).

setext   *Structure-enhanced text.* A method of implicitly marking up text files to make them both easy to read online and readable by special browser software offline.

shareware   A method of software distribution in which the software may be freely distributed, and you may try it before paying. If you decide to keep and use the program, you send your payment directly to the shareware author.

signature   Several lines automatically appended to your email messages, usually listing your name and email address, sometimes along with witty sayings and ASCII graphics. Keep them short, and leave out the ASCII graphics.

.sit   The filename extension used by files compressed with StuffIt.

SLIP   *Serial Line Internet Protocol.* Like PPP, a protocol that lets your Mac pretend it is a full Internet machine, using only a modem and a normal phone line. SLIP is older and less flexible than PPP but currently somewhat more prevalent.

smileys   Collections of characters meant to totally replace body language, intonation, and physical presence. **;-)**

SMTP   *Simple Mail Transport Protocol.* The protocol used on the Internet to transfer mail. Eudora uses SMTP to send mail.

snail mail   The standard name on the Internet for paper mail because email can travel across the country in seconds, whereas my birthday present from my parents took a week once.

soft close   In MacPPP, the method of disconnecting from the Internet in such a way that applications can still automatically connect later on. See also **hard close**.

source   In WAIS jargon, a database of information. Used interchangeably with server in the context of WAIS.

spamming   The act of sending hundreds of inappropriate postings to Usenet newsgroups and mailing lists. Do it and you'll seriously regret it.

Standard File Dialog   The dialog box that appears when you choose Open or Save As (and sometimes Save) from the File menu. Also known as the SFDialog.

Steve Jobs   Cofounder of Apple Computer and father for the NeXT computer, he is legendary for being more interested in doing what he considers the right thing than for doing what makes business sense. Jobs isn't in it for the money; he wants to change the world.

StuffIt   A family of programs originally developed by Raymond Lau and now published by Aladdin Systems. Also the compression format used by those programs.

system administrator   The person who runs your host machine or network. Also known as the *network administrator* or just plain *administrator*. Be very nice to this person.

T

T1   A high-speed network link used on the Internet.

T3   An even higher speed network link used on the Internet.

.tar   The filename extension used by files made into an archive by the Unix tar program.

TCP   *Transmission Control Protocol*. It works with IP to ensure that packets travel safely on the Internet.

TCP/IP   The combination of *Transmission Control Protocol* and *Internet Protocol*. The base protocols on which the Internet is founded.

Telnet   Can refer to a terminal emulation protocol that lets you log in to other machines, or a program that implements this protocol on any of various platforms. On the Mac, NCSA Telnet is the standard.

terminal   A piece of hardware like a **VT100** that lets you interact with a character-based operating system such as Unix.

terminal emulator   Software that allows one computer, such as a Mac, to act like a dedicated terminal, such as a **VT100**.

text   In terms of files, a file that contains only characters from the ASCII character set. In terms of FTP, a mode that assumes the files you will be transferring contain only ASCII characters. You set this mode in FTP with the ASCII command.

thread   A group of messages in a Usenet **newsgroup** that all share the same subject and topic, so you can easily read the entire thread or delete it, depending on your specific newsreader.

TidBITS   A free weekly newsletter distributed solely over computer networks. *TidBITS* focuses on the Macintosh and the world of electronic communications. I'm the editor, so I think it's neat. Send email to **info@tidbits.com** for subscription information.

timeout   After a certain amount of idle time, some connections will disconnect, hanging up the phone in the case of a SLIP connection.

.txt   The filename extension generally used for straight text files that you can read (as opposed to text files that have been encoded by BinHex or uuencode).

U

Ulaw   An audio file format native to Sun workstations but in common use on the Internet. Use SoundMachine to play Ulaw files on the Mac.

Unix   An extremely popular, if utterly cryptic, operating system in wide use on computers on the Internet. Other operating systems work fine on the Internet, but Unix is probably the most common.

UPI   *United Press International*. ClariNet gets much of its news from this wire service.

upload   To send a file to another machine.

upstream   Machines that send you most of your Usenet news are said to be upstream from you. Machines that get most of their news from you are **downstream**.

Usenet   An anarchic network of sorts, composed of thousands of discussion groups on every imaginable topic.

Usenet news   The news that flows through Usenet. Sometimes abbreviated *Usenet* or *news*.

userid   The name you use to log in to another computer. Synonymous with **username**.

username   See **userid**. They're generally the same.

.uu   The filename extension generally used by uuencoded files.

uucode   A file format used for transferring binary files in email, which can only reliably carry ASCII files. See also **uuencode** and **uudecode**.

UUCP   *Unix to Unix CoPy*. UUCP is a small pun on the fact that the Unix copy command is cp. UUCP is a transmission protocol that carries email and news.

.uud   A filename extension sometimes used by uuencoded files.

uudecode   A Unix program for decoding files in the uuencode format, turning them from ASCII back into binary files. Several Macintosh programs can perform this function as well.

.uue   Yet another filename extension sometimes used by uuencoded files.

uuencode   A Unix program that turns binary files into ASCII files for transmission via email. Several Macintosh programs also can create uuencoded files.

V

v.32bis   Currently the fastest standard modem protocol, although others are due to appear soon. Although not required, almost all v.32bis modems support all sorts of other protocols, including v.42 error correction and v.42bis data compression. Don't worry about the specifics; just try to match protocols with the modems you call.

VAT   *Value Added Tax*. A thoroughly unpleasant tax paid by residents of countries such as France and Great Britain. You realize how cheap things in the United States are after hearing about prices in other countries over the Internet.

Veronica   An information agent that searches a database of Gopher servers to find items that interest you.

vi   An extremely powerful Unix editor with the personality of a junkyard dog. Much-beloved by many Unix aficionados.

VMS   DEC's main operating system for their Vax computers.

VT100   Originally, a dedicated terminal built by DEC to interface to mainframes. The VT100 became a standard for terminals, and as a result almost all terminal emulation programs can emulate the VT100. The VT100s make excellent footstools these days and will be outlived only by terminals made long ago by DataMedia that can withstand being dropped out a window without losing a connection.

W

WAIS   *Wide Area Information Servers.* A set of full-text databases containing information on hundreds of topics. You can search WAIS using natural language queries and use relevance feedback to refine your search.

WAN   See **wide-area network**.

wide-area network   A group of geographically separated computers connected via dedicated lines or satellite links. The Internet enables small organizations to simulate a wide-area network without the cost of one.

wildcards   Special characters such as * and ? that can stand in for other characters during text searches in some programs. The * wildcard generally means "match any number of characters in this spot," whereas the ? wildcard generally means "match any character in this spot."

World-Wide Web   The newest and most ambitious of the special Internet services. World-Wide Web browsers can display styled text and graphics. Often abbreviated *WWW*.

worm   A program that infiltrates a computer system and copies itself many times, filling up memory and disk space and crashing the computer. The most famous worm of all time was released accidentally by Robert Morris over the Internet and brought down whole sections of it.

WWW   See **World-Wide Web**.

X–Z

.x   The non-standard filename extension used by SuperDisk self-extracting archives.

Xerox PARC   The Xerox research lab that invented the graphical interface, among many other things, including the mouse and Ethernet.

XMODEM   A common file transfer protocol.

YMODEM   Another common file transfer protocol.

.Z   The filename extension used by files compressed with the Unix Compress program.

.z   A filename extension used by files compressed with the Unix gzip program.

.ZIP   The filename extension used by files compressed into the ZIP format common on PCs.

ZMODEM   The fastest and most popular file transfer protocol.

Appendix

F

Special Internet Access Offer

What would a book about the Internet be worth if it didn't provide some means of getting on the Internet? Not much, to those who aren't already connected. To remedy that, Hayden Books has worked out a deal with Northwest Nexus, Inc., a commercial Internet provider based in Bellevue, WA. This appendix introduces you to both Northwest Nexus and the special offer that Hayden has obtained for readers of this book.

The following section provides general information about Northwest Nexus, some of which won't be relevant if you opt for the special offer. Following that section is offer-specific information, including instructions for how to get online. That part is very important, so make sure you don't skip it!

I'm especially pleased that we were able to work with Northwest Nexus, since I've obtained my Internet access from them for quite some time now. They're good folks, and I've always been happy with their service. Here's what they say about themselves.

Northwest Nexus, Inc.

Northwest Nexus offers a wide range of low-cost options to give both private individuals and companies access to the vast resources of the Internet: millions of people interacting on thousands of subjects, and data available from countless sources, including the U.S. government, universities, research labs, and private corporations.

Our Company

Northwest Nexus was incorporated in Washington state in 1987 and has steadily grown over the years to now serve several thousand accounts. Customers have included such organizations as GTE, Immunex Corporation, McCaw Cellular, Microsoft, Nintendo of America, Traveling Software, US West, and many smaller businesses, professional organizations, consultants, and individuals.

Our current staff has more than 100 combined years of experience in computer and network operations, network engineering, and business. As we grow, we're continually adding staff and equipment to meet your needs.

Although our primary target market is the Puget Sound area, we also serve customers throughout the United States and around the world.

Our Services

Shell Service: Log on to one of our shell servers and you can explore the Internet using either the traditional Unix command line interface or a variety of menu-based interfaces such as Gopher and Hytelnet.

SLIP/PPP Service: With the right software, you can put any computer (including Macs and Windows-based PCs) directly on the Internet—while still keeping your familiar point-and-click interface. Services for both dedicated and dynamic IP address assignment are available.

UUCP Service: Using a pre-set schedule, or whenever required, your computer can connect to our UUCP relay system and collect any mail or other files waiting for your site. A free preassigned `wa.com` sub-domain is included to identify your site. If you would like your own custom domain name, we can arrange it for an additional setup fee.

Dedicated Service: From 56 KB to T-1, we offer reliable, economical high-speed connections using either Frame Relay or dedicated lines. For your convenience, domain name and net number registrations are included. We can also order your circuit for you, if you prefer.

Access to Usenet news is included with all service types. Electronic mail can be set up for all service types and is included free with all accounts except "Classic" (dedicated IP address) dialup SLIP/PPP.

If you're not sure what kind of connection you need, please give us a call and we can help you determine which one will work best and be most cost-effective for you. More detailed information, including pricing, is also available on sheets describing each individual service.

Our Network

Northwest Nexus dial-in lines are a local call from all prefixes in the Seattle metropolitan area, Seattle's Eastside, Everett, parts of Snohomish County, Tacoma, Olympia, and Shelton. New service areas are added periodically. If you are located outside the Puget Sound region, please call our office for available options to standard long-distance charges for your area.

U.S. West Frame Relay service may be used for Frame Relay access to Northwest Nexus within the Puget Sound region. We can also connect with several other carriers in other areas; please call for details.

Our network is monitored 7 days a week, 24 hours a day by professional staff to ensure the reliability of your connection.

What You Need To Connect

Hardware: You can access the Internet through Northwest Nexus from almost any personal computer, workstation, or mini-computer. For shell service, you can even use a simple terminal. For all connections except leased-line service, you will also need a modem and a regular telephone line. Leased-line connections require a CSU/DSU, a router of the appropriate speed and protocol, and a digital circuit of the appropriate speed and type.

Software: Each type of connection requires different software. Shell service is the simplest; unless you have an actual terminal, you can use almost any terminal emulation program (many are free). SLIP/PPP and UUCP services require software that supports these protocols; there are several packages available for many types of computers.

If you're not sure what kind of hardware or software to choose, please give us a call. We can recommend proven combinations to get you started on the net.

We Make Internet Easy

To sign up for Internet service, ask a question or get detailed information and pricing for each service, please contact us by phone, postal mail, or email:

Northwest Nexus, Inc.
P.O. Box 40597
Bellevue, WA 98015-4597
206-455-3505
206-455-4672 (fax)
info@nwnexus.wa.com

Special Connection Offer

So that's what Northwest Nexus says about itself—now let's get into the details.

Folks who purchase this book can take advantage of a special connection, because Northwest Nexus is making dialup PPP accounts available at a special flat rate. This means that you can use MacTCP, MacPPP (or InterSLIP, if you prefer a SLIP account), and the rest of the software on the disk pretty much right away. If you peruse the PDIAL list, you'll see prices as high as $100 for a sign-up fee, and connect rates in the range of $20 per month plus approximately $2 for each hour of connect time. At that rate, your bill can add up fast.

In contrast, Northwest Nexus has created a flat rate SLIP account. You pay $20 to sign up, and $22.50 per month for as many hours as you want to use it each month. (Note that you will be billed in advance on a quarterly basis—they have to keep their overhead low to be able to offer such low prices, and billing monthly is expensive.) In addition, since Northwest Nexus realizes that you should be allowed to try something before buying, they are making the first two weeks available for free. If after two weeks you don't want to keep the account for any reason, just call Northwest Nexus at 206-455-3505 and ask it to deactivate your account, at which point you pay nothing. (It's possible you may receive an automatically generated bill before that time; if that happens, simply call Northwest Nexus and they'll straighten out everything for you.)

There is a catch. There is always a catch. The catch is that you must call Northwest Nexus in Washington State, and that's a long distance phone call for everyone outside of the Puget Sound/Seattle area. In our investigations, we were unable to find a provider that offered SLIP or PPP connections with local numbers throughout the country or via an 800 number (some had 800 numbers but charged $8 per hour or more for you to use them, which is more expensive than a normal long distance call). So with Northwest Nexus, you do have to make that long distance call, but at least you aren't charged additionally for your connect time on their machines.

One way around the long distance charges (and I don't know any details here) is that some specialized telecommunications companies offer deals whereby you pay a certain amount per month that allows you to make a certain number of calls per month (for instance, eight 30-minute calls for $.50 per call). Details will vary widely, but do some poking around and you may find a company in your area that can help. Calling the operators of local bulletin boards is a good place to start. You might also try looking in the Yellow Pages for telecommunications companies. Finally, you may be able to reduce long distance charges through special calling plans offered by your standard long distance provider—call them for details and consult with Northwest Nexus to get it all worked out.

Appendix F
Special Internet
Access Offer

How to Activate Your Account

So, here's how to activate an account. You call a Unix machine called **halcyon.com**, log in, and sign up online by providing your name, address, and other related details. This sign-up process requires a terminal emulation program like ZTerm or MicroPhone that can emulate a VT100 (PC/ANSI also seems to work, but other emulations like TTY, VT52, and VT220 do not work). If a terminal emulator didn't come with your modem, you can call Northwest Nexus's voice number and set up the account with a person, but that will be more of a hassle for everyone. I'll run you through the login process, noting any quirks and making sure you know how to respond to all the prompts. Within three business days, and sometimes sooner, Northwest Nexus will activate your PPP account, at which point you can configure MacTCP and MacPPP as I've outlined here. (Read chapters 12, "MacTCP, PPP, and SLIP," and 13, "MacTCP-based Software," for more details, but the following information is what you must use to configure MacTCP and MacPPP for Northwest Nexus.) If your account isn't active when you call back after three business days, call Northwest Nexus, at 206-455-3505, to check on your account status.

You still *must* return the *original* coupon included in the back of this book to Northwest Nexus via snail mail (that is, regular U.S. Postal Service mail, stamps and all) so it knows that you really bought a copy of the book, but you can do that after going through the initial setup process. Sending in the coupon is important: it indicates that you're a honest-to-goodness purchaser of this book, and that as such, you are entitled to the two free weeks of online service. *So make sure to send in the coupon!*

Once your account is active, you're ready to log in for the first time using MacPPP. I recommend you use TurboGopher or Anarchie for the first test, because they require the least amount of configuration.

Note

Once you install all the software, configure MacPPP, and make the connection to your PPP account, that's when you run the programs to send email, read news, and so forth. MacPPP does nothing more than establish the connection.

Sign-up Process

Note

In the following discussion, italics is used to indicate text that you should replace with your own information. For instance, replace **Sally Q. Public** *with your own name.*

This process requires a terminal emulation program in VT100 emulation mode, but if you have a modem (which it also requires, of course), you almost certainly have a terminal emulation program, and most can emulate a VT100. If by some chance you don't, call Northwest Nexus at 206-455-3505, and it will manually set up your account. Set your program to:

- 8 data bits
- No parity
- 1 stop bit
- VT100 terminal emulation (I hate to harp on this, but if you don't use it, you won't be able to use the sign-up program)

You can use the fastest speed your modem supports, but since Northwest Nexus uses both v.32 and v.32bis modems, if your v.32bis modem connects to a v.32 modem, they talk at the slower v.32, which generally equates to 9,600 bps. After configuring your terminal emulation program, follow the steps provided here exactly, replacing the generic information I've entered with your details. The computer's phone number is 206-382-6245 (the 206 isn't necessary if you're local to Seattle, of course), and that's the same number you'll call with MacPPP to use your PPP account after everything is activated.

Note

Northwest Nexus may modify the screens you see in the sign-up process slightly, so they may not exactly match those in this appendix. Don't worry about it—the basic information will be the same.

First, issue the **ATDT** command, followed by the phone number. (If you must add any prefixes to get an outside line, make sure to add them here, too.)

```
ATDT1-206-455-8455

CONNECT 14400
```

When the modems connect, you see a connect statement similar to the previous one ("**CONNECT 14400**"), although, depending on your modem, the speed may be lower. Press Return to get to the login screen.

```
To set up an account, use VT100 emulation and log in as 'new' (lowercase, no  password)

login: new
```

Log in as **new**, as the onscreen instructions say—you won't need a password at this point.

```
WELCOME to halcyon.com's new user system.

Control-C and Control-Z are used as disconnect sequences.  This
will signal a disconnect from your session.  If you wish to
terminate your session, feel free to use either Control-C
or Control-Z at any time.

When you are prompted to enter information, your DELETE key
or Control-H may be used to backspace over your entry.  A
bell may sound if invalid information is entered or if an
invalid key is pressed.  The arrow keys do not work to move
around in a field.

Only the TAB key may be used to move forward to the next field.

When moving between fields, you will always be given some
information about what might be required prior to entering
that particular area.

If you encounter difficulties in entering information or would
need special help, please contact our staff as indicated below.


PRESS ANY KEY FOR THE NEXT PAGE:
```

At this point, the new user program pauses and tells you to press any key for the next page. You can indeed press any key other than Control-C or Control-Z, both of which close the connection immediately. The reason why the new user program works like this is that it was recently revamped to make it easier to use, and thus it presents only a screen or two of information at a time, allowing you to pause and read everything in between screens. Each part of the process is explained by these informational screens. I won't separate individual screens of informational text again. Now, press any key to move on to the next screen.

```
This system provides a means to access all Internet services, in
addition to providing email and newsgroup capabilities.  Many
applications are available online to assist in utilizing these
services and more.  Halcyon is directly connected to the Internet,
using two high-speed T-1 lines to pass information to other hosts
across the world.

Our current rates are $20 setup + either $200/year or $60/quarter.
A 25% discount is available to K-12 students, schools, group
accounts, etc.  Personal SL/IP or PPP access is available for
$300/year, or $90/quarter.

Our office phone is +1 206 455 3505.  Feel free to call with
any questions.  Requests for information should not be left
with your account request, as it may be overlooked by our
automated validation routines; please call us to discuss
other account options, or send email to info@halcyon.com
for more information.

This is a commercially-operated system.  Users will be billed
for their access to their established accounts.

Thank you for considering halcyon.com as your information gateway.

Ralph Sims, System Administrator (support@halcyon.com)
NWNEXUS, Inc., P.O. Box 40597, Bellevue, WA 98105-4597
+1 206 455 3505 (voice), 455 4672 (FAX)

Would you like an account? [y/n]:
```

Press **Y** to answer the question about opening an account. You do not have to press Return after pressing Y, and in fact, make sure you don't or else you may miss the next informational screen. Also, note the phone numbers and email addresses. After you press the Y key, the new user program immediately tells you about the first field that you must fill in which is the full name field.

```
Please enter your name EXACTLY as you wish it to appear on
outgoing email and news postings.  This will also be what
other users on the Internet will see when they 'finger'
your account, or use other Internet tools to obtain your
name and/or userid (login name).

This field is different from your account name (which may
also be called userid or login or login id or username);
it is probably not a good idea to use nicknames or 'handles'
here, as it may confuse others who may wish to contact you.

If your name is Franklin John Martin, but you prefer to
be known as John Martin, please feel free to do so.  This
information may be changed later on, as you desire (send
email to support@halcyon.com or give us a call, or check
halcyon's help menus for the correct way to do this).

PRESS ANY KEY TO RETURN TO MAIN SCREEN:
```

Once you have read all about the full name field, press any key, and the new user program presents you with the main screen, which has onscreen fields for the information you must fill in. You can only fill in one field at a time, and the cursor should be in the Full Name field. Enter your full name, as I've entered *Sally Q. Public*.

Note

If you make a mistake, you should be able to use the Delete key on your Macintosh keyboard to move back over the error and re-type it. If the terminal emulator just beeps at you when you press the Delete key, look for an option to toggle the function of the Delete key. It may be set to Delete or it may be set to Backspace, and Backspace is probably what you want, although this may vary from terminal emulator to terminal emulator. Also, you have a chance to correct any mistakes at the end of the new user program.

```
Halcyon New User Info Editor. Press [TAB] to move from one field to the next.

Full  Name: [Sally Q. Public                  ]

Login Name: [      ] Password: [            ]
```

```
  Phone Numbers: [(XXX)XXX-XXXX      ] Home
                 [(XXX)XXX-XXXX      ] Work

        Address: [12345 Main St.                 ]
                 [Seattle, WA                     ]
                 [98101                           ]

       Comments: [                                ]
                 [                                ]
                 [                                ]
  Type Of Account (SLIP, PPP, SHELL): [     ]
```

Once you've entered your full name, press the Tab key to move on to the next informational screen.

```
  Selecting a unique login name (also called userid, login, or login id,
  or username), can be difficult (the good ones are probably already
  taken).  You might want to use the first letter of your first name
  and your last name as a combination.  John Taylor might use jtaylor,
  or perhaps johnt, etc.  Nicknames or handles such as 'elvis', or
  'death', or 'hacker' are frowned on, and could result in your
  account not being activated; blatantly objectionable logins will
  not be accepted, and we reserve the right to delay enabling the
  account until questionable matters are resolved.

  Login names are best kept between four and eight characters,
  and must consist of lower case or numerical printable characters
  (no control codes, etc.).  If you enter any username information
  in upper case, it will be converted to lower case, which is what
  the computers use as part of your login routine.  Logins over
  eight characters will not be accepted.

  Your login must be unique to others on the system.  If your choice
  is already in use, you will be asked to select another one.

  PRESS ANY KEY TO RETURN TO MAIN SCREEN:
```

Again, press any key once you've read the informational text about how to select a login name. This the first part that requires a small amount of creativity. You must think of a unique login name here, so using your first name very likely won't work. However, this will also act as your email userid, so make it something intelligible. I first entered **tidbits**, since I know that userid is in use already. The new user program responded with:

```
Please select another login id.  The one you chose is either in
use or cannot be used by the system for one reason or another.

PRESS ANY KEY TO RETURN TO MAIN SCREEN:
```

Oops, press any key to try again. Read chapter 6, "Addressing and Email," for some thoughts on email userids—combinations such as first name and last initial (as I've shown) or first initial and last name work fine and are often unique.

```
Halcyon New User Info Editor. Press [TAB] to move from one field to the next.

Full  Name: [Sally Q. Public                       ]

Login Name: [sallyp  ] Password: [                 ]

Phone Numbers: [(XXX)XXX-XXXX        ] Home
               [(XXX)XXX-XXXX        ] Work

    Address: [12345 Main St.                        ]
             [Seattle, WA                           ]
             [98101                                 ]

   Comments: [                                      ]
             [                                      ]
             [                                      ]
Type Of Account (SLIP, PPP, SHELL): [      ]
```

Once you've entered your desired login name, press the Tab key to move on to the next informational screen.

```
Selecting a good password is not easy.  Passwords must be over five
characters and less than 17 characters.  Passwords should not use
part of your username or family name, or your car's license plate,
etc.  Good system security as well as the privacy of your account
depends on selecting a password that is difficult to guess.

Suggestions are at least six characters, mixed upper and lower case,
interspersed with numbers and punctuation marks.  Our password
```

```
routines will not accept simple, easily guessed passwords, and
you will be prompted to re-enter one that they find acceptable.

The password entries will not echo to your screen, being replaced
with '.' characters.  Do not give your password to someone else
and protect it as you would a credit card number or bank machine
PIN number; you are responsible for the use of your account, and
if someone else uses it, they are doing so in your name, making
you liable for any problems they might create.

Change your password often, once your account is established, to
help us maintain a high level of system security.

PRESS ANY KEY TO RETURN TO MAIN SCREEN:
```

Press any key once you've read the informational text about how to select a password. In the Password field, type your password. It doesn't show up as you type, and bullets replace the letters. I first entered Adam, and the new user program responded with this message.

```
The password routine could not use your choice for one reason or
another.  Select a password of mixed upper and lower-cased letters,
and add in some numbers and punctuation marks; it is useful to
select a password of six to eight characters.

PRESS ANY KEY TO RETURN TO MAIN SCREEN:
```

You see this message if you choose an unacceptable password, or if, during the Verify phase, you don't enter the password in exactly the same way twice. Press a key to return to the main screen and enter your password.

I entered *tmo2tbg*, which seems completely meaningless and is difficult to guess. A mnemonic strategy for thinking of these passwords is to use the first letters of a phrase like "Take me out to the ball game," which translates to *tmo2tbg*. You must enter the password twice to make sure you've got it right, so after you enter it the first time and press Tab, the field name changes from Password to Verify, and you must enter your password again, exactly the same.

Write it down after the first time to make sure you don't forget, especially since you need it later. Without this password, you won't be able to log in again.

```
        Halcyon New User Info Editor. Press [TAB] to move from one field to the next.


        Full  Name: [Sally Q. Public                    ]

        Login Name: [sallyp  ]   Verify: [.......        ]

        Phone Numbers: [(XXX)XXX-XXXX        ] Home
                       [(XXX)XXX-XXXX        ] Work

            Address: [12345 Main St.                     ]
                     [Seattle, WA                        ]
                     [98101                              ]

           Comments: [                                   ]
                     [                                   ]
                     [                                   ]
        Type Of Account (SLIP, PPP, SHELL): [      ]
```

Once you've verified your password successfully, press Tab to continue to the next informational screen.

```
    Enter the phone number in the (XXX)XXX-XXXX format, where (XXX) is the
    Area Code (U.S., Canada, etc.) and XXX-XXXX is the prefix and number.
    Local (Seattle area) subscribers should include their Area Code, as
    well.

    Enter both work and home phone numbers; emergencies may occur where we
    need to reach you at any time during the day.  International users
    may use the (XXX) field to enter their Country Code, followed by
    City Code, prefix, etc., such as (031)26-456-78901.

    Type over the template shown, replacing our information with your
    own.

    PRESS ANY KEY TO RETURN TO MAIN SCREEN:
```

Press any key once you've read the informational text about how to enter your phone numbers. Please enter both of your phone numbers here. Northwest Nexus won't call you if they can avoid it, but if you need help setting up your account, they must be able to reach you by telephone.

You do have to enter the parentheses and the dash within the phone number;
the program does not enter those for you.

```
Halcyon New User Info Editor. Press [TAB] to move from one field to the next.

Full  Name: [Sally Q. Public                        ]

Login Name: [sallyp ]   Verify: [.......          ]

Phone Numbers: [(206)555-1234      ] Home
               [(206)555-6789      ] Work

    Address: [12345 Main St.                    ]
             [Seattle, WA                       ]
             [98101                             ]

   Comments: [                                  ]
             [                                  ]
             [                                  ]
Type Of Account (SLIP, PPP, SHELL): [      ]
```

After you enter the first phone number and press Tab, the new user program
immediately lets you enter the second phone number. After you enter that one
and press Tab, you move on to the next informational screen.

```
Type over the information shown, using the format
12345 Main St., Apt. 201-C (Street Address and locator information)
Seattle, WA (City and State)
98101 (ZIP Code or Postal Code)

International users should provide similar information, changing
it to meet your own postal requirements.

Please include any additional address information in the "Comments"
fields, such as billing department, contact person, etc., if
necessary.

PRESS ANY KEY TO RETURN TO MAIN SCREEN:
```

Once you've read the information about how to enter your address in the next
screen, press any key to return to the entry screen. Enter your address in the
form suggested, since otherwise the folks at Northwest Nexus must reformat it
to import it into their database.

```
Halcyon New User Info Editor. Press [TAB] to move from one field to the next.

Full  Name: [Sally Q. Public                     ]

Login Name: [sallyp  ]   Verify: [.......        ]

Phone Numbers: [(206)555-1234      ] Home
               [(206)555-6789      ] Work

   Address: [999 Elm Street, Apt. 333            ]
            [Seattle, WA                         ]
            [98100                               ]

  Comments: [                                    ]
            [                                    ]
            [                                    ]
Type Of Account (SLIP, PPP, SHELL): [      ]
```

After you've entered your address properly, press the Tab key to move on to the next informational screen.

```
If there's any additional information we should know (special billing
requirements, etc.), please use the 'Comments:' section.

Special coupon or promotional offers may require you to provide
specific information—this is the place to do that.

Do not use this section as a place to request or ask for information.
Our validation routines may not pick up your request.  Please contact
us directly if there's something you'd like to discuss or if you
would like us to send you some more information.

Ralph Sims, System Administrator (support@halcyon.com)
NWNEXUS, Inc., P.O. Box 40597, Bellevue, WA 98105-4597
+1 206 455 3505 (voice), 455 4672 (FAX)

PRESS ANY KEY TO RETURN TO MAIN SCREEN:
```

OK, pay attention. This is a free-form entry area, but you *must* enter some specific information to take advantage of the special offer, and to get Northwest Nexus to set up a PPP account for you.

In the first line, enter **ISK Macintosh,** exactly as I have done. In the second line, type **Please set up a PPP account for me**, exactly as I did. If you don't enter this, your PPP account won't allow you access. In the third line, you don't have to type anything, but it's nice to thank people for helping out. Of course, if you don't want a PPP account, change the second line to SLIP or Shell as appropriate and make sure the Type Of Account field matches your choice.

```
Halcyon New User Info Editor. Press [TAB] to move from one field to the next.

Full  Name: [Sally Q. Public                      ]

Login Name: [sallyp  ]  Verify: [.......          ]

Phone Numbers: [(206)555-1234        ] Home
               [(206)555-6789        ] Work

      Address: [999 Elm Street, Apt. 333           ]
               [Seattle, WA                         ]
               [98100                               ]

     Comments: [ISK Macintosh                       ]
               [Please set up a PPP account for me  ]
               [    -Thanks!                         ]
Type Of Account (SLIP, PPP, SHELL): [      ]
```

After you've entered this information, press the Tab key to move on to the next informational screen.

```
Please indicate the type of account desired.

SHELL accounts are often called 'interactive' or 'dialup' or
'UNIX' accounts.

PPP and SLIP are two types of accounts which place YOUR computer
directly on the Internet for the duration of your connection.  These
types of accounts require software other than your modem terminal
(communications) software; PROCOMM, ZTerm, Windows Terminal, etc.
won't work for this type of account.

SLIP and PPP are similar protocols, but require different software
configurations.  Your account must be configured by us for EITHER
one of these protocols; you will not be able to automatically switch
between the two without notifying us first to change your account
configuration.

PRESS ANY KEY TO RETURN TO MAIN SCREEN:
```

Once you've read this, press any key to move back to the main screen. You want a PPP account if you're using the software that the ISKM Installer installs for you with the *Standard Install for Northwest Nexus* option. Only enter Shell or SLIP in this field if you're positive that you know what you're doing and have the software to take advantage of that sort of account. If you enter Shell or SLIP, make sure the second comment line matches your choice, since the folks at Northwest Nexus will go by the Type Of Account field if there's a conflict.

```
Halcyon New User Info Editor. Press [TAB] to move from one field to the next.


Full  Name: [Sally Q. Public                      ]

Login Name: [sallyp ]   Verify: [.......          ]

Phone Numbers: [(206)555-1234      ] Home
               [(206)555-6789      ] Work

   Address: [999 Elm Street, Apt. 333            ]
            [Seattle, WA                          ]
            [98100                                ]

  Comments: [ISK Macintosh                        ]
            [Please set up a PPP account for me   ]
            [   -Thanks!                           ]
Type Of Account (SLIP, PPP, SHELL): [PPP  ]
```

Once you have entered **PPP** in this field, press the Tab key to move on to the confirmation screen.

```
You will now be prompted if you wish to change any of the information
you provided.  If you do, you will be taken to the beginning of the
information screen, where you may TAB to the next field, changing
whatever you need.  You will not be allowed to proceed past the
password entry without re-entering and verifying the password
information (you may also change your password at this time, if
desired.

Just type over the entry you wish to change, replacing the
erroneous data with new information.

PRESS ANY KEY TO RETURN TO MAIN SCREEN:
```

This step enables you to have one last chance to go back and change anything that you may not like; you can use the Tab key to move past the items that you've already entered, with the exception of the Password field, which you must enter again. So when you're done, the screen, should look something like this:

```
Halcyon New User Info Editor. Press [TAB] to move from one field to the next.

Full  Name: [Sally Q. Public                     ]

Login Name: [sallyp ]   Verify: [.......         ]

Phone Numbers: [(206)555-1234       ] Home
               [(206)555-6789       ] Work

    Address: [999 Elm Street, Apt. 333            ]
             [Seattle, WA                         ]
             [98100                               ]

   Comments: [ISK Macintosh                       ]
             [Please set up a PPP account for me  ]
             [   -Thanks!                         ]
Type Of Account (SLIP, PPP, SHELL): [PPP  ]


Is all of the information correct (y/n):
```

If your information is correct, press **Y** to accept it; otherwise press **N** to go back and try again. Once everything is correct, you move on to the final screen.

```
Thank you for selecting halcyon.com as your information provider.
Please limit your online sessions to two hours at a time, with a
suggested two-hour interval between sessions.

Your account should be activated within three business days.  If you
are able to log in with your new userid and password, then everything
has been set up and you are ready to go.  If you are not able to log
in, after three days, call us by phone and we will investigate the problem.
Often, we can get accounts established sooner, often depending on how
easy it is to reach you during daytime hours.

You will be invoiced for a $20 setup charge as well as a pro-rated
amount for access during the first month of service.  Feel free to
use the system for a week, as a 'get acquainted' period; your first
```

```
invoice will reflect a billing for the trial period as part of the
pro-rated figure.  Send email to billing@halcyon.com for more
information.  You MUST call and cancel your account within a week
after it is activated in order NOT to be billed; if you do receive
an invoice after canceling your account, please call us and we
will straighten out the problem.

Our office number is +1 206 455 3505, and is monitored 24 hours
a day for emergency support; please call between 0900 and 1700
Pacific Time for routine inquiries.

Thank you for considering halcyon.com as your information gateway.

Ralph Sims, System Administrator (support@halcyon.com)
NWNEXUS, Inc., P.O. Box 40597, Bellevue, WA 98105-4597
+1 206 455 3505 (voice), 455 4672 (FAX)

PRESS ANY KEY TO RETURN TO MAIN SCREEN:
```

A few seconds later, your modem will hang up, since you can't use anything until Northwest Nexus activates your account. Now you have to sit tight for three business days before you can call back using MacPPP.

Note

Now that you've completed this sign-up process, you never use your terminal emulator to call Northwest Nexus again. You always make the connection with MacPPP.

Configuring MacTCP and MacPPP

Let's jump forward briefly and assume you're ready to configure MacTCP and MacPPP. In chapter 12, "MacTCP, PPP, and SLIP," I mention again and again that you must get a bunch of information from your system administrator. One advantage of working with Northwest Nexus is that much of that information exists in this appendix. I'm not going to explain the process for configuring applications in great detail here—that information is in chapter 13, "MacTCP-based Software"—but I will tell you what information goes where and provide screen shots so you can see exactly how it should be set up.

ISKM Installer

For the current edition of this book, I created an installer using Aladdin's excellent StuffIt InstallerMaker. My goal was to make it as easy as possible to install all of the necessary software, especially things such as MacTCP and MacPPP that require some configuration.

Note

> *If you want to switch from a SLIP account to a PPP account at Northwest Nexus, you must first talk to the folks at Northwest Nexus (email to* **support@halcyon.com** *or call 206-455-3505) and get them to switch your account to PPP. When that's done, throw out MacTCP, MacTCP DNR, MacTCP Prep, InterSLIP, and InterSLIP Control (if installed), and then restart before running the ISKM Installer. All of those files can be found in the System Folder and its sub-folders—when in doubt, use Find from the File menu in the Finder.*

It's also easy to install generic configurations if you so wish—this is primarily for people who want to work with providers other than Northwest Nexus. See appendix G, "The Internet Starter Kit Disk," for the complete details on what's installed where with all of the various Custom options in the ISKM Installer.

Note

> *The ISKM Installer will* **not** *overwrite any existing files. To reinstall MacTCP after removing a corrupted version, make sure to restart after throwing out the old MacTCP, MacTCP DNR, and MacTCP Prep files. Then, run the ISKM Installer. Otherwise, your new version will retain the corruption. The* MacTCP Only *option in the Custom screen is best for reinstalling only MacTCP.*

The *Standard Install for Northwest Nexus* installs the following files on your Macintosh:

- MacTCP: MacTCP is installed in the Control Panels folder and configured for use with a Northwest Nexus Server-addressed account by a MacTCP Prep file installed in your Preferences folder. A Hosts file, listing some Northwest Nexus host machines, is also installed in your System Folder. All of the Northwest Nexus domain name servers are already entered in MacTCP. You should not need to do any additional configuration on MacTCP.

- MacPPP: Config PPP is installed in your Control Panels folder, PPP is installed in your Extensions folder, and PPP Preferences is installed in your Preferences folder. A MacPPP 2.0.1 folder containing documentation is installed in the ISKM Folder that you save on your hard disk. You must still enter the settings specific to your modem, and enter your userid and password in the Connect Script dialog (no need to use the Authentication dialog).

- InterSLIP: InterSLIP is not installed.

- Anarchie: Anarchie is installed in the ISKM Folder that you save on your hard disk. An Anarchie Prefs file is installed in your Preferences folder so you can use it immediately. You should customize the preferences to use your email address.

- Eudora: Eudora is installed in your ISKM Folder. Before using it, you must customize Eudora with your POP Account and Real Name.

- MacWAIS: MacWAIS is installed in your ISKM Folder.

- MacWeb: MacWeb is installed in your ISKM Folder.

- TurboGopher: TurboGopher is installed in your ISKM Folder. A TurboGopher Settings file containing bookmarks for various useful Gopher servers is installed in your Preferences folder.

- Essential Bookmarks: This folder, containing the bookmarks for essential programs stored on **ftp.tidbits.com**, is installed in your ISKM Folder.

Running the ISKM Installer

First, start-up from the hard disk on which you wish to install MacTCP, MacPPP, and the various preferences files, since the ISKM Installer installs those items in the active Control Panels, Extensions, and Preferences folders. Hold down the Shift key as you restart to prevent extensions from loading. (Although this shouldn't matter, it's always best to be safe.)

Insert the floppy disk in your drive. When it comes up, double click on the file called ISKM Installer. You should see the ISKM Installer splash screen. Click on the Continue button. Next, the ISKM Installer presents you with a screen full of text that describes what the various options available in the ISKM Installer do, and offers other useful information (see figure F.1).

Please read this information, and, if you wish, save or print it by clicking on Save or Print. Then, click on Continue. The ISKM Installer presents you with the Standard Install dialog box (see figure F.2).

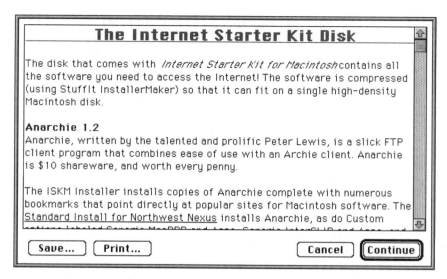

Figure F.1   *ISKM Installer Help Text*

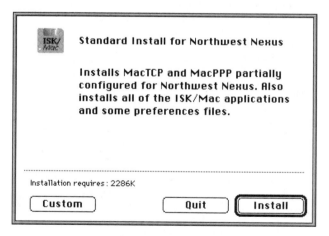

Figure F.2   *ISKM Installer Standard Install dialog*

If you want to perform a *Standard Install for Northwest Nexus*, click on the Install button. The ISKM Installer informs you that you must restart your computer after installing, and asks if you would like to continue (see figure F.3).

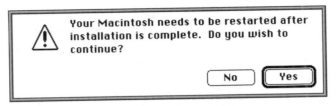

Figure F.3   *Restart question dialog*

If you have any unsaved work open in other applications, click on the No button and then on the Quit button back in the Standard Install dialog. Save your work, quit the other applications, and then repeat the steps to this point. When you are ready to install, click on the Yes button when the ISKM Installer asks about restarting. Next, you're presented with a Standard File dialog that enables you to locate the ISKM Folder anywhere on your hard disk that you like.

Once you choose a location and click on Save, the ISKM Installer proceeds to install everything. When it's finished, it informs you that everything has been installed correctly and forces you to click on the Restart button. Click on it, and after your computer restarts you're ready to configure the software that was installed for you.

Configuring MacTCP

You should not need to configure MacTCP at all, since the ISKM Installer installs a MacTCP Prep file in your Preferences folder that contains the MacTCP configuration for Northwest Nexus. Unless you're re-configuring MacTCP after reinstalling it from scratch, skip to the "Configuring MacPPP" section later on. If you wish to reinstall MacTCP from scratch, see the MacTCP section in chapter 14, "Step-by-Step Internet," for detailed instructions. In summary, though, open the MacTCP control panel and select the PPP icon (if it's not present, install MacPPP before continuing). You don't configure the IP address in the first part of the MacTCP control panel, since Northwest Nexus uses Server-addressed accounts, so that number will change every time you connect.

Note

When you call in with a Server-addressed account, the server assigns you an IP number, something like **198.137.231.51**. It also links a name with that IP address, something like **bellevue.ip51.halcyon.com**. This means that you can use FTP sites like **ftp.apple.com** that require you to have a name and not

continues

continued

just a number, but it also means that you can't easily use Peter Lewis's FTPd or Fingerd to turn your Mac into an FTP or Finger server—no one will know what address you have on any given connection. The only work-around is to log in to **halcyon.com** *using NCSA Telnet, then log out. Then, your friend can finger your email address, something like* **tidbits@halcyon.com**, *and look at the end of the line that says from where you last logged in. That gives the numeric part of the IP, from which your friend can then figure out your current IP address.*

Click on the More button to bring up the Configuration dialog. Here's how I have configured it for Northwest Nexus (see figure F.4).

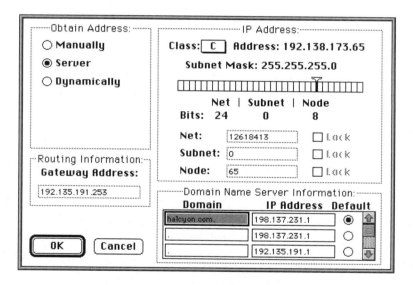

Figure F.4   *MacTCP Configuration dialog*

First, click on the Server radio button to enable Server addressing. Then, you must enter the Domain Name Server Information. Enter that *exactly* as indicated below, making sure to turn on the radio button on right-hand side of the first line.

```
halcyon.com.          198.137.231.1        (•)
      .               198.137.231.1
      .               192.135.191.1
      .               192.135.191.3
```

Don't worry about the large IP Address area in the upper right. When you're done, click on the OK button to save your changes, close the MacTCP control panel, and then restart your Mac.

Configuring MacPPP

Now we must configure MacPPP. The ISKM Installer tries to configure MacPPP for you, but there are some pieces of information that only you know. Open the Config PPP control panel that the ISKM Installer has installed for you in the Control Panels folder (see figure F.5).

If you use a PowerBook internal modem or have your modem connected to your Printer port for some reason, select that port in the Port Name pop-up menu. Then, from the PPP Server pop-up menu, select the modem configuration that most closely matches yours—if none look right, select Hayes-Compatible.

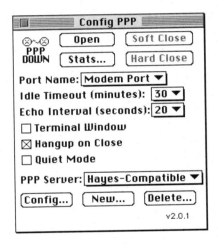

Figure F.5   *Config PPP control panel*

Note

Other users contributed these modem configurations. I cannot guarantee that they work because I don't have most of these modems to test them with. You may have to consult your modem manual to decide on a different modem init string. Make sure your modem init string turns hardware handshaking (RTS/CTS) on and XON/XOFF off.

Click on the Config button to bring up the Server Configuration dialog (see figure F.6).

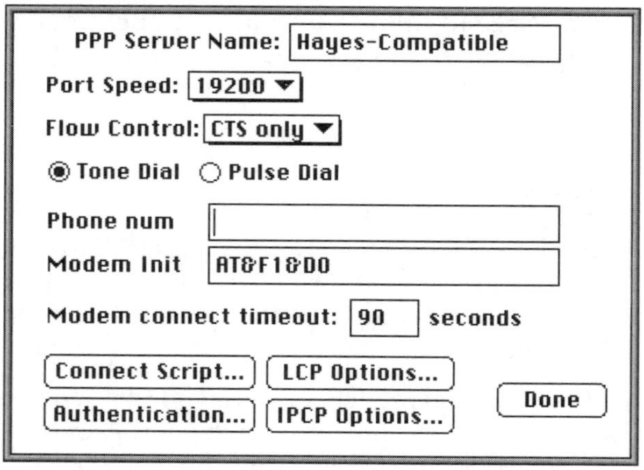

```
┌─────────────────────────────────────────────────┐
│        PPP Server Name: │Hayes-Compatible│       │
│        Port Speed: │19200 ▼│                      │
│        Flow Control:│CTS only ▼│                  │
│        ◉ Tone Dial  ○ Pulse Dial                 │
│        Phone num   │                    │         │
│        Modem Init  │AT&F1&D0│                     │
│        Modem connect timeout: │90│  seconds       │
│        ┌Connect Script...┐ ┌LCP Options...┐       │
│        ┌Authentication...┐ ┌IPCP Options...┐ ┌Done┐│
└─────────────────────────────────────────────────┘
```

Figure F.6   *MacPPP Server Configuration dialog*

If you live within local calling distance of Bellevue, WA, enter **455-8455** in the Phone num field. If you can only call Seattle locally, enter **382-6245** (other numbers are available in Washington State as well). If you must call long distance, enter **1-206-455-8455**. If you don't think the modem init string that's installed for you will work with your modem, enter the appropriate one in the Modem Init field. Check this with your modem manual, or call your modem's manufacturer if you must—don't guess! Click on the Connect Script button (see figure F.7). (Don't forget any special access code you might need to enter, such as **9** to dial out.)

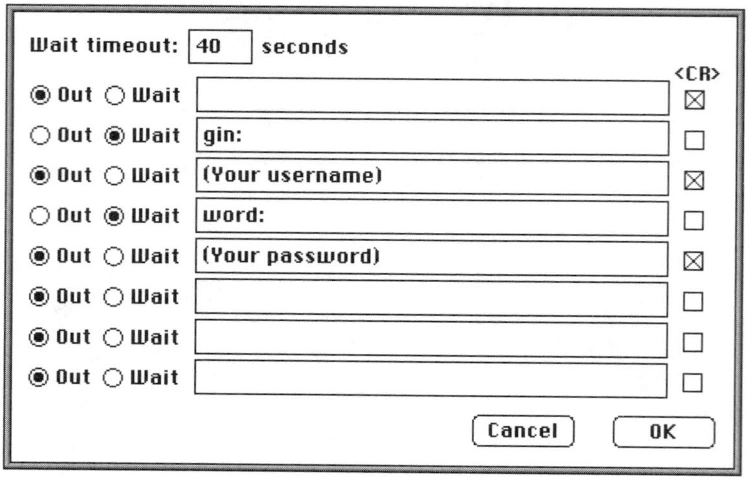

```
┌─────────────────────────────────────────────────┐
│   Wait timeout: │40│   seconds                    │
│                                            <CR>   │
│   ◉ Out ○ Wait │                      │    ☒     │
│   ○ Out ◉ Wait │gin:                  │    ☐     │
│   ◉ Out ○ Wait │(Your username)       │    ☒     │
│   ○ Out ◉ Wait │word:                 │    ☐     │
│   ◉ Out ○ Wait │(Your password)       │    ☒     │
│   ◉ Out ○ Wait │                      │    ☐     │
│   ◉ Out ○ Wait │                      │    ☐     │
│   ◉ Out ○ Wait │                      │    ☐     │
│                            ┌Cancel┐  ┌OK┐         │
└─────────────────────────────────────────────────┘
```

Figure F.7   *MacPPP Connect Script dialog*

Enter your userid and your password in the fields marked for them. Make sure to enter your userid in all lowercase, and your password exactly as you created it online. Click on the OK button to save your changes. Then, back in the Server Configuration dialog, click on the Done button.

Note

You do not have to enter your userid and password in the Authentication dialog box.

You should now be able to click on the Open button in the Config PPP control panel to establish your connection to your PPP account at Northwest Nexus. If you have troubles, first review the sections in chapter 12, "MacTCP, PPP, and SLIP," about setting up MacTCP and MacPPP and on troubleshooting. Try reinstalling everything (making sure to delete all the files that the ISKM Installer has placed in your System Folder and special System Folder folders first).

Configuring Eudora and Email

To configure Eudora for use with your Northwest Nexus account, launch Eudora, and from the Special menu, choose Configuration (see figure F.8).

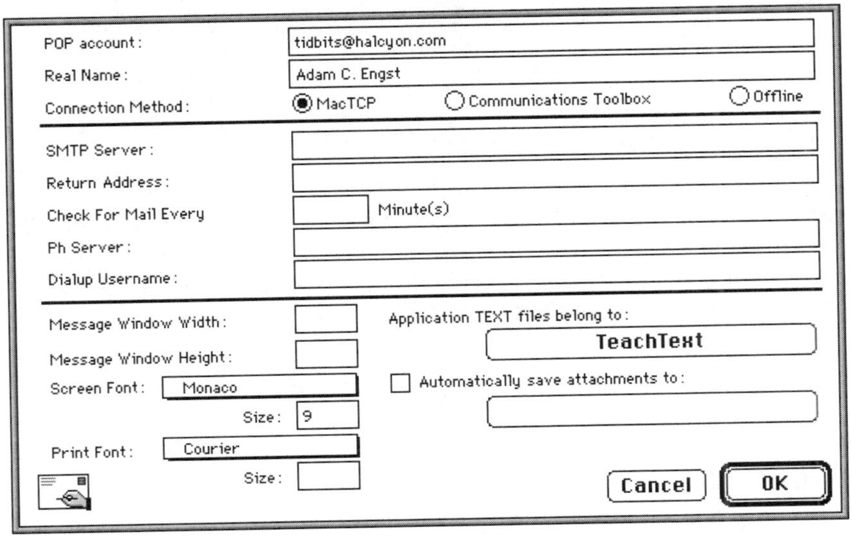

Figure F.8   Configuring Eudora

In the POP account field, enter your userid followed by **@halcyon.com**, as I've done for my **tidbits@halcyon.com** account. This is also your email address, so go ahead and tell your friends. Then, in the Real Name field, type your real name. Other email programs may ask you specifically for your POP server and your SMTP server, or perhaps just your mail server. To each of these questions, the answer is **halcyon.com**.

Configuring Usenet News

To properly use any of the newsreaders, you must know a few pieces of information. Your NNTP server at Northwest Nexus is **news.halcyon.com**, and the Northwest Nexus mailserver is at **halcyon.com**. If you use a program such as Dartmouth's InterNews that requires authentication of some sort, try using POP Authentication with **halcyon.com** as the authentication host and your normal userid and password.

Note

*As this book was going to press, Northwest Nexus added a new news server at **news.halcyon.com**. Although the new name makes much more sense (and the new server is faster), I had no time to redo the screenshots for the book. Thus, if you use Northwest Nexus, please use **news.halcyon.com** as the news server and don't use **nwfocus.wa.com**. Sorry for any confusion this may cause.*

Configuring Anarchie and FTP

Although the ISKM Installer preconfigured Anarchie sufficiently that you can use it immediately, you should adjust the preferences to reflect your email address. Connect to the Internet and launch Anarchie. From the Edit menu, choose Preferences, and in the Anarchie Preferences dialog, enter your email address in the Email Address field (see figure F.9).

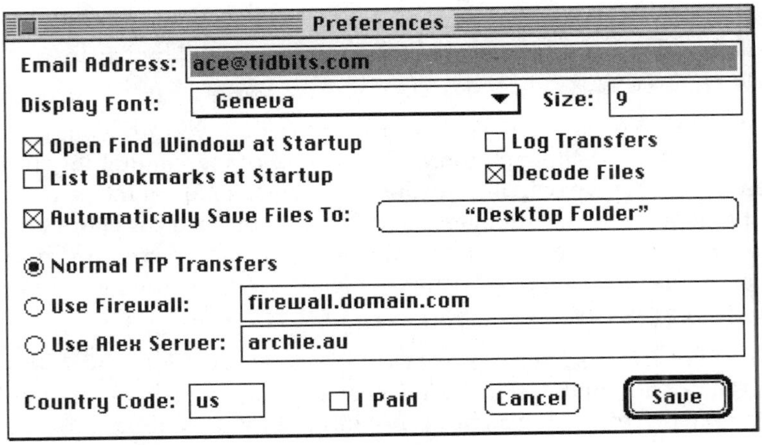

Figure F.9   *Anarchie Preferences dialog*

Configuring Other MacTCP-based Applications

TurboGopher and MacWeb require no configuration at all, although the ISKM Installer installs a TurboGopher Settings file for you. Useful, eh?

That's all there is to it. Enjoy your Internet connection!

Northwest Nexus Terms & Conditions

Terms and Conditions—Effective June 1, 1994

1. You understand and accept these Terms and Conditions and agree to pay for these services according to the Billing Policies currently in effect.

2. If we do not receive your payment when due, your account may be terminated. Termination of your account does not remove your responsibility

under this agreement to pay all fees incurred up to the date the account was canceled including any collection fees incurred by Northwest Nexus Inc.

3. Northwest Nexus Inc. makes no warranties of any kind, whether expressed or implied, including any implied warranty of merchantability or fitness of this service for a particular purpose. Northwest Nexus Inc. takes no responsibility for any damages suffered by you including, but not limited to, loss of data from delays, non-deliveries, mis-deliveries, or service interruptions caused by Northwest Nexus's own negligence or your errors and/or omissions.

4. Northwest Nexus's services may only be used for lawful purposes. Transmission of any material in violation of any U.S. or state regulation is prohibited. This includes, but is not limited to: copyrighted material, threatening or obscene material, or material protected by trade secret. You agree to indemnify and hold harmless Northwest Nexus Inc. from any claims resulting from your use of this service which damages you or another party. At our discretion, we may revoke your access for inappropriate usage.

5. Use of any information obtained via this service is at your own risk. Northwest Nexus specifically denies any responsibility for the accuracy or quality of information obtained through our services.

6. We may list your contact information in relevant directories.

7. If you use another organization's networks or computing resources, you are subject to their respective permission and usage policies.

8. These Terms and Conditions are subject to change without notice. A current copy will always be available online through our "help" facility. Continued usage of your account after a new policy has gone into effect constitutes acceptance of that policy. We encourage you to regularly check the policy statement for any changes. (The effective date at the top will be updated to indicate a new revision.)

9. You will notify Northwest Nexus of any changes in account contact information such as your address.

10. You are responsible for how your account is used. You may allow others to use it, bearing in mind that you are fully responsible for what they do.

11. Per-session time limits are currently set at two hours; you may log back in after a two-hour "off-line" time. This applies to the **halcyon.com** machines only.

12. The use of IRC is not permitted on any of the **halcyon.com** machines. Currently, IRC clients operating on users machines via SLIP/PPP are allowed.

13. Disk storage is limited to 5 megabytes. Excess storage is not permitted on the user drives; use of /scratch for excess files is permitted. This applies only to the **halcyon.com** machines.

14. Northwest Nexus Inc. reserves the right to cancel this service and reimburse you with any unused fees where appropriate on a pro-rata basis.

15. You may cancel your account at any time upon prior written notice to us. You will still be responsible for any fees incurred up to the date of termination of the service. We will reimburse you for any unused fees where appropriate on a pro-rata basis.

16. These Terms and Conditions supersede all previous representations, understandings or agreements and shall prevail notwithstanding any variance with terms and conditions of any order submitted.

17. Some of the information available on our systems, such as ClariNews, is covered by copyright. Unless you have permission from the copyright holder, you are not allowed to redistribute this information to others including use of this information on radio, television, or printed media such as newspapers, magazines, or newsletters.

Appendix F
Special Internet
Access Offer

The Internet Starter Kit Disk

The disk that comes with *Internet Starter Kit for Macintosh* contains all the software you need to access the Internet! The software is compressed (using Aladdin's excellent StuffIt InstallerMaker) so that it can fit on a single high-density Macintosh disk. To install any or all of these programs, double-click on the ISKM Installer icon. See the following sections for a detailed list of what's installed by each option in the ISKM Installer.

ISKM Installer

I designed the ISKM Installer to be as easy as possible to use; I tried to think of the different things you might want to do with the various files on the disk, which is why I created several different installer options.

Note

> *The ISKM Installer will not overwrite any existing files—if you wish to replace a file such as MacTCP, you must throw it away manually first (along with MacTCP DNR and MacTCP Prep). This is imperative if you're switching from SLIP to PPP, or have already used some of this software previously and wish to take advantage of the disk's included preferences and configurations.*

If for some reason your copy of the ISKM Installer is corrupted, you may be able to expand the contents manually with StuffIt Deluxe or StuffIt Lite. Make a copy of the ISKM Installer. Using ResEdit or a similar utility, change the copy's file type to SITD and the creator to SIT! (those are the type and creator of StuffIt archives). Save the file and then open it in StuffIt, which will complain about the archive being corrupted, but which may open it and allow you to expand the contents.

Note

> *If you receive a disk that your Mac rejects, call Hayden/Macmillan Computer Publishing, at 800-858-7674 or 317-581-7674.*

■ If you want to use MacPPP with Northwest Nexus (which is what I recommend), use Standard Install for Northwest Nexus, since it installs all of the applications and MacTCP and MacPPP, partially configured for you. MacTCP and MacPPP are installed in the active System Folder. See appendix F, "Special Internet Access Offer," for the configuration details that remain.

If you're switching from a Northwest Nexus SLIP account, you must first change your account with Northwest Nexus to a PPP account. Before installing, make sure to throw out the old MacTCP, MacTCP DNR, MacTCP Prep, and InterSLIP files.

Note

> *Northwest Nexus is a long distance call outside of the Puget Sound/Seattle area. Sorry, there's no way around that.*

- If you want to use InterSLIP with Northwest Nexus (I recommend this only if for some reason you cannot make MacPPP work, and remember that you must have a SLIP account, not a PPP account), click on the Custom button in the ISKM Installer and select *Generic InterSLIP and Apps.* This installs all of the applications, MacTCP, and InterSLIP, along with the Northwest Nexus gateway script and the Minimal Dialing Script for InterSLIP. I recommend that you check out the detailed instructions for configuring MacTCP and InterSLIP in chapter 14, "Step-by-Step Internet," since those instructions work for Northwest Nexus.

  If you already have a working SLIP account with Northwest Nexus, there's no need to install a fresh version of MacTCP and InterSLIP. However, if you choose this installation, the ISKM Installer will not overwrite your existing MacTCP and InterSLIP files.

- If you want to use MacPPP with another Internet provider, click on the Custom button in the ISKM Installer and select *Generic MacPPP and Apps.* This installs all the applications and MacTCP and MacPPP. A partially configured PPP Preferences file containing some modem configurations is also installed for you. Contact your provider for the information necessary to finish configuring MacTCP, MacPPP, and the rest of the applications. Thoughtful providers may have MacTCP Prep and PPP Preferences files already created for you.

- If you want to use InterSLIP with another Internet provider, click on the Custom button in the ISKM Installer and select *Generic InterSLIP and Apps.* This installs all of the applications and MacTCP and InterSLIP, along with the Northwest Nexus gateway script (as an example) and the Minimal Dialing Script for InterSLIP. Contact your provider for the information necessary to finish configuring MacTCP, InterSLIP, and the rest of the applications. Thoughtful providers may have a version of MacTCP Prep and an InterSLIP gateway script already created for you.

- If you want to install any one or more of the individual programs, click on the Custom button in the ISKM Installer and select the appropriate option. You can select more than one at a time by Command-clicking on them.

Note

Once you install all the software, configure MacPPP or InterSLIP, and make the connection to your PPP or SLIP account, that's when you run the great programs discussed in chapter 13. MacPPP and InterSLIP do nothing more than establish the connection.

Installation Details

Installers are good at putting files in specific places, but they seldom tell you exactly where the various files end up. The following information explains where everything ends up on your hard disk, organized in by installation option and also by program.

Installation Option Details

This section details precisely what each installation option installs and where the files are installed.

Standard Install for Northwest Nexus

- MacTCP: MacTCP is installed in the Control Panels folder and configured for use with a Northwest Nexus Server-addressed account by a MacTCP Prep file installed in your Preferences folder. A Hosts file, listing some Northwest Nexus host machines, is also installed in your System Folder. All of the Northwest Nexus domain name servers are already entered in MacTCP. You should not need to do any additional configuration on MacTCP.

- MacPPP: Config PPP is installed in your Control Panels folder, PPP is installed in your Extensions folder, and PPP Preferences is installed in your Preferences folder. A MacPPP 2.0.1 folder containing documentation is installed in the ISKM Folder that you save on your hard disk. You must still enter the settings specific to your modem, and enter your userid and password in the Connect Script dialog (no need to use the Authentication dialog).

- InterSLIP: InterSLIP is not installed.

- Anarchie: Anarchie is installed in the ISKM Folder that you save on your hard disk. An Anarchie Prefs file is installed in your Preferences folder so you can use it immediately. You should customize the preferences to use your email address.

- Eudora: Eudora is installed in your ISKM Folder. Before using it, you must customize Eudora with your POP Account and Real Name.

- MacWAIS: MacWAIS is installed in your ISKM Folder.

- MacWeb: MacWeb is installed in your ISKM Folder.

- TurboGopher: TurboGopher is installed in your ISKM Folder. A TurboGopher Settings file containing bookmarks for various useful Gopher servers is installed in your Preferences folder.

■ Essential Bookmarks: This folder, containing the bookmarks for essential programs stored on **ftp.tidbits.com**, is installed in your ISKM Folder.

Generic MacPPP and Apps

■ MacTCP: MacTCP is installed in the Control Panels folder.

■ MacPPP: Config PPP is installed in your Control Panels folder, PPP is installed in your Extensions folder, and PPP Preferences is installed in your Preferences folder. A MacPPP 2.0.1 folder containing documentation is installed in the ISKM Folder that you save on your hard disk.

■ InterSLIP: InterSLIP is not installed.

■ Anarchie: Anarchie is installed in the ISKM Folder that you save on your hard disk. An Anarchie Prefs file is installed in your Preferences folder so you can use it immediately. You should customize the preferences to use your email address.

■ Eudora: Eudora is installed in your ISKM Folder. You must customize Eudora with your POP Account and Real Name before using it.

■ MacWAIS: MacWAIS is installed in your ISKM Folder.

■ MacWeb: MacWeb is installed in your ISKM Folder.

■ TurboGopher: TurboGopher is installed in your ISKM Folder. A TurboGopher Settings file containing bookmarks for various useful Gopher servers is installed in your Preferences folder.

■ Essential Bookmarks: This folder, containing the bookmarks for essential programs stored on **ftp.tidbits.com**, is installed in your ISKM Folder.

Generic InterSLIP and Apps

■ MacTCP: MacTCP is installed in the Control Panels folder.

■ MacPPP: MacPPP is not installed.

■ InterSLIP: InterSLIP Setup is installed in your ISKM Folder. InterSLIP Control is installed (in case you're using System 6—System 7 users can remove it) in your Control Panels folder. The InterSLIP extension is installed in your Extensions folder. An InterSLIP Folder is installed in your Preferences folder; it contains a Dialing Scripts folder with Minimal Dialing Script, and a Gateway Scripts folder with the Northwest Nexus gateway script and standard example gateway script. An InterSLIP 1.0.1 folder containing InterSLIP Setup and documentation is installed in the ISKM Folder that you save on your hard disk.

- Anarchie: Anarchie is installed in the ISKM Folder that you save on your hard disk. An Anarchie Prefs file is installed in your Preferences folder so you can use it immediately. You should customize the preferences to use your email address.

- Eudora: Eudora is installed in your ISKM Folder. You must customize Eudora with your POP Account and Real Name before using it.

- MacWAIS: MacWAIS is installed in your ISKM Folder.

- MacWeb: MacWeb is installed in your ISKM Folder.

- TurboGopher: TurboGopher is installed in your ISKM Folder. A TurboGopher Settings file, containing bookmarks for various useful Gopher servers, is installed in your Preferences folder.

- Essential Bookmarks: This folder, containing the bookmarks for essential programs stored on **ftp.tidbits.com**, is installed in your ISKM Folder.

MacTCP Only

- MacTCP: MacTCP is installed in the Control Panels folder. If you use this option to reinstall MacTCP after removing a corrupted version, make sure to restart after throwing out the old MacTCP, MacTCP DNR, and MacTCP Prep. Otherwise, your new version may retain the corruption.

MacPPP Only

- MacPPP: Config PPP is installed in your Control Panels folder, PPP is installed in your Extensions folder, and PPP Preferences is installed in your Preferences folder. A MacPPP 2.0.1 folder containing documentation is installed in the ISKM Folder that you save on your hard disk.

InterSLIP Only

- InterSLIP: InterSLIP Setup is installed in your ISKM Folder. InterSLIP Control is installed (in case you're using System 6—System 7 users can remove it) in your Control Panels folder. The InterSLIP extension is installed in your Extensions folder. An InterSLIP Folder is installed in your Preferences folder. The InterSLIP Folder contains a Dialing Scripts folder holding the Minimal Dialing Script, and a Gateway Scripts folder containing the Northwest Nexus gateway script and standard example gateway script. An InterSLIP 1.0.1 folder containing InterSLIP Setup and documentation is installed in the ISKM Folder that you save on your hard disk.

Anarchie Only

- ■ Anarchie: Anarchie is installed in the ISKM Folder that you save on your hard disk. An Anarchie Prefs file is installed in your Preferences folder so you can use it immediately. You should customize the preferences to use your email address.

Eudora Only

- ■ Eudora: Eudora is installed in your ISKM Folder. Before using it, you must customize Eudora with your POP Account and Real Name.

MacWAIS Only

- ■ MacWAIS: MacWAIS is installed in your ISKM Folder.

MacWeb Only

- ■ MacWeb: MacWeb is installed in your ISKM Folder.

TurboGopher Only

- ■ TurboGopher: TurboGopher is installed in your ISKM Folder. A TurboGopher Settings file containing bookmarks for various interesting Gopher servers is installed in your Preferences folder.

Essential Bookmarks Only

- ■ Essential Bookmarks: This folder, containing the bookmarks for essential programs stored on **ftp.tidbits.com**, is installed in your ISKM Folder.

Program Details

This section details precisely how you can install each of the programs.

Anarchie 1.2

The ISKM Installer installs copies of Anarchie, complete with numerous bookmarks that point directly at popular sites for Macintosh software. The *Standard Install for Northwest Nexus* installs Anarchie, as do Custom options labeled *Generic MacPPP and Apps*, *Generic InterSLIP and Apps*, and *Anarchie Only*. You should adjust the Anarchie preferences to reflect your email address—see chapter 13, "MacTCP-based Software," for details.

Eudora 1.4.3

The ISKM Installer installs Eudora for you with *Standard Install for Northwest Nexus*, or *Generic MacPPP and Apps, Generic InterSLIP and Apps*, or *Eudora Only*, in the Custom installation screen. You must configure Eudora with your POP account and your real name—see chapter 13, "MacTCP-based Software," for details.

InterSLIP 1.0.1

If you use Northwest Nexus, the *Generic InterSLIP and Apps* option in the Custom screen places the necessary Northwest Nexus gateway script in the Gateway Scripts folder. You can also install InterSLIP alone, with the *InterSLIP Only* option in the Custom screen. InterSLIP is installed in the active System Folder. You must configure InterSLIP to match your modem (a file containing modem strings is installed in the InterSLIP 1.0.1 folder) and your account. See chapters 12, "MacTCP, PPP, and SLIP," and 14, "Step-by-Step Internet," for configuration details.

MacPPP 2.0.1

The *Standard Install for Northwest Nexus, Generic MacPPP and Apps*, and *MacPPP Only* options all install MacPPP in your active System Folder and place a PPP Preferences file containing some modem initialization strings in your Preferences folder. You must select or enter the proper modem initialization string for your modem, enter the phone number, and in the Connect Script, enter your userid and password. You need not mess with the Authentication dialog. See chapters 12, "MacTCP, PPP, and SLIP," and 14, "Step-by-Step Internet," for configuration details.

MacTCP 2.0.4

The ISKM Installer installs and configures MacTCP for Northwest Nexus if you perform a *Standard Install for Northwest Nexus*. Clean copies of MacTCP are installed for you if you select *Generic MacPPP and Apps, Generic InterSLIP and Apps*, or *MacTCP Only*. MacTCP is installed in the active System Folder. See chapters 12, "MacTCP, PPP, and SLIP," and 14, "Step-by-Step Internet," for configuration details.

MacWAIS 1.29

The ISKM Installer installs MacWAIS when you select the *Standard Install for Northwest Nexus*, or, in the Custom screen, *Generic MacPPP and Apps, Generic InterSLIP and Apps*, or *MacWAIS Only*.

MacWeb 0.98a

I wanted to give you a special *Internet Starter Kit for Macintosh* home page. To accomplish that, the ISKM Installer installs a customized version of MacWeb that initially points to my *Internet Starter Kit for Macintosh* home page at:

```
http://www.tidbits.com/tidbits/index.html
```

I plan to continually enhance and update my home page to inform you of the latest and greatest Internet applications and happenings, so I think it will be worth visiting regularly. What better way to find out that you should retrieve the latest version of something like Eudora?

A customized copy of MacWeb that points to the *Internet Starter Kit for Macintosh* home page by default is installed for you with the *Standard Install for Northwest Nexus*, and, in the Custom screen, *Generic MacPPP and Apps*, *Generic InterSLIP and Apps*, or *MacWeb Only*.

TurboGopher 1.0.8b4

TurboGopher is installed by the ISKM Installer if you select *Standard Install for Northwest Nexus*, *Generic MacPPP and Apps*, *Generic InterSLIP and Apps*, or *TurboGopher Only*.

Essential Internet Software Bookmarks

The ISKM Installer installs these bookmarks for you with the *Standard Install for Northwest Nexus*, or, in the Custom screen, with *Generic MacPPP and Apps*, *Generic InterSLIP and Apps*, or *Essential Bookmarks*.

The Rest of the Best

I wanted to put more programs on the disk, I really did. But since I seem to have collected about 50M of software in the course of my testing, including even 25 disks would barely have been enough. So, I had a talk with the folks at Northwest Nexus, and they agreed to set up an FTP site for me that everyone on the Internet could access. This way, you will have a single site to visit for all of your Macintosh Internet applications and utilities.

The FTP site is called **ftp.tidbits.com**, and you can use the standard method of accessing an anonymous FTP site. Just use **anonymous** as your username and your email address, and something like **ace@tidbits.com** as your password. If the machine rejects your password, try using just your username and an @ sign, as in **ace@**; sometimes this particular FTP server is a bit finicky.

Here's a quick tutorial on connecting to the FTP site after you have installed and configured MacTCP (and MacPPP or InterSLIP, if necessary). If you are using MacPPP or InterSLIP, connect to your host. Launch Anarchie. From the File menu, choose Get. In the Get via FTP window that appears, enter **ftp.tidbits.com** in the Machine field. In the Path field, type **/pub/tidbits/tisk**, and make sure the Get Listing button is selected (see figure G.1).

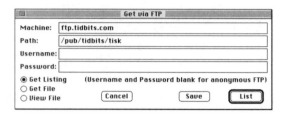

Figure G.1 *Anarchie Get via FTP window configured for* `ftp.tidbits.com`

When you click on the List button, Anarchie connects to `ftp.tidbits.com`, switches into the proper directory, and lists the files. From there you can navigate around in the different folders by double-clicking on them. Double-clicking on a file retrieves it. It's that easy.

Index

Northwest Nexus Terms & Conditions

Terms and Conditions—Effective June 1, 1994

1. You understand and accept these Terms and Conditions and agree to pay for these services according to the Billing Policies currently in effect.

2. If we do not receive your payment when due, your account may be terminated. Termination of your account does not remove your responsibility under this agreement to pay all fees incurred up to the date the account was canceled including any collection fees incurred by Northwest Nexus Inc.

3. Northwest Nexus Inc. makes no warranties of any kind, whether expressed or implied, including any implied warranty of merchantability or fitness of this service for a particular purpose. Northwest Nexus Inc. takes no responsibility for any damages suffered by you including, but not limited to, loss of data from delays, non-deliveries, mis-deliveries, or service interruptions caused by Northwest Nexus's own negligence or your errors and/or omissions.

4. Northwest Nexus's services may only be used for lawful purposes. Transmission of any material in violation of any U.S. or state regulation is prohibited. This includes, but is not limited to: copyrighted material, threatening or obscene material, or material protected by trade secret. You agree to indemnify and hold harmless Northwest Nexus Inc. from any claims resulting from your use of this service which damages you or another party. At our discretion, we may revoke your access for inappropriate usage.

5. Use of any information obtained via this service is at your own risk. Northwest Nexus specifically denies any responsibility for the accuracy or quality of information obtained through our services.

6. We may list your contact information in relevant directories.

7. If you use another organization's networks or computing resources, you are subject to their respective permission and usage policies.

8. These Terms and Conditions are subject to change without notice. A current copy will always be available online through our "help" facility. Continued usage of your account after a new policy has gone into effect constitutes acceptance of that policy. We encourage you to regularly check the policy statement for any changes. (The effective date at the top will be updated to indicate a new revision.)

9. You will notify Northwest Nexus of any changes in account contact information such as your address.

10. You are responsible for how your account is used. You may allow others to use it, bearing in mind that you are fully responsible for what they do.

11. Per-session time limits are currently set at two hours; you may log back in after a two-hour "off-line" time. This applies to the `halcyon.com` machines only.

12. The use of IRC is not permitted on any of the `halcyon.com` machines. Currently, IRC clients operating on users machines via SLIP/PPP are allowed.

13. Disk storage is limited to 5 megabytes. Excess storage is not permitted on the user drives; use of /scratch for excess files is permitted. This applies only to the `halcyon.com` machines.

14. Northwest Nexus Inc. reserves the right to cancel this service and reimburse you with any unused fees where appropriate on a pro-rata basis.

15. You may cancel your account at any time upon prior written notice to us. You will still be responsible for any fees incurred up to the date of termination of the service. We will reimburse you for any unused fees where appropriate on a pro-rata basis.

16. These Terms and Conditions supersede all previous representations, understandings, or agreements and shall prevail notwithstanding any variance with terms and conditions of any order submitted.

17. Some of the information available on our systems, such as ClariNews, is covered by copyright. Unless you have permission from the copyright holder, you are not allowed to redistribute this information to others including use of this information on radio, television, or printed media such as newspapers, magazines, or newsletters.

Northwest Nexus Internet Access Offer

What would a book about the Internet be if it didn't provide some means of getting on the Internet for those people who aren't already connected? Not much, and to remedy that situation, Hayden Books has worked out a deal for readers of this book with Northwest Nexus Inc., a commercial Internet provider based in Bellevue, Washington.

Northwest Nexus has created a flat rate PPP account. You pay $20 to sign up, and $22.50 per month (billed in advance on a quarterly basis) for as many hours as you want to use it each month. In addition, they are making the first two weeks available for free. If after two weeks you don't want to keep the account for any reason, just call Northwest Nexus at 206-455-3505 and ask them to deactivate your account, at which point you pay nothing. (It's possible you may receive an automatically generated bill before that time. Just call Northwest Nexus if that happens and they'll straighten everything out for you.)

One thing to keep in mind is that you must call Northwest Nexus (in Washington State) to connect, and that will be a long distance phone call for everyone outside of the Puget Sound/ Seattle area. However, this is a good deal even with long-distance fees (and you can reduce long-distance calling charges by using discount plans offered by your long distance carrier).

Details for setting up an account are provided in appendix F. The important fact is that after you set the account up, you must send *this page* (not a copy!) to Northwest Nexus to confirm that you bought this book. Just cut out the page, and drop it in the mail. If you don't, you won't get the special deal, so make sure you fill out and send in this page. It's not tough!

Please set up a PPP account for me!

Full Name: _____

Daytime Phone #: _____

Evening Phone #: _____

Address: _____

_____

_____

Requested Login:_____

Please cut out this page (do not send a copy!) and mail it to:

Northwest Nexus Inc.
ATTN: Hayden Books Special Offer
P.O. Box 40597
Bellevue, WA 98015-4597
If you have questions, contact Northwest Nexus at 206-455-3505.

cut here

Internet Starter Kit for Macintosh
Online Information

Hayden Books

MacTCP Account

Addressing Style (Manually, Server, Dynamically): _____	Domain Name Server (default): _____
IP Address (if Manually addressed): _____	Domain Name Server (backup): _____
	SMTP Server: _____
Gateway Address (if Manually addressed): _____	NNTP Server: _____
	POP Account: _____
Network Class (if Manually addressed and necessary): _____	Email Address: _____
	Connection Type (PPP, SLIP, ARA, Network): _____
Subnet Mask (if Manually addressed and necessary): _____	Phone Number: _____
	Port Speed: _____
	Modem Init String: _____

Shell Accounts

Unix Host #1: _____ _____ _____ _____
phone number/speed   userid   password   modem init string

_____
notes

Unix Host #2: _____ _____ _____ _____
phone number/speed   userid   password   modem init string

_____
notes

Bulletin Board Accounts

BBS #1: _____ _____ _____ _____
phone number/speed   userid   password   modem init string

_____
notes

BBS #2: _____ _____ _____ _____
phone number/speed   userid   password   modem init string

_____
notes

UUCP Account

Host: _____ _____ _____ _____
phone number/speed   userid   password   modem init string

_____ _____ _____
mail server name   news server name   Administrator's email address

_____
notes

Note: Storing your passwords here could be a security breach. Only do so if you are sure this won't be a problem.

Internet Starter Kit for Macintosh
Online Information

Hayden
Books

Commercial Online Services

America Online: _____ _____ _____ _____
                      phone number/speed   userid   password   modem init string
_____
                      notes

AppleLink: _____ _____ _____ _____
                      phone number/speed   userid   password   modem init string
_____
                      notes

BIX: _____ _____ _____ _____
                      phone number/speed   userid   password   modem init string
_____
                      notes

CompuServe: _____ _____ _____ _____
                      phone number/speed   userid   password   modem init string
_____
                      notes

Delphi: _____ _____ _____ _____
                      phone number/speed   userid   password   modem init string
_____
                      notes

eWorld: _____ _____ _____ _____
                      phone number/speed   userid   password   modem init string
_____
                      notes

GEnie: _____ _____ _____ _____
                      phone number/speed   userid   password   modem init string
_____
                      notes

MCI Mail: _____ _____ _____ _____
                      phone number/speed   userid   password   modem init string
_____
                      notes

Outland: _____ _____ _____ _____
                      phone number/speed   userid   password   modem init string
_____
                      notes

Prodigy: _____ _____ _____ _____
                      phone number/speed   userid   password   modem init string
_____
                      notes

Note: Storing your passwords here could be a security breach. Only do so if you are sure this won't be a problem.

The Internet Starter Kit Disk

The disk that comes with *Internet Starter Kit for Macintosh* contains all the software you need to access the Internet! To install any or all of these programs, just double-click on the ISKM Installer icon. See appendix G for a detailed list of what's installed by each option in the ISKM Installer. For complete configuration instructions for the various programs on the disk, see chapter 12, chapter 13, chapter 14, appendix F, appendix G, and the ISKM Installer help text.

Anarchie 1.2   Anarchie, written by the talented and prolific Peter Lewis, is a slick FTP client program that combines ease of use with an Archie client. Anarchie is $10 shareware, and worth every penny.

Eudora 1.4.3   Eudora is the most popular program for Internet email on the Macintosh. Created by Steve Dorner of QUALCOMM, Eudora is flexible enough to work via dialup, via UUCP, or via MacTCP. Even better, Eudora comes completely free of charge.

InterSLIP 1.0.1   InterCon Systems won a lot of friends by releasing InterSLIP as freeware for the members of the Macintosh Internet community. Along with MacTCP, InterSLIP enables you to connect to an Internet SLIP account via modem.

MacPPP 2.0.1   MacPPP from Larry Blunk of Merit Network has long been the freeware PPP implementation of choice in the Macintosh world. Along with MacTCP, MacPPP enables you to connect to an Internet PPP account via modem.

MacTCP 2.0.4   Here's the program that makes it all happen—MacTCP, from Apple Computer. MacTCP is necessary to use programs such as Anarchie and TurboGopher on the Internet. If you don't buy this book, you can buy MacTCP direct from Apple for $59.

MacWAIS 1.29   Since its release last year, EINet's shareware MacWAIS has become the *de facto* standard for using WAIS servers from the Macintosh. If you want to search more than 500 full text databases of information, MacWAIS is the way to go.

MacWeb 0.98a   As this book goes to press, EINet's free MacWeb is only in alpha release. However, I wanted to give you a window into the World-Wide Web, and even this early version of MacWeb does an admirable job of that. By the time you read this, there will certainly be a new version of MacWeb—use the Get MacWeb bookmark file to retrieve the latest version.

TurboGopher 1.0.8b4   Last, but certainly not least, comes the free TurboGopher from the Gopher team at the University of Minnesota. TurboGopher enables you to browse the information resources available in Gopherspace, a collection of more than 1,500 information servers around the world. TurboGopher is fast, slick, and it has a great gopher cursor.

Essential Internet Software Bookmarks   The limited size of floppy disks frustrates me to no end, especially when there's great software such as NewsWatcher, StuffIt Expander, NCSA Mosaic, NCSA Telnet, and others that I think every Macintosh Internet user should have. There simply isn't enough room on the disk that comes with this book to include all of them. These bookmarks take you directly to the latest versions of these and much more.

For all the details on the ISKM disk, see appendix G, "The Internet Starter Kit Disk."